ACCOUNTING FOR MANAGERS

ACCOUNTING FOR MANAGERS

FOURTH EDITION

Anne Abraham | John Glynn
Michael Murphy | Bill Wilkinson

SOUTH-WESTERN
CENGAGE Learning

Australia • Brazil • Japan • Korea • Mexico • Singapore • Spain • United Kingdom • United States

Accounting for Managers, 4th Edition
Anne Abraham
John Glynn
Michael Murphy
Bill Wilkinson

Publishing Director: John Yates

Publisher: Pat Bond

Editorial Assistant: Leandra Paoli

Production Manager: Alissa Chappell

Manufacturing Manager: Helen Mason

Senior Production Controller: Maeve Healy

Marketing Manager: Anne-Marie Scoones

Typesetter: Keyword Group Ltd

Cover design: Adam Renvoize

Text design: Design Deluxe, Bath, UK

© 2008, Cengage Learning EMEA

For product information and technology assistance,
contact **emea.info@cengage.com**.
For permission to use material from this text
or product, and for permission queries,
email **clsuk.permissions@cengage.com**

British Library Cataloguing-in-Publication Data

A catalogue record for this book is available from the British Library.

ISBN: 978-1-84480-912-7

Cengage Learning EMEA
High Holborn House,
50-51 Bedford Row
London WC1R 4LR

Cengage Learning products are represented in Canada by Nelson Education Ltd.

For your lifelong learning solutions, visit **www.cengage.co.uk**

Purchase e-books or e-chapters at: **http://estore.bized.co.uk**

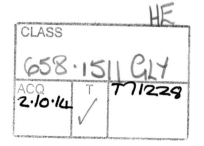

Printed by Seng Lee Press Singapore
1 2 3 4 5 6 7 8 9 10 – 10 09 08

BRIEF CONTENTS

PART **1 - Accounting and the Organisation**

PART **2 - Cost and Management Accounting**

PART **3 - Financial Management**

PART **4 - Financial Reporting**

PART **5 - Issues in Accounting**

CONTENTS

PART 2

PREFACE TO 4TH EDITION

The four years since the third edition of this book was published have been character-ised by a number of changes in accounting. Some of these changes relate to financial reporting, most notably the continuing movement towards the international harmoni-sation of financial reporting for listed companies, in large part driven by the collabora-tion between the IASB and IOSCO, and initial agreement on the implementation of 'core' financial reporting standards. The role of the EU and other regulatory bodies in planning the implementation of such standardisation has also been influential.

Other changes in accounting practice relate to the increasing influence of newer approaches to costing, such as activity-based-costing; and the contributions that accounting is seeking to make to developments in the area broadly described as 'lean management' as well as in the area of social and environmental accounting. Equally, other changes have related to the broadening context of performance measurement (which is, of course, a key function of accounting – at least as it has been traditionally perceived). Of particular importance here is the ongoing, and increasingly vocal, debate about 'corporate governance' and its associated 'values'.

This debate causes a particular problem for the authors of a text such as this – it moves very rapidly, and is perhaps overly reactive to 'scandals' such as Enron, WorldCom and others. However, it needs to be recognised that 'scandals' of this type are not new. The first edition of this book was written following similar UK based 'scandals' such as Polly Peck and BCCI. Similarly, the importance of the work on 'creative accounting' by people such as Griffiths (1995) and Smith (1996) should not be underestimated.

This ongoing debate is sometimes not very well informed, at least from an account-ant's perspective. There can be (and often is) enormous confusion about the distinc-tion between 'business risk' and 'information risk' – accounting is thought (at least by accountants) to be about the latter rather than the former, although it can be difficult to convince a disgruntled investor about this. Investors and managers seek, and perhaps have been led to believe in, accounting certainties, although commercial activities are inherently uncertain – it is a truism that profit is the (potential) reward for taking risks. There are no universal or enduring solutions to these complex problems – instead, as we try to demonstrate in this text, there are underlying principles which need to be applied in particular circumstances. However, such application (inevitably) requires that vast numbers of judgements about past and future economic circumstances have to be made. Some of these judgements will prove to be wrong – what is important is to ensure that they are not made in a biased way.

The question is how to minimise the chance of these judgements being 'wrong', and recognising the potential consequences to stakeholders (internal and external) of wrong information being provided to them by the accounting 'professionals'. In large part, the problem is one of an 'expectations gap' – between what can realistically be expected of corporate financial statements and internal accounting information as compared with what stakeholders might wish for in ideal circumstances.

The challenge faced by management, both in the private and public sectors, is that of planning and controlling the use of resources to achieve organisational objectives. At the same time they have a duty of accountability to the providers of those resources to demonstrate that the resources have been properly applied and that their management has been effective. Accountants have an important role to play in both aspects – they maintain the financial records of an organisation's economic transactions; they prepare regular financial reports based on these records for management; they help management to plan (in part via the budgetary process and the provision of information about costs); and they prepare the external financial statements of the organisation. The work of accountants permeates all aspects of management and the key purpose of accounting is that of providing useful information both for managers and external parties. The more it is able to achieve this successfully, then the more efficient and effective will be the management of organisations and the efficiency with which individuals and society at large allocate resources will be much improved. It is important that accountants and managers understand each other's needs and work together.

In this fourth edition we have attempted to reflect these and other changes by introducing new material as well as revising and updating that contained in earlier editions. In doing this we have been conscious of the need to avoid 'technical overload', as this book is not intended to be a specialist accounting textbook, although it contains much that will be of relevance to mainstream accounting students given its integrated coverage of management and financial accounting.

This book is intended principally for post-experience management students such as those pursuing DMS, MBA and similar qualifications, and for practising managers who need to obtain a better understanding of the work of accountants. No previous knowledge or experience of accounting is assumed. The book explains the conceptual bases of accounting and examines a number of the techniques that have been developed to help accountants provide the useful information which is their raison d'être. Throughout the book we provide illustrations of these techniques, and at the end of each chapter there are exercises and discussion topics as appropriate, as well as suggestions for further reading for those who would like to investigate particular topics in more detail. At the end of the book we also provide a bibliography, of further reading references, and a glossary of accounting terminology, to help demystify the sometimes hieratic language of accountants as well as solution guide notes to selected exercises and discussion topics.

In its first section, the book commences with the nature and purposes of accounting. In this context, the first chapter introduces the distinctive roles of financial accountants and management accountants and the various interfaces between these roles. The second chapter concentrates on the nature of corporate governance and business ethics. The third chapter focuses on the basis of accounting records.

The focus of the second section of the book is accounting systems within organisations and the implications of such systems for effective corporate management, particularly in the shorter term. The first chapter in this section develops the underpinning concepts of costs and their measurement. These underpinnings provide the foundation for the following chapter, which focuses on the analysis and use of costs for management decision taking purposes. The third chapter in this section concentrates on the meaning of working capital and the importance of its effective management in organisational success. The next chapter examines the importance of the budgetary process for effective organisational management and the role of variance analysis in this context. Building on this, the final chapter investigates issues relating to internal performance evaluation and transfer pricing.

The third section of the book, containing four chapters, concentrates on issues relating to longer-term decision making. The first chapter concentrates on the various techniques that accountants have developed to facilitate capital budgeting. The following chapter examines various sources of finance available to organisations to support their investment decisions. This is followed by a chapter which focuses on the relationships between an organisation's capital structure and its dividend decisions. The section concludes with a chapter which examines underpinning principles of business reorganisation decisions.

The fourth section of the book concentrates primarily on the work of financial accountants. The first chapter in this section focuses on the primary financial statements (balance sheets, income statements and cash flow statements). The next chapter examines the regulatory frameworks within which corporate financial statements are prepared. The final chapter in this section addressed the various techniques that are available to users of financial statements to help to interpret the information contained in such statements.

The final section of the book concentrates on a number of emerging issues in accounting and accountability systems. The first chapter in this section looks at issues relating to social responsibility and environmental accounting. This is followed by a chapter addressing the emerging relationship between accounting and supply chain management. The final chapter in this section brings together many of the issues dealt with in earlier chapters under the heading of 'strategic business accounting'.

Many people have helped us in the preparation of this book. In particular our thanks are due to our editors at Cengage Learning for their support and encouragement. Equally, they are due to colleagues at the Universities of Kent and Wollongong for their helpful comments on the manuscript. An enormous debt of gratitude is owed to those people who deciphered our handwriting and prepared the final manuscript.

In conclusion we would like to thank our partners and families, Ross (Abraham), Lourdes (Glynn), Sue and Abigail (Murphy) and Kathy (Wilkinson) for their patience and understanding without which we would have been unable to complete our work.

Anne Abraham
University of Wollongong

John Glynn
University of Wollongong

Michael Murphy
Formerly of the University of Kent

Bill Wilkinson
University of Wollongong

ABBREVIATIONS

ORGANISATIONS

AAA	American Accounting Association
AASB	Australian Accounting Standards Board
ACCA	Chartered Association of Certified Accountants
AICPA	American Institute of Certified Public Accountants
APB	Auditing Practices Board
APC	Auditing Practices Committee
ASB	Accounting Standards Board of the UK
ASC	Accounting Standards Committee of the UK
ASE	Australian Stock Exchange
ASSC	Accounting Standards Steering Committee of the UK
CBI	Confederation of British Industries
CCAB	Consultative Committee of Accountancy Bodies
CICA	Canadian Institute of Chartered Accountants
CIMA	Chartered Institute of Management Accountants
CIPFA	Chartered Institute of Public Finance and Accountancy
DTI	Department for Trade and Industry
EU	European Union
FASB	Financial Accounting Standards Board of the USA
FEE	Federation des Expertes Comptables Europeens
FRC	Financial Reporting Council of the UK
FRRP	Financial Reporting Review Panel of the UK
FSA	Financial Services Authority of the UK
FT	Financial Times Newspaper
IAPC	International Auditing Practices Committee
IASB	International Accounting Standards Board
IASC	International Accounting Standards Committee

ICAEW	Institute of Chartered Accountants in England and Wales
ICAI	Institute of Chartered Accountants in Ireland
ICANZ	Institute of Chartered Accountants of New Zealand
ICAS	Institute of Chartered Accountants of Scotland
IFAC	International Federation of Accountants
IIA	Institute of Internal Auditors
IOSCO	International Organisation of Securities Commissions
LSE	London Stock Exchange
NAO	National Audit Office
NASDAQ	National Association of Stock Dealers Automatic Quotations System
NHS	National Health Service
NYSE	New York Stock Exchange
UITF	Urgent Issues Task Force of the UK

OTHER TERMS

ABC	Activity based costing
ABM	Activity based management
ACT	Advanced Corporation Tax
ARR	Accounting rate of return
CAPM	Capital asset pricing model
CBA	Cost-benefit analysis
CEA	Cost-effectiveness analysis
DCF	Discounted cash flow
ED	Exposure draft
EMH	Efficient markets hypothesis
EOQ	Economic order quantity
FIFO	First in, first out
FRED	Financial reporting exposure draft

FRS	Financial reporting standard
GAAP	Generally accepted accounting principles
GP	General practitioner
IAS	International accounting standard
IFRS	International financial reporting standard
IRR	Internal rate of return
JIT	Just in time
LIFO	Last in, first out
MBO	Management by objectives
MIS	Management information system
NI	National insurance
NPV	Net present value
OED	Oxford English Dictionary
OFR	Operating and financial review
PAYE	Pay as you earn
PB	Programme budgeting
PE	Price/earnings ratio
PPBS	Planning, programming and budgeting systems
R&D	Research and development
RI	Residual income
ROCE	Return on capital employed
ROI	Return on investment
SAC	Statement of accounting concepts
SAS	Statement of auditing standards
SMEs	Small and medium-sized enterprises
SORP	Statement of recommended practice
SSAP	Statement of standard accounting practice
VAT	Value added tax
VFM	Value for money
ZBB	Zero-base budgeting

TABLES AND FIGURES

Tables

Figures

About the Website

Visit the Accounting for Managers 4th edition companion website at **www.cengage.co.uk/glynn4** to find valuable teaching and learning material including:

For students

- Links to relevant websites related to chapter material
- Chapter objectives and overviews, which accompany each chapter of the book
- Multiple choice questions to test your understanding
- Definitions from the International Encyclopedia of Business and Management

For lecturers

- An Instructor's Manual including teaching notes to questions in the text
- PowerPoint™ slides to accompany each chapter of the book

PART 1

This first section comprises three chapters which provide an introduction to accounting and the nature of accounting reports.

The first of these chapters, 'The nature and purpose of accounting', provides an introduction to the roles and activities of accountants, distinguishing between the various roles that accountants play in helping business entities to achieve their objectives, and to report to stakeholders on their success in so doing.

The second chapter, 'Corporate governance and ethics', examines the importance of governance and business ethics to the management of modern business entities and looks at the ways in which the corporate governance debate has developed.

The final chapter, 'Basis of accounting records', looks at the importance of business entities maintaining accurate records of their transactions and how this can be achieved. The contents of this chapter provide the foundations of Part 4 which deals with corporate financial reporting.

Taken together, these three chapters provide a clear introduction to:

- The nature of accounting and what it is trying to achieve.
- The work of accountants, and the important sub-divisions of this work.
- The principles of corporate governance and business ethics.
- The nature and importance of accurate accounting records.

The nature and purpose of accounting

1

Chapter preview

Accounting (or accountancy), like taxation, has been a function of organised society throughout history. Accounting is the recording, reporting and, sometimes, interpretation of all the financial (money-value) transactions and resources of individuals, enterprises and other formal organisations (accounting entities). The main branches of accounting are **financial accounting** and **management accounting**. Financial accounting has as its principal roles the keeping of accurate records of economic events and transactions affecting entities, and their use for the preparation of relevant and useful reports, primarily intended for the benefit of external stakeholders.

Management accounting, often using the same base data/records as financial accounting, but also taking data from other sources, and applying analytic techniques especially relevant to planning, decision taking and control, has the particular role of providing information and advice to managers to aid them in their work. Management accounting has, in large part, evolved from earlier **cost accounting** methods, and the measurement and control of production and other costs remains a major task. Other such tasks include the preparation and monitoring of budgets, capital expenditure evaluation, and participation in **management information systems** (MIS) design and implementation.

The nature of accounting

Accounting has existed throughout history. In all societies, and at all stages of history, accounting systems have been used as a basis for the planning, deciding and controlling of economic activity. Accounting records have been used to provide information for the management of the granaries belonging to the Pharaohs of Ancient Egypt;

to control the tax revenues of the emperors of Ancient China; to ensure the accountability of the stewards of medieval nobility; and to provide information about the activities of modern multinational enterprises in market economies. Throughout history and across all forms of economic structures, accounting has been important.

With the growth of private sector commerce from the Middle Ages onwards, came the need for basic stewardship accounting to develop into a system which would enable merchants and others to maintain control over their trading activities. A major stimulus here was the development of the 'Italian' method of bookkeeping, as exemplified in the work of Luca Pacioli who published a treatise on double-entry bookkeeping in 1494. The continuing development of commerce, combined with the emergence (in the UK) of 'joint-stock' companies, led to accounting occupying an increasingly important role. The Industrial Revolution accelerated this trend, as did (again in the UK) the emergence of company regulation via the Companies Acts of the mid-nineteenth Century.

Although accounting has been present throughout history, it has existed, and continues to exist, in many different forms. The key to a successful accounting system is ensuring that it mirrors the needs of the society and the organisations in which it exists. An accounting system which was appropriate for the monarchs of medieval Europe is unlikely to be appropriate in the twenty-first century. Similarly, an accounting system appropriate for a centrally planned economy is unlikely to be appropriate for a society operating within the disciplines of a market economy. Even within market economies, there are differences in the demands made on accounting, and hence on accounting systems, although there is an increasing emphasis on harmonisation – in part caused by the internationalisation of business throughout the modern world economic environment. Prime examples of this are the work of the International Accounting Standards Board (IASB) and related bodies. However, even within this drive towards harmonisation and standardisation of accounting practice, there is a recognition that different societies are at different stages of development; have different political systems; have different economic infrastructures; and have different histories. The emphasis of harmonisation is on identifying common ground and using this as a basis on which to build, rather than on stating that there is just one correct way to do things. The more that societies move towards common structures and goals, the more this common ground expands and the more a common philosophy of accounting becomes appropriate.

The focus of this book is on the contribution that accounting and accountability systems can make towards the more efficient and effective management of business entities operating in a market economy. It is intended to be of practical use and, as such, contains examples of the ways in which accounting can be used to provide useful information to those concerned with the activities of business entities, whether they operate within or outside such enterprises. However, one book cannot cover all aspects of accounting systems, processes, concepts, techniques and the contribution that accounting can make towards the success of entities. It has been necessary to concentrate on aspects of accounting of particular relevance to management. These are normally termed **financial accounting,** where the focus is on the recording of transactions and the annual financial reporting of enterprises, together with **management accounting** and **cost accounting,** where the focus is on internal decision taking within entities. However, the distinction between these different 'accountings' is not clear cut. Frequently, although they have different emphases, they use the same data as their starting point. These data are those contained in the basic accounting records of the enterprise, and the most common approach to recording these data is that of double-entry bookkeeping. This holds true whether the data are recorded manually in 'books of account' or maintained using modern computer-based systems (see Chapter 3).

It is a feature of all societies that organisations and individuals within them have particular roles and contributions to make towards that society, and that they are provided with resources, of whatever type, to enable them to perform these roles and make these contributions. The possible roles, contributions and resources involved are many and varied. However, a crucial element of the overall process is that the organisations and individuals in question must be **accountable**. This accountability may take a variety of forms: it may relate simply to the safe custody of the resources, or it may relate to the outcomes and outputs of the activities for which managers are responsible while using the resources entrusted to them. The particular contribution of accounting to this process is its focus on the financial consequences of the activities of organisations and individuals.

The need for external financial accounting reports

A feature of modern economic organisation, in whatever form, is that the owners of the resources employed in economic activity frequently do not have direct control over the day-to-day management of these resources. There is a separation between the ownership and the management of resources, and this separation is increasingly common as enterprises become larger. In the case of a small business entity, such as a garage (or service station), there may be only one owner of the entity who also has control over the management of its resources. In such cases there is no separation of ownership and control. Enterprises of this sort are commonly referred to as 'proprietary businesses', as the owner (proprietor) is also responsible for the management. In the case of a business owned by the members of a family, the situation may be different. Perhaps not all the members of the family participate in the management of the business. If this is the case, those who do so will need to account for their management of the business to the rest of the family. To do this they will need to maintain accounting records of the transactions into which they enter on behalf of the business, and of the consequences of their business decisions. These records will then form the basis of 'statements of account', showing the result of their management of the business, which they will then render to the other members of the family. At the same time, the accounting records will help them in their day-to-day management of the business as these will provide information about such items as the costs and revenues associated with different aspects of the business. Thus, the accounting records provide the basis of 'statements of account' (financial reporting) from managers to owners and, at the same time, provide information that managers can use in their management of the business (management accounting).

The separation of ownership and control is at its most noticeable in the case of large business entities where the owners of (shareholders in) the entity appoint professional managers to conduct the activities of the enterprise. There may be many such shareholders. In the case of some previously state-owned entities which have been privatised (e.g. telecommunications, water and electricity companies), there may be millions of shareholders. These shareholders appoint, via a General Meeting, the senior managers (directors) of the company, who are charged with managing the resources of the company to achieve its objectives. However, it is worth noting that it is normally the existing board of directors which nominates replacement or additional directors to such a General Meeting, and these nominations are normally accepted by the shareholders.

In the case of a company, the objectives will typically relate to generation of profit, which can then be distributed to the owners of the enterprise, although there may also be other objectives. For example, a company whose shares are listed on a stock exchange may seek to achieve increases in its share price – this would afford shareholders the opportunity of making capital gains; it might also make the company less vulnerable to a takeover and make it easier for it to acquire other companies. The separation of ownership and control means that there is a need for a formal structure of accountability between the managers of the resources and the owners of these resources, of which annual financial statements are an important, but not the only, element. The larger the entity and the greater the number of shareholders, the more important it is that there is a formal and regulated structure. Virtually every country which operates, or is seeking to operate, a market economy has passed legislation to provide such a formal and regulated structure of accountability, although the detail of the legislation varies from country to country.

There is also a body of accounting theory, **agency theory** (see Chapter 2) which deals with the relationships between the owners of a business entity and those appointed to manage the entity on their behalf. The simple agency relationship between owners and managers summarised above can be expanded to incorporate the many other parties who have an interest in the activities of a business entity. Employees, customers, suppliers, finance providers and society at large all have an interest in the way in which the managers of a business entity use the resources entrusted to them and conduct its business. An alternative viewpoint is that of 'stakeholders' in an entity, whereby the stakeholders are all those groups which society regards as having reasonable rights in, and claims against, the entity and who have corresponding rights to information about its activities. This information is necessary to help them make decisions about their relationships with the entity. In this context, and throughout the rest of the book, a business entity is regarded as being a coherent business unit for which it is appropriate to prepare accounting reports. Such entities can be very diverse, including e.g. sole traders, partnerships, divisions of companies, companies themselves and groups of companies.

The range of stakeholders, their interests in entities and their information needs have frequently been debated in western market economies. Table 1.1 shows extracts

Table 1.1	Stakeholder groups	
Source A	*Source B*	*Source C*
Equity investor group	Investors	Investors
Loan-creditor group	Lenders	Lenders
Employee group	Employees	Employees
Analyst-advisor group		
Business contact group	Suppliers and other trade creditors	Suppliers and other creditors
	Customers	Customers
Government and their agencies	Government	Government
Public	Public	Public

Source: A. ASSC (1975a). B. IASC (1989). C. ASB (1995).

from three influential statements on this subject by major professional accountancy bodies.

It should be noted that none of these statements includes the management of an entity as a user group. This is because the focus of all three statements is upon the external financial reporting of (accountability of) entities and its regulation. This is not to deny the importance of financial information to managers, or their rights to such information. Rather, the focus is on management reporting on the activities and resources of the entity under their control to external stakeholders in the entity. At the same time, managers will be using the services of accountants to provide them with information useful in the operational and strategic management of the entity. The requirements of these different groups for financial information about the activities of an entity can be summarised by considering the types of decision that they have to make about their links with the entity. Table 1.2 provides some examples of the types of decisions these groups may need to make.

Definitions of financial accounting/reporting

We have already seen that many groups have a need for financial information about the activities of business entities and the outcomes of these activities. In market economies the principal but not the only means of providing this information is the annual financial accounts prepared by management. These accounts, which are almost universally required by legislation, are based on the accounting records maintained by an entity and are intended to provide their readers – the stakeholder groups – with the information that they require. They are a vital communication and accountability mechanism in market economies. Unsurprisingly, the structure and objectives of these financial statements have been the subject of much comment. The following quotations are from pronouncements issued by influential accounting bodies about financial statements and the annual corporate reports which contain them:

> The objective of financial statements is to provide information about the financial position, performance, and financial adaptability of an enterprise that is useful to a wide range of users for assessing the stewardship of management and for making economic decisions. (IASB 2006)

Table 1.2	Examples of the differing information requirements of user groups
User group	**Example of decision**
Equity investor group	Buy/hold/sell shares.
Loan-creditor group	Increase/hold constant/reduce levels of credit and loans and on what terms.
Employee group	Submit claims for wage increases; ability to take industrial action.
Analyst-advisor group	Which investments to recommend to clients.
Business contact group	What trade to do and on what terms (e.g. credit).
Government	Central and local taxation and industrial policy, environmental and employment issues.
Public	Assess economic and social impact of firm; policy and implementation issues.

[serving] the informational needs of external users who lack the authority to prescribe the financial information they want from an enterprise, and therefore must use the information that management communicates to them. (ASB 1985)

The fundamental objective of corporate reports is to communicate economic measurements of, and information about, the resources and performance of the reporting entity useful to those having reasonable rights to such information. (ASSC 1975)

As can be seen from these pronouncements, there is a strong measure of agreement about the purposes of the annual financial statement of enterprises. They exist to supply the information requirement of the stakeholders in the enterprise. In most cases these statements are public documents, available for inspection by anyone (although some countries offer exemptions in this respect for smaller companies), and their contents are prescribed by legislation and professional accounting statements. These issues are discussed further in Chapter 14.

Desirable characteristics of accounting information

If annual financial statements are to satisfy the information needs of their users the information that they contain must have characteristics related to the needs of these users. This has been an area of great – and still, to some extent, unresolved – debate. The debate is not so much about what these desirable characteristics are as about the extent to which it is possible to provide accounting information which has all these characteristics. These characteristics will be examined in some detail later in this book. For the present we want simply to identify them and comment briefly upon them. Many desirable characteristics for accounting information have been identified, and to some extent a number of these overlap. It is generally accepted that the main desirable characteristics are that the information should be:

- understandable
- relevant
- material
- reliable
- faithful
- be based on substance over form
- neutral
- prudent
- complete
- comparable
- timely
- balance benefits and costs of preparation
- balance the desired qualitative characteristics
- give a fair ('true and fair') presentation

Table 1.3 summarises these characteristics and the various sources which have, in the past, promoted their importance.

Below we summarise current views on the most important of these characteristics and the way in which they are interpreted for the preparation and analysis of accounts.

1 **Understandable:** If the information contained in the financial statements cannot be understood by the readers of these statements the whole purpose of preparing such statements is rendered futile. Traditionally, financial statements have concentrated on the presentation of information in the form of numerical tables accompanied by some limited explanatory text. Increasingly, it is believed that this should be supplemented by other forms of presentation, including graphs, pie charts, etc., and commentaries on the financial information such that the information is rendered more accessible to readers who have not had formal accountancy training. In addition to the way in which they present information, a major obstacle to the understandability of financial statements is accounting 'jargon'. Accountants, like other professional groups, use language in a very precise way. In particular, they attach very precise meanings to ordinary words. Unfortunately, these meanings are not always those which 'non-accountants' attach to these words. Effectively, accountants use these words as a 'code' which enables them to convey a great deal of information to those who understand the code, but this means that readers who do not know the code can all too easily misinterpret the information that the financial statements are intended to convey. One of the purposes of this book is to provide a decoding manual for non-accountants. It does this in two ways. First, the Glossary at the end of the book provides definitions and explanations of common accounting terminology,

Table 1.3	Desirable characterististics of financial accounting reports			
Characteristsics	*A*	*B*	*C*	*D*
Understandable	y	y	y	y
Relevant	y		y	y
Material			y	y
Reliable	y		y	y
Faithful representation				y
Substance				y
Neutrality				y
Prudent		y		y
Completeness				y
Comparable	y	y	y	y
Timely	y		y	y
Cost/benefit				y
Objective	y	y	y	
Realistic	y	y	y	
Usefulness			y	y
Economy of presentation		y	y	y
Consistent	y	y		y

Source: A: ASSC (1975A). B: Inflation Accounting Committee (1975). C: FASB (1980). D: ASB (1995).

and, second, throughout the book examples and illustrations are given of the practical implementation of accounting terminology.

2 **Relevant:** The purpose of financial statements is to provide information to stakeholders in the entity such that they will be able to make 'informed judgements and decisions' about their financial relationships with the reporting entity by helping them to evaluate past, present or future events or confirming or correcting past evaluations. The information they contain needs to be relevant to those decisions. The problem is that different decisions may require different information and that all decisions ideally require information about the (likely) future consequences of those decisions. Definite information about the future is, of course, not available; we have to predict the future using information about the past (predictive value being another desirable characteristic of financial statements) in conjunction with specific assessments as to how the future may differ from the past. This obviously raises the question as to what information has predictive value, and the balance between predictive and confirmatory value of information. The current position in most market economies is that financial statements must provide information about an entity's assets and liabilities, its revenues and expenditures, and its cash flows. Thereafter, it is up to the readers of the financial statements to make their own assessment in the context of the decisions they need to make.

3 **Material:** While all the transactions of an enterprise must be properly and fully recorded, however small they might be, when it comes to the preparation and publication of financial statements, it is necessary to aggregate these transactions into larger wholes. This inevitably requires that decisions are made about the amount and extent of such aggregation. The problem is twofold: the higher the level of aggregation, the greater the risk of useful information not being disclosed in the financial statements; while, on the other hand, the lower the level of aggregation, the greater the volume of information that has to be disclosed, with all the associated problems of information overload and cost. Materiality is an accounting concept which recognises the fact that it is impractical to record, or at least report, every detail of an enterprise's activities and that to do so would be of little benefit to the users, while acknowledging at the same time that information which is too highly aggregated would be of equally little benefit. A balance has to be struck (ASB 1995a: para. 2.6).

4 **Reliable:** If readers of financial statements are to rely on the information such statements contain in making their decisions, then they must have confidence in that information. In most market economies this confidence is reinforced by a requirement to have the financial statements audited by an independent auditor. The regulations in this respect vary from country to country, but the requirement for such an audit is almost universal. The concept of reliability has been summarised thus: 'Information has the quality of reliability when it is free from material error and bias and can be depended upon by users to represent faithfully what it either purports to represent or could reasonably be expected to represent' (ASB 1995, para. 2.13).

5 **Faithful:** To be reliable information must 'faithfully' represent the transactions and other economic events affecting the reporting entity. The difficulty here is that all financial statements involve considerable amounts of judgement,

by management teams, and by internal and external auditors. The extent of these judgements is frequently not appreciated by financial statement users. However, to achieve this characteristic financial statements need to reflect the economic substance of transactions and other economic events rather than their legal form.

6 **Objective:** The information presented in a financial statement needs to be objective and unbiased if it is to meet the needs of users. It needs to be neutral, in that it should not be biased towards the interest of any one stakeholder group. The principles employed in the preparation of the accounting reports, and the accountants involved in their preparation, must not favour any particular interest group. Historically, there has been a strong tradition in accounting whereby 'objective' has been interpreted as meaning 'verifiable'. According to this tradition, information can not be objective unless it can be independently verified, for example by an independent auditor. This meant that all sorts of potentially useful information which could not be verified in this way was excluded from financial statements. More recently, the emphasis has switched to the view that 'neutrality' is at least as important as 'verifiability'. Financial statements increasingly contain information which, although neutral, is not verifiable in the traditional sense. An example of such information is the inclusion of the values of intangible assets such as 'brand names'. However, the concept of verifiability retains an important influence on the information that is contained in financial statements, particularly where an independent audit is required. The modern view has been expressed thus in the UK (ASB 1995: para. 2.19):

The information contained in financial statements must be neutral, i.e. free from bias. Financial statements are not neutral if they include information that has been selected or presented in such a way as to influence the making of a decision or judgement in order to achieve a predetermined result or outcome.

7 **Prudent:** The nature of financial statements is that they contain information on both complete and incomplete transactions. An incomplete transaction is one in which all of the cash consequences have not yet been realised (for example, a credit sale where the customer has not yet paid for the goods/services as at the date of the financial statements). Because the cash consequences have not been fully realised, there is inevitably an element of doubt as to what these will ultimately be (for example, the customer may be unable/unwilling to pay for the goods or services received). If too optimistic a view is taken as to the ultimate cash consequences, there is a danger that the entity or the stakeholders associated with it will enter into commitments which they will then not be able to meet. The general principle underlying the preparation of financial statements is that they should present a 'prudent' picture of the entity's profit; its assets and liabilities. However: 'Prudence is the inclusion of a degree of caution in the exercise of the judgements needed in making the estimates required under conditions of uncertainty, such that income or assets are not overstated and expenses or liabilities are not understated' (ASB 1995: para. 2.20).

8 **Complete:** If they are to be useful to their users financial statements must contain all the relevant information, subject of course to the requirements of materiality, which suggests that information which would not impact on stakeholders' decisions need not be reported.

9 **Comparable:** Unless the information contained in a set of financial statements can be compared and contrasted with information from elsewhere, its usefulness is greatly diminished. Readers of the information need to be able to compare it with their expectations, with information about the previous performance of the entity, with information about the performance of other entities and with information derived from other sources. There is a need for consistency in the preparation and presentation of financial information. This consistency must apply to the financial statements of an individual entity over time (enabling comparison of current performance with previous and with anticipated performance). Equally, it must apply across different entities (enabling the performance of one entity to be compared with another). This need for consistency has been a major influence in the drive towards the 'harmonisation' and 'standardisation' of accounting practice within and across individual countries. The 'harmonisation' and 'standardisation' movement is a major factor in the work of the IASB, at least as regards 'listed' companies.

10 **Timely:** If the information in financial statements is to have value to its readers, it must be timely. Stale news is no news. If the information is out of date it will not help its readers make sound decisions. Financial statements need to be published as quickly as is consistent with the need for them to be relevant and reliable. If there is undue delay, the information they contain may lose its relevance. In a number of countries timeliness is ensured by legislation; for example, in the United Kingdom a company must publish its financial statements within a specific time of the period to which they relate.

11 **Cost benefit balance:** The maintenance of the detailed accounting records of an entity, the preparation of financial statements and the audit thereof, constitute a costly process. In fact, it is a process the cost of which may often be underestimated. It is necessary to ensure that the benefits derived from this process exceed its costs, as otherwise society will suffer a net loss. The problem is that the benefits and costs of this process are not easily assessed. Thus, there is often a 'political' dimension to decisions about the maintenance of accounting records and the dissemination of financial statements (ASB 1995: para. 2.38):

The evaluation of benefits and costs is, however, substantially a judgmental process. Furthermore the costs do not necessarily fall on those users, who enjoy the benefits … it is often difficult to apply a cost-benefit test in a particular case.

Information is material if it could influence users' decisions taken on the basis of the financial statements. If that information is misstated, or if certain information is omitted, the materiality of the misstatement or omission depends on the size and nature of the item in question judged in the particular circumstances of the case.

12 **Usefulness:** In many ways, this is the ultimate yardstick for the information contained in financial statements. If it is not useful it is not worth preparing. The concept of usefulness goes right back to the definitions of financial statements and accounting which were mentioned earlier in this chapter. It is effectively a conflation of all the other characteristics, and the ultimate question is whether better decisions are made because of the existence and use of the financial statements. The real-world usefulness of financial statements is

inevitably a result of 'trade-offs' between all the characteristics, and perhaps the most important such 'trade-off' is that between relevance and reliability.

The edifice of financial reporting and its desirable characteristics, as outlined above, will be built on sand unless it is based on a reliable structure of financial records which record the economic events and transactions affecting the enterprise. Thus, accountants have two key roles:

1 They must ensure that the entity has in place a system of financial recording that properly records all its trading and other economic transactions. This must be their primary responsibility. In the absence of such records (i.e. a lack of 'proper books of account'), there can be no reliable financial reporting, nor could there be any effective management accounting. Chapter 3 discusses core issues involved in the design and implementation of financial recording systems.

2 They must extract from the financial records the periodic financial statements of the enterprise. Chapter 3 also discusses the essentials of such extraction and provides a basis from which Chapter 13 goes on to discuss the 'primary financial statements' of enterprises. Thus, accountants are traditionally viewed as being responsible both for the maintenance of the core accounting records of an entity and for the preparation of external financial reports based upon these records.

Cost accounting and management accounting

So far we have not presented any precise definition of management accounting or any clear specification of the specific tasks and the boundaries of its role. Some might argue that this is not necessary on the grounds that management accounting is 'what management accountants do'. Management accounting is not defined in law; management accountants do not have to be members of professional accounting bodies (although many of them are) – auditors are the only accountants who have to have appropriate professional qualifications. The tasks, roles and boundaries of management accounting vary from entity to entity. However, a useful definition of the role of management accounting is provided by the IFAC (1987: para. A):

> The process of identification, measurement; accumulation, analysis, preparation, interpretation and communication of information (both financial and operating) used by management to plan, evaluate and control within an organisation and to assure use of an account ability for its resources.

Perhaps the main areas of uncertainty or controversy over the role and boundaries of management accounting relate to how far it should take responsibility for and control of the enterprise's total, or integrated management information system (MIS), and the extent to which the management accountant should have the authority to be proactive – going beyond a purely advisory role towards more interventionist participation in management decision making.

Historically, management accounting has evolved from cost accounting, but with cost accounting remaining a major subordinate component of the management accounting process. Costs have been recorded, reported and controlled since the time of the Pharaohs, and before. However, until modern times 'cost' usually meant simply 'cash expenditures', and, indeed, to this day this remains the case in some parts of the public sector (and in many very small businesses). We shall see in later chapters how many different ways there are of defining and measuring costs.

Modern systems of cost accounting began to develop after the start of the Industrial Revolution, when production processes became more complex, entities grew larger, and top management could no longer maintain awareness and control of efficiency by personal observation and oversight. The First World War encouraged the wider use of cost accounting through the introduction of 'cost-plus contracts', where cost data had to be kept and made available for checking and audit against bills rendered. By the end of the Second World War cost accounting had become more sophisticated and influential, and the terms 'managerial accounting' and 'management accounting' began to be used, especially in the USA and in academic writing. Traditional cost accounting first came under criticism from economists, and then from academic accountants who had a background in economic education (Dean 1951; Solomons 1952) and from management scientists (Goetz 1949). Traditional cost accounting had as its main functions the control of costs in factories, mines, railways, etc. and the provision of cost data for the valuation of stocks. It was the work of critics such as those mentioned above which helped cost accounting evolve into management accounting, with the more intellectual role of helping managers to plan, to evaluate alternative courses of action and investment, and to reach (hopefully) optimal decisions. (For more modern viewpoints on the origins of management accounting, see Johnson and Kaplan 1987; Hopwood 1988.) The contemporary scene in management accounting shows four major developments:

1 There is a growing awareness that simply providing managers with information is not sufficient. Managers have difficulties interpreting accounting information, and may also have personal priorities and agendas which differ from the 'rational' pursuit of optimisation of corporate goals. Thus there is a behavioural dimension to the use of accounting (and other) management information, and approaches are being sought to improve the communication and interpretation of accounting information, and its use in assisting good planning, decision making and control.

2 Some academics believe that much accounting information, far from being objective or neutral, is instead consciously biased or distorted to support narrow managerial objectives which may be against the interest of workers or society (for example, information made available during successive rounds of pit closures in (the then) British Coal). They are working to develop forms and conventions of accounting which might overcome such problems.

3 Traditional cost accounting, and even much modern management accounting, has been fixated mainly on manufacturing and other industrial activity. But modern market economies are characterised by a contraction in industrial employment and the relative expansion of the service sector. (Even ignoring the current recession in manufacturing industry, the rapid spread of automation and robot technology inevitably means a continuing fall in the proportion of the population employed in blue-collar jobs in industry.) So management accountants are working to develop accounting systems which are more tailored to service businesses (including retail operations), professional offices, and public-sector enterprises such as the health services, schools and universities, and local and central government.

4 Given the increasing automation of industry, and the adoption of new forms of management organisation, and of the organisation and control of work (many of these coming from Japan, and some from the USA (Lee 1987)), it is argued that conventional management accounting is today inadequate even for manufacturing industry. This is leading to the development of new accounting technologies and approaches sometimes termed **strategic management accounting.**

The basic problem is that accounting is not an exact science. As we will see in later chapters, many of the precise-looking numbers used in accounting reports are in fact only estimates, or values chosen from a range of alternative measurement methods, each with some validity in a particular context (for example, factual but misleading accounting numbers from past records, as opposed to realistic estimates of present or future costs after allowing for inflation, currency devaluation, market forces, etc.). Good accountants are always in search of the truth, although, if they find it, top management sometimes prevents its disclosure. More often, the problem is that the 'truth' is uncertain and arguable, rather like many cases in a court of law or issues before Parliament. Accounting is a human artifact – different truths lie in the eyes of different beholders. This will become particularly evident when we discuss business reorganisation later in the book.

The tasks (and roles) of management accounting vary from entity to entity, according to the organisational structures and requirements set by top management, but the following comprise the principal ones and closely parallel the tasks of management – this is hardly surprising, as management accounting is intended to help management in the discharge of its responsibilities:

1 *Planning*
- Liaise with other management functions on medium- and long-term (corporate) plans, including capital expenditure proposals.
- Prepare three- to five-year outline medium-term budgets.
- Administer the annual budget cycle, linked to the enterprise's managerial responsibility structure.
- Develop cost and other financial information systems to monitor achievement in realising plans.

2 *Control*
- Measure the outturn (results) of costs, sales, etc. against annual budgets and agree cost and performance 'standards'.
- Prepare cost, sales and budget reports, and circulate them to responsible managers (reports are normally at least monthly, but the goal is real-time systems where up-to-date information is available constantly on managers' terminals).
- Follow up reports with advice, supplementary studies, if helpful, and sometimes pressure to conform to agreed plans, budgets and standards.

3 *Decision making*
- Provide information for decisions (very often the cost and other financial information routinely available for planning and control is not fully relevant for particular strategic or operational decisions – this issue is discussed in later chapters).

- Provide advice and participate in the decision process where multi-function management is an accepted part of the enterprise culture.

4 *Capital projects*

- Participate in planning capital programmes, including liaison with financial management, regarding the raising and timing of capital funds.
- Reconcile the capital programme with corporate plans, and prepare medium-term and long-term capital budgets.
- Prepare detailed cash-flow budgets for capital funding and expenditure for the year ahead.
- Monitor the progress of capital spending against budget.

5 *Performance evaluation*

- Agree procedures with personnel and top management regarding ways to include budgets and other financial measures within the performance evaluation of individual managers, departments, divisions, etc.
- Circulate, explain and follow-up performance reports.

6 *Costs for financial accountants*

- Supply the cost information needed by financial accountants for preparing annual accounts and other external reports (these costs, mainly relating to production operations and stocks in hand, may be measured or classified on a different basis from the relevant costs used for managerial planning, decision making and control).

7 *Wider roles*

- As with other management jobs, management accountants may sometimes expand their roles (or empires!) to take on additional tasks. This may occur especially in small to medium-sized enterprises (SMEs), perhaps because the finance or marketing functions are weak, or if there is no corporate planning function. The management accountant may become involved in tasks such as economic and strategic reviews or management-by-objective programmes.

Accounting and management information systems

Historically, most of the accounting data for production and other operations were collected and entered into records by the cost accounting department. At intervals, these data were transferred to a financial accounting department in full, or in a condensed, aggregated form if that was required. With the spread of large mainframe computers in the 1960s, there was a logic in centralising all accounting data, recording in one computer centre managed by the financial accounting department or by a computer specialist reporting directly to the chief accountant or finance director. Such organisational arrangements have tended to persist, even after the introduction of personal computers (PCs) and diffused networks.

Accounting measurements – or, more precisely, 'money-value measurements' – provide the only common measurement system or common language for business. Costs, revenues and asset values can all be aggregated or compared – in the common denominator of money. In contrast, physical units of output or sales comprising, for example, bolts, nuts, screws, nails and steel girders, provide meaningless disinformation if aggregated together. Nevertheless, this information is essential in its unaggregated form for the accurate measurement of costs. The need is to measure costs per unit or batch of output for separate kinds of product, or the cost or value of each separate kind of asset:

Unit price of inputs x Volume of inputs = Cost
Unit selling price x Volume of sales   = Sales revenue

The accountant has direct access to invoices and price lists for these cost and revenue calculations, but normally must rely on other managers for the accurate collection of data on the volume of sales, inputs and each separate important 'activity' involved in the production or sales processes whose cost needs separate identification and measurement in order to facilitate understanding and control of the efficiency of resource utilisation. Managers themselves also need physical measures of inputs and activities for their own personal use in good management – indeed, many managers prefer to manage mainly on the guidance of the physical measures they collect rather than the accounting measures of these inputs and activities, which may only become available to them after some delay.

As indicated above, there are a number of different types of information which management needs in addition to that relating to cost and revenues – what is sometimes referred to as the 'balanced scorecard' (see Chapter 18). Examples include personnel information regarding skills, training, absenteeism and labour turnover; and quality control and performance information regarding the meeting of completion/delivery dates. If all this information can be combined together in one, normally computer-based, system there exists an MIS, which to be fully integrated must also contain accounting information. A fully integrated MIS is easier to describe than to implement.

The public sector

This book is about accounting for managers. It is expected that the majority of these managers will be in the private sector. However, it is acknowledged that managers in the public sector face similar problems. The phenomenon of the new public management, arising from the introduction of commercial principles (business-style management, contracting, control and accounting methods), wherever possible, into the public sector, emphasises this similarity. For example, hospitals have been expected to account commercially and aim to at least 'break even' (after allowing for financing costs), while 'trading' within the so-called 'internal market' of healthcare, which itself is globally limited by annual government budget allocation. Universities now operate broadly on commercial accounting principles and seek to earn a surplus, or 'profit' (for reinvestment within the university). But there remain large areas of central and local government which are expected to spend all their budget allocation, and thus end the year with no surplus or profit. Here full commercial accounting standards of financial reporting, costing and budgeting are increasingly being demanded and developed.

A manager without accurate, up-to-date and relevant management information is like the captain of a submarine, all of whose navigational and control instrumentation have failed. Such managers are floundering, unlikely to reach their objectives safely, or at least efficiently. Much of the navigational (i.e. planning) and control information needed by managers to aid their decision making and action is provided by accounting. Financial accounting focuses mainly on the information which must be reported externally to satisfy the law, tax collectors, shareholders and major creditors, and maintaining the underpinning accounting records; management accounting exists mainly to provide internal information to assist managers in their planning, decision making, and control of activities, resources and capital projects. There is another element that must be considered: **financial management**, where the core role is that of securing the necessary finance (both long-term and short-term capital, the latter commonly termed 'working capital'). This role involves ensuring that capital is available when needed and balancing the desire to minimise the 'cost of capital', while at the same time minimising the risk of insolvency or loss of credit status. Financial management must establish rapport and trust with major sources of finance, and has to cooperate with financial accounting in deciding the detail and form of external financial reporting and information disclosure.

Financial management

Financial management is often seen as a key 'survival' function of the enterprise, whereas accounting may be viewed as a 'facilitating' function of lower status. Often a finance director will be responsible at board level, not just for finance, but for accounting as well; and the two main branches of accounting may be brought together in larger firms under a chief accountant (often termed 'controller' in American firms and business literature). In smaller firms there may not be enough work to justify the cost of an expert finance specialist and, since most accountants have some expertise in finance, the *de facto* chief accountant will often take on the finance role as well and operate at board level as financial director or controller. In firms large enough to justify a specialist finance department and head of finance (treasurer), the finance director will often be an accountant who has moved across to specialise in finance, although there is an increasing tendency (already pronounced in the USA) to view the finance function as quite separate from accounting, with senior finance staff being recruited from Masters in Business Administration (MBA), postgraduate specialists in finance, or persons trained in merchant banks or other relevant financial institutions.

At board and top-management level, managers will need interface and contact with, as well as information and advice from, all three functions: financial management, financial accounting and management accounting. In contrast, at middle and junior management levels the main contact of the managers will be with management accounting. However, at all levels the accountants – as 'ring-holders' of useful information (which managers may not even realise the accountants hold, or can assemble and provide) – should be proactive in offering information and advice, and in making it clear what aid they can provide to managers.

Interactions in accounting and finance

Figure 1.1 illustrates the interactions, or interdependent interests, in accounting and finance.

The major interactions or interdependent interests, represented in Figure 1.1 by the notation A–D, are summarised below:

A The main link between management accounting and financial management is a shared concern for the efficient and effective use of capital. This is sometimes termed 'resource management'. There is a particular concern for new capital outlays which commit the firm to particular markets, products or technologies for years ahead, and how they are to be financed. The management accountant has to verify all the costs, both of the outlay itself and of the future activities for which the capital outlays will be used. A 'capital appraisal' (termed 'option appraisal' in some public services) must be undertaken to assess whether profitability will be acceptable. In addition, the financial manager will be concerned with the risk or uncertainty involved, and with the timing of cash flows relative to the future needs to meet payment obligations to creditors and shareholders.

B The main link between financial accounting and financial management is a shared concern for the measurement of profit and asset values; for the form and detail of financial reports; and for the impact these will have on interested parties external to the enterprise. One frequent problem here is that financial managers (and the board of directors) may want a more 'rosy' picture of the firm's profits and financial position to be projected externally than a cautious and objective accountant would want to endorse. This puts pressure on accountants, when there are doubts over facts or contingencies – or where there is a choice of accounting methods allowed by professional bodies, government or the Stock Exchange – to report only the most optimistic accounting measurements. This results in what is often termed 'creative accounting' (see Chapter 13).

C The main link between financial accounting and management accounting is the collection of data, maintenance of accounting records and exchange of information relevant to the needs of the two branches of accounting. In particular, the management accountant is typically in charge of the method and detail of collecting data and compiling information on the costs of production, selling and other activities. This information is important for the costing and valuation of unsold stocks of goods for sale (including work still in progress and incomplete), and for the calculation of enterprise profit or loss required from the financial accountant.

Figure 1.1	Interactions in accounting and finance

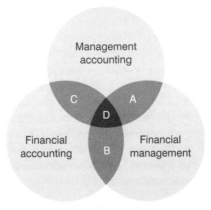

D This is the cross-over area of interests shared by all three of the accounting and finance specialisations. Prominent here is taxation, which affects choices in financing, profit calculation and reporting, and assessment of the effects of both current operations and future choices of operations, other activities and alternative uses of new capital investment. Also important is the measurement and control of cash flow, perhaps with particular concern for the balance between debtor receipts and creditor payments, and the locking up of cash in raw materials, work-in-progress and unsold finished goods relative to the current and foreseeable rate of sales and cash realisation from sales. Again, there is shared concern for the rate of return achieved from existing capital investment and for realistic forecasting of the expected rate of return from new capital investment and the risk associated therewith.

Conclusion

The theme of this chapter has been to introduce readers to the purposes and roles of accounting, to the main branches of accounting and the differences of function between them, and to some of the key tasks they carry out. In essence, the accountant exists to provide information and advice. This book emphasises those aspects of accounting which impinge on the work and understanding of managers. These do not just include management accounting, but also require sufficient understanding of financial accounting and financial management to allow the manager to see how these activities affect the enterprise and the overall management process.

Chapter overview

Accounting has a long history, involving recording and reporting on cash and other property, and amounts owing to and by organisations. From this has grown modern financial accounting, with its particular concern for accountability to various stakeholders, especially the shareholders of public companies, and for financial reporting to stakeholders in accordance with the law and standards set by professional institutes. *Inter alia*, financial statements should be understandable, objective, comparable, realistic, relevant, reliable, consistent, timely, prudent, economical in presentation and material in content.

Earlier systems of cost accounting have come to be incorporated within the much wider approach of modern management accounting, where the objective is to provide information on costs, revenues, the use of capital, in such detail and form as will assist managers in the planning, decision making, and control of their activities and organisational units. Annual budget planning and monitoring have become very important in all entities, but perhaps especially in public sector entities with fixed allocations and no profit to measure or relate to incentives. Management accountants supply advice as well as routine reports, and increasingly their role is proactive, to link up with management information systems and wider management strategy.

Further reading

The International Accounting Standards Board (IASB) in their 2006 set of standards provide professional views on the nature and purposes of financial reporting. Many countries, e.g. EU member states, require that these standards are used in the financial statements of listed companies. Hopwood (1988) discusses the role of accounting within organisations, and Johnson and Kaplan (1987) provide a critique of the development of management accounting practices.

Questions and exercises

Guide notes can be found at the back of the book for all questions marked with an asterisk*.

1* Choose a club or other organisation with which you are familiar. Explain how it discharges financial accountability to members and others through the use of financial statements/reports or other mechanisms. Do you consider that this provides adequate disclosure and accountability – and why, or why not? What improvements would you like to see made in the organisation as regards its accounting or accountability?

2 Explain (a) the common features of, and (b) the distinctive differences between financial accounting and management accounting, as regards their purpose, scope and tasks.

3* Referring to Table 1.3 of desirable characteristics of accounting reports in this chapter, why do you think the terms 'accurate' and 'truthful' do not appear in the list?

4* Why do you think it might be that among all the desirable characteristics of accounting reports and financial statements mentioned in this chapter it has been suggested that the most important 'trade-off' (that is, compromise where separate characteristics may appear to conflict with each other in respect of the accounting measurements or disclosure which would result) is that between relevance and reliability?

5 Some kinds of management decisions can use routine accounting information supplied for control purposes, while other kinds of decisions may need specially prepared accounting (and other) information. Speculate on why this may be true and on what the kinds of decisions are which might benefit from non-routine accounting information.

6* Why is it that management accountants cannot do their job properly without the assistance and cooperation of managers? What kinds of assistance or cooperation do you think accountants may need from managers?

7 What, if any, difficulties or disadvantages might arise if the accounting function takes over and develops the enterprise's MIS? Is there any other organisational framework which would be likely to work better for the corporate benefit – and why, or why not?

8* How do you think financial management imperatives might differ between enterprises in the private and public sectors? To what extent are such differences a function of the differing nature of the accountabilities in these sectors as opposed to anything inherent in the discipline of accounting?

9 Assume you (or your family) comprise an 'enterprise', albeit a domestic one. You want to borrow from the bank for capital purposes, to invest in a car. The bank manager has asked you to submit a financial statement for your domestic enterprise. Prepare an accounting statement to show your revenues, costs/expenses and residual profit/loss (surplus/deficit). You may use disguised or simulated numbers. Think carefully about the amount of detail, the best layout, and the clearest (yet concise) captions to use in order to achieve clarity, to discharge your accountability honestly, and to enable the bank manager quickly to obtain a relevant and reliable understanding of your financial position.

10 'It is not possible to be an effective manager without at least a grounding in accounting because it is the language of business'. Do you agree with this statement?

11* To what extent did global financial scandals, such as Enron and Worldcom, shake investors' faith in accounting practice? What might be done to improve investor confidence in the quality of published financial statements?

12* Why is it possible, with respect to financial and management accounting, that 'different truths be in the eyes of different beholders'? Illustrate your answer with relevant examples of how different stakeholders can have different economic viewpoints based on the nature of the presented accounting data.

13* Do you think that management accounting should be more tightly regulated? Should/could management accounting standards be set? Discuss.

14* Critically discuss, using examples, the relationship between cash and profit.

15 Why are cash and cash-flow analysis so fundamental to many of the techniques adopted by management accountants?

16* Stedry (1960) has concluded that a moderately difficult budgeted standard of performance which is perceived by the budgetee as 'tight, yet attainable' motivates the best performance. Do you agree? Why/Why not?

17 'Traditionally, financial researchers have dealt almost exclusively with data that can be quantified in a predetermined way; in doing so, they have disregarded evidence on the psychological aspects of decision-making'. Discuss.

18* Of what value is 'agency theory' to our understanding of how individuals coexist in an organisation?

19 Use Figure 1.1 to map out the key control systems within an organisation with which you are familiar. Do you consider that this organisation has a sound system of internal control?

20* To what extent do you think that internal management accounting reports have to be reconcilable with external financial statements?

21 What do you believe have been the dominant influences in the design of a management accounting system with which you are familiar?

22 To what extent is it fair to say that control and accountability in the public sector are more difficult to systematise given the conflicting interests of the various interested parties?

23* To what extent do you believe that management accounting systems are overly influenced by financial reporting requirements?

24 'Accounting is too important to be left to accountants'. Do you agree with this statement? If so, why?

Corporate governance and ethics

2

Chapter preview

In this chapter we examine the main principles of corporate governance and business ethics in the light of a number of high profile business failures in recent years. The topics that we cover include:

- The nature of corporate governance and business ethics.
- The relevant economic theories.
- Approaches to achieving effective corporate governance.
- The need for an effective board of directors.
- Executive remuneration.
- Corporate governance and accounting.
- Ethics and corporate governance.

Introduction

In recent years, failures in corporate governance in the UK, USA and Australia have caused major disquiet among the key business stakeholders and shaken the confidence of the public at large in both the corporate sector and the various oversight bodies that are responsible for ensuring effective corporate governance. Scandals such as the demise of BCCI, Barings Bank and the Maxwell media empire in the UK, Enron and WorldCom in the USA and the HIH Insurance Group in Australia, hit the international media because these major business failures have pointed to a lack of leadership from company boards, indifference from institutional investors, ineffective audit procedures and a lack of regularity oversight by a variety of professional, institutional and government watchdogs.

As the Honourable Justice Owen noted in his report into the collapse of the HIH Insurance Group (HIH Royal Commission 2003, p. 23):

> I am becoming less comfortable with the phrase 'corporate governance' – not because of its content but because it has been so widely used that it may become meaningless. There is a danger it will be recited as a mantra, without regard to its real import. If that happens, the tendency will be for those who have to pay regard to it to develop a 'tick the box' mentality. The attitude might be, 'Yes, we have a state-of-the-art corporate model; yes, it is committed to writing; and, yes, the company secretary has checked that each item is in place and has included a statement to that effect in the annual report. Therefore there could be no problem in the corporation'.

> Corporate governance – as properly understood – describes the framework of rules, relationships, systems and processes within and by which authority is exercised and controlled in corporations. Understood in this way, the expression 'corporate governance' embraces not only the models or systems themselves but also the practices by which that exercise and control of authority is in fact affected.

Major corporate collapses merely reawaken concerns about corporate governance. In fact these concerns have been around since the emergence of the joint-stock company with limited liability in the latter half of the nineteenth century and have continued throughout the twentieth century. From the beginning it became clear that stringent mechanisms of corporate governance would be required, reinforced by external regulation, be this by a variety of professional bodies, specialist industry or market regulatory groups or the government itself. In an era of the global economy and multi national enterprises operating across several continents and legal and fiscal jurisdictions, the need for sound and effective corporate governance is needed all the more.

The basic tenet of this chapter is that while a fully implemented and effective system of corporate governance cannot entirely eliminate bad or corrupt business decisions, an applied approach to corporate governance can significantly reduce the incidence of poor management performance and is more likely to ensure that businesses remain profitable and meet the key objectives of their major stakeholders. It is very difficult for those charged with the financial management of an organisation to develop the required control and other reporting systems without the aid of an appropriate system of corporate governance. Such a system defines the rights, key roles and responsibilities of the directors, shareholders, management and employees as well as the system(s) by which the organisation is directed and controlled. This chapter therefore highlights some of the key requirements for effective corporate governance.

Corporate governance defined

Corporate governance is concerned with the exercise of power by corporate bodies. The OECD (1999) definition of corporate governance states that:

> Corporate governance is the system by which business corporations are directed and controlled. The corporate governance structure specifies the distribution of rights and responsibilities among different participants in the corporation, such as the

board, managers, shareholders, and other stakeholders, and spells out the rules and procedures for making decisions on corporate affairs. By doing this, it also provides the structure through which the company objectives are set, and the means of attaining those objectives and monitoring performance.

Authors such as Clarke (2004: 1) consider that the term 'corporate governance' has wider implications to economic and social well-being by:

> . . . providing the incentives and performance measures to achieve business success, and second, in providing the accountability and transparency to ensure equitable distribution of the resulting wealth.

He is supported by Deakin (2003: 584) who states that:

> Corporate governance must no longer confine its analysis to the relationship between managers, boards and shareholders. The narrowness of this focus is a major contributing factor to the present round of corporate scandals of which Enron is the most emblematic.

Enron's spectacular collapse in 2001 sent shockwaves throughout the USA. Enron was seen as a model company whose executives were closely networked with the highest levels of the American political establishment. But this so-called model company created a series of special purpose entities to conceal bad debts in order to maintain the fiction of sustained profits. It also engaged in other accounting frauds and unsavoury business practices, such as the catastrophic power outages in the State of California in order to manipulate the energy market and hype up the cost of electricity to consumers. As Clarke (2004: 19) noted, Enron demonstrates the following failures in corporate governance:

- Systematic failure to disclose to the market significant financial and accounting transactions that substantially impacted on the balance sheet of the company, its reported profitability, debt level, share price and market valuation.
- Systematic failure of transparency that would allow market regulators, investors, creditors and others to understand the financial position of the company.
- Systematic failure of the Chairman, CEO and Board of Directors to exercise their fiduciary responsibilities to investors in ensuring effective financial controls were in place in the company, and effective auditing and reporting procedures completed.
- Systemic conflict of interest on the part of the chief financial officer, and other officers of the company.
- Conflict of interest of the external auditor in receiving extensive consulting as well as auditing fees from Enron, and becoming too closely involved in the management of the company.
- Fundamental failure in the morality and ethical basis of the decision-making of the company, with systematic deception of investors, manipulation of markets, and exploitation of customers.

Senior executives of Enron betrayed their shareholders, their customers and their employees and, for a time, evaded the monitoring efforts of the Enron Board, audit regulators and the market regulators.

Economic perspective

Many of the economic theories that have underlined corporate governance systems have been seen to have contributed to self-interested management running company affairs for their direct benefit at the expense of shareholders and other stakeholders. For example, agency theory, which explains a firm as a nexus of contracts between the major stakeholders; in particular the separation of management and finance, whereby management apply invested funds for economic reward and the rewards are divided between them and their investors. Proponents of this theory, such as Alchain and Demetz (1972) and Jensen and Meckling (1976) see efficient capital markets as key to building the effective relationship between management and investors, thereby allowing for the efficient separation of decision-making and risk-bearing functions.

Since other stakeholders in this nexus of contracts receive the returns for which they have contracted – the employee their agreed wages, the supplier the payment of their invoices, the debt provider the receipt of interest and so on – the shareholder becomes the residuary beneficiary. In order for their return to be maximised it is argued that the contractual rewards to management need to be aligned to those of the shareholders so that their self-interest is also the maximisation of share price. The real concern with this view of the economic world has been that some self-interested senior executives, who have been in receipt of generous share option packages, have been more interested to manipulate short-term financial performance rather than consider improving financial performance over the longer term.

It has also been argued that this strong emphasis on shareholder value created the conditions whereby corporations such as Enron, by focusing almost solely on financial performance, forgot their legal and moral responsibilities to their other stakeholders. Clarke (2004) has the view that if agency theory has been useful in highlighting the self-interest economic inclination of agents it has, at the same time, missed out on one essential ingredient – trust. This has to be worrying given the state of our financial markets which are dominated by powerful executives and institutional investors. Proportionally, individual investors have little impact on markets, indeed the majority of investors are indirect market players as their investments are actually tied up in superannuation or other funds and managed by professional market players.

Approaches to achieving effective corporate governance

Davies (1999: 63) recognises that effective corporate governance needs to be driven by the board of directors and identifies four approaches by which this may be achieved: the Compliance Approach, the 'Best Practice' Approach, the Empowerment Approach and the Stakeholder Approach.

The Compliance Approach focuses on the regulatory requirements for corporate governance such as the Sarbanes-Oxley legislation, arising out of the demise of Enron and WorlCom, along with the other stock exchange listing requirements of the New York Stock Exchange; or the codes of practice required by the listing rules of the London Stock Exchange and the Australian Stock Exchange, both informed by the work of Sir Adrian Cadbury and other authors of Codes of Practice, as well as the findings of various Royal Commissions in some of the more notorious corporate failures.

There is no evidence that the pure compliance approach affords any real competitive advantage to those corporate bodies that institute a code of governance simply because they are required to do so. Mere compliance simply affords stakeholders with a limited assurance that basic codes of governance and business ethics are complied with.

The 'Best Practice Approach' occurs when corporate bodies positively recognise the need for better corporate governance and therefore seek to achieve 'best practice' levels of achievement. Such corporations may feel the need to appoint a corporate governance director, such as instituted by British Telecom. Some corporations have sought to be recognised for their forward approach to achieving improved corporate governance. Companies such as Shell and Astro-Zeneca have also taken this as an opportunity to spell out their commitment to areas such as the environment and health and safety. A key for organisations which follow this approach is to strategically gear 'best practice' to strategies for growing the business.

The Empowerment Approach recognises that corporate governance is concerned with the responsible use of delegated power from the board of directors. This may often be considered necessary in large multinational organisations operating across different continents with divisions subject to a variety of legal and fiscal jurisdictions. Empowerment is really only workable within a framework of shared values. Companies such as the Swedish/Swiss giant Asea Brown Boveri (ABB) or Britain's Morgan Crucible typify companies whose employees, at all levels, share a common vision and culture and who network on a global scale. Davis (1999: 177) quotes Dr Bruce Farmer from Morgan Crucible, who, when asked to whom the company belonged, replied that in Japan it worked for its employees, in Germany for society and in Anglo-Saxon countries for shareholders. Farmer viewed the company as having a tripartite stakeholdership – for customers, for shareholders and for employees. He also recognised that communities were important, especially in some of the countries in which they operated.

The fourth approach, the Stakeholder Approach, is attributed to Nigel and Arthur Kendall (1998), which is seen to comprise both quantitative and qualitative research among stakeholders covering ethical issues, congruence of goals, organisation and reporting. All results are analysed and built into a stakeholder model in order to measure the likely impact of stakeholder views on the company. Such a structured approach is believed to have advantages over the more haphazard approach practised by most companies.

While the above four classifications may provide a useful insight into possible approaches to establishing a corporate governance framework, there is no one perfect approach. What is clear though is that effective corporate governance will need to involve both formal and informal practices. Regulation alone is insufficient, companies need to recognise their moral responsibilities and positively embrace the adoption of effective corporate governance practices and, as stated above, this needs to be initiated and driven by the board of directors.

The need for effective boards of directors

As Mace (1971) notes, the business literature suggests, and the public at large thinks, that boards of directors typically perform three important roles:

- The establishment of basic objectives, corporate objectives, and broad policies on a variety of issues.

- Asking discerning questions of management on all aspects of company performance.
- Selecting the Chair of the Board (or President), the Chief Executive Officer and the Chief Financial Officer.

However, in all too many cases there is evidence that directors are either ignorant of their duties or complacent. As the Honourable Justice Owen noted in his report on the collapse of the HIH Insurance Group (HIH Royal Commission, 2003: 14–15):

> At board level, there was little, if any, analysis of the future strategy … If the HIH board discussed strategy at all, it was in the context of an annual budget meeting. But budget sessions are generally about numbers, there is no indication that the board seriously grasped the opportunity to analyse the direction in which the company was heading.

Owen recognised that, while management were best able to dedicate time to strategic thinking and were more likely to have greater industry knowledge and experience, it was:

> Nevertheless the board's responsibility to understand, test and endorse the company's strategy … As one director conceded, if he had been asked to commit in writing what the long-term strategy was he would have had difficulty doing so; the other directors struggled when asked to identify strategic directions. The chairman of the board maintained that HIH's strategy was international growth and diversification. But the formulation of strategy requires more than just a broad statement of the intended result … A board that does not understand the strategy may not appreciate the risks. And if it does not appreciate the risks it will probably not ask the right questions to ensure that the strategy is properly executed.

Mace (1971) investigated the myth and reality of the powers and responsibilities of company boards of directors in the 1960s and 1970s. He outlined how CEOs in the USA were able to determine board membership, to decide what boards could and could not do, controlled the information and professional advice the board received and determined the salary packages of senior executives, including themselves. He described board membership as more of an accolade than an obligation, describing directors as ornaments on a corporate Christmas tree. Directors were chosen more for whom they knew rather than what they knew, with many boards becoming a sort of old boys' club.

Lorsch and MacIver (1989) have also reviewed the function of boards in the USA in the 1980s and 1990s, noting phases such as in the 1980s when the focus of the boardroom receded, supplanted by the activities of financial markets as the rate of mergers, takeovers and acquisitions increased and the return in the 1990s to greater pressure for more active and independent boards in the wake of a series of major corporate collapses.

So what should the duties of boards of directors be? The American Law Institute (1983, 1984) has produced a useful list of duties:

1 Elect, review the performance of, and if necessary, dismiss the principal senior executives of the company.
2 Oversight of the company's business activities with a view to evaluation on an ongoing basis, ensuring that resources are being managed in a manner consistent with increasing shareholder wealth while also, within the law and within ethical considerations, directing a fair return to other stakeholders and, as possible, allocating resources to public welfare and humanitarian purposes.

3 Review and approve corporate plans and actions that the board and senior executives consider major and changes in accounting principles that the board and senior executives consider material.

4 Perform such other functions as prescribed by law, or ascribed to the board under the company's memorandum and articles of association.

5 Make recommendations to shareholders.

6 Initiate and adopt major corporate plans, commitments and actions, and material changes in accounting principles and practices; and review the actions of any committee, officer, or other employee.

7 Act as to all matters not requiring stockholder approval.

Directors should also be suitably qualified and of the highest integrity. As Colley *et al.* (2003: 55) note:

> The strength of any board correlates with the aggregate abilities of the directors and with their individual capacity for independent action. The latter is difficult to quantify, whereas the former is generally apparent, based on the nominees' career experience and specific skills. The more diverse the background and skill set of nominees, the greater is the likelihood of effective aggregate ability.

Reviews into effective corporate governance invariably recognise the key role that non-executive directors can play. Their role is to act as fully participating members of the board in exercising its various duties and to bring in wider experience and new ideas to its discussions, to monitor and challenge the performance of executive directors and management, and to ensure that there are adequate checks and balances in place in order to protect the company's best interests. As Davies (1999, p. 73) states:

> Non-executive directors have a duty to be independent, challenging and watchful of the personal agendas of their executive directors – they need to generate creative tension, not harmony, in board deliberations.

In the case of the HIH Insurance Group, three of its non-executive directors were former HIH external auditors, while their firm remained as the company's auditors, and a fourth was lawyer who personally provided consulting services to HIH and was a consultant to a law firm engaged by HIH. In noting the need for non-executive directors to be independent, it should be appreciated that some non-executive directors may be appointees of major shareholders and as such they might be in conflict of their legal duty to act in the best interests of all shareholders. This conflict of interest can be further exacerbated by the practice of many companies of briefing their major (institutional) shareholders more frequently than required by the normal reporting dates. It is standard practice that non-executive directors with special interests normally declare them and abstain from voting on issues where those interests may conflict with broader concerns.

Executive remuneration

The topic of executive remuneration, especially that for the Chief Executive Officer (CEO) is hardly ever out of the news. There is near continual discussion on the basis of performance rewards, typically in the form of cash bonuses, shares and share options, and on the large exit payments when senior executives depart their companies. Many of the corporate scandals in recent times have involved CEOs and other senior executives who were in receipt of enormous salary packages and who, all too often, receive large severance payouts despite their incompetence or deceit. In nearly all such instances there have been severe shortcomings in the corporate governance structures in these companies.

At the time of writing, Robert Nardelli's US$ 219 million exit package from Home Depot, America's second-largest retailer, is but the most recent in a line of controversial exit payout settlements. This payout came after only five years with Home Depot, during which Nardelli earned over US$ 63 million. Home Depot's share price was down 8 per cent over this period and sales were down 5 per cent in his final year. During his five year reign Nardelli replaced 98 percent of the senior, experienced, management team, with more than half coming from his previous firm, General Electric. Such huge payments have shocked shareholders, employees and the public at large. Over half of the CEOs in the largest 100 companies in the US have contracts that include large severance clauses. Executives argue that they need such conditions because of the risks involved and it is certainly true that senior executive turnover is at an all-time high. Consultancy Booz-Allen Hamilton noted that roughly a third of departing CEOs in 2005 were forced out of their positions (*Sydney Morning Herald*, January 13, 2007). Critics such as Hodgson 2004, p. 1) note that when:

> The market is up, and the CEO is rewarded with a huge compensation package. The market is down and the CEO is rewarded with a huge compensation package. There's plenty wrong with this picture, not the least of which is the lack of any link between pay and performance, and the absence of any long-term performance measures.

Hodgson is critical that performance measures, particularly in the finance sector, are too simplistic, with indicators such as the return on equity measure being used when this is all too easy to achieve in a rising stock market, or a bull market. Why are such measures not made relative to that of other competitors in the market? It is often stated that up to 80 per cent of any rise or fall in a company's stock price is due to the behaviour of the market rather than the performance of the company, so why is superior performance not required for such generous bonuses? All too often it would appear that the terms of performance reward for senior executives is too loosely defined and as such that there is in fact an incentive to maximise short-term performance at the expense of longer-term performance.

Both annual and long-term incentives schemes need to be properly structured and disclosed and based on real measure of longer-term value creation and not on short-term operational measures, as would appear to be the norm. The latter position must surely point to some weaknesses in the governance framework of such companies. Properly structured, performance reward should be based on a formula that takes into account risk vs. reward vs. time. Performance rewards should be determined at arms-length, which could include some external assistance, and certainly not left to senior executives to tailor their own packages, or to hire their own 'tame' consultant or structure a compensation committee with members of similarly well-rewarded executives, who fear their own packages will suffer when it comes to review time if they don't vote for large increases.

An exemplar of responsible corporate governance is Berkshire Hathaway, whose investment guru CEO Warren Buffett collects an annual salary of US$ 100,000 per year, with no stock options and no bonuses. He also has most of his own personal wealth tied up in the company, which means that he has every incentive to deliver strong results to his fellow shareholders. Buffet (Knowledge@Wharton, 2003) has urged shareholders to resist excessive payments to senior executives. This is sound advice and the only hope for halting such excesses is for shareholders to become more assertive in determining the rewards of senior executives. And there are signs of this happening. Apple Computer's management agreed to a shareholder resolution to count stock options as expenses at the time they are granted, and Alcoa shareholders voted to cap executive severance packages at 2.99 times salary. There are other signs that investors coming together can move for changes and greater accountability – shareholder activism.

For example, the US based Members of the Council of Institutional Investors, an organisation representing more than 130 pension funds with total assets of around US$ 2 trillion, are seeking a change in corporate governance rules that would allow share-holders to nominate directors. Bebchuk (2004), a Harvard Professor and noted critic of American executive remuneration, said that flawed compensation arrangements have been widespread, persistent and systematic, and that they have stemmed from defects in the underlying governance structures of companies that have enabled execu-tive directors to exert far too considerable influence over their boards. Criticism in the US would appear to be equally warranted in the United Kingdom and Australia.

If a company feels it has to have a pay-by-performance scheme and wants one with positive motivational benefits, then the following rules should be applied (adapted from Murray *et al.*, 2006: 84–86):

- Establish that the behaviours being rewarded are clearly linked to overall corporate strategy.
- Ensure that people can see a connection between their own individual work and performance at the team and organisational levels.
- Make sure that incentives are based on objective performance information.
- Do not only use pay; use praise, promotion and other forms of recognition.
- Allow staff a say in what form of performance pay takes, and how it is to be implemented.
- Establish open and transparent policies for the resolution of conflict over such issues as bonuses and termination payments.
- Establish performance pay criteria with the assistance of independent advisors, not nominated by senior executives alone.
- Align performance to teamwork and cooperation wherever possible.
- Establish that performance rewards are set at a sufficient (or meaningful level) so that executives are encouraged to achieve long-term value-added benefits for their shareholders and other key stakeholders.

Ethics and corporate governance

In a very real sense, good corporate governance ought to be seen as promoting an all round ethical climate in business. As Francis (2000: 50) states:

> Ethics may be regarded as knowing what is right, doing what is right, feeling what is right; morals and ethics share these concerns. The term ethics and morals are

sometimes used interchangeably ... More commonly, 'morals' refers to the standards held by the community. 'Ethics', on the other hand, concerns explicit codes of conduct as well as value systems.

Ethical codes in business should be designed to inform all levels of employee in the organisation how to behave in particular situations. Ethics is essentially about human values, but as not all values are shared we are compelled to consider the issues we have in common, and those on which we divide. What may be self-evident in one culture may be ethically repugnant in another. For example, for those working in multinational companies there are often cross-cultural differences of opinion as to what is the difference between a bribe and a gift. The development of ethical codes of practice affords an opportunity to discuss and resolve these human values in a non-threatening frame of reference and to establish, as far as possible, a series of values by which an organisation's employees abide.

In general, codes should be developed and disseminated to all staff, in an open, participative environment. Codes should be sensitive to allow for mitigating circumstances. Referring back to our previous example, it may be policy to refuse all gifts but an exception might be that it could be deemed impolite to refuse a gift when in certain overseas countries. There may, though, also be a policy that all such gifts are to be surrendered once back in the home country. If gifts were expected to be presented when overseas then this might be permitted when the value of the gift was deemed to be within a certain value, set at a level where the gift could only be seen as a token of appreciation or friendship and not of a value that could be thought of being a bribe. This also illustrates that codes need to relate to the social context in which they are to operate. As De George (2006: 207) notes:

> A corporate code can not only guide the actions of employees on legal matters and conflicts of interests, but it can also enable workers and managers to evaluate in moral terms the firm's ends, practices, and actions, to be sure the firm measures up to the code. If management adheres to the code, the code can help develop a moral corporate ethos.

In 1995 the International Federation of Accountants (IFAC) sponsored an empirical study of the ethical codes used in companies. The study reported upon a number of codes developed by a cross-section of companies in a number of countries and provides a useful source of data in support of why ethical codes are used as practical tools of management, and proposes situations when their use might vary. Readers can access a copy of this report – *Codifying Power and Control: Ethical Codes in Action* – by visiting the IFAC web site at www.ifac.org. The Institute of Business Ethics also has a useful website, www.ibe.org.uk, to assist companies with developing a code of business ethics.

When an employee believes or suspects that actions by others within the firm may cause harm, in terms of fraud or other activities that can potentially harm the interests of shareholders, other employees, customers, or the public at large, then such codes should provide, indeed encourage, for these matters to be reported in such a way as they are quickly and fairly addressed. Those who report such matters need to be assured that their actions are seen as a matter of company loyalty and not a process whereby their position or standing is in any was damaged. Such provisions, if effectively implemented, should avoid the phenomenon known as *whistle blowing* – named after the British Bobby's (policeman's) whistle.

All too often companies may not have an appropriate code of business ethics, or if they do, they fail to adhere to its principles in practice. In such circumstances an employee may feel a personal moral obligation to *blow the whistle* either internally or externally. Internally implies that there are no formal channels for such matters to be addressed, but that such reporting will hopefully lead to corrective action that saves the good name of the company. External whistle blowing, to a government agency, ombudsman, professional body or the media, may be deemed necessary because the internal cause of action was ignored and the matter is something that the whistle blower believes is serious and damaging.

While whistle blowing has assisted in the exposure of the corruption within a number of companies, including such well documented case histories as Enron and WorldCom, all too often such actions have led to the whistle blower having their personal career damaged and being ostracized by their colleagues. Increasingly governments are seeking to establish regulations that protect the interests of the whistle blower.

Corporate governance and accounting

Accounting is often described as the language of business, the process by which a company's financial performance is reported both internally and externally to those who have either a right or interest in receiving such information. In larger companies it is usually the Chief Financial Officer (CFO) who is responsible for approving the basis on which the internal (management) accounts are based and the basis by which the external financial statements are prepared that are either reported in the company's annual report or in the various statutory reports to stock exchanges and government agencies, including the various taxation authorities.

There are no accounting regulations, such as standards, that govern the preparation of management accounting reports. Although there are accounting standards, stock exchange listing requirements and a variety of other regulations surrounding the preparation of external financial reports, such standards and requirements do allow for a high degree of interpretation and discretion as to how such information is presented. These requirements are designed, in broad terms, to require senior management to represent the company's financial position as accurately as possible. Management, on the other hand, have the natural tendency to want to present the company's position to its shareholders and the public at large as favourably as possible. This approach is normally as a result of loyalty or obligation to the company but can also be motivated by personal gain if their reward structures are linked to external financial performance indicators. There is therefore often a tension between reporting accurately and favourably.

This tension between reporting accurately and favourably can be misplaced and can lead, if the bias is more towards reporting favourably at the expense of accurately, to misrepresentation which, once exposed, will lead to penalties or damage for the company. For employees involved in the preparation of financial statements there may be occasions when they have concerns about the basis upon which such statements are prepared and whether the intent is to, as the saying goes, present the best picture or to fraudulently mislead. If they believe that such presentation is misleading and, possibly, fraudulent, then they have to decide whether they disregard the situation to follow orders or whether they feel they have a moral obligation to report such matters.

As discussed in the previous section, it would be hoped that in normal circumstances the company had in place a process whereby such concerns could be addressed.

Typically the governance procedures would make this a responsibility of the Audit Committee. If governance procedures are not satisfactorily in place then, again as stated above, this has led to instances of whistle blowing. The primary role of the Audit Committee is to ensure that the balance between presenting information accurately and favourably is, to an objective observer, fair and reasonable. The company, on the recommendation of the Audit Committee, will engage an external audit firm to work with its internal audit team, to independently certify or audit that the company's financial statements and accounting processes conform with generally accepted accounting principles in order to provide confidence to the shareholders and other stakeholders that the information they receive can be relied upon.

This external audit firm is paid by the company but serves a broader societal interest. These firms operate to their own set of ethical standards, supported by the ethical codes of the professional bodies to which their audit staff belong. In the majority of cases audit firms have been held to be independent and not subject to undue influence or pressure from the companies that have appointed them. Differences of opinion are raised and usually satisfactorily resolved. If such resolutions are not possible then the external auditor has a duty to present a qualified audit report, making clear what the matters of concern are. Occasionally audit firms have been more mindful of who writes their cheque than their professional and moral responsibility.

The former international audit firm Andersens presents as a case in point. In both the case of Enron and HIH the firm had too cosy a relationship with their clients that led to concerns, such as maximising consulting fees at the expense of providing critical audit reports (Enron), or outright failures of basic risk management, such as the failure to meet regularly with the consultant actuaries of HIH. Former audit partners of Andersen held senior non-executive positions with both companies. The professionalism of Andersens was clearly compromised and led to the firm's ultimate collapse.

Interestingly, following the demise of Enron, Section 302 of the US Sarbanes-Oxley Act requires both the Chief Executive Officer and the Chief Financial Officer to certify the fairness and accuracy of financial statements and to certify that the board of directors has processes in place to spot problems; that is a direct reference to the increasing importance of internal audit. This section imposes penalties of US$1 million and up to 10 years in prison for 'knowing' about violations, and US$5 million and 20 years for 'wilful' violations and allows civil suits for fraud. It is not a defence for a CEO to plead ignorance of the state of the financial accounts. Section 406 of the same Act requires a company to disclose whether it has a code of ethics for its senior finance officials.

Professional accountants, whether employed in an internal or external capacity, face a numbers of pressures, and the challenge for them is whether the rules by which they practice are sufficient to guide their ethical behaviour. Duska and Duska (2003) and De George (2006) provide useful discussions on this issue from both a UK and USA perspective. Professional accounting bodies also need to be more mindful of public interest considerations and review their own ethical codes of practice. These bodies have been well aware for example, that former auditors often take up senior non-executive appointments with former clients. Why have these bodies not taken the lead and stated that either such practice is unacceptable or introduced rules that state such appointments are not acceptable within, say, five years of ceasing a client relationship. Governments should perhaps ask themselves why professional bodies are not playing a more open and positive role in such matters.

Conclusion

In the last few years, shareholders, the public at large and regulatory authorities in a number of countries, have been seriously misled about accounting irregularities and financial disclosure problems. Although it is easy for those in business to blame such problems on the irresponsibility and greed of the few, the scale of recent business collapses has brought home the need for all companies to take their corporate governance responsibilities seriously.

Processes and structures can only really work if all board members, executive and non-executive members, actively embrace their company's corporate governance processes. Underpinning the corporate governance structures is also the need to establish a code of ethics that establishes and articulates the corporate values, responsibilities and obligations that should be adhered to by all employees. While not explicitly covered in this chapter, it ought to be recognised that many of the duties and issues of governance are equally applicable for not-for-profit organisations, be they structured as corporations, foundations, charitable trusts or associations. There are, though, some subtle differences.

For example, do such organisations have governing boards or advisory boards, both principally relying on the advice of full-time specialist staff? Also, such board members are rarely remunerated, so do they see themselves as having the same statutory and moral responsibilities of director in the for-profit sector? Colley *et al.* (2003: chapter 12) provides a useful discussion on these issues.

Chapter review

Anyone interested in financial management needs to understand that sound and effective accounting practices are more likely to be reliable and accurate when organisations have established effective corporate governance practices. Managers need to understand the benefits that derive from having sound corporate governance practices and be aware of the potential pitfalls that may result from either not having such a structure in place or for paying lip service to the external pressures to put such systems in place without really being committed to them. Managers need to understand their legal, professional and moral responsibilities to their shareholders, their employees, government and the other stakeholders, including the public at large.

Further reading

There are several good text books that deal with corporate governance and ethics. A number of these have been cited in this chapter and full details can be found in the references section of this text. In addition, this is a field of study where students should access the relevant websites of specialist interest groups, professional bodies and government agencies. A useful cross-section of such sites include:

- www.ethics.ubc.ca/, the Centre for Applied Ethics at the University of British Columbia.

- www.managementhelp.org/ethics/ethxgde.htm, to locate a number of useful articles and reports.
- www.ecgi.org/, the website of the European Corporate Governance Institute.
- rru.worldbank.org/Themes/CorporateGovernance/, the World Bank's site for the promotion of governance standards.
- www.corpgov.net, a useful site established in since 1995 to promote improved corporate governance.

Questions and exercises

1* What are the basic responsibilities of the board of directors in the governance of a company?

2* To what degree should government directly intervene in defining and regulating the governance responsibilities of companies? Is this something that can confidently be left to self-regulation?

3* Critically review the findings of the HIH Insurance Royal Commission. What lessons can be learnt?

4 Agency theory is often used as a means of explaining how effective relationships between management and investors can be developed. However, there are those who believe that agency theory actually leads to managers acting in their own self-interest at the expense of shareholders and other stakeholders. Explain what you understand by the term 'agency theory' and discuss whether you agree or disagree with the proposition that agency theory can lead to managers acting in their own self-interest.

5 How should companies determine the proper level and composition of senior executive salary packages, including appropriate severance agreements?

6 'Business ethics can help people approach moral problems in business more systematically and with better tools than they might otherwise use. It can help them to see issues they might typically ignore. It can also impel them to make changes they might otherwise not be moved to make'. Do you agree with that statement? Why or why not?

7 Can ethical codes of practice for multinational businesses be developed and universally applied, or do they need to be contextualised to individual country and societal interests?

8* What do you understand by the term whistle blowing? In what circumstances is whistle blowing morally justifiable?

9 What are the principal roles and responsibilities of a company's Chief Financial Officer?

10   What are the principlal roles and functions of a company's Audit Committee?

11*   Use the internet to find suitable exemplars of companies that have developed and promote their corporate governance structures and their code of business ethics. In choosing your examples, critically evaluate the basis on which you have made your selection.

12*   In what ways are the duties and responsibilities of board members of not-for-profit organisations similar to those of for-profit companies? In what ways are they dissimilar?

Basis of accounting records

3

Chapter preview

This chapter is a transitional one, serving as an introduction to a number of the issues addressed in Part 2 of the book. The second section concentrates on internal accounting processes – accounting for managers, usually termed **management accounting**.

In this chapter, we introduce a number of accounting concepts which underpin the basic financial record-keeping systems of organisations. These underpinnings are essential if the basic accounting records of an organisation are to be fit for purpose – whether that purpose be management accounting or financial reporting.

The chapter discusses the interface between accounting and the functions of management. It summarises the major differences between financial and management accounting, and discusses how management accounting can meet the information needs of management and recognises the behavioural foundations of management accounting.

Financial and management accounting

Both financial and management accounting deal with the reporting of economic events. Each requires the quantification of the outcomes of economic activity, and each is concerned with revenues and expenses, assets, liabilities and cash flows. The major differences between these two forms of accounting stem from the fact that they are intended for different audiences. Financial accounting is concerned with the provision of information to individuals and organisations external to the enterprise. Its reports deal, in summary form, with the organisation as a whole. In financial accounting, costs are usually classified by the *object* or *subject* of the expense (salaries, materials, etc.), or perhaps by the *function* of the expense (cost of goods sold, administrative expenses, etc.)

Management accounting, on the other hand, tends to use more sophisticated cost classifications, including ones based on the *behaviour* of costs (that is, differentiating between costs that change when activity levels vary and ones that do not change regardless of activity levels); the *controllability* of costs (differentiating between the managerial responsibilities for costs); and the *variability* of costs depending on the decisions that managers take. Management accounting can (should) provide reports which are specifically designed for a particular user or a particular decision.

Financial accounting statements tend to concentrate almost exclusively on the results of past decisions, although their preparation does, inevitably, involve management having to make judgements about the future. Management accounting concentrates on what is likely to happen in the future, although this analysis of the future has, in large part, to be based on the past. Managerial accounting is intended to assist managers to make decisions, of whatever sort. Unfortunately, the information that managers ideally want for these decisions, i.e. information about the future, is not available. The best that accountants can do is to provide appropriate information about the past. This can be conflated with information about environmental changes to enable predictions of the future to be made. As Dominiak and Louderback (1988, p. 10) state:

> Managerial accounting has no restrictions such as the generally accepted accounting principles that govern financial accounting. For managerial purposes, relevance is the important concern, and the managerial accountant responds to specific information requirements.

Management accounting exists to serve managers in the differing functional areas of enterprises. They need financial information for planning and control purposes, including decision making and performance evaluation. Management accounting obviously applies to business firms seeking to maximise profit and achieve other economic goals. It applies equally to public-sector bodies (executive agencies, hospitals and the like) and other not-for-profit organisations (such as charities and churches). All these groups need to use their resources economically, efficiently and, above all, effectively.

Whether we are considering meeting the information needs of managers, or those of external users of financial statements, every organisation needs to have sound and effective mechanisms for the recording of its transactions.

The recording of transactions and other economic events

The principles underpinning the **fundamental accounting identity**, and its extensions, provide the conceptual basis for both internal and external accounting reports. This requires an understanding of terms such as asset, liability, equity, income and expenses. Our focus is on the core requirements for the maintenance of an effective system of accounting records. We discuss the distinction between the cash and accruals basis of accounting and the fundamental accounting concepts upon which financial reports (both internal and external) are based.

If accounting is to be of any value whatsoever it must be based on the proper and accurate recording of transactions. Once this basis is established then it can be built on to provide information for both internal and external users. The perspective we adopt in our discussion is that of ensuring the satisfactory recording of the economic activities of an enterprise. Before we can look at the principles underpinning systems of accounting records, we first have to acknowledge two important questions which accounting must address, both of which are implicit in the definitions of accounting discussed in the first chapter of this book. The two questions that must be answered before we can proceed any further are:

1 What should be the focus of accounting records and, by implication, any accounting information (e.g. reports) subsequently based on these records? What is the span (ownership) of activities that the records should cover? The standard accounting response to these questions is that the records should relate to the activities of what is called an **accounting entity**. Such an entity is any unity of economic activity for which it would be helpful to record (or be legally required to record), and subsequently report information for the benefit of interested parties. The range of interested parties is potentially very large (something we discussed in the first chapter with regard to what are commonly referred to as 'stakeholders'). In addition, the different accounting entities about which stakeholders might want information are enormously diverse, ranging from individuals to business units within large multinational corporations, and to the totality of such corporations. There is an equivalent diversity in legal recording and reporting requirements across different countries, although these tend not to cover management accounting reports. There is also a diversity of possible accounting entities across countries, as demonstrated in Table 3.1.

   Accounting makes a major presumption about this diversity of accounting entities – that their activities are separate (should be separable) from those of their owners, and that their accounting records need to reflect this separability. We shall see how significant the implications of this presumption are later in this chapter, when we look at the concept of **ownership interest** in accounting entities For the present, it is sufficient to recognise its existence.

2 What things should be recorded in the accounting records of an accounting entity? The obvious (and glib) answer is 'whatever the users of the information (reports) extracted from such accounting records might want to know'. However, the range of possible such information requirements is vast, something

Table 3.1	Accounting entities
Business entities	**Non-business entities**
Sole trader	Charity
Partnership	Clubs and other associations
Unlimited liability company	Local authorities
Limited liability company	Health authorities
Public limited liability company	Statutory agencies
Group of companies	Educational institutions
Division or other responsibility centre of a company or group of companies	

again reflected on in the first chapter of this book. We need a starting point for our analysis, and conventional wisdom is that most stakeholders are interested (for one reason or another) in those aspects of an accounting entity which are commonly referred to as the **elements of accounts**.

In the following section we adopt the standpoint of the International Accounting Standards Board (IASB) regarding these elements. Other, broadly similar, views to those of the IASB (at least on the surface), are provided by (for example):

- In the UK contest by the Accounting Standards Board (ASB).
- In a USA context, the Financial Accounting Standards Board's (FASB) *Statement of Financial Accounting Concepts No. 6* (FASB 1985).
- In a Canadian context, the Canadian Institute of Chartered Accountants' (CICA) *Handbook Section 1000* (CICA 1988).
- In an Australian context, the Australian Accounting Standards Board's (AASB) *Statement of Accounting Concepts* (AASB 1990).
- In a New Zealand context, the Institute of Chartered Accountants of New Zealand's (ICANZ) *Statement of Concepts for General Purpose Financial Reporting* (ICANZ 1991).

Some of the details of (and rationale(s) for) the differences between these various views are commented on in later chapters. However, this book is intended to support managers in their understanding of accounting's potential impact on, and contribution to, the effectiveness of their managerial efforts. As such, it is not the place for a detailed examination of the minutiae of the differences between different national accounting systems. Instead its focus is on the 'common core' of such systems, albeit with a clear acknowledgement that (at the end of the day) these differing 'minutiae' can have major impacts on the preparation of accounting reports, both internal and external. Readers interested in a more detailed explanation of the differences between these various standpoints are directed to texts such as: Davies, Paterson and Wilson (1999), Alexander and Britton (2004) and Whittred, Zimmer and Taylor (2000).

The core accounting elements are:

1 Those things an entity owns or controls at a point in time and which have a value to the entity, deriving from this ownership or control. Conventionally such things are called **assets**. A more formal definition of an asset is provided by the IASB:

a resource controlled by the entity as a result of past events and from which future economic are expected to flow to the entity;

2 What an entity owes to third parties (i.e. parties other than the beneficial owners of the entity) at a point in time, and the amounts that are owed. Conventionally, these are called **liabilities**. A more formal definition of a liability is again provided by the IASB:

a present obligation of the entity arising from past events, the settlement of which is expected to result in an outflow from the entity of resources embodying economic benefits;

3 What is left over for the beneficial owners of an entity's assets at a given point in time, after all its liabilities have been provided for. Conventionally, this is called **ownership interest** or **equity**. Again a more formal definition is provided by the IASB:

the residual interest in the assets of the entity after deducting all its liabilities.

4 What benefits the entity has generated for its owners from its economic activities over a given period in time (financial period). Conventionally, these benefits are often referred to as **income** or **revenues**, commonly thought of as arising from trading transactions. However, it is possible that an entity will generate benefits for its owners other than via trading transactions, e.g. from the continuing ownership of assets which are increasing in value. Accordingly, the IASB adopts a more general standpoint, that of **gains**.

Increases in economic benefits during the accounting period in the form of inflows or enhancements of assets or decreases of liabilities that result in increases in equity, other than those relating to contributions from equity participants. In this context, 'contributions' arise when equity participants invest new funds into the company.

5 What an entity has had to give up (sacrifice) in order to generate its income (revenues) during a given period of time. Conventionally these are usually referred to as **costs** or **expenses**. However, costs and expenses are often thought of in terms of trading transactions and it is possible that an entity will incur sacrifices other than via trading transactions:

Expenses: These are the obverse of income and represent decreases in economic benefits.

Transfers to owners in their capacity as owners are known as **distributions to owners**.

The foregoing may seem to rely heavily on 'formal' definitions of the elements of accounts. However, we must recognise that it is all too easy for managers to become 'bamboozled' by accounting 'jargon' and therefore it is important to clarify the meaning of these core accounting concepts at the outset. We must also recognise that, while we have defined the above core 'elements' of accounting information, we have not (as yet) commented on how these elements should be recognised or measured in accounting systems. These are important issues we will return to, both in this and following chapters.

Recognition of elements of financial statements

So far in this chapter we have described the qualitative characteristics of financial statements and the principal elements of such statements. We now need to describe the principles on which these elements are incorporated in financial statements. In this context, recognition means that an element should be recorded in the primary financial statements (i.e. Balance sheets, Income statements and Cash flow statements). According to the IASB, an item should be recognised for inclusion in the primary financial statements if:

(a) it is probable that any future economic benefit associated with the item will flow to or from the entity; and

(b) the item has a cost or value that can be measured with reliability.

In applying these principles, a reporting entity will need to use the materiality concept discussed earlier. In addition, it will have to have regard to the probability/reliability concepts referred to in the above recognition requirements. These are both in keeping with the general climate of uncertainty with which all companies operate and recognise that the preparation of financial statements inevitably requires the exercise of 'judgement' by those involved in the process, e.g. company directors and independent auditors. The IASB requires that an entity use the **accruals basis** for the preparation of its financial statements rather than the **cash basis**.

Bookkeeping

A key presumption of accounting reports is that at any point in time the assets of an entity are exactly equal in value to the claims against those assets. It is this presumption which ensures that balance sheets do in fact balance and which ultimately provides the linkage between balance sheets and profit and loss accounts. It is commonly expressed in the form of an equation, which is often referred to as the **fundamental accounting identity**. This equation, in its most basic form is:

$$\text{Assets} = \text{Claims (against the assets)} \tag{3.1}$$

Associated with this key presumption is another, no less important, to which we have already referred. This is that an accounting entity has an existence distinct from that of its beneficial owner(s). We will make use of this presumption in what follows regarding the maintenance of accounting records. We will also revisit it in a different guise in Chapter 14, when we review some of the regulatory requirements of external financial reporting and see how these vary between entities, depending on their precise legal status and the countries in which they operate.

As we have already seen, an asset is something an entity controls (owns) and which has a value. This value derives from the future economic benefits, such as cash inflows, which the enterprise is expected to enjoy because of its ownership of the asset. The range of assets owned by entities is wide, but typically will include items such as cash in hand and at bank, debtors, stocks and work-in-process, plant and machinery, land and buildings, investments, etc. What should be recognised as assets for the purposes of financial reporting and how such assets should be valued are, and have been for some time, major areas of debate in accounting. For the present it is sufficient for us to regard assets as things controlled by an entity which confer economic benefits on it and to which accounting assigns a monetary amount (value).

However, an entity could not have acquired any assets unless it was first provided with the funds to do so. Logically, the providers of such funds must have some claims against the entity, and by implication against its assets, for the repayment of the funds they provided. The detailed terms for such repayment will form part of the contract(s) between the entity and the providers of the funds (in some cases these terms will be the subject of statutory regulation). Thus, given the structure of entities, and the idea of their separate personality, the assets owned by the entity *must by definition* be exactly matched by the claims of the different providers of funds against those assets. This is the basis of the fundamental accounting identity stated in equation (3.1). Broadly, there are two different categories of such claims:

(a) *Liability claims*: the claims of **creditors** for goods, services or money supplied, or lent, to the enterprise, and;

(b) *Ownership claims*: the claims of the **owners** of the enterprise to the residual balance of the assets after all liability claims have been provided for, often referred to as equity claims.

Thus, equation (3.1) can be rewritten as:

$$\text{Assets} = \text{Liability claims} + \text{Equity claims} \qquad \textbf{(3.2)}$$

or, more usually, as:

$$\text{Assets} = \text{Liabilities} + \text{Equity} \qquad \textbf{(3.3)}$$

However, to emphasise the fact that equity is a residual item, left over after all liabilities have been provided for, equation (3.3) is more usually written as:

$$\text{Assets} - \text{Liabilities} = \text{Equity} \qquad \textbf{(3.4)}$$

Individuals, or corporate organisations having liability claims against an entity, are normally referred to as creditors. As is the case with assets, entities can have a wide range of different liabilities, but common examples include: trade creditors, bank loans and overdrafts, other loans, taxation payable, etc. The general accounting principle regarding the inclusion of liabilities in accounting reports is that they should be stated at the amount that will have to be paid to settle them in full, regardless of when payment is actually due, and it is on this basis that they should be incorporated into the accounting records.

Equity is normally regarded as having three components. These are:

(a) The amount of any funds provided by the owner(s) to the entity to fund its activities. In the terminology of the IASB, these are contributions. The accounting representation of these contributions (in the accounting records and any resultant accounting reports) will vary, depending on the nature of the entity in question and the nature of the contribution. In the case of limited liability companies, these contributions will normally take the form of payments to the company from its shareholders in exchange for the purchase of their shares.

(b) The amount of any accumulated surpluses/deficits (profits/losses) resulting from the entity's trading and related activities which have not yet been distributed to its owners.

(c) The amount of any other gains that have arisen since the foundation of the entity and not been distributed to its owners. Such gains might, for example, include surpluses arising on the revaluation of assets to reflect current market values.

The main reason for recording these three components separately, and showing them separately in accounting reports, is derived from the legal regulation of the affairs of limited liability companies. The Companies Acts in the UK and Australia, and similar regulations in other countries, lay down detailed and stringent requirements relating to equity. Equation 3.4 is the basis of one of the primary financial statements of accounting entities, the **balance sheet** or the **statement of financial position**. A balance sheet summarises an entity's assets, liabilities and equity at a point in time. The structure and content of balance sheets is examined in more detail in Chapter 13. For the present it is sufficient to note that a balance sheet is an amplification of the fundamental accounting identity for a given entity at a given point in time. It provides those who read it (and hopefully understand it) with useful information to help them assess their links with the enterprise.

As stated above, equation (3.4) represents a static position; assets, liabilities and equity at a point in time. It can be developed to cover a period of time by focusing on the changes in its components over such a period. Thus, over a particular period in time, a financial year for example:

$$\Delta\,(\text{Equity}) = \Delta(\text{Assets}) - \Delta(\text{Liabilities}) \tag{3.5}$$

Conventionally the symbol Δ is used to indicate a change in the amount of a quantity. Thus, in equation (3.5), Δ (Equity) represents the change in equity over a period in time.

Given the fact that equity is the residual ownership interest, it can be seen that there are three types of events/transactions an enterprise might engage in which could lead to a change in equity during an accounting period.

(a) *Financing transactions*: these are transactions via which owners either invest new equity capital/funds into the accounting entity (i.e. contributions), or withdraw/have returned to them part of their existing equity (i.e. distributions); e.g. by dividend payments out of surpluses (profits).

(b) *Trading transactions*: these are transactions in which the entity buys and sells goods or services (generating revenues and incurring costs), and which result in it making either surpluses (profits) or deficits (losses).

(c) *Revaluations*: from time to time the current value of the assets of an entity will vary significantly from the value at which they are currently shown in the entity's accounting records (and any resultant accounting reports). In these circumstances the entity may, subject to some legal restrictions, restate the assets to their current values (recording gains or losses as appropriate). This will automatically lead to corresponding increase(s)/decrease(s) in the residual equity.

If we assume that an enterprise has had no financing transactions or revaluations during a given financial period then any change in equity during that period must result from its trading transactions. In these circumstances, equation (3.5) can be rewritten as follows:

$$\Delta(\text{Equity}) = \text{Profit/(Loss)} = \Delta(\text{Assets}) - \Delta(\text{Liabilities}) \tag{3.6}$$

This gives us a link between a position statement, the **balance sheet**, and a flow statement which summarises the changes in equity arising from trading transactions during a given financial period. This flow statement is the **income** (or **profit and loss account** or the **statement of financial performance**). The IASB also requires that companies publish two additional statements to the income statement: a **statement of changes in equity**, and a **statement of total recognised gains and losses**. The IASB also requires that reporting entities also publish a **cash flow statement**.

Conventional wisdom tells us that:

$$\text{Profit/(Loss)} = \text{Income} - \text{Expenses} \tag{3.7}$$

The income of an entity comprises the revenues that it is entitled to receive from third parties as a result of its trading transactions. Examples of income include the revenues derived from the sale of goods or services, rents, royalties and other entitlements. The key point is that as a result of the generation of income, the entity, and therefore ultimately its owners/shareholders, are better off. On the other hand, expenses (costs) represent a diminution in the wealth of the entity (and therefore ultimately its owners/shareholders). Normally this diminution will have been accepted in order to obtain resources (goods, labour, knowledge, etc.) which enable the entity to generate future income greater than the amount of the expense incurred to obtain the resources in question.

The relationships between an entity's income and expenses are the essence of an income statement which summarises and analyses the trading transactions of an entity; grouping like items together so as to provide its users with information about the outcomes of the trading transactions during a particular financial period.

However, as indicated above, a change in equity may be the result of the revaluation of assets or liabilities as well as the outcome of trading transactions. In both cases, the end result is that the entity has generated gains or losses resulting in increases or decreases in equity. We can reflect this in our analysis by combining equation (3.7) with equation (3.6) above as follows:

$$\text{Gains} - \text{Losses} = \Delta(\text{Assets}) - \Delta(\text{Liabilities}) \qquad \textbf{(3.8)}$$

However, this analysis ignores the possibility of changes in equity, and hence in assets or liabilities, having arisen as a result of financing transactions. Such changes are either the result of fresh equity capital being introduced into the entity (contributions), or part of the existing equity capital being returned to the owners (distributions). Equation (3.8) needs to be extended to allow for this possibility as follows:

$$\text{Gains} - \text{Losses} + \text{Contributions} - \text{Distributions} = \Delta(\text{Assets}) - \Delta(\text{Liabilities}) \qquad \textbf{(3.9)}$$

We also need to recognise that changes in assets and liabilities can be either increases or decreases, so a fuller statement of equation (3.9) is:

$$\text{Gains} - \text{Losses} = \text{Increases in assets} - \text{Decreases in assets} -$$
$$\text{Contributions} + \text{Distributions} - \text{Increases in liabilities} + \text{Decreases in liabilities} \qquad \textbf{(3.10)}$$

Equation (3.10) can be reorganised in terms of the arithmetic signs of its components as follows:

$$\text{Losses} + \text{Distributions} + \text{Increases in assets} + \text{Decreases in liabilities} =$$
$$\text{Gains} + \text{Contributions} + \text{Decreases in assets} + \text{Increases in liabilities} \qquad \textbf{(3.11)}$$

This extended version of the accounting identity is usually referred to as the **bookkeeping equation** and it is the basis of that system of recording the transactions of accounting entities called **double-entry bookkeeping** on which most modern accounting records and reports are ultimately based. Conventionally items on the left hand side of the equation are called **debits** and items on the right hand side **credits**. Historically, the different items in the equation were recorded by accountants (bookkeepers) in ledger accounts contained, literally, in 'books of account'. However, in more recent times these ledgers have been replaced, first by machine accounting systems, and more recently by computer based accounting systems. Throughout this period of transition the basic principle has remained the same – the bookkeeping equation must remain in balance. Thus, every transaction (economic event) affecting an enterprise must have two sides to it – a debit side and a credit side.

Computer based accounting systems usually consist of **integrated accounting packages** which are broken down into smaller components (or modules) based on the functions they perform. In an integrated system, once transaction data are entered into one module, the computer will generate the related transactions which it then enters automatically into the other modules, thus eliminating the need for the same data to be entered many times by different people (as in a manual system). In addition, accounting reports produced by the system are updated automatically as transactions are entered. Many different modular computerised accounting packages are available in the market.

Accounting records and bookkeeping

It is not the purpose of this book to go into any great detail regarding the operations of either traditional bookkeeping or more modern computerised systems of accounting. Readers seeking more information about bookkeeping are advised to consult a specialist text, such as Bebbington, Gray and Laughlin (2001). However, there are some essential characteristics for any effective system of accounting. These are:

Chart of accounts

The core purpose of any accounting system is to record, in a structured way, the transactions (economic events) affecting the entity to which it relates. This requires a defined structure or framework in accordance with which these transactions can be classified and recorded. Such a structure is normally called a **chart of accounts**. The objective of a chart of accounts is to map out the way in which the enterprise's transactions will be recorded, with like items being grouped together. In countries such as the UK, Australia and the USA, there are no externally imposed requirements for the structure of an entity's chart of accounts. Instead it is down to the individual entity to design its own. In doing this it will be influenced both by its legal obligation (if it is a company) to keep accounting records which must be sufficient to record and explain its transactions and to enable balance sheets and profit and loss accounts to be prepared (UK Companies Act, 1989, s221), and by its own management information requirements. However, in many European countries, companies have to use an approved code of accounts. Thus, subject to the Companies Act requirements (or any other similar national regulation), an entity can itself determine the degree of analytical detail in its basic accounting records. Important considerations in this respect for an entity (and its management) will be:

- *The need to maintain control over its finances*: the level of detail in the accounting records must be sufficient to enable management to discharge its fiduciary obligations with respect to the entity's assets and liabilities.
- *Reporting requirements*: the accounting records must be such as to enable management to prepare proper accounting reports from them.
- *Decision making needs*: the accounting records need to provide information which facilitates managerial decision making, as well as facilitating control over costs and budgetary performance.
- *Cost*: maintaining accounting records is a costly process and the more detailed the analysis provided by these records the more costly maintaining them is likely to be. The cost of accounting should not exceed the value of the management information provided.

The end product of these considerations is a chart (schedule) of accounts with their associated titles and codes. An example is shown in Table 3.2.

The illustration in Table 3.2 is of a very simplified chart of accounts. In reality, even a small business will probably require a much more extensive chart of accounts. Larger businesses are likely to have charts of accounts comprising several thousand,

Table 3.2		Example of a chart accounts
Main code	**Sub-code**	**Account title**
001		**Fixed assets**
	001	Freehold land and building – cost
	002	Leasehold land and building – cost
	003	Motor vehicles – cost
	004	Plant and machinery – cost
	005	Furniture and fittings – cost
	101	Freehold land and buildings – accumulated depreciation
	102	Leasehold land and buildings – accumulated depreciation
	103	Motor vehicles – accumulated depreciation
	104	Plant and machinery – accumulated depreciation
	105	Furniture and fittings – accumulated depreciation
	201	Freehold land and buildings – depreciation charge
	202	Leasehold land and buildings – depreciation charge
	203	Motor vehicles – depreciation charge
	204	Plant and machinery – depreciation charge
	205	Furniture and fittings – deprecation charge
002		**Current assets**
	001	Raw materials stock
	002	Work-in-progress
	003	Finished goods stock
	101	Trade debtors
	102	Other debtors
	103	Prepayments
	201	Cash in hand
	202	Cash at bank
003		**Current liabilities**
	001	Materials suppliers
	002	Other suppliers
	003	Payroll creditors
	004	Taxation payable
	005	Dividends payable
	006	Interest payable
	007	Accruals
004		**Revenues**
	001	Product sales
	002	Service sales
	003	Interest receivable
	004	Other income

Continued

or even more, different 'accounts' because management have decided that they need to have such extensive analysis in order to obtain the information they require to manage the business effectively. A large company organised on a divisional basis might have a chart of accounts structured along the following lines:

Division	Budget Centre	Main Code	Sub-code
01-99	001-999	001-999	001-999

This would result in individual account codes having 11 digits. In practice, the authors have encountered account codes of 17 digits in multinational enterprises. While such an extensive chart of accounts provides the facility for a very detailed analysis of operations, it also carries dangers. The principal of these are an increased opportunity for error (the more the digits in an account code, the greater the likelihood of transactions being miscoded); and of information overload (there is a natural human tendency to ask for all the information that is available, and where extensive analysis is available it tends to be produced, leading to a danger of management being overloaded by detail and unable to see the 'wood for the trees'. Care needs to be exercised to ensure that management, at different levels, are provided with the analysis and information that they do in fact require and are neither overburdened with detail, or provided with insufficient detail. There needs to be effective consultation between management and the entity's accountants to ensure that this does in fact happen and that the chart of accounts, and the reports that are derived from it, are appropriate to the needs of management. Unfortunately, all too often, charts of accounts and accounting reports are designed solely by accountants.

Internal control

Whatever the structure of the chart of accounts decided on by management, it will be important to ensure that it is implemented in practice by the entity and its staff. To achieve this, management need to design and implement detailed financial and

Table 3.2		Example of a chart accounts (Continued)	
005		**Expenditures**
	001	Cost of goods sold
	002	Payroll costs
	003	Premises costs
	004	Marketing costs
	005	Administration costs
	006	Finance costs
	007	Bad and doubtful debts
006		**Equity**
	001	Share capital
	002	Retained profits
	003	Other reserves
007		**Loans**
	001	Long-term loans
	002	Short-term loans

operating procedures. The generic term for such procedures is **internal control** which has been defined by the ASB (1995: para. 8) as:

> All the policies and procedures (internal controls) adopted by the directors and management of an entity to assist in achieving their objective of ensuring, so far as practicable, the orderly and efficient conduct of its business, including adherence to internal policies, the safeguarding of assets, the prevention and detection of fraud and error, the accuracy and completeness of the accounting records, and the timely preparation of reliable financial information.

The modern view is that the installation and maintenance of an adequate internal control system is a key responsibility of corporate management and is part of its corporate governance systems which we discussed in the previous chapter. Within the UK and a number of other countries, it is now standard practice for the directors of a listed company to publish a 'Statement of Directors' Responsibilities' as part of the annual report of their company. Part of this statement will normally confirm that the responsibility for the company having an adequate internal control system is that of the directors, and that the directors have discharged this responsibility properly.

Prime documents

These are the basic inputs into the accounting system of an entity. They are documents that are raised, or received, by the staff of the entity as it engages in economic and other transactions. They are the source material for the whole of the accounting process, and the underpinning of all the accounting records. As such they are crucial to this process and, as part of its internal control system, management need to ensure that they are designed to capture all the information required for accounting purposes; that they are properly prepared in a timely and controlled manner; and that they are transmitted to the accounting function. Examples of prime documents include: goods received notes, stock requisitions, delivery notes, purchase invoices, sales invoices, cheque requisitions, contracts, etc. For example, a sales invoice would need, typically, to record the following information:

- customer name, address, and account number
- quantities, types and prices of merchandise/services
- quantity discounts
- total sales value
- sales tax (e.g. Value Added Tax, Goods and Services Tax)
- settlement terms
- delivery details
- date.

Prime records

These are what were historically called the 'books of prime entry'. They are the first level of accounting records. In practice they may take many forms, but their function is to record the information contained in the prime documents referred to above. Examples of prime records include sales day books, purchases day books, cash payment and cash received records, etc. As well as recording the prime documents, the prime records have another function – they are the first stage in the analysis of the economic transactions. They analyse these transactions into the various categories and classifications specified by the chart of accounts. The information content of a prime record can be illustrated with an extract from a (simplified) cash payment prime record, as shown in Table 3.3.

In real life the analysis of the cash payments would be much more extensive than that shown in Table 3.3, reflecting the (probably) extensive nature of the chart of accounts. Similarly, there will need to be a separate cash payments (and receipts) prime record for every cash fund. Extending the definition of cash to include bank accounts there will need to be a separate prime record for every bank account. An entity will need a number of prime cash payment (cash receipt) records, relating to each of its bank accounts and cash (petty cash) funds. These records are normally referred to as **cash books** (and will normally deal with cash receipts as well as cash payments). The basis for their maintenance are the prime documents referred to earlier and the internal control system, which needs to be such as to ensure that all relevant prime documents (cheque requisitions, cheques, petty cash vouchers, receipts, etc.) are properly recorded in the relevant cash records (or other prime records for other types of transactions/prime documents).

Ledgers

Ledgers are the practical implementation of the chart of accounts. Each of the individual account headings specified in the chart of accounts will have its own ledger account (section) in the accounting records. The purpose of this ledger account is to collect together all the transactions for the account heading in question. Periodically, typically every week or every month, the information from the prime records will be transferred to the ledgers (a process often referred as 'posting'). In a traditional manual system this 'posting' will be done by the physical process of writing the relevant totals from the prime records into the ledgers. Nowadays, with modern computerised systems, the process is likely to be automated. Thus, each ledger account records increases or decreases in the monetary value of the item to which the account heading relates. The ledger as a whole is simply the aggregation of all the individual

Table 3.3	Example of cash payment prime record					
					Analysis	
			Amount	*005-002*	*005-002*	*005-005*
Date	*Ref.*	*Payee*	*£*	*£*	*£*	*£*
1/1/02	00245	Bloggs	156.89		156.89	
2/1/02	00246	Smith	45.21	45.21		
3/1/02	00247	Hill	269.00			269.00
4/1/02	00248	Jones	14.23		14.33	
5/1/02	00249	Hughes	85.11			85.11
6/1/02	00250	Jones	139.84		139.84	
7/1/02	00251	Smith	84.00			84.00
			794.28	45.21	310.96	438.11

ledger accounts. The precise layout of the ledger accounts will vary from entity to entity, depending largely on the technology it employs to maintain the accounting records. However, under the classical manual system of maintaining accounting records, the typical format of a ledger account is shown in Table 3.4:

The double-entry system of bookkeeping (derived from the fundamental accounting identity) requires that for each and every entry there is a balancing entry in the accounting records. The balancing entries in relation to those in Table 3.4 would be:

- Account No. 004-001 (Product sales) a credit entry of £43 241.00
- Account No. 004-002 (Service sales) a credit entry of £9 326.76
- Account No. 002-202 (Bank account – assuming all customer receipts were paid into the bank account) a debit entry of £39 671.07

Within the ledger(s) as a whole there would be many ledger accounts similar to the trade debtors account illustrated in Table 3.4, one for each heading in the chart of accounts. The bottom line is that there should be an individual ledger account for each separable and significant asset or liability, and for each separable and significant category of income or expense. This is perhaps not too great a problem as regards the income and expense categories, depending on the analysis required by management. However, it can be a major problem as regards the individual assets and liabilities.

Debtors can again be used as an example. An entity will need a separate ledger account for each individual customer to whom it offers credit terms. If it does not keep such a separate account, it will not know how much it is owed by that customer at any point in time, and therefore management will have failed in the discharge of its fiduciary duties. Large businesses may have many thousands, even hundreds of thousands, of individual customers; consider for example electricity companies, large retail chains and the clearing banks. Correspondingly, large enterprises may have many different individual suppliers, and may need to maintain complex analyses of their income and expenses from different sources. Such organisations could easily have in excess of a million different individual ledger accounts.

Thus, while the fundamental accounting identity and its derivative, the bookkeeping equation, look very simple in their pure forms, their practical implementation can

Table 3.4	Example of a ledger account		

Account no. 002–101

Account title: Trade debtors

Date	Description	Debit £	Credit £
1/1/02	Opening balance	19 678.95	
7/1/02	Product sales	43 241.00	
7/1/02	Service sales	9 323.76	
7/1/02	Customer receipts		39 671.07
7/1/02	Closing balance		32 575.64
		75 246.71	75 246.71
8/1/02	Opening balance	32 575.64	

be a major problem for organisations. The volume of individual ledger accounts, and the even larger volume of individual transactions that have to be recorded in these ledger accounts, impose great demands on the accounting and internal control systems. Unless these systems are properly designed, resourced, and monitored they are likely to fail. The consequences of such failure can be disastrous. It will not simply be a question of 'the accounts being wrong'. The management of the entity will not know who owes it money, and for how long they have owed it, thus making it very difficult for them to ensure that they collect all the monies due to the enterprise. They will not know to whom the enterprise owes money and when it is due for payment, thus making it very difficult for them to ensure that the entity only pays money to those entitled to such payments. They will not know what the entity is spending money on, what income it is generating, or what expenses it is incurring. Effective management will be impossible and the entity will almost certainly be a rapid candidate for insolvency, and its directors liable for a charge of failing to adequately discharge their fiduciary responsibilities. To prevent this, management must be prepared to invest sufficient resources in the accounting function. It is not good enough to regard the accounting function as an overhead expenditure to be minimised. It is an essential activity for an entity which must be optimised, i.e. it must be adequately resourced to enable it to perform its functions, but, and it is an important 'but', management must ensure that it is getting value-for-money from this resourcing. It must ensure that it is obtaining an appropriate amount of relevant and reliable information from the accounting function. This is an issue to which we will return later.

Journals

While the prime records and associated ledger accounts should automatically record the vast majority of the economic events affecting an entity on a day-to-day basis, there will inevitably be some events with which they are not designed to cope. The range of these is wide, but their frequency limited. Journals are the approach that accounting has developed to cope with events of this type – effectively, journals are a supplementary system of prime records. Examples of the type of economic events recorded via journals include: charging the annual depreciation on fixed assets, providing for bad and doubtful debts, and providing against excess and obsolete stocks. In practical terms, journals serve the same function as prime records; it is their source that distinguishes them from the mainstream system of prime documents being entered in the prime records, and thereafter being posted to the relevant ledger accounts. Because the economic events recorded by journals are outside the day-to-day events affecting the entity, they need to be carefully monitored and controlled. Typically, accounting entries processed via journals require significant amounts of verification and authorisation. Table 3.5 illustrates the usual double entry form of journals.

The journal illustrated in Table 3.5 deals with the annual depreciation charges for an entity. The entries it contains will be the result of detailed calculations based on the types, values and economic lives of the various fixed assets owned by the enterprise. We discuss the meaning of, and methods of calculating, depreciation charges later in this chapter. For the present, it is sufficient to recognise that, while depreciation is a real cost that needs to be reflected in the accounting records and accounts of an enterprise, it is not a cost which emerges from the normal system of prime documents and prime records. Accordingly it requires the preparation of a journal entry. Another item of the same type is the provision for bad and doubtful debts.

All businesses incur bad debts (i.e. customers who, for whatever reason, fail to pay the monies that they owe) and it is normal practice to provide for this. The normal system of prime documents and prime records will ensure that the debt is properly recorded, but will not register the possibility of non-payment. This is a matter of managerial judgement which, once made, needs to recorded. Table 3.6 illustrates a journal entry dealing with bad debt provisions.

Every accounting entity will encounter events/transactions which need to be recorded in the accounting records via journals. The internal control system needs to ensure that all such events/transactions are in fact recognised and recorded; that the journal entries are properly prepared and authorised by responsible personnel; and that unauthorised personnel are not able to initiate and process journal entry transactions.

Trial balance

The volume of ledger accounts, and the even larger volume of individual transactions needing recording, means that there is great scope for unintentional error in accounting records. However, the double entry system also provides quite considerable scope for detecting such errors. This is because of its requirement that the bookkeeping equation always remains in balance. If it is not in balance then an error must have occurred. A trial balance is nothing more or less than a listing of the balances on all

Table 3.5	Illustration of a journal entry dealing with depreciation			
Date	Description	Code	Debit £	Credit £
31/12	Depreciation charge for year on freehold land and buildings	001–201	3 000.00	
	Accumulated depreciation on freehold land and buildings	001–101		3 000.00
	Depreciation charge for year on leasehold land and buildings	001–202	9 000.00	
	Accumulated depreciation on leasehold land and buildings	001–102		9 000.00
	Depreciation charge for year on motor vehicles	002–203	6 500.00	
	Accumulated depreciation on motor vehicles	001–003		6 500.00
	Depreciation charge for year on plant and machinery	001–204	3 700.00	
	Accumulated depreciation on plant and machinery	001–104		3 700.00
	Depreciation charge for year on fixtures and fittings	001–205	8 600.00	
	Accumulated depreciation on fixtures and fittings	001–105		8 600.00
			30 800.00	30 800.00

the individual ledger accounts. By definition each of these balances will be a debit balance (where the value of the debit entries on an individual ledger account exceeds the value of the credit entries), or a credit balance (where the value of the credit entries exceeds the value of the debit entries). The trial balance totals the value of the debit balances and the value of the credit balances. These should be equal. If they are not there must be an error somewhere in the ledger accounts. Examples of such errors include: incorrect arithmetic (where an arithmetical error has been made in computing the balance on a ledger account(s)); single sided entries (where one part of an event/transaction has been recorded in the ledger accounts, but not the other part); and unbalanced entries (where the amount at which the event/transaction has been recorded differs between the ledger accounts in which it has been recorded). Table 3.7 illustrates the structure of a trial balance.

However, even if the trial balance does balance this does not provide a guarantee that the recording of the transactions in the ledger accounts is correct. This is because there are some types of error which do not impact on the balancing of the bookkeeping equation. Examples of such errors include: a debit or credit entry being recorded in the wrong ledger account; a transaction not being recorded at all; a transaction being recorded at an incorrect amount; or the recording of a transaction being duplicated. Thus, while the trial balance provides a valuable check on the integrity of the accounting records it does not provide a foolproof one. This reinforces the need for an adequate system of internal control to ensure that all transactions are recorded; that they are recorded in the correct ledger accounts at the correct amounts; and that they are not duplicated.

On the cash basis of accounting, only cash and cash-at-bank transactions are recorded in the accounting records and recognised in any financial statements based on these records. The only revenues recognised are cash receipts. The only expenditures recognised are cash payments. The only asset (or liability) recognised is cash in hand and at bank (or bank overdraft). No transactions other than those involving an exchange of cash are recognised in the accounting records or financial statements. If an entity has more cash (and cash at bank) at the end of a financial period than it had at the start then it has made a surplus (profit); if it has less it has incurred a deficit (loss). Given the range of assets and liabilities that modern commercial enterprises have and the diversity of the transactions in which they engage, accounting reports prepared on a cash basis can only give a very incomplete picture of their activities. In addition, such reports would be very susceptible to manipulation, e.g. delaying payments to creditors would help to ensure that a better position is reported, although the underlying economic reality would not have changed – the creditors would still have to be paid at some time! The financial picture of an entity could be changed

Table 3.6	Illustration of a journal entry dealing with bad and doubtful debt provisions			
Date	**Description**	**Code**	**Debit £**	**Credit £**
31/12	Bad and doubtful debts charge	005–007	4 500.00	
	Trade debtors	002–101		4 500.00
			4 500.00	4 500.00

dramatically simply by altering the timing pattern of receipts and payments. Nowadays, the use of cash accounting is mainly restricted to some professional practices (where it may be advantageous for taxation purposes) and to various aspects of government accounting where it is supposed to match with the annual governmental budgetary cycle. However, in recent years many governments have sought to move away from cash based accounting, e.g. the UK's move towards what it calls 'resource accounting', which itself is derived from developments in other countries such as New Zealand. Resource accounting is, in essence, the application of the other principal accounting basis (**accruals** accounting) to the public sector.

Nowadays, virtually all financial statements of significant economic entities are prepared on the accruals basis as is required by the IASB. The essence of this basis of accounting is that it recognises the existence of assets and liabilities other than cash. Therefore, it automatically recognises the existence of transactions other than those involving the exchange of cash. Thus, it can accommodate all sorts of credit-based transactions, as well as the fact that a cash (or credit based) expenditure can lead to an entity acquiring a right to future economic benefits (an asset), and it can reflect increases and decreases in the value of such benefits. In fact the accruals basis of accounting goes far beyond simply recording (and reporting) the existence of these factors – it maintains that without doing so it would be impossible for accounting reports to provide an adequate portrayal of the activities of an economic entity, and of the outcomes of these activities. However, this broader approach to the recognition of an entity's assets and liabilities brings with it a problem – when, and on what basis, should changes in an entity's assets and liabilities be recognised in its accounting records, and associated accounting reports. The range of potential assets and liabilities, income and expenses, that can be reflected in such reports prepared on the

Table 3.7	Illustration of a trial balance			
Main code	**Sub-code**	**Account title**	**Debit** **£**	**Credit** **£**
001		Fixed assets		
	001	Freehold land and buildings – cost	67 000.00	
	002	Leasehold land and buildings – cost	85 000.00	
	003	Motor vehicles – cost	32 000.00	
	004	Plant and machinery – cost	49 500.00	
	005	Furniture and fittings – cost	18 700.00	
	101	Freehold land and buildings – accumulated depreciation		9 000.00
	102	Leasehold land and buildings – accumulated depreciation		27 000.00
	103	Motor vehicles – accumulated depreciation		13 500.00
	104	Plant and machinery – accumulated depreciation		11 200.00
	105	Furniture and fittings – accumulated depreciation		14 300.00
		Totals	£	£

accruals basis, is both complex and contentious. There is great scope for differing accounting representations of the same set of economic events and, as we shall see in Chapter 13, there is evidence of use being made of this scope by some managements to prepare financial statements giving rather 'rosy' pictures of corporate performance.

The first step in the accounting recognition of changes in an entity's assets and liabilities on the accruals basis is the initial recognition of such a change with regard to a particular asset or liability. This will usually be the result of some form of exchange transaction such as a sale or purchase taking place. This initial recognition of such an exchange transaction should (normally) be a standard output of the entity's system of internal control and accounting records. The recording in the accounting records will be dated at the time the transaction took place and the amount recorded will (normally) be the monetary value of the transaction, e.g. selling price, purchase price, amount of payment, etc. as shown on the relevant prime document. Conventionally, this initial monetary value is referred to as the **historical cost** of the transaction.

The second step, which will frequently take place as part of the process via which financial statements are extracted from the accounting records, is that of assessing whether or not the monetary value at which an item is recorded in the accounting records is appropriate for the purposes of preparing accounting reports. There are a number of circumstances in which this value may not be appropriate.

For example, while a credit sale may have been made to a customer during the financial period in question and have been correctly recorded in the ledger at the value of the sale, the customer may have subsequently become insolvent and unable to settle the debt. Thus, the debt is not worth the amount shown in the ledger and an adjustment is required. Equally there may be transactions recorded correctly in the ledger which affect more than one financial period. For example, an entity with a 31 December financial year end may on 1 July have paid insurance premiums relating to the coming 12 month period. In such a case the payment recorded in the ledger needs to be apportioned between two financial years when preparing financial statements. Similarly, an enterprise may have paid rent in advance at the end of the financial period. In such circumstances an adjustment, normally called a prepayment, will be required to the core accounting information (trial balance) when accounting reports are being prepared.

There may also be economic events affecting the financial period which have not yet been recorded in the ledger. For example, an entity might not, at the year end, have received an invoice for the electricity it has consumed during the last couple of months of the financial year. Accordingly no expense for this electricity will have been recorded in the ledger. In these, and similar instances, an adjustment, called an 'accrual' (the noun from the verb 'to accrue') will be required to the information contained in the core accounting records before the financial statements can be prepared.

Typically, adjustments for prepayments and accruals are made by journal entries (see earlier discussion) raised at the end of the financial period. Such journal entries are similar to those illustrated earlier regarding depreciation charges and bad/doubtful debt provisions. In the case of a company having paid insurance premiums of £5000 relating to the period 1 July 2006 to 2007 and having a financial year ending on 31 December, Table 3.8 illustrates the relevant journal entry.

As at 31 December 2007, the company has paid in advance for six months insurance and, therefore, the amount of the prepayment was 50 per cent of the premium, i.e. £2500. Within the structure of the company's chart of accounts, insurance premiums are charged to administrative costs. It is relatively easy for most entities to identify their prepayments because their accounting system will have recorded the initial payment and documentation will be available on which to base the computation of the prepayment. In the case of accruals the position may be more difficult. Whereas the entity may recognise the need to make an accrual, e.g. as regards electricity, it may well have to estimate the amount of the necessary accrual in the absence of a supplier's invoice at the time when the accounts are being prepared. In such circumstances it will need to base its estimates on previous invoices, price levels and estimates of consumption. If a company estimates that it needs to accrue £350 for electricity charges then it will need to process a journal entry such as that shown in Table 3.9.

The IASB requirements for the recognition of changes in the elements of financial statements were discussed in Chapter 1 and we will not repeat them here. However, as we shall see in Chapter 13, they provide management with considerable scope in the preparation of accounting reports. Similar principles apply to the subsequent re-measurement of an element or, ultimately, the de-recognition of an element.

Most of the time the prime documents and the resultant prime records and ledger accounts will ensure that the events/transactions that need to be recorded in the accounts will in fact be so recorded. However, as we have indicated, enterprises need to make certain that they have set up internal control systems which will guarantee that *all* events/transactions meeting the recognition criteria are in fact recorded, and this will involve the use of journal entries to supplement the system of prime records. This may well require an extension to the trial balance for the preparation of financial statements. Table 3.10 illustrates such an extension.

The first two columns in Table 3.10 are the trial balance as derived from the core ledger accounts maintained by the entity. The next two columns represent the 'post-trial balance' journal entries needed to comply with the recognition criteria outlined above, and the final two columns represent the final trial balance on which the entity's final accounting reports will be based. Of course, these final adjustments will need, at some point in time, to be incorporated into the ledger accounts of the entity. This is particularly important as the final balances on the ledger accounts will be the starting point on which the accounting records for the next financial year will be based.

Monetary value

As has already been stated, the first stage of accounting is principally concerned with recording the economic events/transactions affecting an enterprise, and in particular recording the monetary values attaching to these events/transactions.

Table 3.8	Illustration of journal entry recording prepayments			
Date	Description	Code	Debit £	Credit £
31/12	Prepayments	002–103	2 500.00	
	Administrative costs	005–005		2 500.00
			2 500.00	2 500.00

Subsequently, and largely based on this initial recording, management information and external financial statements are prepared. This immediately raises the question 'What monetary values should be used for this purpose (as opposed to the initial recording)?' This is a very difficult question to answer, given the various groups interested in accounting information, and their differing information requirements. The identification and reporting of the appropriate monetary value of assets/liabilities/gains/losses is a theme which recurs at many points throughout this book. For the present it is sufficient to recognise that there are different bases for attaching monetary values to economic events/transactions, and to individual assets and liabilities resulting from such events/transactions. The measurement bases that could be used, each having its own advantages and disadvantages in relation to the purposes for which the accounting information is required include:

- **Historical cost:** This is the cash equivalent value attaching to an event/transaction at the time that it took place. Thus, the historical cost of an item of stock, or of a fixed asset such as a motor vehicle, owned by an entity is the amount that it paid to acquire it.

- **Replacement cost:** This is the current cash amount that an enterprise would have to pay to replace an asset that it currently owns. Thus, if it owns an item of stock which it acquired at an historical cost of $100 and it would now cost $150 to purchase a similar item, the replacement cost of the item of stock it owns is $150.

- **Net realisable value:** This is the amount for which an asset could be sold, net of any expenses incurred in the sale.

- **Net present value:** This is a slightly more difficult concept, but one which is closely related to the definition of an asset given earlier. The net present value of an asset is the current value equivalent of all the cash flows that an entity will receive deriving from its ownership of the asset, allowing for the fact that money has a time value; i.e. that money now is worth more than money in the future. The time value of money is a topic that is covered in detail in Chapter 9.

Fundamental accounting concepts

As we pointed out earlier, the accruals basis of accounting is both more complex and contentious than the cash basis and can lead to many different accounting

Table 3.9	Illustration of a journal entry recording accruals			
Date	**Description**	**Code**	**Debit £**	**Credit £**
31/12	Premises costs	005–003	350.00	
	Accruals	003–007		350.00
			350.00	350.00

representations of similar economic events. To help guard against unnecessary diversity in accounting presentation certain **fundamental accounting concepts** have been enunciated. These are contained in the IASB 1, *Presentation of Financial Statements*. Many of these fundamental accounting concepts have been given the force of law, e.g. in the UK via their incorporation into the Companies Acts. The IASB framework contains four fundamental accounting concepts, namely:

1 The **matching concept**: This requires that once any part of a transaction is recognised then all the other elements of that transaction must also be recognised. Thus, if an item of income is recognised in financial records and statements then all the costs of generating that income must be recognised, as must any associated changes in assets and liabilities. For example, a credit sales transaction involving merchandise which the entity previously held in stock will involve the following elements, each of which must be recognised (accounted for):

   - income (the revenue from the sale)
   - an increase in debtors (resulting from the sale)
   - a reduction in stock (resulting from the transfer of the stock to the customer)
   - an increase in costs (the cost to the enterprise of giving up the asset, stock, which it previously owned)

   All of these different elements need to be recorded if the matching concept is to be adhered to. If they were not recorded, then the accounting records and any resultant accounting reports would tell only part of the story.

2 The **going concern concept**: This requires that, in the absence of evidence to the contrary, accounting records should be maintained and accounting reports prepared on the assumption that the entity in question will continue to exist in the future and that it will continue to trade. The implication of this assumption is that the assets of the business will not be the subject of a forced

Table 3.10	Illustration of final trial balance					
	Ledger account balances		Final accounts adjustments		Final accounts balances	
Account code	Debit £	Credit £	Debit £	Credit £	Debit £	Credit £
001–001	XXX				XXX	
001–002	XXX				XXX	
001–003	XXX				XXX	
001–004	XXX				XXX	
001–005	XXX				XXX	
001–101		XXX		XXX		XXX
001–102		XXX		XXX		XXX
etc.	XXX	XXX	XXX	XXX	XXX	XXX

sale, and that any contingent liabilities of the enterprise which would arise if it ceased to trade remain contingent. This is a significant assumption because the forced sale value of the assets of an entity may well be significantly less than their historical cost or other reported value. For example, it is widely recognised that debtors will be difficult to collect and work-in-process difficult to sell in the event of an insolvency.

3 The **prudence concept**: As we saw earlier, the accruals basis of accounting recognises the existence of accounting items other than cash. The ultimate cash value of items recognised in this way must by definition be more or less uncertain. How much can the stock be sold for? Will the entity receive all the money it is owed by debtors? There may be similar uncertainties regarding the amount that will ultimately be paid to creditors. This uncertainty is the focus of the prudence concept which was referred to in Chapter 1.

4 The **consistency concept**: This concept recognises that there are differing accounting bases and policies available to an entity preparing accounting reports. It requires that such an entity be consistent in the bases and policies it adopts. If this were not to be so, then it would be impossible for the users of the financial information provided by the entity to use it with confidence, or to compare information relating to one financial period with that relating to another.

These four 'fundamental concepts', together with the core accounting records based on the fundamental accounting identity and bookkeeping equation, are the underpinning of traditional accounting reports, including the annual financial statements reviewed in more detail in Chapter 13.

Depreciation

At this point we introduce the accounting concept of depreciation. A fixed asset is an asset which an entity intends to employ for the long term in its business activities. Examples of fixed assets include: property, plant and machinery, fixtures and fittings, etc. The use of a fixed asset by an accounting entity in the generation of economic benefits (e.g. from the provision of goods and services) involves a cost which needs to be recognised. This cost derives from the fact that the entity has incurred expenditure on a resource with a long (albeit limited) life during which it will be using it in the entity's operations. The IASB in IAS 16 has defined depreciation as: 'The systematic allocation of the depreciable amount of an asset over its useful life'.

The question to be addressed is how this expenditure should be allocated over the life of the fixed asset, such that each accounting period in which the resource is used bears an appropriate charge for such use. In essence, depreciation is the allocation of expenditure on fixed assets to the financial reporting periods in which they are used – this allocation is referred to as the depreciation charge for the period(s) in question. This can readily be seen from the way in which the most common form of depreciation (**straight-line depreciation**) is calculated:

$$D = \frac{C - S}{N} \tag{3.12}$$

where: D = the amount of the depreciation to be allocated to each year of the
        asset's life;
        C = the original cost of the asset;
        S = the estimated salvage (residual) value of the asset at the time of its
        intended disposal;
        N = the estimated life (to disposal) of the asset in years.

This calculation computes how much of the expenditure on the fixed asset should be charged as a cost in each of the financial periods during which it is forecast that the asset will be used. The charge is based on the overall net cost to the enterprise of the asset (original cost – estimated salvage value) and the number of financial periods that will benefit from the use of the asset. In this way, the requirements of the matching principle are met, with the depreciation charge being included as a cost in the entity's profit and loss account.

Accumulated depreciation

Charging depreciation as a cost in the profit and loss account is only part of the story. It is also necessary to reduce the value at which the fixed asset is shown in the balance sheet by the amount of depreciation that has been charged. This is achieved via the concept of **accumulated depreciation**, which is the sum of all the depreciation charges relating to the asset since it was first acquired. It is shown in the balance sheet as deduction from the expenditure on the asset, i.e.:

	Fixed asset (at original cost)	£XXX
Less:	Accumulated depreciation	XXX
	Net book value	£XXX

In this way, the matching principle is maintained. The **net book value** of a fixed asset is often referred to as its **carrying value**.

Illustration of depreciation charge and accumulated depreciation

Consider the example of Popham Ltd which on 1 January 2004 acquired a fixed asset at a cost of $10 000. Popham forecasts that it will keep (and use) this asset for four years, and that at the end of that time the asset will have a salvage value of $1300. Inserting these values into equation 3.12 gives the following:

$$D = \frac{\$10\ 000 - \$1300}{4} = \$2175$$

Thus, the depreciation charge for each of the four years' ownership of the asset will be $2175. This amount will be shown as a cost in Popham's profit and loss account in each of those years. Table 3.11 illustrates the balance sheet presentation of the asset at the end of each of those years.

As can readily be seen from the foregoing, the assumption of the straight-line method of depreciation is that the (net book) value of the asset declines in a linear fashion, by a constant amount (the depreciation charge) in each financial period. This is illustrated in Figure 3.1.

Alternative approaches to calculating depreciation

The straight-line method of depreciation charges an equal amount to each year of the asset's use. There is a school of argument which maintains that this method fails to reflect adequately the way in which the value of a fixed asset changes over time. This school maintains that the charge for depreciation in any financial period should reflect the decline in an asset's value during that period and that (typically) this decline is greater during the earlier part of an asset's life than in the latter part of its life. Consider, for example, an entity purchasing a new car and how the value of the car will change over the period that the entity owns the car. The reality of the second-hand car market tells us that it is most unlikely that this value will decline in a linear way. It is much more likely to decline in the way indicated in Figure 3.2.

This line of argument is the rationale for the reducing balance method of depreciation which seeks to charge the earlier years of the asset's life with higher depreciation charges (reflecting greater losses in value per year during this time), and the latter years with lower depreciation charges (reflecting smaller losses in value). The greatest annual loss in value will take place in the first year of ownership.

Reducing balance method

In this method of calculating depreciation, an asset's depreciation charge for any financial period is calculated by reference to its net book value at the start of that period. A predetermined percentage (depreciation rate) is applied to this opening net book value to calculate the monetary amount of the depreciation charge for the period. This percentage is calculated using the following formula:

$$D = 1 - \sqrt[n]{S/C}$$

(3.13)

where:　D = the depreciation percentage (rate) per period (of the opening net book
　　　　　value for that period);
　　　　n = the estimated life of the asset;
　　　　S = the forecast salvage value of the asset;
　　　　C = original cost of the asset.

We can illustrate the use of reducing balance depreciation by revisiting the example of Popham Ltd, which acquired an asset costing $10 000, with a forecast life of four years and a forecast salvage value of $1300. Inserting these values into equation 3.13 gives a value for D of 0.40, or 40 per cent. Table 3.12 illustrates how this value is then used to calculate the annual depreciation charges using the reducing balance basis.

Table 3.11	Illustration of straight-line depreciation: Popham Ltd			
	31/12/00 $	**31/12/01** $	**31/12/02** $	**31/12/03** $
Historical cost	10 000	10 000	10 000	10 000
Accumulated depreciation	2 175	4 350	6 525	8 790
Net book value	7 825	5 650	3 475	1 300

As Table 3.12 clearly demonstrates, the annual depreciation charges are higher in the earlier years of ownership of the asset than in the later years, and the net book value of the asset at the end of the fourth year (allowing for a little bit of 'rounding') equals the forecast salvage value of the asset. Table 3.13 summarises the differences between the straight-line and the reducing balance methods of calculating depreciation, using Popham as an example.

As Table 3.13 clearly demonstrates, both methods lead (subject to minor 'rounding' differences) to exactly the same financial position over the life of the asset. Both methods result in a final net book value of $1300 and both methods have charged a total of $8700 depreciation over the four years' ownership of the asset. However, in the first year of the asset's life, the straight-line method results in a depreciation charge of $2175 and the reducing balance method a charge of $4000 – the reducing balance charge is nearly twice that of the straight-line charge. In the final year, the position is reversed, with the straight-line charge remaining at $2175 while the reducing balance charge has fallen to $864. The implications for financial statements are obvious. The straight-line method will result in lower costs (and therefore higher profits and asset values) in the early years of a fixed asset's life than will the reducing balance method.

Usage based methods of depreciation

Apart from the time-based methods of computing depreciation (straight-line and reducing balance), there are a number of other approaches to calculating depreciation charges, mostly based on the extent of the usage of the asset during any given financial period. The underlying principle of these approaches is that of specifying a 'usage capacity' for an asset when it is first acquired. This 'usage capacity' might be

| Figure 3.1 | Illustration of straight-line depreciation |

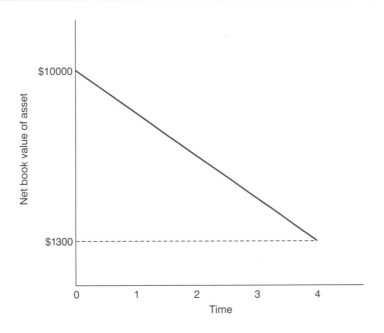

Figure 3.2	Illustration of reducing balance depreciation

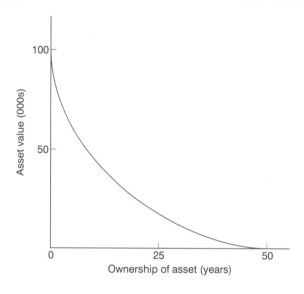

Table 3.12	Illustration of reducing balance depreciation: Popham Ltd

Year ending	Opening asset net book value $	Depreciation charge @ 40% of opening net book value $	Closing net book value $
31/12/00	10 000	4 000	6 000
31/12/01	6 000	2 400	3 600
31/12/02	3 600	1 440	2 160
31/12/03	2 160	864	1 296

Table 3.13	Contrasting straight-line and reducing balance depreciation: Popham Ltd

	Depreciation charge		Net book value	
Year ending	Straight line $	Reducing balance $	Straight line $	Reducing balance $
31/12/00	2 175	4 000	7 825	6 000
31/12/01	2 175	2 400	5 650	3 600
31/12/02	2 175	1 440	3 475	2 160
31/12/03	2 175	864	1 300	1 296

specified as 100 000 miles in the case of a lorry; 40 000 operations in the case of a machine; or 35 000 flying hours in the case of an aeroplane. Using the original cost, an estimate of any forecast salvage value and the estimated 'usage capacity', a usage rate is calculated for each mile driven, operation performed, or hour flown. Thereafter, depreciation is charged in each financial period based on the number of miles driven, operations performed, or hours flown in that period multiplied by this usage rate.

Choice of depreciation method

The IASB does not require that a reporting entity use any particular method, only that it selects that method which most closely reflects the expected consumption of the economic benefits from the asset being depreciated. However, there are countries, in particular a number of continental European ones, in which the methods and rates of depreciation are effectively specified by national legislation. At the end of the day, the directors of a reporting entity have considerable discretion in both how depreciation is calculated (which method to use) and in the parameters (e.g. forecast asset life and salvage value) used in the calculation. This is, of course, subject to the (normal) overriding requirement that the resultant financial statements must provide a reasonable portrayal of the finances of the entity (in the UK, the requirement is that they present 'a true and fair view').

Impact of depreciation method

The choice of method for computing depreciation can have a major impact on the reported profits of an entity, especially one that is capital intensive or growing rapidly. Typically, for newer businesses investing large amounts of start-up capital in fixed assets:

- Straight-line depreciation will equalise the profit and loss charge over the forecast life of the assets.
- Reducing balance depreciation will make the earlier years bear a higher charge than the later years (making it more difficult for the entity to report a profit in those earlier years).
- Usage based depreciation will probably make the earlier years bear a lower charge than the later years, as usage is likely to be lower in the start-up phase (making it easier to report profits in earlier years).

Whichever method is chosen, the computation of the depreciation charges will involve a significant amount of (managerial) judgement in forecasting the:

- Life of the asset (whether in years or usage capacity), particularly as this life should be based on the economic life of the asset rather than its physical life and forecasting the obsolescence of technology is an art rather than a science. This can be a particular problem with new technology assets where the pace of technological change can be very rapid. It is less of a problem with more traditional assets.
- Salvage value of the asset. Again, this is likely to be significantly affected by the pace of technological change and it is likely to be much lower for new technology assets than more traditional ones.

The exercise of this judgement is sometimes a contentious issue as it can be very difficult for auditors, who may (perhaps, inevitably will) lack the technical expertise to challenge these judgements in determining whether financial statements present 'a true and fair view'.

Given the range of different methods available for computing depreciation and the critical importance of forecasts (salvage value and asset life) in this computation, a reader of an entity's accounting reports will not be able to understand its financial state of affairs without knowing on what basis depreciation had been calculated, and what the key estimates used in its computation were. The policies that an entity employs in computing depreciation are (universally) regarded as a significant item of information for the readers of annual corporate financial statements and, as such, have to be disclosed as part of those statements, normally via the supplementary notes.

Meeting the information needs of management

The most important functions of management are to plan and to control the activities of the enterprises they manage. The planning function is the process whereby goals are established and methods developed for achieving them. It includes the important process of operational *budgeting*, formal planning – the relationship between goals and the specific means of achieving them. Managers also have to have information to assist them in *decision making*, often seen as a sub-function of planning. Decision making can be short term, for example deciding whether to subcontract some work as a result of a skills shortage, or longer term, for example deciding when to replace ageing plant and equipment.

The *control function* is the process of assessing whether the established goals are being achieved, and, if they are not, what can be done. Operational questions arise such as: what changes need to be made in order to achieve established goals? Should existing goals be revised? Implicit in the control process is *performance evaluation* – staff managers reviewing the performance of subordinate line managers. Performance evaluation often includes the notion of *management by exception* – that is, highlighting areas of concern rather than necessarily providing too much information, much of which might simply indicate that most areas are in line with expectation. Figure 3.3 illustrates these managerial processes with the corresponding management accounting activities.

A critical issue for the management accountant is the way that information is presented. The question of the extent to which the format and content of management accounting reports influence the actions taken by managers is discussed at length in later chapters. Information *per se* is of little use unless it influences the management decision-making process. Information needs to be communicated and acted upon. If the budgetary (planning, decision-making and control) process (see Chapter 7) is to be a success, line management need to be motivated through:

- Frequent contact about results.
- The use of results in performance appraisal.
- The use of departmental/section meetings.
- The creation of a 'game spirit'. (Hofstede 1968: 247).

A major study of management accounting (AAA 1972) outlined four core objectives of management accounting which are summarised in Table 3.14.

Objectives and goals of organisations

So far, we have touched only briefly on the objectives and goals of organisations. It is commonly assumed that the primary objective of private-sector enterprises is one of profit maximisation. However, this begs the question of what profit and when. An alternative statement of this objective, and one which is widely held within the capital markets, is that private-sector enterprises should act so as to maximise the value of their shares. This is because share prices impute the future earnings stream of an enterprise and the accepted market assessment of the quality/riskiness of this earning stream. More specifically, the share price reflects the market's assessment of the quantity, quality and timing of the future cash flows that will be derived from the enterprise's operations. This approach gives clear guidance to management in its decision making – it should seek to maximise the net present value of the enterprise's future cash flows (for a fuller discussion of the meaning of net present value see Chapter 9), by doing this it will – assuming that the capital markets are efficient – maximise the value of its shares, thereby achieving the best results for shareholders.

What is the relationship between cash flows and profit? This can best be illustrated by considering an enterprise which has a finite life. Consider an enterprise which commenced operations on 1 January 2006 and was wound up on 31 December 2007. On 1 January 2006 the owners of the enterprise subscribed £10 000 in share capital and on that date the enterprise purchased a machine costing £10 000. On the same date it rented this machine to a client on a two-year leasing agreement at an annual rental of £6000. The enterprise forecast that the machine would have a market value of £4000 as at 31 December 2007 and intended to use the straight line basis for depreciation in its profit and loss account. Assuming all transactions are on a cash basis, the enterprise would show the following results for its financial year ended 31 December 2006:

Figure 3.3	Management by objectives and the accounting process

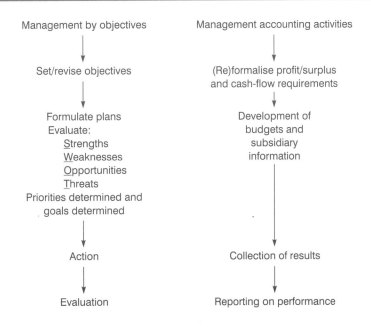

	£
Rental income	6 000
Depreciation (£10 000 – £4 000)/2	3 000
Profit	3 000

Assuming that the forecast market value of the machine as at 31 December 2007 is correct and that the machine is sold for this amount on that date, the profit and loss account for the year ending on that date would be the same as that shown above for the year ended 31 December 2006, i.e. it would show a profit of £3000, and the position over the two years would be:

	2006 £	2007 £	Total £
Rental income	6 000	6 000	12 000
Depreciation	3 000	3 000	6 000
Profit	3 000	3 000	6 000

The corresponding cash flows from the enterprise's perspective would be:

	2006 £	2007 £	Total £
Received from investors	10 000		10 000
Paid for machine	(10 000)		(10 000)
Received from client	6 000	6 000	12 000
Received from sale of machine	0	4 000	4 000
	6 000	10 000	16 000

Table 3.14   Objectives of management accounting

1 Management accounting should be related to the planning functions of the managers. This involves:
   - goal identification;
   - planning for optimal resource flow and their measurement.
2 Management accounting should be related to organisational problem areas. This includes:
   - relating the structure of the firm to its goals;
   - installing and maintaining an effective communication and reporting system;
   - measuring existing resource uses, discovering exceptional performance and identifying causal factors of such exceptions.
3 Management accounting should be related to the management control function. This includes:
   - determining economic characteristics of appropriate performance areas which are significant in terms of overall goals;
   - helping to motivate desirable individual performances through a realistic communication of performance information in relation to goals;
   - highlighting performance measures indicating goal incongruity within identifiable performance and responsibility areas.
4 Management accounting should be related to operating systems management, by function, product, project or other segmentation of operations. This involves:
   - measurement of relevant cost input and/or revenue or statistical measures of outputs;
   - communicating appropriate data, of essentially economic character, to critical personnel on a timely basis.

On its liquidation, the enterprise would be able to pay the investors £16 000, representing a cash gain of £6000 (£16 000 less the original investment of £10 000). That is, the total profit of £6000 shown above is exactly equal to the total cash gain to the investors. However, this profit has been apportioned, using the straight-line depreciation method, equally between the two years involved. This would not be the case if another method of depreciation, such as the reducing-balance method, was used. If this were done the profit and loss account would be:

	2006 £	2007 £	Total £
Rental income	6 000	6 000	12 000
Depreciation	3 680	2 320	6 000
Profit	2 320	3 680	6 000

In this case the profit and loss accounts show a lower profit in the first year, and a higher one in the second year, although the total profit over the two years is the same and equals the total cash gain from the investors' perspective. Ultimately, the investors (shareholders) will be primarily concerned with this total cash gain (receiving it either directly via distributions or indirectly via its being imputed in the share price of the company). Profit is nothing more than a performance measure which allocates this cash gain to individual accounting periods in an attempt to enable shareholders to assess how successfully the enterprise is pursuing the objective of increasing the cash (wealth) ultimately attributable to them. Different accounting bases (e.g. depreciation policies) will result in different allocations of this cash gain across accounting periods – profit can usefully be thought of as 'an intertemporal allocation of cash flows'.

While this is a problem for financial accounting it should not be so for management/management accounting – here the focus should be clearly on cash flows and not on profit. Such a focus will ensure that management orients itself to what is the ultimate objective of private-sector enterprises – increasing shareholder wealth.

In the public sector the notion of maximisation of profit or share value is replaced by a requirement to keep cost to a minimum and to ensure the provision of services which represent value for money (see Chapter 9). In practice, business enterprises have a number of operational goals or effectiveness criteria which include 'maximising' or 'satisfying', profitability, market position, product leadership, throughput and productivity. The purposes of such goals range from the motivation of individuals, the recruitment of capital and other resources, the focusing of attention or direction, to the determination of a rationale or ideal for which the enterprise and the members aim. As these purposes differ problems arise in operationalising them. It is beyond the scope of this book to examine in detail the issues that enterprises face in formulating and operationalising goals or objectives. Useful reviews of these issues can be found in work by Cyert and March (1963), Perrow (1970) and Simon (1957), as well as Freeman (1985), who raises the following questions:

- Should broad abstracts (such as good corporate citizenship) or specific goals (such as to maximise market value) be used ?

- How easy is the measurement of good performance? Broad abstracts are harder to measure than specific goals and therefore more difficult to build into a reward system.

- How congruent and consistent are the various goals (for instance good corporate citizenship versus market value maximisation or short term versus long term)?

- How, and how quickly, do goals change?
- Are goals really determined by the organisation itself, or by its environment or by individuals within the organisation? In the first case the organisation has the power (in terms of competition, bargaining, absorption and coalition) to determine its own goals. In the second case the organisation has no power and so its goals are in direct response to its environment, requiring more cooperation and interaction. In the third case the goals are determined by the informal/formal coalition of its members' goals. Power is determined by dominant members, previous experience and commitment of individuals; bargaining and side payments through the internal and external political process.

Conclusion

Management accounting exists to serve the needs of managers for information to assist them in discharging their planning, deciding and controlling responsibilities. To achieve this, a proper system of recording the transactions of an enterprise needs to be established. The differing nature of enterprises, in both the private and public sectors, means that there is no single universally applicable system of management accounting. Instead, effective management accounting systems reflect their organisational context and the information needs of managers. There is no legal regulation of management accounting, unlike financial accounting. However, it does have an underpinning philosophy – it must be useful and cost effective, and it must provide information about the past, for control purposes, and about the future, for decision-making purposes.

Chapter review

This chapter has recognised that the two major roles of accounting – providing reports on financial performance for external stakeholders (financial reporting) and assisting managers to manage more effectively (management accounting) – require different perspectives. However, the satisfactory discharge of both of these roles requires that an entity have an adequate system for the recording of its economic transactions (events). The orientation of financial reporting is towards the past, with a focus on how much profit an enterprise has generated in a given financial period, and it operates in an increasingly regulated framework. Management accounting needs to have a future orientation, although this needs to be firmly grounded on reliable information about the past. Only by achieving this can it assist management in its various functions. Management accounting needs to reflect the environmental, technological and organisational contexts in which it exists, and to recognise that the focus of management should be the maximisation of the future cash flows which will derive from its decision.

Further reading

There is a vast literature on the subject matter covered in this chapter. The IASB (2006) provides a useful framework. Hofstede's 1968 text is still a valuable read, its title, *The Game of Budget Control,* outlines well the theme of the book. Perkins (1996) is worth a read by those interested in public-sector issues. In addition to the other texts cited in the chapter, Argenti's *Practical Corporate Planning* (1983) provides a useful general background to much of the discussion of this chapter, as does Collier (2003) in the context of a broad range of management decisions. Other useful reference points for further information are the websites of the:

Accounting Standards Board: www.asb.org.uk
Financial Accounting Standards Board: www.fasb.org
Australian Accounting Standards Board: www.aasb.com.au
Canadian Institute of Chartered Accountants: www.cica.com
International Accounting Standards Board: www.iasb.co.uk

Questions and exercises

Guide notes can be found at the back of the book for all questions marked with an asterisk*.

1* The prime records of Suppliers Ltd contain the following summaries of its transactions for the week ending 7 January 2007. These need to be transferred to its ledger accounts. Prepare journal entries which will do this, using the chart of accounts contained in Table 3.2.

(a) Credit sales to customers amounting to $60 000 of merchandise which originally cost $30 000.

(b) Cash sales to customers amounting to $7000 of merchandise which originally cost $3700.

(c) Purchases of materials from suppliers on credit terms amounting to $35 000.

(d) Payments to suppliers for materials supplied on credit terms, amounting to $18 000.

(e) Payments to staff of salaries and wages amounting to $6000.

Required:

Prepare the necessary journal entries.

2* On 1 January 2007 Jehosophat Ltd purchased a new machine for $244 000. The machine was expected to have a useful life of five years and be able during this period to perform a total of 40 000 individual operations. At the end of this time the machine was expected to have a residual value of $24 000. The planned use of this machine during the five year period is:

Year ended 31st December	No. of operations
2007	8 000
2008	12 000
2009	10 000
2010	5 000
2011	5 000

Required:

(a) Calculate the annual depreciation charges for each of the five years during which the machine will be owned on:

   (i)   the straight-line basis

   (ii) the reducing balance basis

   (iii) the usage basis

(b) Plot a graph showing the net book value of the machine at the end of each of the financial years in question.

3   The accounting records of H. Bloggs Plc. contain the following balances as at 31 December 2006.

	Debit £	Credit £
Sales		413 000
Purchases	314 000	
Stock (as at 1/1/06)	45 000	
Insurance	4 000	
Electricity	2 000	
Rent	15 000	
Rates	8 000	
Wages	11 000	
Sundry expenses	8 000	
Freehold land, at cost	13 000	
Equipment, at cost	33 000	
Equipment accumulated depreciation, as at 1/1/2006		11 000
Motor vehicles, at cost	24 000	
Motor vehicles accumulated depreciation, as at 1/1/2006		13 000
Debtors	130 000	
Creditors		65 000
Provision for doubtful debts		1 000
Bank balances		34 000
Share Capital		30 000
Retained profits, at 1/1/2006		40 000
Totals	607 000	607 000

The following factors have not yet been recorded in these accounting records:

(a) The value of stocks as at 31/12/2006 was £52 000.

(b) As at 31/12/2006, there were prepayments on insurance of £1000 and on rates of £3000. There were accruals of £1000 on electricity and £2000 on sundry expenses.

(c) Bad debts of £2000 should be written off and the provision for doubtful debts adjusted to become 3 per cent of the remaining debts.

(d) A vehicle that had originally cost £5000 on 1 January 2005 was sold for £2000 on 31 December 2006, and the sales proceeds were mistakenly credited to the motor vehicles at cost account.

(e) Depreciation should be charged (on a straight-line basis) at a rate of 25 per cent for motor vehicles and 20 per cent of equipment. No motor vehicles or equipment became 'life-expired' during the year.

Required:

Prepare the journal entries needed to adjust the accounting records for the above factors.

4   The final trial balance of A. Business, a general dealer operating as a sole trader, as at 31 December 2005, is shown below. This is the trial balance from which the accounts of the business as at 31 December 2005 were prepared.

	Debit Euros	Credit Euros
Fixed assets at cost	54 000	
Fixed assets – accumulated depreciation		26 000
Bank balance	1 000	
Debtors	23 000	
Creditors		19 000
Stocks	46 000	
Capital		79 000
	124 000	124 000

In the year to 31 December 2006, the business entered into the following transactions:

(a) The owner's personal drawings from the business bank account amounted to €21 000.

(b) Payments to suppliers amounted to €208 000.

(c) Business expenses of €53 000 were paid during the year.

(d) Purchases (on credit) amounted to €220 000.

(e) Sales (on credit) amounted to €385 000.

(f) Additional fixed assets of €4000 were purchased during the year, but these were not paid for until after the year end.

(g) Receipts from customers during the year totalled €387 000.

The following additional information is available:

(a) Fixed assets are depreciated at the rate of 20 per cent per annum of original cost.

(b) Stocks as at 31 December 2006 amounted to €54 000.

Required:

Prepare ledger accounts, and a final trial balance, summarising the transactions of the business for the year to 31 December 2006.

5 On 1 January 2006, J. Smith set up in business as a general dealer. On that day he opened a business bank account with Anywhere Bank PLC in the name J. Smith, trading as Buy It & Sell It Enterprises and deposited $20 000 from his personal resources into this account. At the same time the bank agreed to grant the business a $10 000 overdraft facility, secured on J. Smith's private house. During the following 12 months, Buy It & Sell It Enterprises engaged in the following business transactions:

(i) On 1 January 2006, it purchased for cash (paid from the business bank account) a second-hand van at a cost of $8000. At this time, the forecast useful life of the van was four years with an estimated salvage value of $1000.

(ii) On 1 February 2006 it entered into a rental agreement for a warehouse at an annual rental of $4000 payable quarterly in advance. The rental payments were made on the due dates from the business bank account. At the same time it rented telephone facilities at a quarterly rental of $50 payable in advance.

(iii) On 5 February 2006, it bought goods from an auction sale for $10 000, paid in cash from the business bank account.

(iv) On 9 February 2006, it sold for cash some of the goods it had purchased for $10 000 on 5 February 2006. These goods, which had cost the business $5000, were sold for $9000.

(v) During the remainder of the year to 31 December 2006, it purchased goods at a cost of $100 000 from a variety of sources. $40 000 of these goods were purchased for cash (from the business bank account). The remainder were purchased on credit. Of the credit purchases, $50 000 had been paid for from the business bank account as at 31 December 2006. Of the goods purchased subsequently to 5 February 2006, goods with an original purchase price of $80 000 had been sold by 31 December 2006. These goods were sold for a total of $120 000. $60 000 of these sales were for cash and the balance on credit terms. Of the sales on credit terms, $50 000 had been settled by credit customers as at 31 December 2006.

(vi) From 1 June 2006, it employed a general assistant who was paid a salary of $1000 per month, payable monthly in arrears from the business bank account.

(vii) Paid telephone call charges (i.e. over and above the rental charge) of $750 from the business bank account. As at 31 December 2006, the business estimated that telephone call charges incurred, but not yet invoiced, amounted to some $100.

(viii) At 31 December 2006, the business examined its holding of stock and estimated that stock with a purchase value of $1000 could only be sold for $500. It forecast that all other stock could be sold for more than had been paid for it. On the same date, the business reviewed its debtors and estimated that one customer who owed $2000 would only be able to pay $500. It forecast that all other amounts owed to it by customers would be paid in full.

(ix) During the year, J. Smith transferred $500 per month from the business bank account to his personal bank account to contribute towards his living costs.

Required:

(a) Prepare the ledger accounts necessary to record properly the business transactions of Buy It & Sell It Enterprises.

(b) Prepare a trial balance as at 31 December 2006 for Buy It & Sell It Enterprises, incorporating any necessary year-end adjustments.

6* Using the chart of accounts shown in Table 3.2 design a cash book layout to record the following transactions, and record these transactions in this layout:

(a) The payment of €10 000 for a new delivery van.

(b) The payment of €250 for an advertisement in a local newspaper.

(c) The payment to a supplier of €2500 for goods originally supplied on credit terms.

(d) The repayment of a long-term loan of €10 000.

(e) The receipt of €2000 from a customer who had previously been supplied with goods on a credit basis.

(f) The receipt of €20 000 from the issue of additional share capital.

(g) The payment of wages amounting to €6000.

7 Critically discuss, using examples, the relationship between cash flow and profit.

8* John Smith is about to set up in business as a newsagent in rented premises. He has asked you to help in designing a chart of accounts for this business which will provide him with the information he needs to manage the business in a cost-effective way. Prepare a chart of accounts which would be suitable for a small newsagent business.

9* Makeit Ltd is a small company which specialises in the manufacture of wrought ironwork gates to customer specifications. It employs three specialist blacksmiths, a salesman/negotiator and an office administrator and offers its customers 30-day credit terms. Prepare a schedule listing the prime documents that it needs to have as a basis for the maintenance of its accounting records.

10* Unification Plc is a large, diversified company in the electronics industry. It has a well established accounting and internal control system. However, in preparing its financial statements each year the company finds it necessary to make a number of adjustments to the information recorded in its accounting system. List the areas in which you believe that the company finds it necessary to make such adjustments.

11* It is sometimes said that depreciation is a method of providing for the replacement of fixed assets when they come to the end of their useful lives. Do you agree with this view or not? Justify your answer.

12 Discuss the considerations that management should take into account in determining the design of an accounting system which will satisfy both its own information requirements and its obligation to provide external reports on the entity which it manages.

PART 2

Part 2 of the book contains five chapters, all of which focus (in different ways) on the contribution that accounting (and accountants) can make to the more effective management of organisations.

The first chapter, 'Cost concepts and measurement', develops the underpinning concepts of costs and their measurement. These core principles are then developed further in the next chapter, 'Cost analysis for management decisions', which focuses on the importance of management being provided with useful information to assist them in the measurement of organisational/departmental/product costs and their decision-making and planning processes.

The third chapter in this part, 'Working capital management', focuses on the importance of effective working capital management and the various techniques that accountants have developed to assist in such management.

The next chapter in this part, 'Budgetary planning and control', concentrates on the key role of the budgetary process in the achievement of effective organisational management. This work is built upon in the final chapter, 'Internal performance and evaluation', which focuses on the activities of large multi-divisional organisations.

Cost concepts and measurements

4

Chapter preview

There are many individual concepts and measurements of 'cost', and sometimes these are confusing, or even conflicting. Different costs (or cost information) may be needed for financial accounting and external reporting, for forward planning for short-term as distinct from long-term decision making, and for budgetary and other forms of management control. The objective of this chapter is to clarify this diversity as a background to the topic discussions in the chapters which follow.

Cost is a sacrifice through resource loss, consumption or transformation. The choice of cost concepts and measurements is affected by the type of decision or control situation, by the timespan with which we are concerned, by how identifiable or traceable is the cost data which is available, and by the type of production or other business (or public-service) activity that is being carried out. Here we have a particular concern for opportunity cost, fixed v. variable costs, direct v. indirect costs, and historical and absorption costs v. costs relevant for management planning, decisions and control.

Fundamental concepts

True cost

True cost is a statement or measurement of sacrifice. This sacrifice is the loss, **consumption** or surrender of resources, value, benefit or welfare. The purchase of goods involves the surrender of cash or the taking on of debt. Using raw materials in a factory involves the cost of consumption of the materials, although this cost is then transformed into new value in the production process (after allowing for any process waste, pilferage, etc.). Losing a watch involves cost in the form of the value of the loss, which could be measured by the original price of the watch or by the price of replacing it, according to the context of our concern or the decision facing us. Losing a briefcase may be viewed similarly, but if the briefcase was full of business or personal papers there will be more complex and intangible problems in assessing the total cost, or sacrifice, arising from this loss.

Opportunity cost

Opportunity cost is the measure of benefit forgone by using scarce resources to follow one option to the exclusion of the next-best option. Thus using a limited bank balance to buy a car may make it necessary to forgo a holiday; the opportunity cost is the forgone net satisfaction from the holiday. Using funds from trading profits to increase dividend payments may pre-empt the opportunity to purchase new, cost-saving machinery.

Opportunity cost is an important concept derived from economics. Opportunity costs are not routinely recorded in accounting records or reports. Rather, they arise in the mind, or on the back of an envelope, of the manager or decision-maker. They are often extremely important for good planning and decision making, and the concept helps to emphasise that routine accounting information by itself seldom provides a sufficient basis for forward planning and decisions. Routine accounting records and reports provide information on past costs and revenues, but this is seldom a reliable predictor of the future as it takes no account of choice, inflation, market or technological change, or other uncertainty or risk.

Cash and accrual accounting

Simple accounting systems equate cost with cash expenditure. However, the IASB requires that accrual accounting be employed in the preparation of corporate financial statements.

Under an accrual accounting system the cash or debt outlay costs of resources which are not consumed at time of purchase are debited to asset accounts, e.g. for raw materials stocks, and these asset accounts are then credited or drawn down as the costs of materials consumed are recorded through the year. This is the basis for historical costing methods (see below), which link the financial and management accounting systems for corporate stewardship purposes.

Costs for different purposes

This chapter seeks to demonstrate that cost can be defined and measured in different ways. There is no single 'one correct way'. The most appropriate 'measure of cost is dependent upon the purpose for which it is required' (Parker 1984: 59). The three main purposes for which cost information is required are stewardship accounting, management control, and planning and decision making. Stewardship accounting is accounting recording, and reporting for accountability and information for parties external to management shareholders, creditors, regulators, tax collectors and, sometimes, employees and the general public.

The other two main purposes relate primarily to internal information for management; and they are interlinked. Management control is the function of measuring how well management plans and decisions are being achieved, and of providing guidance for any corrective action needed to improve the achievement of, or to amend, these targeted plans and decisions. Decision making relates to specific problems, opportunities and new plans. In spite of being interlinked, these two main purposes for cost information often require different and distinctive cost concepts and measures to be used. A major reason for this is that cost control information is concerned with the present and the recent past, while planning and decision making information is concerned with the future, sometimes the short term and sometimes the long term. A complication is that many costs have a different significance, or a different measurement, according to the length of the time-horizon relevant to particular management decisions and planning activities.

Costs related to time and activity

Some business costs are constant or 'fixed' over a period of time, regardless of the volume of output or activity, while others will change with normal activity and can be described as 'variable'. In theory, over a long enough period of time, time-related fixed costs can be terminated, so that for the long term all cost may be considered as variable. But most cost analysis is concerned with business behaviour in the short term, both for management control and for decision making, so that the separate identification and measurement of fixed cost and variable cost provide useful information.

Fixed costs

Fixed costs are those costs which are independent of the current level of activity and which are not expected to change in the short term, except for minor revisions for inflation, contract renewal, etc. As in most accounting measurement and reporting, the 'short term' for this purpose is usually taken to mean a period of one year ahead or the current financial and budget year of the firm. Examples of fixed costs include business property taxes, premises rental, equipment lease payments, and the salaries of permanent staff whose work is essential and unrelated to the level of short-term activity; e.g. the managing director, most accounting staff, security staff. Fixed costs are included in the 'overheads' of the business, but there are additional overheads (such as company car expenses) which are at least partly comprised of variable costs. Fixed costs (FC) can be categorised into three main types:

1 Committed costs are costs deriving from ongoing legal or contractual obligations (e.g. rates, insurance premiums, rent, etc.) which typically could not be terminated short of winding up the business.

2 Managed costs include the salaries of staff essential to the continuance of current activity, together with other support costs of the organisation.

3 Programmed (or discretionary) fixed costs include the costs of services not directly linked to current operations or activity but which instead follow policy decisions to support corporate development. Examples include R&D, some personnel and training activities, and some marketing and promotional activities (e.g. sports and arts sponsorship).

Figure 4.1 illustrates these three types of fixed costs.

Committed costs (CC) have a long time-horizon commitment, often for the life of the business. Managed costs (MC) have a shorter time-horizon, although frequently this is greater than a year unless it is upset by deep business recession. Programmed costs (PC), at least in theory, have the shortest time-horizon, being governed by the annual budget cycle for funding renewal; in practice, however, staffing and capital-spending programmes (e.g. in R&D) may make it difficult to cut even this category of fixed cost within as short a period as the next budget year. Programmed costs may also be termed discretionary costs. The distinctions between these three categories of fixed costs may be arbitrary to some extent, but (as can be seen in Figure 4.1) they help to illustrate that all fixed costs do not behave in the same way and that they can have widely different degrees of fixedness through time.

Variable costs

Variable costs comprise those costs which arise, more or less in direct proportion to the level of activity, or the volume of output or of trading, occurring in the firm. The major variable costs are the payroll cost of employees working directly on operations

Figure 4.1	Fixed and variable costs related to time

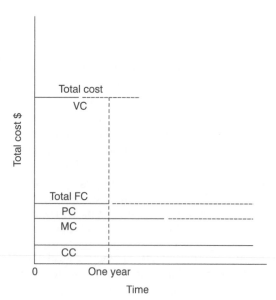

and the costs of bought-in stocks used (whether raw materials, component or finished goods ready for resale). These are the 'prime costs' of the operations of a business, but, additionally, some overhead or indirect cost can be measured and controlled as variable costs because they are directly linked to operational activity; industrial examples include energy, supplies, lubricant and usage-linked equipment maintenance.

Figure 4.1 includes a line for variable cost (VC). Here it is assumed that activity remains at a constant level, so that total VC could, or should, also remain a constant over the short-term planning and budgeting cycle of a typical year. This assumption is usually unrealistic, with total VC changing through the year as activity levels change in response to seasonal, market and other influences.

Mixed costs

Some costs do not fit neatly into either the fixed cost or variable cost categories. These are the semi-fixed costs and semi-variable costs, collectively termed 'mixed costs'. Semi-fixed costs, also called 'step costs', are costs of a fixed or constant character which increase at intervals as activity rises: examples include the need to employ an additional supervisor or to lease an additional machine as output rises. Semi-variable costs are more subtle. At low outputs, labour may be inefficient, especially on new product runs where a 'learning curve' must be experienced before full efficiency is reached. At very high outputs stress, weariness, overcrowding and haste may increase waste and slow the production rate of both labour and machinery.

In Figure 4.2 we bring together the three kinds of time-and activity-related costs previously described. (FC1 indicates the fixed cost, VC1 the variable costs, and MC the mixed costs.) The figure shows the costs as solid lines over the normal range of activity and as dotted lines at the extremes of low and very high activity. An enterprise may have little or no experience of working outside the normal range of activity and therefore no firm evidence of what the costs would be. Another complication is that accountants find it awkward to track mixed costs in routine reporting and they prefer to estimate the semi-fixed costs as if they were fixed, at least over the normal range, and the semi-variable costs as if they were fully variable. The result of this is that the conventional cost-activity diagram does not show mixed costs but, instead, just the subdivision between fixed costs (FC2) and variable costs (VC2), on the basis as if these costs retained the same relationship throughout the entire activity range as they do within the normal range. It follows that conventional accounting estimates of the expected level of 'fixed + variable = total cost' at the extremes of the activity range may not be reliable. This may not be too important at very high levels of activity, where total cost should be well covered by revenue, but it could lead to critical misjudgement by a firm operating at low activity, e.g. during a recession, as regards the hidden 'variable' costs that may be incurred, and also as regards the potential for cutting some 'fixed' costs in the short term.

Figures 4.1 and 4.2 show the subdivisions of total costs in relation to time or activity. But often it is more useful to study the behaviour of unit costs (i.e. cost per unit of activity, be this production, sales or service activity). This is illustrated in Figure 4.3. Once again, the costs are shown by solid lines over the normal range of activity and by dotted lines over the extreme ranges. Unit variable cost is assumed to be a constant value, at least over the normal range of activity. But fixed costs per unit fall as output increases. The same total values of FC2 and VC2 are used for Figure 4.3

as for Figure 4.2; the only difference is that they are displayed on the basis of cost per unit instead of total costs.

Figure 4.3 confirms how unit cost falls as output rises, at least through to the upper end of the normal activity range, and this has important implications for the pricing decisions we shall consider in Chapter 5. Beyond the normal range of activity, for which staffing, equipment and space have been planned, there may arise significant extra semi-fixed and semi-variable cost (i.e. MC), which will need management review of output and pricing policy and decisions.

In Figure 4.3 the FC2 line shows the total of combined fixed and variable unit costs (after subsuming mixed costs). This can be termed 'total unit cost', 'full cost' or 'average unit cost' (ACR). ACR stands for 'average cost, rising', because cost calculations by accountants are usually based on the assumption of stable or rising activity levels. However, activity or output can fall as well as rise, and some of the variable costs and mixed costs can prove 'sticky' or slow in contracting on a downward movement of activity compared to their timing and rate of increase when the activity level is rising. This is a frequent cause of difficulty for firms during a recession or other cause of decline or contraction. This is illustrated in Figure 4.4 by the curve ACF (average cost, falling).

During periods of falling market activity, it is important for managers to be vigilant and keep variable and mixed costs under control so that they remain close to the baseline represented by ACR. In practice, some managements may try to squeeze unit costs below ACR by pressing for higher productivity in variable costs, or by cutting out certain fixed costs. Here the programmed or discretionary costs such as staff training or R&D activity are most vulnerable, but drastic cuts in these policy areas of corporate activity can seriously weaken a firm's long-term capacity for revival and growth.

Figure 4.2   Total costs related to activity

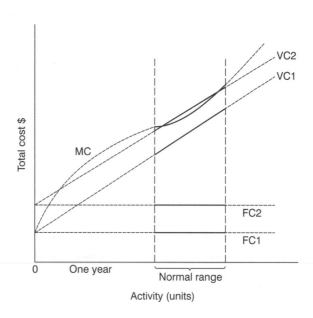

Marginal cost

Accountants sometimes use the term '**marginal cost**' as synonymous with 'variable cost', perhaps especially when using the term in the context of decision making and budgeting, as distinct from routine reporting and control. This can be confusing for readers who have studied economics, where the meaning and measurement of marginal cost is somewhat different. In economics marginal cost is defined as the extra cost of producing one extra unit. In practice this is usually the same, or nearly the same, as the accountant's unit variable cost. However, the economist assumes a continuous curvilinear function for marginal cost, so that the marginal cost of the second extra unit added, or deleted, is always slightly different from that of the first extra unit. In contrast, the accountant, as we have seen, assumes that variable or marginal unit cost remains a constant across a normal range of activity. Of course, for most business decisions, one is not working in the context of making or selling only a single extra unit. Rather, one is considering some larger number of units to fulfil a contract, enter a new market or stock a new branch, etc. For decision making in such situations, one must look out for all costs which may change, including any new fixed or raised costs. This involves differential cost analysis, which we shall consider in Chapter 5. But first we must consider some of the terminology and problems of identifying and tracing cost information.

Cost identification and traceability

Cost is the sacrificed value of resources used or consumed. This value comprises the physical quantity of resources used multiplied by the unit 'prices' of those resources.

| Figure 4.3 | Unit costs related to activity |

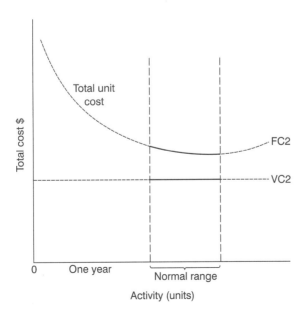

The accountant usually has access to accurate information on resource prices, from invoice files, payroll records, etc. But accountants must depend upon managers for providing accurate information on what resources are used, in what quantity, when, and to achieve what output or other activity. The accountant usually will provide, or help to develop, the necessary data collection and recording systems. Where work is non-uniform and/or there are many separate outputs drawing on common support services, the problems of recording resource use data accurately and tracing them to the correct output are complex.

Recording the quantity of resources used, and when, is fairly straightforward, although it is tedious and requires vigilance to ensure continuing accuracy. The big problem is often to trace the resource usage to a specific output (required for planning and decision making information) and to the accountability of a specific manager (required for the budgetary and management control discussed in later chapters). To achieve this traceability of costs we need to introduce some additional concepts for classifying costs and handling costs information.

Direct costs

These are costs which can be accurately traced to specific activities, output, contracts or decisions (or, in control accounting, to budgetary accountability). The most obvious direct costs are the costs of labour and materials directly used in a specific activity to provide a specific output; these costs are known as 'direct labour' and 'direct materials', and added together they are called 'prime costs'. Sometimes equipment use and some support services are so specific or committed to just one purpose that their costs also can be included as traceable direct costs.

| Figure 4.4 | Average unit costs with activity changes |

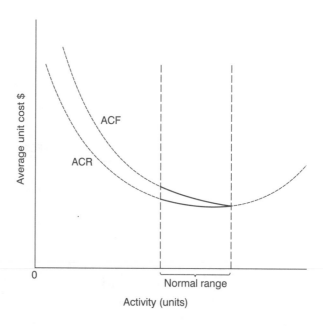

Indirect costs

These comprise all costs and expenses which are not directly traced to specific products, activities or outputs. Common examples include heating and lighting, consumable supplies, equipment and buildings maintenance, and many central services. In practice, the demarcation between direct and indirect cost is as much a matter of convenience and of whether or not more precise information is worth the expense of providing it, as it is a matter of inherent nature. For example, in universities and many other organisations, telephone use was treated as a general overhead expense and was not divided among departments. Then an attempt was made to estimate telephone use for recharge to departmental centres. However, the latter estimates were too tenuous or uncertain to carry conviction for enforcing cost control and reduction. So the final stage, when cost effective technology became available, was to install expensive telephone logging equipment, so that the use, and cost of use, of every separate telephone extension could be recorded and then be recharged as an accountable direct cost to the user departments. Where telephone use cost fell by more than the annualised cost of new equipment and the monitoring and book-keeping involved, then, clearly, converting an indirect cost into a direct cost could prove worthwhile. The detailed metering of energy consumption, especially in factories, provides another example where traditional treatment as an indirect cost can usefully be reorganised to permit recording and charging as a direct cost. In contrast, in a factory producing furniture where pots of glue stand ready beside the work benches, it probably will not be worth the 'cost of costing' to set up a control procedure to allow glue consumption to be charged as a direct cost to each unit or batch of product completed.

Overhead and period costs

The strict definition of 'overhead' or '**overhead costs**' is that this comprises all expenses not charged to output as direct costs (sometimes just direct labour and direct material). More generally, it is widely held that some indirect costs can be traced and estimated sufficiently accurately to be usefully charged to products, activities or at least their host department, and that we should restrict the use of the term 'overhead' to those expenses which are remote from productive activities and remote from any effective control or accountability by the managers of those activities. Examples include rent, property taxes and the costs of head office and central services.

Product costs, both direct and indirect, are carried forward into completed stock/inventory value and should not be recharged against corporate profit and loss until the year in which they are sold. In contrast, the general overheads defined above relate more to keeping the business in being than to specific products or production levels. In this context they are termed 'period costs' and should, in principle, be charged to corporate profit and loss in the year in which they are incurred. This latter group of costs includes the general expenses of promotion, distribution and sales, which are normally very remote from specific production activity, outputs and costs.

Common costs and joint costs

Common costs are defined as 'costs of facilities and services shared by a number of departments' (Parker 1984: 39). Such facilities and services may include a development department, engineering workshops, drawing office, maintenance department, as well as central services such as personnel and training. The use of the term 'common costs' tends to imply that these costs will be treated as overheads, but often they are best charged to user departments as indirect costs, or even as direct costs where a direct linkage can be traced between specific service provision and specific production runs or batches.

Joint costs must not be confused with common costs. Whereas the latter relate to services which back-up the production process, joint costs are the specific costs of production itself. They are the costs of shared resources of material, labour, energy, etc. entering into a production process or series of processes from which emerge two or more saleable products (though these may be saleable only after further, separate processing or after being combined with other product components). The outputs of joint costs production are known as 'joint products' if each is of significant sales value. Joint products of limited sales value are termed 'by-products', but the distinction is often arbitrary. Classic examples of joint product situations include petroleum refineries and petrochemicals, and meat processing (meat, tallow, offal, leather, etc.).

Given the nature of the joint product production process, it is usually impossible to measure and validate a unique cost for each of the joint product and by-product. The problem is exacerbated if varying the proportion of the input or details of joint processing can result in different proportions of volume output of the separate joint product, as in the case of oil refining. The problem is most acute when accountants need defensible costs to use in cost of sales and profit and loss calculations, and in stock/inventory valuation. Here there are several alternative approaches to cost allocation and valuation, of concern mainly to the professional accountant and explained in detail in specialists texts such as that by Drury (2004). Fortunately, the above accounting allocation and valuation problems are not usually important in the control of joint processes, for which physical performance measures and targets can often be used, or in the decision making process, where the main objective will be to maximise the excess of combined sales of all the joint products over and above their combined joint (and separate) costs.

Historical, absorption and variable costing

So far, this chapter has concentrated on concepts and measures of cost which may be relevant for studying problems of planning, decision making or control. These costs are often not immediately available from the firm's accounts but instead may have to be estimated or derived from other sources. Once relevant and accurate data is to hand, cost analysis can often be done 'on the back of an envelope' or, better, on a good PC spreadsheet package. In contrast, there is one form of cost information that is usually readily available from the ongoing accounts or accounting records of the firm. This comprises the historical costs of the enterprise, covering past (i.e. historical) resource purchases, stockholding, use and conversion into outputs.

The main reason for the historical-cost records is to provide a link with the financial accounting system of the firm. These records feed in information needed for periodic determination of profit and loss and of the balance-sheet values of stocks of materials (including components, parts and supplies), work-in-progress and finished goods. In principle, this need applies to all kinds of businesses. In practice, the accounting may be relatively simpler for service businesses which produce no physical product and thus have no physical work-in-progress or finished goods stock. Retailers and wholesalers, by definition, have no physical product conversion processes or work-in-progress, although they do usually carry finished stocks. It is in production businesses where the full complexity of historical costing arises; here the method of charging and recharging production costs is known as 'absorption costing', and this is explained below. An alternative approach, termed 'variable costing', is then compared with absorption costing in an illustrative example, helping to point up some of the weaknesses of historical costing.

Types of production and costing

There are three main types of production. Job (or one-off) production is where a single unit of a given specification is made at any one time. Examples include individual ships, bridges, hospitals and power-station generators. Job production is normally to customer's order and not for stock. Batch (or intermittent) production is where a predetermined number of units are produced at one time, either for stock or to fill a specific customer order. Often the production is on multi-purpose plant, so that time and cost control must allow for 'set-up time' in the changeover from one batch run to another. The third type of production is flow (or continuous) production. This can be a production or assembly line always making the same product. However, more usually it is a flow-line process plant typically producing petroleum or other chemical or mineral products on a continuous basis.

Historical costing, and also costing information for management control, varies somewhat according to the type of production. Job costing and batch costing treat each job or batch as a separate cost unit or cost centre, whereas the process costing used in flow production is more concerned with average costs per unit of output and per unit of plant time. Where process production goes through distinct stages with separable costs it is usual to record the cost at each stage. The slightly different bookkeeping procedures for each type of production are illustrated in specialist costing textbooks.

Historical and absorption cost flow

Figure 4.5 is a highly simplified model or illustration of the flow of resource-use costs through production and into periodic profit and loss calculation. Rectangles are used to indicate balance-sheet accounts, while circles designate cost, expense and revenue account, and transactions. The numbers on Figure 4.5 denote the type of cost calculation being transferred. Direct costs of specific materials and labour (for a known period of time) wholly committed to identified production can be charged to production on a precise, verifiable basis, known as 'allocation'. While the costs of production and other service departments may be direct and traceable when first charged to the control accounts of these departments, their recharge of service provided to benefit specific production jobs, batches, processes, etc. often involves estimation and constitutes indirect cost. Such recharges are known as 'apportionment'. The final recharge of manufacturing overhead to the work-in-progress account is termed 'absorption'; hence 'absorption costing', which will be contrasted with 'variable costing' below. The following paragraphs are keyed by letter to the rectangles and circles on Figure 4.5:

(a)   All central overheads could be recharged, as in (k), to profit and loss. But some central overheads (e.g. personnel and accounting) provide a definite benefit to manufacturing, which can be estimated and apportioned to manufacturing overhead for absorption. Sometimes, expenses such as heating, lighting and cleaning will be controlled and accounted for centrally instead of being separately measured and directly charged to production departments; these too can be apportioned.

(b) Production department costs not directly traceable to production units, batches or runs need to be apportioned to manufacturing overhead for absorption. Often the production overheads are relatively small, but in job production – or where batches or processes are to comply with changing specifications or tight quality standards, etc. – large back-up costs of a drawing office, fitters, quality inspectors, etc. may be involved. The depreciation cost of plant and machinery may be a major element of production overhead.

(c) Raw materials and components are traditionally stocked in secure stores and recorded in account as assets. They are then drawn out on requisitions (which should be closely monitored against waste and pilferage) and at that point become a direct charge to production. If the modern Japanese approach of just-in time (JIT) delivery of component and other materials is adopted material input can be charged to production directly upon delivery and inspection.

Figure 4.5 Historical and absorption cost flows

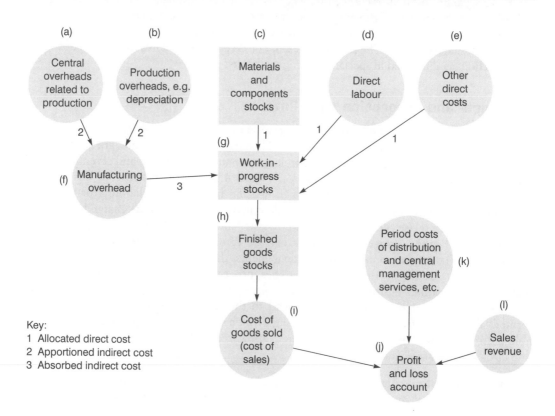

(d)   Labour time working on production is direct labour cost, to be allocated direct to production through the work-in-progress account, like direct materials. But direct workers will have time which is not directly productive, including sometimes maintenance, cleaning, fitting or inspection duties, or idle time because of delay in work flow or waiting for the completion of line reorganisation. These other activities should be separately recorded for charge to appropriate overhead accounts, which should be monitored for control. In practice, it is not always easy to ensure accurate time recording for this control.

(e)   If there are resource costs additional to labour and materials directly traceable to production, these should preferably be charged to production as direct costs instead of being 'lumped in together' with production overheads. Examples include the lease costs of equipment specific to particular production, and energy costs if these are significant (as they are in many process industries) and are metered separately and accurately for direct matching with specific production jobs, batches or runs.

(f)   Manufacturing overhead is used here as a control, or holding account, to bring together (on the debit side) all of the indirect or overhead costs/expenses apportioned to production (work-in-progress). On the credit side of the account will be entered the overhead absorption charges for the degree, or stages, of work completed. One cannot wait to know the final total of apportioned expenses, so one must estimate in advance what these expenses should amount to, or else one must set a target for them (see the discussion of standard costing in Chapter 7). One must also estimate the volume of production. In a multi-product situation one cannot realistically estimate accurately a unique overhead cost for each product, so the absorption recharging is normally based on linking cost absorption (or cost recovery into asset account values) to the particular input deemed to be most directly linked, or correlated, to the main causative influence on the level and/or variability of overhead costs. The absorption base chosen can be direct labour hours (or cost), direct material cost or machine hours (where the pace of production is largely governed by preset machine timings). If production workers effectively determine or fine-tune the production rate, direct labour hours are likely to be the best base for absorption charging. For example, assume that estimated manufacturing overhead for a period is £90 000, and estimated direct labour hours for the same period are estimated at 7500. The overhead absorption charge rate will be £12 per direct labour hour.

(g)   The work-in-progress asset account is debited with all direct and indirect costs as work progresses. Subsidiary account/records segregate the cost of each separate job, batch or process until work is certified complete, at which time the relevant total cost will be transferred to the finished goods asset account.

(h)   The finished goods asset account is debited with transfers from the work-in-progress account (unless the goods have been made to customer order, in which case they may instead be debited direct to the cost of goods sold account).

(i) All costs of output sold during a financial period are accumulated in the cost of goods sold (or cost of sales) account until periodic transfer to the profit and loss account.

(j) The profit and loss account also receives credit for sales revenues, and debit for all non-manufacturing period costs arising from the expenses of distribution, sales, promotion and central services. The residual balance in the account is the net profit or loss from trading/operations. Additional adjustment for interest and other financial corrections may be needed before establishing the final declared profit or loss.

(k) See (j).

Complications in historical absorption costing

It is easier to describe the general principle of the cost apportionment of production overheads and relevant general overheads (see (a) and (b) above) than it is to calculate these overhead costs fairly and reliably, at least when there is more than one department, line or process sharing the use of facilities and support services. For example, an obvious way to apportion costs such as rent, rates, insurance, heating and lighting, and buildings maintenance and depreciation is to base this on the floor area occupied (in square metres). However, this could be unfair to the extent that the age, condition, type of structure, height and insulation of different buildings can vary greatly. Other bases used include capital employed, number of employees using a facility, labour or machine hours of productive work or capacity, number of job orders handled. The key factor is to try to find the basis most closely correlated with the incidence of cost, and which is objectively and reliably measurable and recorded.

With the introduction of more capital-intensive production methods (including automated lines, robots) the proportion of direct labour and materials cost to total cost tends to fall, while the proportion of indirect cost for capital cost and for technical and other back-up services tends to rise. Put another way, the proportion of direct variable cost falls, while the proportion of fixed and indirect variable cost rises. This makes it all the more important to have an accurate understanding of support services and costs for realistic cost apportionment, as well as for the better management control of these often expensive services.

Another problem with support-service departments is that often they provide service to each other as well as to the direct cost production department. These are termed 'reciprocal services'. For example, a factory personnel department serves indirect staff in the stockroom, engineering workshops and other support departments, as well as the production operatives. Personnel department costs could be allocated direct to production, but it may be considered better for sensitive understanding and control of factory cost if the personnel overheads are distributed among all the relevant user departments and staff groups, for later recharge to production as part of the indirect overhead of these department. Yet the personnel department also receives services from some of these user departments. Accountants have several methods for these cost redistributions, or inter-service cost transfers, including the use of simultaneous-equation solutions (see Drury 2004).

A final problem to consider is the value to be placed upon materials when they are taken out of stores and charged into production. If specific materials (including components and parts) are ordered to fulfil a particular job order, then clearly their actual (i.e. invoice) cost should be charged to the direct cost of the relevant job. However, the more usual position for manufacturers, and indeed for retailers and wholesalers maintaining substantial base stocks of goods for resale, is for materials and other goods to have been bought in batches, often at different prices (owing to changes in market forces and inflation). Factory requisitions for production use on batch or process runs will seldom correspond to the exact quantities of materials purchased on particular orders (invoices). Also, if materials are of a standard stock specification, will it always be easy to verify that particular order or delivery? Thus the physical identification of stock becomes detached from the identification of its true cost (or sacrifice value) when that stock is consigned into production. Accountants have three main methods of measuring this transfer of cost.

The first method assumes that the oldest stock received is the first used. It is called 'first-in, first-out' or FIFO. Thus, stock withdrawals will be charged at the oldest invoice price until the relevant quantity is exhausted, and then at the next oldest invoice price, and so on. FIFO is the favoured method of the IASB. The obverse to FIFO is 'last-in, last-out' or LIFO, which works on the basis of charging stock withdrawals first at the most recent invoice price until the relevant quantity is exhausted, and then at the next most recent invoice price, and so on. A compromise approach is to charge out stock withdrawals at the weighted-average price of stock on hand.

It may be argued that the true cost of consuming any resource which has a continuing economic use and value to the enterprise is it replacement cost. LIFO charging is an approximation to the use of replacement cost. Where FIFO charging for materials use has been followed, as the IASB requires, the resultant total production cost figures will understate the 'real' cost of production, and these costs will not be sufficiently accurate or reliable for use in forward decision making, at least during times of substantial inflation, market instability or significant technological change.

Variable costing v. absorption costing

Table 4.1 presents a simplified illustration of the differing figures for net profit and for closing stock (i.e. end-of period finished goods stocks balance) that would arise from the use of historical absorption costing as contrasted to historical variable costing. The illustration is adapted from Drury (1996: 201–2), who goes into much more detail in evaluating the choice between the two costing methods than space permits here.

The variable costs comprise all direct product costs, plus variable indirect (or overhead) production costs. In the illustration we simply have the total of all of these combined. From the information given, the only basis we have for recharging (or recovering) the fixed indirect (or overhead) portions of production cost is to base this charge on each unit of output at the normal output level. Hence, £300 fixed costs at 150 units output yields a unit fixed cost of £2 per unit to be applied to each unit produced under the absorption costing system. When more than 150 units are produced there will be over-recovery of fixed costs (see period 5), and when fewer than 150 units are produced there will be under-recovery (see period 6). In contrast, under variable costing, the fixed production costs are not charged into production cost (or closing stock), but instead are charged below the line of cost of sales, as a period cost.

The data in Table 4.1 covers six periods. The periods could be weeks, months or years. Profit calculation for external reporting is usually yearly or half-yearly, but internal reporting for management control is frequently monthly. Where the periods

Table 4.1	A comparison of variable and absorption costing

The following information is available for periods 1–6 for a company which produces a single product:

	£
Unit selling price	10
Unit variable cost	6
Fixed costs for each period	300

Normal activity is expected to be 150 units per period and production and sales for each period are as follows:

	Period 1	Period 2	Period 3	Period 4	Period 5	Period 6
Units sold	150	120	180	150	140	160
Units produced	150	150	150	150	170	140

There were no opening stocks at the start of period 1 and the actual manufacturing fixed overhead incurred was £300 per period. We shall also assume that non-manufacturing overheads are £100 per period.

Variable costing statements

	Period 1 £	Period 2 £	Period 3 £	Period 4 £	Period 5 £	Period 6 £
Opening stock	–	–	180	–	–	180
Production cost	900	900	900	900	1020	840
Closing stock	–	(180)	–	–	(180)	(60)
Cost of sales	900	720	1080	900	840	960
Fixed costs	300	300	300	300	300	300
Total costs	1200	1020	1380	1200	1140	1260
Sales	1500	1200	1800	1500	1400	1600
Gross profit	300	180	420	300	260	340
Less non-manufacturing costs	100	100	100	100	100	100
Net profit	200	80	320	200	160	240

Absorption costing statements

	Period 1 £	Period 2 £	Period 3 £	Period 4 £	Period 5 £	Period 6 £
Opening stock	–	–	240	–	–	240
Production cost	1200	1200	1200	1200	1360	1120
Closing stock	–	(240)	–	–	(240)	(80)
Cost of sales	1200	960	1440	1200	1120	1280
Adjustment for under/(over) recovery of overhead	–	–	–	–	(40)	–
Total costs	1200	960	1440	1200	1080	1300
Sales	1500	1200	1800	1500	1400	1600
Gross profit	300	240	360	300	320	300
Less non-manufacturing costs	100	100	100	100	100	90
Net profit	200	140	260	200	220	210

Source: Adapted, with permission, from Drury (1996: 201–2).

covered are less than a full year there may be seasonal distortions to sales and/or production volumes.

The most obvious point of attention in contrasting the two statements is that the 'bottom-line' net profit is much more stable under absorption costing than under variable costing. This may represent an acceptable form of 'income smoothing' for external reporting, but it may not send the most useful signals to managers in internal reporting for management control as regards either the setting of production runs or the effort needed in sales promotion.

What absorption costing has done is to transfer into closing inventory that portion of normal unit fixed cost charges which relates to all unsold production, inclusive of production in excess of the normal rate on which the unit fixed cost charge is based. In period 5 this amounts to £40 over-recovery in respect of production of 170 units compared to the normal 150 units. Now, suppose instead that period 5 production had been 200 units, with the same sales of 140 units. In that case, closing inventory value would have been £480, over-recovered overhead £100 and net profit £280. Readers should check these figures for themselves. The effect has been to increase net profit by relieving total cost for period 5 by a notional (unsold) product value of fixed cost contributions carried forward in the end-of-period balance sheet in closing stock. In other words, under absorption costing it is open to production management to manipulate short-term net profit performance by producing goods in excess of current sales requirement. Eventually this distortion will cancel out, so where is the incentive to manipulate? If the periods are a full year, or even a half year, there can always be hope that market changes, inflation, solving technical or efficiency problems in the production process, etc. will provide some relief to front line managers' problems during the next period, so it could well be that some managers surrender to the temptation of this form of gamesmanship. The question remains open whether it is wise to use any accounting system, like absorption costing, which is so prone to yield misleading information and so open to manipulation.

The concerns expressed above regarding absorption cost accounting relate to its use in performance measurement and control. It may be even less relevant for management planning and decision making, to be considered in later chapters.

Further problems in cost accounting

There are many technical and practical problems in cost and management accounting, often with conflicting views on how to deal with them which are beyond the scope of this book (but readers may consult a specialist text such as Drury 2004). However, before moving on, in Chapter 5 and later chapters, to the use of cost and other accounting information in management decision making, we will consider three particular problems of some importance: costing for services, depreciation costs and the transfer of costs between organisational units.

Costing for services

Cost accounting developed originally mainly for application in factories, where hundreds or thousands of identical products are made under standardised work practices. At any one time, a factory worker or machine is usually involved with only a single product. It is therefore relatively easy to trace costs to that specific product. But in many service industries these characteristics do not apply. Sales clerks may sell any combination of hundreds of products in an hour. Bank clerks may process ten different kinds of service transactions in an hour. The work of solicitors, academics or doctors may be even more diffused, with some part of 'professional' activity not traceable to any specific 'product' or even customer, but, rather, committed to general professional learning or updating of skills and to organisational activity. So it becomes difficult to cost many kinds of service work accurately, at least without keeping detailed records of the use of time, which would interrupt the flow of work, or of customer contact and goodwill, and would not be worth the 'cost of costing'.

Responses to this problem vary widely but, in general, service costing aims to follow similar principles to factory costing where work is repetitive and tied to one service output; for example where clerks spend all day inputting into computers the details from cheques, bank slips, credit cards, mail-order forms, etc. The contrast in the work here to that of a secretary or personal assistant is obvious. Supermarket cashiers carry out repetitive duties of a single type also, but these are linked to an enormous variety of products passing through the till. For cost efficiency measurement and control, similar costing methods may be applied as for the clerks inputting into computers. Detailed tracing of the cashier costs to individual products or product lines may not be necessary for wider management control, where the emphasis may be on turnover and profitability per metre of display space. Here, cashier costs will be relatively small and relatively uniform across different products, so that fairly simple apportionments should suffice.

Where it is policy that a full range of products or services should be supplied, the emphasis in costing and cost analysis may not be on individual products or services, but, rather, on the performance of a managerial unit as a whole, whether this is a single department in a department store or each individual branch of a high-street bank.

Where services are non-standard and/or are performed by individuals working in isolation, prices are often charged on an hourly basis, whether for a solicitor or the call-out services of a breakdown engineer. It is assumed that the sum of all the hourly charges (plus any spare parts or extra expense charges) will cover not only the time of the specialist but also the indirect costs and overheads and the target profit margin. If profits turn out too low, manning levels and support costs – and prices if the market permits – will be re-examined, but seldom will this extend to accurate costing of the work of each individual specialist, the solicitor, engineer or whatever.

In both the public and private sectors there appears to be much scope to develop new and better cost information and analysis. The new approach of activity-based costing (ABC), which is introduced in the next chapter, may prove helpful in improving cost and management accounting for services.

Depreciation costs

Depreciation – that is the annualised cost of the wearing out, using up, and/or obsolescence of a fixed asset, spread over the number of years during which economic benefit is obtained from the asset – is usually dealt with in accountancy primarily as a financial accounting topic (as seen in Chapter 3). The purpose of depreciation accounting is to charge against profit and loss a sum sufficient to ensure that the financial capital of a business is retained intact (i.e. reinvested) so that it cannot be declared and distributed to shareholders as dividends, disguised as trading profits. However, in times of inflation it is not sufficient to retain just the annualised financial cost of depreciation, because the new replacement assets needed to retain economic earning power will usually cost more than the original assets. The traditional approach is to charge to production overheads just the annual depreciation on the original purchase price, on the historical absorption costing basis, ignoring inflation effects. Indeed, it would be difficult to do otherwise, given that the cost accounts are expected to reconcile with the financial accounts.

The effects of inflation can be shown in supplementary accounts, bringing in current cost or replacement cost valuations of asset and depreciation, together with other relevant adjustment. These issues are dealt with in IASB 29. However, most entities are able to use the routine historical-costing figures used for valuing the cost of production and the cost of goods sold (for use in the profit and loss account) to include depreciation only on the original cost.

With major capital-intensive plant this practice can give quite misleading depreciation-cost figures, were these to be used in pricing policy and for other management decisions. This is simply one illustration of why routinely available historical or absorption costing figures may not be helpful to management; further illustrations are given in Chapter 5. In separate costing calculations, prepared specifically for use in pricing or other management decisions, it is of course possible at least to approximate the inflation-adjusted current cost of the use of fixed asset.

Transfer of costs

This chapter, and Chapter 5, are written for the basic organisational case of the integrated firm with major planning and control decisions taken by a single manager or management team. This is broadly realistic for most small to medium-sized firms. However, as firms get larger, especially firms which diversify into more than one technology, product line or market, they may adopt decentralised organisational structures, typically identified as operating divisions but sometimes formed as subsidiary companies. These issues are discussed in Chapter 8.

Divisions or subsidiaries may trade with each other as well as with external markets; for example, one division may make castings both for external orders and to supply as components to another division or subsidiary. The spirit of decentralisation requires that intracompany trade should be at fair-market price, or a least a good cost-based estimate thereof, so that each unit of the company can be assessed on its profitability. This internal transfer of cost, often with some profit margin added and then called 'transfer pricing', does, however, give rise to many arguments, sometimes involving conflict between economic theory and organisational theory, and difficulties in cost measurement. Transfer pricing and divisional performance measurement have their own large literature (Emmanuel *et al.* 1990) and the subject is discussed further in Chapter 8 of this book.

Conclusion

There are many concepts of cost and many ways of measuring cost. Further concepts and measures will be explained in Chapter 13. All this involves nuances of meaning, and considerable jargon. Here, the manager is at some disadvantage in communicating with the accountant to obtain the relevant cost information needed for effective control of current operations, and for forward planning and decision making. There is a risk that busy accountants, if left to their own devices and stuck within their own four walls, will seek to answer management questions and requests by using cost information derived directly from their historical absorption-cost records, which are maintained primarily to feed production cost and value information into the financial accounting system.

It is essential for the accountant to be brought into the workplace and into open dialogue with managers so that the real needs of cost information for control, and for planning and decisions, can be established. Only then can the most relevant information be provided. Of the concepts explored in this chapter, perhaps the most valuable are opportunity cost and awareness of how some costs are dependent on volume, while other costs are governed more by other factors. Such other factors could include the passage of time, or the decisions or commitments of managers (sometimes by default rather than by conscious choice and decision) in creating and sustaining an ongoing core structure of costly service organisation and staffing, and of buildings, plant and equipment which may not always be adaptable to meet future needs and opportunities.

Chapter review

This chapter introduced the basic definitions, concepts and measures of business cost. These included opportunity cost, a measure of sacrifice, and the distinction between simple cash costs and the more complicated but accurate accrual costs. It explained how some costs vary with volume of activity, while other costs are largely independent of volume and are fixed during a period of time. Some costs combine variable and fixed elements, and of course over a long enough period of time all costs can be made variable (or at least avoidable) by management choice and action. The bases for identifying costs as fixed or variable, and as direct, indirect or overhead, were outlined.

The traditional ongoing system of cost recording and reporting in business, historical absorption costing, was explained, and some of its weaknesses for providing useful information to management were explored. Further weaknesses, together with alternative approaches to costing and cost analysis to provide better information for management decisions, will be explained in subsequent chapters.

Further reading

For a classic historical view of the issues, see Solomons (1952). For contemporary views and detail, see Drury (2004) or Homgen *et al.* (2002). Other useful texts include Elliot and Elliot (2003) and Alexander and Britton (2004).

Questions and exercises

*1 Bashers Ltd is a small metalworking business. For the month of September the total works overhead cost was £10 000. During that month only three jobs were worked on. All were started and completed within the month, and the following data is supplied.

	Job no. 1 £	Job no. 2 £	Job no. 3 £
Direct materials	5 000	2 000	1 000
Direct labour cost	7 500	5 000	500
Direct expenses	500	1 000	300
Prime cost	13 000	8 000	1 800
Direct labour hours	1 500	1 500	150
Machine hours	500	300	100

Required:

(a) Identify four different bases for calculating an overhead absorption rate for the work of the period, and calculate what the rate would be under each of the four bases.

(b) State whether the data and your results suggest which of the four bases is likely to be the most appropriate for use in this company? If so, explain why. If not, explain what additional information you would seek in order to choose the best overhead absorption basis.

*2 The Elite Shoe Company manufactures two grades of shoes, A and B. Manufacturing costs for the year ended 31 March were:

	$000
Direct materials	1000
Direct wages	560
Variable production overhead	140
Fixed production overhead	160
	1860

There was no work-in-progress at the beginning or end of the year. It is ascertained that:

(a) direct materials in grade A shoes cost twice as much as in grade B shoes (per pair);

(b) direct wages for grade B shoes were 60% of those for grade A shoes (per pair);

(c) fixed production overhead was the same per pair of A and B grade shoes, while variable production overhead was apportioned on the basis of direct wages;

(d) administration overhead for each grade of shoe was 50% of direct labour cost;

(e) selling cost was $1.75 per pair for each grade of shoe;

· (f) production during the year was:

- grade A, 40 000 pairs, of which 36 000 pairs were sold,
- grade B, 120 000 pairs, of which 110 000 pairs were sold;

(g) factory prices were $25 per pair for grade A and $15 per pair for Grade B.

Required:

Assuming that all costs were exactly measured in the direct and indirect costs listed above, prepare a statement showing:

(i) the total costs of production and sales for each grade of shoe,

(ii) the unit costs and profit for each grade of shoe, and

(iii) the balance sheet value of finished stocks at year-end.

*3 Hi-Tech Ltd is a small manufacturer of precision instruments. For the latest trading year its summary accounts, prepared on the absorption costing basis, are as follows;

	€000
Opening stock	200
Prime cost	1400
Variable production overheads	200
Fixed production overheads	400
Less closing stock	(600)
Cost of sales	1600
Sales	2300
Gross profit	700
Variable admin and sales overheads	(150)
Fixed admin and sales overheads	(300)
Net profit	250

Required:

(a) Recast the above summary accounts using the alternative approach of variable costing. You will need to know that if the company had used variable costing in the previous year the opening stock balance at the beginning of the latest year would have been €150 000.

(b) Comparing the two sets of accounts, identify what inferences you can draw regarding the financial position of the company, and what advantages or disadvantages you see in the two alternative accounting and valuation approaches?

4 Machinations Ltd buys in steel strip for stores, and it machines this to a variety of specifications in batch runs to customer order and for holding a range of standard stock. We will look at its use of material and the flow of material cost to cost of sales. We are given the following information for the month of November (all figures are in $million and relate solely to the materials component of each control account).

Opening materials	1000
Opening work-in-progress	1200
Materials purchased	2000
Cost of materials in finished goods sold and delivered	3000
Ending balances: materials	600
work-in-progress	1400
finished goods	700

Required:

(a) From the given information, calculate the values for materials requisitioned from stores to work-in-progress; for the material component of work-in-progress passed to finished goods, and for the opening balance of the finished goods account. (Hint: it may be helpful to link your calculations to the cost flows in Figure 4.5 and to use 'T' accounts and/or lay out your solution in tabular format.)

(b) Consider and then concisely suggest how you might deal in the cost flow accounts with the following complications arising during November: the price of steel strip rose by 10% early in the month, a physical stock count at the end of the month showed $50 000 of strip to be missing from the materials store, and during the month 4% of steel strip in progress was wasted owing to machining errors (as against a normal wastage of 2%).

5   Jock, Sam and Lee (JSL) are starting up a new business assembling and marketing commercial security systems. As a start-up, they cannot afford to buy new company cars, but they need to agree on a fair scheme for reimbursing the use of their own existing cars when used on company business. Sam, in charge of design and assembly, expects to use his car very little for the company, whereas Lee, head of marketing and sales, expects to drive a great deal. Jock, the CEO, expects to drive an intermediate distance. Cash flow is tight during start up, and JSL do not want to pay out more than is fair and necessary to cover costs. The cost of fuel is £0.70 per litre. The scheme is to cover the first year of the new business, and the following forecast information has been provided:

	Jock	Sam	Lee
Estimated kms on company business	10 000	3 000	40 000
Estimated kms in private driving	20 000	27 000	20 000
Kms per litre of respective cars	12	15	13
Age of cars, years	1	4	2
Estimated remaining useful life of cars, years	4	3	4
Original price of cars, £	20 000	14 000	18 000
Current resale values of cars, £	15 000	7 000	13 000
Estimated scrap values at end of useful lives, £	5 000	3 000	4 000

Annual cost of licence, £	200	200	200
Annual cost of insurance, £	800	300	900
Estimated costs of oil, tyres, etc. per km, £	0.02	0.015	0.03
Estimated annual cost of services and repairs, £	300	400	600

Required:

(a) Ignoring taxation problems and any inflation, calculate what you consider would be the fairest rate or rates of car-use reimbursement for JSL to apply in its first year.

(b) What, if any, are the arguments which might be raised by Jock, Sam or Lee for some alternative rate or rates of reimbursement? How do the distinctions between fixed or period costs, and directly variable costs, assist in resolving such arguments?

6 The Exxell Corporation has established a new division to produce and market a new type of machine for the extrusion of aluminum alloy materials for the building industry. There are uncertainties as to the demand for this product, and so the divisional general manager has asked for an engineering estimate of the expected costs of production at a variety of possible market demand levels. The cost engineers have supplied the following data:

	Production volume (units)			
	3000	4000	5000	6000
Production costs:	$000	$000	$000	$000
Supervisory labour	30	30	40	60
Plant-hire rental charges	60	80	80	100
Plant operators' direct labour	150	180	240	280
Materials and components used	300	400	500	600
Plant lubricants and cleansers	15	18	21	24
Energy	60	75	90	105
Buildings rent and maintenance	60	60	60	60

Required:

(a) Make a new schedule of the above costs subdivided by headings for variable costs, fixed costs and mixed costs.

(b) Identify any evidence of 'step costs' in the mixed costs, and briefly suggest what might cause or explain them.

(c) Can you identify the fixed-cost component in any of the mixed costs?

(d) Calculate the average unit costs at each of the production volumes shown, and briefly comment on whether or not the costs differences are large enough to be significant when deciding prices for the new machine.

*7 Define and explain 'opportunity cost' and explain also why opportunity cost is seldom mentioned or measured in routine cost measurement and reporting systems. Suggest how the opportunity cost concept could be given explicit use or recognition in cost information for management.

*8 Draw a graph to display total unit cost related to activity (measured in volume of units produced or sold). Include in your costs variable costs, fixed costs and step-type (or semi-fixed) mixed costs. (NB: graph paper need not be used for this question.) How far do you think the existence of mixed costs limits the usefulness of the conventional simplification of all costs into the two categories of fixed and variable?

*9 It could be argued that total fixed costs broadly equate to total indirect costs, and that total variable costs broadly equate to total direct costs. Explain how and why the foregoing simple matching breaks down, and why it is important to use both of these two different cost-classification systems.

10 In the absence of inflation accounting or asset revaluation adjustments, cash accounting and accrual accounting should lead to the same total profit (or loss) over the lifetime of a business'. Explain why you agree or disagree with this statement. Does it matter which of these two systems we use for the purpose of providing information for management planning and control?

11 There is a choice in product costing between the absorption (or historical) costing method and the variable (or period) costing method. Speculate on the relative advantages and disadvantages of each of these two methods in respect of:

(a) the valuation of finished stocks;

(b) periodic profit or loss measurement;

(c) control of production operations;

(d) planning changes in product mix or volume.

12 How does depreciation cost for buildings and equipment differ in its nature and measurement from other production costs, and how might such differences affect the measurement and reporting of product costs for planning and control?

Cost analysis for management decisions

5

Chapter preview

Many management decisions involve both short-term and long-term implications, but for the purposes of analysis it is helpful to examine these separately. Short-term decisions are mainly concerned with making the most cost-effective and profitable use of existing resources, while long-term decisions typically revolve around the best use of new capital investment. This chapter concentrates on the understanding and analysis of accounting information which is most relevant to short-term decisions on the best choice of inputs, volumes of outputs and pricing.

We will examine the decision-relevance of different types of cost information, in particular absorption costs, attributable costs, activity-based costs and differential costs. Methods of cost estimation are illustrated, and cost-volume-profit and contribution analysis are explained. Even though final decisions on production, marketing and pricing must be taken in the light of commercial strategy and market conditions, costing information can provide helpful guidance on product mix, volume and pricing.

Planning, control and decisions

Business planning looks forward, sets objectives and targets, and develops detailed operational plans. The financial parts of these plans are termed 'budgets', and we will examine these in Chapter 7. Business control comprises monitoring and correcting current business performance in production and sales, and in cost-efficiency and profitability. This chapter also discusses control in the particular context of standard costing and performance-variance analysis and also explains how budgets link ongoing planning with control with effective action to remedy control problems (e.g. inefficient use of labour or materials) requiring management decisions. Selecting, amending or updating plans and budgets requires decisions. More generally, rather like driving a car, or steering a ship, there is a need in management for constant alertness, simultaneously implementing control, making choices, updating plans and generally adapting as optimally as possible in the current environment while moving towards agreed business goals. All this involves making decisions.

Whereas control is largely reactive, positive business management is mainly proactive, making decisions concerned with change, choices, risk and uncertainty. Longer-term decisions usually involve the investment or disinvestment of capital, and we look at these in Chapter 8. Here we concentrate on short-term decisions, typically focused on what to make and sell, how to make it efficiently, and what price to seek or accept. Here cost information can be a valuable aid or it can be seriously misleading. We must have cost information which is relevant to each specific decision situation confronting us.

Relevant costs and costing systems

We have seen that routine, day-to-day cost recording and reporting systems are designed primarily to meet the requirements of financial accounting – essentially to capture all historical costs of production activity and to allocate or apportion these fairly between the cost of goods sold and the cost of goods in unsold stock or inventory. The costing method usually employed is historical absorption costing, which is discussed in the previous chapter. This is normally based on the absorption of all production costs (i.e. costs incurred up to the point where goods are ready for sale), both fixed and variable. There is an alternative viewpoint that only variable costs (i.e. direct materials, direct labour, and direct or traceable variable overheads) should be charged to product costs, with the remaining overheads charged as period costs direct to current profit and loss, and thus not entering into finished stock or inventory values. However, it has been questioned whether or not either of these routine costing approaches provides the information which managers need to make decisions on sales and production strategies involving linked decisions on product mix and volume, sales and pricing policies, etc.

There has been continuing controversy regarding what alternative method of costing should be used for decision making. Economists have argued their general case that rational firms should go on producing until marginal revenue falls to equal rising marginal cost. In other words, firms should ignore fixed costs and cut the prices of output as necessary to meet market conditions until the price for disposing of any extra output falls to equal the marginal costs of extra production. However, if this brings down the general price level firms may be unable to recover their fixed costs from the market. This tends to happen during recession and in export markets when a country is suffering high inflation without compensating exchange-rate adjustments; empirical observation suggests that following this guideline increases the risks of business failure and liquidation. Instead, there must be a much more fundamental and rigorous challenge of production methods and structures, and, indeed, of product designs and marketing.

Modern thinking (e.g. as reviewed in Lee 1987) points out that as and where production becomes increasingly automated and computer controlled, and the production labour force shrinks in number but becomes more highly trained, 'white collar' and fixed in cost over time (ignoring major shakeouts during recession or reorganisation), the only major remaining fully variable cost is materials (including parts and components). Although there may be many exceptions in the older industries, the modern, growth, high-tech industries often, if not typically, operate with a high value-added cost and profit margin over and above the variable costs of their material inputs. Thus, it is argued, it will be very misleading to base volume, product mix and pricing decisions on an information system focused mainly on tracing and reporting variable (or marginal) cost.

Activity-based costing (ABC)

Recently some academics and consultants have been promoting an alternative system of production costing known as **activity-based costing** (ABC). The initiative for this has come from the USA (Cooper and Kaplan 1988), where there has perhaps been greater awareness than in the UK and other countries regarding the survival need to improve manufacturing methods, structures and information systems in order to compete successfully in the world marketplace. Historically, the Anglo-American approach has been to concentrate cost control and information on direct labour (i.e. the people actually working hands-on in the production line or process plant). However, with increased automation in production occurring at the same time as the movement to more complicated and frequently changing product design, innovation and technical complexity, labour employment and the associated overhead cost related to space, equipment, training and IT support, etc. have often shifted greatly from the production line to the production planning and support services (including R&D). Given these changes, it has been argued that traditional historical absorption costing discloses misleading information both for control and for planning/decision making.

ABC advocates do not claim that ABC systems routinely measure and report all the costing information which managers need for decisions, but nevertheless ABC information should prove to be more decision-relevant and help managers more often to identify problems and to ascertain what further information they will need to make decisions (e.g. using the differential costing approach described below). Absorption costing collects all production overheads into overhead department control accounts, and then it apportions this cost to production according to which of the main production indicators – machine hours, labour hours or materials used – appears to be the most reliable measure of productive work, i.e. achieved production volume. The ABC approach rejects the logic of this.

Under the ABC approach, the primary concern is for the study and understanding of each kind of support activity generating overhead cost. An activity-based costing system includes the following stages:

1　Identify the major activities supporting production (and the method can be extended to distribution as well).
2　Determine the 'cost driver' for each activity.

3 Set up an account (as a 'cost centre' or 'cost pool') to collect the cost of the activity.

4 Trace the cost of the separate activities through to individual products (i.e. to specific jobs, batches or process segments), using the cost-driver measures as indicators of the volume of each activity consumed on behalf of each individual product.

Activities may include design, purchasing, tooling, scheduling, set up engineering, quality inspection. **'Cost driver'** is a jargon term for the event, forces or transactions which cause or build up the total costs of the activities. 'Activities' may or may not match up closely with single departments as used in conventional factory overheads costing and budgeting. But clearly, cost drivers will often involve work, and therefore costs, from more than one traditional department. For example, a close study of resource consumption and cost may show that purchase orders often cause work in design and engineering, and in stores, stores inspection and accounts, as well as in the purchasing department proper. Careful tracking of the cost drivers may provide a much truer picture of the cost incurred by an individual product than traditional absorption costing based on apportioning departmental costs. However, if factory budgetary control is based on departmental costs while production control is based on cost-driver-led activity costs, there could be conflict and confusion in management control in the factory. One solution could be to reorganise factory management so that it is based on activity centres and flows rather than on traditional functional departments.

In its basic concept, ABC seems no more than common sense. However, it is being promoted, like most new systems, with a distinctive literature, its own jargon and detailed suggestions for implementation. All this is well explained by Drury (2004). One situation where ABC advocates claim a clear advantage for their method is where a firm uses common production facilities to make the same or similar product for production orders and runs of widely differing quantities. It is alleged that traditional absorption costing will tend greatly to understate the true costs of small production quantities and overstate the true cost of large quantities. This is because traditional costing will average out all the support costs across all the units produced, whereas these costs are disproportionately caused by the small production orders and runs. This could lead to errors in pricing and, depending on market forces, including the pricing behaviour of competitors, it could lead to the firm building up low-profit business at the expense of being priced out of high-volume, high-profit business.

Another situation where ABC information may be valuable is where the firm supplies various products making quite different levels of demand upon support services. Table 5.1 provides an example of this. The example is very much simplified, but the firm prints two kinds of publications: one is trade catalogues (A), including many photos and drawings, while the other is community magazines (B), comprising mainly simple typesetting but also a few drawings. It can be seen from the table that unit production costs for the two types of work can vary between the ABC method and the traditional absorption method by a substantial amount, in this case by more than the probable net profit margin on sales.

In summary, activity-based costing seeks to focus management attention on production overheads, and to trace these through to unit and order costs on a basis much more sensitive to the impact of support activities and costs, and the length of production runs, than is achieved through conventional absorption costing. ABC can be carried out as a one-off analysis study, or it can replace absorption costing as the routine ongoing recording and reporting system for production (or distribution) operations.

Table 5.1 PrintPublish Ltd Product costs, 20xx

Costs in £000

	Total costs	Absorption costs				ABC				Attributable costs			
		FC		VC		FC		VC		FC		VC	
		A	B	A	B	A	B	A	B	A	B	A	B
Materials (paper, covers, etc.)	300			100	200			100	200			100	200
Labour:													
Artwork, negotiation and set-ups	150	60	90			135	15			100	10		
Printing and binding (direct labour)	200			80	120			80	120			60	90
Supervision	50	20	30			25	25			10	10		
Premises (rent, rates, energy, etc)	150	60	90			60	90			20	30		
Depreciation of equipment	100	40	60			40	60			30	10		
Accounts, purchasing and stores	60	24	36			30	30			10	10		
Central overheads (excluding marketing and distribution)	90	36	54			45	45			20	20		
Total FC and VC product costs		240	360	180	320	335	265	180	320	190	90	160	290

Continued

Table 5.1   PrintPublish Ltd Product costs, 20xx—cont'd

Costs in £000

	Total costs	Absorption costs				ABC				Attributable costs			
		FC		VC		FC		VC		FC		VC	
		A	B	A	B	A	B	A	B	A	B	A	B
Add VC to FC costs:	1100	420	680			515	585			350	380		
Total production costs		400	2000			400	2000			400	2000		
Units produced (000s of items)													
Average production cost per unit		£1.05	£0.34			£1.29	£0.29			£0.88	£0.19		

Notes:

FC = fixed costs; VC = variable costs.

The columns headed 'A' relate to trade-catalogue products; the columns headed 'B' relate to community-magazine products.

The table uses the simplifying assumptions that there is no beginning or ending inventory of unfinished work-in-progress, and that all indirect and overhead costs are wholly fixed costs. In the Absorption costs columns all indirect and overhead costs are recharged to products as a function of production-line activity, in this case proportional to direct labour cost.

In the ABC (activity-based costs) columns all indirect and overhead costs are charged to products (or product lines) by the use of cost drivers counting number of transactions, or use of activity time, relating to each product. For example, supervision cost is allocated by number of orders, set-ups and runs; artwork costs are allocated by the number of photos and other illustrations processed.

In the Attributable cost columns one can trace the indirect and overhead costs using either the absorption or the ABC approach, the key difference here being that the only costs charged products will be those for resource use or expenditure which could be avoided or terminated if a product is discontinued (after a reasonable planning lead-time). This leaves, the remaining overhead costs unallocated to products; instead they will be charged to profit and loss as 'period costs' together with the costs of distribution (i.e. promotion, marketing, and physical distribution hexpenses).

It could be argued that the absorption unit costs are inaccurate and misleading for pricing related decisions, while ABC unit costs should come close to accuracy and relevance for long-term pricing and product-mix decisions. Attributable unit costs indicate prices for continued production and sales unless and until a more profitable use for available resources is found.

Avoidable and attributable costs

Avoidable cost is a useful decision-relevant concept of cost. Avoidable costs are those costs which will be avoided, or saved, if a new project is not undertaken or, more usually, if an existing product or activity is abandoned. This approach involves a critical study of overheads, as well as direct cost, to see where savings can be made or commitments avoided. It has some similarity to 'differential costing', which we consider in greater detail below. Applying the approach can make good use of the cost insights available from a rigorous activity-based costing system such as previously discussed.

'Attributable cost' is a structured approach to defining, collecting and using available cost data. This cost concept was originally put forward by Shillinglaw (1963). Here attributable cost is defined as the cost per unit which could be avoided, on average, if a function (or activity or product) were discontinued entirely without changing the supporting organisation structure. The assumption here is that the core of the organisation, and the related fixed or period cost, will continue. Any non-core function, or any product or commercial activity which could be separately abandoned, should be retained only if it generates more income than its attributable cost. Alternatively to abandonment, the approach can provide guidance on pricing policy, quantity discounts, delivery and customer service policies, etc.

Attributable costs clearly include all relevant direct variable costs, and also all traceable and avoidable variable overhead costs. They can include fixed costs which could be avoided given time for management planning and action. This involves unitising some fixed (i.e. period) costs to derive average unit (attributable) cost – which figure becomes the minimum price or revenue return to justify continuation of the product or activity. So, in a sense, this is a specific measurement of long-run marginal cost, although we include it in this chapter because it has application in the continuing (i.e. short-term) decision and performance review process, and because the method stops short of explicit consideration of the time-value of capital, the essence of the investment (or disinvestment) problems discussed in Chapter 9 on long-term decisions.

A simplified example of attributable costing is included in Table 5.1. It is assumed that there are just two separable elements to be costed, trade catalogues and community magazines as individual product lines. As should be expected, the average unit cost is less under attributable costing than under absorption costing or ABC, since core organisation costs have been excluded from allocation to product. Yet this total attributable cost per unit is higher than unit marginal/variable cost, and it may be argued that it provides a more realistic minimum price for individual sales transactions or for keeping resources devoted to that product line instead of being disinvested. However, it tells us nothing about the opportunity cost, or the possibilities of other, more profitable lines or products.

In summary, absorption costing, activity-based costing and avoidable/attributable costing can all provide information that can be helpful for decision making, as well as for performance monitoring and control. But since this information is based on existing activities and products, using past or historical data, the decision-relevance is limited to what could be described as the fine-tuning of the status quo. Ideally what we need is information relating to probable future costs and revenues, and to the choices of product, production or distribution methods, and markets. For this we need to employ 'differential analysis', but before discussing that approach we need to consider the problems of cost estimation and of cost volume-profit analysis.

Cost estimation

Cost estimation is used when the information from routine costing systems – mainly designed for the financial accounting purposes of stock valuation and historical profit or loss determination, and/or designed for short-term cost-control use (see the discussion of standard costing in Chapter 7) – is not relevant for decisions on future action. Cost-estimation techniques have a particular concern for the separation of fixed (period) costs from variable (volume-related) costs. There are five main approaches: the engineering method, account inspection, visual fit, the high-low method and linear regression anaysis.

Given concern for the different total costs – and therefore different average unit costs – of production or supply at different volumes, it is often useful to study cost behaviour graphically. The relationship between fixed and variable costs can be summarised by the equation below:

$$Y = a + bX \tag{5.1}$$

where: Y = total cost;
X = volume of activity;
a = fixed costs;
b = unit variable cost.

Figure 5.1 illustrates the form of linear cost volume relationships related to this equation. The practical problem, of course, is to obtain relevant and reliable measures and estimates of the values of a and b. Of the alternative techniques, the engineering method can and should be carried out as much as possible using data independent of the historical accounting system. The other four approaches normally derive their data from the historical records, so therefore they should always be challenged as to their robustness for use in forward decision making. Even so, evidence of past cost performance offers some baseline of guidance (after adjustment for inflation) towards likely future experience.

Accounts inspection

The accountant can be asked to inspect the detail of the cost accounting records for specified products (or sales lines, markets, branches or services), to determine all the chargeable and relevant costs, to analyse these as between fixed and variable, and then to aggregate them to a determined total cost at a specified volume level. From this can be derived the average unit cost at that volume level. A cost determined in this way can vary considerably from the average unit cost routinely provided from an ongoing absorption costing system. However, it relies on subjective judgement in discriminating between fixed and variable costs and it may not give reliable guidance for the extrapolation of cost performance to unusually high (or low) volume levels.

Repeating the accounts inspection analysis at times of differing volumes can provide a series of 'snapshots' of cost experience which can be analysed by the next three techniques below, possibly to yield a more sensitive and reliable feel for the relationship of fixed and variable costs to volume. These techniques can be applied also to data obtained directly from the routine cost absorption accounts. Both sets of data must be treated with some caution, partly because of the subjective nature of much of the data classification, partly because the effects of raised costs may be sporadic and not directly detected, and partly because of the effects of inflation on performance results recorded at different times (although generally the inflation distortions can be corrected by appropriate index adjustments).

Visual fit

The 'visual-fit' technique involves entering on a graph, known as a 'scattergram', the historical values of total costs recorded (Ys) for different volumes experienced (Xs). A line is then drawn through the scatter of points so that it best weights their representation as a linear function of total cost to volume. If the scatter of points departs widely from the average line the results may be of limited validity, because of errors in the input cost data, random raised costs which have not been identified or poor management control of operations. If the scatter of points is skewed at either end of the average line this could indicate significant raised or step costs needing further investigation, or else that the cost function is inherently non-linear. In any case outlier values which are widely divergent from the average line (as determined ignoring those values) may be ignored for purposes of drawing the line of visual best fit, although these and any other widely divergent values could form the basis of supplementary enquiry seeking explanation of variation in management performance.

Figure 5.2 is a scattergram graph on which have been marked with crosses the recent experience of total costs of trade catalogues produced at PrintPublish Ltd, at

| Figure 5.1 | A linear cost-volume relationship |

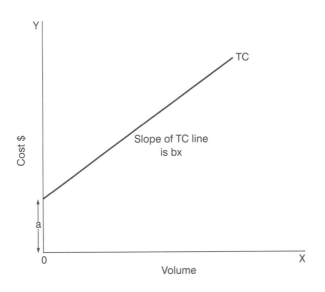

different volume levels. A visual line of best fit has been entered. The line (i.e. the upper line) is shown as a solid line only through the range of volumes experienced. The extensions of the solid line are shown only as dotted lines, to emphasise that they represent volumes outside the normal range where, at least in the short term until management changes have been effected, the 'normal' fixed-to-variable cost relationships might not be valid. However, at least as regards the normal volume or activity range, where the line intersects the vertical axis determines the approximate value of total fixed costs a, while the slope of the line determines the unit variable cost b.

High-low method

An alternative simple method of fixed and variable cost estimation is known as the high-low method. It also uses a scattergram and the same data as for the visual-fit method. Again we use Figure 5.2 and the same data for illustration. This method works by using the cost figures for the highest and lowest activity volume levels in the data set used, and connecting these to determine the cost-fit line. If the highest and lowest volume cost are markedly out of line with a linear function as a whole, these outliers should be ignored in favour of cost points nearer to a linear function but as close as possible to the extremes of the experienced volume range.

| Figure 5.2 | Scattergram for visual fit and high-low, PrintPublish (20 XX monthly figures) |

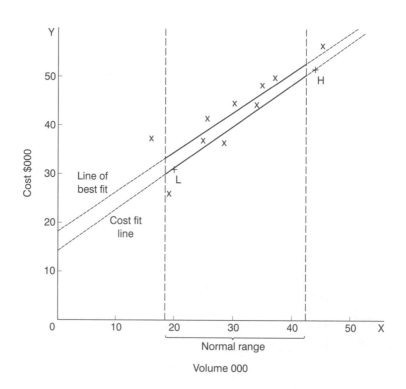

Volume 000

Following the above precept, we have selected point H and L in Figure 5.2 to give us what appears visually to be the most realistic cost-fit line between two high-low volumes. Drawing the line, and again showing it dotted outside the range of experienced or normal production volumes, we can determine the estimated fixed costs from the intercept point on the vertical axis and the variable cost rate from the slope of the line; or we can calculate these two costs arithmetically.

The data recorded in Figure 5.2 is taken from monthly cost reports during 20XX. For month L the total costs are £30 000 for a volume of 20 000 units, and for month H the total costs are £50 000 for a volume of 45 000 units. Taking our assumption of linearity, which includes the assumption that all mixed or step costs become averaged out over a larger volume, the increase in total costs between points L and H is taken to consist wholly of variable costs. The increase is £20 000 for 25 000 units, or £0.80 variable cost per unit. Returning to our basic cost equation, $Y = a + bX$, this can be restated as $a = Y - bX$ to solve for fixed costs. From this, and taking our values from either L or H, it will be seen that the indicated fixed cost is £14 000 per month.

Note the difference between the high-low method fixed costs of £14 000 as compared to the visual-fit indication of £18 000 per month. Which is correct? We do not know and we cannot prove an answer. Fixed costs at zero output are a notional concept, and fixed costs within our normal or experienced output range are influenced by raised or stepped costs. In any event, we are probably more often interested in measuring the variable cost per unit.

From Table 5.1 we know that the volume of trade catalogues printed in 20XX was 400 000. Taking the figures from our high-low solution, this would indicate total variable cost of f320 000, with total fixed costs of £168 000, giving a total overall cost of £488 000. Comparing these figures with Table 5.1 it appears that our total falls between the total costs recorded for absorption costing and activity-based costing. However, the subdivision of total cost as between fixed and variable is very different, and this could be the basis for an enquiry or engineering method study of the underlying resource uses and costs. (NB: Many indirect and overhead costs may be variable.) Alternatively, one could submit the data in our scattergram to the further test of simple linear regression analysis.

Linear regression analysis

Simple linear regression analysis and the least-squares method of finding a line of best fit can be used to derive a more scientific subdivision between fixed and variable cost than is possible by the visual-fit and high-low methods. The mechanics of the method are illustrated in detail in specialist management accounting texts such as those by Drury (2000) and Horngren *et al,* (2002). With access to appropriate PC software, this mathematical solution may be the quickest as well as the most 'precise' solution available. We use the word 'precise' advisedly, rather than 'accurate' or 'true', because no mathematical solution can resolve abnormalities in the underlying data, whether arising from poor management control in the periods from which the data is drawn or from inherent mixed or stepped costs. Perhaps the best solution of all would be to have a computer graphics system on which the raw data and the least squares regression solution are displayed, and where there is the further facility to generate visual best fit lines for comparison with the regression solution. However, managerial experience of past events and awareness of the kinds of situations (e.g. particular volume levels or speeds of change to higher or lower volume levels) relevant to decisions pending, may often be at least as significant in identifying relevant information as would be any mathematical or computer outputs applying 'precision' analysis to historical costs whose 'relevance' may be uncertain.

The engineering method

At its best, the 'engineering method' of cost estimation ignores historical costs, or else considers them only to the extent that they provide an alternative set of data for cross-checking the credibility of the data generated for the engineering method exercise. The engineering method can be used not only for cost estimation for decision making and planning, which is our present concern, but also for establishing accurate standard costs for use in management accounting control systems.

In spite of its name, the engineering method of cost estimation can be carried out by any accountant or manager with expert knowledge of the production or distribution processes involved. The method is especially appropriate when new products, processes or distribution channels are being introduced – with historical costs of little relevance - but it can also be used for periodic reviews of the continuing accuracy and credibility of the historical costing of continuing products, processes and distribution, perhaps on a three to five year cycle of rolling review.

The point of naming this method of cost estimation the 'engineering method' is that the critical skill needed is the ability to understand the technicalities of the production or distribution process involved, and to measure accurately the physical resources consumed from materials, labour and equipment. These physical measures of resource consumption, or real cost, can then be converted into money cost by the accountant multiplying the physical resource measures by their unit input prices. The method works best when the proportion of direct costs (including direct fixed costs as well as variable costs) is high relative to the indirect or overhead costs, because it will be obvious that the estimation and apportionment of the latter is a matter of 'expert opinion', with uncertainty, likely wide errors of judgement and therefore the potential for unconscious or even wilful distortion of the apportionment in favour of the cost estimates for which the accountants or managers may be hoping.

Time-and-motion studies and other careful study of work methods and flow are often important for the success of the engineering method, although these activities may require negotiation with trade unions or, at the least tactful approaches to ensure the cooperation of workers, both from the general objective of sustaining employee morale and because uncooperative workers can lead to 'rubbish readings' in respect of work-study measurement of potential productivity.

The engineering method is especially appropriate where a change in products, production volumes, distribution methods, etc. is under consideration. It is also in this type of circumstance that differential costing, discussed in the next section, is most useful. The cost figures used in Table 5.2 are therefore obtained by using the engineering method.

Differential cost and revenue analysis

Differential cost analysis is the study of the results of changes in costs, or in revenues, arising from taking up one particular opportunity. It is a way of operationalising 'opportunity cost'. Even when one is studying only one specified new course of action, there is the opportunity cost involved of otherwise doing nothing, just maintaining the status quo. Given that we are looking at change, at future possibilities, it follows that we should use future costs and revenues, not the historical figures obtainable from absorption costing records. Also, we should be using up-to-date information on current technology, attainable efficiency in production and distribution activities, and the current market prices of input; in short, the kind of information obtainable from good engineering methods cost estimation.

Differential analysis can be used to study the effects of volume changes (downwards as well as upwards), the introduction of new products or other changes in the product mix, or the introduction of new technology or change in the methods of distribution and marketing.

Often, differential analysis will consist entirely, or almost entirely, of the cash-flow changes expected to result from a particular course of action. Non-cash accrual costs, notably depreciation, may be omitted either because they already exist and will not change or because any needed new plant or equipment, or building space, can be leased or hired without long-term capital or contractual commitment. Existing capital and other costs, which will not change in amount in the decision situation we are studying, can be ignored in the differential analysis. These costs are known as 'sunk costs'. But, of course, if old buildings or plant and equipment assets are made redundant by the new decision initiative, these may have a cash resale or salvage value which should be taken into account in the differential analysis.

Table 5.2	Absorption costs and differential costs compared – PrintPublish Ltd new product annual cost and profit or loss			
			Differential costs	
	Absorption costs	Method A £	Method B £	Difference £
Annual fixed costs:				
Staff (to edit and obtain entries and orders)	60 000	50 000	60 000	10 000
Equipment leasing costs	10 000	10 000	20 000	10 000
Equipment maintenance contract	4 000	4 000	5 000	1 000
Premises costs	20 000	6 000	6 000	–
Total fixed costs	94 000	70 000	91 000	21 000
Variable cost per unit:				
Direct materials	1.00	1.00	1.20	0.20
Direct labour (printing and binding, etc.)	5.00	5.00	3.00	(2.00)
Total unit variable cost	6.00	6.00	4.20	(1.80)
Estimated sales (10 000 units at £14.95)	149 500	149 500	149 500	–
Less variable costs (10 000 units)	60 000	60 000	42 000	(18 000)
Contribution	89 500	89 500	107 500	18 000
Less annual fixed costs	94 000	70 000	91 000	21 000
Projected profit or (loss) on annual sales	(4 500)	19 500	16 500	(3 000)

Differential analysis is primarily an approach for short-term decisions. Most long-term decisions involve the commitment of investment capital, and their assessment requires the use of the investment appraisal methods explained in Chapter 9. Even when formal investment appraisal is required, however, this will be based on careful cash-flow forecasts, which should be prepared on the same rigorous basis as the differential analysis described here.

It should be emphasised that in differential analysis we are studying all costs that change as a result of a particular decision. Thus, if costs conventionally classified as 'fixed' in routine cost recording and reporting are expected to increase, or decrease, as a result of the specified decision situation, it is essential to include in the differential analysis the amount of the change in fixed costs as well as the true variable costs.

Using differential cost analysis

Table 5.2 presents information for a business opportunity being considered by PrintPublish Ltd. Until now, in spite of its name, the company has worked only as a printer. Management seeks to expand, and is attracted by diversification into publishing to spread commercial risk and achieve hoped-for increases to value added. The proposition is to fill a market gap by publishing a good business directory for the company's region, South Anglia. Following an engineering-methods-type study, it has been established that there is sufficient space in the existing offices and workshops to house the new project, but new, specialised typesetting and printing equipment will be needed. The latter can be obtained on annual lease with all maintenance covered under annual contract. Based on the technical information supplied to him, the accountant has drawn up a summary of the costs which he considers should be properly chargeable to the new project. This is shown in the Absorption costs column of Table 5.2. Management estimates the sales potential of the directory at 10 000 copies per annum if it is priced at £14.95. On that volume, total revenue would be £149 500, as against total costs of £154 000, giving a loss of £4500 per annum. The chief executive is surprised, and he discusses with the accountant the basis of the costs used.

The discussion reveals that the accountant has included in the staff costs £10 000 of existing staff pay for time which he understands would be diverted to selling space in, and copies of, the new directory. However, he accepts that the extra work would largely be taking up slack and that none of this £10 000 would consist of extra cash cost. It also turns out that the £20 000 premises charge was mainly an allocation of existing overheads on a basis of estimated space to be used for the new product. Only £6000 of this charge was for additional out-of-pocket cash-flow costs. It thus appears that £24 000 of the product costs in the first column of Table 5.2 were simply book-keeping reallocations and not true differential costs. Adjusting for this in the second column of Table 5.2 changes the projected loss to a projected differential profit of £19 500. Given that this profit would be achieved with no investment of company capital beyond working capital for work-in-progress and any stocks of unsold directories, this might be seen as a satisfactory return, at least for the first year. On the other hand, it is not an enormous profit margin for a product not sharing in the full recharge of corporate overheads, and this profit could be very sensitive to any short-fall in the predicted sales volume, especially as fixed costs comprise more than half the total costs on the predicted sales volume. We shall look at this uncertainty in more detail in the next section, on cost volume-profit (CVP) analysis.

Subsequent to the above review, the technical director found a new desk-top publishing system which he thinks could give the firm better value in publishing the new directory. This allows us to show another application for differential costing, the case of comparing two mutually exclusive alternatives means to meeting an agreed need.

In Table 5.2 the original proposal is shown as method A and the desktop publishing alternative as method B. The fixed-cost figures entered have all been corrected for the differential-costing mistakes made in the data entered in the left-hand column. Looking at the differential costs between methods A and B, the total fixed costs for B are £21 000 greater than for A, but the variable cost per unit under method B is £1.80 less. At the expected production and sales level of 10 000 directories, method B will cost £3000 more, thus yielding £3000 less profit. But how will profits be affected if sales are significantly less than or greater than 10 000? This is one question that cost volume-profit analysis helps to clarify, so we shall return to this example in the next section.

Cost-volume-profit analysis (CVP)

In Chapter 4 we looked at the relationship of fixed and variable costs to changes in the volume of activity using graphical display. This was shown to be a helpful exercise, although one must be cautious about making judgements on the levels of costs at activity volumes which are outside the 'normal range' of operational experience. If data on sales revenue are included in the graphical analysis, in addition to data on costs, then the effect of changes in volume on profits can also be displayed and studied. Profit, of course, equals total revenue less total costs at any indicated level or volume of activity.

Break-even graph and profit graph

Figure 5.3 illustrates a conventional break-even graph. This takes its name from the critical volume level of sales at which total sales revenue and total costs chargeable against sales are exactly equal. Above **break-even** point (BEV) there is profit; below it there is a loss. Critical interest should focus on the behaviour of both costs and revenue across the entire realistic range of operating volumes. The graph provides only a starting point for sensitive understanding. Especially when considering operating at volume levels near or outside the margins of the normal range, it becomes important to ask for specific cost-study information on how costs, especially fixed costs, could be controlled to maximise the benefit at any given revenue activity level.

Some managers prefer to focus just on the relationship between sales revenue volume and profit, and for them the relevant data in the break-even graph can be simplified to display as a profit graph (see Figure 5.4). This display loses the information on variable costs, which is made possible because of the assumption that variable cost per unit is constant and is a constant proportion of sales price, throughout at least the normal volume range. However, this is an assumption which should perhaps be kept visible and explicit, as in the break-even graph, if only so that managers are

Figure 5.3 Break-even graph

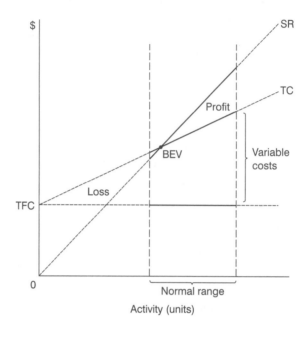

Figure 5.4 Profit graph

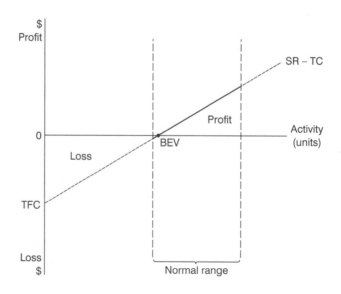

reminded to challenge the assumption from time to time, and to seek efficient means of reducing variable costs and thus further enhancing profit.

Contribution analysis

'Contribution' is defined as the excess of sales price over unit variable cost, or the excess of sales revenue over total variable cost (see Table 5.2). The concept and measurement of contribution can be applied when studying the pricing or marketing of individual products (including services, and retail and wholesale distribution), including the potential of new products and also reviews considering whether or not to drop existing products. It can additionally be used to study the overall performance of the firm. As volume increases from zero, all contribution is applied initially to recover fixed costs (and thus reduce loss) up to the break-even volume.

Beyond break-even all contribution received becomes profit. However, when seeking to expand sales beyond the existing or normal range it may be necessary to spend disproportionate extra funds on marketing (including promotion, sales staff time, discounts, etc.), so that measurement of incremental contribution should be taken not from the graphs of the firm as a whole, but instead from one-off calculations using data (such as from engineering-method studies) explicitly tailored to the particular product(s) and market circumstances.

To illustrate some of the problems and methods of using CVP/break-even analysis and contribution analysis let us return to PrintPublish Ltd's pending decision whether or not to start a line in regional business directories and, if so, whether to produce these using method A or method B. The terminology and notation we will use for this are summarised in Table 5.3, together with the equations for key relationships of data. The data we will use is displayed in Table 5.2. The applications of the concepts and equations to the choice between method A and method B are summarised in Table 5.3.

Unit contribution and contribution ratio

Unit contribution, or sales price less unit variable cost, is shown in Table 5.4. Method B offers the prospect of an extra £1.80 per unit for every extra unit sold. This benefit will be reflected in the contribution ratio, 0.719 for B as against 0.599 for A, showing the proportional contributions to profits once the break-even point has been passed. But if sales fall below the break-even point, losses will be greater the higher the contribution ratio. This can be shown graphically, as in Figure 5.5, using data from Tables 5.2 and 5.3. Method A gives a break-even of 7821 units, compared to 8465 units for method B. The difference between break-even and a (realistic) sales volume is called the margin of safety: this is 2179 units (or 21.8%) for method A and 1535 units (or 15.4%) for method B. This suggests method B is higher risk.

One further test illustrated by Figure 5.4 is the 'indifference volume' (IV); that is, the volume at which total costs will be equal between the alternatives being compared, so that total profits will also be equal at that volume. In our example the IV is 11 667 units, well above the expected sales volume. Until sales volume reaches this level, profit will be less under method B than method A, but beyond this level they will be greater under method B.

Profit sensitivity analysis

'**Sensitivity analysis**' is not an analytical technique particular to accounting, but rather a general approach to subjecting operational data to testing to see what would or might be the likely outcomes resulting from a change in key variables affecting a decision. In our PrintPublish example we could test for differences in unit variable costs or in total fixed costs (including changes in the assumptions as regards including only incremental fixed costs or, alternatively, a proportional share of existing plus incremental fixed costs). For the present purpose of illustrating CVP analysis, however, it will suffice to show the effect on profits of different assumptions regarding the market sales volume. The results of this are shown at the bottom of Table 5.4. Method B will generate significantly greater profit at high sales volume, but also the trading loss will be much greater if there is a large shortfall in sales volume. The credibility of the sales forecast of 10 000 units should be re-examined. Even if credibility is confirmed uncertainty remains, and many, if not most accountants would tend to recommend the risk-averse alternative of choosing method A, arguing that avoiding large losses is more important than gambling on larger but uncertain profits. Here, of course, is where managers rather than accountants must take the final decision – and the accountability!

One could also ask, what if a cautious or even realistic sales forecast were only 6000 units, what then would be the break-even price (BEP) for the new directory? Using the BEP equation from Table 5.3, we obtain the results shown near the bottom of Table 5.4; that is, the BEP would be £17.67 under method A and £19.37 under

---

Figure 5.5   Frequency volume for alternative production method (See Table 5.4)

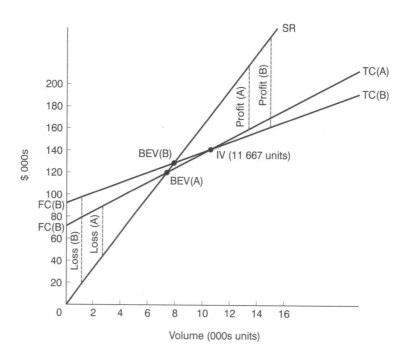

NOTE: FOR KEY TO NOTATIONS ON GRAPHS, SEE TABLE 5.3.

method B. Whichever method is chosen, and unless there is high credibility for the sales forecast of 10 000 units, a cautious approach would suggest that the price should perhaps be set higher than the £14.95 proposed, unless it is thought that the market will be price-resistant (including concern for any direct market competition from other publishers).

Limiting factors

In our PrintPublish example we have assumed that management has the time to take on the introduction and marketing of a new product range, that there was space and skill to undertake new production and that the extra production would be supplied on newly leased equipment. However, many decision situations will not be so straightforward. Indeed, for illustration, let us consider that in the PrintPublish example, while all the typesetting and printing will be done on new, leased equipment, the binding is to be done on the existing bindery production line. We shall have to accommodate all

Table 5.3	Notation and equations for cost-volume-profit and differential analysis

CU	=	contribution per unit sold at a given price
CT	=	contribution total for a given volume of sales
CR	=	contribution ratio or percentage of sales
UVC	=	unit variable cost
UFC	=	unit fixed cost
TVC	=	total variable cost
TFC	=	total fixed cost
TC	=	total (fixed and variable) cost
SP	=	sales price (per unit)
SR	=	sales revenue (for specified number of units)
SV	=	sales (revenue) volume, in units
BEV	=	break-even volume, in units
BEP	=	break-even price, for a specified volume in units
MS	=	margin of safety, in units
MSR	=	margin of safety ratio or percentage
IV	=	indifference volume (of sales in units)
CU	=	SP − UVC
CT	=	SR − TVC
CR	=	CU ÷ SP or CT ÷ SR
BEV	=	TFC ÷ CU
MS	=	SV − BEV
MSR	=	MS ÷ SV
IV	=	Differential TFC ÷ Differential UVC
Profit	=	SR − TC = SR − (TFC + TVC) = SR − (TFC + (SV)(UVC))
BEP	=	(TFC ÷ SV) + UVC

Note: see Table 5.4 and Figures 5.3, 5.4 and 5.5.

three of the company's products in the bindery: trade catalogues, community magazines and the new business directory. The bindery is nearing its maximum production capacity and new equipment cannot be leased but, instead, can only be purchased as a capital outlay, for which the company presently has no spare cash or any spare credit capacity (in the opinion of its bankers). It is therefore pertinent to ask, in view of this limited capacity (or **limiting factor**), how the firm should best use, or ration, its capacity to maximise total contribution and profits.

The relevant data is summarised in Table 5.5. The object of the analysis is to determine which product produces the highest contribution per unit of scarce resource, or limiting factor, consumed. In theory, the output of the product with the highest contribution per unit of limiting factor should be maximised until that product's market is saturated. In this example the optimal bindery product turns out to be the trade catalogues. The reason for this is probably that a high proportion of the cost and value in this product derives from the artwork and photo reproduction, while the binding costs are relatively small.

Limiting-factor analysis can be conducted at a more sophisticated level by the use of linear programming (see Wilson and Chua 1993). While this analysis may indeed lead to optimal product-mix decisions in the very short term – or during a recession or crisis, when new investment is barred by top-management policy decisions – it may be more constructive in typical circumstances for management to focus its energies on removing the limiting factor, rather than just accepting this and constraining its output and its ability to meet customer requirements. In PrintPublish, for exam-

Table 5.4	Cost-volume-profit and differential-cost calculations for PrintPublish Ltd – proposal to produce and sell 10 000 directories at £14.95

	Method A	*Method B*
CU	=	£14.95 – £6.00 = £8.95	£14.95 – £4.20 = £10.75
CR	=	£8.95 ÷ £14.95 = 0.599	£10.75 ÷ £14.95 = 0.719
BEV	=	70 000 ÷ 8.95 = 7.821 units	91 000 ÷ £10.75 = 8.465 units
MS	=	10 000 – 7821 = 2179 units	10 000 – 8465 = 1535 units
MSR	=	2179 ÷ 10 000 = 21.8%	1535 ÷ 10 000 = 15.4%
IV	=	£21 000 ÷ £1.80 = 11 667 units (see Figure 13.5)	

BEP if sales, e.g. only 6 000 units

(70 000 ÷ 6 000) + £6.00 = £17.67 (£91 000 ÷ 6 000) + £4.20 = £19.37

Sensitivity at selected volumes	£ *Profit*	£ *Profit*
6 000 units	(16 300)	(26 500)
8 000	1 600	(5 000)
10 000	19 500	16 500
11 667	34 422	34 422
14 000	55 300	59 500
20 000	109 000	124 000

Note: For key to notation, see Table 5.3.

ple, the limiting-factor constraint might be removed simply by putting on an extra shift or half-shift in the bindery.

CVP in perspective

CVP, including contribution analysis and limiting-factor analysis, and preferably based on decision-relevant differential costs rather than historical absorption costs, offers powerful tools for short-term business decisions. These decisions include the solving of problems regarding pricing, new products, keeping or dropping existing products, production-mix and sales-mix planning, altering plant layouts and work flows, changing material-input mixes or process flows and output mixes, choices of distribution channels and promotional activities, and so on.

Nevertheless, the CVP and related analytical methods have their limitations. Their conclusions are no more reliable than the quality of the assumptions and parameters supplied by management, or the appropriateness of the physical resource use and cost data available to, or chosen by, the accountant. Both management and accountants need to communicate openly about their problems concerning objectives and data limitations in order to minimise the limitations and obtain the best decision-relevant advice.

Decisions on inputs and outputs

This chapter has been concerned with explaining the types of cost information and cost analysis which should prove helpful to management decision making in specific circumstances. The key criterion, it is argued, is not precision or even accuracy, but relevance. Management science and production management textbooks abound with methods of analysis seeking to optimise the choice and use of inputs. The choices available relate to the use of alternative materials (e.g. steel v. aluminium tube), standard parts (for economy) v. tailor-made parts (for 'perfection' in design or performance); to questions of the substitution of higher-cost materials for labour costs involved in 'making do' with lower-cost, lower-grade materials; and to the merits of substituting capital-intensive methods of production for traditional, craft skilled,

Table 5.5	PrintPublish Ltd limiting-factor analysis		
	Trade catalogues	*Community magazines*	*Business directories*
Sales price per unit (SP)	£1.20	£0.40	£14.95
Less variable cost (VC)	0.45	0.16	4.20
Contribution per unit (CU)	£0.75	£0.24	£10.75
Divide by bindery time per unit (hours)	0.002	0.001	0.035
Contribution per bindery hour	£375.00	£240.00	£307.14
Limiting factor contribution ranking	1	3	2

high-cost, labour-intensive methods. The latter issue involves the 'time value of money' and the capital-investment decision considered in Chapter 9.

If non-relevant costs are fed into decision making on production-input decisions such as the above examples, 'rubbish' solutions will result. The manager must not just ask the accountant for the cost of a particular input, process or output. Rather, given that, as we have seen, there are many alternative measures of cost for any particular resource or activity, the manager must make clear to the accountant exactly what kind of decision-situation he needs decision-relevant cost information for.

The above examples typify the kinds of decision which should be taken before production begins, or perhaps even before there is a commitment to produce a particular product. There are other kinds of decision situations which relate to ongoing management performance; these overlap between the topic areas of management planning and decisions, and management control. An example is the problem of determining what is the optimal stock to maintain of raw materials, parts and components, of work-in-progress, and of finished goods ready for sale and delivery. There is a well-established operations research technique for solving this problem: the economic order quantity (EOQ) model, which is discussed in Chapter 6.

There is an approach, however, which could make the use of the EOQ redundant in many industries. This is the Japanese-inspired just-in-time (JIT) approach to disciplining both external suppliers and internal production lines to complete deliveries precisely on time to meet both production-line requirements for inputs and customer delivery requirements for outputs (Lee 1987). In practice, it will clearly be easier to apply the JIT approach to a plant with a limited range of regularly produced products, such as a bakery, than to a factory producing a thousand different lines of hardware, many in small quantities.

Conclusions

Routine costing systems provide information appropriate for valuing work-in-progress and stocks to meet financial accounting requirements, and also information useful in the day-to-day monitoring of shop-floor performance or in assisting budgetary control (especially in service organisations and the public sector).

However, the most important management decisions involve seeking out and assessing possible changes, in products or product mix, in technologies or production methods, and/or in markets or distribution methods. For these decision situations routine cost accounting information is of little help, and management must demand relevant cost information and explain the nature of the decision situation and choices under consideration to the accounting staff so that they can help provide relevant information and analysis.

For some decisions, activity-based costs or attributable costs, unlike conventional absorption costs, may provide sufficiently relevant information. But where decisions involve the possibility of substantial changes in the volume or scale of operations, or in products or product mix, then *ad hoc* cost studies, often involving the so-called engineering method, and also more sophisticated analysis, will be needed. Here the concepts and methods of cost estimation, differential costing, and contribution and cost-volume-profit analysis should be employed. Business and financial risk must also be considered, and where decision situations involve significant capital outlays the 'time value of money' must additionally be brought into the decision process (this is discussed in Chapter 9).

Chapter review

This chapter has explained cost concepts and forms of cost analysis which are useful to managers in making short-term decisions. It was necessary to consider some of the limitations of traditional absorption cost accounting, and how that approach might be modified and improved through activity-based-costing (ABC) and attributable-costing methods. At the heart of many business decisions is change – of product or product mix, or of technology or market. Assessing the consequences of change requires a clear separation of fixed or period costs, especially the core costs of the organisation, from the variable costs attributable to individual products (or services or markets) and to changes in their volume.

Methods of cost estimation for identifying fixed and variable costs were discussed. This led on to the concept of contribution and to methods of differential costing and cost-volume-profit analysis, including sensitivity and limiting-factor calculations

Further reading

See Arnold and Turley (1996), Drury (2000) or Horngren *et al.* (2002).

Questions and exercises

*1   Dryways Ltd makes a single product, a dehumidifier. The price to wholesalers and direct to some large customers is normally £100. Recent years' sales have ranged between 20 000 and 35 000 units. Variable costs are currently £70 per unit and total fixed costs are £700 000.

Required:
Draw one or more break-even or CVP graphs to display your findings (graph paper is helpful but not essential). You may find it useful to check your graph solutions by using some of the notation and equations in Table 5.3.
(a) Determine the break-even volume under the company's existing pricing policy and price structure. Also determine at what volume profit will equal a 10% return on sales.
(b) During a recession it is forecast that only 20 000 units can be sold at the normal price. However, it appears that up to a further 15 000 units could be sold through large mail-order distributors if the price were cut to £80.
(c) Alternatively to (b), the company could attempt to enlarge its normal market by reducing its normal price, as a result of product redesign to reduce material and labour costs, and of leasing new automated plant to further cut labour requirements. It is estimated that variable cost could be cut to £50 per unit but fixed costs would rise to £900 000. At what volume would management be indifferent between alternatives (c) and (a) or (c) and (b)?
(d) What other factors should be taken into account before a choice is made between alternatives and what additional information would you seek before making a decision?

*2 Tork Ltd produces a single line of powered heavy-duty torque wrenches. Its budget profit and loss summary for a normal six months' trading is as follows:

	€000
Sales (2400 units)	840
Direct labour	192
Direct materials	180
Variable production overhead	72
Fixed production overhead	120
Variable admin and sales overhead	36
Fixed admin and sales overhead	96
Total costs	696
Profit before tax	144

A foreign government has invited the firm to tender for a special order of 500 torque wrenches. The following additional information is supplied.

(a) The customer requires variations of product and delivery specifications whereby direct labour costs would be 12.5% above normal, direct material costs would be 20% above normal, sales overheads (transport) would cost €35 per unit more than usual; and special tooling costs of €10 000 would arise (and the tooling would have no certain value after completion of the special order).

(b) The customer requires completion of the order within six months of confirmation of the order.

(c) The firm does not want the investment risk of enlarging its premises, but present facilities can be used to produce up to 450 units per month. All units beyond 400 per month incur an overtime premium of €20 per unit.

Required:

(a) Apply differential cost analysis to the special order.

(b) Calculate the tender price which would leave the total company profits for six months unaltered, also calculate the tender price which would earn the same profit margin on sales as in the budget above, on the enlarged volume sold during the six months of the special order, and recalculate and show the six months' budget on this tender basis.

(c) Comment on any simplifying assumptions you may have had to make in this exercise and on any other financial complications to be considered or any additional information needed before a final decision.

*3 Information is supplied in Table 5.6 on the year's accounting results for a division of Tinbrass Ltd supplying four hardware products.

Required:

(a) Calculate the numbers to fill in the blanks left in the list in Table 5.6, and study the completed list for what you can learn or infer about the products and their cost, price and profit characteristics.

(b) Assuming spare capacity, suggest which product(s) should be given the greatest sales promotion effort. What would you advise if, instead, the firm is at full capacity and the sales of one product can be increased only at the expense of another?

4* Chippers Ltd trades under the motto 'Anything with chips', and it supplies a wide range of electronic components to the automotive and other industries. It works to the designs of both its own staff and major customers. It does not carry out any basic manufacture, but instead buys all its parts and sundries from specialist manufacturers, often from low-cost overseas sources. All incoming parts are tested to high standards, and Chippers is proud of the quality and inspection standards of its own main work, which is the precision assembly of electronic components and systems as finished products.

Chippers has four main departments assembly, marketing, administration and design. The purchasing function is located within the assembly department, but for quality-control reasons the design department is responsible for the technical specification in purchase orders, for listing approved suppliers, and for quality inspection and testing of incoming purchases (and of completed assembly work). The assembly department is responsible for stock availability and storage, and it controls the timing and quantities for purchase orders (and for assembly production orders).

Chippers has used an absorption costing system to assign overheads (together with direct costs) to profit-contribution accounts for each final product. It is now considering changing to an ABC system.

Overhead	Absorption basis		Cost in Month	Hours of ABC time
Purchasing	Materials value	£1 000 000	£30 000	1200
Production control	Direct labour hours	100 000	18 000	800
Inspection and testing	Materials value	£1 000 000	£15 000	400
Design services	Direct labour hours	100 000	£25 000	500

Preliminary enquiry finds that numbers of transactions will not provide a useful ABC cost driver, but that recording service activity time traceable to each product (and reallocating all general service office time in proportion to each product) should produce a fair cost driver. ABC-relevant chargeable time and absorption values are given below for two products for the month under study:

	Product A	Product B
Value of material issued to product	£100 000	£50 000
Direct labour hours in assembly department	15 000	5 000
Overhead activity for each product:		
Purchasing	100	80
Production control	110	70
Inspection and testing	40	30
Design services	20	6

· *Required*:

The chief executive has asked you to prepare a concise report:

(a) To show a comparison of the cost allocations as between absorption costing and ABC,

(b) To comment on any differences and why the figures under one or the other system may be more true or more helpful to management

(c) To explain briefly whether your findings have any implications for Chipper's pricing policies (where it is a price maker) or for its willingness to accept orders (where it is a price taker).

Hint: First calculate the cost/absorption-driver rates for the two methods and then apply the two sets of recharging rates to each product for interpretation and any comparisons possibly relevant to your report.

5* Cozee Bedrooms Ltd sells complete bedroom remake packages, comprising bought-in furniture, fabrics, wallpapers, etc, customised and installed within a range of choices in each package. There are four standard, fixed-price packages: Countess, the cheapest, Duchess, Princess and Empress. You are the company manager and your accountant has just informed you that in his/her opinion the Countess package should be discontinued because it is making a loss. He/she has given you the following updated figures for the Countess:

	£	£
Countess package fixed price per sale		1 995
Less average costs per package completed:		
Purchases of beds and other furniture and fittings	850	
Purchases of fabric and decorative materials	250	
Direct labour to customise, make up and install	350	
Overheads	650	2 100
Loss on each Countess sale		(105)

You are surprised by the loss and by the overheads charge as you know that, company-wide, the overheads are a little under 25% of sales revenue. You ask the accountant for an overheads breakdown. The accountant is surprised in his/her turn and perhaps a little peeved. He/she suggests that the overheads appear proportionately larger on the Countess only because the furniture and other materials used in the package are so relatively cheap. He/she supplies the following breakdown of estimated Countess overheads:

	£
Selling expenses (the same average cost as calculated for all four product packages on number of sales completed)	230
Workshop (indirect) labour (for customizing furniture, making up curtains, etc, based on average of sampled job sheets)	120
Energy, rent, rates and other premises costs (apportioned on a basis proportional to direct labour)	110
Transport (apportioned on a basis proportional to direct labour)	100
Administration (apportioned on the basis of total Countess revenue as a proportion of total company sales revenue, per unit)	90
Total overheads per Countess sale	650

Required:

(a) On the evidence available, would you discontinue or retain the Countess sales package? What are the arguments for and against?

(b) Briefly assess the decision-relevance of each of the five overhead categories and the cost allocation or apportionment bases used.

(c) What further accounting and/or other information would you wish to have in the real world before making a final decision on the Countess package?

6 Aus Wings Ltd (AWL) supplies long-haul holidays, especially to and from Australasia. It arranges tailor-made travel, but mainly operates organised package tours with tour leaders. It markets tours under two separate brand names, the two being slightly differentiated in price and content. One brand name is marketed solely through travel agents, while the other brand name is marketed exclusively through advertising and direct mail. Each holiday tour is managed as a profit centre, as are the two brands at a higher level of aggregation.

AWL is organised into three main departments, which are the principal cost and budget centres for all direct costs, advertising and promotions. Marketing is responsible for market research, advertising and promotions, direct mail, telephone and agency bookings, and customer services. Operations researches, plans and organises travel and tour itineraries and facilities, and recruits and supervises tour leaders. Administration provides computer, clerical, accounting, foreign-exchange, insurance and other services to, or through, the other two departments.

Administration is not charged direct to profit centres, but instead to the other two departments. Here, routine services are charged monthly, based on the achieved volume percentage of the agreed annual budget extra or special services are charged at estimated full cost. All overhead recharges to the profit centres arise from the other two departments; they are calculated on the basis of distribution to tour/brand profit centres in proportion to the monthly share of total bookings revenue achieved by each separate tour. The only direct costs charged or recharged to profit centres comprise the airline and other travel and accommodation expenses, and the pay and expenses of the tour leaders incurred for each tour.

While the external auditors see no problem affecting profit determination for the company as a whole, they have criticised the present overhead accounting arrangements as possibly giving rise to misleading information for internal management and have suggested the company introduces ABC systems.

Required:

(a) Write a concise report explaining (i) all the likely weaknesses of the present system of overhead allocation, relevant to management needs and (ii) the probable advantages and/or disadvantages of a change to using ABC.

(b) Outline the sequence of steps/actions you would undertake in order to install, operate and benefit from a new ABC system, bearing in mind managerial and behavioural issues as well as technical accounting requirements.

7* Briefly explain the principles and method of differential-cost analysis and suggest for what types of decision situations it may have the greatest advantage over analysis based on CVP (cost volume-profit) studies derived from historical absorption costs.

8 (a) Why may any single given concept or measure of cost not be suitable equally for use in the separate exercises of planning, decision-making and control?

(b) How does the time-horizon of forward planning and decisions affect the classification or measurement of costs?

9 Although strictly 'overheads' is a narrower concept or classification than 'indirect costs', the label of overheads has come to be applied to almost all costs not charged as direct costs to marketable end-products or end-services. Concisely, suggest possible reasons for this and also discuss why accounting for overheads has attracted increasing concern and importance in recent years.

10 'Attributable costing may be more relevant than either absorption costing or differential costing to many decisions involving marketing, pricing, and product range and product abandonment problems.' Explain why you agree or disagree with this statement.

11* Concisely outline the distinctive features of ABC and explain its main differences from aborption costing.

12 Why are pricing decisions more difficult for firms with multiple products than for firms with single products? Also, to the extent that prices are based on or related to costs, can you suggest any one concept or measure of cost that is generally most relevant to pricing decisions? Explain this viewpoint.

Working capital management

6

Chapter preview

In this chapter, we focus on working capital and explain why its effective management is important to the financial success of entities. We also look at the concept of the cash-conversion cycle and its component elements. Emphasis is placed on the need for efficient management of the cash-conversion cycle with particular attention being paid to the management of inventories, debtors and creditors. A number of techniques that can be employed to help in this regard are discussed.

The meaning and importance of working capital

Nature of working capital

Working capital is the name given to the short-term resources (**current assets**) owned by an entity, and the short-term funding (**current liabilities**) that it uses to finance these resources. Typically, the value of the current assets of an entity will exceed the value of the current liabilities, leading to working capital representing a net investment. As with any other investment, an entity should only invest in working capital insofar as such an investment will lead to returns greater than those that could be obtained from alternative forms of investment. Working capital can be analysed into four main constituent elements, as shown by the following equation:

$$\text{Working capital} = \text{Stock} + \text{Debtors} + \text{Cash} - \text{Creditors} \qquad \textbf{(6.1)}$$

Stock (inventories), debtors and cash are the most common forms of current asset, and the term creditors is used as a shorthand representing all forms of current liabilities. Later in this chapter we discuss the management of each of the different components of working capital in some detail. However, before doing so we need to summarise the reasons why entities invest in the asset components of working capital and use the liability component as a source of finance. We will do this by looking at each of the components in turn.

Stock (inventory) It is important to recognise that accounting entities are likely to hold different types of inventory. A core distinction is that between production/service delivery related inventories and support service related inventories. The former are directly related to productive/service delivery processes, while the latter are related to various overhead/support functions, e.g. maintenance and office supplies. For many entities, production related inventories will include stocks of raw materials, work-in-progress and finished goods. If an entity did not hold stocks of raw materials it would be entirely dependent on the timely delivery of such materials from its suppliers to enable the production/service delivery process to continue (although proponents of just-in-time management would argue that this is exactly what an enterprise should seek to arrange with its suppliers). Work-in-progress represents inventories where the transformation from raw material to final product has commenced but not yet been completed. Finished goods represent inventories of finished product not yet sold (delivered) to customers. They also include inventories purchased simply for resale, e.g. by a wholesaler or retailer. In all cases, the investment in inventories is made to support the commercial activities of the entity, whether they be production processes (e.g. raw materials), sales activities (e.g. finished goods), or support activities (e.g. maintenance stocks). The level of the inventory held for each purpose needs to be sufficient to ensure that the activity in question generates the necessary contribution to the overall profitability of the entity, but no more than that.

Debtors (accounts receivable) In the main, these are the result of an entity selling goods or services on credit terms to its customers who have not (as yet) paid the amounts that they owe the entity resulting from these sales. However, debtors may also result from other forms of transactions such as the granting of short-term loans. Entities generally offer credit terms to their customers to secure sales that they might not otherwise have been able to obtain. The extent, and the terms of credit, that entities offer to their customers are (should be) the result of explicit market positioning decisions, and will frequently be influenced by the customary practice of the industrial/commercial sector in which the entity operates. The balance to be struck by an entity is that between the additional profits generated by the extra sales resulting from offering credit and the costs of financing the resultant investment in debtors, including the potential cost of default by customers.

Cash Entities need ready access to cash to enable them to fund their day-to-day payment obligations, and to deal with unexpected contingencies. However, maintaining liquid cash resources (including bank current accounts) means that these resources are not being used for alternative investments, and are not generating any of the returns that might derive from such investments. Alternative investments in this context include not only productive investments but financial investments such as deposit accounts. The balance that has to be struck is between the benefits of the liquidity and flexibility afforded by cash against the associated costs, and in particular the opportunity costs of the forgone returns from alternative investments.

Creditors (accounts payable) These are the obverse of debtors. They represent the short-term funding that an entity has obtained. A major element of this is likely to be the amounts owed to suppliers for purchases that the enterprise has made on credit terms, although creditors may also include short-term finance from lenders (e.g. bank over-drafts) and monies due to state agencies. For example, in the UK the monies are payable to the HM Customs and Revenue for such things as: PAYE, National Insurance and VAT; while in Australia, the Australian Taxation Office expects to receive payments for both PAYG and GST. There may be a short period of time during which this credit appears costless, but there are often hidden costs, e.g. to do with the overall relationships with suppliers, which need to be taken into account. Management need to balance the costs of short-term funding, both apparent and hidden, against those of other types of funding and the returns that are generated from the investments that these funds support.

Core principles of working capital management

The core principles on which the management of working capital should be based are easily stated:

(a) Entities should invest in current assets, so long as the return from such investment exceeds the cost of the capital used to fund them, and;

(b) Entities should make use of short-term funding, so long as it has a lower cost than other sources of funding and can be used to make profitable investments, after allowing for the cost of the funding.

However, the implementation of these principles in practice is normally rather more problematic. Most entities have well-defined procedures for the analysis and monitoring of investment in large-scale capital projects. These may include the use of discounted cash flow analysis, or other techniques such as the payback method, for investment appraisal (see Chapter 9) and will typically require a clear specification of the benefit to the entity of undertaking the investment. There will normally be clearly specified levels of authorisation, frequently involving senior management, required before an entity commits itself to undertaking such an investment.

This tends not to be the case with working capital. Even accepting that all organisations have (should have) internal control systems designed to prevent unauthorised expenditures, the same level of attention is not normally paid to investments in working capital. In part, this is because of the amounts involved in individual working capital investment decisions. While the overall investment in inventories or debtors may be significant, such investments are the outcome of many different individual decisions and transactions, each of which may in its own right appear to be relatively immaterial to the finances of the entity. Many different individuals in many different organisational functions, and at many different levels of seniority, are likely to be involved in these decisions and transactions. The interests of all these individuals are likely to differ, and few of them will view working capital as an investment. Typically, they will be more concerned with operating within their own expenditure and revenue budgets and with discharging their own management responsibilities satisfactorily. Sales staff are going to focus on generating sales without regard to the costs of financing the resultant debtors; maintenance staff will want to ensure that they have a stock of spare parts sufficient to deal with any breakdowns; production staff will want to ensure that they have a sufficient stock of raw materials. There are understandable motives to have more rather than less, and this can easily result in an entity's investment in working capital becoming out of control, particularly in entities where departmental budget holders are not charged with the cost of their departmental investments in working capital. All too often, such costs are hidden and departmental managers have no incentive either to recognise or minimise them.

To summarise, decisions which impact on the effectiveness of an entity's working capital management are taken all the time, and at all levels of the organisation, by staff and managers who, all too often, are not aware of the financial impact of their decisions or held accountable for this impact.

Need for working capital management policies

The amount invested in working capital will vary from entity to entity, and from economic sector to economic sector. However, in many sectors/entities it might well be of the order of 25–40%, or more, of net assets. Thus, it represents a major investment and one which needs careful management attention but, for the reasons outlined above, it does not always receive this attention – often to the ultimate cost of the entity's financial performance. Management needs to institute clearly stated policies for the management of working capital, and ensure that all staff appreciate the importance of adhering to these policies in their day-to-day decision making. It needs to have clear strategies for the implementation of these policies, and mechanisms for monitoring this implementation. These policies need to be an integral part of overall financing and financial management strategies. In formulating these policies and strategies, regard needs to be had to the following:

1 Optimisation of investment in working capital involves issues of both efficiency and scale. For any given level of efficiency in the management of working capital, a change in the scale of activities of the entity will lead to a change in the quantum of the appropriate investment. If the level of business activity increases, and there is no change in the level of efficiency, the amount of investment will need to increase. Correspondingly, if the level of efficiency of working capital management changes, then for any given level of business activity the investment in working capital will also change. In planning its working capital management, and the associated level of investment, management needs to consider both efficiency and level of activity. All too often companies plan expansion without considering the consequences for their investment in working capital. In extreme cases, this can result in **overtrading** (having insufficient funding to support the working capital investment implicit in the higher level of activity), perhaps leading to insolvency.

2 The speed with which levels of investment in working capital can change with improvements or deteriorations in its management needs to be acknowledged. Working capital comprises short-term assets and liabilities. As such, its investment cycle is a short one and improvements in management will have a rapid impact. Equally, so will deteriorations. The planning of working capital management should involve the setting of performance targets, which should be regularly monitored to detect any deterioration at an early stage, so that corrective action can be taken and the achievement of the benefits of improvements identified.

Working capital management is an all too often neglected facet of financial management, but one which can play a major part in the overall financial viability and success of an entity. Enterprises need to develop and implement clearly defined working capital management policies. In the remainder of this chapter, we discuss the factors that should be taken into account by management in identifying management strategies for the different components of working capital.

The flow of working capital

Effective management of working capital needs to reflect its dynamic nature and its individual components. The composition of working capital as a whole, and of its component elements, is constantly changing. This can be illustrated by considering the individual asset and liability categories:

(a) **Inventories.** Individual items of raw materials are purchased as the first step in the manufacture and ultimate sale of products. As these are used in the transformation process, they are converted first into work in progress and then into finished goods. To enable the transformation process to continue, these raw materials have to be replaced by fresh ones. Similarly, as the stock of finished goods is reduced by sales to customers it is constantly being replenished by the transformation of new raw materials, or the purchase of new finished goods. The individual components of inventory are continually being diminished and replenished.

(b) **Debtors.** Individual debtors arise from sales on credit terms. However, they only exist as assets until the customer settles the debt. At this point they disappear and are replaced by another element of working capital – cash. However, in the meantime it is likely that further credit sales will have been made, resulting in the creation of new debtors.

(c) **Creditors.** Individual creditors are created by individual purchases on credit terms, or other funding transactions. However, they only remain as liabilities until they are settled, resulting in a change to another component of working capital – cash. In the meantime it is likely that other credit purchase/funding transactions will have taken place, resulting in the creation of new creditors.

(d) **Cash.** Cash and bank balances are constantly changing as a result of all the entity's payments and receipts. Many of these are associated with changes in other components of working capital (most notably debtors and creditors), although they are also associated with other events as well (e.g. new long-term funding, purchase of fixed assets, etc.).

The challenge facing management is that of controlling all the constantly changing individual items comprising working capital and, thereby, controlling working capital as a whole. There is a continual circulation of current assets/liabilities through the business, and it is useful to think of this circulation in terms of the business cycle of the enterprise. This business cycle commences with the purchase of resource inputs, whether on cash or credit terms, and continues via the various transformation processes through the sale of the finished goods or services to the ultimate receipt of cash from the customer. This business cycle can be analysed into a number of component elements relating to the movements in the various elements of working capital. This is illustrated in Figure 6.1.

The cycle illustrated in Figure 6.1 demonstrates the linkages between the elements of working capital in the overall business cycle of the enterprise. The starting point is the purchase of the input resources which represents the start of two elements of the cycle (the inventory transformation period and the creditor deferral period). The elements of the cycle are:

(a) **Inventory transformation period.** This is the period of time from the purchase of the input resources (e.g. raw materials, or labour), through the transformation process (manufacturing and holding of finished product), to the point where the finished product is sold to the customer. This period will vary from sector to sector – it could be very short, particularly where the life of materials is an important factor (e.g. a restaurant which promotes itself on using only fresh produce, where the inventory transformation period might be less than 24 hours for much of the inventory), through to the construction industry, where it might be several years before a major construction project is completed. The end of the inventory transformation period (the sale of the finished goods) represents the commencement of another element of the cycle.

(b) **Debtor collection period.** This is the period of time between the point of sale and the receipt of cash from customers. In the case of cash sales, this period will effectively be zero. In the case of credit sales, it can be substantially longer, depending, at least in part, on the customary terms of trade in the particular industrial sector.

(c) **Creditor deferral period.** This is the period of time between the purchase of the resource inputs and the payment to the supplier. In the case of credit

---

Figure 6.1   The working capital cycle

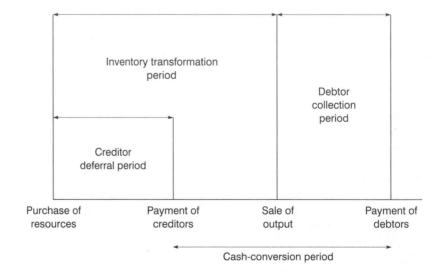

purchases, it is effectively zero. In the case of credit purchases, it may represent a substantial period of time. In the UK, companies often take two to three months, or more, to pay their suppliers. The end of the creditor deferral period, with the outflow of cash to the supplier, is the commencement of the final element of the working capital cycle.

(d) **Cash conversion period**. This represents the period of time between the outflow of cash to suppliers and the inflow of cash from customers.

The analysis shown in Figure 6.1 is obviously somewhat idealised. In real life, businesses will have many different types of inventory having different transformation periods; different payment terms with its suppliers (ranging from cash purchase to purchase on extended credit terms) and different terms of sales to its customers (again ranging from cash sales to sale on deferred credit terms). However, it does focus attention on the key issues involved in managing working capital as a whole, and on the importance of the different elements of the cycle, thereby giving management a start towards effective working capital management. An equation can be derived from the diagram in Figure 6.1:

$$\begin{array}{llll} \text{Cash} & \text{Inventory} & \text{Debtor} & \text{Creditor} \\ \text{conversion} = & \text{transformation} + & \text{collection} - & \text{deferral} \\ \text{period} & \text{period} & \text{period} & \text{period} \end{array} \qquad \textbf{(6.2)}$$

In general terms, an entity will prefer to have a shorter rather than a longer cash conversion period, because by doing so it will reduce the time that it has cash invested in short-term assets. This will enable it to use the cash that is thereby freed up for other profitable investments. However, as we shall see later in the chapter, it would be overly simplistic to state that the core objective of the management of working capital must be the reduction of the cash conversion period. Although this is an important objective, it must be tempered by other objectives relating to the reasons why inventory is held, why credit terms are given to customers, and why credit is taken from suppliers. Effective working capital management requires a conflation of these objectives with that of reducing, wherever possible, the cash conversion period so as to maximise the overall profitability of the enterprise. In many ways, the essence of working capital management is that of questioning why things happen (Why do we hold the stocks we do? Why do we give/receive credit to business partners in the way we do?) and ensuring that the answers to these questions reflect the overall objectives of the enterprise.

We stated earlier that an entity's working capital requirements were a function of two things – the efficiency with which it managed its working capital, and the scale of its operations. We can use equation (6.2) above to demonstrate this. Consider a business with the following characteristics:

(a) Current annual sales of £288 000 with a gross margin of 50% (i.e. cost of sales of £144 000 p.a.).

(b) An inventory transformation period of 3 months.

(c) A debtor collection period of 2.25 months.

(d) A creditor deferral period of 1.5 months.

The current working capital requirements of such a business can be calculated as follows:

		£
		£
Inventory	£144 000 × (3/12)	36 000
Debtors	£288 000 × (2.25/12)	54 000
Creditors	£144 000 × (1.5/12)	(18 000)
		72 000

The impact of scale can be examined first. If the volume of activity were to increase by 10%, with no change in any of the other parameters, then the working capital requirements could be restated as:

		£
Inventory	(£144 000 × 1.1) × (3/12)	39 600
Debtors	(£288 000 × 1.1) × (2.25/12)	59 400
Creditors	(£144 000 × 1.1) × (1.5/12)	(19 800)
		79 200

Thus, the overall working capital requirement has risen by £7200 (i.e. 10% of the original £72 000). The message is a clear and simple one. If the scale of the business (sales volume) increases, and everything else remains the same (profit margins and working capital conversion periods), then a business will have to be able to finance an increase in working capital if it is to survive, and the proportion of this increase will be exactly the same as the proportion of the increase in business activity. Unfortunately, all too many businesses focus on growth – however it is measured (increases in sales revenue, increases in market share, etc.) – without recognising that such growth has a consequence for the amount of working capital they require. This is particularly true of smaller businesses, which, when organising their finances, tend to concentrate on how the bigger individual items such as plant and machinery are to be financed. They tend to ignore the requirement to provide increasing amounts of finance for working capital as they expand, and may even grow beyond their ability to finance such increases. Technically, such growth beyond the ability to finance working capital requirements is called 'over-trading' and can in extreme circumstances lead to an inability to pay creditors, resulting in insolvency. Many are the profitable and growing businesses which are forced into insolvency because they did not plan and manage their working capital requirements. One way out of this problem is to seek and obtain additional sources of finance. Another way is to improve, wherever possible given the prevailing terms of trade, the day-to-day management of working capital. This can also be illustrated using the above example.

We will continue to assume a sales growth of 10%, but in addition to this we will also now assume that the inventory transformation period is reduced by one week, that the debtor collection period is similarly reduced, and that the creditor deferral period is increased by one week. In these circumstances, the working capital requirement becomes:

		£
		£
Inventory	(£144 000 × 1.1) × (2.75/12)	36 300
Debtors	(£288 000 × 1.1) × (2/12)	52 800
Creditors	(£144 000 × 1.1) × (1.75/12)	(23 100)
		66 000

In this case, the business has grown by 10% but, despite this, the amount it needs to invest in working capital has actually declined (from £72 000 to £66 000) because of the more effective working capital management. This is obviously a constructed example, but it does illustrate the impact that attention to the management of working capital can have on a business's finances. Growth of 10% without any change in the effectiveness of working capital management requires a commensurate growth in the financing of working capital, i.e. £7200 (10%). It may be possible to achieve the same level of growth, and at the same time reduce the investment in working capital, by improving the effectiveness of working capital management. The extent to which this is in fact possible will, of course, depend not just upon management actions but also on the commercial circumstances in which they find themselves operating. However, it does suggest a focus for their attention.

Inventory management

Earlier in this chapter we suggested that a prime reason for a business to hold inventories was to enable it to service the needs of its production/transformation/sales processes and, thereby, to meet the needs of its customers, and to generate profit from so doing. If asked, most managers will advance this as the reason why they do in fact hold inventories. However, if the question as to why inventories are held is pursued further a number of different motives for holding inventory will start to emerge. The principal of these are:

(a) **Transactions motive**. As described above, this relates to the holding of inventories in order to meet anticipated production/sales and service delivery requirements. It is, or should be, based on budgeted levels of production/ sales and service delivery. However, all too often these requirements may not be clearly specified or managers may not trust the budget. This leads to a second motive for holding inventory.

(b) **Precautionary motive**. Here the managers involved do not want to be 'caught short'. They deliberately hold more inventory than the budgets and forecasts indicate that they need, so that they can cope with any underestimates of demand that may have been made. Their aim is to avoid any loss of production/ sales by ensuring that they have a margin of safety. The problem that this can, of course, cause is that different managers may have different estimates of the level of safety that they require and that these may lead, not just to an entity holding excessive stocks, but to it holding an uncoordinated pattern of stocks leading to ineffectiveness. The precautionary motive is a perfectly reasonable motive for an entity to hold stocks beyond the level it forecasts that it needs. However, this needs to be done in a coordinated fashion.

(c) **Speculative motive**. Here the managers involved are speculating that there will be increases in the future prices of the items of stock, and that by buying items now and holding them in stock they will be able to save money, in terms of purchase prices. Again, this is a perfectly rational motive for holding stocks, provided that the costs of holding such stocks as well as any future price savings are taken into account. Unfortunately, all too often this is not the case, as the managers involved are not charged with the costs associated with holding the larger amount of stock.

(d) **Budgetary motive.** This is a rather more difficult issue and relates to the issues discussed in Chapter 7 regarding the way in which an organisation implements its budgetary process. It is, perhaps, at its most pointed in the public sector although it also applies to the private sector. A typical situation is one where a manager has a given expenditure budget for a financial period (year) to support a particular service/activity and, based on past experience, knows that if the budget is underspent it is likely that it will be reduced next year. Thus, *ceteris paribus*, the manager has an incentive to spend to the limit of the budget. One way that this can be done is to purchase more inventory (particularly if the budget is based on simple expenditure rather than costs which reflect changes in inventory levels). Managers may feel that they gain in two ways by doing this. Firstly, their expenditure is up to budget and this may help them in negotiating next year's budget. Secondly, the inventory that they have acquired will be available to support service provision next year and, thereby, provide them with something of a buffer against problems that they may encounter.

The amount of inventory that entities hold will depend in part on the nature of their activities (bakers will tend to hold less inventory than manufacturing companies), and in part on the scale of their activities (larger companies will tend to hold more inventory than smaller companies). It will also depend in part on the balance between the various motives for holding inventories outlined above, and in part on the attention that is devoted by management to inventory levels and the effectiveness of the policies that they implement for such management. In all cases, the actual amount of inventory held will be the result of many different factors and of 'trade-offs' between these factors. Ultimately, the determination of appropriate policies for the management of inventories requires some form of cost-benefit analysis (such analysis may in practice be more or less sophisticated). Unfortunately, all too often the benefits (real or potential) are emphasised and the costs de-emphasised. We have already discussed some of the benefits of holding inventories and these can be summarised as:

(a) Holding inventory reduces the uncertainty of operations. It enables a business to cope with unexpected demands, either from customers (thereby avoiding the loss of potential sales), or from the production process itself.

(b) There is a possibility of obtaining discounts from suppliers for purchasing in bulk, thereby reducing the cost of materials.

(c) There is a possibility of purchasing in advance of anticipated price rises, thereby keeping costs lower than they might otherwise have been.

(d) Holding large levels of inventory may facilitate large production runs, thereby reducing the impact of set-up costs.

However, these benefits have costs associated with them and not only may these costs be very significant, they may not be charged against the budgets of those who make the decisions regarding the levels of inventory that are to be held. Such costs are normally considered under two headings – the costs of acquiring the inventory and the costs of holding the inventory. Frequently, these costs will be charged against the budgets of other managers who may have little or no influence on stock-holding/purchasing decisions. In many ways, this problem is similar to that discussed in Chapter 7 regarding the use of standard costing and variance analysis, and which managers should be held accountable for which variances. We can illustrate this by reviewing the costs associated with the acquisition and holding of inventories in a typical manufacturing company and considering in which managers' budgets these costs might actually accrue. Table 6.1 does this.

As can be seen from Table 6.1, many of the costs associated with the ordering and stockholding decisions of a particular department/function may never in fact be charged to that department/function. They will be borne by the budgets of other departments. Moreover, for the entity as a whole, acquisition costs and holding costs will tend to move in different directions. Lower levels of inventory imply that an entity will make more frequent purchase orders and, conversely, higher levels of inventory imply that it will make fewer orders. Thus, there is a trade-off to be made between the two types of costs. This leads to a concept called the **economic order quantity** (EOQ), which is an approach to inventory acquisition that seeks to minimise the combination of acquisition and holding costs. Assuming that the quantum of both these types of cost can be identified, that they are relatively constant, that there is no buffer stock (i.e. there is no defined minimum stock level above zero) and that there are no significant seasonal variations in the pattern of trade, then there is a well-defined model for minimising these costs and determining the EOQ for any type of inventory. The notation for this model is:

C = Carrying cost per unit of inventory
S = Sales volume
O = Cost of processing a purchase order
Q = Number of units of inventory per purchase order

Given these assumptions, the total carrying cost of inventory is: Average inventory level (in units) × carrying cost per unit, or:

$$\frac{Q}{2} \times C \qquad\qquad\qquad \textbf{(6.3)}$$

Table 6.1	Costs associated with holding inventories
Type of cost	**Possibly charged to**
Acquisition costs	
Ordering costs	Purchasing department budget
Handling costs	Stores budget
Holding costs	
Opportunity costs of financing inventories	Finance department budget
Obsolescence and deterioration	Stores budget
Insurance	Finance department budget
Labour and equipment costs	Stores budget
Administration costs	Various departmental budgets

The total ordering cost is: Sales volume (in units) × cost per order divided by number of units per order, or:

$$\frac{S}{Q} \times O \tag{6.4}$$

Therefore, summing equations (6.3) and (6.4), the total cost (of carrying and ordering) inventory is:

$$\text{Total cost} = ((Q/2) \times C) + (S/Q) \times O)) \tag{6.5}$$

If this equation is reorganised and differentiated with respect to Q, and the derivative set to 0, then the value of Q which minimises the total inventory costs (the EOQ) is obtained and this can be stated as:

$$\text{EOQ} = \sqrt{(2SO/C} \tag{6.6}$$

This EOQ model leads, as can be seen, to a classic square root formula, and is useful insofar as it prompts management to focus on important issues associated with inventory management. However, its practical utility is limited by the assumptions that it makes (e.g. as regards the constancy of ordering and holding costs and the pattern of inventory usage) and that the necessary information is available. It is also a linear model. Operational researchers have developed numerous other models for inventory management which may prove more appropriate in particular cases. Moore (1976) provides a useful review of these. Despite this, the value of requiring management to ask themselves the right questions, even if they find them difficult to answer, should not be underestimated. It would also be impractical to expect management to focus to the same extent on all the different elements of inventory. A medium sized manufacturing entity may well hold several hundred (or more) different lines of inventory. To expect it to monitor, and manage, all these different lines of inventory to the same degree of detail would almost certainly be a waste of management time. Instead, management needs to concentrate on those areas of inventory where it can have the most impact on the overall financial performance of the entity.

One commonly used concept used for this is that of **usage value**, combined with the Pareto relationship. Usage value is defined as:

$$\text{Usage value} = \text{Usage (in units)} \times \text{Cost (per unit)} \tag{6.7}$$

Thus, usage value focuses directly on the amount of money that an enterprise is spending on the consumption of any given line of stock as part of its commercial activities. The Pareto relationship is a common pattern of the balance between the number of individual stock lines and their relative usage values. Table 6.2 illustrates a typical set of such relationships:

While the relationships portrayed in Table 6.2 might not apply in precise detail to the usage values in every individual entity, the message is a clear one. Something like 10% of the individual lines of stock will account for in the region of 60% of the usage value (the category A items). Careful attention to the management of these items is likely to be very rewarding. Conversely, the majority of the individual lines of stock (60%) will probably account for a rather small proportion of usage value (10%), and detailed management attention is likely to be correspondingly less rewarding. The use of the principles of the Pareto relationship will help management to focus its efforts where they are likely to be of most value.

In planning its inventory management policies, an enterprise needs to have regard to issues other than simply identifying the EOQ. It also needs to have regard to other motives in relation to holding inventories. Of particular importance is the need to avoid running out of stock (avoiding a stock-out). Stock-outs fall into two main categories: those that are the result of poor management planning and those that are the result of failure to purchase raw materials (finished goods in the case of wholesalers/retailers) in time to meet anticipated levels of activity. Good management should easily prevent stock-outs of this type using three key concepts. These concepts are:

(a) **Usage rate**. This is simply the number of units of inventory required in any given period to meet production/sales requirements. This is often expressed as the number of units per day or per week.

(b) **Lead time**. This is the period of time needed to acquire new stocks from suppliers. It is likely to vary significantly from industry to industry, and perhaps from supplier to supplier. In some commercial sectors it could be as little as a few hours, while in other sectors, such as the perfumery industry, it could be as much as 12 months.

(c) **Re-order level**. This is a function of the usage rate and the lead time, and is the stock level at which it is necessary to place a fresh purchase order so as to have new stock arriving before existing stocks are exhausted. For example, if a particular item of inventory has a usage rate of 1000 units per week and a lead time of two weeks then it will be necessary to place a fresh purchase order whenever inventory levels decline to 2000 units. This should ensure that just as the existing stock (re-order level) of 2000 units is exhausted (i.e. after two weeks), the new supplies of inventory arrive (again after two weeks).

The strategy described above is likely to be somewhat risky. However well management understand their business, and however well they budget and plan, they are doing so in a climate of uncertainty. This means that there is a danger that their plans and budgets may not, in the event, reflect what actually happens. There may be a higher level of activity (usage) than they anticipated, or it may take longer to acquire the fresh inventories than they expected. These uncertainties need to be taken into account in determining inventory management policies because of the financial consequences of potential stock-outs. The danger against which they need to guard is that, in the case of finished goods stocks, they may not have enough to meet customer

Table 6.2	The Pareto relationship	
Stock category	**Proportion of total usage value**	**Proportion of number of stock lines**
A	60%	10%
B	30%	30%
C	10%	60%

demands, thereby losing sales and profit, and in the case of raw materials stocks that production will have to cease, leading to production problems and inefficiencies, and perhaps to lost sales. A commonly adopted approach to prevent this happening is the holding of **buffer stocks** (safety stocks). These are stocks, above those specifically required to meet planned activity levels, intended to provide a margin of safety against uncertainties.

There are a number of sophisticated techniques, largely derived from operational research, which are intended to help management decide on appropriate levels of safety stocks, which are beyond the scope of this book. In the main, these techniques ask management to determine the financial costs of a stock-out and then use probability based approaches to balance these against the financial costs of holding different levels of safety stock. Although a number of organisations, particularly larger ones, do employ such techniques, many organisations adopt rather more pragmatic approaches. These approaches tend to be based on rather subjective assessments of the variability of the pattern of trade of the entity and the nature of its relationships with its suppliers. However, at the core remain the key concepts of usage rates and lead times.

In recent years, some management literature has focused on the concept of just-in-time management (JIT). This is a management philosophy which requires that inventory should be available 'just in time' to meet the purpose for which it is required. It is a philosophy which seeks to minimise inventory levels and, therefore, the costs and risks of holding inventories and is frequently presented as an approach which was developed by successful Japanese companies, accounting, at least in part, for the competitive advantages that they appear to have enjoyed in recent years. To some extent, this is true and reflects the lack of attention that many UK companies paid to working capital management up until the 1970s and 1980s, although there have been notable exceptions. The implementation of JIT requires an entity to establish very close relationships with its suppliers, involving rapid and effective communication of production planning and scheduling information. The motor vehicle industry is often cited as an example of this – a car may start its way down the production line before its seats have been made, let alone delivered to the car manufacturer. At the time the seats are required to be fitted, their supplier should have completed their manufacture and delivered them to the appropriate location. This is a rather extreme example, but one which encapsulates the core principles of JIT. The principal of these are:

(a) **Reliability**. The manufacturer must be able to rely on supplies being delivered at the right time, to the right place, and being of the right quality.

(b) **Sharing of information**. The supplier must know what is expected at all times.

(c) **Flexibility**. Both the entity and its supplier must be able to respond to changes in the pattern of demand.

Suppliers in this context may be external or internal. The example of the motor industry used an example of an external supplier. However, exactly the same principles apply to internal suppliers. Thus JIT principles apply both within and across organisations. In many ways, the successful implementation of JIT principles involves a blurring of organisational boundaries. In the case of external suppliers, it depends on establishing and maintaining relationships between separate entities which are similar to those which should exist between units within the same entity. The financial benefits that can be obtained from the implementation of JIT principles are significant. However, such implementation carries a risk – that the 'partner' entity may fail to deliver. Thus, adopting a JIT philosophy is not something which should be done lightly. It requires a very careful appraisal of the potential advantages and the potential partner's capacity to meet the demands placed on it. For a more detailed explanation of JIT see Bailes and Kleinsorge (1992).

Managing debtors

In broad terms, entities sell on credit to their customers so as to generate higher levels of sales than they would otherwise have achieved, thereby increasing their overall profitability. In deciding to do this, they need to balance the profit they expect to be generated from the additional sales against the costs associated with having granted credit. The principal costs are likely to be those involved in financing the investment in debtors (this will be a function of the anticipated level of debtors and the enterprise's cost of capital); the administrative costs of maintaining the necessary accounting systems; and those associated with default by customers (i.e. uncollectable debts). Before offering credit to its customers, an entity needs to be assured that this balance will be in its favour. Having said this, it must be recognised that the granting of credit to customers is a very pervasive feature of commercial activity in the UK and elsewhere. Accordingly, for most companies the question is not one of whether or not to offer credit to their customers, rather it is one of how to maximise the benefits and minimise the costs associated with offering credit. To achieve this, and thereby ensure the effective management of its debtors, an entity needs to have a clearly defined credit policy, and this policy needs to cover a number of key aspects of debtor management. These are:

(a) A clear statement of the general terms on which it is prepared to grant credit to customers.

(b) Credit rating procedures.

(c) A credit management system.

General terms of credit

These terms will be dictated in part by the overall financial management strategies of an entity, and its ability to finance debtors without harming its overall financial soundness. It needs to plan the amount of debtors in the light of the other demands on its long- and short-term capital funding resources. However, decisions on this cannot be taken purely from an internal financial management perspective. They also need to reflect the competitive environment within which the entity operates, and in particular the terms of credit that are being offered by its competitors. The terms of credit that an entity offers its customers are an interface between its financial management and its marketing management as part of its overall strategic decision-taking process. As such they need to have regard to the following:

Linkages between credit terms and pricing policies An entity may be able to charge its customers higher prices than its competitors if it offers reasonably generous credit terms. Alternatively, it might decide to offer very restrictive credit terms, but price its products/services very competitively. Thus, credit terms are an important part of the market positioning of an enterprise.

Custom and practice in the relevant industrial/commercial sector(s) As part of its market positioning an entity must have regard to what is normal practice within the sector in which it operates, and this can vary considerably. In this respect, regard needs to be had not just to the formal position but also to what actually happens. It is not at all uncommon for the formal (contractual) terms of credit to be 30 days from invoice date, but the actual period of credit being taken by customers to be nearer 60 or 70 days.

Cash settlement discounts It is common practice in a number of sectors to offer customers a discount for prompt settlement. Thus, for example, an enterprise might offer customers 30 days credit (from invoice date), but also offer a settlement discount if the invoice is settled within seven days. Such a discount might be of the order of 2% to 5% of the invoice value. Again, this is part of the market positioning of the entity as, effectively, such discounts offer a price advantage to those customers who are able to settle their bills promptly. Their financial consequences for the enterprise itself also need to be analysed. Suppose that a company has annual credit sales of £1 560 000, and that its average level of debtors is nine weeks' sales, despite the fact that its terms of trade are that customers (in theory) are allowed only four weeks' credit. The company has to borrow money to finance the investment in debtors at an annual interest rate of 12%, and is considering introducing a cash settlement discount for customers who settle their invoices within seven days. It has estimated that this will lead to one-third of the customers taking advantage of the cash settlement discount. Table 6.3 illustrates the likely financial impact of offering the cash settlement discount.

As Table 6.3 indicates, there would be no advantage to the company in offering the cash settlement discount – in fact there would be a net cost of £2200. In such circumstances, the company would probably be better advised to concentrate on using other measures, such as tighter credit control, to reduce its average debtor collection period of nine weeks. However, as offering a cash settlement discount is effectively offering a price reduction to those customers who settle their invoices promptly, it is possible that offering such a discount might lead to increased sales. If we assume that the company's gross profit margin is 25%, then if offering the discount led to an increase in sales (paid for within the discount period) of more than £8800 (£2200/0.25) offering the discount would be financially advantageous.

The likely/acceptable level of bad debts The potential impact of bad debts on the financial soundness of the entity and on the extent of the enhanced profitability to be

Table 6.3	Appraisal of cash settlement decision
Current average debtors: (£1 560 000 × 9 / 52)	£270 000
Forecast average debtors after offering the cash settlement discount:	
(£1 560 000 × 6 / 52) + (£1 560 000 / (3 × 52))	£190 000
Forecast reduction in debtors: (£270 000 – £190 000)	£80 000
Forecast saving in financing costs: (£80 000 × 12%)	£9 600
Cost of settlement discount: (£1 560 000 × 0.025 / 13)	£13 000
Net cost of settlement discount: (£13 000 – £9 600)	£2 200

obtained from offering credit terms must be assessed. The level of bad debts will be the result of the combination of factors. Some business sectors traditionally have a higher level of bad debts than others; entities with a large number of small debtors (e.g. a departmental store) are less at risk of financial failure resulting from an individual bad debt than those with a small number of high value debtors (e.g. the construction industry). However, the potential impact of a large number of small bad debts should not be underestimated – both on overall financial soundness and on the additional profits expected to be derived from offering credit.

Credit rating procedures

Once it has determined its basic terms of credit, an entity needs to install processes aimed at identifying those potential credit customers to whom it is in fact prepared to offer credit. In essence, this involves making an assessment of the likelihood of a potential customer defaulting on the debt. Like many other aspects of management, this involves forecasting the future using information about the past and, as such, is inevitably subject to uncertainty. However, there is a wide range of potential sources of information that can, and should, be used to help make credit rating decisions. These include:

(a) **Bank references**. Entities should, as a matter of course, ask potential customers to supply details of their banking arrangements. Historically, it has been quite common to ask a customer's bank to provide a reference as to the customer's creditworthiness. In practice, a bank is not going to guarantee that a customer will settle outstanding debts and the wording of bank references is usually rather bland and non-committal. However, information about the present, and past, state of a customer's bank accounts and of the period of time that banking arrangements have been in force (assuming the bank is willing to provide such information) can be very helpful in making a credit rating assessment.

(b) **Company accounts**. Reference should be had to the financial statements of potential (corporate) customers for recent years. Analysis of these can help to detect trends in the financial position of the customer, and to appraise its solvency at the last balance sheet date.

(c) **Trade references**. Potential credit customers should be asked to supply references from other suppliers who already supply them on credit terms. Again, these references should indicate the length of the trading relationship and how reliable the potential customer has been in adhering to agreed terms of credit.

(d) **Credit rating agencies**. These provide information about the past credit performance of both corporate entities and individuals. Reference to them is virtually standard practice when dealing with consumer credit applications.

Use can also be made of 'informed trade gossip' and articles in trade journals and the wider press. However, at the end of the day a judgement has to be made. Is the customer to be granted credit and, if so, for how much (the **credit limit**) and on what exact terms? The responsibility for such a decision will normally rest with an entity's credit control function, following guidelines laid down by senior management, and where large amounts are involved, having reference to senior finance department staff. Once the judgement is made, it is important that it is promptly notified to all interested parties as quickly as possible. Principal among these are the customer, relevant sales department staff, and the credit control department itself. A similar process needs to be gone through whenever a customer seeks a change in credit terms, whether a change in credit limit or a change in settlement terms.

Credit management system

The essence of a credit management system is that of ensuring that, as far as practicable, all credit customers adhere to the terms of credit which were offered to them. A successful credit management system will need to have regard to the following:

Credit authorisation procedures. The authorisation of credit terms for a customer is simply the first stage in an ongoing process. Thereafter, a procedure needs to be in place for the authorisation of individual credit sales transactions with the customer. An extreme example of this might be that any credit sale, of whatever value, requires specific authorisation, such authorisation normally coming from a credit control function within the entity. However, this might be thought unduly burdensome and therefore some upper limit might be placed for each customer on the amount of credit sales that can be made without seeking such specific authorisation. Sales below this value can proceed without seeking credit control approval; sales above it require specific approval.

Credit authorisation procedures can often lead to tensions in businesses. Sales staff are eager to secure sales (and perhaps earn commissions), whereas credit control staff are charged with ensuring that customers adhere to specified credit terms. It is important to ensure that credit control staff are given, and accepted as having, the power to refuse further credit to a customer unless and until the customer is adhering to the specified terms.

Information systems. The effective management of debtors requires that adequate information is available to all staff involved with customers, whether they be sales staff negotiating with the customer, or credit control staff monitoring the customer's credit performance. The core requirements of such a system are that it shows, on a timely basis, the current credit terms being offered to that customer and how well the customer is adhering to those terms. This requires what is normally referred to as a **debtor ageing analysis**, which analyses the amounts currently owed by customer(s) on the basis of how long they have been outstanding. Typically, such an analysis would contain the information shown in Table 6.4.

The 'ageing analysis' identifies, in aggregate terms, the amounts owed by the customer and for how long they have been outstanding. It enables a reader to identify readily whether or not a customer is adhering to the agreed credit terms. In the example contained in Table 6.4, the customer is not adhering to the specified terms. While the total debt of $8490 is within the agreed credit limit of $10 000, the settlement of amounts outstanding is not within the specified 30-day limit. The sum of $4200 falls within the 31–60-day analysis, i.e. beyond the agreed 30-day limit. Unfortunately, such a situation is all too common. Many credit customers will stretch their credit beyond the agreed terms. In some sectors, although it is never formally agreed, 30 days is taken to mean 60 days. In addition, a monthly ageing is something of a blunt instrument – it might be the case that this $4200 has only been outstanding for, say, 35 days and is likely to be settled shortly. However, a credit control department would need to monitor the position closely. Thus, backing up an ageing analysis of the type illustrated in Table 6.4, an entity needs a more detailed analysis on an invoice-by-invoice basis.

In monitoring the behaviour of debtors, an entity needs to pay careful attention to changes in the pattern of settlement by a credit customer. Some customers will always go beyond the agreed terms and settle their accounts after the due dates. If they are good customers in other respects – purchasing reasonable volumes of merchandise with good profit margins – then an entity might well be prepared informally to accept this state of affairs. What would, however, be worrying is a situation where a customer who had previously settled accounts on time started not to do so. This might indicate that the customer was having cash flow or other problems, and that the entity needs to take rapid action to collect the monies due to it and stop making further credit sales. An 'ageing analysis' can also help to reveal disputes between customers and suppliers. In the case of Bloggs Engineering Ltd, there is an amount of $890 which has been outstanding for over 120 days. Given that there is nothing outstanding in either the 61–90 or 91–120-day categories, this would seem to indicate a problem. There may be a dispute about the delivery or quality of the goods leading to Bloggs refusing to pay. Whatever the reason, the 'ageing analysis' indicates that there is a problem which needs to be referred to the appropriate department – probably the sales department in the first instance.

The example in Table 6.4 relates to an individual customer. An entity will also require aggregate information on the ageing profile of its debtors. Such information will help its financial managers assess the overall efficacy of debtor management policies and practices. However, if such information is to be useful, both at an aggregate and individual customer level, it needs to be up to date. Timely processing and presentation of information is needed to ensure that management needs for decision taking are met. However, it goes further than this – the more rapidly a customer receives an invoice, the more rapidly it is likely to be settled, as many customers will settle their invoices in calendar order. Similarly, the more rapidly a customer's payment is recorded the less likely it is that he will be refused credit, thereby avoiding the loss of goodwill and potential sales. As Figure 6.2 illustrates, there are a number

Table 6.4	Debtor ageing analysis
Customer name	Bloggs Engineering Ltd
Account number	0227635
Credit limit	$10 000
Credit terms	7 days settlement discount 2.5%, 30 days net
Outstanding items	
1–30 days	$3 400
31–60 days	$4 200
61–90 days	$0
91–120 days	$0
Over 120 days	$890
Total	$8 490

of different stages in the debtor management process, each of which needs to be performed on as timely a basis as possible.

As discussed earlier in this chapter, the process illustrated in Figure 6.2 is likely to involve a number of different functions and staff within the entity – sales staff, credit control staff, warehouse staff, invoice clerks, sales ledger staff, and cashiers. These staff will be involved in discharging their own responsibilities and providing information to enable others to discharge theirs, e.g. the cashier's staff informing the sales ledger staff that cash has been received from a customer so that they can record this. The entity needs to ensure that all the individual functions and staff involved are aware of this interdependence, and the importance of the rapid discharge of their functions and the transfer of information to others.

Debt collection procedures These follow on naturally from the other elements of the credit management system. They will, typically, comprise a series of increasingly purposeful steps towards the recovery of monies from the customer. The first step could be a telephone call to the customer for a fairly informal reminder that a debt is overdue. After this, a series of letters are likely to be sent at predetermined intervals. These would start with ones simply pointing out that the customer has overdue invoices, through to ones demanding payment and threatening, and then implementing, steps such as the cessation of supplies and court action. Normally these would emanate from the credit control department. However, this department should not act independently. It needs to liaise closely with the marketing/sales department to

| Figure 6.2 | Stages in the debtor management process |

enlist the help of their staff who may be in regular contact with the customer, and to ensure that there are not valid reasons for non-payment, e.g. a dispute over delivery or quality.

Core objectives

The core objective of an entity with regard to debtors should be to optimise the benefits it derives from offering credit to its customers. Each of the three elements of: specifying the general terms on which credit will be offered; carrying out a credit rating for each customers; and thereafter managing the ongoing credit relationships with customers, has a part to play in this optimisation process. The benefits and costs associated with each of these different elements needs to be taken into account. Unfortunately, all too often the benefits are assumed to exist and the costs are not identified. Whereas trade practice cannot be ignored in a competitive market place, it should not be accepted as 'holy writ' and alternative debtor strategies, such as **factoring** and **invoice-discounting**, should always be considered.

Managing accounts payable

Trade creditors, i.e. suppliers who offer entities supplies of goods and services on credit terms, can be major sources of short-term finance. Such creditors are the obverse of an entity's own debtors, and it needs to be recognised that these suppliers will have exactly the same management concerns as does an entity itself in managing its own debtors. All too often entities regard trade credit as a readily available and costless source of finance. This view can lead to abuse of trade credit as a source of finance, rooted in the idea that the suppliers are keen to obtain business and that they will overlook any delays in settlement, at least within reason, because they don't want to lose that business. This is a naive view which needs to be guarded against. Entities should recognise that the credit they obtain from their suppliers is the counterpart of the credit that they give to their customers and it needs to be managed with exactly the same considerations. Thus, regard needs to be paid to the following:

(a) **Terms of trade**. As with selling on credit, an entity should pay attention to industry practice when purchasing on credit. By doing this, it will ensure that the terms which it is able to negotiate with its suppliers are at least comparable with those being offered to its competitors, thereby avoiding any loss of competitive advantage.

(b) **Loyalty of suppliers**. Entities all too often fail to recognise the extent of their dependence on their suppliers, focusing instead on trade credit as a 'free' source of finance. In part, this can be a reflection of the problem referred to earlier – different parts of an entity having different functional interests. The accountancy/finance department may be focused on the deferral of payments to suppliers because of cash flow considerations. The purchasing/production functions may focus on obtaining supplies of merchandise of appropriate quality and quantity at the appropriate time and at a competitive price. These focuses may conflict. If the finance department regularly delays payment to a supplier, this may make it much more difficult for the purchasing function to negotiate competitive prices.

Suppliers will tend to favour those customers who keep to their credit terms in matters of preferential pricing and delivery. 'Trade gossip' will also spread information about entities which are 'poor payers', thereby making it more difficult for such entities to establish credit relationships with suppliers.

(c) Settlement discounts. Such discounts are a fairly common feature throughout the economy. However, many purchasers, particularly smaller entities, do not take advantage of them because of cash flow considerations. Typically, such entities are undercapitalised and rely on the availability and flexibility of trade credit as an essential part of their financial management. However, obtaining finance by deciding not to take advantage of settlement discounts may be a very expensive approach. Consider the case of an entity which purchases goods from a supplier who offers credit terms, including a 2% cash settlement discount for payment within ten days of invoice date and 30 days net. If the enterprise does not take advantage of this settlement discount, it is financing that part of its business via credit from the supplier in question at a very high effective annual interest rate. The annualised cost of the interest can be computed using the following formula:

$$\text{Cost} = \frac{\text{Discount \%}}{(100 - \text{Discount \%})} \times \frac{365}{(\text{Final due date} - \text{Discount period})} \tag{6.8}$$

Thus, for the example of 2% for settlement within seven days:

$$\text{Cost} = \frac{2}{(100 - 2)} \times \frac{365}{(30 - 10)} = 44.56\%$$

In this case, the entity would clearly be better off (given the general structure of financing costs) to obtain an alternative form of finance and take advantage of the settlement discount on offer. While trade credit is fairly readily available, it has the disadvantage that it is essentially very short-term in nature and easily withdrawn by suppliers, with potentially disastrous effects. It is also potentially very expensive. Entities would, in general, be better advised to seek more secure, and cheaper, forms of short-term finance. Possible sources of such finance are discussed in the next section.

As is the case with debtors, an entity needs to pay careful attention to the recording of the amounts due to suppliers and to the management of the purchasing and payment procedures. Figure 6.3 illustrates the stages involved in these processes.

Figure 6.3 illustrates that, as with debtors, many different functions and staff are involved in the process of managing creditors, and that the challenge which management faces is one of integrating these different activities, and the associated decisions, into a coherent framework which ensures that duly authorised payments are made on a timely basis.

Managing cash

So far in this chapter, we have discussed the cash conversion cycle and the management of inventories, debtors, and creditors. Cash is the lifeblood of any commercial entity – without access to cash it will be unable to meet its existing liabilities, or to engage in new and profitable ventures. At the same time, it needs to ensure that its cash resources are employed as efficiently as possible. This requires that an entity:

- Plans and monitors the flows of cash associated with its day-to-day activities. As we have seen, this requires the determination and implementation of appropriate policies for the management of inventories, debtors, and creditors.
- Plans and monitors the sources of long- and short-term finance it employs to fund its activities, having due regard to its cash flow position.

There are a number of sources of short-term finance, other than trade credit, available to commercial entities. These include the following:

(a) **Bank borrowing.** This can be via a bank overdraft or a short-term loan. Overdrafts have the advantage of flexibility, i.e. the entity has access to funds up to an agreed limit, but does not have to use them if it does not need to. Thus, it has (at least in theory) guaranteed access to finance, but only pays for that amount of finance which it actually uses. However, short-term bank finance can have its disadvantages – banks will often seek security for their advances and may want to charge premium interest rates. In addition, overdrafts are repayable on demand, thus exposing entities to the risk of bankers foreclosing, as has been the case with many smaller enterprises in recent years, and they can be costly in terms of interest and other bank charges.

Figure 6.3 Stages in the creditor management process

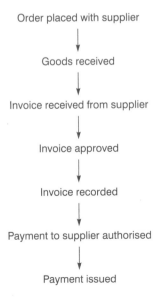

(b) **Instalment credit.** There are a number of options here. In essence all of them are aimed at enabling an entity to acquire an asset on deferred payment terms. Thus, the principal orientation of instalment credit is normally towards the acquisition of fixed assets. The main types of instalment credit are leasing and hire purchase.

(c) **Financial instruments.** There are numerous types of these, but their essence is that of providing an entity with something which it can use to obtain cash in the financial markets. A common sort of such an instrument is a 'bill of exchange', which effectively is a promissory note, normally issued by a customer, which an entity can sell on to a finance house at a discount and receive cash in exchange. The better the reputation of the customer and the nearer the due date of the bill, the greater the proportion of the face value of the bill that the entity will receive.

(d) **Factoring.** In essence, factoring involves an enterprise handing over its debtors to a factoring company. The factoring company pays the entity the face value of the debtors, less a discount, and recoups this by collecting the debts. Factoring debtors can provide an entity with an immediate boost to its liquidity. There are several different methods of factoring, the principal distinctions involving the extent to which the factor has recourse to the entity (if the debts prove uncollectable), and the extent to which the factor takes over the administration of the entity's sales ledger (thereby saving it administration costs). These differences will be reflected in the discount at which the factor accepts the debts. Factoring is now a major source of finance, particularly for smaller entities.

These different sources of short-term finance have differing advantages and disadvantages, including availability, cost and flexibility. In deciding whether or not to use finance of this type, and to what extent, management need to ensure that it is more relevant to their needs and cheaper than other (e.g. longer-term) sources of finance. Whatever sources of finance an entity uses, it needs to manage its day-to-day cash flows within the constraints that its financial structure imposes. In particular, it needs to pay careful attention to the detailed management of the monies it receives from customers and other sources and the payments it makes to its suppliers. This requires clearly defined banking strategies including:

(a) **Number and location of bank accounts.** Maintaining a bank account has costs associated with it. A bank will seek, and increasingly so these days, to levy charges for the services it provides (apart from interest on any overdrawn balances) and these charges are likely to be higher for an entity which maintains a number of different bank accounts. A further issue is that of **cleared balances**. Simply depositing a cheque from a customer into a bank account does not mean that the entity is immediately credited with that amount. Only when the cheque has been 'cleared' by the customer's bankers will the entity finally receive credit for it. Typically, such clearance will take about three days. However, it may take longer if an entity deposits monies at a branch other than the one at which its account is maintained. This can be a particular problem for entities having a number of geographically dispersed locations.

Such entities need to discuss the problem with their bankers, and ensure that arrangements are made which reduce any delays in 'clearance' of deposits to a minimum.

(b) **Frequency of banking.** An entity should always deposit monies with its bankers as soon as possible. Doing this will minimise the security risks of holding cash, help to reduce any interest charges on overdrawn accounts, and help to generate interest on interest bearing accounts. However, the act of banking itself has costs. These include any transaction charges made by the bank together with the entity's own administrative costs. These differing costs and risks need to be balanced in determining a policy dealing with the frequency of banking.

(c) **Use of cash and bank balances.** Cash, including credit balances on current accounts, is an unproductive asset – it is not generating any return. Entities should use their cash resources in ways which do in fact generate returns, while having regard to their liquidity requirements. Doing this successfully means that they should prepare cash flow forecasts and monitor the outturn of these forecasts closely. By doing so, they can identify when they are likely to have cash surpluses and plan for the investment of such surpluses. There are a wide range of financial investment opportunities available, ranging from the overnight money market to longer-term fixed interest accounts. Failing to do this can result in the entity incurring large opportunity costs in terms of forgone interest.

Conclusion

For many companies, particularly manufacturing ones, working capital (defined as current assets minus current liabilities) represents a major part of their resources. Many staff are engaged in making decisions which affect the level of an entity's investment in working capital. However, all too often these decisions are made with a narrow departmental/functional focus, lacking any strategic direction. The core principles of managing an entity's investment in working capital are relatively straightforward (invest in short-term assets as long as they generate a return greater than their cost of capital, and use short-term sources of finance as long as they have a cost lower than other sources of capital). There are a number of decision models available to help managers utilise these principles. In practice, the management of working capital tends to be much more diffuse, involving numerous trade-offs, frequently based on rather ill-defined judgements.

Chapter review

In this chapter we have discussed the meaning of working capital, and emphasised that it comprises the short-term assets and financing of an entity. We have also emphasised the importance of its effective management to the overall financial health of the entity. The concept of the cash conversion cycle was introduced and, based on this, we reviewed a number of concepts that can be used to improve the management of the components of working capital, i.e.

- Inventory
- Debtors
- Creditors
- Cash

Further reading

Samuels, Wilkes and Brayshaw (1999) provide a detailed analysis of a number of approaches to the management of working capital within the broader context of financial management, as do Block and Hirt (2002). Hill and Sartoris (1995) focus entirely on short-term financial management, albeit in an American context. The monthly publication *Business Money Facts* and its associated website provide useful information about the current availability, and cost, of a wide range of financial management opportunities.

Questions and exercises

Guide notes can be found at the back of the book for all questions marked with an asterisk*.

1* Torment Ltd is a manufacturer of electronic components located in the countryside. All its sales are on credit terms and all its customers settle their accounts by cheque posted to Torment's premises. Because Torment is several miles from the nearest bank, its cashier banks the cheques received from customers on Friday lunchtimes, after Friday's post has been opened.

A chief accountant who has recently been appointed by Torment has asked you, as cashier, to prepare a report for him reviewing its current banking policy. He has suggested that you consider three options:

(a) daily banking
(b) banking twice per week (on Tuesdays and Fridays)
(c) continuing the existing banking practice.

You have collected the following data relating to Torment's receipts from customers and banking arrangements:

(i) Forecast receipts for the coming 12 months are £25 480 000.

(ii) The anticipated pattern of receipts is that they will be evenly spread throughout the year.

(iii) Typically twice as much is received each Monday and Tuesday as is received on the other days of the week.

(iv) Torment makes extensive and continued use of its overdraft facility for which the current interest rate is 10% per annum.

(v) Each visit to the bank and banking costs Torment £50.

Required:

Prepare the report requested by the chief accountant comparing the three banking strategies.

2* At a recent board meeting of Merchant Trading plc an animated discussion took place about the company's trading prospects. Although Harry Sleeze, the marketing director, was happy to state that 'our sales are up 25% on the previous year, therefore we are definitely in a healthy state and our shareholders ought to be well pleased with our efforts', the distribution director, Henrietta Ford, was more cautious, stating, What I don't understand, therefore, is why I have finished goods staying in stock longer'. The finance director, Martina Bianca, stated, 'Profitability might well have gone up marginally on the increased volume of sales but, given that we are only just coming out of the recession, I pay greater attention to our liquidity'. George Giorgiou, the managing director, shares Bianca's concerns, stating, 'I agree. In last month's *Management Today* it said that "all too often businesses fail to pay sufficient attention to their cash operating cycle"'. The meeting ended with Bianca agreeing to make a short presentation on Merchant's cash operating problems at the next board meeting in two weeks' time.

However, Bianca is scheduled to take ten days' holiday and gives you the following information, so that she can have a memorandum on her desk when she returns, commenting on Merchant's cash operating cycle and outlining suggestions on how it might be improved.

	Year to 31/12/20×1 £000s	Year to 31/12/20×2 £000s
Stocks: raw materials	80	108
work-in-progress	56	72
finished goods	64	96
Purchases	384	520
Cost of goods sold	560	720
Sales	640	800
Debtors	128	192
Creditors	64	78

Required:

Prepare a memorandum for Martina Bianca and include as an appendix your calculations of the length of Merchant's cash operating cycle. Be sure to explain all terms used and, as requested, provide ideas on how Merchant's cash operating cycle might be improved.

3* Jason Ltd is a manufacturer of hardware which it sells on credit terms to wholesalers. Its current credit terms are 30 days net, with no discount for prompt settlement. Currently the average period of credit taken by customers is 73 days.

Its board of directors is considering introducing a 2½% cash discount for customers who settle their invoices within seven days. The marketing director has estimated that this will lead to an increase in sales of 5% (from their current level of £2 million) and that these sales will generate the same gross profit margin (20%) as existing sales. He also estimates that 25% of customers would take advantage of the discount. Jason currently operates using a substantial bank overdraft on which pays interest at a rate of 12%.

Required:

Write a report for the board assessing whether or not it would be financially advantageous to offer the discount.

4 Jakers Ltd is a small family company which was formed four years ago to manufacture and distribute, via wholesalers and retailers, a new novelty board game. Besides its founders, Jean and Jan Jakers, it has three other part-time employees involved with purchasing, despatch and invoicing. Its annual turnover is steady at about £600 000. The cost data for each game are:

Unit selling price	£36
Variable costs	£18
Fixed costs apportionment	£ 6
	£24
Profit	£12

The current cost of capital of the company is 15% per annum.

The management of Jakers want to expand its market penetration and believe that they can achieve this if they offer their customers better credit terms. At present customers take, on average, 30 days to pay and all sales are on a credit basis. The company is considering three options as regards a new credit policy. These are:

	Option 1	Option 2	Option 3
Increase in average collection period (days)	10	20	30
Forecast increase in sales (£s)	30 000	45 000	50 000

To help finance this increased level of debtors, the company is also reconsidering its policy towards paying its suppliers of raw materials. Raw materials account for £12 of the unit variable costs of the company's product. At present the company pays its suppliers at the end of a ten-day period from invoice date to obtain a 2.5% settlement discount. It is considering delaying payment until the end of either a 30 or 45-day period after invoice date, when it will pay the full amount of the invoice.

Required:

(a) Advise the company whether, and if so how, it is worth changing the terms of credit that it gives to its customers.

(b) Advise the company whether, and if so how, it is worth changing the way it pays its raw materials suppliers.

(c) Comment on any reservations you may have regarding the advice you have given at (a) and (b) above.

5. Shoppers Ltd is a wholesaler of hardware. It has just prepared its cash budget for the coming financial year and has predicted a serious deficit arising because the required level of working capital has increased. It is necessary for the company to reduce its budgeted deficit by at least £50 000 at the end of the first month of the coming financial year and by at least £30 000 (which is not additional to the sum of £50 000) by the end of that year. The company's bankers have indicated that they are not prepared to increase its overdraft facilities. Two approaches are being considered by the company's management:

(a) The provision of an incentive to encourage debtors to pay promptly by giving a discount of 2.5% on payments made one month after invoice date.

(b) The issue at the start of the new financial year of long-term unsecured loan stock amounting to £50 000 and bearing interest at the rate of 20% per annum, payable annually in arrears.

Shoppers has recently had a steady sales turnover of £100 000 per month and it expects to maintain this level for the forseeable future. The present pattern of payments by debtors is that 20% pay exactly one month after invoice; 70% pay exactly two months after invoice and the remainder pay exactly three months after invoice. If the cash discount were offered it is estimated that 80% would pay one month after invoice and 10% at the end of two and three months. All invoices are despatched on the last day of the month in which the goods are sold. The rate of interest on the company's overdraft is 15% per annum, payable at six monthly intervals (halfway through and at the end of the company's financial year). The overall cost of capital is estimated at 25%.

Required:

Ignoring taxation and using monthly calculations, identify which alternative is to be preferred.

6 ToyTown Ltd manufactures several types of novelty items which it sells to a variety of retail outlets. The company expects to suffer a temporary shortage of funds during the first three months of 2007 and its directors are considering three alternative means of meeting the shortfall, as follows:

(a) Delaying payments to trade creditors in respect of raw material purchases. At present, ToyTown receives a cash discount of 2.5% in return for settlement of creditors' invoices within one month of the invoice date. It currently takes advantage of this discount in respect of all invoices received. The proposed policy would involve payment of 50% (by value) at the end of two months and 50% at the end of three months.

(b) Offering settlement discounts to trade debtors. At present ToyTown offers no cash discount for early settlement of invoices. On average, 10% of debtors pay one month after the invoice date; 36% two months after invoice date and 50% three months after invoice date; 4% of trade debts are bad. The proposed policy would be to offer a discount of 3% for payment within one month of invoice date. If the policy were implemented, the directors expect that 50% of debtors would pay one month after the invoice date; 22% two months after the invoice date, and 25% three months after the invoice date; 3% of trade debts would be bad.

(c) Undertaking short-term borrowing. Overdraft facilities are available from the company's bankers at an interest cost of 1% per month. Short-term borrowing could be undertaken to meet all the expected shortfall or just the shortfall remaining after the implementation of either or both of the two alternatives described above.

If either of the first two alternatives were adopted, it would be applied only to the invoices received or issued in January, February and March 2007. Thereafter ToyTown would revert to its existing policies. The actual and expected sales of ToyTown for the nine months from October 2006 to June 2007 are as follows:

			£
Actual sales:	October	2006	250 000
	November	2006	250 000
	December	2006	200 000
Expected sales:	January	2007	200 000
	February	2007	160 000
	March	2007	140 000
	April	2007	140 000
	May	2007	140 000
	June	2007	160 000

Raw materials are purchased, and the manufacture of the products takes place, in the month before sale. For all types of products, the cost of the raw materials is equal to 30% of the selling price. All invoices for sales or purchases are issued or received by ToyTown on the last day of the month to which they relate.

Required:
(a) Prepare calculations showing the cash flows of ToyTown on a month-by-month basis if the company:

    (i) delays payments to creditors in respect of January, February and March purchases;

    (ii) offers discounts to trade debtors in respect of January, February and March sales.

(b) Prepare calculations showing whether either delaying payments to creditors or offering discounts to debtors is worthwhile.

7   Outline the main reasons why many entities are unable to manage their working capital effectively.

8* Explain what is meant by 'over-trading' and what its likely consequences are for a business.

9* Analyse the principal motives a manufacturing company may have for holding high levels of stock.

10 Outline the principal elements of a successful credit control system.

11 'Delaying payments to creditors may lead to short-term savings in a company's interest bill, but a longer-term cost-deterioration in its relationships with its suppliers'. Discuss.

12 It is often said that the availability of bank credit is more important to small- and medium-sized firms than it is to larger ones. Why might this be so?

Budgetary planning and control

7

Chapter preview

Budgets are financial plans. Checking performance against plans assists managerial control. As budgets are normally identified with accountable managers, budgeting is sometimes described as responsibility accounting. Good budgeting is especially important where outputs are diverse, or non-standard, as in a factory research and development department, an advertising agency or, within the public sector, a school, hospital or social services department.

This chapter explains how budgets link financial accountability with the management organisation structure, how they are constructed, and how follow-up reporting and corrective action is needed. Some budgets are 'fixed' for the year, and some need to be 'flexible' to allow spending to reflect achieved activity volumes and costs. The budget cycle and timetable are explained, and the components of the 'master budget', which shadows the annual financial accounts of the organisation, are examined. The behavioural problems in achieving effective budgeting are considered, together with some specialised applications of budgeting, including both private- and public-sector service organisations, budgeting for capital, and the management-by-objectives (MBO) approach to stimulating improvement in management performance.

The chapter then concentrates on the ways in which accounting can contribute to enhancing control within the enterprise, beginning with an examination of the key considerations that need to be taken into account if an organisation is to implement an effective internal control system, particularly with respect to the accounting aspects of that system. It then discusses a major accounting control technique known as standard costing or variance analysis, building on the introduction to flexible budgeting provided earlier.

Within the broader framework of management control we need also to appreciate that not all controls are quantitative controls and that, indeed, not all quantitative controls are accounting controls. Variance analysis is not always appropriate, and in certain instances in the public sector the budgetary control framework may be supplemented by the use of performance indicators, some of which may have an economic value but may, if necessary, include related issues such as the output, efficiency or effectiveness of a particular management strategy.

The nature of budgeting

Budgeting is any formalised system of forecasting, planning, monitoring and controlling the use of resources. Budgets can be prepared in physical units of inputs, outputs or sales, but normally this is followed by 'pricing' each unit in order to express the final budgets and budget reports in financial terms.

Sometimes budgets are set in the first instance in financial terms, providing limits to spending and leaving it to managers to determine subsequently how to subdivide the monetary resource allocation among different physical resources, comprising employees, premises, equipment, etc. This latter alternative applies especially to budgeting in the public sector.

The term **budget** derives from the public sector. A *bougette* (OED; from the French) is a small leather bag or case. At least by 1733 (OED), and probably earlier, the Chancellor of the Exchequer would bring his proposals for collecting and spending public revenues to the British Parliament in a *bougette*. Opening his bag and revealing his proposal papers led to the expression 'to open the budget', a tradition carried on to this day with the familiar red dispatch box used in the House of Commons.

Given that public spending involves the allocation of finite funds from taxation (and sometimes, more controversially, from government borrowing), it is natural that budgets for public services are set as limits to spending. Thus 'control' will be exercised as much by prohibition of overspending as by any later review of the wisdom of how funds were spent or of the results achieved. Although budgetary practice in the public sector is today coming closer to that in the private sector, there remain some distinctive problems and features, to which we return later in the chapter.

In private business the firm's spending and commitments must be responsive to changes in the marketplace, as well as to longer-term objectives of business development. Budgetary planning and control are typically more complex in the business firm than in government, so we shall take business budgeting as our general model in the chapter. Emmanuel *et al.* (1990) suggested five main functions or roles for budgets:

- a system of authorization
- a means of forecasting and planning
- a channel of communication and coordination
- a motivational device
- a means of performance evaluation and control, as well as of providing a basis for decision making.

These functions will arise for discussion in different contexts throughout this chapter. First, let us clarify the meanings of certain words as they will be used in the discussion of budgeting. Some of these words have alternative meanings or nuances in other contexts; it is just unfortunate that the terminology, or jargon, of accounting is composed largely of words with everyday meanings!

- **Estimates** are approximations of what might happen under specified assumptions. Often alternative or multiple assumptions will be specified. There may be a form of search or even sensitivity analysis to help focus choice.

- **Forecasts** are predictions of what will happen under a chosen alternative set of assumptions or, occasionally, of what would happen under alternative assumptions. Forecasts, like estimates, are often linked with the study of uncertainty, and uncertainty is usually greatest when studying markets, likely sales, technological change and political environments (e.g. interest rates, exchange rates, the trade policies of foreign governments). It is often useful to have independent outside experts as advisers on key issues of forecasting, and market research is often used to help with the making of predictions.

- **Plans** are the details of intended future operations which, once agreed or approved, form commitments to future action. However, there should be known channels and procedures for reviewing, updating and revising any plans which are made.

- **Budgets** are a specialised type of plans, usually in financial rather than physical resource terms. Budgets link together all the parts of the organisation, in the common denominator of cost and revenue flows, and their interdependencies.

Managers who accept and administer budgets are called 'budget holders'. Budget holding is a major managerial responsibility. The accounting and reporting procedures developed for budgets are often called responsibility accounting systems. This is linked with agency theory. An agency relationship involves an actual or implicit contract under which one or more persons (i.e. the principals) engage another person (i.e. the agent) to provide some service or function on their behalf, with some degree of delegated powers in carrying out that service or function. Agency costs can arise because the agent may not always act in the best interests of the principal(s) – in this case the business organisation and its official objectives, plans and budgets. Failure to act in the best interests of the organisation can result from lack of experience, bad luck, slackness or conflict of interests. The latter two causes are behavioural problems which we consider later in the chapter. First, we consider the normative model of how budgeting should work in an ideal situation with goal congruence and with the budgets providing a kind of financial mirror-image to the formal organisation structure and objectives of the enterprise.

Drury (2004) provides a useful overview of the overall budgetary process, identifying a number of key stages.

These include:

- *Identification of objectives*: ideally, this requires that the planning objectives should be congruent with the overall goals of the organisation. Obvious as this may seem, there is frequently confusion in this regard – are the objectives to be the maximisation of corporate profits? It should be noted that some commentators (e.g. Simon 1959) believe that management may operate under a system of what is sometimes called 'bounded rationality'. This can lead to management being content to focus on generating satisfactory rather than maximum profits. In these circumstances, management may simply pursue the first acceptable solution rather than continuing to review all the available solutions so as to find that which maximises profit. This is frequently described as the planning process satisfying (as opposed to maximising) corporate profits.

- *Search for alternative courses of action*: this stage of the planning process involves management seeking those corporate strategies which will (are likely to) lead to the achievement of corporate objectives. In the real world management will be faced by many possible strategies, principally involving the selection of marketplaces in which to operate and the range of products to offer in these marketplaces. Cyert and March (1969) outline a number of the issues associated with this search process.

- *Gathering data about alternatives*: this involves management in seeking to gather data about the likely outcomes of the identified alternatives. Inevitably, this will require management to make judgements about the future – 'what do we think (believe) will happen if we select alternative A'? Some of these judgements will have a short-term focus and some a longer-term focus, depending on the nature of the alternatives being considered.

- *Selecting alternative courses of action*: this process follows on from the previous one and involves a choice between the alternative courses of action investigated in that process.

- *Implementing the chosen courses of action*: an important part of this stage of the overall process is the preparation of detailed budgets for these courses of action, a process described in greater detail in Chapter 5.

- *Comparing actual and planned outcomes and responding to differences between these*: this process forms part of the control system of the organisation. It involves the preparation of performance reports (covering the responsibilities of various managers within the organisational hierarch). Various actions may result from this process, including, for example, making changes to the original plans (budgets) to account for changes in the business environment or making changes to the ways in which these plans are being implemented.

Budget organisation

Managerial responsibility is the role situation of exercising authority over specified and often limited resources to be used in pursuit of agreed organisational goals, with accountability for the results. Accountability involves disclosure of performance, for evaluation and performance appraisal, and for any rewards or penalties that might result. Budgeting is a financial information system which exists to:

- help managers reach their goals and discharge their responsibilities;
- make managers fairly accountable for their performance.

Achieving these objectives requires that budgeting should be relevant, accurate and prompt in reporting any performance problems and assisting with explaining their cause. We shall return to these aspects later. The key point for the moment is to high-light that, given the description of budgeting set out above, it should be clear that budgets should reflect the organisational chart structure of the firm (or public-sector body) – and therefore be a mirror-image of that structure.

Budget centres

An organisational chart is pyramidal, and the chart of budgets must reflect this (see Figure 7.1). Major accounts for bringing together the costs, revenues, etc. associated with a particular activity, product or service, or with the area of respon-sibility of a particular manager, are termed 'centres' (and this term combines both the focus of managerial accountability and the gathering of relevant financial information). Let us illustrate this by reference to the four levels of budget account-ability in Figure 7.2.

- **Investment centre:** level A, at the top of the organisation, is where the budget holder is responsible for capital investments and the rate of return earned on capital, as well as for the supporting pyramid of profit or loss comprising the total revenues less total costs. This budget holder would be the chief executive of the company, a subsidiary company, or a division organised on the basis of delegated or decentralised control over and accountability for the level of investment and the rate of return earned.

- **Profit centre:** shown at level B, the profit-centre budget holder will typically be a general manager in charge of a department or division, with responsibility for both revenue-earning and cost-incurring activities. Sometimes he/she could be a 'brand manager' or 'product-line manager' with only notional real control

Figure 7.1   Long and short term planning

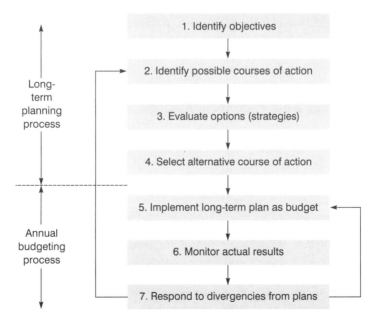

over resources, but with responsibility for planning and coordinating the marketing (and sometimes the production) requirements for a particular brand or product line. Below the level of a divisional general manager, a budget holder's control over fixed costs or overheads and their apportionment or absorption between different activities, outputs or organisational units may be weak, so that it could be quite unfair to try to hold the manager accountable for precise measures of profit. Here it would be better to designate a 'contribution-centre' budget, based on the excess of revenues over variable or attributable costs; and here the manager's objective is simply to maximise contribution.

- **Budget centre:** in the wider sense, all financial information accounts centres are 'budget centres', assuming they are used for financial planning, monitoring and control, and not just for collecting data for historical accounts. However, the term is used here in the narrower sense, in level B, to identify budgets which are normally 'fixed' in maximum spending limits (see below); examples include research and development, personnel, finance, public relations.

- **Revenue centre:** revenue centres are shown at level C. These show sales or other income as compared to budgeted targets for revenue. Revenue budget holders could be general managers, marketing managers, sales managers or brand managers.

- **Cost centre:** cost centres, shown at both level C and level D, are the basic collection accounts for recorded costs, whether related to activity (i.e. inputs), outputs or authorised spending against fixed budgets. Thus a budget-centre manager may have a number of cost-centre budgets beneath his/her overall budget; for example, a public relations manager may have separate cost budgets for conference expenses, for printing, and for departmental staff and expenses. A manager whose primary role is as a revenue budget holder may also have cost budgets; for example, a sales or brands manager may hold the advertising and promotions expense budget for relevant brands, products or markets. A manager whose primary role is as a cost-centre budget holder may also hold subsidiary cost budgets; for example, a warehouse manager whose overall budget is for stock-handling cost may have subsidiary budgets for premises and equipment maintenance.

Budgets and decentralisation

Good budgetary planning and control facilitate the decentralisation of a corporate organisational structure where this is desired. Decentralisation can take various forms, based on geographical units, markets served, products or technologies, or simply parallel and competing enterprises. There are many ramifications – the subject matter of business organisation textbooks – but for our purposes the key point is that an essential prerequisite of decentralisation, devolution and the delegation of effective operational authority and responsibility to subordinate units (be these known as departments, divisions or subsidiary companies) is that central management has access to high quality and timely management information in order to monitor performance, and to be able to intervene and take corrective action in the case of serious failure or major deviation from agreed strategies and plans. The budgeting system can and should provide this information.

It is a task for senior management policy making to decide the degree to which decentralisation and authority delegation should be employed. Thus, for example, a division could be run as an investment centre, with divisional management empowered to take the lead in capital-investment planning and decisions, and to be held accountable for the return on capital achieved. Alternatively, the same division could be run as just a profit centre, with investment decisions retained at central-management level and the divisional manager held accountable only for optimising profit, or profit contribution, from the use of the capital assets with which he/she is provided. Divisionalisation is further discussed in Chapter 8. Similarly, at lower management levels the more accurate, detailed and timely the budgetary reporting system is, the greater will be the degree of decision-making authority which may safely be delegated. The degree is a matter of senior management choice.

Budgeting based on costing

Revenue budgets are based on targets and forecast of sales volume and prices, and they are inevitably subject to the vagaries of the marketplace. But most budgets are for costs and expenses, and here management has greater control. Budgets are built upon forecast costs at specific volumes of activity, and subsequent budgetary performance reports compare these budgets with the output derived from actual cost at actual volumes of activity. So cost information forms the 'building blocks' both for realistic budgets and for accurate budgetary performance reports. It follows that it is impossible to have a high-quality budgetary planning and control system unless the organisation's costing methods and systems, as discussed in previous chapters, are also of a high degree of relevance and accuracy, with data available promptly. And the quality of costing data, in its turn, is dependent not just, or even mainly, on the work of accounting in 'pricing' units of inputs or activity, but rather on the relevance and accuracy of the departmental recording, both of the use of physical resource inputs and of the outputs achieved.

Figure 7.2	A pyramid of budget centres

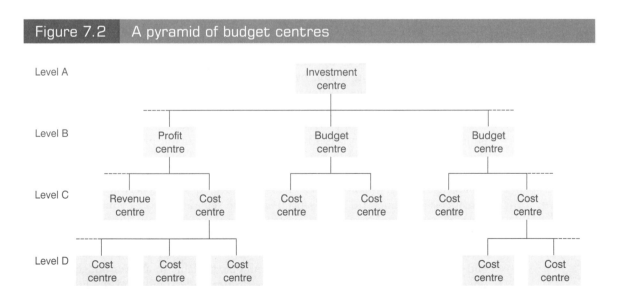

The budget cycle and administration

This section explains the time-cycle of budgeting, the forms of control which budgeting can provide, and some of the administrative arrangements for effective budget planning and control.

The time-cycle of budget planning and control

Most budgets are managed on an annual basis to coincide with the corporate financial year. But for each year's budgets planning must begin in the preceding year, while the annual end-of-year 'post-mortem' review and final corrective action can extend well into the following year. This cycle of planning and control is summarised in Table 7.1. The table is simplified in that it shows only the activity related to one year's budgets, year 2 in the example. In practice, work is going on simultaneously on the adjoining years' budget planning and control follow-through.

In year 1, the year preceding our illustrative budget, preparatory work is needed before individual budgets can be drawn up. The detail and thoroughness of this preparatory work will vary greatly between organisations, but, in general, the larger and more complex the organisation, the greater the degree to which it is decentralised, and the more dynamic the markets in which it operates then the more important it is that the preparatory work is comprehensive. This may begin in the middle of the financial year, or even earlier, commencing from the completion of the control 'post-mortem' review on the previous year's performance.

The work in year 1 should comprise a strategic review of the firm's markets, capacity, technology, capital-investment programme and objectives. From this review initial budget guidelines should emerge for use by the budget staff in helping managers draft individual budgets. These draft budgets are then combined into an overall 'master budget' (see below) to see if the 'sum of the parts' really adds up to fulfilment of the corporate objectives. If it does not, individual budgets must be revised, iteratively, and/or the corporate objectives and strategy must be amended, until an optimal but realistic set of budgets is obtained and agreed. This budget planning sequence can take several months, and it should be completed at least a month or two before the start of the new budget year so that managers have a lead-time to organise the implementation of the budget. In the public sector there is an occasional complaint because budgets are not always finally determined before the start of the new budget year, owing to late notification by government of the allowed total funding or to other delays in the resource-allocation decision process.

Moving to year 2, cost accountants and budget staff work to collect all relevant cost (or revenue) data, usually bringing these together in monthly summaries or budget performance reports (see below), to be made available promptly to each budget holder. As is summarised in the Control column of Table 7.1, the monthly budget reports are intended to be studied by managers for evidence as to how well they are achieving budgetary plans/targets. To assist in this, differences between budgeted and actual costs/revenues are usually printed out in separate report columns. These differences are termed 'budget variances'; variance accounting is illustrated in detail later in the chapter in the specific context of standard costing, a costing approach often used in combination with budgeting to improve the quality of reporting and control information. Budget staff should be available to answer budget holders' queries regarding any budget results they do not understand, and the budget staff should themselves take the initiative to work with management budget holders to find the causes of significant unfavourable variances and to take corrective action (which could include amending the budget should this be found to have been genuinely unrealistic).

At the start of year 3, all the individual budgets, together with the overall master budget, should be subjected to a close review. Sometimes this may be linked with the annual performance reviews or assessments of managers, although, clearly, budgetary performance forms only one part of a much wider range of assessment criteria. But always this annual review, or 'post-mortem' on the previous year, should be used positively to provide feedback of information and insight to assist the monitoring of current budgets and the preparation of the next strategic review.

Feedback and feedforward control

Figure 7.3 provides an overview of the budget feedback process, emphasising the importance of regular comparisons of budgets with the associated outturns.

Planning and control may be likened to two sides of the same coin. They should match, in size and worth. That is, assuming our plan is optimal given the state of knowledge and uncertainty, our object with control systems is to ensure that performance matches or achieves the plan. Broadly, two main control concepts or types of control systems are identified and developed in the literature (Emmanuel *et al.* 1990; Wilson and Chua 1993): feedback control and feedforward control.

Feedback is the traditional control system, historically associated with budgeting. Performance would be recorded, accumulated on file and then assembled in reports to managers, typically monthly but sometimes more frequently. If reported performance showed unfavourable variances from plan, corrective action would be taken.

Feedforward is the more modern approach to control systems. The object is to control performance in real time, as it happens; or, even better, to achieve control through prediction and anticipation of what action is needed to achieve plans or other targets or criteria of good performance. Modern technology of instrumentation and computer control makes the feedforward approach feasible and valuable in

Table 7.1	The time-cycle of budget planning and control	
Time	*Budgeting*	*Control*
Year 1	Strategic review	
	Set budget guidelines	
	Draft individual budgets	
	Assemble master budget	
	Adjust or reiterate until all budgets are optimal	
Year 2	Collect cost, revenue, etc, data by budget centre and prepare progress reports for managers, including variance analysis	Reports and variance analysis flag problems for corrective action
		Budget staff and higher management follow up major budget problems
Year 3		Postmortem analysis of prior budget year, with feedback into the next strategic review

many productive operations, for example in helping to eliminate rejects and waste in production lines by sensing machine deviation from the set specification. This leads either to machines correcting themselves or at least to the production line stopping if human corrective intervention is needed. Real-time control has other applications also, such as in the stock-control distribution and ordering arrangements for supermarket chains. Feedforward control is usually applied using physical resource measures rather than cost data. In such situations the budget objectives are sought through optimising control of the physical surrogates for financial targets. Periodic budget reports may become less important, or certainly less urgent or critical in their control role, but will remain essential for monitoring to check that the performance of individual operations and departments, when expressed in money terms for combination with other activities in the overall master budget, is on course to meet the financial targets and objectives of the enterprise as a whole.

The principle of feedforward control is important, and management should seek to implement feedforward control whenever it is feasible and cost-effective, especially the aspects of anticipation and prediction to avoid problems or unfavourable deviations from plan before they begin to bite. Nevertheless, there remain many areas of activity where automatic feedforward control systems cannot be used (as yet) and where traditional **budgetary control** feedback reporting systems remain the major form of financial control. These areas are typically where work is not routine or standardised, or where work cannot be planned in detail in advance but must evolve under management discretion stage by stage. Examples here include much of the work of commercial marketing and research and development, many professional services, university research projects, and much of the work of the social services and health services.

Feedforward control is but one example of the expanding ways in which information technology (IT) is contributing to improved budgeting and financial management. Other examples include financial modelling, analysis for risk and uncertainty or probability, and the general ability to employ sensitivity analysis in financial and budgetary planning. In a budgeting context, sensitivity analysis involves the quantification of a wide range of different permutations of production mix, costs, prices and marketing mix in search of the most favourable of profitable prospects.

Figure 7.3   The budgetary control process

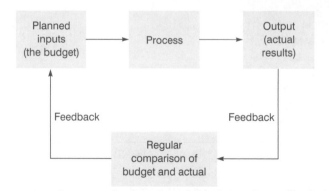

Budget administration

In many large organisations a specialist budget director is appointed, reporting to the finance director or controller. In smaller organisations the role may be combined with that of the chief management accountant. Again, larger organisations are likely to have a budget committee composed of senior executives to review financial strategy, set budget guidelines, study main budget proposals, review and approve main budgets and the master budget, adjudicate any disputes between budget holders and budget staff, and generally monitor the effectiveness of the budgetary planning and control system.

Organisations of any size will provide budget manuals giving detailed instructions on the layout of budget, what to include and where, the routines to be followed, and the coding system for matching resource use and costs (or revenues) with the specific inputs, activities, outputs, items of stock, items of sales, or organisational units and activities whose budgets should be charged (or credited). Good design of the coding system is of the highest importance, both so that it is comprehensible to the clerks and other workers who have to enter activity data by code, and so that the data can be manipulated by computer into all the various combinations of cost, budget and revenue analysis report which may be required.

A key issue in budget administration is whether budgets should be drafted by budget or accounting staff, and then discussed with budget-holding managers and amended as necessary, or whether budget holders should be given a blank budget form, together with copies of current budget guidelines and last year's budget for reference, and be told to get on with drafting their own budgets. Opinions differ. Practice differs. The nature of the business and the culture of the organisation are important factors in how to proceed on this. There are also important behavioural factors to consider in budgetary planning and control, which will be discussed in a separate section later in this chapter.

An important aspect of budget administration is the arrangement for amending or updating budgets if and when circumstances change during the budget year. There should be clear procedures for amending budgets – or making budget revisions, as they are often called, especially in the public sector. One form of amendment may involve no change in the total budget, but rather the switching of planned expenditure from one budget heading (or resource category) to another. Budget rules in the business world may often give managers substantial discretion as regards switching, whereas the tradition in the public service sector has been to set tight rules (here a particular term, 'virement', is used to identify the process of switching funds from one budget heading to another).

Budgets and budget reports

Budgets are required for every element of cost, expense and revenue for all the financial flows represented in the periodic operational profit and loss accounts or income statements. They are also required for all the asset and liability categories represented in the balance sheet. There are also budgets which link these two sets, perhaps most importantly the purchases budget, which effectively authorises expenditure on materials, parts and components for production or on finished goods for distribution. The purchases budget is extremely important, because it must meet the needs of sales plans (and thus of production plans in manufacturing businesses), yet also be reconciled with the firm's cash position and overall credit and working capital plans and limits.

Operational budgets

We set out below a list of the main budgets, or control budgets, for a typical manufacturing firm. It must be remembered that supporting each of these main or control budgets there will be separate subordinate budgets for each cost or revenue category – or centre – which is of sufficient importance to be managed as a budget centre in its own right, with a designated and accountable manager as budget holder.

- **Sales budget**: this might be subdivided or segmented in one or more of the following ways: product, area, brand, class of customer, exports, divisions, branches, etc.
- **Production budget**: this might be subdivided by plant or technology, and/or match the subdivisions in the sales budget. Both the production and sales budgets may be set out in physical volume terms as well as money costs and revenues.
- **Purchases budget**: this links the forecast requirements of sales and production with other interlinkages mentioned in the preceding paragraph.
- **Personnel budget** (sometimes called the labour budget or manpower budget): this may classify requirement by skills, grades or types of labour. Supporting expense budgets may cover recruitment, training, welfare and redundancy.
- **Marketing budget**: this is linked to the sales budget, and includes the expenses of marketing planning and administration, advertising and promotion (including sponsorships of sporting and cultural activities).
- **Capital budget**: this shows the amount and timing of approved major capital (fixed assets) expenditure over the budget year. Minor plant, equipment and vehicle expenditure may be included in other operational budgets, especially for production.
- **Cash budget**: this summarises all cash receipts and disbursements arising from trading, and also often includes cash flows arising from the capital budget and any new funding. Seasonal and other factors may result in periods of negative cash balances; these must be reconciled to overdraft limits and other borrowing arrangements. At other times there may be cash surpluses in excess of operational requirements, and how these should be invested profitably but safely in the short term needs to be planned.
- **Budgeted working capital** or **sources and application of funds statements**: these link with financing plans and the cash budget, as well as with the budgeted profit and loss and balance sheet (see below).
- **Budgeted profit and loss** or **income statement** or **statement of financial performance**: this draws together all revenue, cost and expense budget totals to derive the budgeted, or expected, profit and loss for the (usually) annual budget period.
- **Budgeted balance sheet** or **statement of financial position**: this draws together the effects of all the above budgets on the expected end-of-period values of the firm's assets, liabilities and residual capital balances.

The master budget

The term 'master budget' is used in two ways. Usually, it designates the key budget at the top of the pyramid of budget planning – for profit and loss and the balance sheet – which must be approved by top management before all the subsidiary budgets can be accepted as firm and approved. If these key budgets are not acceptable – or indeed if the cash or working capital budgets are not viable or are too risky – the entire budget planning process may have to be reiterated until the impact on the master budget becomes acceptable. There is, of course, the risk of junior managers 'fudging' some budgets against their realistic expectations or intuitive judgement in order to accommodate this reiteration exercise.

Once agreed, the above master budget becomes a firm plan and commitment for management. By extension, the term 'master budget' is sometimes used to identify the final, agreed form of each and every subordinate budget as well. In this context, all such master budgets are apparently 'fixed' in character; we shall consider the differences between 'fixed' and 'flexible' budgets further below.

Budget reports

Main budgets are usually made on an annual basis, but normally subdivided by months (or sometimes into 13 four-week periods to facilitate inter-period comparisons). Monthly or four-weekly periods are the traditional intervals for which to issue budgetary control progress reports. However, for some budgets thought critical at particular stages of business – often cash budgets – reports may be issued more frequently, and with modern computer systems it is increasingly common for managers to check their budget positions at any time between the formal reporting and review dates.

Table 7.2 provides a simplified example of a monthly production department budget report. The budgets agreed before the start of the year, or with any approved amendments, are shown for the current month and for the year to date for each main category or **cost centre** within the budget. Against each budget are set the actual costs

Table 7.2	Production department budget report

Department Q – month 3

Current month					Year to date		
Budget	Actual	Variance	Costs	Code	Budget	Actual	Variance
£48 000	£46 400	£1 600 F	Direct materials	801	£144 000	£145 400	£1 400 U
18 000	18 800	800 U	Direct labour	802	54 000	56 200	2 200 U
10 000	10 000		Fixed overheads	803	30 000	30 000	
6 000	6 300	300 U	Variable overheads	804	18 000	18 600	600 U
£82 000	£81 500	£500 F	Totals		£24 6000	£250 200	£4 200 U
4 000	3 800	200 U	Units produced		1 2000	11 500	500 U
£20.50	£21.45	£0.95 U	Unit production cost		£20.50	£21.76	1.26 U

Notes: U = unfavourable operating variance; F = favourable operating variance.

charged to the cost centres for the periods concerned, and the differences between these two figures are then displayed in the **variance** columns.

Supporting each of the main budget cost centres there may be a whole series of subordinate cost centres with supporting detail. Direct materials, for example, may be supported by separate cost accounts for each major item or type of material, part and component used. Often many more cost categories will be shown than in our example but there is a view that many managers are too busy to be able to scrutinise detailed budgets properly, and that it is preferable that summary budget reports should be restricted to such detail as can be displayed on a single sheet.

There are two important simplifying assumptions in Table 7.2. First, it has been assumed that the budget is identical for each month, implying a continuously stable rate of production, and thus probably of sales. Often, though, seasonal patterns of demand, planned promotion or product innovation, or forecast expansion or contraction of markets, as well as closures for holidays or plant overhaul or replacement, will result in variations in planned output and authorised budget from month to month. Second, our example shows actual fixed overheads as identical to budget. In real life this will happen sometimes, but not always. Whether it happens or not, there is a school of thought which holds, that where fixed overheads are not under the control of the budget holder, variances arising should not be included in that budget holder's report (possibly distorting or at least confusing his/her accountable performance). Proponents of this viewpoint would prefer to see the fixed overhead variances carried to a separate account for which top management would be accountable. Of course, proponents of variable costing or contribution costing would anyway wish to see fixed overheads wholly excluded from the production budget and unit cost calculations, on the grounds discussed in previous chapters.

The variance figures in Table 7.2 are net variances, and supplementary analysis may be needed to explain their full causes and significance. Take the apparently favourable variance of £1600 on direct materials. Yet output was down by 200 units, or 5%, on budget. *Prima facie*, direct-materials cost should also have fallen by 5%, or £2400. Thus, the budget holder has actually incurred materials costs £800 greater than expected, an unfavourable variance. This may have been caused by wastage owing to poor quality of material or to production errors, or it may be due to higher material prices than forecast when the budget was set. *Ad hoc* enquiry or supplementary analysis, can explain the true nature of, and accountability for, the overall net variance. However, our first distortion, owing to the deviation in production volume, can be resolved by using the flexible budgeting approach described below in place of fixed budgets. And the second distortion, or uncertainty as to the cause(s) of the remaining variance, may be more easily explained by linking budgetary reporting with the routine use of standard costing and standard cost variance analysis, as explained later.

Flexible budgeting

True fixed budgets set out absolute limits to expenditure, although sometimes these can be amended to allow for the effects of inflation on input costs beyond the control of the budget holder. Fixed budgets are used in the private sector when there is no direct linkage between expenditure and (at least short-term) market performance. This applies to many administrative costs, and to what are known as 'policy costs', including outlays on research and development and some parts of outlays on marketing, market research, promotion, sponsorship and public relations.

Most public-sector budgets are fixed budgets, since they represent maximum expenditure allocations from central or local government. In the UK prior to 1976 many of these fixed budgets were automatically uplifted for inflation as the budget year progressed, funded by supplementary votes in Parliament. From 1976 the 'cash-limits' system was introduced, whereby initial budgets were fixed to include forecast inflation, with, normally, no subsequent uplift allowed. However, the governmental allowances for inflation were often 'wishful thinking' underestimates of the actual inflation, so that public-sector funding became constricted in 'real terms'; that is, in the purchasing power for real resources which government cash limits have covered.

Where production or selling activity is demand-led or market-led, budgets should be flexible to reflect the levels of expenditure (and revenue) needed to cover the volume of activity meeting demand. Even in demand-led circumstances one could use fixed budgets, but they would never give realistic guidance on expenditure. There would often be large variances, which would have to be analysed to establish what part of the variances were caused by volume changes from the baseline used for the fixed budget, as distinct from variances for efficiency and the prices of resource inputs.

Flexible budgets are illustrated in Table 7.3. Section A shows a basic or traditional form of flexible budgeting. Here it is assumed that both direct materials and direct labour are fully variable, i.e. that direct material and labour cost is a linear function, with a constant cost per unit regardless of the volume level. However, as discussed in previous chapters, this is an unrealistic assumption, at least in the short term when management may be unable to reduce the workforce quickly, or indeed recruit and train new workers quickly. There may also be inherent technical features of the production process which cause step-costs (i.e. **semi-fixed** or **semi-variable** costs) in the

Table 7.3	Flexible budgets of production department		
	8 000 units £000	10 000 units £000	12 000 units £000
A Traditional allocation:			
Fixed overheads	80	80	80
Direct material (£10 per unit)	80	100	120
Direct labour (£8 per unit)	64	80	96
Variable overheads (£4 per unit)	32	40	48
Total cost	£256	£300	£344
Unit cost	£32	£30	£28.67
B Alternative allocation:			
Fixed overheads	80	80	80
Direct material (£10 per unit)	80	100	120
Direct labour			
core/fixed (7–14 000 units)	60	60	60
variable (0–11 000 units; £2 per unit)	16	20	22
variable (11 000 + units; £4 per unit)	–	–	4
Variable overheads (£4 per unit)	32	40	48
Total cost	£268	£300	£334
Unit cost	£33.50	£30	£27.83

use of direct labour at different production volumes. In Table 7.3 it is assumed that 10 000 units constitute the standard output for the budget period and that if a single fixed budget were used this would be the middle column in Section A.

Flexible budgets calculate the expected cost (or revenue) at alternative, relevant volume levels. Monthly or other periodic budget reports can show the precise combination of fixed costs plus aggregate unit variable costs for the actual volume achieved. The type of multiple-column, alternative-volume layout shown in Table 7.3 would be prepared before the start of the year to give managers guidance in short-term planning of resources and expenditure. The flexible budgeting process also allows calculation of the unit production costs that are expected at each volume, which should provide helpful information for marketing decisions on product pricing.

Section B of Table 7.3 illustrates the alternative approach of recognising that, while direct materials may be a fully variable cost, direct labour usually is not fully variable. Analysis of production can determine a core of staff needed for essential skills and for minimum manning of separate workstations, which defines the minimum workforce for continuing, efficient operations. This part of labour cost can then be seen for budgetary purposes as a fixed cost (as shown in Table 7.3). There then follows a more genuinely variable element of labour cost, comprising the result of marginal expansion or contraction of the labour force, ordinary overtime, use of casual labour, etc. Finally, beyond a certain volume (11 000 units in our illustration) excess overtime and/or subcontracting out part of the work will cause short-term unit variable cost to rise for the 'excess' production.

It is interesting to note the differences in unit costs disclosed by the two approaches to flexible budgeting in Table 7.3. These differences reflect the economies of scale from higher output made evident by departing from a simplistic assumption that direct labour is a fully variable cost (and this is an insight which may be obtained also from ABC, discussed previously). Even so, the differences in unit costs disclosed between the two approaches may not be so great as to alter company pricing and production plans in most business situations. In contrast, the differences in expected expenditure on production between the alternatives – e.g. showing that total production cost would be expected to be £12 000 higher at 8000 units, but £10 000 lower at 12 000 units – are quite substantial sums of expenditure in the context of budgetary reporting, accountability and control. At the lower volume level, the budget holding manager might be wrongly accused of inefficiency or overspending, while at the higher volume level a flexible budget based simplistically on the approach in section A of the table could serve to conceal inefficiency. It is of the essence that budgets and budgetary-control reports must be relevant, realistic, accurate and fair if they are to be effective aids to management. Where they fail to meet these requirements, as often happens, budget holders will resist the discipline of the budget and engage in counterproductive behaviour. This will be considered further in the next section.

Budgets and behaviour

There used to be two sets of convenient assumptions about accounting information and its use, including budget planning and control. The first assumption was that accounting and budgeting normally provided information which was objective, accurate and relevant, and which all managers should accept as rational guidance for positive action in the corporate interest. The second assumption was that all managers (and indeed all accountants) shared goal congruence in the corporate interest and would prepare and use budget information solely, or at least mainly, to that end. We now know that both assumptions are often wrong.

There is not space here to go into behavioural issues in detail, but much of the mainstream literature on business organisation and organisational behaviour applies. The classic organisational study of the behavioural problems of budgeting is by Hofstede (1968). Emmanuel *et al.* (1990) develop a comprehensive overall review of the role and use of accounting in management control.

Behavioural problems

Among the key problems identified by the authors mentioned above are: budget slack, pumping and overreaction.

Budget slack: where managers propose their own budget, or even where they simply feed in non-financial resource data to a budget officer or accountant to draft the formal budget, there is a great temptation for managers to overstate their resource needs. This could be to provide a safety margin against uncertainty and/or to secure some spare funding which they may later be able to divert to a spending interest which would not obtain approval if disclosed in advance at the budget planning and review stage (e.g. to pay for some extra equipment, maintenance or travel). This is a natural human reaction: even as individuals within a family discussing our personal budget, we may, for example, exaggerate the amount we expect to need to service the car in the year ahead, hoping for some slack which could be diverted to buying golf clubs, or to extra visits to the theatre or pub!

The temptation to budget holders to build slack into their budget will be greatest where one or more of the following circumstances apply:

1 There is great pressure (and possible sanctions) not to overspend budget, sometimes even when the operational situation has changed from that which was planned or expected. This can happen if fixed budgets are used when operational conditions would be more realistically reflected by flexible budgets. Of course, in the public sector the use of fixed budgets may often be unavoidable given public spending (cash) limits.

2 There is no efficient machinery for review, updating or amendment of budgets after the start of the budget year.

3 The budget controller, or senior management, is concerned only with compliance with total budget limits, and if the latter are achieved there is no enquiry into the detail of spending from the budget.

4 Budget holders are dealt with individually, in isolation, so that budgeting is seen as a game between the individual and the corporate bureaucracy. The alternative is to develop 'team budgeting', a consensual approach to resource planning, and a climate of interdependence and shared responsibility. Unfortunately, this is time-consuming and requires skilful leadership.

Pumping: 'pumping' occurs if one manager passes on a cost from his/her own budget to another manager's budget. This is most likely to occur between production departments or divisions where there is process or sequential work flow and multiple products. For example, if a budget holder has several jobs or batches of work on hand and knows the costings are more generous on some than on others, he/she may depart from the optimal production timetable and produce more than is currently needed of the products on which he/she knows the input cost budget can be beaten. This leaves the next department with a currently unwanted stock charge, not to mention possible congestion from storing the extra stock until it is needed and possible shortages of other stock.

Overreaction: in some organisations, 'achieving the budget' has been given a degree of pre-eminence in assessing managerial performance, possibly beyond its true importance, and often beyond the relevance and credibility of the data included in budget charges (especially where a high proportion of the charges are indirect or for overheads, or result from decisions taken elsewhere in the organisation). The problem is exacerbated if budget achievement is used as a key factor in performance reviews or in performance-related pay.

Some budget holders may expend precious time trying to find faults or errors in their budgets (and, if they succeed, this, while constructive in one sense, will also serve to further reduce morale and confidence in the 'management information system', of which budgeting is meant to be a major component. Other budget holders may fall back on devious excuses, or simply seek to ignore the problem. None of this contributes to better management.

Effective budgeting and management by objectives (MBO)

It is easier to specify the conditions for effective budgeting as an information aid and tool for good management than it is to achieve them. The first need is for good management leadership from the top, with an open willingness to discuss choices, problems and objectives with the lower tiers of managers who are the operational budget holders. The second need is for accurate, relevant and timely information on resource use and on who is properly accountable for that use. Here first-class computer support is essential and the objective should be to provide managers with terminals and systems allowing budget holders to monitor regularly their resource use, commitments, costs (and revenues, where relevant). The third need is for budget staff who interact frequently, openly and constructively with budget holders to assist understanding, facilitate team working and goal congruence, and sort out any budget uncertainties or conflicts quickly and fairly.

Top down or bottom up?

There are two basic approaches to the preparation of budgets for individual managers. The top-down approach involves the budget officer or accountant in preparing a draft budget for each manager, drawing on his/her knowledge of agreed strategic plans, forecasts of sales and production, etc. for the coming year or other budget period. Many budgets interact; that is, their resource use and output assumptions are interdependent; so these must be reconciled as consistent. The budget officer circulates the draft budgets to managers and should then follow through by discussing and explaining the draft with each manager to obtain his/her agreement that this is a feasible plan for which he/she accepts responsibility – or else to clarify what changes in the draft he/she needs or seeks before giving commitment to the budget.

The bottom-up approach operated by the budget officer provides the manager with a budget form with money figures not yet entered, together with a copy of last year's budget, and a summary of relevant strategic and forecast factors. The manager may then be left to work up the budget on his/her own, or the manager can do this with the budget officer in attendance for supplementary information or advice. In theory, this bottom-up approach should introduce greater realism, accuracy and commitment into the budget. In practice, budgeting will often take place as some mixture of or compromise between the two approaches.

Budgets for managers will have to be approved by their senior managers. Often this may involve only nominal or cursory attention from the senior manager, in conjunction with the budget officer. However, for budgets to be taken seriously, with full commitment at each management level, it can be argued that each manager should agree and accept his/her budget in the presence of the senior manager after appropriate discussion of any uncertainties, with the advice of the budget officer in attendance. This three-way commitment is often recommended for use in MBO systems.

Management by objectives (MBO)

Budget systems are concerned with the totality of cost, expenditure or revenue for a specified budget centre or budget holder. It is not easy to focus budgetary control on one management issue in isolation for concentrated attention. Also, whereas in theory budgets can be expressed in physical units rather than money measurement, in practice nearly all managerial budgets are financial. Thus, to supplement budgeting it is useful to have a technique widely known as management by objectives (MBO).

MBO involves setting individual managers one or more operational objectives for which to seek measurable improvement over a period, typically of 6 to 12 months. For example, improving staff morale may be a worthy objective, but improvement could be difficult to measure objectively. In contrast, labour/staff turnover is measurable, or quantifiable, and it could serve as a partial surrogate for 'morale'. Moreover, while high labour turnover clearly incurs costs – in severance, temporary manpower shortages, recruitment and training – these costs are not clearly isolated in departmental budgets, so that management attention is not focused on the underlying problem. But an MBO exercise can focus on the problem. The manager can be set the specific objective of reducing his/her department's labour turnover by 20%, or whatever, over the budget year or some shorter period.

Conventional guidelines for MBO systems recommend that just one important objective, or one problem inhibiting achievement of objectives, should be tackled by a manager at any one point in time. There should be an MBO officer, who could be, but need not be, the budget officer or accountant, and who is held responsible by higher management for running and reporting on the MBO projects. The objective or problem for improvement must be quantifiable, and progress in the MBO task must be measured and reported periodically. At intervals, or certainly at the end of the MBO assignment, the MBO officer should meet with the manager and with his superior to review and evaluate progress and to consider what the next-stage MBO assignment should be. Thus, the model for running an effective MBO system is very similar to that discussed previously for effective budgetary planning and control systems. That is, effective commitment and discipline in achieving budgetary and other corporate objectives is very dependent upon personal accountability and responsibility between each manager and his superior, with the role of the MBO/budget officer or accountant being that of facilitator, providing timely information and technical advice as needed.

Budgeting in the public sector

Historically, public-sector budgeting has been dominated by the need to account to various levels of government for the expenditure and use of the cash spending authorised by government. Budgets solely or mainly to allocate and control cash are technically simple. The intellectually interesting input has come at the budget-planning stage from the economists and the politicians. However, in recent years the public sector has been forced to change.

In the UK this started over four decades ago with many other countries eventually following a similar path. The 1974 reorganisations of local government and the National Health Service (NHS) marked the beginning of a period of major, ongoing, change. In 1974 the new regional water authorities were formed from services previously under local government control, and these new water authorities were enjoined to adopt commercial financial and budgetary practices, and to keep and report their financial accounts under 'best commercial practice'. The NHS was told to improve its costing and budgeting systems, although progress was slow. After 1979 the process of change accelerated. The introduction of the 'internal market' in health care, and of the NHS Trusts, forced the NHS to move largely to commercial accounting methods, even though it remained the case that the underlying cost information on the enormous number of diverse services provided did not yet enable highly accurate costings for budgetary management to be effected at the disaggregated level of the workload of individual hospital doctors, or even of teams of doctors working together in 'specialties' (e.g. orthopaedics). However, cost information for budgeting and control continued to improve gradually in the NHS, and even though the 1997 Labour government undertook to reform the NHS 'internal market' – based on individual Health Trusts acting as separate profit and investment centres and 'selling' their services to purchasing authorities – it seems likely that continuing shortages of funding will mean that costing and budgeting systems will continue to be developed and to be used ever more rigorously in the NHS, as also in other cash-limited public services.

Table 7.4 illustrates a form of budget report for an NHS hospital specialty or 'team'. Although based on a public service, the report illustrates features which could be applied equally in the private sector, especially for a service department inside a larger enterprise where the department works to a fixed budget and does not market its output outside that enterprise. First, the section captions are 'user-friendly' and avoid accounting jargon. Second, the budget costs are classified logically to reflect the degrees of financial accountability expected from the team or it leader. The first item, medical salaries, is the only cost wholly controlled by the team. The second category of other expenses controlled by the team includes the volume-related or variable direct cost of other resources used at the team's discretion. The subtotals that follow this indicate budget expenditure for which the team has primary accountability (even though it has no control over the ordering or pricing of the drugs and consumables listed). The third category combines some variable costs over which the team does not have primary control (e.g. ward consumables controlled by nurses) and the fixed costs or overheads (including salary allocations) of other service departments on which the team draws; these together comprise the indirect costs, in this case being outside the accountability of the team but subject to the influence of the team's behaviour, in that, in the longer term, planning and joint agreement with the team could serve to alter the staffing establishment and fixed costs. The last category comprises central overheads entirely outside team accountability or influence. Finally, the report

Table 7.4   Budget report for surgical team

Current month				Year to date		
Budget £	Actual £	Variance £		Budget £	Actual £	Variance £
10 998	10 697	−301 U	Medical staff costs	54 990	53 166	−1 824 U
			Other expenses controlled by team			
12 499	12 014	−485 U	Prescribed drugs	62 495	58 712	−3 783 U
290	248	−42 U	Histopathology – consumables	1 450	1 193	−257 U
7 679	9 016	1 319	Radiology – consumables	40 837	44 808	3 971 F
7 283	7 892	609 F	Operating theatre – consumables	36 415	38 878	2 463 F
38 767	39 867	1 100 F	Total costs controlled by team	196 187	196 757	570 F
			Costs influenced by team			
4 166	5 152	986 F	Ward – consumables	20 830	22 584	1 754 F
83	149	66 F	Outpatient – consumables	415	495	80 F
11 572	10 983	−589 U	Ward – overheads	57 860	58 592	732 F
41	193	152 F	Outpatient – overheads	205	452	247 F
1 565	1 782	217 F	Pharmacy – overheads	7 825	8 571	746 F
833	814	−19 U	Histopathology – overheads	4 165	4 046	−119 U
8 208	7 932	−276 U	Operating theatre overheads	41 040	40 463	−397 U
4 107	4 182	75 F	ECG – overheads	20 535	21 916	1 381 F
15 485	15 654	169 F	Physiotherapy – hydrotherapy	77 425	75 296	−2 129 U
46 060	46 841	781 F	Total costs influenced by team	230 300	232 595	2 295 F
			General services overheads			
2 499	2 261	−238 U	Unit administration	12 495	11 236	−1 259 U
973	1 028	55 F	Catering	4 865	5 386	521 F
1 219	817	−402 U	Domestic	6 095	3 932	−2 163 U
832	946	114 F	Linen/laundry	4 160	4 701	541 F
7 499	6 753	−746 U	Estate management	37 495	35 388	−2 107 U
13 022	11 805	−1 217 U	Total general services overheads	65 110	60 643	−4 467 U
97 849	98 513	664 F	Total costs for team	491 597	489 995	−1 602 U
			Memorandum statistics			
857	878	21 F	Inpatients – days	4 285	4 382	97
148	193	45 F	Outpatients – attendances	740	849	109
499	296	−203 U	Histopathology – tests	2 495	2 650	155
473	682	209 F	Radiology – tests	2 801	3 690	889
599	634	35 F	Operating theatre – hours	2 995	3 286	291

Source: draft for a report, with simulated cost figures, from a Clinical Accountability, Service Planning and Evaluation Project at a London hospital, by permission.
Notes: ECG = electrocardiograph, Minus signs indicate underspend of cash budget. U = unfavourable operating variance; F = favourable operating variance.

concludes with selected workload statistics which may roughly correlate with service output and which serve as a kind of surrogate for a marketed output.

Overall, the distinctive features of public sector accounting – and thus of budgeting, which is essentially the forward-looking mirror image of (cost and management) accounting – have become blurred or diluted. Commercial systems of accounting and budgeting are likely to be increasingly encouraged. However, there are two post-war developments in public-sector budgeting which have had some wider impact. These are PPBS and ZBB.

Planning, programming and budgeting system (PPBS)

PPBS is a method of planning, resource allocation and budgeting originally developed in the USA, in the Department of Defense during the Cold War. Nowadays, the approach is more generally known as programme budgeting. Programmes are targeted on objectives, outcomes or outputs for specified groups of clients or beneficiaries (or customers). Thus, a government may decide to target the 'elderly' as a specific group to receive maximised benefit within the resources available. A national programme of benefit or care for the elderly will involve resource use (and budgets) in health services, social security, local social services, and voluntary and private-sector elderly care homes. Coordinating such disparate bodies is almost impossible in the real world of politics and management competition. Even taking the much more limited objective of a programme budget for the elderly within the public health service (such as the NHS in the UK), there remain major problems.

Elderly people are treated within the NHS geriatric services but they also form the largest group of patients in most other NHS specialties and in NHS community-care facilities. They also comprise the largest group taking up the time and resources of NHS family doctors. All these budget holders are on different lines of resource funding, detailed planning and managerial accountability. Effective operational budgeting depends on clear accountability to one manager, or at least to one organisational source of control and discipline. Thus programme budgeting (PB) fails the test of being an effective operational budgeting system. However, the PB, or PPBS, approach is important in that it involves separate organisations joining together in the generalised planning of the distribution, use and target objectives of public resources, even though it cannot be applied effectively in the detailed administration of budgetary control. There may be few opportunities for the application of PB/PPBS in the private business sector, but sometimes the concept can be applied, as for example in overviewing the planning and budget funding of a new product, combining research and development, pilot production and market testing, and the main product launch and its promotion.

Zero-base budgeting (ZBB)

Again of American origin, **zero-base budgeting** (ZBB) is a technique designed to escape from the traditional approach to public-sector budgeting, **incremental budgeting**. Incremental budgeting is found also, all too frequently, in the private business sector. It involves the assumption by managers that last year's budget, plus adjustment for inflation, provides the baseline for negotiating the next year's budget. That is, it is assumed that the budget planning debate is concerned largely with how much extra or incremental funding the budget holder can get and how it should be applied. ZBB challenges this assumption.

ZBB operates on the basis that a manager should justify all expenditure in order to get his/her budget renewed. To do this is difficult unless one can somehow relate expenditure to the outputs, outcomes or benefits obtained for service objectives or client groups. To this end, the ZBB approach requires that managers allocate their resources and expenditure between separate 'decision packages', on the assumption that if a particular decision package is not yielding benefit greater than its cost it could be deleted from future budget funding. Obvious problems here are the apportionment of common or joint cost among the decision packages on a basis which is realistic as regards what could be saved if specific service activities were to be withdrawn, and also the degree of job security and narrowly specific (professional) skill training of public employees. Also there is the intractable problem of evaluating the benefit obtained from using resources in each decision package. In theory, this could be achieved using the economist's method of **cost-benefit analysis** (CBA), but in practice the priorities, prejudices and current 'fashions' of politicians and senior management will usually prevail.

For example, no British public body has ever formally adopted ZBB as a routine resource-allocation system. The system requires a large investment of the time of senior management, accounting and other expert staff and consultants, so doubters challenge whether it is cost-effective. Annual repetition of the ZBB exercise would cover the same ground again and again, and budget holders would become increasingly 'streetwise' in structuring and defending their decision packages so as to make cuts unlikely. However, discussions with many senior public-sector accountants show that they are attracted by the ZBB approach as a concept, and that they have been influenced by it in the way they negotiate with budget holders. Perhaps the nearest equivalent to ZBB in the private business sector is when firms, during recession or other times of crisis, embark on major cost-cutting exercises to scale down or eliminate staff activities deemed to be of low marginal benefit to (at least short-term) commercial operations.

Budgeting in service organisations

Manufacturers, farmers, wholesalers and retailers supply products. Most of the examples of costing and budgeting in this book are based on products or production activities. Supplying products is a 'service'. By the term 'service organisations' we mean more specifically those organisations whose outputs are not tangible, physical products. Service organisations typically are labour intensive; they apply specific labour skills to the particular requirement or problems of individual clients or customers. The police, universities and hospitals are service organisations, as are stockbrokers, advertising agencies and hairdressers. The question is whether there are distinctive features of service organisations, compared with product-based organisations, which need different kinds of budgetary (and/or costing) planning and control systems.

Arguably, however, the main distinction between organisations for budgetary and costing purposes is not whether they are product-based or service-based or whether they are in the public sector or the private sector, but rather whether they are trading in a genuine market or, instead, supplying a free or subsidised service or other output for which the market is not providing an independent validation of value. In the public health service in the UK, where an internal-market separation of healthcare 'purchasers' and healthcare 'providers' exists, no clear success has been demonstrated in replicating 'genuine market' behaviour. There remains the major problem, in the NHS, as in many private-sector service businesses, that the outputs marketed are diverse, while many of the resource inputs are in the form of common costs or joint costs, so that direct linkage between expenditure budgets and market performance is tenuous. This is an area awaiting new research and information-systems development.

Included within this may be the extension of ABC or standard costing and variance analysis, as discussed elsewhere, to wider application in service businesses.

Capital budgeting

The capital budget was mentioned briefly earlier in this chapter. **Capital budgeting** is a major topic in its own right. It involves most of the characteristics and problems outlined in this chapter. It comprises the search for capital-investment opportunities, the evaluation of alternative investments, the planning of investment programmes (including linking the timing of finance with the timing of capital-expenditure payments), control of the implementation of capital programmes, and post-mortem audits or reviews of the success of individual programmes. Of these five stages, it is the evaluation stage which attracts the most attention in textbooks (see Chapter 9, on longer-term decisions), probably because of the analytical interest involved in discounting for the time-value of money and in the associated analysis for risk and uncertainty.

It has been argued, however, that it is the first stage, the search for opportunities (e.g. new technologies, products and markets), which is most often neglected and which may be the weakest link in the decision-making chain. It is also very likely that the evaluation and decision variables for investment (e.g. cost estimates for new products and for capital development, and marketing, sales and price forecast) are often estimated too roughly, too optimistically, and without adequate market research and professional advice. These are, of course, areas of action and responsibility for management; not the accountant. The accountant can calculate discounted cash flows and risk analysis with computer programs but cannot supply most of the forecast data. To paraphrase: garbage data in, garbage solutions out. Capital budgeting deserves better than this; it is crucial to the firm's survival and growth.

The need for effective control systems

The essence of accounting control is feedback – the comparison of actual performance with planned performance. Techniques such as flexible budgets, standard costs and performance indicators are major attention-directing techniques for future planning and day-to-day operational control. They form part of the overall internal control system of an organisation, which operates at three basic levels (De Paula and Attwood 1982):

- management controls
- organisational controls and segregation of duties
- accounting controls.

A key feature of any system of effective internal control is that senior management should systematically review the organisation's financial operations and production/service delivery levels at regular and frequent meetings, aided by periodic financial statements, operational summaries, statistical and other appropriate information. In addition to regular reviews, management may also institute special reviews which constitute another, perhaps more strategic, instrument of control. In many large organisations a key feature of an effective internal control system is often the internal audit department. Principally concerned with accounting controls, the internal audit staff has the task of assuring management of the efficient and effective design and operation of internal checks within the financial and management accounting systems.

Organisations should have hierarchy charts or similar mechanisms that clearly show the extent to which authority and responsibility have been appropriately allocated in a clear reporting structure. If this is done, accountabilities and individual responsibilities are less likely to be confused. Accounting controls should ensure that transactions have been:

- authorised and approved
- correctly recorded
- appropriately reported.

A good **responsibility accounting** system should report only on factors that management can control. Thus, non-controllable costs either should not appear in performance reports or should be carefully segregated so as not to form part of the evaluation of a manager. As Dominiak and Louderback (1988: 362) state:

> Most of the major problems in developing an effective responsibility accounting system are behavioural. Managers must trust the reporting system; they must believe that it accurately depicts their performances. Managers must also believe that the system is fair. Accordingly, the evaluation system should use performance evaluation criteria that are under the control of the managers. But if the system is to perform its function for the company as a whole, the feedback provided, and the criteria used for evaluating the managers, should also motivate them to act in such a way as to advance the overall goals of the firm.

Organisational structures influence reporting systems. This is because different organisational structures result in different groupings of management responsibilities. For example, in a divisionalised company the marketing activity may be devolved to individual operating divisions or it may remain a main board responsibility.

Within the broader framework of management control it must be appreciated that not all controls are quantitative controls and not all quantitative controls are accounting controls. Amey and Egginton (1975) pointed out that the latter, when coupled with planning, are the most important subset if they are effective and operate to increase efficiency. They suggest that the major control devices used within an organisation 'constitute a continuum', ranging from tight to loose control, depending upon the amenability to control of the activities in question. Feedback controls can be listed or ranked in descending order of degree of control, as illustrated below:

- **automatic:** for example, mechanical systems, such as a steam valve, or electronic devices for measuring tolerances etc.;
- **statistical:** for example, quality control and consumer surveys;
- **technical standards**: for example, the minimum composition of base metals in an alloy, or staffing requirements in an NHS clinic;
- **performance standards:** for example, output per hour or, in the public sector, numbers of unemployed youths obtaining employment after receiving training, via resource allocation: for example, research and development or training budgets;

- **profitability measures**: for example, departmental contribution;
- **investment-centre measures**: for example, divisional return on investment (discussed in Chapter 8).

The continuum relates both to the degree of control that can be exercised and the degree of responsibility delegated, as Amey and Egginton (1975: 392) state:

> As a very broad generalization it might be said that, as firms succeed in moving more activities and problems towards the 'tightly controlled' end of the spectrum, there is a tendency for new 'loosely controllable' activities to appear at the other end, such things as multinational activities, diversification, and more complex technologies which are only partially understood by top management.

The two principal accounting control techniques in this regard are known as budgetary control and standard costing/variance analysis. Budgets were discussed earlier in the chapter; in the next section we discuss how flexible budgets form the basis from which variances can be analysed. This process involves determining internal standards of performance and feeding back to those concerned comparisons of their actual result with these predetermined targets or norms. In budgetary control and standard costing as normally practised, the boundary of control is co-extensive with the boundaries of the firm.

Organisational management control structures can, in general terms, be characterized as **centralised** or **decentralised**, depending on the extent of responsibilities delegated to individual managers. Managers who have a good deal of authority and can take a number of key decisions – such as pricing and production levels and even, perhaps, investment decisions – without the approval of higher levels of management – tend to belong to decentralised organisations, whereas managers who have little scope to invest on their own initiative tend to belong to centralised organisations. As mentioned above, we consider the question of decentralisation and its associated control problems in Chapter 8.

All too often, organisations establish management accounting control systems that violate the principle of devolved management controllability because there is an overriding desire by senior board members to concentrate their attention on making calculations of and drawing attention to the **full cost** of an activity provided by a production or service department. In part, this is because of the need to evaluate the performance of the division as well as that of the manager. Recall that full cost represents a combination of costs that are both directly traceable to the activity under consideration and indirectly apportioned to it, based on some 'fair share' of apportioned/absorbed cost from elsewhere in the organisation. Whatever the plan for segmenting an organisation for reporting purposes, individual managers should be held responsible only for that which they can control. If this is not the case, managers will, naturally enough, tend to act in their own interests, and this may be dysfunctional for the organisation as a whole.

Variance analysis

In most manufacturing enterprises standard costs, i.e. the costs per unit of activity, form part of the basis on which the overall budget is constructed. Standard costs should represent anticipated target cost and are based on either historical records or, preferably, engineered standards. Engineered standards involve the collection of a great deal of information about a product's technical specification, ideal production pattern and so on. Standard costs based on historical records assume or imply a level of operational efficiency which may not have occurred. Drury (2004: 732) points out that standards are normally classified into three broad categories:

- basic standard costs
- ideal standards
- currently attainable standards.

Basic standard costs tend to be left unchanged over long periods and to be used as a planning tool for plotting trends in efficiency. Ideal standards represent the minimum operational costs expected under the most efficient production erudition. In practice, ideal standards are rarely used since management can be demotivated if asked to achieve what are virtually unobtainable results. Currently attainable standards are the most commonly used form of standards, and represent difficult targets but ones that ought to be capable of achievement by management. Standards are only of use if they motivate the desired behaviour by management. It is therefore important that management is fully involved in the standard-setting process, along with management accountants and supported by the technical expertise of production engineers, operations researchers and so on.

A standard cost is produced by the multiple of a unit(s) of productive input (materials, labour or overhead) and unit costs or rates. Once calculated, standard costs can be utilised to compare planned with actual performance. The core model for all productive variance analysis is based on the following set of expressions:

1   Standard cost (SC) = Standard price (SP) × Standard quantity (SQ)   **(7.1)**
2   Actual cost (AC) = Actual price (AP) × Actual quantity (AQ)   **(7.2)**
3   Total variance = (SP × SQ) – (AP × AQ)   **(7.3)**
4   Price/rate variance = (SP – AP) × AQ   **(7.4)**
5   Quantity variance = (SQ – AQ) × SP   **(7.5)**

To understand the application of expressions 7.3 to 7.5 above, let us consider the following example. Elexitron Digital Instruments PLC manufactures a particular product that requires four printed circuit boards at a cost of £5 each, a total of £20 per unit manufactured. When it came to evaluate actual production costs it found that the particular circuit boards specified were in short supply and that it had been necessary to substitute these circuit boards with an alternative of lesser specification. In practice, this meant using five of the inferior circuit boards, at a cost of £4.50 each, i.e. a total cost of £22.50. This variance can be analysed as follows:

3   Total variance = £20 – £22.50 = – £2.50 (unfavourable)
4   Price/rate variance = (£5 – £4.50) × 5 = £2.50 (favourable)
5   Quantity variance = (4 – 5) × £5 = –£5.00 (unfavourable)

Several issues are highlighted by this basic illustration:

- The analysis of the total variance recognises that, inevitably, different managers have different areas of responsibility. Typically, as regards materials, the purchasing function is a separate function from the production function. As regards labour the personnel department would be responsible for the relevant pay rates but line management would be responsible for the deployment of the mix of staff available to them, including the use of overtime.

- In most computerised standard costing systems, the price (for materials) and the rate (for labour) variances would be calculated first. This makes sense, since to be of use variances should be produced in as timely a way as possible. If one considers materials, it is more relevant to calculate the price variance at the time of acquisition. The materials are then entered into stock at the standard price and charged out to production at the standard price. Subsequently, when production has taken place, the quantity variance can be calculated.

- The variances above have been termed either favourable or unfavourable. These terms are used only to denote the direction of the variance. Other texts may use alternative terminology but all point out that it is the analysis of the variance that is important.

- Some variances can be further subdivided. For example, the quantity variance could, if appropriate, be further subdivided into a yield and a mix variance. Such subdivision depends on the individual circumstances of particular enterprises. A yield/mix division would, for example, be an appropriate sub classification in the chemical or plastics industry.

- Many books favour a long list of formulae for variances. For managers we think this is unnecessary; instead, they should be conversant with the principles of variance analysis so as to be able to define the type of information that they expect their management accountant to prepare for them. Table 7.5 lists the relevant expressions for the production variances used in this text. There are two points to note: first, the expressions for labour, material and variable overheads all follow the same pattern; second, fixed overheads are classified only as expenditure variances. This is because we do not see the relevance of further disaggregating these items of expenditure. Other texts do disaggregate fixed overheads. We discuss this issue again later in the chapter.

Table 7.5	Operational production variances	
Labour:	Total	(Standard hours × Standard rate) – (Actual hours × Actual rate) $(SH \times SR) - (AH \times AR)$
	Rate	(Standard rate – Actual rate) × Actual hours $(SR - AR) \times AH$
	Efficiency	(Standard hours – Actual hours) × Standard rate $(SH - AH) \times SR$
Materials:	Total	(Standard price × Standard quantity) – (Actual Price × Actual quantity) $(SP \times SQ) - (AP \times AQ)$
	Price	(Standard price – Actual price) × Actual quantity $(SP - AP) \times AQ$
	Quantity	(Standard quantity – Actual quantity) × Standard price $(SQ - AQ) \times SP$
Variable overheads:	As per the three labour expressions above	
Fixed overheads:	Total	Actual fixed overheads – Budgeted fixed overheads AFO – BFO
	Expenditure	AFO – BFO

Standard costing can be implemented only in organisations which already have a sound budgetary control system. When preparing variances it is not sufficient simply to compare the original budget with actual results. To do so would produce variances that muddled both planning and operating variances, and though the figures produced could be reconciled they would produce relatively meaningless figures by which to manage. In order to compute meaningful operational variances budgets must be flexed to reflect the actual level of activity achieved in a period. This is necessary if we are to look at operational performance on a comparative basis. It could be, for example, that a firm had planned to produce 1000 items per month, but in fact, due to the high demand for its products, production was 20% higher, at 1200 units per month. Simply comparing the original budget with actual performance would produce a string of unfavourable variances and little attention would be paid to the efficiency of actual production, since everyone would expect actual performance to produce these slightly absurd results. The question, in reviewing actual production, is how well production management has done relative to the standards expected of it. We need, therefore, to compare the fixed budget with a flexed budget. This will identify planning variances at the flexed budget level with actual results. By comparing the flexed budget with actual results we can compute operational variances (see Figure 7.4).

As explained above, the purpose of this part of the chapter is to introduce managers to the basic constructions of variance analysis. That is why, for simplicity, we have flexed the fixed budget using the original standard cost. In practice, standard cost would of course be periodically updated and revised. This would mean that an analysis of the planning variances would not just identify, as outlined above, planning efficiency or quantity variances, but also allow for the preparation of planning-rate and price variances.

Purposes of variance analysis

Using the discussion to date, we can summarise the four principal purposes of variance analysis as being:

1 **Comparison of actual performance with standard performance for a given level of activity.** This can provide meaningful variances based on both value and volume changes that assist managers by:

Figure 7.4   Planning variances and operational variances

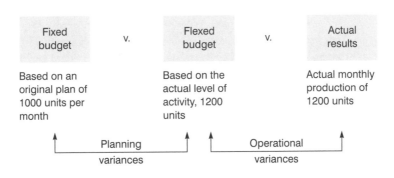

Fixed budget	v.	Flexed budget	v.	Actual results
Based on an original plan of 1000 units per month		Based on the actual level of activity, 1200 units		Actual monthly production of 1200 units

Planning variances   Operational variances

- providing control information on those aspects of activities where operations are not proceeding according to plan;
- evaluating the performance of individual functions in the organisation (e.g. purchasing, production, service delivery, administration and so on);
- providing information useful for future planning.

2 The production of periodic performance reports and variance information on bases, which to be effective must be:

- behaviourally sound: they should incorporate the notion of responsibility accounting and should 'map' the pattern of the firm's organisational structure. Variance analysis is of little use for budgetary control unless it 'fits' the organisational structure of the particular firm. As with other internal accounting systems, a classic failure is framing the reporting system around the external accounting reporting system.

- appropriately produced: as we have often stated throughout this text, reports must be relevant, timely, accurate and cost-effective. Most variance analysis systems are not cheap to implement and run, and variance analysis is of use only if it changes planning and operational behaviour. A costly system that does not provide for this is clearly a drain on valuable resources, time and effort, and is entirely demotivating. Indeed, it could be argued that for some line managers, variances would be more appropriately reported in terms of hours or units of input/output. Consider, for example, a production manager. Is it helpful to him/her to have to consider variances presented in monetary terms or would he/she be better served by receiving information in terms of the mix of labour hours, including overtime, and units of inputs/outputs in terms of kilograms, etc?

- based on flexible budgeting principles that reflect real levels of activity.

3 **The setting of standards to encourage managers to understand more fully the cost structures of those parts of the organisation that they manage,** thereby enhancing their managerial effectiveness by:

- saving valuable management time by identifying for their attention areas where planned performance is not being achieved;
- facilitating management by exception, as many systems will only report significant variances rather than all variances – also, as discussed later, many variances are interrelated and the correction of one will often impact on others.

We are now in a position to consider a slightly more comprehensive illustration of variance analysis based on the principles so far outlined. Let us consider the case of Fizzer Plc. Fizzer Plc manufactures and distributes an industrial bonding agent known as Bondlite. The standard direct costs per cylinder of Bondlite are:

Material	50 kg of A at 40p per kg
	100 kg of B at 50p per kg
Labour	5 hours at £1.80 per hour
Variable overheads	Recovered on the basis of labour hours
	at a rate of 50p per hour

The budgeted monthly production/sales level is 750 cylinders and the selling price is £100 per cylinder. Budgeted fixed overheads of £5000 per month are anticipated. The following details relate to production in month 3, when 800 cylinders of Bondlite were produced and sold:

	£
Sales	79 400
Materials used:	
A (44 000 kg)	16 720
B (75 200 kg)	39 104
Labour:	
3750 hours	7125
Variable overheads	2250
Fixed overheads	5600
Total costs for month	70 799
Profit	8601

George Snelling, the managing director, is surprised at the attitude of some of his colleagues, who see little to worry about as the actual profit generated was only about 3% below that anticipated when the original budget was set. Are these other managers being complacent?

An examination of the analysis presented in Table 7.6 shows that, in fact, compared to the standard for this level of production the profit is 12% below what would have been anticipated. But what of the individual line item variances? Material A indicates a favourable price variance of £880 but an unfavourable quantity variance of £1600. Why? There are several possible reasons. One could be that an inferior quality was purchased which meant a lower price, but that a larger quantity was needed. Perhaps an opposite explanation could be given for material B. Is the labour variance worth investigating? After all, the total is only £75 favourable. However, this variance is the net of an unfavourable rate variance of £375 and a favourable efficiency variance of £450. What caused this? Was this due to an underestimation at the time the original budget was set of the pay scales for labour, countered by too lax an estimation of the labour hours required? Alternatively, did the hourly rate paid constitute an incentive that resulted in better than standard productivity? The principal difference with the variable overheads seems to have been an underestimation of the hourly recovery rate. The variable overhead efficiency variance is, for obvious reasons, in line with the labour efficiency variance.

The fixed overhead adverse expenditure variance was £600. Note that this was not flexed. If the cost accounting system used in the organisation was based on absorption-costing principles (see Chapter 4) this expenditure heading might have been flexed. However, our view is that, although this can be done and expenditure and efficiency variances produced, little practical information is achieved, other than that the computation produces an over- or under-recovery of expenditure. In our opinion, it is of no practical use to calculate variances unless they actually provide meaningful information on which management can act. The reality is that the budget for fixed overheads was understated, and it is this that requires investigation.

Table 7.6	Fixed Plc – analysis of production variances			
	Fixed monthly budget (750 cylinders) £	Fixed monthly budget (800 cylinders) £	Actual results for month (800 cylinders) £	Total operational variances £
Sales[1]	75 000	80 000	79 400	600 (U)
Material A[2]	15 000	16 000	16 720	720 (U)
Material B[3]	37 400	40 000	39 104	896 (F)
Labour[4]	6 750	7 200	7 125	75 (F)
Variable overheads[5]	1 875	2 000	2 250	250 (U)
Fixed overheads[6]	5 000	5 000	5 600	600 (U)
	66 125	70 200	70 799	599 (U)
Profit	8 875	9 800	8 601	1 199 (U)

Key (U) = unfavourable operating variance (column 2 – column 3)
(F) = favourable operating variance (column 2 – column 3)

1 Analysis of the sales variance is provided in Table 5.4.
2 Material A:

Total variance:	$(SQ \times SP) - (AQ \times AP)$	= £720 (U)
Price variance:	$(SP - AP) \times AQ$	
	$(40p - 38p) \times 44\,000$ kg	= £880 (F)
Quantity:	$(SQ - AQ) \times SP$	
	$(40\,000$ kg $- 44\,000$ kg$) \times 40p$	= £1 600 (U)

3 Material B:

Total variance:	$(SQ \times SP) - (AQ \times AP)$	= £896 (F)
Price variance:	$(SP - AP) \times AQ$	
	$(50p - 52p) \times 75\,200$ kg	= £1504 (U)
Quantity:	$(SQ - AQ) \times SP$	
	$(80\,000$ kg $- 75\,200$ kg$) \times 50p$	= £2400 (F)

4 Labour:

Total variance:	$(SH \times SR) - (AH \times AR)$	= £75 (F)
Rate:	$(SR - AR) \times AH$	
	$(£1.80 - £1.90) \times 3\,750$ hours	= £375 (U)
Efficiency:	$(SH - AH) \times SR$	
	$(4000$ hours $- 3750$ hours$) \times £1.80$	= £450 (F)

5 Variable overheads:

Total variance:	$(SH \times SR) - (AH \times AR)$	= £250 (U)
Rate:	$(SR - AR) \times AH$	
	$(50p - 60p) \times 3750$ hours	= £375 (U)
Efficiency:	$(SH - AH) \times SR$	
	$(4000$ hours $- 3750$ hours$) \times 50p$	= £125 (F)

6 Fixed overheads: Note: not flexed due to change in activity: the £600 (U) variance is solely due to expenditure.

The reasons given for the variances of Fizzer Plc are only speculative. In practice, variances indicate only of which manager enquiries should be made. This example has been constructed simply to demonstrate that, although overall the target profit was close to that expected, this result is far from satisfactory and further investigation is indeed called for. However, the need to investigate variances is not always self-evident. While the accounting system will quantify the size and classification of a variance, management should be concerned about the cause as well as the size. Clearly, in an 'on-line' situation managers need to weigh up the costs and benefit of further investigation but should not base such decisions simply on whether a variance is favourable or unfavourable. To help with this, some standard costing systems use statistical techniques, often derived from the techniques of engineering quality control analysis.

So far in this discussion we have not commented on sales variances. The principles on which they are based are similar to those of production variances except that actual sales margins are determined based on the original budgeted margins. This is only equitable since the sales function would typically be expected to achieve a budgeted profit or contribution margin and it is not their responsibility if production costs were more or less than was budgeted for. Table 7.7 provides the relevant expressions for the calculation of sales margin variances and a simplified illustration and Table 7.8 provides the analysis of the Fizzer Plc sales variance. Note that, as presented, the overall operational sales variance will be due to differences in the sales price obtained.

The exercises at the end of this chapter provide further illustrations of variance analysis. Note that the analysis of these questions can be based on either an absorption or a contribution-based cost accounting system. Given the earlier discussions in this chapter, and examining the illustrations at the end of this chapter, readers should appreciate that, whichever system is in operation, the basic technique for the analysis

---

Table 7.7   Sales margin variances – general expression and illustration

Sales margin variance analysis assumes that all production casts are at standard. This is sensible since the sales activity of an organisation is relatively independent of production or service activities. By convention, therefore, sales variance analysis assumes that the cost price of all units sold is at standard cost; the actual costs do not enter the analysis at all.

Total sales margin variance	(Actual sales – Standard cost of sales) – (Budgeted sales – Standard cost of sales) $(AS - SCS) - (BS - SCS)$
Sales margin price variance	*either* (Actual margin per unit – Standard margin per unit) × Actual sales units $(AMU - SMU) \times ASU$ *or** (Actual sales price – Standard sales price) × Actual sales units $(ASP - SSP) \times ASU$
Sales quantity	(Actual sales variance – Budgeted sales variance) × Standard margin per unit $(ASU - BSU) \times SMU$

Note: It is possible to further subdivide the sales quantity variance into miscellaneous and yield variances. This would be necessary only in certain instances, such as in the chemical industry.
* Both formulae give the same result; this is because the AMU is derived by deducting the standard cost of sales from the actual sales price and this is a constant term because the SMU also uses this value.

of variances remains unchanged. For sales variances the difference between the actual profit contribution margin and the budget profit/contribution margin under both approaches is the same, since the fixed cost element is a common term for the determination of both the budgeted and the actual profit margins. These exercises also include a public-section illustration, St Margaret's Hospital Trust. Although it is a relatively simple example, it highlights that several possible applications of this approach to variance analysis are available in the public sector.

To conclude this section, we can say that there are probably four major causes of variances:

- inefficient operations
- incorrect original plans and specifications
- poor communication of standards and budgetary goals
- failure to take interdependencies into account when setting standards and preparing a budget.

With respect to inefficient operations we would want to know whether the variance was controllable by management and, if so, whether its cause could be identified. Often, as previously stated, variances can be the result of interdependencies. For example, as illustrated above, when variable overheads are based on a labour-hour recovery rate, was adverse performance in one productive department the result of bad management in that department or a technical fault in another department? It could be that because a particular job arrived behind schedule in one department overtime had to be worked. The reason for the delay could have been poor scheduling earlier in the production cycle or, perhaps, an earlier machine failure. For planning, we need information on market effect charges and we would need to know if

Table 7.8	Fizzer Plc – analysis of sales margin variances*
Total sales margin variance	$(AS - SCS) - (BS - SCS)$ $= (\pounds79\,400 - \pounds70\,200) - (\pounds75\,000 - \pounds66\,125)$ $= \pounds9\,200 - \pounds8\,875$ $= \pounds325\,(F)$
Sales margin price variance	*either* $(AMU - SMU) - ASU$ $= (\pounds17.75 - \pounds18.50) \times ASU$ $= \pounds600\,(U)$ *or* $(ASP - SSP) \times ASU$ $= (\pounds99.25 - \pounds100) \times 800$ $= \pounds600\,(U)$
	$(ASP = \pounds79\,400 \div 800\ units = \pounds99.25;\ AMU = \pounds99.25 - \pounds81.50 = \pounds17.75;$ $SMU = \pounds100 - \pounds81.50 = \pounds18.50,$ where $\pounds81.50$ is the standard cost per unit before fixed costs.)
Sales quantity variance	$(ASU - BSU) \times SMU$ $= (800 - 750) \times \pounds18.50$ $= \pounds925\,(F)$

Note: In Table 7.6 the sales variance shown was £600(U); this is because under this approach to flexible budgeting we are comparing actual sales with a budget which is flexed relative to actual sales activity. The full analysis is provided here.

variances are persistent in order to determine whether our overall long-term plan needs changing. Also, importantly, we need feedback from those responsible for planning, since it takes much longer to rectify planning failures than operational failures.

Performance indicators

Although the concern with economy, efficiency and effectiveness (the three 'Es') is not new to the British government (or other governments), its emphasis was given a boost following the public-sector crisis of the mid-1970s and the return of the Conservative Party to government in 1979. A series of reforms gave pre-eminence to the gospel of the new public management in central government; the efficiency movement began with the Rayner scrutinies and was followed by the Financial Management Initiative (FMI), with its emphasis on accountable management and information systems, and the more recent development of executive agencies, each with its service and resource targets. Local government, the NHS and other parts of the public sector have not been immune. Indeed, they have often been at the forefront of development, including the Citizens' Charter movement, which reflect the increasing concern, not just with the economical management of resources, but also with the efficiency and effectiveness of service delivery.

Public-sector organisations have to operate in a strict financial climate that includes the use of cash limits, cash planning and the development of performance indicators intended to demonstrate whether the public at large receives value for money from the services provided. The use of performance indicators is seen as a vital part of internal control, and they are also used in annual reports as an important supplement to financial information. As Glynn states, 'Accountability in the public sector occurs when both politicians and the public at large are assured that public funds are being spent **efficiently, economically** and on programmes that are **effective**' (Glynn 1985: 18). Performance indicators are concerned with demonstrating that services are provided efficiently and that the output from any activity/service is achieving the desired result.

Efficiency indicators refer to the productive use of resources. In order to produce such measures managers need to be able to identify and measure both programme outputs and programme inputs. In order to define suitable efficiency measures it is necessary to assess five factors:

1 The suitable delineation of individual departmental or programme goals to all levels of the organization.
2 The adequacy of controls and systems used by management in monitoring and measuring both the efficiency and the level of service they offer.
3 The level of efficiency currently attained, as well as measures of comparable results (if available).
4 The efforts taken to improve methods of operation in order to improve efficiency.
5 Whether efficiency measures are feasible and, if not, the reasons why.

The term 'efficiency' is often wrongly confused with the term 'productivity'. Productivity is simply the ratio between output and input, whereas efficiency is the relationship of actual output and input (productivity) to a performance standard.

Efficiency can be measured in terms of a rate of return of production, the work content measured over time, or the unit cost of an output. Consider the following example (based on Glynn 1985) in relation to the dispensing of prescriptions by a hospital pharmacy.

A hospital employs two pharmacists who each work a 35-hour week. The *standard rate of production* is six prescriptions/hour, which in terms of work content in time is ten minutes/prescription. Each pharmacist is paid £8.40 per hour, so that the *unit cost per prescription* is £1.40. Statistics show that, on average, 924 prescriptions are dispensed each month. Efficiency can be measured as follows:

$$\frac{\text{Actual rate per hour}}{\text{Standard rate per hour}} = \frac{6.60}{6} \times 100 = 110\%$$

$$\frac{\text{Standard time (minutes)/prescription}}{\text{Actual time (minutes)/prescription}} = \frac{10}{9.09} \times 100 = 110\%$$

$$\frac{\text{Standard cost (£)/prescription}}{\text{Actual cost (£)/prescription}} = \frac{1.40}{1.27} \times 100 = 110\%$$

Various points arise from this example. In comparing actual costs with standard costs, management should first consider the economy of operations. Efficiency measures are only possible when outputs can be separated from each other and possess uniform characteristics. A repetitive process, as in our example, meets these criteria. There are instances when efficiency measures are either not practicable or not possible. Consider the potential difficulties associated with attempting to measure the efficiency of a community-policing programme. Though tasks may be clearly stated for the officers concerned (school visits, handling crime-prevention enquiries, maintaining and developing contacts with ethnic minorities, etc.), outputs, not necessarily being tangible, cannot be measured easily, if at all.

When an agreed standard of performance does not exist it might, in the first instance, be useful to compare present performance with some previous base period (e.g. the same month last year). Such a base output/input ratio is termed a historical standard or target. This assumes that past performance is an appropriate comparison for future performance; this may not always be so. For instance, if a new service is building up a client base one would naturally expect the efficiency ratio to improve over time. Hatry (1979) provides a useful list of efficiency indicators, in six categories:

1 Comparisons over *time*.
2 Measurements compared between geographical areas.
3 Comparison of actual performance with *standards*, particularly in relation to standardised procedures.
4 Comparisons of actual performance with that *targeted* at the beginning of the year.
5 Comparisons with similar *private-sector* activities.
6 *Inter-authority* comparisons.

Clearly the purpose is not to measure efficiency for efficiency's sake – improving efficiency is the objective. By developing appropriate efficiency indicators management can contribute to improving efficiency and to determining the expected gains from suggested improvements. The 1981 *Canadian Audit Guide* (Canadian Government 1981: 5) discussed the importance of efficiency measures in the following terms:

Standards and performance data are used for different purposes in various information and control systems. These are to:

- demonstrate achievement of results by comparing performance data to standards, target and goals;
- plan operations and budget resource requirements by providing data for comparing present and proposed methods and procedures;
- provide a rational basis for pricing goods and services (when charges are made);
- make trade-off decisions between efficiency and the level of service; and
- indicate to employees and supervisors what results are expected.

The key elements for management that arise from adopting efficiency measures are therefore:

1 An awareness of, and the determination to accomplish, programme goals in the most economical and efficient manner.

2 The need to plan operations as efficiently as possible for a given level of resources (or budgeted level of income if a statutory authority is expected largely to generate its own income).

3 The need to have a structured organisation whose administration should follow prescribed work measures and procedures in order to avoid duplication of effort, unnecessary tasks, idle time, etc.

4 The provision of work instructions, in sufficient detail, to employees who are suitably qualified and trained for the duties they are required to perform.

As the report of the Layfield Committee (1976: 95) stated:

The best way of promoting efficiency and securing value for money by external means is through the dissemination of comprehensive but intelligible information on the methods employed by local authorities and the result they achieve.

By contrast to measuring efficiency, the notion of effectiveness is probably the most important yet least precise element of the three Es. Consider the following definitions:

[Effectiveness is] The extent to which the objectives of a policy are achieved. The most effective policy is one which achieves all it objectives. (HM Treasury 1988: 28)

Effectiveness means providing the right services to enable the local authority to implement its policies and objectives. (Audit Commission 1986: 8)

Ensuring that the output from any given activity is achieving the desired result. (Price Waterhouse 1990: 4)

The definitions contain a variety of terms and implications but share a common view of effectiveness: it is a value given to the relationship between an activity and its effect. Glynn *et al.* (1992) believe that there is something of a conventional wisdom about what different effectiveness measures can be. These can be measured in terms of:

- *output* – unit of goods or services produced

- *outcomes* – externalities to the activities themselves
- *impacts* – the ultimate policy effect of a programme, project or policy.

Of these three measures, outputs are the most easily measured. Output performance indicators relate to the direct product of management processes, such as numbers of young persons on training schemes, housing units built, etc. Outcomes represent direct and measurable consequences of an activity, for example the proportion of training scheme recipients obtaining vocational qualifications or employment and the reduction in homelessness. Impacts are much harder to report in terms of performance indicators since impacts tend to be associated with the more abstract notion of 'quality of life'; that is, the broader impact of training schemes and crime-prevention campaigns on the quality of life of citizens.

The production of performance indicators is a relatively new concept, albeit one increasingly used since the late 1980s. Performance indicators are quantitative expressions of various characteristics or consequences of an activity. Indicators are, as the word implies, *indicative* of performance, and thus attempt to portray the achievement of an activity where actual output or impact is difficult to measure. There are essentially two classes of effectiveness indicators: absolute indicators, which report volume or incidence (e.g. numbers of university graduates obtaining first class degrees), and indices, which report relative achievement (e.g. percentage of university graduates with first class degrees). Both classes focus on descriptions of aggregate activities. Thus their function is primarily descriptive, but they may, in a limited way, also address normative and prescriptive questions. They are unlikely, however, to provide explanations of what they reveal and they do not always measure effectiveness directly. Nevertheless, they often have to be used as proxies for effectiveness, because it is difficult to identify and measure outcomes and impacts themselves.

Although this section of the chapter has dealt with public-sector issues, it should be obvious to the reader that in service-sector industries the development of performance indicators is probably more to be commended than the development of flexible budgets and detailed variance analysis.

Conclusion

Some of the comments above concerning capital budgeting apply similarly, if not always so critically, to annual cost and revenue budgeting, as discussed more generally in this chapter. The mechanics of preparing budgets and budget reports can be tedious, like the time managers may have to spend in committees planning or reviewing budgets. But budget mechanics are of secondary importance compared to two other aspects. First, in the budget-planning stage, are the alternative uses of resources fully explored and rigorously assessed with realistic estimates of efficiency, cost and related revenue? Second, is the organisational culture and climate and management leadership properly developed to make use of budget systems and information as a powerful tool of management planning, coordination and control?

For effective budgeting, managers must be able to see their budgets, not as some sort of independent fiefdom, but, rather, as a piece in the jigsaw of the organisation as a whole. Debate about issues raised by budget planning and control should be as open and wide as possible, and this may be assisted if top management makes it clear that rigidly following budgets and achieving them is not directly linked to pay and promotion. There must be discipline in budgeting, but, beyond that, it should be primarily a system to aid managerial learning, choosing and improvement.

Part of this process should be recognition of the fact that management has a need for control information to help evaluate performance against budgets, standards and targets. A common accounting technique for the provision of such information is that of standard costing. When combined with flexible budgeting, a standard costing approach enables the identification of planning variances (focusing on the impact of a differing actual level of activity from that originally budgeted for) and operational variances (focusing on the extent to which actual operational performance met the standards – targets – underpinning the budgetary process). However, this analysis has a strong financial orientation. As such, it may well require supplementation by (integration with) non-financial performance measures if effective control is to be achieved.

Chapter overview

Budgets are plans, usually expressed in money terms. Once agreed, they are also used for coordination and control. Budgets should mirror the structure of the organisation and provide accountability covering all of its resources and activities. There are different kinds of budgets and budget centres, for investment, profit, sales or revenue, and costs and expenses. Most budgets are for costs, generally derived from the historical cost accrual accounting system, but sometimes (especially in the public sector) they are based on cash expenditure. Performance against budgets should be monitored at least monthly, with progress reports supplied promptly and significant variances checked out for any corrective action which may be needed. Many budgets are fixed, but flexible budgeting is better when output or sales fluctuate with market demand.

Budgets can be seen as a straightjacket on managers, but the ideal is for them to be seen as a self-help information system for managers' use to improve the management of their own responsibilities and their coordination with other parts of the organisation. In reality, however, there are important behavioural problems associated with budgeting, notably the temptation to build in 'budgetary slack' and the failure to undertake adequate budgetary planning, which leads to managers blaming poor performance on failings or unfairness in the budgets. Nevertheless, budgeting is necessary and relevant in all types of organisation – industrial, retail and service – and it is especially prominent for activities (such as many public services) where total expenditure is strictly limited.

An important element of the budgetary process is the contribution that it can make to management control. This contribution was explicated in the parts of the chapter dealing with control systems in general and the nature of the standard costing approach in particular. It was later recognised that, in many instances, most notable in the public sector, budgetary information needs to be supplemented by the development of performance indicators, which should assist management in monitoring and reporting on the efficiency and effectiveness of programmes.

Further reading

For classical insights into the behavioural and organisational contexts and problems of budgeting, see Argyris (1964) and Hofstede (1968). For greater detail on the structure of budgets and budget reports, see Arnold and Turley (1996: chs 15, 16) or Drury (2004: chs 15 to 19). For a comprehensive view of budgeting and control in all their contexts, see Emmanuel *et al.* (1995). Drury (2004) also provides ample illustrations of applied approaches to standard costing and variance analysis. Readers might also refer to relevant journals, including: *Journal of Business Finance and Accounting, Accounting and Business Research,* and *Accounting, Organisations and Society.*

Questions and exercises

Guide notes can be found at the back of the book for all questions marked with an asterisk*.

1*   Metalfab Ltd has adopted a budgetary system in which budget centres are charged only with direct or indirect costs which their budget holders can control or strongly influence. The information below is for use in a flexible budget for the supervisor of Metalfab machine shop.

   (i)   Work is machine paced and capacity is limited by the available machine time. There are 12 machines, each needing one operator. The standard working week is 40 hours, with a maximum of 14 hours of overtime available. The factory works a 48-week year and budgets are based on four-week periods of 'months'. Public holidays are ignored.

   (ii)   There are 12 operators, plus the supervisor. Eight operators and the supervisor work full time, while four operators are 'casual' and work only as required. All operators cost £7 per hour, inclusive of national insurance and other payroll-linked expenses, or £9 on overtime. The supervisor costs £10 per hour, or £12 on overtime.

   (iii)   Normal working is 85% productive time and 15% for set-ups, maintenance and stopped time. Non-productive labour time is recorded and charged to budget as a separate cost category and is monitored for control. The same hourly charge rates are used for both productive and non-productive time.

   (iv)   Heating and lighting averages £80 per week over the year.

   (v)   Power costs £0.50 per productive machine hour.

   (vi)   Breakdown and repair costs average £0.60 per productive machine hour.

   (vii)   Lubricants and sundries cost £0.40 per productive machine hour.

   (viii)   Depreciation charges are £35 000 for the year.

   (ix)   Materials wastage and spoilage varies, but experience suggests the equivalent of £2 per productive machine hour as a realistic target. All wastage and spoilage are costed and charged against budget.

   (x)   Materials costs (other than wastage and spoilage) are not charged to the machine-shop budget. Instead, these are charged to the budget of the head of purchasing and production scheduling on the grounds that this is where control and responsibility resides. In addition, materials costs, machine shop and other service department costs are all charged to individual job sheets, whose total for open jobs is summarised in the work in progress control account.

(xi) The machine-shop budget uses productive machine hours as its activity unit for flexing the budget. The activity range to be considered is that between 1000 and 2000 productive machine hours per four-week budget period.

Required:

(a) Make the necessary calculations and draft a four-week flexible budget for the Metalfab machine shop, spanning the activity range given above.

(b) Comment on any shortages or weaknesses in the available information, and/or comment on any further improvements you might envisage for the effective budget management and control of the machine shop.

2* As a consultant you have been assigned to a budget project at Tweedshire Council (TC), which is too short-staffed to cover the introduction of improved budgets in all council services. Your project includes preparing a new budget for the next year for Tweedshire Libraries (TL). TL has had a single, cash-limited, departmental budget. Nine months into the current year it is forecast that the year's budget will probably just be met, albeit only by postponing some orders for books, equipment and maintenance. The budgeted costs for the year were as follows:

	£
Staff costs (full and part time and casual)	250 000
Purchases of books and periodicals, new bindings, etc.	125 000
Purchases of CDs, records, tapes, software, etc.	60 000
Furnishings, fittings and equipment (FEE) including computers	70 000
Rent charge by TC for premises used	50 000
Maintenance of premises and of FEE (and energy costs)	40 000

The control budget is on a cash basis. Pending actual transfer to accrual accounting, depreciation (covering all assets other than premises) is shown as a footnote to the budget. For the current year, depreciation was set at 20%, on estimated year-end historical-cost asset values of £600 000.

The improved budget for next year is to reflect new operational objectives assigned to TL management. Books and periodicals are to operate as a cost centre, fully funded (NB fines and charges, being negligible, can be ignored). Services relating to CDs, records, tapes, software and public use of computers, etc. are to operate as a contribution centre (and, at the least, to break even, partly so as not to provide unfair competition to local private businesses). Target revenue for these services next year is to be set at 10% above budget costs (with any profit contribution to be divided equally between TC general funds and TL funds for carry-forward for extra spending in the following year).

Next year's total budget will be the same as for the current year, except for uplift of 3% in line with the general inflation forecast. However, average hourly pay is expected to increase by 5%, and to cover for this staff hours will be cut by 1%, and purchases of books and periodicals will be cut by 2%. All other cost categories are expected to rise in line with general inflation. The proportions of budget headings chargeable to the new contribution centre are forecast to be as follows:

Staff	40%
FEE spending	60%
Rent and maintenance (proportional to space)	30%

Required:
You are required to draft a budget for TL for next year. The budget statements should be constructed with user-friendly captions, and should reflect controllability and operational objectives.

3* Eastbrook Ltd manufactures a revolutionary insulating material which is marketed under the brand name Cosiwrap for £5.40 per roll. Originally, the company had planned to manufacture 100 000 rolls per month on the basis of a standard marginal unit cost, computed as follows:

	£
Material A (2 kg @ 40p)	0.80
Material B (2 kg @ 50p)	1.00
Material C (4 kg @ 30p)	1.20
	3 00
Labour (15 minutes)	0.75
Variable expenses	0.25
	4.00

Fixed expenses were estimated at £80 000 per month.

Unfortunately for Eastbrook, there has been severe market competition for insulating material and the actual results for the last month were:

Production and sales (rolls)	80 000
Sales	£392 000
Material A (128 000 kg)	57 600
Material B (256 000 kg)	115 200
Material C (256 000 kg)	76 800
Labour (16 000 hours)	54 400
Variable expenses	18 400
Fixed expenses	82 000
	404 000
Loss	12 400

Required:
Although the managing director is aware that his product has many competitors and that there have been problems with the supply of materials, he is amazed by the company's poor performance. Thus, he has asked you to prepare a short report.
(a) that reconciles actual and planned performance by analysing all important variables;
(b) that provides a commentary on the results for the month.

4 Wollongong Equipment Ltd manufactures specialist electrical equipment. It employs a standard costing system using a contribution approach and operates a just-in-time management system such that it holds no stocks of raw materials, work in progress, or finished goods. The standard costing information for one of its products is as shown below:

Unit selling price	$90.00
Direct materials:	
Iron (5 sheets @ $2.00)	10.00
Copper (3 reels at $3.00)	9.00
Direct labour (4 hours at $7.00 per hour)	28.00
Variable overheads (at $3.00 per labour hour)	12.00
	$59.00
Unit contribution	$31.00

The normal and expected monthly capacity is 4000 direct labour hours per month. Variable overheads are expected to vary with the number of direct labour hours actually used.

During May 2007, only 800 units of product were produced and sold (as opposed to the 1000 expected). This shortfall was the result of a labour dispute which occurred during contract negotiations with the workforce. Once this dispute was settled, overtime was worked in an attempt to catch up to expected production levels.

The company's accounting records show the following information in relation to the month:

Sales:	800 units @ $90.00
Iron purchases:	3900 sheets @ $2.00
Copper purchases:	2600 reels @ $3.10
Direct labour:	
Regular time	2000 hours @ $7.00
Overtime	1400 hours @ $7.20
Variable overhead expenditure:	$10 000

Required:
Prepare a report for the management of the company which:

(a) Identifies the budgeted contribution for the month

(b) Identifies the actual contribution for the month

(c) Reconciles (a) and (b) above, identifying any differences arising from:
  (i) Planning variances
  (ii) Operating variances

(d) Comments on the managerial accountability for these variances

5 Chememulsions Ltd makes three domestic cleaning products for distribution through supermarkets and shops. The following data have been prepared in connection with the marketing director's annual presentation of the advertising and promotion budget requests. 'Profits' and 'losses' are shown below at values before charging expenditure on advertising and promotion (A&P); all figures are in thousands of dollars.

A&P is a fixed budget which must be renegotiated annually and needs justification by evidence of results achieved.

| | | SKWEEZ Detergent | | | PHOAMY Detergent | | | SACHET Car Wash | |
Date	Sales	Profit	A&P	Sales	Profit	A&P	Sales	Profit	A&P
2001	500	100	20	500	50	40	–	–	–
2002	450	80	20	560	68	50	–	–	–
2003	420	68	20	600	80	56	–	–	–
2004	400	80	20	700	110	60	40	(12)	10
2005	410	84	25	750	125	70	100	0	12
2006	320	48	25	710	113	75	150	10	15
Budget									
2007	310	50	30	800	140	71	250	30	20

Required:
Evaluate the given data, state any conclusions and/or implications that may derive from your analysis, and state what further data the budget controller should request or what enquiries he/she should make. Assume that sales prices per unit and total fixed costs have not changed over the time-span under review.

6   In 2007 the St Margaret's Hospital Trust started promoting its new Sports Injuries Clinic. The clinic specialises in the treatment of athletic injuries. The budgeted and actual financial data relating to the three months ending December 2007 are as follows:

	Budget		Actual	
	£	£	£	£
Fee income		75 000		82 500
Physiotherapists' salaries	25 000		27 500	
Bought-in services from other departments	12 500		14 950	
Clinical facilities	28 750	66 250	30 000	72 450
Surplus		£8 750		£10 050

The following additional information is available:

(i)   The actual unit fee of £75 was the same as that budgeted.

(ii) X-rays and other bought-in services are paid for on a unit-cost basis. Overall, the unit manager, Mrs T, states that usage of these services was 15% higher than budgeted and that the unit price was, on average, 4% higher than budgeted.

(iii) Sessional physiotherapists' time was at the volume budgeted. However, the budget had only allowed for a 5% pay rise from 1 October, whereas the actual pay rise was 10%, compared with a national average of 8%.

(iv) Clinic facilities represent allocated costs incurred by the clinic. These include a secretary/receptionist and a full-time staff nurse. It was expected that this charge would also be sufficient to cover other establishment costs.

Required:

Prepare a short report for the finance officer in a form that most clearly sets out an analysis of variances between budgeted and actual results. In this report also include recommendations on how this information might more usefully be presented in the future.

7* Briefly list and explain the features of an effective system of budgetary performance and reporting and control.

8* 'The weakest link in any system of budgetary planning and control is human behaviour'. Defend or refute this statement with reasoned argument.

9* Both the top-down and bottom-up approaches to budgetary planning have good arguments in their favour. What may these arguments be, and how should the choice of approach be decided?

10 Outline what you consider to be the main features of an accounting control system.

11 Discuss the advantages of flexible budgeting when it comes to preparing performance reports.

12 'Because of its emphasis on comparison between the actual results and the original plans, the traditional standard costing system does not yield useful information for decision-making'. Discuss.

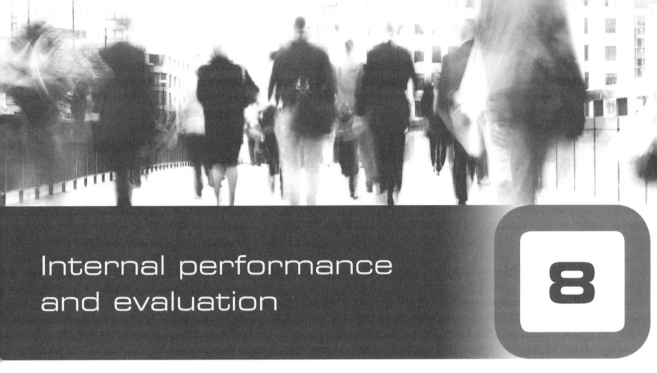

Internal performance and evaluation

8

Chapter preview

This focus of this chapter is responsibility accounting, with particular reference to divisionalised organisations. Within such organisations the management control process is important in ensuring that overall goal congruence is achieved, while at the same time promoting and maintaining divisional autonomy. All too often organisations institute performance criteria for managers which evaluate short-term performance at the expense of longer-term objectives.

We will examine the arguments for and against a divisionalised organisational structure. Depending on the type of divisional structure adopted, particular performance measures are either more or less appropriate. The responsibility accounting system must parallel the structure of the organisation. This structure depends on the nature of the organisation's operations and on the attitudes and management styles of its senior management. The reporting segments of this type of responsibility accounting system may be cost centres, profit centres (either natural or artificial) or investment centres.

We will examine each of these segments and analyse what may be appropriate performance measures. We will also discuss issues relating to internal transfer prices – the selling prices established for trading between artificial profit centres – as problems may arise if the bases on which these prices are determined either motivate or demotivate the managers concerned.

Divisionalisation

If managers are to be held accountable for their performance they must have clearly defined areas of responsibility – activities over which they can exercise control. Such defined areas of responsibility are to be found in any decentralised organisation. At its simplest this can be a functional department or cost centre where financial accountability is achieved by keeping expenditure within agreed budget limits. In highly decentralised organisations operational units may well be termed **divisions**. Within a divisionalised organisation there is usually an additional element to a manager's financial accountability, i.e. the concept of delegated profit responsibility. As Solomons (1983: 3) states:

> A division has been defined as a company unit headed by a person fully responsible for the profitability of its operations, including planning, production, financial and accounting activities, and which usually, although not always, has its own sales force. The division may be a unit of the parent company or it may be a wholly or partially owned subsidiary.

Divisional management responsibility covers not only how operations should be carried out but also, within prescribed limits, what those operations should be. This discretion will cover such areas as what products or services to sell and at what price; what manufacturing operations are to be performed within the division and what might be bought in from outside (including other companies/divisions within the group); and sales and research strategy. Divisions are often termed, for accounting control purposes, either as profit or investment centres.

A **profit centre** can be either natural or artificial. A natural profit centre operates in external markets, whereas an artificial profit centre sells its output to other divisions within the organisation. It is also possible to have divisions that sell both externally and internally. The notion of artificial profit centres is becoming more popular, not just in industry, but also in the public sector. A local authority direct labour organisation is an example of an artificial profit centre (see Glynn 1993). Internal selling prices are usually termed **transfer prices**; these are discussed later in this chapter.

An **investment centre** is a division in which the divisional management controls not only revenues and costs but also investment. Rather than simply evaluating managers in terms of profit, it is more usual to evaluate the performance of investment centres in terms of a return on investment (ROI).

For profit centres to operate fully in the spirit set out by Solomons (above) it is preferable that divisional managers should have full (delegated) authority and control over the resources and decisions involved in divisional management. At the least, they should have primary influence (in the absence of ultimate control responsibility) over these resources and decisions. This is because of the guiding principle, based on our understanding of human behaviour, that managers can be held accountable effectively only for what they can realistically control. Where divisional managers are obliged to 'sell' goods to other divisions within the company at prices and volumes which they do not decide, or to use goods and services from other parts of the company at costs or input prices which they do not decide (or at least very strongly influence), the divisional (financial) autonomy is indeed artificial, and it may be preferable to plan, budget and assess performance on the basis of **contribution centres** rather than profit centres. That is, contribution (as defined in earlier chapters) should be used to strike the bottom line on which divisional (managerial) performance is assessed. Below this line, head office can add in the further costs and revenues outside the control and accountability of divisional managers in order to derive a final net profit figure. This final net profit then represents the 'economic performance' of the division.

Economic performance is crucial to group-management strategic decisions affecting divisions, especially decisions on new investment, sale of the division or closure. Here, final net profit usually needs to be related to capital investment, in order for the profit return to be meaningfully compared with cost of capital, competitors and the opportunity costs of alternative investments. However, while it is important to calculate and report the return on investment centrally, it should not be used for managerial-performance control unless divisional managers have primary influence, even if not full control, over the level of divisional investment and its composition. As Dominiak and Louderback (1988: 360) state:

> The choice of a type of responsibility centre for a particular activity (or group of activities) is unique to each firm. Such factors as size, industry, operating characteristics, and managerial philosophy influence organisational structure … An important characteristic of good responsibility reporting is that its reports include only controllable costs. Whether or not a particular cost is controllable – and hence includable in the report to a particular manager – depends on the level of that manager in the hierarchy.

Having outlined what is meant by the term division, we come to the question of what advantages there are for an organisation that has a divisionalised structure. The answer is that seven key advantages are potentially to be obtained:

1 Giving divisional managers autonomy with accountability should lead to them being better motivated. Research in the behavioural sciences suggests that individuals who are involved in the entire production process take more interest in their work and perform better than those who merely perform the same operation repeatedly. Similarly, a manager who is responsible for most operational aspects of a division may feel more in control of his/her performance than if he/she were responsible for only one core activity.

2 Divisionalisation facilitates diversification. Many organizations operate in a number of markets or technologies and it is not possible for the central corporate management team to have detailed knowledge about the operational aspects of each division. For example, a pharmaceutical company could have a number of divisions, dealing with medicines, agricultural pesticides and so on. Each aspect of the organisation, represented by its operational divisions, has to develop products for what are essentially very different markets, each with their own particular business risks.

3 Divisionalisation can reduce the need for complicated internal communications between the central corporate management team and the divisional managers. This, in turn, can lead to an improvement in the time taken over decisions and prevent a communications overload.

4 Because divisional managers have an intimate knowledge of their division they are more likely to understand and be able to resolve issues affecting their division.

5 Central corporate management will have more time to concentrate on overall corporate strategy and problem divisions, and management-by-exception principles can be applied.

6 Performance measures can be produced which should lead to goal congruence between individual divisional managers and the organisation as a whole.

7 Divisionalisation provides a training environment which enables future senior managers to 'cut their teeth' on smaller identifiable business units.

Decentralisation can also have its problems. The major and most worrying factor is that managers who operate in near autonomy may make decisions which harm the organisation as a whole. The challenge for central corporate management is to achieve overall goal congruence, while at the same time promoting and maintaining divisional autonomy. There are a number of prerequisites for successful divisionalisation, and if these are not present problems will inevitably occur. They are:

1 Successful operating divisions need a sufficiently independent existence to make delegated profit responsibility a reality. Not all organisations can achieve this. Independence requires some clear organisational separateness of markets, of technology and/or of geographical location, as well as managerial structures and financial information systems supporting autonomy.

2 While key resources and decision areas must be delegated in order to achieve effective divisional performance, some common services may need to be centralised for economies of scale essential to overall optimum profitability. However, all such core common services must be responsive to divisional needs, and they must be 'charged for' at costs or internal prices which optimise corporate performance (see later section on transfer prices).

3 There should be an appropriate managerial-performance assessment and reward system, reflecting contributions to corporate as well as divisional profitability, and to other strategic objectives and performance criteria.

4 Divisional managers should be closely involved with the development of a sound participative budgetary system, and of internal relationships, information exchanges and transfer prices conducive to goal congruence.

5 There should be a recognised and supportive corporate culture which helps to foster unity within diversity.

6 No division should be able to increase its profits (or its return on capital) at the expense of reducing overall corporate profitability. This relates both to the management of internal service and trading relationships, and to the informational and motivational signals provided by the internal financial reporting (and budgeting) systems used to inform the allocation of resources between divisions and the assessment of divisional performance in annual reports (and in any more frequent interim progress reports from divisional to central management).

Internal financial reporting for divisionalised organisations

By convention, divisional managers tend to have their performance evaluated by measures that closely correspond to the organisation's overall financial reporting structure. The reasons for this are varied and include the following:

1 **Pressure on management:** professional investors tend to look for short-term financial profit performance, as this directly influences share market prices.

Directors need to fulfil their accounting responsibilities under the Companies Acts, which are becoming increasingly onerous. Recall that many divisions may be corporate entities in their own right. Additionally, there is a need to produce regular periodic reports on accounting profits. For example, interim reports for Stock Exchange purposes, profit and cash flow forecasts for bankers and others, briefings for brokers, analysts, etc.

2 **Background of managers:** senior managers are increasingly aware of the need to use and relate to financial performance measures that are 'transferable' and understood by potential new employers. Rightly or wrongly, accounting profit is regarded as a universally transferable comparator of performance. It should also be remembered that many bonus schemes are also linked to accounting profit.

3 **Pressure from auditors:** auditors are always keen to see that financial accounts should be integrated with, or at least agree with, the management accounts. Aligned with this is the auditors' concern that a key aspect of internal control is that financial accounts should be positively traceable back to the accounting database.

Return on investment

By far the most common measure used to evaluate divisional managers is the return on investment (ROI). This measure closely approximates to the return on capital employed (ROCE), discussed in Chapter 15. ROI is the ratio of some measure of profit to some corresponding measure of divisional investment capital. Many UK companies use the following definition:

$$\text{ROI} = \frac{\text{Net profit}}{\text{Investment in net assets}} \times 100 \qquad \textbf{(8.1)}$$

This measure has the distinct advantage of assessing profit, not in isolation, but relative to a division's capital base. ROI therefore makes it possible to compare the efficiency of different-sized divisions by relating output (income/profit) to input (the capital investment base). As with the ROCE definition discussed in Chapter 15, the ROI measure can be restated as:

$$\text{ROI} = \frac{\text{Net profit}}{\text{Sales}} \times \frac{\text{Sales}}{\text{Investment in net assets}} \times 100 \qquad \textbf{(8.2)}$$

This subdivision helps to focus management's attention on the components of ROI. The first element of this revised expression focuses on the return-on-sales ratio; the second, on capital turnover. From this subdivision it is clear that an increase in sales, by itself, will not increase ROI because sales cancel out. But a decrease in investment, with other factors staying constant, will increase ROI. There is also scope for a manager to consider the impact on ROI of a decision that is expected to change two factors. For example, suppose that return on sales is currently 16% and that investment turnover is two times; ROI is therefore 32%

(16% × 2). What is the likely impact on ROI if the manager considers changing the product mix to items with lower sales margins, say an average of 12%, which should increase capital turnover to three times? The outcome is that the ROI would rise to 36% (12% × 3).

The values of the components of ROI can often provide clues as to the kinds of strategies used by group management when they evaluate its different divisions or subsidiaries. Consider a retail company which operates both departmental and discount stores. Both kinds of store might earn the same ROI, but by adopting different strategies. Let us assume that the following information relates to two of the group's stores:

	The Debonair departmental store	*The Thrifty discount store*
Sales	£1 000 000	£1 200 000
Divisional profit	£ 120 000	£ 96 000
Divisional investment	£ 500 000	£ 400 000

The two ROI computations are:

$$\text{Debonair} = \frac{£120\,000}{£1\,000\,000} \times \frac{£1\,000\,000}{£500\,000} = 24\%$$

$$\text{Thrifty} = \frac{£96\,000}{£1\,200\,000} \times \frac{£1\,200\,000}{£400\,000} = 24\%$$

As can be seen, the Thrifty discount store, while producing a lower return on sales, obtains a higher sales volume for each pound invested.

Given that ROI is a ratio, it is important to ensure that the basis used for calculating the investment in net assets is compatible with the measure used for profit. In particular, if a 'controllable' measure is used for calculating profit, then a 'controllable' measure should be used for the measurement of net assets. Three alternative measures of net assets are net book value, gross book value and current value. Net book value creates a problem because the impact of depreciation is such that, for a given set of physical assets, a constant level of profit will produce, year by year, an increasing ROI. In difficult trading times divisional managers might be persuaded to keep assets beyond their useful economic life. A secondary problem is that assets are stated at historic values which do not measure their true opportunity value.

Gross book value removes the problem of depreciation but still relies on historical cost as a measure. Current value would produce a much more meaningful valuation of assets, if reliable figures could be obtained. However, as discussed in Chapter 13, there are a number of problems associated with the use of current values for accounting purposes. Even if current values were used for measuring a division's asset base we would still have the problem of historic-cost profit. Ideally we would want to have both profit and asset base stated in current terms. However, given the rather sorry history of current-cost (value) accounting in the UK, this is likely to remain a pipe-dream.

There are two principal difficulties relating to divisional profit measures for ROI. The first difficulty relates to the situation of measuring revenues and costs when different divisions trade with each other. The (transfer) price at which this trade is carried out can have a significant impact on the profit of the divisions involved. As discussed in the next section, it is important to develop appropriate mechanisms for the setting and agreement of transfer prices. If this is not done and the (transfer) price is 'wrong', then:

- if volumes are large, relatively small changes in the transfer price can lead to big differences in the profits of the trading divisions;
- there can be significant impacts on the motivation of divisional managers, leading to a loss of some of the advantages of divisionalisation;
- the financial performance measures (e.g. ROI) may lead senior managers into thinking that divisions are more or less profitable than is really the case.

The second difficulty relates to the identification of the true costs of running a division. Two issues are particularly relevant:

1 To what extent should a division be charged with a share of expenses (most commonly head office/group expenses) the benefits of which are enjoyed by all parts of the company?
2 There is a cost of capital associated with the net assets employed by the division. Should a financial charge be made for this?

Most divisional managers rapidly become aware of the potential flaws associated with the use of ROI to assess their performance. In order to prevent them exploiting the flexibility afforded by historic cost accounting conventions, e.g. by exercising 'accounting judgement' with respect to items such as provisions for doubtful debts and depreciation rates, group management needs to lay down explicit accounting rules and regulations. Nevertheless, the 'artful' divisional manager might seek to reduce discretionary expenditure, such as that on training and research and development. This is short-sighted and group management might seek to counter this by also instituting the use of non-financial (supplementary) performance measures; for example, with respect to training, an expectation that particular grades of staff should have a prescribed number of days' training each year. Divisional managers night also seek to adjust the asset base of their division by techniques of sale and lease-back and off-balance sheet finance. Here again, group management may wish to exercise some general control on the degree of discretion afforded to divisional managers.

Despite the difficulties associated with using the historical-cost convention to measure ROI, we can summarise four main advantages of using ROI as a performance measure:

1 It is a relative measure which reflects both the profit generated by the division and the resources (net assets) employed to generate those profits.
2 It can be subdivided into a hierarchy of other measures and ratios which can be used to appraise divisional performance at a more detailed level if necessary.
3 It mirrors a commonly used measure of overall corporate performance – ROCE – and as such can help develop goal congruence.
4 It uses data compatible with those contained in the financial accounting data base and the external financial reports which a company needs to use.

Residual income

A second commonly used measure of divisional performance is residual income (RI). It is a measure of the amount of income that a division produces in excess of the minimum desired (sometimes called target) rate of return. This desired target rate of return is generally determined by group management, since such management has overall responsibility for the long-term financing strategy of the group. The target set is usually equal to or greater than the organisation's cost of capital. In general, RI is computed as follows:

$$\text{RI} = \text{Income} - (\text{Investment} \times \text{Target ROI}) \tag{8.3}$$

The argument for using RI as a measure of divisional performance is that it measures the amount of profit that the division provides to the enterprise over and above the profit to be expected (the minimum required) for the amount invested. RI has an important advantage over ROI as a measure of divisional performance. It allows for the fact that a division with a higher ROI may be less valuable to the organisation as a whole than one with a lower ROI. Consider the following situation. Division A produces £400 000 profit on an investment of £2 000 000, an ROI of 20%. Division B earns a profit of £3 000 000 on an investment base of £20 000 000; ROI is 15%. The contributions of each division to the organisation as a whole will appear quite different, depending on the desired ROI for the organisation as a whole. Let us consider two possible scenarios, ROI of 10% and ROI of 18%. The RIs for each division are calculated as follows:

	Scenario I Required ROI 10%		Scenario 2 Required ROI 18%	
	A	B	A	B
Investment base	£2 000 000	£20 000 000	£2 000 000	£20 000 000
Divisional profit	£400 000	£3 000 000	£400 000	£3 000 000
Desired minimum return (investment × minimum required return)	£200 000	£2 000 000	£360 000	£3 600 000
Residual income	£200 000	£1 000 000	£40 000	(£600 000)

As can be seen, if the minimum desired ROI is 10%, division B makes a greater contribution to the organisation than does division A, despite the fact that division B's ROI is lower. Division B is therefore the more valuable to the firm. However, if the minimum desired ROI is 18% this situation is dramatically reversed and division A is much more valuable to the organisation. As Dominiak and Louderback (1988: 410) state:

> Generally speaking, using RI as the criterion for evaluating divisional performance, the division rated highest is the one with the greatest positive difference between profit and the minimum desired return. In some ways it is similar to the use of net present values (NPVs) as the criterion for evaluating capital expenditure. Under that criterion, the most desirable (valuable) capital project is the one with the highest net present value after discounting future returns at the cost of capital.

The above quotation links the RI approach both to evaluating current divisional performance and to making capital-expenditure decisions. Chapter 9 provides a fuller description of the analysis required for investment decision. The data in the above example of scenarios 1 and 2 was given in the context of past performance. If the RI is to be used to assess divisional economic performance data should be inclusive of all costs, and similarly with managerial performance (provided that all the costs included in arriving at divisional profit were controllable, or at least could be strongly influenced, by the divisional management). The same numbers could have been cited in a different context, future investment selection, where the 'investment base' represents forecast future capital outlays proposed, and the 'divisional profit' is the forecast profit from such new investment. The same RI figures would have been derived in this alternative context showing to us the changing attractiveness of new investment in the two divisions as the test rate of desired minimum return is altered. If divisions A and B have an absolute ability to obtain new capital from the centre each division will seek to invest up to the level of whatever target rate of RI (or of ROI) has been set for it. However, in the more usual situation of capital rationing at some stage affecting the corporate entity as a whole it is likely that an absolute right or ability to access new long-term capital cannot be granted to divisions. In this event corporate management must take responsibility for allocating capital, in order to optimise corporate profit. In severe cases of capital rationing it may be a misleading fiction to label divisions 'investment centres', and it may be fairer and more realistic to treat them as just profit centres (for assessing managerial performance, as distinct from economic performance).

Where divisions realistically can be managed as investment centres, and with largely delegated decision-making on investments, the RI approach will give decision signals consistent with corporate objectives, at least so long as:

1 Net cash flows are constant year on year (where they are not the NPV test must always be used).

2 The minimum desired (or target) rate of return has been set at the optimal rate.

The optimal target rate of return can be described (but not always easily measured) as the opportunity rate of return on new capital for the best alternative investment allowing realistically for comparative risk. However, it has often been suggested that British management, suffering repeatedly form stop-go economics, volatile interest and exchange rates, etc., has become excessively risk averse, leading it too often to set unrealistically high target rates of return for investment. To illustrate, our example above was designed to show how the higher 18% target rate dramatically alters the apparent performance of the two divisions. But the 18% rate should not be used simply because it appears to offer a desirable 'motivational' target. It should be used only if it is the company's realistic risk-weighted opportunity return or its realistic marginal cost of capital (which should, in itself, include allowance for average corporate risk).

It has been suggested that the majority of divisionalised companies prefer to use ROI, rather than RI, as their primary indicator of divisional performance. This is understandable to the extent that managers think of ROI as the normal basis for assessing performance, especially as they wish to compare their performance against other (independent) businesses. Although the foregoing discussion suggests that the use of ROI is theoretically undesirable, it can be argued that in the common situation where divisions do not control their capital (or at least decisions on increments of capital) ROI leads to the same correct decision-signals as RI: this is because if the ROI is maximised on a given/fixed amount of capital the absolute return will itself also be maximised. However, even where ROI may be reliable for assessing the performance of divisional management operating *de facto* as a profit centre, central management may still need to look at RI for guidance on investment (or disinvestment) decisions.

It may be human nature to focus on a single performance variable – be this ROI, RI or any other – but also it may be wiser to draw attention to a wider range of performance measures. These involve other financial indicators, including the financial ratios discussed in Chapter 15. They can include additionally a wide range of quantified indicators relating to the use of inputs or to achieved physical outputs. The public sector has pioneered a diversity of performance measures; the NHS, for example, has developed over 450 measures. Such a large number of measures may be excessive for strategic overview, but even in private businesses divisional reporting may usefully include additional selected measurements considered to be significant indicators of organisational health or performance. These might include some of the following:

- market share
- sales turnover per employee
- profit per employee
- labour turnover rates
- average labour remuneration
- expenditure on staff training, and on research and development
- number of customer complaints received.

Because calculating RI involves the same factors as those used in ROI above, similar questions arise about what elements and bases should or should not be included in computations, especially as regards asset valuation, depreciation and capital charges, and fair and relevant transfer prices and central services costs.

Transfer prices

As work progresses through an integrated organisation, the costs of the work flow in parallel, transferring from cost centre to cost centre. These costs could be called 'transfer costs'. But when the flow of work is between profit centres rather than mere cost centres and these profit centres are under more or less autonomous management, often organised as corporate divisions, the transfer of costs is termed 'transfer prices' to reflect that some form of internal market exists within the overall enterprise. Moreover, these transfer prices in internal markets need not be the same amounts as simple historical cost transfers. In general they should normally be higher than that because otherwise the supplying division receives no revenue above cost to contribute to its own profits and viability, and thus no incentive to cooperate with the receiving division. On the other hand, if the receiving division is overcharged for internal supply it may be unable to compete in its end-product market, and the total corporate sales and profits will be reduced. The problem is to find a basis of transfer pricing which:

- optimises resource allocation and use for the total enterprise; and
- does not undermine the autonomy of individual divisions nor result in an unfair or demotivating attribution of profits between them.

In the extreme case, all divisions are operationally self-contained and also can sell all their output to external customers at a prevailing market price. In this case inter-divisional transfer pricing need not be a big issue. If for any reason any two of such divisions wished to trade with each other the transfer price should be at the external market price – otherwise, total earnings of the overall corporate enterprise would be reduced. Even in this case, however, there may be central or common services shared by the operating divisions and charged for by transfer pricing (see below).

In the more general case, there is a degree of interdependence and internal trading between divisions. For example, one division may make castings and both sell its output into external markets and supply it internally to another division of the company which uses the castings as a component in an end product. If the castings sold externally and internally are of similar specification, and if the external market is reasonably perfect, once again the external market price will be the optimal transfer price internally. Reasonably perfect markets require a number of competitors, active competition (i.e. not just a series of contractual, tied relationships at *ad hoc* bargained prices) and reasonably 'perfect information' (i.e. reliable information on prevailing market conditions). Frequently these conditions cannot be met, there is no stable, unequivocal 'market price', and so companies must consider alternative bases for transfer prices.

A further widely encountered case is where a large company is organised into divisions by function, so that there are one or more product divisions and one or more marketing/sales divisions. Here product divisions may sell exclusively to the internal marketing divisions, or at least sell mainly internally, simply 'flogging off' any periodic surplus capacity at the best bargaining price available. This periodic bargaining price will often have been struck on the basis of a short-term balance between demand and supply, and it may not itself be a realistic price to use in ongoing transfer pricing. Alternative information on a genuine market price may often be unavailable, so again one may need to turn to other methods to determine internal transfer prices between the divisions. Moreover, one may ask whether or not there is any real logic, or benefit, in having a divisional structure where some of the divisions are so internally dependent and inevitably are only artificial creations, albeit called 'autonomous profit centres'. The answer here appears to be that many top managements (and management consultants) feel that even artificial profit centres/divisions help to generate greater managerial motivation, to attract or hold better calibre managers, and to encourage the constant search for efficiency, innovation, sales growth and diversification. The point is that the effect of any improvement or problems will show up more dramatically, and with more motivational impact, in profit-and-loss figures than when buried in aggregates or traditional cost or revenue information.

Economic theory teaches us that profit is maximised when volume reaches the point where (rising) marginal cost equals (falling) marginal revenue. Thus marginal cost is the key internal signal for corporate profit maximisation, and this is (theoretically) true whether the corporate business is integrated or divisionalised. It therefore follows that, ideally, each end-product division selling into external market should be able to obtain internal supplies of goods and services at their marginal cost to the corporate entity. However, economic marginal cost changes with each volume change, and the exact value of marginal cost is often unknown – and accounting variable cost may be only a rough approximation. Moreover, transferring goods or services only at variable cost leaves the supplying division with no revenue to set against its fixed costs or to contribute to a profit; this is demotivating and goes against the spirit of divisional profit centre accountability. Of course, where reasonably perfect external market prices exit for each division these can be used and will satisfy the theoretical requirement for optimisation, provided that savings of marketing and transport expense, etc. are deducted from the external price used by the supplying division as its transfer price to the receiving division. The theoretical and practical complexities of transfer pricing are perhaps best explained in the classical work of Solomons (1983).

Given that, frequently, some divisions do not have genuine external markets or valid external market prices, and also that true marginal cost is frequently unknown or could only be used in a way that would demotivate the supplying divisions, let us consider the other methods used for setting transfer prices:

1 **Cost-based prices**: many accountants seem to prefer to use full costs plus some small excess for profit contribution. For good discipline, budgeted or standard cost should be used in preference to actual outturn costs. However, full-cost-plus transfer pricing may not give the correct signals to the receiving division for its role in optimising corporate sales volume and profit. The alternative of variable cost-plus transfer pricing is probably seldom used, if only because it undermines the supplying division's profit centre status. Whatever cost-plus charging system is used, it runs the risk of including within its variable costs some element of central service costs and overheads which are actually a fixed cost in the overall context of the corporate group. Thus transferred variable costs could actually be significantly higher than the theoretical optimum marginal cost, resulting in sub-optimisation.

2 **Negotiated prices**: transfer prices can be negotiated between divisions to reach agreement or, failing agreement, they can be mediated by central management. There is a risk here of transfer prices being determined more by the bargaining positions and skills of the negotiators than by rational economic information. Negotiators may introduce into the negotiating process estimates of true market price, various measures of cost and threat of turning to external suppliers. Of course, external suppliers in an imperfect market may be offering reduced 'penetration prices' which could later be raised if the company scrapped its internal supply and became dependent on the external suppliers. Where sensible agreement cannot be reached, so that mediation becomes involved or a central decision has to be imposed, the managerial autonomy and sense of personal responsibility of divisional management are undermined.

3 **Two-part tariff prices**: this method charges receiving divisions with the budgeted or standard variable cost per unit of the intermediate good or service transferred, plus an annual 'block' charge (probably payable in monthly instalments) to cover approved fixed costs and a small margin for profit contribution. In effect, the block charge represents a form of contract whereby the receiving division undertakes responsibility for purchasing a given proportion of the supplying division's capacity in the year ahead. Central mediation will often be required. Supplying divisions will be free to seek external sales for surplus (i.e. uncontracted) capacity, but will be under moral pressure to supply additional units above contract levels if the receiving division encounters unexpectedly high (and profitable) sales opportunities. To discourage receiving divisions from the gamesmanship of understating future requirement (so as to minimise the

block charge), the contract may impose extra charges for volumes above contract. For this method to work well there needs to be thorough advance planning of sales and of production resources as part of an integrated corporate budget, but arguably this is beneficial on balance in spite of any interference with real or imagined divisional autonomy.

In conclusion, external market prices should be used if all divisions can sell all output in external markets. Aside from this rather limited case, and if viable profit centres and reasonable divisional autonomy are to be maintained, the two-part tariff could be the best method. But this involves extra effort and central mediation, so perhaps too often in the real world recourse is made to transfer pricing based on full-costs-plus, or on negotiated estimates of fair market prices, even when either of these methods may well lead to sub-optimal sales (and profit) performance for the divisions and for the corporate entity as a whole.

Before leaving this section, we should note one specialised situation where transfer pricing allegedly often departs from the above economic and operational criteria. This is in international trade, between divisions (typically organised locally as companies) supplying or receiving materials, components or finished products across national boundaries. Here, the overriding object may be to minimise total group taxation and to minimise the accumulation of profit-derived cash flows in countries with exchange controls preventing or delaying the outward transfer of profits or investment funds. Also, if transfer prices need in any way to come under regulation or audit for fairness in international trade, cost-based transfer prices will usually be the easiest to justify and document. This still begs the question of how far 'creative accounting' can alter systems of defining, measuring and charging cost within a plausible range of practices, yet still carry conviction of reasonableness as well as 'objectivity' in justifying sometimes much higher transfer prices than would be considered optimal between divisions operating within a single country.

Transfer pricing for services

Corporate central services are not usually organised as separate 'divisions' and they need not even be designated as profit centres. They rarely trade externally, so seldom have the direct comparator of trading successfully at the current external market price. Even so, especially if they are large, costly or can easily be compared to external market prices and profit, they may be designated as divisions to enhance management motivation. Whatever the organisational name, these services generate costs which convention argues should be recharged to user divisions receiving benefit. However, if user divisions have no control or influence over service efficiency and no authority to seek alternative external suppliers, there can be problems. Group management has an overall responsibility not to sanction transfer-pricing policies that provoke dysfunctional management behaviour by those operating at the divisional level. The case of Valleta Ltd illustrates this point.

Valleta Ltd has three operating divisions, X, Y and Z, and a transport division, T. Divisional managers are free to choose whether or not to use the company's own transport facilities, but T division has neither the marketing nor the administrative facilities to deal with customers outside the group. T division has entered into an annual rental agreement with a hire company, under which ten vans are supplied to the division at a fixed rent of £2750 per week. If more vans are required, these can be hired at £50 per day. Other costs are expected to be £50 per vehicle per day up to ten vans and £150 per vehicle thereafter, plus fixed costs of £4560 per week. Divisions X, Y and Z have budgeted weekly requirements for vans during the next three months as follows:

	Monday	Tuesday	Wednesday	Thursday	Friday	Saturday	Total
X	5	5	5	4	4	3	26
Y	4	4	4	4	4	4	24
Z	1	3	3	1	1	1	10
	10	12	12	9	9	8	60

Actual requirements are often greater or less than budget. Divisions are charged £200 per vehicle per day at the end of each month for the vehicles which are actually used. The management of Y division is considering whether to make an alternative arrangement outside the company, which would cost £3840 per week for a maximum of four vans per day, payable whether this number of vans was fully utilised or not. Should the management of Y be permitted to trade outside the company? What are the implications of the pricing policy adopted by T division? Clearly, a number of behavioural and economic consequences arise, depending on the strategies adopted by each of the divisional management teams.

The first thing we can do is to construct T division's weekly budget in order to understand its charging policy:

	£
Fixed rent for 10 vans	2 750
Other fixed cost	4 560
	7 310
Four extra vans (Tuesday and Wednesday)	200
Other variable costs	
56 vans per week at £50	2 800
4 vans per week at £150	600
	10 910
Charges to X, Y and Z (60 @ £200)	12 000
Profit	1 090

It seems obvious that T division is charging the other three divisions on the basis of cost plus 10%. Questions need to be asked about this policy. Is this cost-plus policy in fact group policy or a policy established by the management of T division? As it stands, Y division would gain if it has the ability to accept the outside contract. The current charge to Y division by T division is £4800 (24 @ £200). The cost of external supply is £3840, a saving to Y division of £960 per week. However, whilst this may be advantageous to Y division it is not sensible from the overall group company point of view. There is, in fact, a net cost to the group because only certain of the costs currently incurred by T division can be avoided. Recall that T division has total weekly fixed costs of £7310. The cost to the group as a whole of T division accepting the outside contract can be calculated as follows:

Savings by T division:	£
Extra vans on Tuesday and Wednesday no longer needed	200
Other variable costs saved	
4 vans at £150	600
20 vans at £50	1 000
	1 800
Cost of external supply	3 840
Net additional cost to the group	2 040

This illustration highlights a not untypical situation where a divisional manager feels driven to obtain a particular service or product externally. Three options seem to arise from this illustration:

1 Enquiry might establish that the prevailing market price for van use is well above the £3840 quoted to division Y by the outside supplier. This would suggest only a temporary cost saving to division Y, which might have to pay more later; yet meanwhile the company's own fleet would have been cut back, with likely morale problems and fixed costs to be divided among a smaller number of vans. Therefore Y could be instructed not to contract with the outside supplier, although this would interfere with divisional autonomy,

2 Alternatively, Y could be charged internally the same low price currently available from the external supplier, and T would then at least still receive some contribution above variable cost. However, this might create ill will with the other user divisions.

3 Division T could be closed down, with all vans hired externally in future, on the presumption that T is uncompetitive. But first, however, the external price of £3840 needs validating as a sustainable ongoing price. Also, the fixed cost of £4560 charged to T needs checking to discover how far these are controllable by T's manager and unavoidable to the group (e.g. allocation of rent for space in a large shared building) even if T division is closed down. These enquiries could lead to a conclusion that T should be retained but that fixed cost charges should be reduced, with internal transfer prices reduced proportionally. This would alter T's status from a full profit centre to that of a controllable profit contribution centre, but, although departing from the classic divisional model of full cost and (notional) full autonomy, the result might actually be to increase the motivation and sense of accountability felt by the manager of T. The latter change could be combined with altering the transfer price into a two-part tariff, which would give user divisions a better understanding of the true cost of any incremental use of the van fleet.

With respect to the general problem of intercompany services, Solomons (1983: 205) notes that most service departments are almost, by definition, not market oriented:

There is, then, much to be said for a two-part tariff as a means of charging divisions for their services. The divisions should tend to demand services up to the point where the incremental value of the services equals the incremental cost of providing them. Each division will bear its proportion of the service centre's fixed costs, but not in such a way as to affect its judgement as to how much of its services to take. Ideally, this should ensure that an optimal amount of services will be provided and used within the firm.

Public-sector transfer pricing

The previous discussion has been set in a private sector business context. However, transfer pricing has become increasingly important in the public sector as well, not for it own sake, but as an inevitable consequence of the attempt to achieve greater efficiency in many parts of the public sector by introducing a business culture, subdividing work into operational profit centres, and therefore needing relevant costs for the interdivisional supply of goods and (mainly) services. While the main objective may have been to encourage managerial efficiency by delegating focused responsibility and exacting tighter accountability, it appears that a secondary objective was to facilitate benchmarking and to test whether public services were viable for privatisation – or, if not, to consider contracting out those services if more economical.

The services given greatest attention for more accurate costing and setting fair (full-cost) transfer prices were initially those services where the work and skills were most closely comparable with the private sector, e.g. laundry, cleaning and catering in the NHS, and (building and maintenance) works services in local government. Interestingly, government has typically accepted the theoretical case (rejected in private business) that depreciation should be based on current cost rather than historical cost, while rejecting the theoretical case for variable-cost plus or two-part tariff transfer prices in favour of full-cost transfer prices often uplifted by target returns on assets employed (valued at net current replacement cost or value). Target rates of return have typically been at 5% or 6%; this may seem modest, but can be burdensome when based on realistic current values and when required to be included in internal price quotations, sometimes judged in competition with private contractors completely free to offer prices on a marginal-cost plus or market penetration pricing basis.

Whereas in local authorities the use of transfer pricing has been mainly in the context of charging out central services at market prices or at full cost-plus target ROCE, and intended to approximate to market prices, the NHS in the 1990s used transfer prices more in the competing divisions model, with the so-called internal market in healthcare delivery. Central NHS funding was allocated by demographic formula to local health authorities, who, *de facto*, acted as purchasing divisions to buy or commission hospital and related services from the local NHS Trust, the latter acting as supply divisions. The geographically based trusts could also trade among themselves either to obtain extra specialised services or to take advantage of any transfer prices which may be below their own internal cost. In addition, some NHS funding was allocated direct to the budget of many general practitioners (GPs) for the purpose of allowing them to 'shop around' among trust (and private hospitals) so as to purchase the most cost-effective healthcare at the best prices on offer.

Its sponsors thought that the NHS internal market would lead to an active market in which NHS Trusts actively competed, both on price and quality (i.e. value for money), to attract and treat extra patients from other health authorities. In practice this was not widely achieved, at least outside the largest cities, where hospitals are reasonably close together. This may have been partly because of local loyalties; partly because of concern that long travel journeys have high ambulance costs and high social costs for patients (and for their families to visit hospitalised patients); and partly because the requirement to price services at full cost-plus target ROCE was too inflexible to give much encouragement to relocate treatment from local hospitals. Thus the internal market in the NHS failed to develop into anything like a real or reasonable 'perfect' market in the commercial sense of developing active competition on the basis mainly of price or value for money. On the other hand, it did increase cost awareness, and intensify enquiry into the detail and nature of costs and the underlying resource use.

Conclusion

There is a deceptive simplicity in the application of financial performance measures such as profit or profitability in evaluating the performance of profit centres and divisions. As we have seen, this simplicity masks a number of real problems regarding the measures of profit and, for divisions, net investment. There is also the danger commented on by Johnson and Kaplan (1987) of an overemphasis on financial accounting based measures at the expense of more useful management information. However, such financially based measures are, unquestionably, widely used.

Chapter review

As organisations grow and their activities become more complex it may be more useful to decentralise decision making as much as possible. One option is to create divisions which become, in effect, quasi-independent businesses. The managers of these divisions ought then to be evaluated on the basis of the effectiveness with which they deploy the assets in their charge. The test of effectiveness is not the absolute size of divisional income or profit.

The most frequently used test of effectiveness is ROI. However, as an overall measure of performance ROI has its problems. Some relate to the definition of the profit numerator and the capital denominator. Other problems can relate to the way in which divisional managers attempt to 'manipulate' accounting policies with respect to items such as depreciation, provisions and so on. The use of RI can overcome some, but not all, of these problems.

When divisions (or other forms of profit or investment centre, including in the public sector) trade internally it is necessary to establish internal (transfer) prices which, as fully as possible, both motivate managers and achieve optimum returns. If an external competitive market exists the optimal price would be the market price less any savings on internal trade. Failing near-perfect markets, theoretically optimal approaches such as marginal or opportunity cost would be best in terms of overall group returns. However, in practice these approaches are not widely accepted, so that it may be necessary to use techniques such as cost-plus or negotiated prices, or the two-part tariff – but these alternatives may lead, from the overall group point of view, to suboptimal returns, and/or to some reduction of divisional autonomy and divisional management motivation and accountability.

Further reading

For the classic view of divisional performance and transfer pricing, see Solomons (1983). For alternative contemporary views, see Arnold and Turley (1996: ch. 18), Drury (2004: chs 20, 21). For a wider discussion of the topics, see Emmanuel *et al.* (1995). For an American view, see Horngren *et al.* (2005: chs 18, 19).

Questions and exercises

Guide notes can be found at the back of the book for all questions marked with an asterisk*.

1* The manager of the Invicta Division of PFF Plc has given you the following information related to budgeted operations for the coming year, 200X:

Sales (100 000 units @ £50 each)	£5 000 000
Variable costs (@ £20 per unit)	2 000 000
Contribution (@ £30 per unit)	3 000 000
Fixed costs	1 200 000
Divisional profit	1 800 000
Divisional investment	£8 000 000

PFF has stated that the minimum desired return on investment (ROI) is 20%.

Required:

(a) Determine Invicta's expected ROI and residual income (RI).

(b) Invicta's management has just been approached by a new, potentially major, customer to sell an additional 10 000 units at £45 each. While unit variable costs are expected to remain unchanged, fixed costs would increase by £100 000. Additional investment of £500 000 would also be required to cover necessary extensions to productive capacity and additional working-capital requirements. If this order is accepted, what is the impact on Invicta's ROI and RI measures?

(c) Of the total budgeted volume of 100 000 units, Invicta expects to sell 20% to the Wessex Division of PFF Plc. However, Invicta's management has been informed by Wessex that an external supplier is willing to supply them at £42 per unit. Unless Invicta agrees to match this price, Wessex will terminate its current agreement. If this happened Invicta would save £250 000 in fixed costs as a result of reducing its estimated production to 80 000 units. If Invicta refuses to lower its internal transfer price to Wessex, evaluate what would be the impact for Invicta, Wessex and for PFF Plc as a whole.

2* Carlton Plastics, a division of Harkness Plc, has prepared the following profit plan for 200X.

Sales	£2500 000
Variable costs	1250 000
Fixed costs	750 000
	2000 000
Gross profit	500 000
Assets employed by the division	£2000 000

The entire company has projected a rate of return of 15%. The cost of capital of the company is 12%.

The division is considering the following investment in new machinery for a new product line:

Cost of equipment	£100 000
Expected annual sales	£150 000
Variable costs	40% of sales
Annual fixed costs (including depreciation)	£70 000

Other divisions of Harkness Plc have also submitted proposals for new projects that will provide a return on investment of approximately 15%.

Required:

(a) As a manager of Carlton, would you accept or reject the proposal?

(b) As a main board member of Harkness Plc, would you want Carlton to accept or reject the proposal?

(c) What would you advise in order to avoid problems of this nature in the future?

3* Foolem Plc is a large advertising and marketing promotions agency providing service outputs through television and other visual media. The agency has a cost of capital of 10%, but its target rate of return is a minimum 12%. Foolem has a divisional structure to incentivise management. Division A is biggest, sells only externally and is well known, with a good market share. It plans, organises and assembles promotional campaigns, and buys in specialist services both externally and from Division B. B is a technical support division with good skills and equipment for art and design, graphics and animations. B's sales are divided equally between Division A and a number of external customers. Both divisions sell externally on negotiated contract prices, as there are no list prices for their types of tailor-made services. Jobs are charged internally on the basis of the 'chargeable hours' of prime staff. Both divisions, especially B, are operating below the capacity of their space, equipment and management, allegedly because too often external contract quotations are too high priced.

Division C supplies the usual central services but also has a Property Section controlling the firm's large London head office. Rent (proportional to average value of space allocated) is charged to A and B, like other central services, on the basis of block (fixed) charges negotiated in the annual budget.

$ million per annum (unless otherwise stated)

	Division A	Division B	Division C	Property
Other external sales	200	40	–	–
Divisional variable costs	120	20	5	15
Depreciation transferred in (out)	5	10	(20)	5
Rent for space allocated per budget	20	40	–	10
Other central transfer service charges	10	10	–	–
Divisionally controlled fixed costs	20	10	–	20
Divisionally controlled capital employed	10	30	90	10
Chargeable hours of total sales time (000s)	200	200	–	–

The divisional variable costs of A include $40 million of internal sales from B, currently transferred at negotiated prices.

Required:

(a) Bearing in mind the company's circumstances, what alternative transfer prices might be considered for division B, and why?

(b) Show calculations for possible transfer prices for B based on (i) full-cost-plus, (ii) relevant-cost-plus and (iii) a two-part tariff.

(c) Briefly note any other issues, calculations or needs for further information.

4 Puppy Plc is the parent company of a group of companies that for management purposes operate as a set of autonomous, profit-motivated divisions. There are four such divisions: P, Q, R and S.

Division P proposes to place a contract for a sub-assembly it requires and, in accordance with group policy, it has circulated contract specifications both inside and outside the group.

A non-group company, External Ltd, has quoted an amount of £3600 for each sub-assembly, in part based on a quotation it has received from Division R of the Puppy group. This quotation is for 1000 units to supply the necessary electrical components for each sub-assembly.

Division Q has also submitted a quotation to supply the sub-assembly. Its quotation, which is for £4500 per sub-assembly, is in part based on a quotation it has received from Division R. The specifications are identical to those that External received from that division. It is also, in part, based on a quotation of £800 per sub-assembly from Division S for carrying out some specialist machining.

Further investigation reveals the following:

(a) The variable cost to Division R of the electrical components is £700 per sub-assembly.

(b) The contribution/sales ratio of Division S is 40%.

(c) When preparing quotations, Division Q bases these on its variable costs plus 20%.

(d) Whatever sourcing is used for the sub-assemblies will have no impact on fixed costs within the Puppy group.

Required:

(a) Identify which quotation is likely to be accepted by Division P, and which quotation it would be in the best interests of the group to accept assuming that:

(i) Spare capacity exists in all divisions.

(ii) There is heavy demand from outside the group for the machining services of Division S.

(b) How might any conflict revealed by your answer to (a) above be resolved via changes to internal pricing mechanisms within the Puppy group?

(c) Briefly summarise the principal advantages and disadvantages of return on investment and residual income as measures of divisional performance.

5   Jurassic Plc's business is organised into divisions. For operating purposes, each division is regarded as an investment centre, with divisional managers enjoying substantial autonomy in their selection of investment projects. Divisional managers are rewarded via a remuneration package which is linked to a Return on Investment (ROI) performance measure. The ROI calculation is based on the net book value of assets at the beginning of the year. Although there is a high degree of autonomy in investment selection, approval to go ahead has to be obtained from management at head office in order to release the finance.

Division X is currently investigating three independent investment proposals. If they appear acceptable, it wishes to assign each a priority in the event that funds may not be available to cover all three. Group finance staff assess the cost of capital to the company at 15% p.a. The details of the three proposals are:

	Project A	Project B	Project C
	(£000)	*(£000)*	*(£000)*
Initial outlay on fixed assets	60	60	60
Net cash inflow in year 1	21	25	10
Net cash inflow in year 2	21	20	20
Net cash inflow in year 3	21	20	30
Net cash inflow in year 4	21	15	40

Depreciation is charged on a straight-line basis over asset life, which is four years in each case. Residual values and taxation should be ignored.

Required:

Give an appraisal of the three investment proposals from a divisional and from a company perspective and explain any divergence between these two points of view.

6   From a management accounting perspective an organisation may determine its operational units to be classified as cost centres, profit centres or investment centres. Indeed, all three classifications might, as appropriate, be used by the one organisation. Explain each of these classifications and describe in which situation each is most appropriately adopted.

7* 'The most suitable income figure for use in appraising the performance of divisional management, and also for use by divisional executives in guiding their decisions, is controllable residual income' (Solomons 1983: 83). Discuss.

8* (a) What are the main methods that are used to evaluate the performance of managers of divisionalised organisations?
(b) What are the main criteria that group management need to consider when establishing accounting control systems for evaluating the performance of their divisional colleagues?

9* Within any large and diversified organisation conflicts can arise between the aims of the group as a whole and the aspirations of individual divisional managers. What kinds of conflict might arise? How can the accounting function help resolve such conflicts?

10 Choose an organisation with which you are familiar and critically evaluate the accounting control mechanisms by which management's performance is evaluated. What, if any, recommendations would you make regarding the way in which management performance is evaluated?

11 'Accounting treatments of interdependence in multidivisional organisations must be as concerned with the behavioural effects of transfer prices as with their ability to secure possible solution'. Discuss.

12 Set out in outline the questions you would investigate before giving advice to a large divisionalised enterprise as regards the basis or method(s) of transfer pricing which it should adopt.

PART 3

The focus of this section, which contains four chapters, is on investment decisions and their evaluation. The first chapter, 'Capital budgeting' looks at the theory and processes making long-term investment decisions. The following chapter, 'Financing business operations', looks at the types of long-term finance that entities can raise, and the costs of such finance. The third chapter, 'Capital structure and dividend decisions', develops these discussions further, raising the question of whether or not there is such a thing as an optimal capital structure. The final chapter, 'Business reorganisation' focuses on how firms can restructure their activities, either by the acquisition of other companies or changing their capital structure.

Capital budgeting

9

Chapter preview

This chapter looks at the contribution that can be made to effective long-term decision making by the use of capital budgeting techniques and contrasts the effectiveness of discounting and non-discounting techniques in this regard. The taxation implications of capital investment are reviewed, as are the benefits that can be derived from the post-completion audits of capital projects.

The background to capital budgeting

The (normally assumed) principal financial objective of management in the private sector is the maximisation of the overall value of the company. In practical terms this equates to the maximisation, over time, of dividend payments to shareholders. The more successful the company is in generating cash inflows, the greater the productive investments that it can undertake. This, in turn, should lead to the prospect of increased dividend payments in the future and a rise in share price.

Investment appraisal is equally important in the public sector, even though some commentators have argued that private sector approaches are inappropriate as the majority of public sector investments do not produce commercially sold outputs. This view is quite wrong. Outputs can sometimes be valued, even when they are not sold commercially. Investment appraisals where such values are regarded as very important (such as the siting of an airport/hospital or the routing of a bypass) are called **cost-benefit analysis** (CBA). Even if outputs cannot be satisfactorily valued, investment appraisal can still show the cheapest way of providing a given level of output; this is called **cost-effectiveness analysis** (CEA).

This chapter is principally devoted to the use of **discounted cash flow** (DCF) techniques for the proper evaluation of potential investments. It is a technical chapter that describes criteria to be used in assessing whether an investment is worth undertaking; assessing which of mutually exclusive projects is to be preferred in ranking the acceptability of projects when investment funds are limited; and deciding when the economic life of a project has come to an end. However, it needs to be stressed that the process of evaluation, as described in this chapter, is but one stage in the overall process of deciding whether or not to undertake a particular project. Pinches (1982) warns against focusing too much attention on the selection phase of this process to the exclusion of the identification, development and control phases. Simon (1957) and Ansoff (1965 and 1968) both provide useful insights into the general framework of decision theory.

In the first section of the chapter we briefly consider non-discounting appraisal techniques. The next section considers the principles associated with discounted cashflow techniques and concludes that, of the two methods discussed, the **net present value** (NPV) method is theoretically superior to the **internal rate of return** (IRR) method. The following section continues the discussion by demonstrating that in many practical situations the NPV approach is also practically superior to the IRR approach. The impact of taxation on investment appraisal is discussed in the subsequent section. We then consider investment appraisal in the public sector before looking at empirical evidence about the application of these various techniques in practice and setting out a framework for the establishment of **post-completion audits** of capital projects. The final section reviews the main themes of the chapter and provides a brief guide to further reading on this important area. This chapter builds on the principles set out in Chapter 5 to consider decision making in circumstances when it may take some years to assess whether funds have been prudently invested.

Non-discounting appraisal techniques

Though the concern of this chapter is with the net cash flows generated by alternative projects over time, we start by briefly discussing two traditional, non-discounting appraisal techniques as historically they have been commonly used in business. The two techniques are the accounting rate of return (or return on capital employed), which is discussed further in Chapter 15, and the payback method.

Accounting rate of return method

Accounting rate of return (ARR) is also commonly referred to as the return on investment (ROI). There are many ways in which this measure can be derived, its base form being the ratio of some measure of accounting profit to a corresponding measure of capital outlay. One of the more common ways of deriving this ratio for decision making is to calculate a project's average profit after depreciation, but before any allowance for taxation, and divide this by the average capital employed during the life of the project. If significant, it would also be usual practice to include in capital employed any increases in working capital required should the project be accepted. Let us consider a simple example: a project requires an initial capital outlay of $500 000 and has a life of five years, at the end of which it can be sold as scrap for $50 000. The expected annual profits over this period for the project are:

Year	$
1	40 000
2	100 000
3	160 000
4	120 000
5	30 000

(a) Average annual profit:

$$\frac{(40\ 00 + 100\ 000 + 160\ 000 + 120\ 000 + 30\ 000)}{5} = \$90\ 000$$

(b) Average capital employed:

$$\frac{\$500\ 000 - \$50\ 000}{2} = \$225\ 00$$

(c) Accounting rate of return (ARR):

$$\frac{\$90\ 000}{\$225\ 000} \times 100\% = 40\%$$

Note that the denominators for the first two stages of this calculation were 5 and 2, respectively. In (a), 5 was used to give the average annual profit, while in (b), 2 was used to give the simple average of capital employed throughout the entire five-year life of the project.

Once the ARR has been determined a simple accept/reject decision is then made on the basis of the percentage return achieved. Providing the ARR, which in this case was 40%, exceeds some predetermined 'target' rate of return, the project is accepted; otherwise it is rejected. In the case of competing projects the decision rule is to accept the one with the higher accounting rate of return, provided that it is larger than the target rate.

The advantages of this technique are its ease of calculation, the fact that it considers the accounting profit flows throughout the life of the project, and that it produces a percentage rate of return which is a ratio commonly used by market analysts and others when measuring the profitability of a company. The disadvantages do, however, outweigh these advantages. As alluded to earlier, there is no standard measure of capital employed or profit. Since this is an accounting ratio, non-cash items such as depreciation are included. The production of a ratio in percentage terms fails to reflect the absolute size of investment and, although the whole life of individual projects are considered, this method fails to distinguish between the differing lives of mutually exclusive projects. Finally, and most fundamentally, the ARR method ignores the *timing* of the earnings streams of projects. An illustration of this is provided in Table 9.1, which compares two projects each having a five-year life, and requiring an initial investment of £200 000 with an anticipated scrap value of £0.

Table 9.1	Illustration of accounting rate of returns

Year	Project A	Project B
1	£10 000	£50 000
2	£20 000	£40 000
3	£30 000	£30 000
4	£40 000	£20 000
5	£50 000	£10 000
Which project is preferred?		
The result with the ARR is inconclusive:		
Average annual profit	£30 000	£30 000
Average capital employed	£100 000	£100 000
ARR	30%	30%

Both projects have the same ARR, although the earnings of project B arise earlier than those of project A. Most people would prefer project B on this basis, although ARR fails to distinguish between them.

The payback method

The second commonly used non-discounting appraisal technique is the payback method. Strictly speaking, this method is more of a liquidity measure than a profitability measure. For all organisations, it is important that they remain 'liquid' in cash terms (see Chapters 8 and 15 for more detailed discussions of liquidity). As with the ARR, the payback calculation is simple, but it concentrates on cash flows and not accounting measures. Individual projects are accepted provided that they 'pay back' their investment within a specified target period, while mutually exclusive projects are ranked by speed of repayment. Let us consider two further projects, C and D:

	Project C £	Project D £
Initial investment (t_0)	−20 000	−20 000
Net cash flows each year:		
1(t_1)	+ 12 000	+ 8 000
2(t_2)	+ 8 000	+ 8 000
3(t_3)	+ 8 640	+ 4 000
4(t_4)		+ 8 000
5(t_5)		+ 6 000

For ease of expression, initial investments are denoted as being made at time t_0. Thereafter, cash flows are treated as arising at the end of each year, commencing at t_1. Investments and net negative cash flows are denoted by a negative (−) sign, while net positive cash flows are denoted by a positive (+) sign. This notation will be used throughout the remainder of this chapter. If the target cut-off payback period was three years both projects would be acceptable. If, however, projects C and D were mutually exclusive, project C would be preferred to project D since its payback period is two years compared to D's three-year period, despite D's larger net cash flow surplus.

The payback method can also be discredited because it fails to take account of any cash flows arising after the payback period and, like the ARR, it ignores the time value of money. A variation of the payback method is the discounted payback method, based on the principles set out below. While this method is an improvement, in that it discounts cash flows in calculating the payback period, it still ignores cash flows arising thereafter.

The theory behind discounted cash-flow appraisal techniques

For many private sector managers the overall corporate goal of maximising the value of the firm may initially appear vague. We begin this section by examining a normative model which, under a series of restrictive assumptions about the real world, illustrates the microeconomic theory underpinning the principles of investment appraisal. It is based on a two-period graphical analysis, first suggested by Hirshleifer (1958), which adopts the principles laid down by Fisher's (1907, 1930) work on the theory of interest.

Net present value method

Broadly, two categories of investment opportunities are available to firms: to invest in the external capital market or to invest in internal productive opportunities. It could, of course, be argued that if no productive opportunities are available the firm should repay its funds to its shareholders and allow them either to deal directly with the capital market or to reinvest in other firms. With respect to investment in internal productive opportunities, this means investment in a range of tangible assets such as buildings, plant and machinery, or in intangible assets such as patents and licences. Productive opportunities are clearly more attractive than investing in the capital market if they provide a greater return.

The theory outlined by Hirshleifer (1958) is presented by means of a simplified numerical example. Let us assume that a firm has recently been established with a share capital of $1 million (distributed as $1 nominal value ordinary shares). The firm is also able to borrow, or lend, on the capital market at a rate of 15% per annum. Various other assumptions have been made to produce Figure 9.1. Figure 9.1(a) explains the structure of the graph, while Figure 9.1(b) records the transactions in terms of dollars.

Having studied the parameters of the graph presented in Figure 9.1(a), examine the results presented in Figure 9.1(b). The management has $1 million to invest. Its first task is to decide on which productive opportunities to undertake. From the graph it can be seen that $0.5 million invested in productive opportunities at t_0 will yield $0.94 million at t_1. All productive opportunities, as stated in Figure 9.1(a), lie along a concave curve, ranked in terms of their return, beginning with the largest return. Investing in productive opportunities beyond point I_0 is unwise as the returns offered are less than those available on the capital market. The firm should therefore invest the balance of its funds, $0.5m, in the market at 15% to earn $0.575 million at the end of the period t_1.

This strategy of investing half of the available funds internally on productive opportunities and half externally on the capital market returns a total of $1.515 million

Figure 9.1 (a) Illustration of a two-period investment decision. (b) Illustration of a two-period investment decision (continued)

(a)

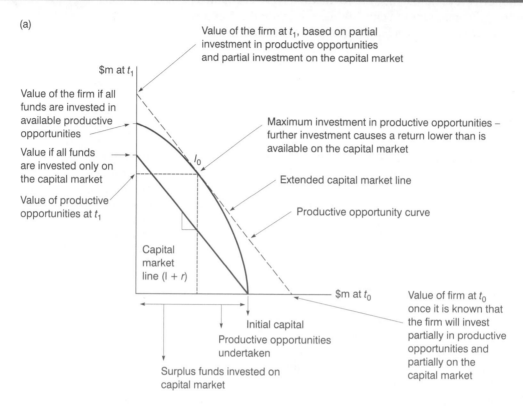

Value of the firm at t_1, based on partial investment in productive opportunities and partial investment on the capital market

$m at t_1

Value of the firm if all funds are invested in available productive opportunities

Value if all funds are invested only on the capital market

Value of productive opportunities at t_1

Maximum investment in productive opportunities – further investment causes a return lower than is available on the capital market

Extended capital market line

Productive opportunity curve

I_0

Capital market line (l + r)

$m at t_0

Value of firm at t_0 once it is known that the firm will invest partially in productive opportunities and partially on the capital market

Initial capital

Productive opportunities undertaken

Surplus funds invested on capital market

Note that:

The downward sloping line of the capital market line represents the rate of exchange $(1 + r)$ on the capital market, where r denotes the rate of interest over this period.

Productive investment opportunities are represented as a concave investment opportunity which offers the largest return, thus:

(b)

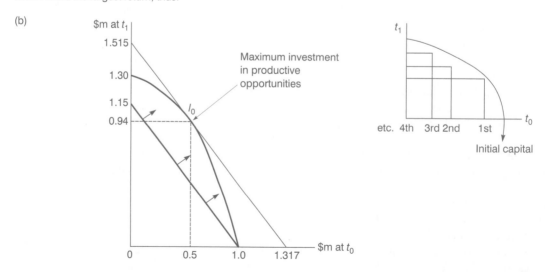

$m at t_1

1.515

1.30

1.15

0.94

Maximum investment in productive opportunities

I_0

$m at t_0

0   0.5   1.0   1.317

t_1

etc. 4th 3rd 2nd 1st

t_0

Initial capital

to the firm at t_1. Under the efficient-markets hypothesis (EMH – see Chapter 10) the current value of the company, at t_0 will rise from $1 million to $1.317 million, i.e. the future value available to the firm of $1.515 million discounted at the external capital market opportunity cost of 15%:

$$\frac{\$1.515m}{1.15} = \$1.317m$$

At this point, two issues need to be noted. The EMH states, in broad terms, that the current value of the firm will rise once the market becomes aware of the investment and financing strategies adopted by the firm. The EMH is further discussed in the 'Glossary of terms' at the end of this book. The use of the term 'external capital market opportunity cost' is discussed in more detail in Chapter 11. Recall that the definition of an opportunity cost is 'the cost of the best opportunity forgone', and the opportunity forgone by investing in internal productive opportunities is that available from lending in the external capital market.

The illustration in Figure 9.1 demonstrates what has become known in the finance literature as the *separation theorem* (Tobin 1958). It is a theorem that has two propositions:

1 Management should invest in all productive opportunities that yield a return greater than that available on the capital market.

2 Shareholders should borrow or lend on the capital market to produce the cash flows that meet their own individual needs.

The market value of the firm illustrated in Figure 9.1 today (at t_0) is $1.317 million. The shares issued at a nominal value of $1 therefore have a market value of $1.317. Examine Figure 9.1(b) again. It is drawn to scale. Is there any alternative strategy to be followed? We think not. The shareholders could sell all/some of their shares for an immediate capital gain, or they could stay with the firm and receive a dividend at t_1 from the profits that the firm decides to distribute and increased capital gains as the remaining funds are reinvested in further productive opportunities. The nature of this scenario is that the firm's management seeks to ensure the best interests of its shareholders. This investment strategy is one that serves all their interests.

The foregoing analysis assumed that borrowing and lending rates on the capital market were equal. As we know, in reality borrowing rates in the market are higher than lending rates. Management must still decide on the optimal selection of productive opportunities. Productive opportunities should first be selected by reference to the (higher) borrowing rate. If available funds are insufficient to accept all available opportunities, then additional funds can be borrowed, as productive opportunities will produce returns more than sufficient to cover the cost of borrowing. If, however, the firm has surplus funds available after this exercise, management should then evaluate all remaining opportunities at the lending rate, as these additional productive projects will earn a return greater than is available on the market.

The two-period analysis illustrated in Figure 9.1 can be further developed to accommodate longer time horizons. In fact, it is the theoretical basis on which the NPV discounted cash flow approach to investment appraisal depends. As Bromwich states (1976: 7):

A project with a positive net present value covers the opportunity cost of both internal and external funds. Its acceptance, therefore, makes the shareholders better off.

Looking at it another way, the net present value of the project is the price at which the firm (and its shareholders) could sell the opportunity to undertake the project to someone else and be no worse off.

As stated above, this approach is normative, based on how rational managers and shareholders (investors) should act given the stated assumptions. It presents a logical structure for the management of the financial affairs of enterprises and a link to the pragmatic business environment that operates in the real world. Thus, financial theory lays a foundation for sound corporate financial management. To this it is necessary to add the constraints of the present-day business environment as provided by government fiscal policy, financial institutions, legislation and practice. Further support for this theoretical approach to financial management is supplied by corporate legislation (e.g. the Companies Acts in the UK, commonly state that directors of companies are expected to run them in the best interests of the shareholders).

In a multi-period situation NPV can be found by the following expression:

$$NPV = \frac{Cf_1}{(1+r)^1} + \frac{Cf_2}{(1+r)^2} + \frac{Cf_3}{(1+r)^3} + \dots + \frac{Cf_n}{(1+r)^n} - Inv_{t0} \qquad (9.2)$$

or:

$$NPV = \sum_{t=1}^{t=n} \frac{Cf_t}{(1+r)^t} - Inv_{t0}$$

where: Cf_t = the net cash flow at the end of year t;
Inv_{t0} = the initial investment outlay at t = 0;
r = the discount rate based on the opportunity cost of capital;
n = the project's expected life-cycle.

The NPV imputes a known discount rate, which is based on the market-determined opportunity cost of capital. Projects that have a positive NPV using this approach are worth accepting. The net cash flow for each year is expressed in present value terms by dividing by $(1 + r)^t$ as appropriate. The following illustration represents the present-value factors for a discount rate of 10% over a five year period:

$$\frac{1}{(1+r)} = \frac{1}{(1.1)} = 0.909$$

$$\frac{1}{(1+r)^2} = \frac{1}{(1.1)^2} = 0.826$$

$$\frac{1}{(1+r)^3} = \frac{1}{(1.1)^3} = 0.751$$

$$\frac{1}{(1+r)^4} = \frac{1}{(1.1)^4} = 0.683$$

$$\frac{1}{(1+r)^5} = \frac{1}{(1.1)^5} = 0.621$$

In simple terms, a return of $100 in five years' time is today worth $62.10 at a market opportunity cost of 10% per annum. This is simply the application of compound interest in reverse, since $62.10 invested today at 10% per annum would yield $100 in five years' time.

At this point it might be useful to reconsider the cash flows associated with projects C and D, introduced earlier in the chapter. Let us assume that the relevant opportunity cost of capital for C and D is 10%. This would probably, in practice, be based on some weighted-average cost of capital (WACC), as further discussed in Chapter 11. The relevant calculations for C and D are now:

	Project C				Project D		
	$	PVF (10%)	PV ($)		$	PVF (10%)	PV ($)
t_0	−20 000	1.000	−20 000		−20 000	1.000	−20 000
t_1	+12 000	0.909	+10 908		+8 000	0.909	+7 272
t_2	+8 000	0.826	+6 608		+8 000	0.826	+6 608
t_3	+8 640	0.751	+6 489		+4 000	0.751	+3 004
t_4					+8 000	0.683	+5 464
t_5					+6 000	0.621	+3 726
		NPV	$+4 005			NPV	$+6 074

(PVF = present value factor; PV = present value.)

Both projects have positive NPVs, but if they were mutually exclusive project D would be preferred. This is the reverse situation to the advice given by the payback method. The difference between these two methods is that the NPV approach takes into account those cash flows arising after the payback cut-off period and also considers the time value of the funds so invested.

The appendix to this chapter introduces the reader to Tables 9.A.1 and 9.A.2: one provides present-value factors and one provides cumulative present-value factors. Both tables greatly facilitate calculations of the NPV. The relevant figures are provided at yearly intervals since this coincides with the usual convention that all costs occurring during a year are accumulated and discounted at the year end. In practice it is possible to have other values at shorter intervals if this is deemed useful. In financial leasing, for example, monthly and quarterly rates are often used.

Internal rate of return method

The second discounted cash flow technique is the IRR method. This technique calculates that discount rate which equates the present value of future cash flows to the cost of the initial investment, i.e. which equates all the cash flows associated with a project to a net present value of zero. Providing that the IRR for a project exceeds a known predetermined hurdle rate the project is accepted, in the absence of limits to the supply of capital (known as 'capital rationing'; see below). Often the hurdle rate set is the opportunity cost of capital. The IRR can be found by solving for i in the following expression:

$$\text{Inv}_{to} = \frac{Cf_1}{(1+i)^1} + \frac{Cf_2}{(1+i)^2} + \frac{Cf_3}{(1+i)^3} + \frac{Cf_n}{(1+i)^n} \qquad (9.3)$$

or:

$$Inv_{to} = \sum_{t=1}^{t=n} \frac{Cf_t}{(1+i)^t} \qquad (9.4)$$

where: Cf_t = the net cash flow at the end of year t;
Inv_{to} = the initial investment outlay at t = 0;
n = the project's expected life-span;
i = that discount rate that equates the sum of future cash flows to Inv_{to}

While the calculation of IRRs may call for the solution of complex polynomial equations, there are several computer software packages that can expedite their solution. An alternative approach, which provides a good approximation of a project's IRR, can be found by using the mathematical technique of linear interpolation. We can calculate the IRR for project C by means of linear interpolation as follows:

(a)   let i = 20%

	$	PVF (20%)	PV ($)
t_0	−20 000	1.000	−20 000
t_1	+12 000	0.833	+9 996
t_2	+8 000	0.694	+5 552
t_3	+8 640	0.579	+5 003
		NPV	$+551

This result indicates an IRR greater than 20%.

(b)   let i = 25%

	$	PVF (25%)	PV ($)
t_0	−20 000	1.000	−20 000
t_1	+12 000	0.800	+9 600
t_2	+8 000	0.640	+5 120
t_3	+8 640	0.512	+4 424
		NPV	$−856

This result indicates an IRR less than 25%.
With these two results we can now interpolate to find the exact value:

$$0.20 + \frac{551}{551 + 856} \times (0.25 - 0.20) = 0.22, \text{ or } 22\%.$$

We can now test the 'soundness' of our approximation by letting i = 22%:

	$	PVF (22%)	PV ($)
t_0	−20 000	1.000	−20 000
t_1	+12 000	0.820	+9 840
t_2	+8 000	0.672	+5 376
t_3	+8 640	0.551	+4 761
		NPV	$−23

Only a small rounding difference of $23 is left.

Readers can confirm their familiarity with the technique of linear interpolation by calculating the IRR for project C. The result should also work out at 22%, meaning that if these two projects were mutually exclusive management might be indifferent between them. It could be argued that marginal preference be given to project B, since it has the shorter life-cycle, and because the further into the future we go, the more difficult it is to forecast cash flows with relative precision.

While it is usually true that the NPV and IRR approaches produce the same recommendation, there are important occasions when these two approaches can provide conflicting advice. Bromwich (1976; 87) states that 'knowledge of a project's internal rate of return is neither necessary nor sufficient for optimal investment decisions'. On its own the IRR of a project gives no information about either a project's present value or the effect of its acceptance on the value of the firm. Whereas the NPV provides an absolute value, the IRR does not. The above consideration of projects C and D is a case in point. While the NPV approach favours project D, with an absolute value of $6074, the IRR approach was indifferent between the two. We can summarise our discussion on the NPV and IRR techniques as follows:

1 The NPV rule is sufficient in itself, whereas the IRR rule does not make economic sense, knowledge of a project's IRR is neither necessary nor sufficient for optimal decisions.

2 IRR on its own gives no information about either a project's present value, an absolute measure, or the effect of its acceptance on shareholder's wealth.

3 The two techniques have different reinvestment assumptions. Implicit in the NPV rule is that any positive cash flows occurring during the project's life can be reinvested at a rate of interest equal to that used as the discount rate. By contrast, the IRR decision rule assumes that the cash flows resulting during the

Table 9.2 Comparison of net present value and net terminal sum

Consider a project that requires an initial investment of £1000 and returns net cash inflows in each of the subsequent three years. The relevant opportunity cost of capital can be assumed as 10%. The NPV of this project is £492. There is a net terminal surplus (NTS) of £655, being the increase in value over and above the opportunity given up in the capital market of £331. The relevant figures are set out below.
Interest received on surpluses reinvested at 10%

	Cash flows	Year 2	Year 3	Terminal value	DCF(10%)	PV
t_0	(1000)			(1000)	1.000	(1000)
t_1	600	60	66	726	0.909	545
t_2	600		60	660	0.826	496
t_3	600			600	0.751	451
	Net terminal value			986	NPV	492*
	less opportunity cost of capital					
	1000 at 10% for 3 years			331		
			NTS	655		

Note: *The NPV of the NTS is £655 × 0.751 = £492, allowing for rounding differences in the calculations.

life-cycle of a project have an opportunity cost equal to the IRR that generated them. The theoretical basis for the NPV approach is that the discount rate used is determined by the capital market. No such theoretical basis exists for the IRR approach. Can we really suppose that surplus cash flows arising from one investment will earn the same IRR in the next investment?

Table 9.2 illustrates that notion of opportunity cost associated with the NPV.

Practical issues surrounding the application of the NPV and IRR appraisal techniques

In this section we consider technical issues surrounding the application of the NPV and IRR techniques. In each instance we demonstrate that the NPV technique is, in practice, the preferred technique. Our discussion continues under the following headings:

Mutually exclusive investments

As is stated above, it is often the case that capital resources are limited and that competing projects are therefore mutually exclusive. For example, if a construction company had a particular development site various development options might be available but only one proposal could ultimately be undertaken. These proposals are therefore mutually exclusive. Consider two mutually exclusive projects, E and F, with the following pattern of cash flows:

	t_0	t_1	t_2	t_3	NPV (10%)	IRR
Project E	$(1000)	475	475	475	181	20%
Project F	$(500)	256	256	256	137	25%

Whereas the NPV approach favours project E, the IRR approach favours project F. Some authors, for example Levy and Sarnatt (1986), suggest that this conflict in advice can be solved using the 'incremental yield approach'; that is, by evaluating the incremental project, in this case E – F. The resultant cash flows are:

	t_0	t_1	t_2	t_3	NPV (10%)	IRR
Project (E–F)	$(500)	219	219	219	44	15%

If, as in the case in point, the incremental project produces a positive net present value and an IRR greater than the opportunity cost of capital (here 10%) the larger project, project E, should be accepted. The Levy and Sarnatt (1986) approach ignores the unrealistic reinvestment assumption implicit in the IRR approach. Further, as we need to calculate the opportunity cost of capital in order to assess the incremental project, why not simply use the NPV approach in the first place?

Multiple rates of return

The IRR approach is unable to provide solutions to those potential projects that have unconventional cash flows. In such situations an IRR may not exist, or, if it does, it may not be unique. Such situations could occur, for example, when a project has an expansion option phased into it which could lead to an overall net cash outflow a few years into the life of the project, before potential (and increased) cash flows resume. Another example occurs in the extractive industry when net cash outflows occur at the end of a project's life, due to landscaping and other rectification costs incurred to restore the environment. Levy and Sarnatt (1986: 87) provide an illustration of a non-conventional cash flow that has no IRR. The numbers are $t_0 = +\$100$, $t_1 = -\$200$ and $t_2 = +\$150$. Rather than waste time in calculations, we can accept their assertion that no solution is to be found. Interestingly this sequence of cash flows, if discounted at 10%, produces a positive NPV. An alternative sequence of $t_0 = -\$20\,000$, $t_1 = +\$51\,000$ and $t_2 = -\$31\,500$ produces two IRRs, 5% and 50%. Bromwich (1976: 103) provides further analysis and discussion of this phenomenon. Suffice it to say, for our purposes, that where multiple rates of return exist there are no mathematical or economic grounds for specifying any one IRR over another.

Timing of cash flows

Consider two further projects, G and H, with the following patterns of cash flows:

	t_0	t_1	t_2	NPV	IRR
Project G	$(1000)	1000	200	76	16.67%
Project H	$(1000)	200	1100	95	15.42%

Here again we have conflicting advice, with the NPV approach favouring project H, when a 10% discount factor is used, and the IRR approach favouring project G. This case is different to that illustrated by projects E and F, in that this conflict in advice cannot be resolved via incremental analysis since both projects require the same capital outlay. The problem here lies with the underlying reinvestment assumptions between the NPV and IRR approaches and the differences in the timing of the receipt of the post-investment cash flows that result. This problem is illustrated in Figure 9.2. The curves associated with both projects approximate the net present values at different rates of interest. The NPV rule would advise project H if the firm's cost of capital is below 13% and project G if it is higher. As the opportunity cost of capital is less than 13%, project H is to be preferred.

Uneven project lives

One final problem with the IRR approach is that it is impossible to use it when projects have different lives (see Cooke and Glynn 1981). Typically, asset replacement decisions fall into this category of appraisal. Plant and machinery, for example, cannot be kept indefinitely; as their age increases so do their operating and maintenance costs, while their residual value declines. Management needs to decide when to replace an existing machine with a new one and also to have some notion of the expected optimal life of its replacement. Not only capital outlay costs need to be considered, but also any difference that arises in working capital requirements between operating and maintaining current equipment compared to using replacement technology. The concern of such calculations is therefore to determine the 'economic life' of an asset rather than its physical life.

Figure 9.2	Comparison of NPV and IRR

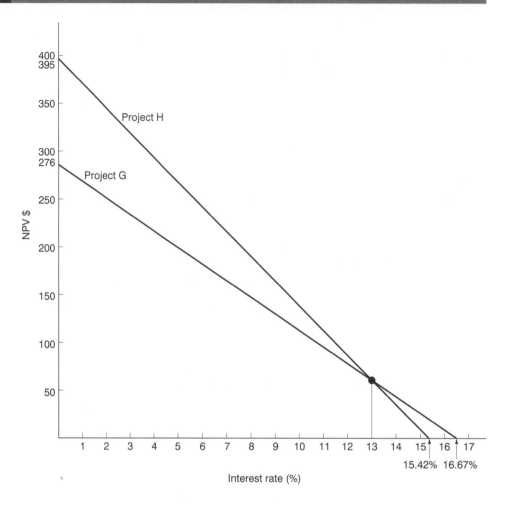

Consider the everyday problem of having to replace a car. Let us consider, for simplicity, that our choice is between the two propositions:

- buying a new car at a net (of trade-in allowance) cost of $2000, keeping it for four years and then replacing it;

- buying a one-year-old car of the same model at a net (of trade-in allowance) cost of $1600, keeping it for three years and then replacing it.

The pattern of running costs for this make of car is:

Annual running costs ($)

Year 1 of life	600
Year 2 of life	800
Year 3 of life	1 000
Year 4 of life	1 600

We cannot simply calculate the NPV of each alternative since the new car will be kept for four years and the second-hand car for three years. We need some way of equating the alternatives. There are four principal approaches to solving this sort of problem.

The first would be to impute a resale value for the new car at the end of year 3 and discount both alternatives over the same three-year time horizon. This approach is difficult in that one would need to be fairly confident about calculating the market value of the new car at the end of year 3. Another approach would be to consider repeating both alternatives within a common time horizon. The least common multiple associated with these two alternatives is 12 years. The new car would be replaced three times over this time horizon whilst the second-hand car would be replaced on four occasions over the same period. To calculate this approach one simply multiplies the NPV associated with the new car by 3, and the NPV associated with the second-hand car by 4. Again, this is not a very practical approach.

The two remaining approaches are more common: the perpetuity approach and the annuity approach. In order to consider each of these approaches we need first to calculate the NPV associated with each alternative. If we assume an opportunity cost of capital of 15%, we have the following results:

	PV New car ($)	PV Second-hand car ($)
t_0	−2 000	−1 600
t_1	−600	−800
t_2	−800	−1 000
t_3	−1 000	−1 600
t_4	−1 600	−
NPV (15%)	−4 699	−4 104

With the perpetuity approach we assume a chain of replacements starting now and taking place every three or four years. The present value of the four-year replacement cycle of the new car is:

$$\frac{\$-4699}{(1-0.5718)} = \$-10\,974$$

The present value associated with the three-year replacement cycle of the second-hand car is:

$$\frac{\$-4104}{(1-0.6575)} = \$-11\,982$$

By this approach we have determined that an investment outlay of $10 974 is required in order to buy a new car, run it for four years and then replace it. The sum of $10 974, if invested at 15%, would provide sufficient funds to meet the annual cash outflows identified above. In similar fashion an investment outlay of $11 982 is required in order to buy and run the second-hand car. Therefore it is prudent to buy the new car.

The annuity approach is to calculate the annual equivalent cost of operating either choice. We have found in practice that it is this approach that managers most readily understand. The relevant calculations are:

New car $$\frac{\$-4104}{(2.855)} = \$-1\,646$$

$$\text{Second-hand car } \frac{\$-4104}{(2.283)} = \$-1798$$

The denominators are cumulative net present-value factors from Appendix 9.A2. Again, the new car alternative is preferred as it has the lowest annual equivalent cost.

In summary we are able to point to four practical problems associated with the IRR approach:

1 It can give different advice due to the time pattern of cash flows (i.e. the time crossing of present values).

2 Problems can arise due to multiple roots.

3 It has a different (unrealistic) reinvestment assumption which assumes intermediate cash flows can earn a return equal to the project's IRR.

4 It cannot be applied to problems associated with different economic life-cycles.

Risk and uncertainty

Having demonstrated that the NPV is the preferred technique for investment appraisal, we have to recognise that the future is not certain. The techniques that firms use to evaluate risks range from traditional methods, such as simulation and sensitivity analysis, through to market-oriented techniques, such as the capital asset-pricing model (CAPM – see below). In some instances even cruder approaches have been adopted, such as simply increasing the discount factor by an amount as a 'hedge' against future uncertainties. This latter approach has little merit since it unrealistically presupposes that risk is compounded over time.

The advantage of simulation analysis is that it compels project planners to review carefully the key relationships that affect the projected cash flows. Brearley and Myers (2003) consider that model-building leads to a deeper understanding of the project. Particular simulation techniques such as Monte Carlo simulation analysis require the construction of probability distributions for each factor that influences the capital-investment decision. Sensitivity analysis enables managers to assess how responsive the NPV is to changes in the variables which are used to calculate it. This approach requires that the NPVs are calculated under alternative assumptions to determine how sensitive they are to changing conditions; that is, it indicates why a project might fail. Drury (2004) provides useful illustrations of these techniques but it should be noted that these techniques rely on discounting the cash flows at a risk-free rate.

The CAPM, although still not widely used, has become one well-recognised technique that provides a risk-adjusted discount rate based on the principles of portfolio analysis. Risk is measured by a beta factor, which measures the sensitivity of the return on a quoted share with the movement of the market as a whole. The values of betas for all UK quoted companies are published by the London Business School and Datastream. These values are used in a formula developed by Sharpe (1964):

$$Erj = rf + \beta j(Erm - rf) \tag{9.5}$$

where: Erj = the expected return of the share;
        rf = a risk-free return (typically equated to the return on government bonds);
       Erm = the expected return on the market as a whole;
    $(Erm - rf)$ = the market premium;
       $βj$ = the risk of the share j relative to the market index.

For a fuller discussion of the application of this technique, see Collier *et al.* (1988).

In concluding this section, brief mention should be made of how the impact of *inflation* should be taken into account. Two basic approaches can be adopted. First, a market-determined discount rate can be used to discount inflation-adjusted cash flows. These cash flows should not be revised in line with a general index of inflation; rather, specific inputs should be uprated using specific indices. The second alternative, though less practical, is to exclude the impact of inflation from the discount rate and discount what economists term 'real' cash flows.

Taxation and investment appraisal

So far in our discussion we have ignored the impact of taxation. Chapter 14 provides a detailed analysis of taxation systems. Here we consider how taxation can be incorporated into NPV calculations. The approach to adopt is fairly straightforward; it is to incorporate the impact of taxation into the incremental cash flows arising from the investment and to discount the resultant net cash flows by a net-of-tax discount rate. The discount rate should reflect the tax advantage of the deductibility of debt interest. This process is illustrated by the example of Strathmore Ltd.

Strathmore Ltd is considering whether to purchase some additional machinery that will cost £250 000 and should contribute additional cash flows of £125 000 per annum for four years. The net-of-tax cost of capital is 10% per annum and corporation tax is at the rate of 31%. The machinery is eligible for 25% annual written-down allowances. It is anticipated that the machinery can be sold at the end of year 4 at its written-down value for taxation purposes.

Table 9.3 contains the necessary calculations. As Chapter 14 points out, depreciation is not a cash flow and should not appear in the calculation. In Section A the written-down allowances are calculated. In Section B we can see the additional corporation-tax liability that arises from the anticipated incremental cash flows. In Section C the net present value is calculated, but note the timing of the tax payments. Tax payments have been assumed to be payable in the year following the receipt of the additional cash flows. As there is a net present value of £127 948 this project should be accepted. Again, as Chapter 14 discusses, had the machinery been projected to be sold for a figure greater than its written-down value a 'balancing charge' would have had to be included in the calculation to recoup excess capital allowances.

Investment appraisal in the public sector

The rationale behind the use of the NPV approach in the private sector is accepted by most governments as being exactly analogous to that in the public sector. This is because

Table 9.3   Illustration of taxation in investment appraisal

A

End of year £	Written-down allowance (25%) £	£	Written-down value carried forward
0	0		250 000
1	62 500	(25% × 250 000)	187 500
2	46 875	(25% × 187 500)	140 625
3	35 156	(25% × 140 625)	105 469
4	26 367	(25% × 105 469)	79 102

B

	Year 1 £	Year 2 £	Year 3 £	Year 4 £
Incremental cash flows	125 000	125 000	125 000	125 000
less writing down allowance	62 500	46 875	35 156	26 367
Incremental cash flows subject to taxation	62 500	78 125	89 844	98 633
Incremental tax (31%)	19 375	24 219	27 852	30 576

C

Year	Cash flow £	Taxation cash flow £	Net factor £	Discount value £	Present £
0	− 250 000	0	− 250 000	1.000	250 000
1	+ 125 000	0	+ 125 000	0.909	+ 113 625
2	+ 125 000	− 19 375	+ 105 625	0.826	+ 87 246
3	+ 125 000	− 24 219	+ 100 781	0.751	+ 75 686
4	+ 125 000	− 27 852	+ 97 148	0.683	+ 66 352
	+ 79 102[a]		+ 79 102	0.683	+ 54 027
5	0	− 30 576	− 30 576	0.621	− 18 988
		Net present value			£ + 127 948

Note: [a]Projected sale of machinery at the written-down value for tax purposes. All calculations are rounded to the nearest whole £1. This example is based on UK capital taxation principles.

'jam today is worth more than jam tomorrow' (HM Treasury 1984: 14) since, just as in the private sector, 'more weight is given to earlier than to later cost and benefits'. The discount rate for use in the public sector is often referred to as a test discount rate (TDR). The TDR was first introduced, in the UK, in the early 1960s as a means of promoting consistent investment appraisal by nationalised industries. Its use subsequently spread to other areas of the public sector, both in the UK and other countries. Since 1978 the discount rates used by nationalised industries have not been set centrally but have been a matter of individual consultation between each industry and its sponsoring department. Again, this is also the process used in many other countries. Typically, public sector capital appraisals are expected to be based on the basis of *real cash flows* using a *real discount rate*.

In many instances public sector capital projects are similar in character to those carried out in the private sector. Often, though, the emphasis is on cost-effectiveness rather than overall profit maximisation. On occasions social costs and benefits may be incorporated into the calculation. Consider the building of a hospital. With respect to its location, social benefits could arise in terms of the time saved in travelling by out-patients (particularly emergency cases) and visitors. Conversely, social costs can arise in addition to the direct cash outlays associated with the construction of the project. As Glynn (1987: 88) states:

> The accountant engaged in a CBA project is not, in essence then, asking a different sort of question from that being asked by the accountant of a private firm. Rather, the same sort of question is being asked about a wider group of people – who comprise society – and is being asked more searchingly.

Mishan (1971) provides several examples of the application of CBA to public-sector capital investment.

Project appraisal in practice

This chapter has concentrated on the preferred approach to project appraisal – the net present-value approach. In practice this approach has been slow in gaining popularity and, when used, has often been used in conjunction with one of the other approaches referred to earlier. Why is this? Traditionally, management has not seriously considered the importance of investment appraisal, or else it has paid too close attention to short-term measures rather than taking an economic approach. The ARR is used, as stated, because it is a simple technique; second, it is similar to the accounting ratios used by market analysts, and it has to be recognised that (as discussed in Chapter 15) financial accounting communicates important information externally and some managements may feel that it is important to undertake projects that confer 'relevant' information to the market. This, we would argue, is far too short-sighted. Accounting cannot supplant the long-term need of companies to generate surplus cash flows. Likewise, the payback approach may be used when funds are in limited supply or as a crude measure of risk. However, such an approach is not a maximising one; it is an optimising one, given limited funds for investment.

Several surveys have been carried out regarding the capital budgeting practices of private firms and public sector bodies. Surveys by Pike and Wolfe (1988), McIntyre and Coulthurst (1986), and Drury *et al.* (1992) show that, despite earlier criticisms, the payback method is the appraisal technique most frequently used by firms. However, many firms in these surveys did appear to use a combination of the evaluation methods discussed in this chapter. Despite its theoretical and practical drawbacks, the IRR is still preferred to the NPV in many firms. In discussing these results, Drury considers that 'financial measures of performance evaluation place undue emphasis on the short term and may not be consistent with DCF decision making models' (Drury 1996: 402). Lapsley (1986) reports research which shows that in the public sector a number of investment appraisal techniques are used, despite the government's preference for the NPV technique.

In concluding this section it is apt to return briefly to an issue raised earlier, that of 'capital rationing'. Capital rationing, a restriction on the funds available for reinvestment, quite often exists in organisations. Capital rationing may apply only in a particular year (single-period rationing) or there may be a limit on funds over several years (multi-period rationing). In the case of single-period capital rationing the preferred approach is to rank competing projects in terms of the NPV contribution per £1 or $1 of outlay. This is easily done by dividing a project's NPV by the initial investment sum. In situations of multi-period capital rationing mathematical programming needs to be employed. Carsberg (1969) provides a useful introduction to mathematical programming, while Mepham (1980) provides a guide to the detailed application of linear and matrix algebra.

Post-completion audits of capital projects

Once a decision has been made to undertake a particular project it is sound management practice to compare the actual results with those forecast in the investment appraisal. Important questions need to be asked; for example, was capital expenditure as budgeted? Were anticipated costs and benefits as anticipated? Despite the uniqueness of many projects, a 'post-completion audit' can provide important information for management. As Drury states, 'a record of past performance and mistakes is one way of improving future performance and ensuring that fewer mistakes are made' (Drury 2004). Pike and Wolfe (1988) found that ex-post monitoring of capital investment decisions operates in almost all the major UK companies. Lapsley (1986) reported that 47% of public sector organisations conducted post-completion audits.

The objective of capital budgeting is, in the private sector, to maximise shareholders' wealth. In the public sector the objective is to undertake cost-effective projects. Of the four techniques reviewed, the NPV approach is regarded as being both theoretically and technically superior. The other three techniques, despite their frequent use in practice, are theoretically unsound.

Conclusion

As we have emphasised in this, and the preceding chapters, the objective of long-term investment decisions in the private sector is that of maximising the wealth of the equity holders. In the public sector it is that of undertaking the most cost-effective investments. Of the various techniques that we have reviewed in this chapter, there is no doubt that the discounted cash flow techniques are the best, and that of these techniques the one to be preferred is the net present value approach.

Chapter review

In this chapter we have built upon the foundations laid by the two previous chapters to identify the most economically rational approach to evaluating potential investment projects. Of these, the technique to be preferred is that of the net present value approach. However, as we have seen, for a variety of reasons this approach is not always employed in practice. The other techniques we have discussed all suffer from drawbacks which mitigate against the making of economically rational decisions.

Further reading

For those wishing for further illustrative examples of project appraisals we would suggest Drury (2004) and Lumby (1991). Both texts are popular with students and are regularly updated. Another useful text is that by Butler (1993), which is based upon a study of strategic investment decisions in a wide range of UK and international companies. The authors examine these decisions from the perspective of organisational decision-making theory and find that investments are made not only by the application of formal quantitative procedures but also involve the more qualitative processes of judgement, negotiation and inspiration.

Questions and exercises

Guide notes can be found at the back of the book for all questions marked with an asterisk*.

1* The board of directors of Porterhouse Ltd is considering whether or not to launch a new product which has been subject to extensive research and development. It is expected that this new product will have a market life of ten years, with sales running at 40 000 units annually at a unit selling price of £90. The expected unit costs of the new product are:

	£
Direct materials	28
Direct labour	12
Manufacturing overheads	22
Selling and administrative costs	12
Total unit costs	£74

To manufacture this new product will require an immediate investment in plant and machinery of £2 million. The anticipated scrap value of this equipment will be £100 000. In addition to the investment in plant and machinery, it is expected that the company will need to increase its working-capital investment by £1.8 million because of the increased levels of stock and debtors associated with the new product.

The manufacturing overheads include an allocation of existing costs to the new product of £300 000 but make no allowance for depreciation. The remaining manufacturing costs are variable.

The selling and administrative costs represent an allocation of the company's overall costs in these areas to the new product on the basis of anticipated sales value. Included in these overall costs is the £4 per unit sales commission which will be payable to sales agents who will be responsible for the sales of the new product. This commission is the only incremental selling and administrative cost likely to be associated with the new product. After reviewing the above details the managing director says:

We have already spent £1 million on research and development for this product, and we are now being asked to invest £3.8 million further in its production.

This would bring our total investment to £4.8 million, and for what? On the information we have it is only going to generate an annual profit of £640 000 before taxation. Remember that corporation tax will swallow up one-third of this profit. This is a rate of return of just under 9%, as compared with our cost of capital of 15%. In my view, every product should pay its own way, cover its own costs and give us a decent return. This one will not, so we should not go ahead with it. We should write off the research and development to experience and learn from our mistake. Do you all agree?

Required:

Respond in clear, non-technical language to the managing director's statement, saying whether or not you agree with his analysis and recommendation.

2* The directors of Dobson Ltd are considering whether to accept one of two mutually exclusive projects and, if so, which one to accept. Each project involves an immediate outlay of $1 million, and the estimates of the subsequent cash inflows are as follows:

	Project A $	Project B $
Net cash inflow at the end of:		
Year 1	800 000	100 000
Year 2	500 000	300 000
Year 3	300 000	1 500 000

The directors of Dobson Ltd do not expect capital or any other resource to be in short supply during the next three years, and taxation can be ignored.

Required:

(a) Prepare a graph to show the functional relationship between the net present value and the discount rate for the two projects.

(b) Use the graph to estimate the internal rate of return of each project.

(c) On the basis of the information given, advise which project to accept if the cost of capital is (i) 10% and (ii) 20%.

(d) Describe briefly any additional information that you think would be useful in choosing between the projects.

3* The Midshire Community Trust is considering establishing its own pathology services facility, for which it currently contracts with the St Bottomley Hospital Trust. Midshire's board of management believes not only that establishing its own facilities will lead to a cheaper and more efficient service, but that additional income could be earned by offering its own service to other health-service trusts and GP fundholders. You have been asked to prepare a brief report for a forthcoming board meeting which should appraise the two alternatives of negotiating a new three-year contract with St Bottomley and establishing this facility inhouse. The finance director has provided you with the following information:

(i) The capital cost of establishing a pathology laboratory for Midshire would be £250 000, and the estimated total annual running costs for the first three years are estimated, respectively, at £650 000, £750 000 and £800 000.

(ii) The annual charges for pathology services proposed by St Bottomley's for the next three years are, respectively, £750 000, £850 000 and £900 000.

(iii) If the new pathology laboratory is built it will be on land owned by Midshire that is currently rented out to a road-haulage contractor for warehousing at an annual rent of £15 000.

(iv) If Midshire has misestimated the success of establishing its own facility it ought to be able to sell it off on a 99-year lease for £100 000 at the end of three years.

She has further suggested that you use 6% as an appropriate discount factor, but you are concerned that 12% seems more like a rate at which money might be borrowed from a bank or other financial lender.

Required:
Prepare a brief report for the board of management of the Midshire Community Trust which clearly outlines the financial feasibility of establishing an inhouse pathology service. Be sure to state any assumptions that you have made and to raise any additional considerations not covered in your calculations that you feel the board should consider. Attach your calculations as an appendix to your report. Any implications regarding taxation should be ignored.

4 Your friend, who is the senior engineer of a local factory, Jackson Limited, is seeking your advice on the replacement of some machinery. He states, 'At a recent seminar I learned that it is the economic life of an asset that is important and not its physical life. I really am somewhat confused about this concept. How does it apply to my company's circumstances?'

He says that the machines the company is currently using could be sold now for £30 000 each and estimates that in a year's time they would realise £15 000 each; in two years' time, £6000 each. He also estimates that each machine's operating costs would be:

Year 1	£40 000
Year 2	£60 000

The replacement machines that he is considering have a purchase price of £120 000 each and he estimates that their operating costs (including any adjustments to working-capital requirements) would be:

Year 1	£24 000
Year 2	£30 000
Year 3	£34 000
Year 4	£39 000
Year 5	£45 000
Year 6	£59 000

These new machines are expected to have a residual (net resale) value of £60 000 at the end of one year; £36 000 at the end of two years; £32 000 at the end of three years; £22 000 at the end of four years; £16 000 at the end of five years; and £12 000 at the end of six years.

The company's cost of capital is 12% per annum.

Required:
Using the information given above, advise whether the present series of machines should be replaced by more modern machinery. In your analysis, be sure to explain why it is the economic life of a machine that is important rather than its operational life.

5 A friend seeks your advice. She has recently become a project manager for a construction company and is a little confused with some of the information she is receiving. By way of an example she explains that the management accountant gave her some calculations relating to an investment appraisal. The relevant cash flows showed a positive net present value of $350 000 for a five year project when discounted at 12% which she was informed 'was the rate charged on the bank loan raised to finance the investment'. She also noted that the appraisal calculations did not appear to include any considerations of the effects of inflation nor was there any form of risk analysis.

Required:
(a) Explain the meaning of a positive net present value of $350 000.
(b) Comment on the appropriateness or otherwise of using 12% as the discount rate.

6* 'Post-completion audits for all major capital investment projects should be the norm for all companies.' Discuss this proposition.

7 'The main reason that many firms choose not to use the discounted cash flow approach to investment appraisal is the unreality of the assumptions underlying the relevant theory.' Discuss.

8* The rationale behind the use of the net present value approach to project appraisal in the public sector is accepted by government as being exactly analogous to the private sector. Explain this rationale and consider any contentious issues that arise when applying this technique in practice.

9 Empirical studies suggest that there are major differences between current theories of investment appraisal and the methods which both private and public sector organisations actually use in evaluating long-term investments. Why is this so and what can be done to improve the financial management aspects of long-term decision-making?

10 Accounting rate of return and payback are widely used by firms in the capital investment process. Suggest reasons for their widespread use. Do you agree with these reasons?

11 Outline how risk might be taken into consideration when using the net present value approach to project appraisal.

12* Explain how the impact of taxation is incorporated into investment-appraisal decisions. Indicate the effects which a lack of taxable profits may have on investment decisions and comment on the main possibilities open to a firm to overcome such effects.

APPENDIX 9.A.1

Present value factors

Table 9.A.1 | The table gives the present value of a single payment received in *n* years in the future discounted at *x*% per year. For example, with a discount rate of 7% a single payment of £1 in six years time has a present value of £0.6663 or 66.63p.

Years	1%	2%	3%	4%	5%	6%	7%	8%	9%	10%
1	0.9901	0.9804	0.9709	0.9615	0.9524	0.9434	0.9346	0.9259	0.9174	0.9091
2	0.9803	0.9612	0.9426	0.9426	0.9070	0.8900	0.8734	0.8573	0.8417	0.8264
3	0.9706	0.9423	0.9151	0.8890	0.8638	0.8396	0.8163	0.7938	0.7722	0.7513
4	0.9610	0.9238	0.8850	0.8548	0.8227	0.7921	0.7629	0.7350	0.7084	0.6830
5	0.9515	0.9057	0.8626	0.8219	0.7835	0.7473	0.7130	0.6806	0.6499	0.6209
6	0.9420	0.8880	0.8375	0.7903	0.7462	0.7050	0.6663	0.6302	0.5963	0.5645
7	0.9327	0.8706	0.8131	0.7599	0.7107	0.6651	0.6227	0.5835	0.5470	0.5132
8	0.9235	0.8535	0.7894	0.7307	0.6768	0.6274	0.5820	0.5403	0.5019	0.4665
9	0.9143	0.8368	0.7664	0.7026	0.6446	0.5919	0.5439	0.5002	0.4604	0.4241
10	0.9053	0.8203	0.7441	0.6756	0.6139	0.5584	0.5083	0.4632	0.4224	0.3855
11	0.8963	0.8043	0.7224	0.6496	0.5847	0.5268	0.4751	0.4289	0.3875	0.3505
12	0.8874	0.7885	0.7014	0.6246	0.5568	0.4970	0.4440	0.3971	0.3555	0.3186
13	0.8787	0.7730	0.6810	0.6006	0.5303	0.4688	0.4150	0.3677	0.3262	0.2897
14	0.8700	0.7579	0.6611	0.5775	0.5051	0.4423	0.3878	0.3405	0.2992	0.2633
15	0.8613	0.7430	0.6419	0.5553	0.4810	0.4173	0.3624	0.3152	0.2745	0.2394
16	0.8528	0.7284	0.6323	0.5339	0.4581	0.3936	0.3387	0.2919	0.2519	0.2176
17	0.8444	0.7142	0.6050	0.5134	0.4363	0.3714	0.3166	0.2703	0.2311	0.1978
18	0.8360	0.7002	0.5874	0.4936	0.4155	0.3503	0.2959	0.2502	0.2120	0.1799
19	0.8277	0.6864	0.5703	0.4746	0.3957	0.3305	0.2765	0.2317	0.1945	0.1635
20	0.8195	0.6730	0.5537	0.4564	0.3769	0.3118	0.2584	0.2145	0.1784	0.1486
21	0.8114	0.6598	0.5375	0.4388	0.3589	0.2942	0.2415	0.1987	0.1637	0.1351
22	0.8034	0.6468	0.5219	0.4220	0.3418	0.2775	0.2257	0.1839	0.1502	0.1228
23	0.7954	0.6342	0.5067	0.4057	0.3256	0.2618	0.2109	0.1703	0.1378	0.1117
24	0.7876	0.6217	0.4919	0.3901	0.3101	0.2470	0.1971	0.1577	0.1264	0.1015
25	0.7798	0.6095	0.4776	0.3751	0.2953	0.2330	0.1842	0.1460	0.1160	0.0923
26	0.7720	0.5976	0.4637	0.3607	0.2812	0.2198	0.1722	0.1352	0.1064	0.0839
27	0.7644	0.5859	0.4502	0.3468	0.2678	0.2074	0.1609	0.1252	0.0976	0.0763
28	0.7568	0.5744	0.4371	0.3335	0.2551	0.1956	0.1504	0.1159	0.0895	0.0693
29	0.7493	0.5631	0.4243	0.3207	0.2429	0.1846	0.1406	0.1073	0.0822	0.0630
30	0.7419	0.5521	0.4120	0.3083	0.2314	0.1741	0.1314	0.0994	0.0754	0.0573
35	0.7059	0.5000	0.3554	0.2534	0.1813	0.1301	0.0937	0.0676	0.0490	0.0356
40	0.6717	0.4529	0.3066	0.2083	0.1420	0.0972	0.0668	0.0460	0.0318	0.0221
45	0.6391	0.4102	0.2644	0.1712	0.1113	0.0727	0.0476	0.0313	0.0207	0.0137
50	0.6080	0.3715	0.2281	0.1407	0.0872	0.0543	0.0339	0.0213	0.0134	0.0085

Table 9.A.1 (continued)

11%	12%	13%	14%	15%	16%	17%	18%	19%	20%	Years
0.9009	0.8929	0.8850	0.8772	0.8696	0.8621	0.8547	0.8475	0.8403	0.8333	1
0.8116	0.7972	0.7831	0.7695	0.7561	0.7432	0.7305	0.7182	0.7062	0.6944	2
0.7312	0.7118	0.6931	0.6750	0.6575	0.6407	0.6244	0.6086	0.5934	0.5787	3
0.6587	0.6355	0.6133	0.5921	0.5718	0.5523	0.5337	0.5158	0.4987	0.4823	4
0.5935	0.5674	0.5428	0.5194	0.4972	0.4761	0.4561	0.4371	0.4190	0.4019	5
0.5346	0.5066	0.4803	0.4556	0.4323	0.4104	0.3898	0.3704	0.3521	0.3349	6
0.4817	0.4523	0.4251	0.3996	0.3759	0.3538	0.3332	0.3139	0.2959	0.2791	7
0.4339	0.4039	0.3762	0.3506	0.3269	0.3050	0.2848	0.2660	0.2487	0.2326	8
0.3909	0.3606	0.3329	0.3075	0.2843	0.2630	0.2434	0.2225	0.2090	0.1938	9
0.3522	0.3220	0.2946	0.2697	0.2472	0.2267	0.2080	0.1911	0.1756	0.1615	10
0.3173	0.2875	0.2607	0.2366	0.2149	0.1954	0.1778	0.1619	0.1476	0.1346	11
0.2858	0.2567	0.2307	0.2076	0.1869	0.1685	0.1520	0.1372	0.1240	0.1122	12
0.2575	0.2292	0.2042	0.1821	0.1625	0.1452	0.1299	0.1163	0.1042	0.0935	13
0.2320	0.2046	0.1807	0.1597	0.1413	0.1252	0.1110	0.0985	0.0876	0.0779	14
0.2090	0.1827	0.1599	0.1401	0.1229	0.1079	0.0949	0.0835	0.0736	0.0649	15
0.1883	0.1631	0.1415	0.1229	0.1069	0.0930	0.0811	0.0708	0.0618	0.0541	16
0.1696	0.1456	0.1252	0.1078	0.0929	0.0802	0.0693	0.0600	0.0520	0.0451	17
0.1528	0.1300	0.1108	0.0946	0.0808	0.0691	0.0592	0.0508	0.0437	0.0376	18
0.1377	0.1161	0.0981	0.0829	0.0703	0.0596	0.0506	0.0431	0.0367	0.0313	19
0.1240	0.1037	0.0868	0.0728	0.0611	0.0514	0.0433	0.0365	0.0308	0.0261	20
0.1117	0.0926	0.0768	0.0638	0.0531	0.0443	0.0370	0.0309	0.0259	0.0217	21
0.1007	0.0826	0.0680	0.0560	0.0462	0.0382	0.0316	0.0262	0.0218	0.0181	22
0.0907	0.0738	0.0601	0.0491	0.0402	0.0329	0.0270	0.0222	0.0183	0.0151	23
0.0817	0.0659	0.0532	0.0431	0.0349	0.0284	0.0231	0.0188	0.0154	0.0126	24
0.0736	0.0588	0.0471	0.0378	0.0304	0.0245	0.0197	0.0160	0.0129	0.0105	25
0.0663	0.0525	0.0417	0.0331	0.0264	0.0211	0.0169	0.0135	0.0109	0.0087	26
0.0597	0.0469	0.0369	0.0291	0.0230	0.0182	0.0144	0.0115	0.0091	0.0073	27
0.0538	0.0419	0.0326	0.0255	0.0200	0.0157	0.0123	0.0097	0.0077	0.0061	28
0.0485	0.0374	0.0289	0.0224	0.0174	0.0135	0.0105	0.0082	0.0064	0.0051	29
0.0437	0.0334	0.0256	0.0194	0.0151	0.0116	0.0090	0.0070	0.0054	0.0042	30
0.0259	0.0189	0.0.139	0.0102	0.0075	0.0055	0.0041	0.0030	0.0023	0.0017	35
0.0154	0.0107	0.0075	0.0053	0.0037	0.0026	0.0019	0.0013	0.0010	0.0007	40
0.0091	0.0061	0.0041	0.0027	0.0019	0.0013	0.0009	0.0006	0.0004	0.0003	45
0.0054	0.0035	0.0022	0.0014	0.0009	0.0006	0.0004	0.0003	0.0002	0.0001	50

APPENDIX 9.A.2

Present value factors

Table 9.A.2	The table gives the present value of *n* annual payments of £1 received for the next *n* years with a constant discount of *x*% per year. For example, with a discount rate of 7% and with six annual payments of £1, the present value is £4.767 (reproduced from Drury 1992).

Years 0 to:	1%	2%	3%	4%	5%	6%	7%	8%	9%	10%
1	0.990	0.980	0.971	0.962	0.952	0.943	0.935	0.926	0.917	0.909
2	1.970	1.942	1.913	1.886	1.859	1.833	1.808	1.783	1.759	1.736
3	2.941	2.884	2.829	2.775	2.723	2.673	2.624	2.577	2.531	2.487
4	3.902	3.080	3.717	3.630	3.546	3.465	3.387	3.312	3.240	3.170
5	4.853	4.713	4.580	4.452	4.329	4.212	4.100	3.993	3.890	3.791
6	5.795	5.061	5.417	5.242	5.076	4.917	4.767	4.623	4.486	4.355
7	6.728	6.472	6.230	6.002	5.786	5.582	5.389	5.206	5.033	4.868
8	7.652	7.352	7.020	6.733	6.463	6.210	5.971	5.747	5.535	5.335
9	8.556	8.162	7.786	7.435	7.108	6.802	6.515	6.247	5.995	5.759
10	9.471	8.983	8.530	8.111	7.722	7.360	7.024	6.710	6.418	6.145
11	10.368	9.787	9.253	8.760	8.306	7.887	7.499	7.139	6.805	6.495
12	11.255	10.575	9.954	9.385	8.863	8.384	7.943	7.536	7.161	6.814
13	12.134	11.348	10.635	9.986	9.394	8.853	8.358	7.904	7.487	7.103
14	13.004	12.106	11.296	10.563	9.899	9.295	8.745	8.244	7.786	7.367
15	13.865	12.849	11.938	11.118	10.380	9.712	9.108	8.559	8.061	7.606
16	14.718	13.578	12.561	11.652	10.838	10.106	9.447	8.851	8.313	7.824
17	15.562	14.292	13.166	12.166	11.274	10.427	9.763	9.122	8.544	8.022
18	16.398	14.992	13.754	12.659	11.690	10.828	10.059	9.372	8.756	8.201
19	17.226	15.678	14.324	13.134	12.085	11.158	10.336	9.604	8.950	8.365
20	18.046	16.351	14.877	13.590	12.462	11.470	10.594	9.818	9.129	8.514
21	18.857	17.011	15.415	14.029	12.821	11.764	10.836	10.017	9.292	8.649
22	19.660	17.658	15.937	14.451	13.163	12.042	11.061	10.201	9.442	8.772
23	20.456	18.292	16.444	14.857	13.489	12.303	11.272	10.371	9.580	8.883
24	21.243	18.914	16.939	15.247	13.799	12.550	11.469	10.529	9.707	9.985
25	22.023	19.523	17.413	15.622	14.094	12.783	11.654	10.675	9.823	9.077
26	22.795	20.121	17.877	15.983	13.375	13.003	11.826	10.810	9.929	9.161
27	23.560	20.707	18.327	16.330	14.643	13.211	11.987	10.935	10.027	9.237
28	24.316	21.281	18.764	16.663	13.898	13.406	12.137	11.051	10.116	9.307
29	25.066	21.844	19.188	16.984	15.141	13.591	12.278	11.158	10.198	9.307
30	25.808	22.396	19.600	17.292	15.372	13.765	12.409	11.258	10.274	9.427
35	29.409	24.999	21.487	18.665	16.374	14.498	12.948	11.655	10.567	9.644
40	32.835	27.355	23.115	19.793	17.159	15.046	13.332	11.925	10.575	9.779
45	36.095	29.490	24.519	20.720	17.774	15.456	13.606	12.108	10.881	9.863
50	39.196	31.424	25.730	21.482	18.256	15.762	13.801	12.233	10.962	9.915

Table 9.A.2	(continued)									
11%	*12%*	*13%*	*14%*	*15%*	*16%*	*17%*	*18%*	*19%*	*20%*	*Years 0 to:*
0.901	0.893	0.885	0.877	0.870	0.862	0.855	0.847	0.840	0.833	1
1.713	1.690	1.668	1.647	1.626	1.605	1.585	1.566	1.547	1.528	2
2.444	2.402	2.361	2.322	2.283	2.246	2.210	2.174	2.140	2.106	3
3.102	3.037	2.974	2.914	2.855	2.798	2.743	2.690	2.639	2.589	4
3.696	3.605	3.517	3.433	3.352	3.274	3.199	3.127	3.058	2.991	5
4.231	4.111	3.998	3.889	3.784	3.685	3.589	3.498	3..410	3.326	6
4.712	4.564	4.423	4.288	4.160	4.039	3.922	3.812	3.706	3.605	7
5.146	4.968	4.799	4.639	4.487	4.344	4.207	4.078	3.954	3.837	8
5.537	5.328	5.132	4.946	4.772	4.607	4.451	4.303	4.163	4.031	9
5.889	5.650	5.426	5.216	5.019	4.833	4.659	4.494	4.339	4.192	10
6.207	5.938	5.687	5.453	5.234	5.029	4.836	4.656	4.486	4.327	11
6.492	6.194	5.918	5.660	5.421	5.197	4.988	4.793	4.611	4.439	12
6.750	6.424	6.122	5.842	5.583	5.342	5.118	4.910	4.715	4.533	13
6.982	6.628	6.302	3.002	5.724	5.468	5.229	5.008	4.802	4.611	14
7.191	6.811	6.462	6.142	5.847	5.575	5.324	5.092	4.876	4.675	15
7.379	6.974	6.604	6.265	5.954	5.668	5.405	5.162	4.938	4.730	16
7.549	7.120	6.729	6.373	6.047	5.749	5.475	5.222	4.990	4.775	17
7.702	7.250	6.840	6.467	6.128	5.818	5.534	5.273	5.033	4.812	18
7.839	7.366	6.938	6.550	6.198	5.877	5.584	5.316	5.070	4.843	19
7.963	7.469	7.025	6.623	6.259	5.929	5.628	5.353	5.101	4.870	20
8.075	7.562	7.102	6.687	6.312	5.973	5.665	5.381	5.127	4.891	21
8.176	7.645	7.170	6.743	6.359	6.011	5.696	5.410	5.149	4.909	22
8.266	7.718	7.230	6.792	6.399	6.044	5.723	5.432	5.167	4.925	23
8.348	7.784	7.283	6.835	6.434	6.073	5.746	5.451	5.182	4.937	24
8.422	7.843	7.330	6.873	6.464	6.097	5.766	5.467	5.195	4.948	25
8.488	7.896	7.372	6.906	6.491	6.118	5.783	5.480	5.206	4.956	26
8.548	7.943	7.409	6.935	6.514	6.136	5.798	5.492	5.215	4.964	27
8.602	7.984	7.441	6.961	6.534	6.152	5.810	5.502	5.223	4.970	28
8.650	8.022	7.470	6.983	6.551	6.166	5.820	5.510	5.229	4.975	29
8.694	8.055	7.496	7.003	6.566	6.177	5.829	5.517	5.235	4.979	30
8.855	8.176	7.586	7.070	6.617	6.215	5.858	5.539	5.251	4.992	35
8.951	8.244	7.634	7.105	6.642	6.233	5.871	5.548	5.258	4.997	40
9.008	8.283	7.661	7.123	6.654	6.242	5.877	5.552	5.261	4.999	45
9.042	8.304	7.675	7.133	6.661	6.246	5.880	5.554	5.262	4.999	50

Financing business operations

10

Chapter preview

The purpose of this chapter is that of providing a general background to the financing of business operations. All managers need to have, at least, a basic level of financial literacy. They need to understand the importance of financial markets, the basic sources of funds available to their businesses and the costs of such finance. The whole of financial theory is predicated on the fact that management and investors are able to raise funds and buy and sell securities by transactions in efficient financial markets. We discuss the importance and role of **stock exchanges** and whether stock exchanges are indeed efficient. In discussing efficiency we consider to what degree market speculators are able to beat the market and whether management are able to overstate their firm's financial performance by means of **creative accounting**. Whilst this chapter is mainly concerned with the financing of long-term operations it is also necessary to recognise that short to medium sources of funds are also important to the firm and we briefly review the main sources of these funds and their advantages and disadvantages.

Introduction

Up until this point in the text, we have said little about the long-term financing of firms other than to indicate, in broad terms, that their funding is composed of two elements – equity and debt. In addition to being able to interpret financial reports (whether prepared for management or external users of financial statements) all managers need to be broadly financially literate. That is, they need to have a broad understanding of the importance and functioning of the various sources of funds available to them, and how to determine their individual costs. This background is important in order for managers to determine how to meet their overall needs for capital and the timescales of such funding, over the short to medium term and the longer term. Without this background they will not be able to appreciate the importance of the firm's overall **capital structure** and the importance of its **dividend policy**. These topics are discussed in Chapter 11. Managers will not fully appreciate why, for investment purposes, it is important to apply an overall **weighted average cost of capital** when undertaking the type of investment appraisals discussed in Chapter 9. The whole business-economic framework is indeed predicated on satisfying the needs of investors who, from time to time, trade their investments in well-functioning and reasonably efficient **capital markets**.

Not all business investment is undertaken internally. Firms may seek to invest externally by means of an acquisition or merger with another firm. They may also wish, for a variety of reasons, to divest part of their operations. These issues are addressed in Chapter 12. Such key business decisions simply underpin the need for managers to be financially literate, since much of the pricing of such opportunities relies on market-based proxies.

The importance of stock exchanges

Stock exchanges provide two important services. Operating as a **primary market**, they provide the opportunity for firms and government agencies to raise capital by issuing securities. Buyers of such securities may also wish to sell their investments from time to time to other investors. Stock exchanges also provide a market for these transactions, operating as a **secondary market**. Securities traded on a stock exchange fall into two broad categories – equity based securities and debt securities.

Stock exchanges operate in well over 80 countries. Since the 1980s stock exchanges have emerged in many developing and newly industrialised countries, including ones which had historically operated as command economies. Stock exchanges are a key part of the private enterprise system, which underpins the concept of property owning democracies. The World Bank has been a leading advocate of such development, pointing to the success of such countries as Hong Kong, Malaysia, Singapore and South Korea. The advantages of stock exchanges to domestic economies can be summarised as:

- redirecting and encouraging new savings into the corporate sector;
- attracting foreign inward investment;
- assisting in the privatisation process of government enterprises;
- providing a market mechanism that rewards financially efficient firms and penalises inefficient firms.

For individual firms, the advantages of having their securities listed (quoted) on a stock exchange include:

- access to new lines of capital funding;
- the opportunity to enhance their business activities by means of external growth;
- a means of benchmarking financial performance;

- the possibility of improving the level of their financial gearing (leverage);
- recognition of their standing both nationally and, perhaps, internationally.

Investors, by trading on stock exchanges, are able to spread the risk of their investments by the development of portfolios that provide a risk-reward trade-off. The secondary market function of stock exchanges means that investors can trade in and out of investments easily, and can liquidate them when they desire.

Table 10.1 lists the 12 most important international stock exchanges, together with their web-mail addresses. Readers can access these sites for up-to-date information on market size, turnover, other trading statistics, listing and other regulatory requirements. The London Stock Exchange, which dates back to the seventeenth century and is the oldest and one of the largest in the world, has more overseas companies listed than any other market; roughly double the number on the NASDAQ. These companies comprise the leading multinationals, whose market value in fact exceeds the total market value of the domestic (UK) listed companies by a factor of around 3:1. Loan capital and public sector securities each account for less than 10% of the total market capitalisation of the London Stock Exchange. Whilst London has more companies listed than New York, the total market value of the listed companies in New York is higher.

In recent years, moves in the USA and by the European Union (EU) have been designed to attract even more foreign firms to seek listings on their stock exchanges. Such moves have further increased the globalisation of stock market trading. An investor wishing to trade in the shares of a major international company, and finding the London Stock Exchange closed, might just as easily trade in New York. If New York was also closed then, once again switching time zones, Tokyo or Sydney might be tried. Within the EU, policies (termed Directives) have been implemented that should lead to the mutual recognition of each member country's stock exchanges. For example, listing requirements have been harmonised such that all new entrants to an EU stock exchange must have a minimum of a three-year trading record. Previously the London Stock Exchange required a five-year trading record.

Table 10.1	The top 12 international stock exchanges in terms of the market value of listed equities	
Austral-Asia	**Europe**	**North America**
Australia www.asx.com.au	Frankfurt www.deutsche-boerse.com	NASDAQ www.nasdaq.com
Hong Kong www.hkex.com.hk	London www. londonstockexchange.com	New York www.nyse.com
Korea www.krx.or.kr	Luxembourg www.bourse.lu	Toronto www.tsx.com
Tokyo www.tse.or.jp	Paris www.euronext.com	
	Vienna www.wienerboerse.at	

This globalisation of stock market trading, and the need for a commonality of information, was a major factor in the collaboration between International Oraganisation of Security Commissions (IOSCO) and the International Accounting Standards Board in the development of an agreed set of standards for financial reporting. This collaboration is discussed in more detail in Chapter 13.

As indicated above, a quotation on a stock exchange adds to the reputation of a firm. Typically, large investors prefer to invest in quoted companies because of the marketability of both their equity shares and debt securities. Although many governments actively try to attract the smaller investor to the stock exchange, the truth is that it is the large institutional investors, such as insurance companies, pension and trust funds, that dominate the trading activity on stock exchanges. Most of us, even if not direct personal investors, are therefore often third-party investors on the market by proxy.

Although individual rules vary, in terms of detail, all leading stock exchanges require their listed companies to make annual financial disclosures, as well as publishing relevant information at other times, such as when a new issue of capital is to be made or a take-over bid is to be announced. This information is required in order to provide investors with the fullest possible knowledge about each listed company's business activities, profit record and future prospects for earnings and dividends. Other information will also include disclosure of major shareholder and director share interests.

The costs of obtaining a listing on a stock exchange are high. First, there are the costs of gaining an initial listing; secondly, the costs of meeting all the relevant auditing and financial reporting requirements. The initial listing costs will vary depending upon the type of listing sought. For example, a **placement,** which is a private sale to clients of an issuing house or broker, which is much cheaper than an **offer for sale.** An offer for sale is made to the public at large, via a **prospectus,** with the price per share being stated. Well-established private companies, or those already listed on another stock exchange, wishing to gain a listing rather than, at this point in time, seeking to raise additional capital, may apply for what is termed a **stock exchange introduction.** In such cases the relevant stock exchange will normally only permit an introduction if it is satisfied that there will be, over time, a free market in the shares.

Stock market efficiency

From a financial economics perspective, the efficiency of financial markets is key to the optimal allocation of available funds across the variously traded securities. For this to happen, investors wishing to either buy or sell securities need to feel confident that market prices fairly represent their underlying value. This notion of market efficiency is also important to managers hoping to raise funds in the market at a cost that fairly reflects the risk-return trade-off of the projects for which funding is sought. It is also important in terms of the market being able to evaluate a firm's financial performance such that its quoted share price is deemed to be a fair one.

For a considerable period of time, academics (and others) have sought to test this notion of market efficiency with respect to the pricing of equity shares. What has been termed the **efficient markets hypothesis** (EMH) has been tested at three levels:

1 *Weak form tests* – which attempt to ascertain whether a knowledge and analysis of past price data of securities can successfully be used to predict future prices.

2 *Semi-strong form tests* – which attempt to examine whether the knowledge of all publicly available information is encapsulated in the market price of a share.

3 *Strong form tests* – which consider whether all knowledge, whether in the public domain, or internal to the company, is reflected in the market price of securities.

With regard to weak form tests, research shows that if this were all the information available to financial analysts, then they would not be very successful in forecasting future prices. Most research supports the semi-strong form test of the EMH. That is that current market prices tend to reflect all publicly available knowledge about quoted companies and that these market prices adjust quickly when new information becomes available. Note that when we talk about all public knowledge, or information, we do not just mean financial information relevant to a particular company or industry sector. Information can be as diverse as, for example, the death of a key director, a corporate scandal, the impact of new government legislation or a macroeconomic event such as the impact of rising world crude oil prices.

Fama *et al.* (1969) were the first to show that markets in the USA tended to operate to the semi-strong form of the test. Firth (1977) and Marsh (1977) showed that the price of shares in the UK performed entirely consistently to the semi-strong form of the EMH. The importance of this research is that no one group of investors can be said to use this information to attain an abnormal gain; that is, on average, to outperform the market.

Strong-form tests involve examining whether professional analysts or company insiders have access to privileged information that affords them an (unfair) advantage in the market. With respect to insiders, legislation attempts to protect other investors from **insider trading**. Informed investors, such as investment fund managers, do sometimes appear, in the short term, to outperform the market but in the longer term they appear not to consistently outperform the market.

As Samuels *et al.* (1995: 400) state:

> Why insider dealing is an important issue from the point of view of stock market efficiency is because the strong form of the test of the market efficiency is concerned with price movements in response to any information. That is information whether publicly available or not. It has been found that within limits share prices in the market reflect all publicly available information. They do not, however, reflect information not available to the public. People with access to non-public information (insiders) can therefore make above average returns. If 'insider dealing' is known to be taking place in the stock market, it will frighten investors without insider knowledge and keep them out of the stock market. The view is taken therefore in most stock markets that an individual may not deal in securities of a company if he or she has price-sensitive information, which is held by virtue of being a connected person or having obtained inside information from such a person. Similarly, an insider must not counsel or procure others to act on inside information and must communicate such information to anyone else.

Insider trading, in most countries, is subject to both statutory and non-statutory regulation. Non-statutory regulation involves, for example, breaches of stock exchange rules and the ethical codes of practice of relevant professional bodies. Despite increasing penalties, it has to be said that the practice of insider dealing does not appear to be on the decline; and despite also the large body of empirical evidence in support of stock market efficiency doubts persist. Again to quote Samuels *et al.* (1995: 404):

> These tests indicate that the EMH cannot be rejected on the basis of the data being used – this does not mean that the tests prove that the market is efficient.

> The empirical tests in fact can neither confirm nor disconfirm that stock markets are efficient. The tests do not establish that a stock market is efficient. All they show is that it cannot be proved that it is inefficient.

Most of the empirical research has been carried out in the USA and care needs to be taken when assuming that the findings automatically apply to the efficiency of stock exchange trading in Europe or the Austral-Asian region. Another basic problem is that the valuation models commonly employed for valuing shares (see later) are based on a number of simplifying assumptions that are only as good as their underlying relevance.

In 1986, the internationally renowned US financial economist, Black, told the American Finance Association that he thought US markets were efficient almost all of the time. By that he meant 90% of the time, which leaves plenty of room for market speculation.

We also know that, since the 1980s there have been a spate of scandals with listed companies seeking to manipulate the earnings figures that they publish in order to deceive the market about the 'true' state of their financial performance. Cases such as Enron, HIH Insurance, Rank Xerox and Worldcom have all been the subject of investigation (and in some cases criminal prosecutions) and subject to international media attention. Sadly in such cases it is not only senior management who have been involved, but also external financial advisors and auditors. Creative accounting practices have shaken the faith of many investors in their belief that markets operate efficiently. In Chapter 12 we provide an example of one such practice, the manipulation of earnings-per-share figures in respect of one aspect of a business reorganisation strategy.

Smith (1996) has listed 12 possible accounting techniques that have been used by listed companies as a means of creatively raising their profits. These are:

1 Write down of pre-acquisition costs and potential future costs.
2 Profits on disposal of a business.
3 Deferred purchase consideration.
4 Extraordinary and exceptional items of income and expenditure.
5 Off-balance sheet finance.
6 Contingent liabilities.
7 Capitalisation of costs.
8 Brand accounting.
9 Changes in depreciation policy.
10 Convertible securities.
11 Pension fund accounting.
12 Treatment of foreign currency items.

When Smith wrote the first edition of his book, he was working as a market analyst for UBS Philips and Drew in London. Being a professional analyst, his book received widespread publicity and Smith was featured in a BBC television documentary. Of the 12 areas of accounting manipulation cited, Smith had identified one listed company that had actually adopted nine of these ploys, two companies that had adopted eight, four that had used seven and 15 that had used six. Because Smith dared to go public and reveal some of the accounting scams used by well-known corporate bodies he was sacked.

Manipulation of accounting reports can occur for a number of reasons. For example, directors' remuneration may be linked to company earnings; or perhaps, following a takeover, directors wish to impress their existing shareholders with their performance. In any event the current trend of monitoring earnings (sometimes referred to as the bottom-line) would appear to be a cause for some unscrupulous board members to try to pull the wool over the eyes of some of their colleagues, their shareholders and the market at large. Capital markets appear to be far less concerned with monitoring stewardship and much more fixated with the earnings per share and price-earnings ratio as the main criteria for measuring corporate performance. In fairness, it must also be pointed out the various bodies responsible for issuing statements dealing with financial reporting standards have, in recent years, taken on board many of these issues and have promulgated financial reporting standards to deal with them. This was undoubtedly one of the motivations behind the collaboration between IOSCO and the IASB referred to above.

To conclude this section, we can state that in many respects the leading stock markets do appear to operate efficiently. Despite the reservations just highlighted, it is important that researchers continue to investigate market efficiency. There are no doubt anomalies that do occur, some shares may, from time to time, be overvalued or undervalued. Speculators may make short-term gains, but research does tend to show that overall, and over time, price movements are random and that it is not possible to consistently outperform the market. For management, market prices can generally be taken to be a fair reflection of the value of equity shares and other quoted securities.

The valuation of listed securities

In this section we outline the basic methods for valuing shares, bonds, debt and other securities. We commence with the valuation of equity.

The valuation of equity shares

The most traditional way of measuring the market price of a share is to use the **dividend valuation model**. This model recognises the fact that shares are in themselves **perpetuities**. Once listed, individual investors buy and sell them, but only exceptionally are they actually redeemed by the company. In this model, the current value of a share (P_0) is taken to be the present value of the expected future stream of dividend payments. Those not familiar with the concept of present value and the time value of money should briefly refer to the Appendix to this chapter before continuing with this topic. The relevant expression can be written thus:

$$P_0 = \frac{d_1}{(1 + K_e)} + \frac{d_2}{(1 + K_e)^2} + \frac{d_3}{(1 + K_e)^3} + \text{into perpetuity } (\infty) \qquad \textbf{(10.1)}$$

where: d_n = expected future dividend at time n,
K_e = the required rate of return on equity.

This expression can, fortunately, be simplified to (see note 1)

$$P_0 = \frac{d_1}{K_e} \qquad \textbf{(10.2)}$$

By way of illustration, let us suppose that a share has a current market value of $2 in a static economic environment where a constant annual dividend of 20 cents is anticipated. Rearranging equation 10.2, we are able to find the cost of equity as follows:

$$K_e = \frac{d_1}{P_0} = \frac{\$0.20}{\$2.00} = 0.1 \text{ or } 10\%.$$

As in any simple algebraic expression, if we know any two of three component items then we can calculate the third. For example, if in this case the next anticipated dividend was not to be paid as expected but reduced to 15 cents, and if investor expectations (requirements) remain at 10%, then we would expect a downward adjustment to the current share price, thus:

$$P_0 = \frac{d_1}{K_e} = \frac{\$0.15}{0.10} = \$1.50.$$

The dividend valuation model therefore states that the current share price is totally determined by the anticipated future flow of dividends, discounted by the investor's required rate of return. It is a model that, since listed share prices are quoted, can be related to future dividends and shareholders' expected returns.

This basic model can be further developed to allow for growth in the future expected dividends stream. In similar fashion to the stages first outlined, this perpetuity valuation model reduces to (see note 2):

$$P_0 = \frac{d_1}{(K_e - g)} \tag{10.3}$$

and the cost of equity capital becomes:

$$K_e = \frac{d_1}{P_0} + g \tag{10.4}$$

where: g denotes the anticipated growth factor.

Continuing with our illustration, if dividends are expected to grow by about 5% compound per annum, then the equity cost of capital becomes:

$$K_e = \frac{d_1}{P_0} + g = \frac{\$0.20}{\$2.00} + 5.5 = 0.15 \text{ or } 15\%.$$

For K_e to be realistic, market expectations must be such that dividends are believed to grow at a rate of g. One method of projection would be to examine the past history of dividend payments in an attempt to gain an insight into future dividend expectations. Such an approach would mean that investors expect past performance to provide a suitable proxy for future performance. There is of course no real rational basis for assumption, dividends could easily rise or fall in the future. If anything other than a constant growth of dividends is expected in the future, the model must be sub-divided into time periods, each spanning an expected growth pattern. More sophisticated models have been developed to cope with such forecasts but we will stick with the basic model for the purposes of further discussion.

Dividends are paid periodically on shares. The dividend valuation model assumes the next dividend is due in 12 months time. During the period prior to the payment of a dividend, the market price of a share rises in anticipation of the payment. At this stage (from the Latin) the price is said to be *cum div*. After the dividend is paid the share price is quoted (again, from the Latin) *ex div* and the price drops. In our illustration the *cum div* share price would be $2.20 and the *ex div* price would drop to $2, once the dividend of 20 cents was paid. Readers should note that in practice shares go *ex div* shortly before the dividend is actually paid. Any new investor acquiring shares at this point in time will not receive the dividend, which will be paid to the previous owner. The rationale for this is based on the fact that it can take time for a company to amend its register of members and it is therefore logical to have a cut-off date sometime before the actual date of payment of the dividend.

Whilst few would disagree with the basic premise of the dividend valuation model, that is that the value of a share relates to its future (dividend) income stream, the major weakness of the model stems from limitations in determining the relevant input data. Based upon our previous analysis of market efficiency, we can state that any difference between an investor's calculation of a share's 'true worth' and its quoted market price probably represents an error in the forecasts (d and K_e) used in the computation rather than the share being over or under priced. P_0 could also be susceptible to short-term influences, such as rumours of a takeover bid or an announcement of an unsuccessful business venture.

The version of the model incorporating the growth factor (g) is generally regarded as more realistic, if only because growth is likely to occur because of inflation. However, perhaps unrealistically, it must be remembered that this growth factor is growth into perpetuity. The logic of the model is that, just as dividends grow, so too will the share price over time. From our illustration, we should expect the $2 share to rise to $2.10 in a year's time ($2 $\times$ 1.05).

The **capital asset pricing model** (CAPM) can also be used to estimate the value of K_e, the equity cost of capital. As explained in Chapter 9, this model provides a measure of equity return that allows for the **systematic risk** in the market. Systematic risk is based on factors external to the firm, caused by underlying movements in the economy. This risk cannot be diversified away by an investor and is measured by what is known as a **beta factor** (β). It is this risk measure that provides for a premium to be paid for equity investment over and above the rate of return of a virtually risk free investment, such as provided by government bonds. The assumption here being that governments rarely, if ever, default on their payments.

The dividend valuation model is often used for the valuation of shares in **unquoted companies** by applying the required rate of return for a **quoted company** in a similar line of business to the dividend forecasts of the unquoted firm. There is though one major problem. Shares in unquoted firms are not easy to sell. Potential buyers will therefore expect to pay perhaps considerably less than the price of an equivalent quoted share, unless they can identify a clear exit strategy. Therefore, any computed value obtained by using the required rate of return for quoted companies in the dividend valuation model must be scaled down to factor in this lack of marketability. The extent of such scaling is, inevitably, subjective. It must also be recognised that the dividend distribution policies of unquoted companies will frequently reflect the income needs and taxation position of dominant (often family) shareholders.

We can illustrate the nature of this problem by considering the case of Barter Ltd, an unquoted family owned and managed company that is forecasting a dividend of $0.30 per share in 12 months time, and a growth rate of 5% per annum in dividends. Smarter Ltd is a quoted company in a similar line of business. Its shares are valued at $1 each *ex div* on the basis of a forecast of 15 cents per share dividend next year, and a forecast growth rate of 5% per annum. The managing director of Barter is willing to sell some shares in the company to a relative who wishes to have a stake in the family company. The question is what should the price be?

From the information available we can first estimate the rate of return offered by Smarter to its existing shareholders. Utilising equation 10.4:

$$K_e = \frac{d_1}{P_0} + g = \frac{\$0.15}{\$1.00} + 0.05 = 0.20, \text{ or } 20\%.$$

If we were to apply this rate of return to the dividend forecast of Barter then utilising equation 10.3:

$$P_0 = \frac{d_1}{(K_e - g)} = \frac{\$3.30}{(0.20 - 0.05)} = \$2.00.$$

On this basis, the value of Barter's shares are double those of Smarter. This makes little sense given the advantages commonly attributed to owning shares in listed companies as opposed to unlisted companies. Clearly the model has taken account of the fact that Barter pays a dividend double that of Smarter. However, it could be argued that the reason for this is the higher risk that might be associated with a smaller, unquoted, family business. In order to get a realistic price for Barter's shares there is a need to scale down (albeit subjectively) the computed price. Such an 'adjusted' price would presumably be based on a price less than that currently quoted for Smarter. In the end, however, the ultimate price that will be agreed – between the managing director of Barter and his relative – will depend on the outcome of negotiations between them.

An alternative approach to valuing shares is based on the use of a multiple of the company's earnings per share (EPS). The normal multiplier employed is a price-earnings (P/E) ratio. Both of these concepts are discussed in more detail in Chapter 15. As that chapter discusses, the P/E ratio for a listed company is the current quoted price for an equity share divided by the latest, most recent reported EPS. The reciprocal of the P/E ratio is called the **earnings yield**. The popularity of this approach can be attributed to the fact that many daily newspapers (e.g. *The Financial Times*) regularly publish the P/E ratios of major quoted companies in their financial or business news section. A high P/E ratio indicates that the market thinks that a particular company has good growth potential and/or a high quality earnings stream. To illustrate, if the EPS for a listed company was 35 cents and its P/E ratio was 5, then its share price would be $1.75 ($0.35 × 5).

As with the dividend valuation model, this approach to the valuation of shares in unlisted companies has its limitations. Firstly, what denotes an appropriate P/E ratio? Using the information published in the financial press, should we use an industry average P/E ratio, or that of a specific company? The core of the problem is that no two firms are exactly alike, and issues such as the extent of diversification need to be taken into account. Secondly, when it comes to determining the earnings figure to be used in the calculation, do we take the most recent reported figure at face value, or adjust it for factors such as unusual earnings? Thirdly, should allowance be made for the fact that the current share price might be the result of abnormal market conditions? These are major difficulties. However, an undoubted merit of the P/E ratio approach to valuation is its ease of calculation, but its underlying assumptions mask the real world complexities of valuing shares.

In practice shares in unquoted companies are frequently valued by applying an agreed P/E ratio to an agreed figure of 'maintainable' earnings, for example in takeover situations. To illustrate, Carter Ltd, an unquoted company, has generated earnings of $250 000 this year. A quoted company in a similar line of business,

Jupiter Ltd, has a market price of $4 per share and an EPS of 40 cents, giving it a P/E ratio of 10. To arrive at a value for Carter's shares we could multiply its earnings by the P/E of Jupiter as follows:

$$\$250\ 000 \times 10 = \$2\ 500\ 000$$

As indicated earlier, such a 'benchmark' valuation really needs adjusting to reflect the difference in the marketability and benefits attaching to shares in quoted as opposed to unquoted companies – in reality such an adjustment will almost certainly be downwards. We might (subjectively) feel it appropriate to revise the relevant P/E ratio downwards to, say, 6 (rather than the original 10), which would give the lower valuation of $1 500 000. Once again, the final price will be a matter of negotiation between the relevant parties.

The cost of preference shares

The cost of a **preference share** is closely related to its stated preferential dividend entitlement, even though such dividends are still paid at the discretion of the directors. If a $1 nominal value preference share, listed on a stock exchange, has a (fixed) preferential dividend entitlement of 7.5% and a current market value of $0.90, then its equivalent cost of capital would be:

$$K_p = \frac{d_p}{P_{po}} = \frac{7.5}{90} = 0.833, \text{ or } 8.33\%.$$

where: K_p = the cost of the preference share,
d_p = the fixed dividend based on the nominal value,
P_{po} = the current market price of the preference share.

Over recent years, as part of a general trend towards the simplification of companies' capital structures, there has been a marked slump in the popularity of preference shares on the part of issuing companies. For this reason we will not discuss them further.

Cost of debt finance

Traditionally debt finance, especially long-term debt finance, has been subject to fixed interest rates and raised on the stock market by the sale of securities, typically corporate **loan stock** or **debentures**. The basis of the valuation of this form of debt finance is fairly straightforward, being based on the dividend valuation model, allowing for the fact that most debt finance has a fixed repayment date and therefore (on the face of it) does not involve a perpetuity. Thus:

$$D_0 = \frac{I_1}{(1 + K_d)} + \frac{I_2}{(1 + K_d)^2} + \ldots + \frac{I_1 + D_n}{(1 + K_d)^n} \tag{10.5}$$

where: D_0 = current market price of debt,
I_n = interest payment at time n,
D_n = amount payable on redemption,
K_d = cost of debt capital.

Suppose a debenture has a fixed interest rate of 8% and was issued at a price of $100 and that it will be redeemed in ten years' time. Shortly after it was issued the market price of the debenture dropped to $90. What should the market cost of this debenture be revised to? Utilising equation 10.5 we need to find the value of K_d:

$$\$90 = \frac{8}{(1 + K_d)} + \frac{8}{(1 + K_d)^2} +...+ \frac{(8 + 100)}{(1 + K_d)^{10}}$$

We can use interpolation to find the relevant value for K_d, which turns out to be just above 10%. Those not familiar with the application of discounted cash flows might like to read the relevant section in Chapter 8 in order to better understand how this result was obtained.

Interest charges are a tax deductible expense for corporation tax purposes in most countries, but any K_d computed should not be adjusted to a net of tax basis. This is because the tax advantage of debt is reflected in the cost of equity, because dividends and retained earnings are higher than would otherwise be the case.

Whilst individual debt instruments are repaid from time to time, a company normally replaces, or rolls over, this debt capacity with the issue of new debt securities to maintain its desired overall debt/equity capital structure. In such instances, the appropriate formula for calculating the cost of debt is in the form of a perpetuity and becomes (see equation 10.2 for the analogy):

$$K_d = \frac{I_n}{D_0} \tag{10.6}$$

To illustrate this formula, suppose that an irredeemable debenture, with a $100 nominal value, pays a nominal rate of 5% per annum. If the required return on the market for this type of security is currently 12.5%, then at what price will this debenture be traded? Rearranging equation 10.6 we have:

$$D_0 = \frac{I_n}{K_d} = \frac{\$5}{0.125} = \$40.$$

If the current interest rates rise further to, say, 15% per annum, then one would expect this security to further drop in price:

$$D_0 = \frac{I_n}{K_d} = \frac{\$5}{0.15} = \$33.33$$

This demonstrates the principle that the values of fixed interest stock will fall when interest rates are expected to rise, and vice versa.

In more recent times other forms of debt instruments have been devised, such as convertible debentures (or loan stock) and warrants. **Convertible loan stock** is loan stock that at the option of the holder may be converted into ordinary shares, under specific conditions. **Warrants** are options to buy shares in a company at a given price within a given period. They can be traded on the market and are sometimes issued alongside loan stock as an additional incentive to the lender. Two simple examples illustrate the pricing of each of these instruments:

- Heart Ltd has 8% convertible loan stock in issue. The conversion terms are 80 ordinary shares for every $100 of loan stock, otherwise the loan stock will be redeemed at par. If today is the last date for conversion or redemption, above what price is it worth converting to shares as opposed to receiving the proceeds on redemption?

Solution:

Redemption proceeds	$100
Therefore, 80 shares at $1.25	$100

   To gain a benefit by conversion the shares must be trading above $1.25.

- Spade Ltd has issued warrants to subscribe for ordinary shares at an **exercise price** of $1.25 per share. What is the value of this warrant if the current share price is (a) $1.40, and (b) $1.20?

Solution:
(a) Value of warrant: $1.40 – $1.25 = $0.15.

(b) Value of the warrant: Zero, it is not a negative value as the holder of the warrant has an option, not an obligation, to subscribe.

Costs and sources of short- and medium-term finance

All too often management concentrates on the longer-term sources of finance available to enterprises. However, for many businesses short- and medium-term finance is of great importance, particularly the management of what is commonly called 'working capital' (an issue which is focused on in Chapter 6). At the end of the day, a business needs access to short-term funding to settle its immediate liabilities. Some types of businesses, e.g. in the retail sector, traditionally rely to a greater extent than others on short-term finance. This is usually because they have relatively large amounts of short-term assets and are matching their finance to their asset holding. Correspondingly, with a relatively high proportion of long-term (fixed) assets tend to have a higher proportion of long-term (equity or debt) finance.

There is a wide variety of short and medium sources of finance available to business entities and the terms on which such finance is available can vary enormously. However, the principal forms of such finance are: trade credit; bank overdrafts; factoring and invoice discounting; rental/lease agreements; short-term bank borrowing; bills of exchange; acceptance credits and sale and leaseback arrangements.

Trade credit

In essence this involves suppliers providing goods/services to the enterprise on credit terms, e.g. payment being due 30 days after invoice date. Access to such finance is usually a function of the perceived 'creditworthiness' of the enterprise, i.e. how confident are suppliers that they will (ultimately) get paid what they are owed and what are the benefits to them of offering credit? Historically, there has not normally been an explicit finance charge for the provision of such credit. This has been because the provision of the credit has been seen as being part of the overall 'terms of trade' offered by the supplier, and the cost to the supplier of providing the credit has been built into these terms. However, some suppliers will offer a 'cash settlement discount' for early payment, and purchasing enterprises which do not take advantages of such discounts may well incur significant short-term finance costs. This is an issue that is discussed at greater length in Chapter 6. In some countries, there is also an increasing trend for suppliers to charge (attempt to charge) interest to enterprises that do not adhere to their specified trade credit terms – e.g. if such terms are payment within 30 days of invoice date, suppliers may state there will be an interest charge of 1% per month (or part thereof) for overdue payments. It is not clear how effective such attempts to charge interest are – much will depend on the broader commercial relationships between the enterprise and its supplier.

Bank overdrafts

These are a common form of short-term finance. However, there are some important features to note about overdrafts:

(a) They normally involve a business entity agreeing an overdraft facility with its bankers. Interest is only payable on the actual amount of the overdraft borrowing (normally computed on a daily basis). However, the bankers will normally seek to impose some form of 'arrangement' fee for agreeing to the overdraft facility.

(b) In theory, and sometimes in practice, overdrafts are repayable on demand by the bankers. As such they may, depending on the relationship between an enterprise and its bankers, be a rather insecure form of finance.

(c) The interest rates that banks charge on overdrafts may be rather high – perhaps 1.5 to 2 times higher than they charge on loans.

(d) As with any other form of bank finance, the providers (bankers) may only provide such finance if the borrower is able to offer them adequate security, e.g. charges over property assets.

Flexibility is the major advantage of a bank overdraft facility. It enables the company to match its immediate cash needs with its borrowing. If it does not need to borrow, it does not. If it does need to borrow, it borrows the amount needed on a day-to-day basis, up to the limit of its overdraft facility and only pays interest on the amount borrowed and not on the total amount of the facility. However, there is a price to pay for this flexibility.

Factoring and invoice discounting

A number of enterprises, especially smaller rapidly growing ones, seek to raise finance based on their debtors. In recent years, this has been a rapidly growing source of finance. It takes a variety of forms, depending on the circumstances of the particular enterprise but will (typically) incorporate a mixture of the following features:

(a) A finance house will advance money to the enterprise as and when the enterprise makes credit sales. Typically, the amount of the advance will be 80–90% of the value of such sales.

(b) The finance house will charge the enterprise interest (normally on a monthly basis) for the finance advanced. There may also be some form of management charge.

(c) The finance house will collect the money from the credit sale customers, deduct its charges and pass the balance over to the enterprise.

(d)   The advance may be with recourse (i.e. if the customer defaults the finance house can recover the outstanding balance from the enterprise) or without recourse.

(e)   In extreme cases, the process may effectively involve the finance house taking overall responsibility for the management of the enterprise's credit customers.

Rental/lease agreements

In these cases, enterprises obtain access to the operating capacity they need on deferred payment terms. Rental agreements are fairly straightforward commercial arrangements between someone owning an asset and an enterprise that wants to make use of that asset – perhaps the simplest example is that of a car rental. However, there can be much more to such agreements, effectively involving a finance house funding the acquisition of an asset by an enterprise. For example, a hire purchase agreement, while legally a rental agreement with an option to purchase, is to all practical effect a purchase on credit terms. A key distinction is between an **operating lease**, which is simply a rental agreement (in which there is never intent that title to the underlying asset pass to the lessor) and a **finance lease** via which the lessor is effectively purchasing the underlying asset. A difficulty that such leases can cause for accounting is that, while the legal form of the agreement between the lessor and the lessee is that of a rental agreement, the economic substance is that of a purchasing transaction. Accounting prefers to deal with economic substance and such transactions have to be incorporated in financial statements on that basis. The terms of such leases are a matter of negotiation between the finance house and the lessor. The economic significance of such leases should not be understated, e.g. many airlines acquire their aircraft via finance leases rather than via outright purchase.

Short-term bank borrowing

This does not differ greatly in principle from longer-term bank borrowing (or other forms of debt finance). The key difference is that the duration of the loan is shorter, typically no more than two years.

Bills of exchange

A **bill of exchange** is defined as 'an unconditional order in writing addressed by one person to another signed by the person giving it requiring the person to whom it is addressed to pay on demand, or at some fixed or determinable future time, a sum certain in money to or to the order of a specified person or bearer' (s.3(1), Bills of Exchange Act 1882). In essence, a bill of exchange is rather like a post-dated cheque. The person receiving the bill can either hold it to maturity and present it for payment on the due date or sell it on to a finance house for cash, less a discount. The amount of the discount will depend on the perceived risk of the ultimate collection of the bill, the period of time till the due date and prevailing interest rates. Bills of exchange used to be a very common means of financing commercial transactions. However, as the banking system became more sophisticated and the range of short-term financing opportunities wider, they have become much less common and these days are principally used in connection with overseas trade. In essence, they allow the seller of the goods to receive immediately a negotiable instrument (the bill of exchange) which can be used to obtain cash immediately, albeit at the cost of a discount, and the purchaser of the goods to defer the actual payment for the duration of the bill, typically 60 to 180 days.

Acceptance credit

This is a variant on a bill of exchange. The difference is that the bill of exchange is accepted by a bank, which thereby commits itself to the ultimate settlement of the bill – in effect, it guarantees payment which, of course, makes the bill much more negotiable. The company which draws the bill has to satisfy the bank of its creditworthiness, i.e. its ability to settle the bill on the due date. Acceptance credits have an advantage over bank overdrafts as they form a secure means of credit to the company, at least until the due date of settlement. Having obtained the acceptance from the bank, the company does not have to use it immediately – it can use it as part of a broader set of credit facilities as and when required as a means of deferred payment to suppliers. The amounts involved in acceptance credits are usually relatively large and they are a popular means of finance, mainly because they can prove cheaper and more certain than bank overdrafts.

Sale and leaseback

This is another form of financing which seeks to release cash tied up in assets to the company so that it can be used for other purposes. The assets involved are most commonly property assets. In a sale and leaseback arrangement the company will sell, for cash, the assets (e.g. a building) to a third party, normally a financial institution such as an insurance company, for its current market value and take out a long-term lease at a commercial rental on the asset. The advantage from the company's perspective is that it retains the operating capacity associated with the asset (via the lease) and realises the market value as cash which can be used for alternative investments, or to reduce its debt burden. The downside from the company's perspective is that it is committed to the future rental payments, normally with periodic rent reviews, and will not share in any increase in the market value of the building. The amounts that can be raised by sale and leaseback arrangements are, of course, sensitive to movements in the property market and the timing of a sale and leaseback agreement can be of crucial importance.

Conclusion

One thing that management needs to guard against is the use of short-tem finance to fund the acquisition of long-term assets. The danger is that if they cannot 'roll-over' the short-term finance or obtain alternative long-term funding they may find themselves having to dispose of an asset in distress circumstances. This may undermine the financial viability of the enterprise. Management needs to plan its financing carefully, ensuring that it has an appropriate meld of long- and short-term financing to match its operational needs and investment plans.

Chapter review

Because we live in an uncertain economic environment, different sources of investment capital have different costs due to their different risks. Long-term capital for investment is either generated internally, from retained earnings or capital gains, or raised externally through the medium of the various forms of security available on the stock market. Managers needs to understand the market influences on each source in order to attract new investors, retain the interest of present investors and perceive why other investors have moved their funds elsewhere. They also need to employ a suitable mixture of long- and shorter-term financing opportunities.

Further reading

There are a number of good texts on corporate finance, including Ross *et al.*, *Fundamentals of Corporate Finance* (2001); Brealey and Myers, *Principles of Corporate Finance* (2003); and Samuels *et al.*, *Management of Company Finance* (1999).

Questions and exercises

Guide notes can be found at the back of the book for all questions marked with an asterisk*.

1* The Orion Games Company, a market leader, announces that it is to produce a new interactive computer game. It was not known before this announcement that the company had exceeded its expectations in secret pre-launch test marketing of a prototype which suggests that this will be their best ever game launch. The price of an equity share in Orion before the announcement was $6.90. Consider the following three scenarios:

   (a) Following this announcement the price of an equity share in Orion jumps to $9, and then over the next week drops back to $8.10.

   (b) Following this announcement, the price of an equity share jumps to $8.10 and stays there.

   (c) Following the announcement the price steadily climbs over a number of days to $8.10.

   Required:
   Which scenario indicates an efficient market? Which does not? Why?

2* Company X has 4 million shares in issue and Company Y has 10 million shares in issue.

   On day 1:   the market value per share is £1 for X and £2 for Y.

On day 2:   the directors of Y decide to make a cash takeover bid for X at a price of £1.50 per share. They predict the takeover will produce large operating savings with a present value of £3.2 million.

On day 4:   Y publicly announces an unconditional offer to purchase all shares in X at a price of £1.50 with settlement on day 15. Details of the operating savings are not public knowledge.

On day 10: Y announces details of the anticipated operating savings which are anticipated to arise from the takeover.

Required:
Determine the day 2, 4 and 10 share prices of X and Y if the market is

   (i)   semi-strong form efficient and

   (ii) strong-form efficient.

Ignore tax and the time value of money between days 1 and 10 and assume that only the information provided has any impact on the share prices of X and Y.

3* (a)   A company's last dividend was €0.25. Dividends are expected to increase by 10% per annum. The expected rate of return on shares in the same risk class is 20%.

Required:
   (a)   What is the market value of an equity share in this company?

   (b)   A company has recently paid a dividend per share of €0.10. The price of a share on the stock market is €2.00. The par (nominal) value of the share is €0.50, and they had initially been sold to shareholders for €1.00. The company's policy is to increase dividends by 8% per annum.

   (c)   What is the cost of equity capital to the company?

4   Harkness Ltd, a private company, is considering applying for a stock market listing. The managing director sees that a key benefit of this strategy is the opportunity for existing shareholders to sell their shares while allowing Harkness to raise additional funds for a new capital expenditure programme. The earnings of Harkness over the next financial year are expected to be about £4 million, dividends will be limited to £1 million and £3 million will be reinvested in the business. As it is intended to spend £5 million on new investments next year it is planned to raise £2 million from a new issue of shares. Over the next three years dividends will be limited to 25% of earnings as opportunities to earn above normal rates of return from new investments are anticipated. No further new issues are planned and it is expected that all investment after next year will be financed out of retained earnings. While the expected rate of return on shares with a similar risk is around 10%, the board of Harkness anticipate an average rate of return on new investments planned for the next three years of 20%. From year four onwards it is anticipated that Harkness will continue to grow at above the average rate, but new investments are not expected to yield more than the industry average of 10% per annum and the board plans to revert to a 50% payout ratio.

Required:
(a) Estimate what the market value of Harkness should be at the end of year three.

(b) What is the appropriate market value of Harkness today?

(c) What proportion of the market value today is due to growth opportunities?

Ignore taxation.

5 Blanco Ltd is an unquoted family owned and managed, company that is forecasting a dividend of $0.25 per share in 12 months' time, and a growth rate of 5% per annum. Arthur is the principal shareholder and he is shortly seeking to retire. He hopes to sell his shares to the remaining family members. Because Blanco is an unquoted company, Arthur's financial adviser has suggested to the rest of the family that an acceptable price could be benchmarked against that of a similar, but quoted, company, Vende Ltd. Vende's shares are currently valued at $100 each *ex div* on the basis of a forecast of a 15 cents per share dividend next year, and a forecast growth rate of 5% per annum.

Required:
Suggest, on the basis of the information provided, what might be deemed a fair price for Arthur to receive. Are there other ways in which Arthur might arrive at an alternative estimate of the worth of his shares?

6 Canter Ltd has a 7% redeemable debenture in issue, quoted at €14. It is redeemable in six years' time at €160. It also has a 10% convertible debenture, which has six years to run. The terms of the conversion are 30 shares per €100 debenture. If the debenture is not converted, it will be redeemed at €106.

Required:
At what current share price would a debenture holder be indifferent between converting the debenture now, or holding onto it?

7 Describe the efficient markets hypothesis and distinguish between its three forms. Discuss the relevance of this hypothesis for the internal management of publicly quoted companies.

8* Discuss why it is important to legislate against insider trading even if current penalties seem not to fully prevent this sort of behaviour. Illustrate your answer with relevant examples.

9* What advantages might arise to a medium-sized company from seeking a listing on a stock exchange?

10 Choose a recent case of privatisation, or a situation whereby a listed company seeks to raise additional equity from the market. Write up a short case-history report that pays particular attention to the determination of the share price. What lessons have you learnt from this case-history?

11* What are the attractions of convertibles as a source of finance?

12 How dangerous can it be to use short-term sources of finance to fund the acquisition of long-term assets?

Notes

1 Proof: $P_0 = \dfrac{d_1}{(1 + k_e)} + \dfrac{d_2}{(1 + k_e)^2} + \dfrac{d_3}{(1 + k_e)^3} + \dots \infty$

(a) rewrite $P_0 = d\left[\dfrac{1}{(1 + k_e)} + \dfrac{1}{(1 + k_e)^2} + \dfrac{1}{(1 + k_e)^3} + \dots \dfrac{1}{(1 + k_e)^t}\right]$

(b) multiply both sides by $(1 + k_e)$

$$P_0(1 + k_e) = d\left[1 + \dfrac{1}{(1 + k_e)} + \dfrac{1}{(1 + k_e)^2} + \dots \dfrac{1}{(1 + k_e)^{t-1}}\right]$$

(c) Subtract (b) from (a)

$$P_0(1 + k_e - 1) = d\left[1 - \dfrac{1}{(1 + k_e)}\right]$$

(d) as $t \to \infty$, so $(1/(1 + k)^t$ approaches 0,
therefore (c) approaches $P_0 k_e = d$ and $P_0 = d/k_e$

2 $P_0 = \dfrac{d_0(1 + g)}{(1 + k_e)} + \dfrac{d_0(1 + g)^2}{(1 + k_e)} + \dots \dfrac{d_0(1 + g)\,\infty}{(1 + k_e)\,\infty}$

Multiply both sides of the equation by $(1 + k_e)/(1 + g)$ and subtract from the product:

$$\dfrac{d_0(1 + k_e)}{(1 + g)} - P_0 = d_0 - \dfrac{d_0(1 + g)\,\infty}{(1 + k_e)\,\infty}$$

Because k_e is greater than g, the second term on the right hand side of the above equation will be zero. Consequently:

$$\dfrac{P_0(1 + k_e)}{1 + g} - 1 = d_0$$

$$P_0(k_e - g) = d_0(1 + g)$$

$$P_0 = \dfrac{d_1}{(k_e - g)}$$

APPENDIX Ch. 10

The concept of the time value of money

Money has a time value associated with it and therefore a dollar received today is worth more than a dollar received at some future date. Simply speaking, if an investor wishes to invest $1000 for a period of, say, three years he or she would hope for a return, or *future value*, that would compensate for the sacrifice of not being able to access this money during this period. For the purposes of illustration, let us assume that this investment will earn 10% interest per annum. The relevant expression for this type of investment is that of a simple compound interest formula:

$$FV = PV \times (1 + i)^n$$

Where FV is the future value, PV is the present value, 'i' is the interest rate and 'n' represents the number of years. With the information provided the future value of this investment is:

$$FV = \$1000 \times (1 + 0.10)^3$$
$$FV = \$1000 \, (1.10)^3$$
$$FV = \$1331$$

The term in brackets $(1.10)^3$ is the short form of multiplying $1000 three times by 1.10, thus:

$$\text{Year 1}: \$1000 \times 1.10 = \$1100$$
$$\text{Year 2}: \$1100 \times 1.10 = \$1210$$
$$\text{Year 3}: \$1210 \times 1.10 = \$1331$$

The *present value* is the exact opposite of the future value and works on the principle of compound interest in reverse. Based on our previous illustration we could ask the question, what would $1331 due in three years time be worth today if our cost or opportunity cost of capital is 10% per annum? The formula for the present value is derived from the original formula above:

$$PV = FV \times \frac{1}{(1+I)^n}$$
$$PV = FV \times PV_{if}$$

where PV_{if} represents the present value interest factor. The relevant interest factors for 10% over three years are:

$$\frac{1}{(1+i)} = \frac{1}{(1.1)} = 0.909$$

$$\frac{1}{(1+i)^2} = \frac{1}{(1.1)^2} = 0.826$$

$$\frac{1}{(1+i)^3} = \frac{1}{(1.1)^3} = 0.751$$

Since the relevant interest factor for year three is 0.751, we can rework the present value formula as follows:

$$PV = \$1331 \times 0.751$$
$$PV = \$1000$$

Continued

APPENDIX Ch. 10 cont'd

The concept of the time value of money—cont'd

Present value interest factors are provided in tabular form for ease or calculation. Financial calculators also have relevant factors built into their programmes. Cumulative present value factors are also provided in tabular form. These factors are useful in annuity calculations. An annuity calculation is one where there are a series of equal annual sums.

At this point in the text it is only necessary that readers understand the concept of the time value of money. More applied uses of concept of the time value for money are covered in Chapter 18 (Accounting and longer term decision making). The appendix to Chapter 18 provides tables for present value interest factors and cumulative present value interest factors. Any factors used in illustrations in this chapter are drawn from those tables.

Capital structure and dividend decisions

11

Chapter preview

Following on from the discussion in the previous chapter, we now discuss three key issues for firms. Firstly, we consider how the overall cost of capital for a firm is determined and why this is important. The combined current, and future, projects of the firm must together earn at least this level of return if the various contributors of capital are to remain satisfied with its financial performance.

This leads into the second major area of discussion, the optimal capital structure debate. Whilst recognising that there can be an advantage to equity investors from having part of a firm's long–term capital needs funded in the form of debt, the question we consider is: to what degree does debt finance provide such a benefit? Much has been written about this debate but, as we will see, there is no magic formula for determining what capital structure best serves the needs of the various stakeholders. Some level of **gearing**, or **leverage**, is advantageous, but at excessive levels these advantages are lost.

Allied to this debate is a related issue, our third main area of discussion – the dividend policy debate. Should firms reinvest all their available earnings in productive opportunities which generate acceptable rates of return, leaving only any residual balance to be distributed in the form of dividends; or should they, as often observed in practice, first determine their dividend distribution policy using only residual internal funds for reinvestment and, if necessary, approaching the capital market for additional funds?

Background to the capital structure and dividend decision

As was made clear in the introduction to this text, an essential factor in the financing decisions of the firms is their cost of capital. From the previous chapter, we learned that firms have a broad range of sources of finance available to them and how to measure the costs of these different sources of finance. In this chapter we consider how a firm determines its overall cost of capital in order to identify successful investment strategies. We will see that the overall cost of capital of a firm is in fact a **weighted average cost of capital** (WACC), based on the financial structure deemed most appropriate.

The financial structure of a firm has two principal components: equity capital, including retained (undistributed) reserves, and debt capital. So a key question is how should a firm structure its capital profile between these two elements?

Debt finance is typically cheaper than equity finance but there are relatively few instances of firms that are primarily financed by debt. As a generalisation, Japanese firms tend to have capital structures that include a high level of debt finance, sometimes as high as 80% of total finance. The proportion in many EU countries is around 60%, with the UK and USA being slightly lower at around 50%. Many Australian firms have even lower levels of debt. Once a firm has decided upon its optimal capital structure, it must decide how much equity it will obtain externally through the issue of new equity capital, and what proportion internally through the retention of earnings and utilisation of capital gains. This is an important area of discussion since retained earnings constitute by far the largest single proportion of funds used by established firms.

A firm's retention policy is the counterpart of its dividend policy, which is the concluding area of discussion in this chapter. We will consider whether a firm should reinvest available earnings in productive opportunities, leaving only a residual balance to be distributed as dividends, or whether it should first decide upon its dividend distribution strategy, using only residual funds for reinvestment.

Measuring the overall cost of capital

Part of the discussion in Chapter 10 related to the individual costs of the different types of capital. In this section we recognise that these individual costs must be combined in order to obtain the firm's overall cost of capital. This is its weighted average cost of capital (WACC) which is the average cost of all of the firm's various sources of finance, weighted according to the proportion each element contributes to the total funding.

When it comes to issues of investment appraisal, it is generally regarded as impossible, and indeed unwise, to allocate specific funds to specific projects. Rather, funds for projects are thought of as coming from a central pool. To this extent it is common practice to use the WACC for project evaluation purposes. In this way, as we will shortly see, the firm maintains its key financial objectives of servicing its debt commitments and providing the level of return its shareholders expect.

A firm's WACC can be measured by using either balance sheet (historical) values of the different types of finance, or by using their market values (for listed companies). To illustrate and to consider whether one approach is preferable to the other, let us consider the case of Qualitas Ltd, whose balance sheet reveals the following capital structure:

	$
$1 nominal value ordinary shares	4 000 000
Reserves	6 000 000
Total equity capital	10 000 000
Debt (10% debenture stock)	2 000 000
	12 000 000

Let us assume that the current market value of Qualitas shares is $3.20 and that the debenture stock is valued at $80 per $100 nominal value. The cost of equity is estimated to be 18% and the cost of debt is estimated to be 12.5%. The WACC based on **book values** is calculated as follows:

	$	%
Equity capital (issued share capital plus reserves)	10 000 000	83
Debt capital	2 000 000	17
Total capital	12 000 000	100

WACC: (0.83 × 18%) + (0.17 × 12.5%) = 17.07%.

The WACC based on **market values** is calculated as follows:

	$	%
Equity (4 000 000 shares @ $3.20)	12 800 000	89
Debt (2 000 000 @ $0.80)	1 600 000	11
Total capital	14 400 000	100

WACC: (0.89 × 18%) + (0.11 × 12.5%) = 17.34%.

As can be seen in this instance, both calculations produce similar results. Frequently, a WACC based on book values will indicate a lower overall cost of capital, as the proportion of the equity capital will typically be smaller. Book values depend upon the historic accident of when particular securities were issued and the accounting policies applied to the valuation of reserves. Obviously for non–listed companies there is no alternative other than to use book values. However, in the case of listed companies it is always advisable to use market values, since these incorporate the current expectations of both shareholders and the providers of debt finance. Using the market value for equity capital has the clear advantage of also encompassing any value attributable by the capital market to the retained earnings of the firm.

Use of an appropriate WACC as a cut–off rate for project evaluation best satisfies the expectations of all investors. This can be simply illustrated by reference to the illustration of Torros Ltd. Let us suppose that the following data applies to Torros:

	Market value	% of total capital	Cost of capital (%)
Equity	$10 million	50	12
Debt	$10 million	50	8

From this information the WACC can be calculated:

WACC = (0.50 × 12%) + (0.50 × 8%) = 10%.

If Torros earns an overall average annual return of 10% all of its investors will be satisfied, thus:

	$m
Total capital employed, $20 million at 10%	2.00
Less debt interest, $10 million at 8%	0.80
Balance available to equity investors	1.20

Return to equity investors: $\dfrac{\$1.20 \text{ million}}{\$10.00 \text{ million}} \times 100\% = 12\%$.

Thus a WACC of 10% enables the providers of debt to receive interest at 8% and the equity investors to receive a return of 12%. The WACC of 10% is the correct cut–off rate to use for the evaluation of new investment projects provided that, over time, Torros intends to maintain its current level of gearing at 50/50 and provided that Torros does not diversify its current business activities. Diversification may alter the risk profile of the firm, which, in turn, may increase or decrease the rate of return required by equity investors. This aspect of project evaluation was discussed in Chapter 9.

Should Torros decide in the future to change its capital structure, then its WACC will change to reflect the change in the proportions of equity and debt. Let us suppose that Torros determines that it will expand its capital base by the addition of $4 million debt and maintain this higher level of gearing for the foreseeable future. We will assume that individual costs remain as before. In this case the revised financial structure is:

	Market value	**% total capital**	**Cost of capital (%)**
Equity	$10 million	41.67	12
Debt	$14 million	58.33	8

The revised WACC can be calculated thus:

WACC = (0.4167 × 12%) + (0.5833 × 8%) = 9.67%.

The advantage of additional debt in the capital structure has, in this illustration, marginally reduced the WACC. Readers should note that in real terms, such a significant change in gearing might make equity investors more risk averse and they might marginally increase their cost of capital. This is an issue we will return to shortly, but first we will conclude this current illustration. If Torros now earns an overall average annual return of 9.67% then, once again, the interests of all investors will have been satisfied. Thus:

	$m
Total capital employed, $24 million at 9.67%	2.32
Less debt interest, $14 million at 8%	1.12
Available to equity investors	1.20

$$\text{Return to equity investors: } \frac{\$1.20 \text{ million}}{\text{million}} \times 100\% = 12\%.$$

We stated earlier that the convention for investment appraisal calculations was to pool all funds and thus determine a WACC. The importance of this statement can be appreciated if we revisit the situation where Torros revised its capital structure by acquiring $4 million of debt. Let us assume, again for the purposes of discussion, that Torros had only contemplated earning a return on this additional sum sufficient to meet its additional debt interest payments.

We now have a situation where the original $20 million of capital funds earn an average return of 10%, whilst the additional $4 million only earns a return of 8%. Such a situation will still provide equity shareholders with a 12% return since the additional income earned is simply paid out as interest. But one really needs to question whether this is a wise strategy. The overall level of gearing has increased, making the residual return to equity investors riskier, with no compensating increase in the return. As we have earlier stated, there would shortly come a point, as gearing increases, where the equity shareholders would demand a return in excess of 12% and in such a case Torros has no funds available to meet such a request.

Our discussion so far has illustrated that the use of a WACC as a cut–off rate for project evaluation has the advantage of simplicity, but the assumptions, which underlie its application, should not be forgotten. First, there is the assumption that all projects are in the same risk class. It may be that a firm which is diversifying its activities should require different rates of return for each distinct division of business activity, reflecting the differential risks. Second, there is the assumption that, over time, the firm seeks to maintain constant proportions of debt and equity. Changes in the capital structure of a firm may alter the financial risk of individual sources of capital as well as altering the relevant weights of each individual source. Third, it is dangerous to fund certain projects with cheaper finance since this can seriously impact on the risk of the return available to equity investors being maintained. The investment decision should always precede any individual financing decision for individual projects. An appropriate WACC should ensure that equity investors gain the advantages of cheaper sources of finance yet maintain their desired level of investment return.

Given the real world scenario of economic risk and uncertainty, a judicious mix of equity and debt can, as we have seen, result in a lower overall cost of capital than if the firm had been financed solely by equity capital. The standard academic approach to financial gearing, or leverage, is to state that the optimal degree of financial gearing is that which minimises the WACC. This is a compatible objective with maximising the market value of shares for a firm's equity investors.

Consider an all equity–financed firm, Petros Ltd, which currently has 1000 shares outstanding with a market price of $10 and earnings of $1000 per annum. Earnings per share (EPS) are therefore $1. Suppose that Petros wishes to embark upon a major investment project costing $10 000 and expects annual earnings to double from $1000 to $2000. Should Petros issue an additional 1000 shares at the current market price, or raise $10 000 of 8% loan stock? (For simplicity of illustration, and as stated earlier in this chapter, we are ignoring the impact of corporate taxation.) The choice of finance is as follows:

	Equity financed	Equity/debt financed
Number of shares in issue	2 000	1 000
Debentures, at 8% interest per annum	–	$10 000
	$	$
Earnings	2 000	2 000
Less interest	–	800
	2 000	1 200
EPS	$1.00	$1.20

Shareholders are therefore better off if loan stock is issued. Note that if earnings exceed expectations and increase further, the interest charges will take an ever-decreasing proportion of earnings and the attraction of debt finance is further enhanced. However, what if earnings fail to reach their expected level? In this case debt financing will take an increased share of the firm's profits and EPS would be reduced. If the earning forecast of Petros dropped substantially, say by 50%, from $2000 to $1000, then the EPS for the all equity financed position would also drop 50% to $0.50 and drop over 80% to $0.20 for the equity/debt financed position. The relevant calculations are as follows:

	Equity financed	Equity/debt financed
Number of shares in issue	2 000	1 000
Debentures, at 8% interest per annum	–	$10 000
	$	$
Earnings	1 000	1 000
Less interest	–	800
	1 000	200
EPS	$0.50	$0.20

Although the example of Petros is somewhat simplified, it does serve to illustrate that it is desirable for managers to understand the dynamics of how the financial structure of a firm can impact on the income received by its equity investors.

The optimal capital structure debate

Much has been written on the effect that capital structure has on the cost of capital. There is in fact a rather complex relationship between a firm's capital structure and its cost of capital. If the cost of capital is to be based on some weighted average of a number of sources, each with a different cost, does one suppose that different structures lead to different overall costs? It is perhaps useful to recall that the costs of the various components of capital depend upon market factors, which in turn take account of commercial and financial risk.

Whilst at first sight it might appear that firms should go for as high a level of gearing as possible, this ignores the effect of gearing on the risk borne by equity investors, as mentioned earlier. As illustrated in the example of Petros, as gearing increases there is the potential that earnings available to equity investors can become increasingly more variable, or risky. To compensate for this risk equity investors, being the residual beneficiaries, will expect to be rewarded by higher returns. This increase may well cancel out any benefits derived from cheaper, tax deductible, debt. Two theories provide insights into the optimal structure debate. These are:

1 The *traditionalists' view*, sometimes referred to as the net income view. This holds that the judicious use of debt finance can lower the WACC until an optimum level is reached. However, increased gearing beyond that level will push the cost of capital back up again.

2 The *Modigliani and Miller view*, sometimes referred to as the net operating income view. This holds that the cost of capital is unaffected by gearing.

The traditionalists' viewpoint is argued more from empirical observation than from any rigorously tested model. Traditionalists contend that, to begin with, gearing should be increased by the introduction of debt finance, because the initial financial risk caused by the introduction of this source of finance is more than compensated for by the gains to the equity investors from its use. The two principal gains are the lower cost of debt finance and the fact that interest is a tax-deductible expense. As debt is added to the firm's financial structure, the average cost of capital will fall.

Later, as the proportion of debt increases, the cost of equity will increase to take account of the increasing risk arising from the employment of debt and will offset any previous gains. This stage will vary between firms, because of individual differences in their business and financial risk. Beyond this point the cost of equity will rise rapidly, as will the cost of debt, so that the overall cost of capital likewise increases. Figure 11.1 illustrates the traditionalists' view of the capital structure debate. The implication of this theory for the management of a firm is that they will need to try and identify this optimal position and ensure that they maintain the firm's capital structure at this level.

Figure 11.1   Traditionalists' view of the cost of capital

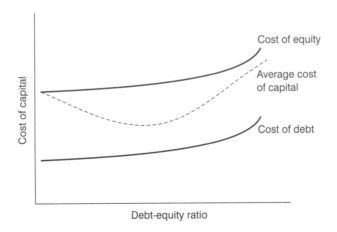

Modigliani and Miller (1958), using the principles of normative economics, were the first to challenge the traditionalists' approach to the capital structure debate and they created a lively academic debate that has continued ever since. Their view stated, in summary, that given the conditions of a perfect capital market, two firms in the same industrial sector and with the same productive potential, yielding identical cash flows and of the same risk complexion, must have the same aggregate capitalised value, regardless of their capital structure. They further assumed that distortionary taxes did not exist, in the sense of favouring one source of capital over another. A market mechanism called **arbitrage** was expected to interpose, such that rational investors would act so as to equate the values of the two firms in all respects, except that of gearing. Arbitrage, in this sense, can be defined as the switching of funds by an investor from one investment to another so as to obtain a better return for the same level of risk. The attraction of this theory is that the WACC, being constant, could be used as an accepted discount factor for project appraisal.

In the perfect market envisaged by Modigliani and Miller, information is freely available to all investors. Further, they are expected to act in a rational manner and have similar expectations. All investors are expected to agree on the expected future stream of cash flows for each firm. With these assumptions, Modigliani and Miller derived three propositions:

1 The total market value of a firm is independent of the proportion of debt in its capital structure.

2 As gearing increases, the equity cost of capital of a geared firm will rise in order to offset the advantages following from the lower cost of debt relative to equity.

3 In order to maximise equity holders' wealth, the firm should use its WACC as an investment cut-off rate.

The essence of this somewhat theoretical argument hinges on the assumption, examined below, that arbitragers are able to substitute personal gearing for corporate gearing. Before examining these three propositions further, let us consider the following numerical illustration. Alpha Ltd and Beta Ltd are two firms in the same class of business risk and both have similar market shares. Both firms have annual earnings before interest of $1 million but different capital structures. Let us assume that the two firms are currently valued on the market as follows:

	Alpha Ltd $m	Beta Ltd $m
Equity	5.00	4.00
Debt, at 10% interest per annum	–	1.00
Total market value	5.00	5.00

With this information let us consider the position of Martina who currently has a 1% interest in the equity of Beta. Her annual income can be determined thus:

	$m
Beta's earnings	1.00
Less debt interest at 10%	0.10
	0.90 × 1/100 = $90 000

If Martina were a rational investor, and informed about the trading position of Alpha, she would sell her equity investment in Beta for $40 000 (1% of $4m), borrow, pro-rata, $10 000 in the market at 10%, the same rate as applicable to corporate borrowers, and invest $50 000 in Alpha's equity. She would now have a 1% interest in Alpha, maintaining her total level of risk at the same level, but her income will have increased by 10%, thus:

	$
Alpha's earnings	1 000 000
Martina's income (1% of Alpha's earnings)	100 000
Less interest on personal loan at 10%	1 000
Revised net annual income	$ 99 000

As Alpha is financed solely by equity, it can be readily appreciated that the cost of its equity capital is 20% ($1m earnings/$5m market value of equity). And hence its WACC is also 20%. Given that the market value of Beta's debt is given as 10% we can calculate the cost of its equity share capital:

	$
Beta's earnings	1 000 000
Less interest on debt capital at 10%	100 000
Available to equity investors	$900 000

Return to Beta's equity investors: $\dfrac{\$0.90}{\$4.00} \times 100\% = 22.5\%$

The WACC for Beta is therefore: (22.5% x 0.80) + (10% x 0.20) = 20%.

We can therefore appreciate Modigliani and Miller's line of argument when they state that the WACC is the same irrespective of the level of gearing and is equal to the equity rate of return of an ungeared firm. Further, the value of a firm in a particular industry risk class is equal to the annual cash flow income discounted at the required rate of return required from an ungeared firm. In the case of Alpha and Beta:

Total market value = $1 000 000 income $\times \dfrac{100}{20}$ = $5 000 000.

Figure 11.2 shows graphically the Modigliani and Miller view of gearing.

Under the restrictive assumptions developed by Modigliani and Miller, their conclusion that gearing cannot affect the total market value of two similar firms must be true. It also follows, therefore, that the overall cost of capital will remain constant. Such assumptions are, though, too restrictive for applicability in the real world. It is in this area of applicability that most attacks have been made against Modigliani and Miller's propositions.

Modigliani and Miller, in their original study, ignored the distortionary effect of corporation tax, whereby debt (because interest is an allowable business expense) is more favourably treated than equity. They later (1963) accepted this point when they decided that, owing to this tax advantage, the WACC would continuously decline as more and more debt is added to a firm's capital structure.

Could it then be argued that, given the tax deductibility of debt interest, firms should strive to use as much debt finance as possible? Most authorities would say not,

Figure 11.2 Modigliani and Miller view of the cost of capital

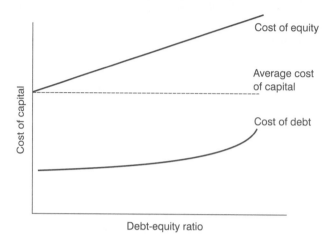

suggesting instead that the cost of debt is more likely to rise to a level that outweighs its attractiveness over equity if excessive leverage is pursued.

Criticism is also raised against Modigliani and Miller's assumption with respect to the arbitrage process. No difference is drawn between corporate debt and personal debt; that is, the inference that personal and corporate gearing is equivalent. Can it really be true that individuals have the same ready access to all funds available as corporate bodies? Is it also true that individuals and firms are equally risky? Transaction costs can also be significant for the personal investor. Certainly individuals could never have as high a credit rating as large corporations. The limited liability that firms enjoy means that for the investor it is safer if the firm (effectively) borrows debt capital on his/her behalf. If, as is the practice, firms can secure larger amounts of debt capital and borrow at lower rates than individuals, then the notion that personal gearing can replace corporate gearing collapses.

Another issue ignored by Modigliani and Miller was that of financial distress, or bankruptcy. Clearly as gearing increases, not only does the risk of the equity investors increase, but also those of succeeding providers of debt. For example, there is less and less security available as the level of debt rises. It is quite probable that the marginal cost of debt will therefore rise to offset this disadvantage. Financial distress can increase owing to the fact that, as gearing increases, fixed interest payments must be made annually whatever the profit or cash flow position of the firm. It is only possible to postpone a dividend payment. We briefly re-visit the issue of financial distress in Chapter 12 when we discuss business reorganisation.

So what have we learnt from these two opposing theories on the optimal capital structure debate? Empirical studies have been carried out but these have been largely inconclusive. Perhaps one important issue arising out of the work of Modigliani and Miller is that, despite the limitations of their model, we do at least arrive at a check-list of important factors which all contribute to management's deliberations on the capital structure of their particular firm. Equally, traditionalists would nowadays accept that Modigliani and Miller's view that capital structure, while important, is not the only overriding determinant of the cost of capital. As Samuels *et al.* (1995: 663) suggest:

> Large companies using tangible saleable assets and having a low earnings volatility might be expected to have a higher level of debt than a smaller company with intangible assets and a high earnings volatility.

As the authors recognise, these are broad categorisations, but the main purpose of their example is to highlight some of the factors that one might expect affect a firm's debt strategy.

To conclude this section we introduce readers to the earnings per share (EPS)/ earnings before interest and taxes (EBIT) chart. Such a chart allows management to map out the impact of various capital structure scenarios. In order to best understand how such a chart is developed, consider the case of Endon Ltd.

Endon Ltd currently has no debt in its capital structure. The financial director is considering a capital restructuring that would involve the issue of debt which, in turn, would be used to buy back some of the outstanding equity. The current market value of Endon is $10 million, comprising 500 000 shares in issue at a market price of $20. The proposed debt issue would raise $5 million at an annual interest rate of 10% and this would enable Endon to revise its capital structure to 50% equity and 50% debt. The debt/equity ratio would be 1 and we will assume that the share price would remain at $20.

To investigate the impact of this proposed restructuring we can consider its impact on shareholders (in terms of EPS) by considering the pre- and post-restructuring positions given three possible levels of EBIT: $0.5 million: $1.00 million and $1.5 million. The results are as follows:

Pre-proposed restructure (100% equity)

EBIT	$500 000	$1 000 000	$1 500 000
Interest	0	0	0
Net profit	$500 000	$1 000 000	$1 500 000
EPS	$1	$2	$3

Post-proposed restructure (50% equity/50% debt)

EBIT	$500 000	$1 000 000	$1 500 000
Interest	500 000	500 000	500 000
Net profit	$0	$500 000	$1 000 000
EPS	$0	$2	$4

A quick review of these figures shows that at a level of $1 million EBIT there is indifference as regards EPS between whether Endon's capital structure is composed of 100% equity or 50% equity/50% debt. Figure 11.3 plots all six EBIT/EPS relationships and confirms that $1 million is the break-even point. EBIT beyond this point provides a letter EPS return to shareholders in the geared company. Notice that the with-debt line is steeper than the without-debt line, this is because EPS, in this case, is twice as sensitive to changes in EBIT because of the level of debt employed. Also notice that the with-debt line descends as far as EPS – $2. EPS is negative if EBIT is zero. This is because $0.5 million of interest is still due and if there are 250 000 shares in issue the EPS is therefore –$2.

Figure 11.3 Endon Ltd EPS/EBIT chart

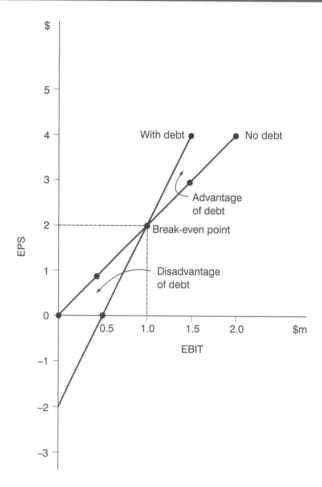

The use of such a chart reveals the effect of financial gearing on Endon's EBIT. When EBIT is relatively high, gearing is beneficial. The chart maps out the impact that financial gearing has on both the expected return to shareholders and highlights the riskiness involved with alternative capital structures.

The optimal dividend policy debate

In the introduction we stated that by far the greatest source of investment funds for the firm are those generated internally within the business. The firm's retention policy is linked to its dividend policy. In this section we again consider two theories, whether a firm should either reinvest all available earnings in productive opportunities, leaving any residual balance to be distributed as dividends, or whether, as is often the case in practice, the firm firstly decides upon its dividend distribution strategy and then uses residual funds for reinvestment. The first of these two theories is an extension of the views of Modigliani and Miller and could result in a wide fluctuation in the level of dividend payments from one year to the other.

As with the capital structure debate, it is impossible to devise precise rules on a dividend policy which could be universally applied by all firms. Instead, our discussion will isolate the basic elements, which will underpin the choice of the most favourable dividend policy. We begin by reviewing the debate on whether or not dividend policy affects the market value of a firm's equity shares.

The more traditional school of thought maintains that dividend policy plays a vital role in determining the market value of the firm. This school contends, for a variety of reasons, that dividends are preferred by shareholders to capital gains. Proponents such as Gordon (1959) and Lintner (1956), suggest that capital gains, which arise when retained earnings are reinvested in the firm, are seen as more risky than present dividends. Walter (1967) states that dividends have an effect on equity share prices because they communicate information about the firm's profitability. If a firm has a stable dividend policy and this is altered, investors could interpret this as signalling a change in management's expectations for the future and the market price of the shares will adjust accordingly. A reduction in the level of dividends declared could, for example, be thought to be a reflection of pessimism about future business prospects. However, analysts are not easily fooled when management determine to maintain their dividend strategy despite a decline in financial performance. Shares could easily be marked down if, for example, it was recognised that this policy would impact negatively on scarce reserves.

The alternative school of thought was developed by Modigliani and Miller (1961). This holds that dividends should only be considered as a passive residual. They argued that in a tax-free world the market is indifferent between receiving a specific sum of money in the form of dividends or capital gains. In other words, dividend policy is irrelevant. What is important, in conformity with their thinking on the capital structure debate, is the net operating earnings of the firm. In conditions of certainty and perfect capital markets it is expected that the firm undertakes what it believes to be its optimal investment policy and that the investor will enter the market if he or she wishes to generate a cash flow different from that offered by the firm. More specifically their assumptions are:

- Perfect capital markets in which investors trade in a rational manner. Information is available to all investors at no cost, transactions are instantaneous and without cost, securities are infinitely divisible, and no investor is large enough to distort market prices.

- An absence of floatation costs on securities issued by the firm.

- An absence of distortionary taxes.

- A given investment policy for the firm, not subject to change.

- Perfect certainty by every investor as to future investments and profits of the firm.

As previously, it is best to illustrate Modigliani and Miller's view by means of an example. Logistica Ltd, an all equity firm, has in issue 2 million shares of $1 nominal value each. These shares are currently quoted at $3 *ex div*. The dividend proposed for the current year is 30 cents per share. No increase in dividend is expected unless new projects are accepted. Logistica can invest surplus funds at 10% per annum at the same level of risk as current operations. With this information we can consider four scenarios:

(a) a continuation with the current dividend and investment policy;

(b) retaining an extra $0.50 million, investing at 10% and paying out the subsequent returns as additional dividends;

(c) retaining an extra $0.60 million, investing at 10% and paying out the subsequent returns as additional dividends;

(d) paying the usual dividend, and raising an additional $0.50 million for investment at 10% by means of a rights issue to current shareholders.

Taxation and transaction costs will be ignored for ease of explanation. From the above information, we can assume that any new investment is not expected to alter the firm's risk profile, since (using the dividend valuation model from Chapter 9):

$$k_e = \frac{d}{P_0} = \frac{\$0.30}{\$3.00} = 10\%$$

Under scenario (a) we can calculate the total wealth of the firm as being $6.6 million. We know that the total market value of the shares is $6 million (2 million shares at $3) to which we add the current total dividend paid by Logistica, $0.60 million (2 million shares at $0.30).

Under scenario (b) the retained earnings will generate $50 000 ($0.50 million at 10%) so that the future dividends will rise to $0.65 million ($0.60 million + $0.05 million), giving at 10% a capitalised market value of Logistica's shares of $6.5 million. The current dividend we will assume would be reduced to $0.10 million ($0.60 million − $0.50 million) which, added to the revised market value of the shares, gives us an overall total measure of wealth of $6.6 million.

Scenario (c) considers the situation where no dividend is currently paid and the whole of the proposed $0.60 million is invested at 10%. In this case subsequent future dividends would rise to $0.66 million, being the original level of dividend $0.60 million plus $60 000 from the new investment ($0.60 at 10%) which, capitalised at 10%, gives us a market value of total wealth of $6.6 million.

In the financial situation, scenario (d), we earn the same additional return as under scenario (b), $50 000. New future dividends would again rise to $0.65 million and the new market value of the shares would again be capitalised at 10% to give a projected market value of $6.5 million. In order to estimate the total wealth generated under this strategy we need to add to the capitalised value of the current dividend $0.60 million ($60 000 at 10%) less the cost of the rights issue, $0.50 million, a net figure of $100 000. The total wealth is therefore once again $6.6 million.

Under all four scenarios the shareholders' wealth was shown in all cases to be the same. From this illustration we have illustrated two important issues:

● Provided any cash retained is invested at the shareholders' required return, any reduction in dividend should not adversely affect the investor since current income lost is compensated for by an increase (capital gain) in the share value.

● In theory, it makes no difference whether the new investment is funded by retained funds or via the issue of new equity shares.

What if, instead, under scenario (d), of raising additional equity, an equivalent amount of debt was raised? Dividend policy is again irrelevant as, under Modigliani and Miller's certainty assumption, the cost of debt must also be 10% per annum.

As Bromwich (1976) has pointed out, this rather academic debate is not about whether investors use dividends or earnings figures in their valuation models. Rather it is whether a given sum of money is valued differently when paid out as dividends or realised as a capital gain. Real world complications and market imperfections cause dividend policy to affect the wealth of equity investors. The most obvious of these issues is that of risk. There are those who argue that, if a present dividend is 'safe', that is, certain, and a capital gain, to be realised at some future date, is 'risky', it is preferable to receive a current dividend – the 'bird in the hand' argument. Gordon (1959) contends that investors, being risk–averse, are willing to pay a higher price for equity shares that offer a greater current dividend, all other things being equal. Modigliani and Miller would counter that as long as investment policy and borrowings are held constant, a firm's cash flows are the same. It is distant earnings, they contend, that are uncertain, and this uncertainty will be the same whether earnings are distributed as dividends or capital gains.

Modigliani and Miller have also been accused of ignoring problems with regard to differential corporate and personal tax structures. The individual tax positions of equity investors can greatly influence their desire for dividends, their desire being to receive the largest possible net of all taxes return. There can often be a bias by some investors in favour of capital gains as these are almost invariably taxed at a lower rate than dividends. Moreover, capital gains tax is deferred until such time as the investment is sold and the gain realised. Of course when it comes to matters of taxation managers need to recognise that, in practice, the majority of equity investment comes from financial institutions, rather than individuals.

As with the earlier discussion on the optimal capital structure debate, investors have been assumed to be able to freely borrow and lend in the market in order to obtain a desired personal income pattern. This may not be so in reality and transaction costs may not be insignificant. There is also the assumption that all equity investors are in agreement as to the risk class and future prospects of the firm. In the real world, some investors may either have access to different information and/or may evaluate such information differently.

Apart from the unresolved academic debate, other considerations have also to be taken into account by management when deciding the level of dividends to distribute. These include: the legal framework, the firm's desired payout ratio, its liquidity position, the level of fixed interest payments and so on. It is generally accepted that, while profits may fluctuate considerably, dividends are usually paid at a fairly constant and conservative level. The general contention of managers is that equity investors prefer a steady progression in the level of their dividends. Usually, growth in the level of dividends tends to lag behind growth in the level of earnings. Dividends are only increased once a sustained increase in earnings is discernible. When a firm retains a proportion of its earnings, equity investors tend to value their shares more highly if they anticipate that current reinvestments will lead to larger dividends in the future. A stable dividend policy encourages this anticipation.

So does dividend policy really matter? Dividend policy is basically a trade-off between retaining earnings for further reinvestment within the firm or else paying out cash dividends and seeking to raise additional equity or long-term debt. One unresolved consequence of dividend policy is the effect on the market for equity shares caused by announcements of dividends. In large part, the valuation debate hinges on the degree to which market imperfections impinge on the valuation process. It is generally recognised that sudden changes in dividend policy can cause sudden changes in equity share prices. Accordingly, it would seem to make sense for firms to follow a conservative approach in determining the dividends that they will pay. Dividend policy may affect the financial structure, the flow of funds, the firm's liquidity, share prices and investor satisfaction. As such, it is an important aspect of the financial management of any firm.

Conclusion

This chapter has discussed issues related to a firm's capital structure and its dividend policy. Different sources of funds, by having different costs, present management with the problems of how best to attain some optimal balance of funds – capital structure.

Chapter review

Modigliani and Miller have provided, via their theoretical approach, an important checklist of factors for us to consider. Market analysis provides an insight to possible capital structures in different industry sectors. Internationally we also know that some firms are more or less highly geared depending on which country they operate in. The debate on whether it is possible to determine an optimal capital structure remains open. Dividend policy is basically a trade-off between retaining earnings within the firm or else paying out cash dividends and seeking to raise additional external capital. One unresolved consequence of dividend policy is the effect on the market for equity shares by such announcements. The valuation debate hinges on the degree to which market imperfections impinge. It is generally recognised that sudden changes in dividend policy can cause sudden changes in share price.

Further reading

There are a number of good texts on corporate finance, including Ross *et al.*, *Fundamentals of Corporate Finance* (2001); Samuels *et al.*, *Management of Company Finance* (1999); and Brearley and Myers (2003).

Questions and exercises

Guide notes can be found at the end of the book for all questions marked with an asterisk*.

1* Serendipity Ltd employs two types of funding: equity shares and 6% irredeemable debentures. The market values of these funds are:

Sources of funds	Market value $m
Equity shares	20
Debentures (6%)	10
	30

The debentures are currently quoted at $80 per $100 nominal value. The firm earns profits of $3.6 million before interest. After the interest is paid Serendipity distributes surplus funds as dividends. Although expecting no growth in profits, the management of Serendipity believe that they will be able to maintain the current level of profits for the foreseeable future.

Required:
Ignoring the impact of taxation:
(a) Calculate the cost of equity capital and the cost of debt capital for Serendipity.

(b) Compute the WACC for Serendipity using the given market values as weights.

(c) Compute the overall cost of capital for Serendipity by comparing total annual profits distributed to debt and equity with the total market value of the funds employed.

2* Exe Ltd and Wye Ltd are two firms that operate in the same industry sector and are considered to be in the same business risk class. Both firms have a gross operating profit of £250 000 per annum. Exe relies solely on equity funding whilst Wye utilises both equity and loan finance. The capital structures of the two firms are as follows:

Exe Ltd:	Equity (market value)	£1 750 000
Wye Ltd:	Equity (market value)	£1 000 000
	Debt (8%), currently traded at par	£1 000 000
		£2 000 000

At present Liam holds 4% of Wye's share capital. Assume that both companies pay out all their profit after any interest as dividends.

Required:
Ignoring the impact of taxation:

(a) Determine the WACC of these two firms; then comment whether these two firms' equity shares are in equilibrium or not.

(b) Show how Liam may gain from arbitrage whilst keeping his current level of financial risk constant. Assume that he can borrow money at an annual rate of 8%.

3 Suppose Marta owns 6% of the equity in an ungeared company, Portos Ltd. The total market value of the shares of Portos is $2 500 000 and the expected annual

operating earnings are $225 000 into the foreseeable future. Marta has realised that there is another firm, Qudos Ltd, which is identical in every way to Portos except that it has a geared capital structure with a debt-to-equity ratio of 1:2. The expected annual operating earnings of Qudos are also $225 000, before the deduction of debt interest, and the current market value of its equity is $1 500 000. The debt of Qudos is in the form of $750 000 of 6% debentures, currently trading at par. Assume that both Portos and Qudos pay out all available earnings as dividends.

Required:
(a) Show how Marta could increase her current dividend expectation, without changing its risk. Note any assumptions that you need to make in calculating this.
(b) What are the implications of the transactions that all rational investors would make in this situation? What is their importance for capital budgeting?

4* Sparta Ltd has just paid a dividend of €0.10 per share. The market expects this dividend to grow in future years at a constant rate of 6% per annum. The cost of capital for Sparta is currently 8% per annum. Soon after the most recent dividend was paid, the board of Sparta decided to finance a new project by retaining the next three annual dividend payments. It is anticipated that the market will see this project as being in the same risk category as Sparta's existing activities. It is further expected that the dividend declared at the end of the fourth year from now will be €0.125 per share and that dividends will grow thereafter at a rate of 7% per annum.

Arthur holds 1000 shares in Sparta and his personal circumstances require that he receive at least €100 per year from this investment.

Required:
(a) Assuming that there is a perfect market for Sparta's shares, and that the capital market uses the dividend valuation model to value shares, show how the market value of Sparta's shares will be affected by the board's decision.
(b) Show how Arthur can still achieve his desired income pattern in the first three years, whilst improving his expected dividend stream from then on.

5 Two years ago, Asia-Pacific Shipping Ltd, a large and well-established firm, was forced to cease dividend payments because of its poor financial performance. Now, following considerable reorganisation and new investment, Asia-Pacific is once again efficient and operating at a profit. The board is currently considering recommending the renewed payment of dividends. At a recent board meeting three main views were put forward:

- A stable dividend policy should be introduced as soon as possible.
- Dividends are basically an irrelevance to our shareholders.
- Dividends should only be paid once Asia-Pacific has no further investment opportunities which promise a return equal to, or greater than, that required by shareholders; this latter position being unlikely to arise for several years.

Required:

In a report to the board, outline, and explain the importance of, the key issues that should be considered when they next meet to further discuss the possible resumption of dividend payments. In particular you should address each of the three viewpoints put forward at the previous meeting.

6 Hargreaves and several associates are considering establishing a company. In their discussions to date they have considered two possible capital structures: either $5 million in debt and 10 million in shares which they anticipate will sell for $4 each, or $25 million in debt and the balance in shares. In both proposals the cost of debt is anticipated to be 12% per annum. The second capital structure proposal is expected to increase the return to the equity investors.

Required:

If taxes are ignored, what is the minimum level of earnings before interest and taxation (EBIT) that can be expected to derive from this company?

7* 'The ideal mixture of debt and equity for a firm, its optimal capital structure, is the one that maximises the value of the firm and minimises the overall cost of capital'. Discuss.

8* Critically evaluate the contribution of Modigliani and Miller to the optimal capital structure debate.

9* 'By the standards of 1961 M and M were leftist radicals, because at the time most people believed that even under idealised assumptions increased dividends made shareholders better off'. What was so radical about M and Ms' views on dividend policy?

10 Choose a company and analyse its dividend strategy over the last five years. From this analysis what lessons have you learnt about the importance of this firm's dividend policy?

11 Illustrate the use of an EPS/EBIT chart. How useful is the use of such a chart for determining the optimal capital structure of a firm?

12 Choose a company from each of three distinct industry sectors (e.g. retail, manufacturing, service sectors). Analyse both the capital structures and dividend policies of each company. What lessons have you learnt from this analysis?

Business reorganisation 12

Chapter preview

In this chapter we recognise the fact that firms are not limited to expanding and contracting the scale and nature of their business activities by internal, organic, means. There are occasions when it will make good economic sense to expand a business by means of an external investment, such as in an acquisition or a merger. There are also occasions when it will make good economic sense to divest some parts of the business and concentrate on core business activities.

Both of these scenarios presuppose that a firm is in a relatively good trading and financial position, but sadly there are occasions when a firm may face insolvency and the only hope of survival is a reorganisation via which the relevant stakeholders agree to revise their claims and expectations, as a better option than filing for bankruptcy.

In considering these various forms of business reorganisation, it should be noted that the principal objective that management need to pursue remains the best interests of their shareholders. This chapter therefore builds upon the earlier discussions in Chapters 8 and 9 and extends the discussion of the previous chapter, Chapter 11.

Business reorganisations of whatever type involve investment appraisal considerations. As we will see, in practice, there is often a lack of necessary financial data and, for this reason, a number of adjustments and approximations need to be made as part of the appraisal. Most business reorganisations involve a large amount of discussion and debate and inevitably a lot of subjectivity enters into the terms of any final agreement. The aim of this chapter is to provide managers with an overall framework for the various processes involved. Even though this is an area were a number of external advisors will inevitably be involved, managers cannot abdicate their responsibility to have an understanding of the basic tools and assumptions that they will be presented with.

Why do businesses reorganise?

In Chapter 9 we considered the basic mechanisms of investment appraisal. Projects are undertaken to achieve the key objective of maximising the wealth of the firm's equity investors. Such projects might include the acceptance of a major new customer order or the determination of whether or not to establish a new product line. In this chapter we broaden this discussion in two respects. Firstly, we consider mergers and acquisitions – that is, firms seeking business growth externally rather than internally. There are several reasons why a firm might seek to merge with, or acquire another business and we examine these. Central to our discussion will be how to determine what price should be paid in the case of an acquisition, or what is an appropriate exchange rate for shares in a combination of two firms whose markets, share prices and internal accounting policies may differ significantly.

The second section of the chapter considers business divestment. It is a sad fact that many firms run into trading difficulties and therefore it is equally important to consider various strategies that may assure the ongoing viability of businesses. Business units, such as divisions, may need to be sold off or capital reconstruction schemes introduced as an alternative to the possibility of bankruptcy. It is as well that managers understand the potential for business failure in order to react quickly to the warning signs and to come up with appropriate rescue strategies.

Throughout the latter part of the twentieth century, and indeed right up to today, we have witnessed business cycles that have seen mergers and acquisitions take place not only on a national scale but also on an international scale. We have also witnessed cycles of business downturn and restructuring in a wide range of industries. ICI floated off Zeneca which ended up being a much bigger entity than its parent. In Australia, BHP and Billiton merged to become BHP Billiton and this group then floated off BHP Steel as it determined to concentrate its core activities in the mining and extractive industry sectors. The pages of the financial press, e.g. *The Financial Times* and *The Wall Street Journal*, are replete with stories about possible merger and acquisition activity and the restructuring of corporate enterprises.

Mergers and acquisitions: advantages and disadvantages

Mergers and acquisitions occur when a firm seeks to expand externally. The exact distinction between a merger and an acquisition (takeover) is perhaps of little significance, since few examples of a true merger tend to exist. Usually there is one dominant party to the arrangement. From a textbook point of view, a merger tends to suggest that two firms of approximately the same size and value come together to provide synergistic benefits to both groups of shareholders. An acquisition, on the other hand, implies that one of the parties will be larger and more dominant. On many occasions any attempt at an acquisition will be contested by the threatened, or target firm.

Mergers and acquisitions often involve firms in the same business sector (horizontal growth). They can also occur when a firm decides to expand either up or down the supply chain (vertical growth). For example, a retailer might merge with, or seek to acquire, a key supplier. Conglomerate growth occurs when a firm determines to broaden its portfolio of activities into new, and often unrelated, lines of business.

Merger activity tends to be significantly higher in countries such as the USA, UK and Australia, than in countries such as Germany and Japan. In Germany, despite a developing stock exchange, there is only limited merger activity. Germany has a fairly unique corporate governance structure that tends to discourage mergers. Further, in Germany and in Japan banks tend to be key investors in firms so that gearing ratios tend to be higher than in the USA, UK and Australia, where institutional equity investors such as insurance companies, unit trusts and pension funds, rather than banks, tend to dominate. Institutional investors have a tendency to sell off shares they believe are under-performing, or if they are offered a significant premium over the current share market price. Bidding firms often tend to offer substantial premiums over the current market value of target firms. This latter point is important because it reflects the overall conclusion of many empirical research studies into mergers and acquisitions – the most consistent beneficiaries tend to be the shareholders in the target firm whilst the most consistent losers tend to be the shareholders of the acquiring firm.

Whether via a merger or an acquisition, any new business combination is formally recognised by either a transfer of assets or shares between the parties. In the case of a merger, where, for example, A and B merge to form C, with C either acquiring assets from, or shares in both A and B in exchange for shares in itself. The businesses of A and B will be folded into C or continue to trade individually, albeit now in much closer collaboration.

The rationale of two businesses combining their resources is to achieve some form(s) of synergy. Synergy occurs when the combined market value of the two firms is greater than the sum of their individual market values. Management will hope such synergies can arise because of economies of scale, in areas such as production, marketing and distribution, increased market power or financial gains. Increased market power may be subject to government monopoly regulation. Other financial benefits may be less obvious. For example, the acquiring (profitable) firm may be interested in taking over the accumulated tax losses of another firm in order to offset them against its own taxation liabilities.

Whatever the form that a merger or acquisition takes, financial reporting regulation generally requires that 'group' financial statements, reflecting the overall financial position and performance of the economic entity that is the group, should be prepared. The preparation of such group financial statements, often referred to as consolidated accounts, is discussed in Chapter 13.

Despite the potential advantages of mergers and acquisitions, investors need to be wary of management who promote diversification for its own sake, or who are simply attempting to manipulate the firm's earnings per share (EPS). Diversification may be argued for as a way of reducing overall business risk, but sometimes such diversification may be more of interest to managers than their shareholders. An attempt to manipulate EPS, without any obvious synergic benefits, is sometimes termed **bootstrapping**. Consider the case of Weston Creek Wineries Ltd.

Weston Creek Wineries Ltd has a price-earnings (P/E) ratio of 20, and operates in the wine making sector. Its current annual earnings are $4 million and it has 20 million ordinary shares in issue, with a current market value of $4 each. Its management have targeted Furniture-4-U (F4U) Ltd as a potential target for a takeover. F4U, which operates in the furniture manufacturing sector, has a current P/E ratio of 10. Its current annual earnings are $20 million and it has 25 million ordinary shares in issue, with a market value of $8 each.

Assuming that Weston Creek succeeds in acquiring the shares of F4U by issuing an additional 50 million of its own shares at $4 each in exchange for the share capital of F4U, what would the position be?

The combined earnings of the two firms would be $24 million. Weston will now have 70 million shares in issue so that its EPS will be:

$$\frac{\$24 \text{ million}}{70 \text{ million shares}} = \$0.34$$

Previously Weston Creek's EPS would have been:

$$\frac{\$4 \text{ million}}{20 \text{ million shares}} = \$0.20$$

The acquisition has raised Weston Creek's EPS by over 70% (from $0.20 to $0.34). In addition, if investors still believe that Weston Creek's P/E ratio should be around 20, then its share price might be expected to rise from $4 as shown below:

$$P/E \times EPS = 20 \times \$0.34 = \$6.80$$

However, we need to think about this further. This takeover involves two firms in completely different industries – wine making and furniture manufacture. We might therefore suppose that there are no real business synergies arising from the combination. If this is true, the combined value of the two firms should only be the sum of the two parts, their previous individual valuations totalling $280 million, that is:

	$m
Weston Creek: 20 million shares at $4	80
K4U: 25 million shares at $8	200
	280

Weston Creek's share price should therefore have remained unchanged:

$$\frac{\$280 \text{ million}}{70 \text{ million shares}} = \$4$$

and its P/E ratio should simply have been the weighted average of the two original businesses:

$$\text{Weston Creek's P/E} \times \frac{\text{Weston Creek's Earnings}}{\text{Combined earnings}} \times \text{K4U P/E} \times \frac{\text{K4U Earnings}}{\text{Combined earnings}}$$

$$20 \times \frac{\$4 \text{ million}}{\$24 \text{ million}} + 10 \times \frac{\$20 \text{ million}}{\$24 \text{ million}} = 11.67\%.$$

What we can see from this illustration is that a high P/E in the acquiring firm is not (of itself) a cause for an increase in value of the capitalised earnings of the acquired firm. In an efficient market, increases in value will be caused by other factors.

If no other such factors are identified then the new P/E ought to be simply the weighted average of the two individual P/E ratios, as no synergistic gain has occurred.

The strategies and processes of mergers and acquisitions

Once a firm has decided upon acquired growth as its strategy, it needs to identify and appraise possible target firms. A business case will need to be made in each instance. If, for example, the firm is seeking horizontal integration via acquisition it will need to assess the target firm's turnover and market share. It will also need to assess the target's financial strengths and weaknesses, as well as the commercial benefits that might be offered by the target firm's management, employees, etc. Another key issue to be addressed is the ownership of the target firm: is it indeed feasible to plan to obtain control? Are there, for example, strategic portfolios of shares held by third parties which could be purchased as a prelude to an all-out attempt to gain control?

The nature of potential target firms varies enormously. At one extreme the target might be a large and ailing firm, ripe for new investment and restructuring. On the other hand it might be a smaller company with a dynamic group of managers and workforce lacking the funds to expand from their current operational base.

In seeking targets and determining strategies for a merger or acquisition, there are no end of 'experts' in the market offering their advice and expertise. Accountants, lawyers and investment bankers are all keen to offer their services, helping to develop strategies and advising on the costs and methods of securing the chosen business combination. It is far from unknown for such advisers to come to a company with suggestions about possible acquisitions. In every country there are rules and regulations that govern the processes of mergers and acquisitions. As indicated above, the first stage might be tactical purchases of parcels of shares. This might be followed, in the case of a quoted company, by a **dawn raid**. As the name implies, this is a swoop on the stock market by the acquiring firm. However, legislation will usually (at least in part) regulate this process. For example, in the United Kingdom, a purchaser must inform the stock exchange when it holds 5% or more of another company's shares. When it holds 30% or more, the UK's City Code on Takeovers and Mergers obliges it to make an offer to the remainder of the shareholders.

The purchaser successfully gains control of the target company when more than 50% of the voting shares of the target company have been acquired. If the purchaser succeeds in obtaining 90% of the target company's shares then it can compulsorily acquire the remaining 10% of the shares, or equally the remaining shareholders can insist that their shareholdings be bought out by the acquiring company.

Valuing businesses

There are two principal approaches to the valuation of shares:

(a) *Income-based approaches*, which include:
   - present value
   - dividend valuation model

- price-earnings ratio.

(b) *Asset-based approaches*, which include:
- adjusted book value
- replacement cost (deprival value)
- cessation (break-up) value.

In practice a purchaser may look at a number of valuation approaches to provide a guide to a range of possible valuations. Equally, the target firm's management will be hoping to ensure that they obtain the highest possible price for their shareholders. Table 12.1 summarises some of the key issues relevant to the valuation of shares using the above approaches.

In order to amplify this discussion, consider the case of Engadine Ltd, which uses five of the above valuation methods, the exception being the present value method.

Table 12.1	Bases of share valuation

Income-based approaches

From a theoretical point of view, the net present value is the only approach that needs to be considered. However, given the information likely to be available to the purchaser, this model may be impossible to apply in practice, because of the difficulties inherent in estimating future cash flow streams and in the determination of an appropriate discount rate. In practice therefore surrogate methods such as the dividend valuation model or the P/E ratio approach may need to be used. Other factors to be taken into consideration include:

(a) *Present value*: In addition to the issues outlined above, this approach should only be considered if a controlling interest is being sought, as only then are the hoped for synergies likely to be realised.

(b) *Dividend valuation model*: As with all valuation problems, the key issue is to obtain relevant input data Dividend valuation approaches should only be considered when valuing relatively small parcels of shares. If a controlling interest is sought then the acquirer has the power to influence future dividend streams. To use this model for the valuation of shares in an unquoted company requires the introduction of proxy input measures, perhaps based on finding a quoted company of similar size and involved in the same line of business. Even then it would be appropriate to adjust the input data to allow for the fact that such shares are not marketable. Shareholders in quoted companies might normally be expected to accept a lower return on their shares because their shares can more easily be disposed of.

(c) *P/E ratio*: The same basic issues apply as for the dividend valuation model.

Asset-based approaches

These approaches are considered to be appropriate when shareholdings of greater than 50% are to be valued.

(a) *Adjusted book value*: A fairly meaningless figure for valuation purposes since it will be based on historic cost valuations.

(b) *Replacement (deprival) value*: This provides a maximum price since it represents the amount required by the acquirer to build up the business from scratch, as if the target did not exist. However, the major element of any business valued on a going-concern basis is goodwill – the income value of the business less tangible assets. As such this valuation cannot be taken in isolation but needs to be considered alongside an income-based valuation.

(c) *Cessation (break-up) value*: This should provide the lowest value since net assets are valued on a distress basis, rather than on an ongoing basis.

Engadine Ltd has for some time been seeking horizontal growth and its directors have identified Tankerton Ltd., an unquoted company, as a possible target. Table 12.2 shows financial data which Tankerton's directors have provided to Engadine's management.

With the information contained in Table 12.2 it is possible to value the equity of Tankerton on the following bases:

(a) adjusted book value

(b) replacement cost

Table 12.2   Summarised financial data for Tankerton Ltd

Summarised Balance Sheet

	$000	$000	$000
Assets:			
Production equipment (net book value)			2610
Raw materials stock	500		
Finished goods stock	1564		
Debtors	2980		
Bank and cash balances	632	5676	
Less:			
Creditors	3014		
Short-term bank loans	3452	6466	(790)
			1820
Financed by:			200
Equity share capital			1620
Reserves			1820

Summarised income record:

	2001 (estimate) ($000)	2000	1999	1998	1997
Net income	212	192	200	276	124
Extraordinary items	20	(40)		(10)	
	232	152	200	266	124
Dividend	100	100	100	90	82
Retained income	132	52	100	176	42

Additional information:
(a) Production equipment has an estimated replacement value of $3 million and a sale value of $2 million.
(b) Raw material and finished goods stocks have a combined estimated replacement cost of $2.4 million and a sale value of $2.2 million.
(c) The industry standard level of bad debts is 2% of sales value. Estimated sales income for 2001 is $2.8 million.
(d) A similar quoted company in this industry sector might be expected to have a PE ratio of 10 and a cost of equity capital of 12%.

(c) cessation (break-up) value

(d) dividend valuation model

(e) price-earnings ratio.

We can consider each of these valuation bases in turn.

(a) Adjusted book value:	*$000*
Balance sheet value (as given in Table 12.2)	1820
Less estimated bad debts ($2.8 million × 2%)	(56)
Adjusted balance sheet value	1764

(b) Replacement cost:	*$000*
Adjusted balance sheet value	1764
Add increased valuation in equipment ($3m – $2.61m)	390
Add increased valuation of stocks ($2.4m – $2.064)	336
Replacement cost value	2490

(c) Cessation (break-up) value:	*$000*
Adjusted balance sheet value	1764
Less reduced value of equipment ($2m – $2.61m)	(610)
Plus increased value of stocks ($2.2m – $2.064m)	136
Cessation value	1290

(d) Dividend valuation model:

Dividends have remained static for three years. However, comparing the dividend paid in 1997 with that estimated to be paid in 2001, we could estimate that there has been an approximate year-on-year increase of 5% over these five years. We can then apply the formula for the dividend valuation model:

$$\frac{\text{Dividend} \times \text{growth rate}}{\text{Cost of equity} - \text{growth rate}} = \frac{\$100\,000\,(1.05))}{(0.12 - 0.05)} = \$1.5 \text{ million.}$$

(e) Price-earnings ratio:

This is found by taking the profit, before any adjustment for extraordinary items, and multiplying by the relevant P/E ratio:

$$\$212\,000 \times 10 = \$2.12 \text{ million.}$$

However, it should be noted that it is usually recommended that, when using a quoted company's P/E ratio to value shares in an unquoted company, the quoted P/E ratio be lowered to allow for the lower liquidity of an investment in an unquoted company. If we suppose that the P/E ratio should be reduced to 8 then:

$$\$212\,000 \times 8 = \$1.696 \text{ million.}$$

We therefore have a range of valuations for Tankerton, from a low of $1.29 million to a high of $2.49 million.

As indicated earlier, the first of these valuations has little to recommend it, being based on historical accounting and relatively arbitrary accounting regulations effecting items such as depreciation and stock values. The break-up value provides a useful bottom line valuation, whereas in practice the replacement cost relies to a great degree on specialist assistance in trying to provide necessary valuations. Tankerton is clearly a manufacturing business with largely tangible assets and that does at least make such a valuation easier than if it were a service sector enterprise with significant intangible assets. We can therefore say that the replacement cost approach is only likely to be applicable to asset intensive businesses. But, then again, even asset intensive businesses still have some degree of intangible assets that may need to be accounted for, such as brand names and the fact that a skilled workforce is already in place.

The dividend valuation approach could be said to be the most useful of the five approaches since it operates on the basis that Tankerton's value is determined by the future cash flow stream (dividends) likely to be paid to its shareholders. However, the limitations with this model are the estimates of future dividends that have to be made and the determination of a relevant cost of capital. The P/E approach is quite widely used but here again the limitation is the determination of the P/E multiple itself. The P/E multiple is supposed to be a function of two characteristics – future earnings growth and the uncertainty surrounding future earnings. The problem is that there are no set guidelines as to how these two elements combine within a single P/E multiple. So we are left with a problem – to what degree does the benchmark of 10, provided in this illustration, actually represent the expectations of the current owners of Tankerton.

Given the range of values produced in this illustration and given some of the practical problems associated with some of the calculations, one might suggest that negotiations centre in the range of $1.5 million to $2.12 million. That is the dividend and P/E related valuations as they fall within the two extreme valuations. What is clear is that such valuations are not a precise science. They provide a framework within which to debate and negotiate. What we do know is that the empirical evidence often points to the acquirer paying too much for the target firm such that there are winners and losers. The winners being those shareholders being taken over, since they gain from any premium paid over and above a reasonable market value, whilst the losers are often those in the acquiring firm.

For example, suppose that Delta Ltd, valued at £10 million, sought to acquire Celta Plc which has a market value of £9 million. If we assume a small amount of anticipated synergy arising, then we might suppose that the combined value of these two firms might rise to, say, £19.5 million. That is, a £0.5 million additional gain due to synergistic advantages. If Delta pays more than £9.5 million for Celta then its shareholders lose. If Delta pays no more than £9 million then its shareholders gain from the synergies. What if Delta paid £10 million for Celta? The loss to Delta's shareholders can be calculated thus:

	£m
Combined market value of Delta and Celta	19.5
Original value of Delta	(10.0)
Price paid to Celta	(10.0)
Loss to Delta's shareholders	(0.50)

Celta's shareholders gain a premium of £1 million, being the difference between the price paid and the estimated market value of Celta.

To end this section, we can draw the following conclusions:

1 External growth may prove to be a useful, and perhaps necessary, alternative to internal growth.

2 Some merger and acquisition business combinations have proven to be very successful, but research shows that the majority of benefits tend to flow to the shareholders of the target firm.

3 Firm valuation is far from being a precise science. Models provide indicators of value since, in practice, research again tends to show that the acquirer pays too much of a premium to secure control of the target firm.

Business divestment

Divestment occurs when management withdraw investment from a business. This is usually achieved either by selling a business to a third party, or by selling parts of the business (perhaps a division) in a more piecemeal fashion. Divestment can often be seen as a crisis response in a turbulent and uncertain economic environment. In such conditions a parent company may decide to sell off less viable subsidiaries and concentrate on what might be termed 'core business activities' to the best advantage of the group's shareholders. In the most extreme of circumstances liquidation may occur either by selling the business as a going concern or by selling off assets at distress values. The reasons for divestment are many. Table 12.3 lists some of the more common reasons. De-merger activity tends to be cyclical, following on from the cyclical waves of merger and acquisition activity.

An interesting example with respect to the fourth point in Table 12.3 arises with the success of AstraZeneca Plc, a textbook case of the creation of value through its de-merger from ICI Plc in 1991.

Table 12.3	Possible reasons for divestment

1 Subsidiaries that are peripheral may be sold off in order to concentrate group investment in core business activities.
2 Peripheral subsidiaries may be sold off to raise funds as part of a recovery strategy when there is an overall group-funding crisis.
3 Some subsidiaries are sold off because they were part of a package in an earlier acquisition and their business activities have little interest to group management.
4 Some business conglomerates decide to split because there may be no real advantage of staying as the one group. Business growth is achieved by providing the respective management teams with more autonomy.
5 A subsidiary may be sold off because it is either unprofitable or not profitable enough in the eyes of group management. It may be sold either to another organisation which can make better use of its resources, or perhaps become the result of a management buyout by the subsidiary's own management team because they believe they can run the business more effectively if it is independent of the group.
6 A subsidiary may be sold off because its operating risk is too high for the group as a whole.

Just as with mergers and acquisitions, divestment, from a financial viewpoint, is all about determining exchange prices that are perceived to be to the benefit of both parties, the vendor and the purchaser.

Management buyouts

By way of illustration we might concentrate on one particular form of divestment, the **management buyout** (MBO). MBOs occur for a variety of reasons, in line with those provided in Table 12.3. The parent may have financial difficulties. The business unit (division) might not 'fit' within the group's overall strategy. It might be loss making and selling it to management might be a cheaper alternative to putting it into liquidation, particularly when redundancy and other wind-up costs are considered. MBOs may be attractive to managers since it is quicker than starting their own business from scratch and they have independence of direction. In addition, by being autonomous, the new owners can determine their own financial structure and cost strategies that may be less onerous than when they were part of a larger group. MBOs often occur with the managers acquiring the bulk of the equity share interest but with a high degree of debt financing being provided by **venture capitalists**. Such MBOs are termed **leveraged buyouts**.

The case of Merchant Ltd provides a useful review of key issues associated with an MBO. Table 12.4 summarises relevant financial information about one of its divisions and its relation to its parent company. Table 12.5 outlines the proposed financial arrangements to make the MBO effective. These arrangements require the MBO team to work with a venture capitalist, New Venture Finance Ltd.

With this information we can consider a number of issues. We can start by considering whether the $15 million purchase price is likely to be acceptable to the MBO team and their financial backers. Calculations using three valuation models are possible:

(a) Dividend valuation model:

$$\frac{D_1}{K_e - g} = \frac{\$212\,000}{0.22 - 0.2078^*} = \$17.38 \text{ million}$$

(* Average over five years but declining by year 5. If reworked using a growth term of, say, 18% then the value drops to $5.3 million.)

(b) P/E ratio:

$$\$1.059 \text{ million} \times 14 = \$14.83 \text{ million}.$$

Note: for the calculation of the earnings figure see Table 12.6 (a).

It could be argued that the P/E multiple could be lower as the division is currently not listed.

| Table 12.4 | Financial details relevant to Merchant Ltd and the MBO team |

Summarised balance sheets

	Year ended 31/12/2002		Year ended 31/12/2001	
	$000	$000	$000	$000
Property[a]		2 640		2 520
Plant and equipment		4 008		4 320
		6 648		6 840
Stocks	5 490		4 320	
Debtors	3 480		2 820	
Cash and Bank	120	9 090	261	7 401
Less				
Creditors	2 160		2 040	
Share of group taxation	618		561	
Bank overdraft	960	(3 738)	–	(2 601)
		12 000		11 640
Financed by[b]:		8 400		8 160
Equity		3 600		3 480
Debt		12 000		11 640

Summarised profit and loss accounts

	Year to 31/12/2001 $000	Year to 31/12/2001 $000
Turnover	25 500	24 300
Earnings before interest and tax	2 838	2 874
Interest[c]	(1 560)	(1398)
Attributable taxation[d]	(618)	(561)
Earnings after tax	660	915

Notes:
(a) The division's property is estimated to have a market value 30% higher than its book value.
(b) Financing is based on the same proportions as the book value of the group's equity and debt captial. The group has provided all external financing for the division, with the exception of the bank loan.
(c) This represents an annual payment by the division to the group to cover the amount of long-term finance allocated and to pay the interest on the bank overdraft. The cost of long-term finance provided by the group is based on the group's WACC of 12% per annum.
(d) The division is allocated a taxation charge by the group according to the percentage of group earnings before interest and tax generated by the division.

Table 12.5	Proposed financial arrangements for the MBO

By the group:

- The purchase price has been set at $15 million.
- The group will repay the bank overdraft and there will be no outstanding long-term liabilities, including tax liabilities, at the time of purchase.

By the MBO team:

- Management is to contribute $1.5 million in return for 1.5 million $1 ordinary shares.
- Corporation tax is assumed to be payable at a rate of 35% in, for simplicity of calculation, the year the profit is earned.
- Earnings before interest and tax are predicted to increase by 8% per year.
- No further capital issues or major purchases or disposals of fixed assets are expected over the next five years.
- Dividends based on 20% of earnings are expected to be paid.
- Financial advice suggests that the cost of equity capital should be set at 22% per annum and that the average PE ratio for a similar listed company is of the order of 14:1.

By New Venture Finance:

- Provision of $13.5 million funding as follows:
  - $1.2 million in ordinary shares.
  - $4.5 million in fixed bonds at 1.3% per annum.
  - $3.0 million in subordinate debt at 14% per annum.
  - $4.8 million as 9% convertible loan stock. Conversion is at the rate of shares every $100 loan stock, and may occur at any time after six years.
  - The $4.5 million and the $3 million loans are both to repaid by a series of equal payments (including both interest and principal) over five years.
- Shareholdings (but not convertible loan stock) to be disposed of in a little over five years' time when it is hoped the division will have its own listing on the stock exchange and with a market value of equity at least as great as the book value of equity, including retained earnings, at that time.

(c) Asset value:	$000
Property	3 432
Plant and equipment	4 008
Stock	5 490
Debtors	3 480
Cash and Bank	120
Less Creditors	(2 160)
	14 370

All these valuations are not too far off the $15 million asked for by Merchant. Much of the discussion will depend upon what both parties ultimately agree is fair. For Merchant, the issue is whether this price is fair in relation to the alternative of a sale in the open market, taking into account the likelihood of higher disposal costs. From the MBO perspective, the deal has to be weighed against the costs of the team having to set up independently, including the cost of re-engaging staff, re-establishing a new customer base, etc.

Note also that the MBO team will gain control of the new company by only investing one-tenth of the total capital. Most of the financial risk is with their venture capital backer, New Venture Finance. Usually venture capital rates will be higher than normal costs of capital to reflect the substantially higher risk associated with such a high level of gearing. A feature of a leveraged MBO is that such buyouts are indeed extremely highly geared in the initial years of establishment. Table 12.6 (f) reveals that the MBO will start with a gearing level in excess of 80%. Given that venture capitalists only invest in the short to medium term it is necessary for the MBO team to meet the stringent conditions of their loan arrangements and reduce their gearing to 34% by the end of year 5.

Table 12.6 Calculations pertinent to the MBO proposal

(a) Estimated retained earnings for the first five years if the MBO proceeds.

Year	1 $000	2 $000	3 $000	4 $000	5 $000
Earnings before interest and tax[1]	3066	3309	3576	3861	4170
Interest[2]	1437	1286	1109	910	686
Taxable earnings	1629	2023	2467	2951	3484
Taxation (35%)	570	708	863	1033	1219
	1059	1315	1604	1918	2265
Dividends (20%)	212	263	321	384	453
Retained earnings	847	1052	1283	1534	1812

Notes:
1 Increases at 8% per annum.
2 Based on calculation (b) below.

(b) Calculation of loan interest and repayment schedules:

(i) The 13% and 14% loans are repaid by five equal instalments. This is found by dividing the principal sum of each loan by the relevant present value factor of an annuity for five years.
13% loan = $4.5m/3.517 = $1279 500 per annum; 14% loan = $3m/3.433 = $873 870.

(ii) 13% loan schedule:

	Interest $000	Principal $000	Year end balance $000
Year 1	585	695	3805
Year 2	498	785	3021
Year 3	393	887	2134
Year 4	277	1002	1132
Year 5	147	1132	

Table 12.6	Calculations pertinent to the MBO proposal—cont'd

(iii) 14% loan schedule:

Year 1	420	434	2 546
Year 2	356	517	2 029
Year 3	284	590	1 439
Year 4	201	672	767
Year 5	107	767	

(c) 9% convertible debenture:

$$\$48 \text{ million} \times 9\% = \$432\ 000$$

(d) Interest payable:

	13% $000	14% $000	9% $000	Total $000
Year 1	585	420	432	1 437
Year 2	498	356	432	1 286
Year 3	393	284	432	1 109
Year 4	277	201	432	910
Year 5	147	107	432	686

(e) Estimate of book value of equity:

Years	0 $000	1 $000	2 $000	3 $000	4 $000	5 $000
	2 700	3 547	4 595	5 882	7 416	9 228

(f) Change in gearing/leverage over first five years of new company trading:

Years	0 $000	1 $000	2 $000	3 $000	4 $000	5 $000
Equity, from working (e)	2 700	3 547	4 595	5 882	7 416	9 226
Opening debt	12 300	12 300	11 171	9 869	8 392	6 718
Principal repaid		1 129	1 302	1 477	1 674	1 899
Closing debt	12 300	11 171	9 869	8 392	6 718	4 819
Gearing (D/(D+E))	82%	76%	68%	59%	48%	34%

Venture capitalists will usually take a relatively small equity interest in the MBO. In this case they have taken only 1.2 million shares. If New Venture Finance sticks with its plan to dispose of these shares in five years time then their predicted net return would be:

Disposal of shares ($9.229 million × 1.2/2.7)	$4101 333
Initial share investment	$1200 000
Projected gain (circa 27% compound growth)	$2901 333

The gearing could drop to zero if New Venture Finance decides at some point to convert the loan stock to shares.

The MBO team themselves need to be extremely focused and motivated in order to achieve significant gains. As stated, the MBO illustrates one important approach to divestment. They are risky and are quite often prone to failure or a takeover in their early years. Managers risk losing their jobs as well as their personal wealth. However, although the risks are high, so are the potential rewards.

Capital reconstruction schemes

Finally in this chapter we briefly consider capital reconstruction schemes. These are usually undertaken for one of two reasons. Either the firm is in dire financial difficulties, possibly facing liquidation, or it is seeking to improve the mix of different types of capital and the timing of available funds.

In the first instance the firm may propose a capital reconstruction scheme as being a better alternative to liquidation, where the distress sale proceeds may not be sufficient to settle all liabilities, including workers' benefits, and the shareholders will usually have lost their investment. Such schemes require a balance such that all stakeholders realise that their best interest lies with allowing the firm to continue trading. This will normally require stakeholders to accept a lower claim. Business failures such as these occur for a variety of reasons, starting with bad management decisions. Bad management decisions can arise because of a dominant individual, such as a chairman who combines this position with that of chief executive and by having an unbalanced board of directors, including too few (independent) non-executive directors, is able to follow personal whims, issues which are considered in Chapter 2 which deals with corporate governance issues.

When there is bad management, poor business decisions may be taken, for example, over expansion. As matters get worse there is pressure to try to hide some of the negative results by, perhaps, manipulating the financial statements by the use of 'creative accounting', as discussed in Chapter 10. Readers will be aware of a number of well documented instances of such behaviour.

In order to re-float the firm an injection of new management, as well as a capital reconstruction, may well be needed in order to regain shareholder confidence. In terms of financial data, stakeholders are usually provided with various financial statements that would typically include:

- a statement of the likely outcome if the firm were to be liquidated, including a schedule of predicted disbursements;
- a proposal for a revised balance sheet, post re-floatation, which would not only deal with the proposed funding arrangements but would also re-express key asset values such as property;
- a forecast of future profits.

Some providers of debt, for example, might be asked to waive outstanding current interest, either entirely or in exchange for shares, and a renegotiation of the terms associated with the loan. If the debt providers agree to accept such an arrangement it will be because it would be preferable to what they might lose in the event of a winding up of the business. Shares may be offered as an additional inducement, such that, if the firm expands in future years, there will be capital gains to be realised.

Ordinary shareholders cannot be forgotten. Although they are the residual beneficiaries, if their interest is entirely written off they could simply exercise their voting power to close the firm down and enter into formal bankruptcy proceedings. Whilst in a capital reconstruction they may only receive a fraction of their current assets, this is better than nothing and may be sufficient to gain their consent to the rearrangement scheme. As Samuels *et al.* (1994: 924) note:

> In the UK it was certainly the case in the late 1980s and early 1990s that the larger the company the greater the chance of survival once the company became insolvent. Only 13% of insolvent companies with a turnover of less than £1 million were saved and only 28% of those with a turnover of between £1 million and £5 million. This contrasts with 30% of insolvent companies with a turnover of between £5 million and £15 million being saved and 64% of companies with a turnover of £15 million or more being saved.

From the 1990s the Bank of England in the UK has tried to encourage debate among stakeholders involved with firms in severe financial distress. Banks and other creditors are encouraged to collaborate in order to reach a collective view on whether, and if so how, a firm should be given further financial support. The key being that workable proposals maximise the value due to creditors. In the USA, Chapter 11 legislation (of the Bankruptcy Code) allows directors to apply for protection from its creditors. The role of Chapter 11 is to allow directors to reorganise the firm. In practice only around 10% of firms survive once this legislative provision is invoked.

In the final analysis, if a scheme of arrangement is not successful, the firm will have to cease trading and be liquidated. Most countries have legislation that penalises directors for knowingly continuing to trade when their firm is insolvent. In the UK, directors who become bankrupt as a result of an insolvency are usually discharged after a couple of years and the balance of any debts written off. In most of the rest of the EU directors remain bankrupt until they are fully able to discharge all outstanding debts. Equally, some EU member states give a higher priority to employee rights than do other others. Space prohibits a detailed discussion of the various processes by which liquidations take place.

Concluding example

We conclude this element of our discussion by illustrating a relatively simple scheme of arrangement. Let us consider the case of Shaky PLC. Table 12.7 summarises the latest balance sheet of this company.

In recent years Shaky PLC has suffered a series of trading losses which have brought it to the verge of liquidation. The firm's financial advisers estimate that a distress sale of the assets will realise the following amounts:

	£
Freehold premises	4 000 000
Machinery	2 000 000
Stock	3 400 000
Debtors	3 400 000
	12 800 000

Table 12.7	Latest balance sheet of Shaky PLC		
	£000	£000	£000
Fixed assets (net book value)[1]			11 400
Current assets			
Stock and work in progress		7 000	
Debtors		3 600	
Less current liabilities		10 600	
Unsecured creditors	8 000		
Bank overdraft (unsecured)	3 200	11 200	
			(600)
Total assets less current liabilities			10 800
Longer term liabilities – 10% secured debentures[2]			(6 000)
Net assets			4 800
Represented by:			
Called up share capital[3]			8000
Profit and loss account			(3 200)
			4800

Notes:
1 The fixed assets comprise freehold property with a book value of £6 million and machinery with a book value of £5.4 million.
2 The debentures are secured on the freehold property.
3 8 million £1 ordinary shares issued and fully paid.

In addition the costs of liquidation are estimated to be £1.54 million, leaving net funds of £11.26 million to settle £17.2 million of liabilities due to creditors, bankers and debenture holders. Clearly nothing would be available to the shareholders.

Let us assume that a new board of directors believe that it is possible to turn the company around. However, this will require an injection of an additional £5 million for new machinery. The firm's financial advisers concur that if this investment is made the firm should return to profitability with annual profits, before interest, in the order of £3.5 million. The key question is: will the creditors decide to put the company into liquidation or will they be prepared to agree to a scheme of arrangement whereby, in the longer term, they will be more financially advantaged? To be accepted, any scheme of arrangement must be acceptable to all parties involved, including the shareholders. Shaky's financial advisers have suggested the following reconstruction scheme:

(a) Freehold premises should be written down to £4 million, the machinery to £3.2 million, stocks and work in progress to £5.4 million and debtors to £3.4 million.

(b) Ordinary shares should be written down to £2 million and the accumulated losses in the profit and loss account written off.

Table 12.8 Some consequences of the scheme of arrangement

- For the current ordinary shareholders:

		No. shares:
Existing shareholdings reduced to		2 000 00
Assume rights issue exercised (40%)		2 000 000
		4 000 000
Shares taken up by secured debenture holders	3 000 000	
Assume rights issue exercised (60%)	3 000 000	
		6 000 000
Revised shares on issue (£1 par)		10 000 000

	£
Revised profit forecast	3 500 000
Less interest (£5m debt @ 14%)	700 000
	2 800 000
Earnings per share	£0.28

- For the secured debenture holders

	£
Net funds from liquidation	11 260 000
Less value of secured property	4 000 000
Available to unsecured creditors	7 260 000

Unsecured creditors:	£
Balance due to secured debenture holders	2 000 000
Other unsecured creditors	8 000 000
Bank overdraft	3 200 000
	13 200 000

This means a distribution of only £0.55 per £1 outstanding.

Return to debenture holders on liquidation is therefore:	£
Secured on property	4 000 000
Unsecured payout (£2m × 0.55)	1 000 000
	5 100 000

If the scheme of reconstruction is accepted then:	£
Cash forgone from liquidation	5 100 000
Additional cash invested re rights issue	3 000 000
	8 100 000

Projected annual return in cash terms:	£
Interest (£3 million at 14%)	364 000
From equity (6 million shares at £0.28)	1 680 000
	2 044 000

Projected annual return in % terms:

$$\frac{£2\ 044\ 000}{£8\ 100\ 000} \times 100$$

25.23%

- For the bank

The cash forgone from the liquidation is £1.76 million. The annual returns would be £336 000 (£2.4 million 14%) which as a return on the cash forgone is:

$$\frac{£336\ 000}{£1760\ 000} \times 100 = 19.1\%$$

(c) The secured debenture holders would exchange their debentures for £3 million ordinary shares and £2.6 million 14% unsecured loan stock repayable in five years' time.

(d) The bank overdraft should be written off and the bank should receive £2.4 million of 14% unsecured loan stock payable in five years' time in compensation.

(e) Unsecured creditors should be written down by 25%.

(f) A rights issue of 1 for 1 at par value is to be made, affecting the share capital after the above adjustments have been made.

(g) £5 million will be invested in new machinery.

If this scheme is accepted the existing shareholders will have to provide an additional £2 million of share capital in accordance with the terms of the rights issue. If the projected profit forecasts are correct, then earnings per share would be of the order of £0.28, which should permit Shaky to start paying a dividend and thus providing some return to shareholders again. By returning to profitability it should also be possible to resume trading in the shares, which at present must be almost impossible. With liquidation the existing shareholders receive nothing. In this scheme of arrangement they control only 40% of the equity, as shown in Table 12.8.

The secured debenture holders are owed £6 million, secured on the freehold property, but a forced sale will only realise £4 million. In addition, they would rank alongside the bank and other creditors for repayment of the outstanding £2 million balance. Under the proposed scheme the debenture holders are being offered £5.6 million (£0.933 in the pound) in the form of capital rather than cash. As can be seen from Table 12.8, acceptance of this scheme provides a projected return of 25.23%, which is likely to be well above that which could be earned elsewhere, thus making the scheme attractive to the debenture holders. For this the debenture holders have to forgo their security on the property and rank partly with the unsecured creditors and partly with the equity.

The bank overdraft is unsecured and could only be repaid at £0.55 in the £1. In the event of a liquidation the bank would therefore recover £1.76 million and have to write off £1.44 million. In the reconstruction the bank would have to write off £0.8 million immediately, but would receive 14% per annum on the outstanding balance with repayment of the balance in five years' time. This represents a return on the incremental investment of 19.1%, which is probably well in excess of current overdraft rates (see Table 12.8).

Finally, if Shaky goes into liquidation the unsecured creditors will only receive £0.55 in the £, but if they accept the scheme of arrangement they will receive £0.75 in the £1.

As such, this proposed scheme of arrangements would appear to offer benefits to all the parties concerned. In the final analysis it is all a matter of the confidence that the various parties have in the plans and projections of the new board and their financial advisers.

Table 12.9 provides the restated balance sheet of Shaky PLC on the assumption that the scheme of arrangement proceeds.

Table 12.9	Revised balance sheet of Shaky PLC (post-reconsilation)		
	£	£	£
Fixed assets (£11.4 million –£4.2 million +£5 million)			12 200
Current assets			
Stock (revised)		5400	
Debtors		3400	
		8800	
Less current liabilities			
Creditors	6000		
Overdraft	–	6000	
Total assets less current liabilities			2 800
14% loan stock			15 000
			(5 000)
			10 000
Represented by:			
Called up share capital			10 000

Conclusion

Business reorganisations occur for a variety of reasons, some positive and some negative. Such reorganisations draw together many of the principles involved in business planning and the valuation of the firm. In terms of mergers and acquisitions, there is often a failure by management to adequately integrate the activities of the two firms after the merger or takeover has taken place, depending upon the nature of the merger or takeover; for example, horizontally, vertically, or as part of a diversified conglomerate. There may be a need to redefine corporate objectives and develop strategic plans in order to harmonise the aspirations of both parties. However, as we have seen, not all reorganisations involve growth by the company; they may involve management buy-outs or capital reconstructions. To be successful, all of these require a skilled management team who must pay close attention to the 'human factor' in order to avoid loss of direction and motivation.

A post-reorganisation (restructuring) audit is often a good idea. Such an audit can identify any post-merger (post-restructuring) problems for management and act as a deterrent to carrying out unwise reorganisations. Such audits will clearly examine the forecasting accuracy of the management team so that lessons can be learnt for the future.

As we have seen, not all business reorganisations relate to an expansion of activities, although many (e.g. mergers and acquisitions) do. Others can relate to a reduction of corporate activities and a restructuring of such activities. Business demergers relate to the sub-division of a corporate body. Often these occur because of an unprofitable subsidiary which ought to be sold off, or because of a subsidiary not involved in 'core business' and as such does not fit into the overall group strategic plan. And, finally, we have also come to appreciate that not all business ventures are successful. Firms can get into difficulties and, despite reasonable future prospects, face the prospect of going into liquidation. Sometimes all is not entirely lost if it is possible to attract an injection of fresh capital and to persuade creditors to renegotiate their claims. It may be possible to achieve a capital reconstruction which allows the firm to continue trading and prosper in the future.

Further reading

Most mainstream business finance texts provide further information about the issues discussed in this chapter. Useful sources include: Ross *et al.*, *Fundamentals of Corporate Finance* (2001); Samuels *et al.*, *Management of Company Finance* (1999); and Bearley and Myers (2003).

Questions and exercises

Guide notes can be found at the back of the book for all questions marked with an asterisk*.

1*   Consider the following information which relates to two all-equity firms, A and B:

	Firm A	Firm B
Issued shares	1 000	500
Price per share	$10	$6

Firm A estimates that there might be a synergistic benefit of $400 if it were to acquire Firm B. Firm B indicates that it would be prepared to accept a cash purchase offer of $7.00 per share.

Required:
Advise Firm A whether it should proceed and purchase Firm B.

2* Consider the following information for two all-equity firms C and D:

	Firm C	Firm D
Total earnings	$2 000	$800
Issued shares	1 000	800
Price per share	$16	$5

Firm C has agreed to acquire Firm D by exchanging 250 of its shares for all the shares in D.

Required:

(a) Calculate the cost of the merger if the merged firm is expected to be worth $22 000.

(b) Explain what will happen to firm C's earnings per share (EPS) and its price earnings (P/E) ratio.

3* You are asked to value a 60% and a 5% holding in Bright Ltd for the purposes of a share transfer. The company manufactures plastic garden furniture, and is well known in this field.

The management of the company has always been regarded as satisfactory, having passed from the hands of the original founding family (a senior member of which is selling her shares) into the hands of a professional management team. The continuity of management is, at present, well organised. Extracts from recent financial statements of the company are shown below:

Profit and dividend record

Year to 31 January	Turnover	Pre-tax profit		Dividend
	£000	£000	%	£
2005	1 800	300	5	15 000
2006	2 000	330	10	30 000
2007	2 400	410	12	36 000

Net asset position, per Balance Sheet, at 31 January 2007

	£000	£000	£000
Fixed assets			
Freehold land and buildings at cost			860
Plant and machinery, at cost less			
accumulated depreciation			120
			980
Current assets			
Stock		400	
Debtors		700	
		1 100	
Current liabilities			
Creditors	330		
Taxation	160		
Dividends	36		
Overdraft	40	566	
			534
			1 514
8% Debenture 2009			100
			1 414

Additional information:

(i) A note to the accounts indicates that the freeholds have this year been revalued, on an existing use basis, at £1 200 000.

(ii) Share capital at 31 January 2007 consists of 150 000 £1 nominal value ordinary shares.

(iii) Assume the corporation tax rate on income and chargeable capital gains is 30%.

(iv) The following data was obtained from the *Financial Times* share indices:

	Dividend yield	P/E ratio
500 share index	6.2	9.7
Consumer goods (non-clearable)	6.7	10.0
Garden furniture	8.1	6.6

Required:

Indicate how you would value:

(a) a 60% holding

(b) a 5% holding.

4   Azul Ltd wishes to acquire Blanco Ltd. The directors of Azul are trying to justify the acquisition to the shareholders of both companies on the grounds that it will increase the wealth of both sets of shareholders. The supporting financial evidence produced by Azul's directors is summarised as follows:

	Azul $000	Blanco $000
Operating profit	12 400	5 800
Interest payable	4 421	2 200
Profit before tax	7 969	3 600
Tax	2 789	1 260
Earning available to ordinary shareholders	5 180	2 340
EPS (pre-acquisition)	$0.1480	$0.2925
Market price per share (pre-acquisition)	$2.22	$3.22
Estimated market price (post-acquisition)	$2.40	
Estimated equivalent value of one old Blanco share (post-acquisition)	–	$3.60

Payment is to be made with Azul ordinary shares, at an exchange ratio of 3 Azul ordinary shares for every 2 Blanco shares.

Required:

(a) Show how the directors of Azul produced their estimates of post-acquisition value and, if you do not agree with these estimates, produce revised estimates of post-acquisition values. State clearly any assumptions that you make.

(b) If the acquisition is contested by Blanco, using Azul's estimates of its post-acquisition market price calculate the maximum price that Azul could offer without reducing the wealth of its shareholders.

5 The following information relates to the proposed financing scheme for a management buy-out of a manufacturing firm.

	%	000
Ordinary share capital held by:		
Management	40	200
Institutions	60	300
		500
10% redeemable preference shares		
(redeemable in 10 years' time)		2400
		2900
Loans		1400
Overdraft facilities		1400
		5700

Loans are redeemable over the next five years in equal instalments. They are secured on various specific assets, including properties. Interest is 12% per annum.

The manufacturing company to be acquired is at present part of a much larger organisation which considers this segment to be no longer part of its core business interests. This is despite the fact that the company in question has been experiencing a turnover growth in excess of 10% per annum.

The assets to be acquired have a book value of 4 500 000 but the agreed price was 5 000 000.

Required:
Write a report to the buy-out team which appraises the proposed financing scheme.

6 Dire Ltd has suffered trading losses for the last three years. Its balance sheet as at 31 December 2006 shows:

		$	$
Fixed assets:	Land and buildings		386 492
	Equipment		121 508
	Short term investments		54 000
			562 000
Current assets:	Stock	240 494	
	Debtors	141 384	
		381 878	
Current liabilities:	Creditors	224 494	
	Interest payable	25 600	
	Overdraft	73 426	
		323 520	
Net current assets			58 358
			620 358
Long term liabilities: 8% debentures (2009)			(160 000)
			460 358
Represented by:			
Ordinary shares on issue $1 nominal value			400 000

5% Cumulative preference shares $1 nominal value	140 000
Profit and Loss account	(79 642)
	460 358

Sales have been difficult to achieve throughout 2007 and stock levels are very high. Interest has not been paid for the last two years. The debenture holders have demanded either a scheme of arrangement or else they threaten to place Dire into liquidation. In response, a meeting of directors and shareholders has proposed the following scheme of reconstruction:

(i) Each $1 ordinary share to be redesignated as a $0.25 share.

(ii) The existing 140 000 preference shares to be exchanged for a new issue of 70 000 8% cumulative preference shares of $1 each and 280 000 ordinary shares of $0.25 each.

(iii) Ordinary shareholders are to accept a reduction in the nominal value of their shares from $1 to $0.25, and subscribe for a new issue on the basis of 1 for 1 at a price of $0.30 per share.

(iv) The debenture holders are to accept 40 000 ordinary shares of $0.25 in lieu of interest payable. It is a condition that the value of the interest liability is equivalent to the nominal value of the shares issued. The interest rate on the debentures is to be increased to 9.5% and the repayment date deferred for a further three years. A further $18 000 of this 9.5% debentures is to be issued and taken up by the existing holders at $90 per $100.

(v) The profit and loss account balance is to be written off.

(vi) The investment is to be sold at the current market price of $120 000.

(vii) The bank overdraft is to be repaid.

(viii) 10% of the debtors are to be written off.

(ix) The remaining assets have been professionally valued at:

Land	$160 000
Buildings	$160 000
Equipment	$60 000
Stock	$100 000

(x) It is anticipated that net profit before interest will be around $100 000 per annum.

Required:

Ignoring the impact of corporation tax:

(a) Advise whether the shareholders and debenture holders should support this scheme.

(b) Prepare a balance sheet for Dire Ltd post reconstruction.

7*   Consider the position where your firm is subject to an unexpected takeover bid by a rival company. You and your fellow directors determine to reject the bid as insufficient.

    Required:
    Outline and discuss what strategies you and your fellow directors could adopt in order to deter your rival from further attempts to take over your firm. At what stage would it become unethical for you to continue to oppose this acquisition.

8*   With respect to a merger or takeover, what are the advantages and disadvantages of a cash offer as opposed to a share-for-share exchange?

9   Write up a case-history of either a merger or a takeover. Analyse the relative successes or failures from the point of view of shareholders in both of the original companies. What lessons have you learnt from this case history? To what extent could your case history be said to be a typical or atypical illustration of the empirical evidence on the winners and losers in mergers and takeovers?

10*   Management buyouts have become increasingly popular in recent years. What are the advantages and disadvantages to the buyout team?

11   What do you understand by the term 'capital reconstruction scheme'? What general principles need to be devised if such a scheme is to be successful?

12   Investigate a well-reported business reorganisation. Determine the reasons for this reorganisation and the impact on the key stakeholders. Write up your findings in the form of a case history.

PART 4

The focus of this part, which contains three chapters, is on the preparation and evaluation company financial statements. The first chapter, 'External financial reporting', looks at the types and structures of the primary financial statements of business entities, paying particular attention to the requirements of the International Accounting Standards Board. The second chapter, 'Regulations, audit and taxation', examines the principal sources of the regulation of financial statements, the need for and the nature of these statements to be independently audited, and the bases on which corporate taxation liabilities are calculated. The final chapter, 'Financial statement analysis', looks at the various techniques that accountants have developed to enable financial statement users to interpret the information that these statements contain.

External financial reporting   13

Chapter preview

In this chapter we examine the structure and content of the primary financial statements. Originally these were the balance sheet and, later, the profit and loss account. However, in more recent years cash flow statements have also come to be regarded as one of the principal accounting statements. We will see that the purpose of these primary financial statements is that of providing information to their users about the financial position, performance and adaptability of the reporting entity. We will base our discussions on the provisions of the 2006 IASB financial reporting standards.

Attention will be paid to the ways in which accountants classify and present information in financial statements – including the distinction between fixed and current assets in balance sheets, and the debate regarding the nature and disclosure of unusual items in the profit and loss account.

Reference will also be made to the regulation of financial statements, via influence of legislation and the (influential) statements of professional accountancy bodies. Emphasis is also placed on the need for financial statements to provide an effective communication channel accessible to interested parties and the concept of financial adaptability.

The primary financial statements

The primary financial statements are the principal means via which the managers of (business) entities communicate (are required to communicate), information about the financial position and performance of their entities to the differing stakeholders associated with them. They are derived from the accounting records of these entities, the bases of which were described in Chapter 3, and are required to comply with relevant local regulation. Normally, they focus on three main aspects of the financial affairs of reporting entities (although they are often accompanied by significant amounts of supplementary information, principally in notes to the financial statements); these main aspects are:

(a) The resources employed by the entity and how these resources are funded – this is the focus of the **balance sheet**, also referred to as the **statement of financial position**.

(b) Performance in terms of the increases (gains) or the decreases (losses) in ownership interest over a financial period – this is the focus of the **income statement**, the **statement of changes in equity** and the **statement of total recognised gains and losses**.

(c) The sources of the entity's cash inflows and the ways in which this cash flow has been applied – this is the focus of the **cash flow statement**.

The objective of these financial statements is (IASB):

... to provide information about the reporting entity's financial position, performance and changes in financial position of an entity that is useful to a wide range of users in making economic decisions.

Normally these primary financial statements form part of an entity's (company's) annual report. Such reports can be voluminous documents, containing a variety of information in addition to the primary financial statements. The structure and content of **annual reports** is covered later in more detail in the next chapter. Most listed companies post their annual reports on their websites, frequently in a section of the website called 'investor relations'.

Taken together, the primary financial statements can provide a rich source of information for assessing the financial affairs of reporting entities, particularly when utilised in conjunction with other available sources of information. However, for this to be achieved the statements must be readily understandable. The IASB emphasise the importance of effective communication via financial statements. In presenting information in financial statements, the objective is to communicate clearly and effectively. Financial statements should be as simple, straightforward and brief as possible while retaining their relevance and reliability.

Balance sheets

A balance sheet is a statement of the financial position of the reporting entity at a given point in time. It should contain IASB (2006):

. . . current and non-current assets, and current and non-current liabilities, as separate classifications on the face of its balance sheet.

In this context a current asset or liability is one which is expected to be realised either in the entity's normal operating cycle or within the next 12 months. Broadly speaking, balance sheets are balance sheets wherever in the world they are produced. However, their detailed layout and content will vary, e.g. depending on local legislation and whether they relate to private or public sector entities. In what follows we will concentrate our discussion on a 'generic' framework for balance sheets, ignoring local variations. In large part, the detail of this framework will be based on that recommended by the IASB.

The essential structure of a balance sheet, based on the fundamental accounting identity discussed in the previous chapter, is shown in Table 13.1.

The balance sheet structure illustrated in Table 13.1 is obviously a simplified one, intended to highlight the core features of a balance sheet. Using such a simplified structure is particularly relevant given the increasing tendency of many large listed companies to keep their balance sheets free from what they regard as 'unnecessary detail'. Such companies seek to emphasise the key elements and relationships in the balance sheet and to provide more detailed information in the supplementary notes to the financial statements. This style of financial reporting is potentially very useful because it provides informed readers with key figures on which they can concentrate. However, it can also be argued that it might lead to important issues being relegated to the supplementary notes, which may not be read by many users of the financial statements. The issue of the balance between the information content of the primary financial statements themselves and that of amplifying/supplementary information is considered in more detail later. However, the key point is that such supplementary disclosures should only serve to provide additional information, expanding on and consistent with the core information disclosed in the primary financial statements themselves. They should not contradict or otherwise be at variance with the information in the primary financial statements.

Table 13.1   Framework of a balance sheet

XYZ plc
Balance Sheet as at 31 December 2007

	2007 £000s	2006 £000s
Fixed assets		
Intangible assets	XXX	YYY
Tangible assets	XXX	YYY
Investments	XXX	YYY
	XXX	YYY
Current assets		
Stocks	XXX	YYY
Debtors	XXX	YYY
Cash in hand and at bank	XXX	YYY
	XXX	YYY
Creditors: amounts falling due within one year	XXX	YYY
Net current assets	XXX	YYY
Total assets less current liabilities	XXX	YYY
Creditors: amounts falling due after more than one year	XXX	YYY
Total net assets	XXX	YYY
Capital and reserves		
Called up share capital	XXX	YYY
Reserves	XXX	YYY
	XXX	YYY

The structure in Table 13.1 demonstrates the following key features of balance sheets:

(a) *Titles*: the title clearly states the name of the reporting entity and the point in time to which the balance sheet relates. Without this information the statement would be useless. It also reinforces the fact that the balance sheet is a position statement showing the assets, liabilities and equity of a specific entity at a specific point in time.

(b) *Comparatives*: the balance sheet contains values relating to the financial year being reported on and the previous one. Stakeholders in the entity will want to know how the structure of its assets, liabilities and equity has changed during the period to which the financial statements relate. The provision of comparative figures enables them to do this. In practice, particularly for larger companies which have their shares listed on a stock exchange, a separate part of their annual report will be a **financial review** showing comparative data for 5, 10 or 20 years – enabling trends in the financial structure and performance of the company to be identified.

(c) *Core items* being reported on, i.e. the elements of the fundamental accounting identity described in Chapter 3. It is these elements which will form the main focus of this section.

- Assets – divided into fixed assets and current assets.
- Liabilities – divided into current and long-term liabilities.
- Ownership interest – equal to the total net asset value, and divided into capital and reserves.

As can readily be seen from the above, balance sheets seek to distinguish clearly between the short term and the long term. For financial reporting purposes, the short term is the entity's normal operating cycle or the 12-month period following the date of the balance sheet. Thus, liabilities (creditors) which will be settled within this period are classified as short-term (current) liabilities, others as long-term liabilities. Similarly, assets which the entity intends to keep for longer than 12 months are classified as long-term (fixed) assets, others as short-term (current) assets.

Fixed assets

Like any asset, a fixed asset is something owned or controlled by an entity from which it is expected that future economic benefits will be derived. The distinctive features of a fixed asset are that:

- the entity intends to own it for the long term (i.e. more than one financial period);
- the reason the entity owns the asset is to use it to generate economic benefits, rather than to achieve such benefits by selling it at a profit.

In the context of financial statements, the determining feature of a fixed asset is not the physical nature of the asset, but the economic rationale for owning it – the generation of economic benefits, e.g. by using the asset to produce goods or services (over a number of accounting periods) which will then be sold to customers, thereby generating revenues for the entity. It might be the case that an entity owns two physically identical assets, one of which will be classified as a fixed asset and one of which will not. Consider a motor dealer owning two physically identical vans. One van may have been acquired with a view to using it in the business over a long period of time – for carrying spares, making deliveries, etc. This van would be classified as a fixed asset. The other van may have been acquired with a view to making a profit from reselling it as soon as possible. Such a van, which will typically spend a short period of time with the entity, perhaps in a showroom until it is sold, would not be classified as a fixed asset – it would be classified as a current asset. Common examples of fixed assets include land and buildings, plant and machinery, furniture and equipment, motor vehicles, etc.

The economic rationale for the ownership of fixed assets creates a difficulty for accountants. The matching concept requires that once any aspect of a transaction is recognised in financial statements then all other aspects of that transaction must also be recognised. If the economic benefits generated from using fixed assets in a given financial period are to be recognised, then the cost of this use must also be recognised. The way in which this is achieved in financial statements is via the concept of **depreciation**, discussed in Chapter 3.

Fixed assets are generally stated in balance sheets at their original (historical) cost (or sometimes a subsequent **revaluation**) less **accumulated depreciation**. This amount is called the **net book value** of the asset. The starting point in the recording of fixed assets, as for other assets, is the historical cost at which the asset was first acquired by the reporting entity. This will be recorded in the core accounting records in the normal way. Frequently, it will also be recorded in a subsidiary register (**fixed assets register**), where the physical details and location of the asset (as well as its cost and accumulated depreciation) will be shown.

So far we have implicitly assumed that fixed assets are tangible, i.e. having a physical presence. However, a company may also have intangible fixed assets, e.g. patent rights. Intangible fixed assets are the subject of IAS 38.

Fixed asset carrying values

Another difficulty that financial reporting can (and frequently does) face in relation to fixed assets is that the application of 'the historical cost' principle (with its associated depreciation charges) can easily lead to the carrying (net book) value of fixed assets differing significantly from their current market (net realisable) value. In such cases, the reported total net asset value of (and therefore the reported ownership interest in) the entity may increasingly diverge from commercial reality. Such divergence can be the result of either general, or asset specific, price level changes.

Traditionally, accountants were wedded to the stewardship view of accounting – i.e. that financial reporting should focus on the consequences of transactions entered into by entities, and particularly the monetary consequences of such transactions. According to this view, financial reporting should concentrate on what can be determined as having happened (as evidenced by contractually based and legally enforceable transactions with determined monetary values). Some accounting theorists attempt to justify this divergence of 'values' on the grounds that an entity does not intend to sell its fixed assets. Therefore, in their view, the current market (net realisable value) of such assets is not a significant piece of information and does not need to be reported. However, an important consequence of this divergence is that the balance sheet will (in times of inflation) understate the 'true' value of the assets that a firm is using in its business. This can lead to overestimates of the profitability of the firm (defined as profit divided by the value of the assets used to generate that profit) – there is something of a double 'whammy' here as the use of historical cost will lead to lower depreciation charges (and thus higher profits) while the value of the assets is below their 'true' economic worth. Management may, thus, be tempted not to revalue. However, the understatement of 'asset' values may make a firm vulnerable to acquisition and asset-stripping, something unlikely to appeal to existing corporate management.

To counter these dangers, it is common practice in a number of countries for companies periodically to revalue their fixed assets – i.e. to state them at their current market value in their balance sheets. However, in other countries such revaluations (particularly upward ones) are not permitted. The use of revaluations naturally introduces a degree of subjectivity into the financial statements (the value can really only be determined by selling the assets in question). Historically, revaluations have been most common for property assets where it is (usually) relatively straightforward to obtain professional valuations from professionals such as estate agents and surveyors.

Consider the case of a company which on 1 January 1999 acquired a 50-year lease on its factory premises at a cost of £1 000 000. On 31 December 2006 the company employed professional property valuers to assess the value of the remaining term of its lease on an 'open market' basis. They assessed this value as being £1 200 000. Ignoring this valuation, the leasehold property would be shown in the balance sheet of the company as follows:

	Leasehold property at original cost	£1 000 000
Less	Accumulated depreciation (10 × £20 000)	200 000
	Net book value	£800 000

Thus, the carrying value of the property on a historical cost basis is some £400 000 below its open market valuation. The directors of the company decide that they should incorporate the property in its balance sheet at the open market valuation. This will result in the property being shown in the balance sheet as:

Leasehold property at valuation	£1 200 000

The notes to the balance sheet would show the date of the valuation, the identity of the valuers and the basis of the valuation. However, having increased the carrying value of the asset by £400 000, the matching principle requires a corresponding entry. This will be in the ownership interest (equity) section of the balance sheet, which will show:

Revaluation reserve	£400 000

This will be referred to the note giving details of the revaluation. In most countries, a revaluation reserve is not available for distribution (as dividends) to shareholders. This is because it is an unrealised gain and most countries only permit dividends to be paid out of realised gains. The final part of the revaluation process comes with the depreciation charges after the revaluation. These will be based on the revalued amount and the remaining life of the asset after the revaluation. In our example, this will be £30 000 per year (£1 200 000 / 40), compared to the annual charge of £20 000 (£1 000 000 / 50) prior to the revaluation.

A logical consequence of permitting revaluations is that, if the current market value of the revalued assets falls below their balance sheet carrying value, then the assets must be revalued downwards – something that managers are not always very keen on. Technically, this is referred to as 'impairment' of asset values and is the subject of 1AS 36, which requires that management regularly review the value of its assets to identify (and report in the financial statements) where impairment has occurred.

Current assets

These are the short-term assets of the reporting entity, i.e. those assets which it is expected that the entity will realise (convert into cash, or an equivalent short-term asset) within 12 months of the balance sheet date or within its normal operating cycle. Typically, such assets fall into one of following categories:

(a) **Cash** and cash equivalents (e.g. bank balances).

(b) Monies (**receivables**) owed to the reporting entity, which it expects will be settled (paid) by the **debtors** (the individuals/organisations owing the money) within the next 12 months. Such debts will (typically) be the result of sales transactions (on a credit basis) to customers of the entity, or it having lent money to third parties on a short-term basis. An alternative name for debtors that is used by many companies is **accounts receivable**;

(c) Prepayments of business expenses, where the economic benefit of the prepayment will be realised within the next 12 months (the concept of prepayment of expenses was discussed in the previous chapter). Within balance sheets, prepayments are usually incorporated with debtors (the 'old-fashioned' balance sheet terminology was 'debtors and prepayments').

(d) **Stock** or **inventory** – in essence, this is money that has been spent by the reporting entity on physical resources which it expects to consume in the short term. This may be via sale of the resources to customers or in otherwise supporting the operations of the entity. Typically, the major element of stock is that which will be used in the supply of goods/services to customers. For a manufacturing entity, this is likely to include raw materials, part-finished goods (**work-in-progress**) and finished goods (ready for sale to customers). For a retail organisation, it will be the merchandise purchased from suppliers (manufacturers and wholesalers) for onward sale to customers. Stock will also include other items such as stationery and maintenance stores.

The old-fashioned (Victorian) name for current assets was **circulating assets**. This rather descriptive term emphasises the way in which current assets circulate through the entity – cash is used to purchase stock (or to pay creditors if the stock is purchased on credit terms); this stock is then sold resulting in debtors; these debtors then pay what they owe resulting in the circle coming back to cash.

As for fixed assets, current assets will initially be recorded, and reported, at their historical cost. Thus, stock will be stated 'at the cost of bringing it to its present condition and location' (IAS 2). Similarly debtors will initially be stated at the monetary amount owed to the entity. However, the expectation is that current assets will be recycled into cash in the short term. Because of this, unlike fixed assets, the current market (cash equivalent) value of current assets is likely to be an important piece of information for appreciating the financial affairs of an enterprise – it indicates how much cash the entity is likely to realise (as a minimum) from these assets. We say 'as a minimum' because of the fundamental accounting concept of prudence. As we saw in Chapter 1, this requires that financial statements are prepared on a prudent basis, i.e. one which does not anticipate profits until their ultimate cash realisation is reasonably certain. This is particularly relevant in the case of stocks. Stocks may have a cash equivalent in excess of their original cost *assuming they can be sold for this amount*. However, the fact that they are stocks (at the date of the financial statements) indicates that they have not as yet been sold and, therefore, it is not certain that they will ultimately realise current market prices when sold. Accordingly, their carrying value (historic cost) is not revalued upwards to such market prices and profits are not anticipated.

The concept of prudence goes further than this. It not only requires that profits are not anticipated, but also that potential losses are anticipated. This means that, if the market (net realisable) value of a current asset falls below its original cost, then for financial reporting purposes the monetary value of the asset must be reduced from original cost to market value. This is usually referred to as the 'lower of cost and market value' rule. For example, if it seems that a debtor will be unable to pay the whole of the amount owed, then (in financial statements) the monetary value of the debt should be reduced to the amount that it is estimated will ultimately be received from the debtor. Similarly, if the market value of an item of stock falls below original cost, then its monetary value for the financial statements should be reduced to its estimated realisable value. The core concept underlying the monetary valuation of current assets in a balance sheet is that of trying to provide readers with a prudent statement of the amount of cash which the enterprise is likely to have available to it, in the short term, resulting from its ownership of these assets.

However, this requires those responsible for preparing the financial statements (usually, the managers of the reporting entity) to make extensive judgements about the 'value' of current assets. For example, with respect to debtors, they must judge (at least in theory) whether the entire 'face' value of each individual debt will be recovered. If it is thought that the total amount will not be recoverable then a bad debt provision needs to be made. Ideally, a specific bad debt provision should be made for every debt which may not be fully collectable – this would probably involve reviewing the debtor's financial position and previous payment record. This is a time-consuming process and one which it would be unrealistic to expect of a business having many thousands of (or perhaps even more) individual debtors. In such cases it is more usual to make a general bad debt provision, based on the entity's past experience of the proportion of debts that prove uncollectable. Inevitably, the result is an opinion rather than a fact.

The judgements required with regard to stock are even more complex. Decisions have to be made with regard to the accounting bases that will be used in measuring the (original) cost of items of stock. This is a particular problem for manufacturing entities as there are a number of different ways in which the 'original' cost of processed products can be computed. The general, underlying principle of measuring such costs is that they should be based on the direct costs of production (typically, the labour and materials costs) plus an 'appropriate' share of production overhead expenditure. These costing issues are considered in more detail in Chapter 5, where we looked at the computation of product costs for management purposes. In addition, decisions (assumptions) have to be made about the time pattern of the flow of stocks through the reporting entity. The two principal bases (assumptions) employed in this regard are the First In First Out (FIFO) method (which effectively assumes that the oldest items of stock are those disposed of first) and the Last In First Out (LIFO) method, popular for taxation reasons in the USA (which assumes that the newest items of stock are those that are disposed of first). The IASB require that the FIFO method be used. The impact of this choice can be illustrated with a simple example. Consider a company with the following transactions:

1 January:	Purchase of 100 widgets at a unit price of £100
8 January:	Sale of 75 widgets at a unit price of £150
15 January:	Purchase of 50 widgets at a unit price of £110
22 January:	Sale of 50 widgets at a unit price of £160
31 January:	Purchase of 75 widgets at a unit price of £120
	Sale of 50 widgets at a unit price of £170

The company has purchased a total of 225 widgets and sold a total of 175 widgets during the month. Thus, at the end of January it has 50 widgets remaining in stock. FIFO would assume that the widgets are sold in the order in which they are purchased, i.e. that the ones remaining in stock were those purchased last. This would indicate a stock value of £6000 (i.e. 50 widgets at a unit cost of £120). LIFO would assume that the widgets remaining in stock were those that were first purchased. This would indicate a stock value of £5000 (i.e. 50 widgets at a unit cost of £100). Thus, FIFO produces a value for stock at the end of the month which is £1000 higher than the corresponding LIFO valuation, a difference of 20% in value. Naturally, associated with this difference in the valuation of the stock of widgets is a difference in the accounting profit for the month. Under both methods, the sales revenue would be £27 750 and the amount spent on purchasing the widgets would be £24 500. The cost of the widgets sold can be calculated by deducting the closing stock value from the purchase cost of widgets. On a FIFO basis, the cost of widgets sold is £18 500 (£24 500 – £6000). On a LIFO basis, it is £19 500 (£24 500 – £5000). Thus, on a FIFO basis the company's profit for January is £9250 (£27 750 – £18 500). On a LIFO basis it is £8250 (£27 750 – £19 500). This is the normal pattern of difference between the use of FIFO and LIFO. FIFO leads to higher stock values and higher profits. LIFO leads to lower stock values and lower profits.

Investments

Investments in financial instruments (e.g. shares and bonds) are normally fairly easy to fit into the accounting model. There will be a historical cost, the price paid to acquire the instrument and (in the case of listed instruments) an easily ascertained current market (net realisable) value. In the case of unlisted instruments an assessment (more or less reliable) can normally be made of a net realisable value. Given this, the principles we have already discussed for the valuation of fixed and current assets can readily be employed in the valuation of investments, albeit with a degree of judgement. Whether investments are shown as fixed or current assets in a balance sheet depends on the reporting entity's intentions regarding them. If they are long-term, strategic investments, they will be shown as fixed assets. If they are short-term investments, they will be shown as current assets.

Current liabilities

As can be seen from Table 13.1, these are creditors falling due for payment within one year or within the entity's normal operating cycle. As we have already seen, a liability is an amount of money owed to a person or organisation who has either lent the entity money, or who has supplied it with goods or services on a credit basis, and who has not yet been paid. These are the most common types of **creditors** of an accounting entity. However, entities will often have other types of liabilities in addition to creditors. The most common of these are amounts owed to government (for taxation arising from the entity's activities), and amounts due to shareholders for dividends approved but not yet paid. In some ways, these are complete opposites. The other most common form of liability is short-term loan finance from a bank or similar financial institution.

The financial reporting of current liabilities is, in principle, reasonably straightforward. They should be stated at the amount of money that the enterprise expects to have to pay to its creditors during the course of the 12 months following the date of the balance sheet. There should be none of the valuation problems involved with the balance sheet valuation of fixed and current assets.

Net current assets

By showing the net current assets of an entity (current assets minus current liabilities), the balance sheet is directing the reader's attention to what is often thought of as a key indicator of the entity's financial well-being – whether or not it will be able to meet its short-term liabilities from its short-term assets. If it cannot, then it may have to resort to further borrowing to settle these liabilities, or it may have to contemplate fixed asset disposals, thereby reducing its operating capacity. This is an issue which was looked at in Chapter 6, where we saw that different types of enterprise have different patterns of net current assets, depending on their trading and financing structures and relationships. For the present, we need to note that it is a key measure, highlighted by the balance sheet, and as with all financial measures it needs to be interpreted in the light of other available information.

Another term for net current assets is **working capital**. This reflects the fact that, while the fixed assets of an entity provide it with its long-term operating capacity, it is the short-term assets and liabilities which are often the day-to-day working focus of management. In exactly the same way that investments in operating capacity (fixed assets) should be justified and evaluated in terms of their contribution to the overall profitability of an enterprise, so should its investments in short-term assets.

Long-term liabilities

These form part of the longer-term financing of the reporting entity and comprise liabilities that are not due for settlement by the enterprise within the 12 months following the balance sheet date. Typically they will be medium- or longer-term loans provided by financial institutions. The range of terms on which such medium- to long-term finance is available are very wide. It is important that users of financial statements have a full understanding of the financing structure of the entity. Accordingly, the financial statements, or their supporting notes, need to provide full details of the terms of all long-term loan finance. These details should provide information on when the loan finance is repayable, the interest rates which are being charged, and what security, if any, has been pledged to secure the loans. The due dates for the repayment of loan finance need to be continually reviewed, to ensure that any amounts which are in fact repayable within 12 months of the date of the financial statements are included in current rather than long-term liabilities.

Provisions

The foregoing discussion of liabilities (both current and long-term) presumes that the amount which will have to be paid to settle the liability is in fact known at the date of the financial statements. There will be some circumstances where the existence of a liability at balance sheet date is known but the amount of the liability is not. Equally, there may be circumstances in which the existence of a set of liabilities is known but the individual liabilities are not. This is common in the insurance industry, where at the end of the financial year an insurer knows that there will be claims from policy-holders in relation to a particular line of business but does not at that time know the number of outstanding claims or their amount. In such circumstances, the insurer has to estimate the potential liability for such claims (based on past experience and knowledge of recent events). Liabilities of this type, where the entity knows that a liability exists but does not know the amount, are incorporated in the balance sheet as **provisions,** and they can be substantial in some industrial/commercial sectors. The notes supporting the balance sheet should explain the nature of the provisions and the bases on which they have been calculated.

Contingent liabilities

There may be situations of even greater uncertainty than those requiring provisions to be made, e.g. where an entity is aware that a liability might exist but is not sure what one does, or for how much. This might be the case where the entity is involved in a legal action – if it loses the action, it might have to pay damages. Another example might be where the entity has given a guarantee – it may or may not be called upon to honour this guarantee, depending on future events. This is a very common situation in the financial services sector, where giving guarantees on behalf of customers is a common event. Potential liabilities of this type are called **contingent liabilities.** Such liabilities are not included in the balance sheet because of the degree of uncertainty surrounding them. However, stakeholders do need to be aware of them because they can be very substantial. Accordingly, information about them is provided in the amplifying notes to the financial statements.

Ownership interest

The ownership interest (often referred to as equity) in an entity is the residual amount after its liabilities have been deducted from its assets. It is the amount that the owners of the entity would be entitled to if all the assets of the entity were sold, and all its liabilities settled, at their balance sheet values. This residual nature of ownership interest is emphasised by the fundamental accounting identity:

$$\text{Equity} = \text{Assets} - \text{Liabilities} \qquad\qquad (13.1)$$

There are two principal components of equity:

- the funds contributed to the entity by its owners; and
- gains and losses made by the entity.

The focus in financial statements is on providing an analysis of these two components, particularly in the case of companies.

Contributions from owners

In the case of companies, the contributions from owners come via their subscribing for shares in the company, either at the time that the company is first set up, or a later date.

Companies have legal constitutions (in the UK and Australia, their Articles and Memorandum of Association). They are also subject to nationally determined company law, which will often specify at least part of the contents of their individual constitutions. *Inter alia*, these constitutions will often (as for example in the UK and Australia) set out the value of the share capital that the company is authorised to issue (its authorised capital). They may also set out how many shares the company is authorised to issue and the **nominal value** (par value) of each share. For example, the authorised capital of a company (Makeham Ltd) might be: £1 000 000 divided into 100 000 ordinary shares of £10 each.

Companies can have quite complex capital structures involving a number of different classes of share with each class of share having different rights (e.g. as to voting entitlements at general meetings, payment of dividends and repayment of capital). However, there must always be a class of ordinary shares which are the ultimate risk capital of the company. In recent years, in part because of pressure from stock exchanges, there has been a trend towards companies having simpler capital structures than used to be the case in the past. However, there are still some quite complex ones around.

In its financial statements, or the amplifying notes, a company is required to show:

- its authorised capital, and how this is made up (numbers and types of shares); and

- its issued capital, and how this is made up (numbers and types of shares and whether these shares have been issued fully or part paid (in relation to the nominal value).

This information will only change if a company increases its authorised capital (with the approval of shareholders in general meeting), issues additional shares (from its authorised but not issued capital) or redeems or otherwise reconstructs its share capital (normally with the sanction of the courts).

The nominal value of a share is exactly what it says – nominal. It has no necessary bearing on the economic value of a share. Thus, a company may issue its shares to the capital market at a price higher than the nominal value – if the capital market is willing to pay this price. This excess (of issue price over nominal value) is called a **share premium**. Share premiums are shown separately in balance sheets and are effectively part of the contributions from owners. Share premiums are normally regarded as being non-distributable reserves. Similarly, there is no necessary link between the issue price of a share and the current market value of a share (as, for example, listed on a stock exchange) – as a number of dot. coms clearly demonstrated. The market value of a company's shares, while of undoubted interest to shareholders and directors (and others) does not feature in a company's balance sheet – the focus of the balance sheet is the original (and any subsequent) contributions from the shareholders (made up of the nominal value and any share premiums).

Consider the example of Makeham Ltd, assuming that it issued 50 000 shares at an issue price of £15 per share, fully paid. The relevant section of its balance sheet (or of the notes to the accounts) would look like:

Share capital		
Authorised:	100 000 ordinary shares of £10 each	£1 000 000
Issued:	50 000 ordinary shares of £10 each, fully paid	£ 500 000
Share premium account		£ 250 000
		£ 750 000

Gains/losses and reserves

Gains and losses can arise in a number of different ways and the focus in the financial statements is on identifying the source of the gain/loss. This is important because only some gains are legally available (within the UK) for distribution as dividends to shareholders. Gains/losses are shown as part of the **reserves** element of ownership interest. The principal categories of reserves are:

- Non-distributable reserves
- *Share premium account*: this represents the gain a company makes when it is able to issue shares at a price above their nominal value. In effect, it forms part of the contribution from shareholders and, on that basis, as with the share capital itself, dividends cannot be paid out of it. It is part of the 'locked-in' long-term capital of the business.

- *Revaluation reserve*: a revaluation reserve arises when a company revalues its assets (e.g. land and buildings). The general principle is that dividends can only be paid out of realised gains and a gain is not realised until an asset is disposed of. Thus, revaluation reserves are non-distributable until the underlying asset is disposed of.

- *Distributable reserves*: effectively, these are all the realised gains that a company has made since its formation, which have not yet been paid out as dividends to shareholders. Their most common source of these reserves will be the profits that the company has made from its trading operations – i.e. retained profits.

Balance sheet summary

The 'bottom-line' is that, whatever it may achieve in terms of a 'stewardship' model of financial reporting, a balance sheet cannot, except in the most unusual circumstances, show the value of a business. This is because the net assets (equity) shown in a balance sheet:

- exclude many potentially valuable economic assets such as goodwill, non-separable intangible assets and internally generated intangible assets;

- have historic cost rather than current market value as their principal measurement basis for the assets that are recognised (although, as we have seen, there is some scope for revaluations upwards and downwards);

- include a considerable amount of 'judgement' in the computation of items such as depreciation and provisions;

- are based on past transactions and other economic events, rather than future events likely to impact on the value of the business; and

- are prepared, typically, once per year and as such the information they contain may be considerably out of date.

Statements of financial performance

The second main category of primary financial statements is that of **statements of financial performance**. These statements are concerned with reporting the outcomes of an entity's activities over a period of time (typically a financial year), with particular emphasis on the increases (decreases) in ownership interest; (profits/gains) resulting from such activities. They aim to provide an explication of the significant elements of such changes for the benefit of the users of the financial statements. Whereas balance sheets are position statements (concentrating on a particular point in time), statements of financial performance are flow statements (reporting the value changes in key accounting elements over the period to which they relate). Exactly the same fundamental accounting principles as apply to balance sheets (going concern, matching, prudence and consistency) apply to statements of financial performance. **Income statements** (profit and loss accounts) are commonly regarded by the capital markets as providing key indicators of financial performance, because they (are supposed to) show how successful a (business) entity has been in the achievement of its core objective – making profits for its owners.

It is generally accepted that statements of financial performance perform two key functions:

(a) Reporting on the past performance of entities – thereby enabling users of the financial statements to assess historic corporate and managerial performance and to make decisions based on this past performance.

(b) Helping users of the financial statements to predict the future financial performance of entities – such predictions will (inevitably) be, in large part, based on information about past performance. Therefore, the information contained in statements of financial performance should be aimed at facilitating such predictions, and decisions (by stakeholders) about their ongoing relationships with the entity.

In recent years, the focus has increasingly moved to the importance of helping users of financial statements predict future financial performance. In the words of the ASB (1999c: para 15):

Users of financial statements require information on the entity's financial performance because such information:

(a) assists users in assessing the capacity of the entity to generate cash flows from its existing resource base and in forming judgements about the effectiveness with which the entity has employed its resources and might employ additional resources, and

(b) provides feedback to users so that they can review their previous assessments of the financial performance for past periods and can modify their assessments for, or develop new expectations about, future periods.

The content and structure of statements of financial performance have been the subject of considerable debate in recent years. This debate arises (in part) from two contrasting views as to the purpose of profit and loss accounts:

1 The **comprehensive income** view: Comprehensive income has been defined FASB (1985: para 70) as:

> The change in equity of a business enterprise during a period from transactions and other events and circumstances from non-owner sources.

Under this view, an entity's reported net profit (loss) for a period should include all the transactions for that period affecting the entity's net equity, other than contributions or distributions. The rationale for this view is that a profit and loss account prepared on this basis is less susceptible to manipulation and variations resulting from the applications of subjective judgements. In addition, such a profit and loss account will provide users with better information on which to base their assessment of the entity's financial performance. It also ensures that, over time, there is a congruence between the periodic reported profit of the entity and changes in its net asset values.

2 The **current operating performance** view. Under this view the emphasis in the profit and loss account should be on the ordinary, recurring operations of the reporting entity. The inclusion of other items in the profit and loss account 'might impair the significance of net income to such an extent that misleading inferences might be drawn' (APB 1966: para. 10). Under this view, transactions which are not part of the ordinary, recurring operations of the entity should not form part of the profit (loss) for the period. Instead, they should be reported as adjustments to **retained profits**, i.e. reserves. Proponents of this approach to the reporting of profit (tend) to claim that concentrating on current operating performance will enable readers of the financial statements to make better predictions of the future financial performance of the entity, because of the focus on the type(s) of transactions which might reasonably be expected to continue in the future – the ordinary, recurring ones. The danger of this approach is that it is not always easy to judge what are ordinary, recurring transactions. Managers might be tempted to identify favourable items as resulting from ordinary, recurring operations and include them in reported profit; equally they might be tempted to identify unfavourable items as not resulting from such operations and exclude them from reported profit, instead adjusting retained profit for them.

This difference in approach has significant implications for the reporting of financial performance. Under the current operating performance approach, an entity needs two different financial statements to report on changes in its equity. These are:

(a) A profit and loss account, which summarises the outcomes of the ordinary, recurring operations and provides a figure for the final (retained) profit (loss) for the financial period arising from these operations.

(b) A supplementary statement which summarises all the changes in the entity's equity for the period, including the retained profit for the period (from (a) above) and the impact of any 'non-recurring' transactions. One name for such a statement is a **statement of total recognised gains and losses**, as required by IAS 1.

Under the comprehensive income approach, only one statement is required (at least in theory) – an all-encompassing profit and loss account.

Framework of a profit and loss account

Table 13.2 provides an illustration of the structure of a 'traditional' (non-comprehensive income) profit and loss account. As can be seen, such a profit and loss account summarises all the principal components of the trading activities of an entity for a financial period (year).

As for a balance sheet, the profit and loss account commences with an identification of the reporting entity and the financial period to which it relates. Similarly, it shows figures both for the current and a comparative period. The rationale here is the same as that for the balance sheet – to enable comparisons to be made and trend analysis started. The concept of consistency is obviously of great importance here. If the financial statements have not been prepared on a consistent basis, a true comparison will be difficult, if not impossible.

The IASB permits two different approaches to the preparation of income statements: the first is the nature of expense method and the second, more commonly used, is the functional method. In the example shown in the Table 13.2 we have used the latter method.

The profit and loss account starts with the sales turnover (trading revenue) of the entity for the relevant financial period, stated net of any sales taxes (e.g. Value Added

---

Table 13.2   Frameworks of a profit and loss account

XYZ Plc
Profit and Loss Account for year ended 31 December 2007

	2007 £000	2007 £000	2006 £000
Turnover		XXX	YYY
Cost of sales		XXX	YYY
Gross profit		XXX	YYY
Distribution costs	XXX		YYY
Administration costs	XXX		YYY
		XXX	YYY
		XXX	YYY
Other operating income		XXX	YYY
Operating profit		XXX	YYY
Interest on loans		XXX	YYY
Profit before investment income and taxation		XXX	YYY
Income from investments		XXX	YYY
Profit before taxation		XXX	YYY
Taxation		XXX	YYY
Profit after taxation		XXX	YYY
Dividends		XXX	YYY
Retained profit for year		XXX	YYY

Tax, Goods and Services Tax, etc.). From this it deducts the cost of sales (i.e. the costs of supplying goods and services to customers), again net of sales taxes to give the **gross profit** of the entity. In essence, this first section of the profit and loss account focuses on how successful the entity has been at trading in the market places in which it operates. This is because it relates the revenues obtained from selling goods and services in such markets to the costs incurred in obtaining (producing) these goods and services. Frequently, the relationship between gross profit and sales revenue is expressed as a percentage, called the gross profit percentage. Changes in this percentage over time will indicate changes in the success of the entity and its management in operating in these markets (both buying and selling).

The next part of the profit and loss account summarises the expenses that the entity has incurred in supporting its trading activities. In Table 13.2 these are shown as distribution and administrative costs. The amounts of any other operating income (e.g. property rents) earned by the entity is then added to arrive at 'profit before investment income and taxation'. This is frequently referred to as **operating profit**, commonly regarded as a key performance indicator, especially under the current operating income approach. This is because it encapsulates the financial outcomes of the entity's trading activities and its use of resources (irrespective of the financing of these resources). The amount of detail shown in this part of the profit and loss account is to some extent a matter for managerial judgement. For the annual financial statements of companies, national legislation (e.g. the Companies Acts in the UK) will normally lay down a minimum standard of disclosure. In practice, much of such disclosure (e.g. regarding depreciation charges, directors' remuneration, etc.) will be provided in the supplementary notes to the financial statements. For (internal) management accounts the level of detail could be extensive, depending on the amount of analysis management feel they need for decision taking and control purposes.

From this operating profit are deducted the interest charges on any long-term loan finance to arrive at the entity's 'profit before investment income and taxation'. Thereafter, investment income is added to arrive at the overall 'profit before taxation', from which any taxation payable is deducted to arrive at the amount of the 'profit after taxation' for the period in question. The computation of taxation payable on profit is something which is (understandably) dependent on national legislation. In some countries (where taxation legislation has a major influence on financial reporting practices) there will be a close relationship between the nominal rate(s) of corporate taxation, the 'pre-tax' profit and the taxation charge. In other countries (e.g. the UK, the USA and Australia) where financial reporting practices and taxation legislation are largely independent of each other, there will be no readily identifiable relationship between these factors.

The final section of the profit and loss account deals with the disposition of the 'profit after taxation'. It shows how much of these profits have been (will be) distributed to shareholders (as dividends) and how much is being retained by the entity to support its ongoing activities.

The profit and loss account illustrated in Table 13.2 contains no indication as to whether or not it is based on the ordinary, recurring operations of the entity, or whether it includes other elements as well. Thus, it leaves the user in a bit of a quandary when it comes to assessing past (and potential future) corporate performance. At the very least, the reader would want to look at the 'movements in reserves', typically shown as a supplementary note to the corresponding balance sheet to detect any changes in equity value not reflected in the profit and loss account. However, even doing this would not help the reader detect the impact of any unusual items which had been subsumed into the profit and loss account headings.

It is commonly thought that such unusual items fall into two categories:

(a) **Exceptional** items: defined as (ASB 1992: para. 5) as:

Material items which derive from events or transactions that fall within the ordinary activities of the reporting entity and which individually or, if of similar type, in aggregate, need to be disclosed by virtue of their size or incidence if the financial statements are to give a true and fair view.

(b) **Extraordinary** items: The IASB states that no such items can be shown, either on the face of the income statement or in any accompanying notes.

Information as to the extent of exceptional items contained in an income statement is potentially very valuable to the users of financial statements. By definition, exceptional items are a part of normal operations and, as such, rightly belong within the mainstream content of an income statement. Users of the financial statements need to know about them (because of their 'one-off' monetary significance) if they are to be able to assess historic performance and predict future performance in a realistic way. An example of an exceptional item might be an unusually large cost for bad debts arising from the insolvency of a major customer. The normal way of providing this information is via the supplementary notes to the financial statements.

Statement of total recognised gains and losses

Table 13.3 provides an illustration of a statement of total recognised gains and losses.

The purpose of this statement is that of helping to reconcile the equity 'value' of an entity at the start of a financial period and that at the end of the period. It does not do this explicitly, primarily because it does not incorporate the opening and closing equity values. However, this should not be a major problem for readers of the financial statements, especially as the IASB as the IASB requires the publication of a **statement of changes in equity.**

Table 13.3	Specimen statement of total recognised gains and losses

XYZ plc
Statement of total recognised gains and losses for year ended 31 December 2007

	2007 £000	2006 as restated £000
Profit for the financial year	X	X
Unrealised surplus on revaluation of properties	X	X
Unrealised gain on trade investment	X	X
	X	X
Currency translation differences on foreign currency investments	X	X
Total recognised gains and losses relating to the year	X	X

Cash flow statements

These are the subject of IAS 7 which permits two different approaches to their preparation: the direct and the indirect methods. Frequently, which method a company chooses will depend on the adequacy of its accounting records. As we have already pointed out, a positive cash flow is (ultimately) crucial for the continuing success and existence of business entities – they will become insolvent if they run out of cash to pay their bills. The accounting profession was initially rather slow in requiring the provision of cash flow information in financial statements, perhaps because of a reluctance to abandon profit as the 'ultimate indicator' of corporate performance (although profit is, in essence, nothing more than an inter-temporal allocation of cash flows, actual and predicted). In the words of Hendriksen (1982: 236):

> In the final analysis, cash flows into and out of a business enterprise are the most fundamental events upon which accounting measurements are based and upon which investors and creditors are assumed to base their decisions.

The position now is that cash flow statements are regarded as 'a primary financial statement', because of the importance of the information that they provide and are a specific IASB requirement. This is because users need information about cash inflows and outflows to help with assessments of liquidity, solvency and future cash flows and to provide feedback about previous assessments. A statement of cash flows provides useful information about an enterprise's activities in generating cash through operations to repay debt, distribute dividends, or reinvest to maintain or expand operating capacity; and about its investing and financing activities, both debt and equity, insofar as they relate to receipts and payments of cash. Important uses of information about an enterprise's current cash receipts and payments include helping to assess factors such as an enterprise's liquidity, solvency and financial adaptability, the way in which profits are converted into cash and risk.

Table 13.4 provides an illustration of the layout and information content of a cash flow statement based on the requirements of the ASB.

The IASB in IAS 7 identifies four major components of cash flow which will help users of the financial statements appreciate the financial performance and position of the reporting entity. These are:

1 **Net cash flow from operating activities**. This is the cash flow that the entity has generated (incurred) during the financial period from its operations, independently of how long-term finance has been provided for these activities and incorporates the taxation charge for the year. As such it is a prime indicator of how successful the entity has been in managing these activities, and their cash flow consequences. The amount of the cash flow from operating activities, while a prime performance indicator, should not be looked at in isolation. As with many other items of information contained in financial statements, it should be interpreted in conjunction with other information, both from the financial statements and from elsewhere.

2 **Cash flows from investing activities**. The focus here is the amount of cash that the enterprise has spent on fixed assets during the financial period and the amount that it has recouped from the sale of such assets. In general, successful, thriving entities will invest cash in acquiring operating capacity via a continuing investment programme in fixed assets, while declining enterprises may seek to

stabilise themselves via the sale of fixed assets. However, it should be noted that fixed assets, or more generally operating capacity, can be acquired other than by cash purchase, e.g. by purchase on deferred payment terms or by leasing. This, again, emphasises the point that items of information contained in financial statements, in this case information about net cash outflow on investing activities, need to be interpreted in the light of other relevant information.

3 **Cash flows from financing activities.** This is the net cash flow resulting from the costs of the finance (other than equity finance) that the entity has employed during the year, together with any interest that it has been able to generate from the management of its cash resources. Its focus is essentially the cash flow cost (typically interest payments or dividends) of the entity's finance. As such it is information which helps users of financial statements to assess the consequences of financing and financial management decisions.

4 **Net increase in cash and cash equivalents.** This represents the change in these balances over the financial period and is the final element of the cash flow statement.

Overall a cash flow statement is potentially a significant source information about the activities of an entity:

(a) It complements the information contained in the balance sheet and income statement.

Table 13.4	Illustration of a cash flow statement

XYZ plc Cash Flow Statement for year ended 31 December 2007	
	£000
Net cash inflow from operating activities	X
Reconciliation of operating profit to net-cash flow from operating activities	
Operating profit	X
Depreciation charges	X
Loss/(profit) on sale of fixed assets	X
Decrease/(increase)in stocks	X
Decrease/(increase) in debtors	X
Increase/(decrease) in creditors	X
Returns on investment and servicing of finance	X
Taxation	X
Capital expenditure	X
	X
Equity dividends paid	X
	X
Management of liquid resources	X
Financing	X
Increase/(decrease) in cash	X

(b) It focuses on the flow of cash through the enterprise and addresses key issues such as:

- How successful is the enterprise in generating cash flows from operating activities?
- What investment activities has it undertaken?
- What are the cash costs of its financial structure?
- What are the taxation cash flows associated with its activities?

In summary, the cash flow statement directly addresses the cash flow/financial management decisions of the entity and their consequences for its financial health.

The concept of financial adaptability

Modern commercial enterprises exist in a fast-changing competitive environment. One has only to consider the rapid advances in technology in recent years, the political changes that have taken place in Central and Eastern Europe, and the economic crises in various regions of the world to recognise the pace and scale of change in the commercial environment. These changes present new opportunities for enterprises and new threats to them. New product and market opportunities are continually emerging and old products and markets are disappearing. To remain successful, enterprises need to be able to respond to these changes – they need to be adaptable. In part, this adaptability will be a function of corporate visions and cultures, of management's styles and abilities. However, it will also in part be a function of their finances. Is their financial structure, the pattern of their resources and liabilities, and the pattern of their cash flows such as to enable them to respond to challenges and opportunities? If so then, ceteris paribus, they will be more successful. Users of financial information will seek to assess the financial adaptability of enterprises and each of the primary financial statements has a role to play in this. The balance sheet provides information on the pattern and amounts of assets and liabilities; the statements of financial performance show how successful the enterprise has been in the past in generating gains from its activities, and the cash flow statement provides information about the flow of the ultimate resource, cash, through the enterprise. In the words of the ASB (1995: para 1.13):

> Financial adaptability consists of the ability of an enterprise to take effective action to alter the amount and timing of cash flows so that it can respond to unexpected needs, events and opportunities. All the primary financial statements provide information that is useful in evaluating the financial adaptability of an enterprise.

Professional statements and financial reporting

Increasingly the IASB has become the primary source of these, in part because of its link with IOSCO, and its most recent set of standards are those issued in 2006. Most jurisdictions, e.g. all EU member states and those in a number of other countries, require that IASB pronouncements are adopted for the annual financial statements of all listed companies. Some go even further than this, although many offer smaller companies exemptions from the full rigour of the IASB statements. We have already described some of the IASB's pronouncements. In the next chapter we will look at them in more detail.

Conclusion

In this chapter we have identified that the major purpose of external financial statements is to provide useful information to stakeholders about the financial affairs of enterprises. The principal way in which they achieve this is via the primary financial statements themselves, together with any supplementary notes. The extent to which these statements in fact achieve their objective of the provision of useful information is a matter of continuing debate. The primary financial statements are the balance sheet, the income statement, the statement of changes in equity, the statement of total recognised gains and losses and the cash flow statement. All of these statements are subject to (at least some) degree of regulation, and the principal sources of regulation are typically statute law (e.g. the *Companies Acts* in the UK); the requirements of stock exchanges (for listed companies) and accounting 'standards' issued by bodies such as the IASB.

Chapter review

Financial statements are intended to provide their readers with useful information about entities so as to help them assess their economic and other relationships with such entities. The principal financial statements are:

- The balance sheet – this is a position statement intended to show, at a specific point in time, the resources owned by an entity (its assets) and how these resources have been financed by liabilities and equity. The historical cost basis of accounting, which is the normal basis on which financial statements are prepared, although it may be adjusted by the use of revaluations, means that balance sheets are not statements which show the current value, either of the entity in total, or of its individual assets.
- Statements of financial performance reflect the financial performance of an entity over a period of time, normally a financial year. They summarise the entitiy's trading activities, providing information about its sales revenues and the costs that have been incurred to generate these revenues, and other significant changes in ownership interest.
- The cash flow statement – this is a flow statement summarising the receipts and payments of cash by an entity during a given time period, normally a financial year. It analyses these receipts and payments according to their economic purpose and origins, providing information such as the net cash flow generated from operations and from the raising of additional long-term finance.

Taken together with other information available to users, such as that contained in the directors' report and the financial and operating review, the primary financial statements help users to assess the financial adaptability of an enterprise – its financial ability to respond to new opportunities and to meet challenges.

The primary financial statements (and their contents) are the subject of quite a high degree of regulation, the detail of which will vary from country to country. However, common sources of regulation include: local statute and case law, the requirements of stock exchanges, taxation legislation and professional statements on accounting principles and presentation, such as those of the IASB.

Further reading

Alexander and Britton (2004) provide a useful discussion of financial reporting principles, as do Elliot and Elliot (2003). The pronouncements of accountancy bodies and accounting regulators provide professional views on the purposes and processes of effective financial reporting. Notable amongst such bodies are the IASB, the FASB and the ASB, whose websites provide useful sources of information.

Questions and exercises

Guide notes can be found at the back of the book for all questions marked with an asterisk*.

1* The accounting records of Hendy Ltd contained the following balances as at 31 December 2007.

	Debit £	Credit £
Cash and bank balances	1 000	
Debtors	17 158	
Creditors		9 538
Stocks	19 431	
Fixed assets (at cost)	65 098	
Fixed assets (accumulated depreciation)		16 751
Depreciation for year	6 984	
Bank overdraft		7 423
Credit sales		89 649
Cash sales		47 053
Cost of goods sold	76 030	
Operating costs	41 582	
Loan repayable 31 December 2012		10 000
Share capital		30 000
Retained profit as at 1 January 20X1		6 689

Required:
Using the balances shown above, draft a Balance Sheet and Income Statement for Hendy as at that date.

2* The balance sheets and income statements of Liquidity Plc for the years ended 31 December 2006 and 2007 are shown below:

Balance sheets

	2007 £000s	2006 £000s
Fixed assets		
Freehold land and buildings		
Cost	1 600	1 600
Accumulated depreciation	256	224
	1 344	1 376
Plant and vehicles		
Cost	2 385	1 012
Accumulated depreciation	1 027	495
	1 358	517
	2 702	1 893
Current assets		
Inventories	554	338
Debtors	330	191
Cash at bank and in hand	2	8
	886	537
Current liabilities		
Creditors	350	280
Taxation	226	58
Dividends	104	84
	680	422
Net current assets	206	115
Long-term loans	178	158
Total net assets	2 730	1 850
Share capital	1 500	1 000
Retained profits	1 230	850
	2 730	1 850

Income statements

	2007 £000s	2006 £000s
Sales	8 756	5 941
Cost of sales	6 113	4 568
Gross profit	2 643	1 373
Operating expenses	1 895	1 035
Operating profit	748	338
Interest payable	38	23
Profit before taxation	710	326
Taxation payable	226	58
Profit after taxation	484	268
Dividends payable	104	84
Retained profit	380	184

The following additional information is also available:

(a) During the year plant and vehicles with an original cost of £300 000 and a net book value of £100 000 were sold for £80 000.

(b) During the year the following amounts of depreciation were charged: Land and buildings £32 000; Plant and vehicles £732 000.

Required:

Using the information provided above, prepare a cash flow statement for liquidity for the year ended 31 December 2007.

3 Imagination Ltd is a company which commenced operations on 1 January 20XX. During its first year of operations it engaged in the following transactions:

(a) Incurred expenditure on the following items:

	£000
Direct materials	200
Manufacturing labour	100
Manufacturing overheads (excluding depreciation on plant and equipment)	200
Factory administration	100
Head office administration	50
Selling and distribution costs	50
	700

(i) The cost of direct materials increased by 50% halfway through the year.

(ii) 20% of the year's production of 8000 units remained unsold at the year end.

(iii) At the year end there were no unused materials or work in progress.

(b) Purchased the following assets:

(i) Freehold land for a cost of £100 000. One quarter of this land was resold immediately for £60 000 as it was surplus to the company's requirements.

(ii) A leasehold building on a 20-year lease for a cost of £400 000. The market value of this building at the end of the year was £500 000.

(iii) Plant and equipment with a cost of £300 000, an estimated useful life of five years and an estimated residual value of zero.

(c) Spent £200 000 on research and development.

(d) Generated £1 050 000 revenue from the sale of goods.

Required:

Using GAAP, compute the highest and lowest profit figures that Imagination could incorporate in its financial statements.

4   Redhead is proposing to start his own business on the basis of the following estimates:

(a) He will use £20 000 of his own money to provide capital for the business and will use this to buy stock costing £8000 and fixed assets costing £12 000 which are expected to last for five years.

(b) Sales will be made on credit, with payment being received in the month following the month of sale. Sales for the first month will be £2000 and will increase by £1000 each month until they level off at £8000 from the seventh month onwards.

(c) Sales will usually be made at cost price plus 100%, but from the seventh month onwards 10% of sales revenue will come from goods sold at 'half price', i.e. at cost price so as to break even on the sale.

(d) At the end of each month, goods will be purchased, if necessary, to bring stock up to twice the cost of goods sold in the latest month; these purchases will be paid for in the month following that in which they are purchased.

(e) Other expenses will average £2200 per month.

(f) Redhead will draw £500 per month out of the business for personal expenses.

Required:
Prepare a budgeted income statement for the first year of the business and a budgeted balance sheet at the end of that year.

5   The inventory transactions of Amusing Ltd for the month of December 2007 are summarised below:

Date	Receipts Quantity Units	Receipts Price £s	Issues Quantity Units
1/12	20	15	
5/12	40	18	
7/12			10
9/12	20	15	
12/12			20
16/12			40
19/12	30	18	
20/12	20	20	
27/12			30
29/12	20	22	

Required:
On the assumption that Amusing had no stocks at the start of the month, calculate the value of the closing stock for the month on:

(a) FIFO basis.

(b) LIFO basis.

(c) Average cost basis.

6   Seamus O'Glynn is trying to make his way as a theatrical impressario but is at the very early stages of his career. For the last couple of years he has, as a sole proprietorship business, been operating out of a rented theatre in Margate. He opens for business during the summer season and again over the Christmas period when he stages family entertainment. Recently, he has not been doing too well and is looking to obtain a bank loan to finance the next Christmas production. To this end he has prepared the following balance sheet as at 30 September 2007.

Seamus O'Glynn Productions
Balance sheet as at 30 September 2007

	£	£
Fixed assets		
Theatre building		54 000
Lighting equipment		9 800
Furnishings		56 000
Vehicle		30 000
Props and costumes		6 000
		155 800
Current assets		
Debtors	110 500	
Cash at bank	21 900	
	132 400	
Current liabilities		
Trade creditors	12 000	
Salaries payable	29 200	
	41 200	
Net current assets		91 200
Total net assets		247 000
Ownership interest		200 000

The following additional information is available:

(a) Seamus rents the theatre from the local council, at a monthly rental of £6000 per month. The £54 000 shown in the balance sheet is the rent he paid for the 12 months to 30 September 2007.

(b) Seamus purchased the lighting equipment on 20 September 2007 at a cost of £9800, expecting it to last four years. However, Anne O'Grady, the stage manager at the theatre, is on record as saying that the equipment is totally unsuitable for the theatre – her exact words were 'its not worth scrap'.

(c) The furnishings cost £56 000 two years ago when Seamus first acquired use of the theatre. Being specific to the theatre, they have no residual sales value. They are now beginning to show their age and Seamus would like to replace them. Catalogue prices from theatrical suppliers indicate that around £120 000 would be required to replace them with up-to-date furnishings.

(d) The props and costumes are for the intended production of 'Tony and the Seven Spin Doctors'. They were purchased on 10 September 2007, via a cheque for £6000 from Seamus's business bank account. Seamus agreed to pay the balance of £30 000 by 31 March 2008.

(e) The vehicle is Seamus's own Aston Martin which he purchased three years ago for £16 000. He recently saw a similar car advertised in a car magazine for £30000. He uses the car mainly for personal use, although he occasionally ferries actors and dignatories between the theatre and the local railway station.

(f) The debtors' figure of £110 500 includes £14 000 owed by Thanet Theatricals for ticket sales relating to the summer 2007 season. The remaining £96 500 represents expected advance bookings for the forthcoming Christmas season. This figure is based on the position at the same time last year, because printing problems mean that tickets for the forthcoming Christmas season have not gone on sale yet.

(g) Trade creditors include £7800 owed to Italian Ices who operate the theatre's refreshment kiosk. The remaining £2400 is the balance on Seamus's personal VISA card.

(h) Salaries payable includes £25 000 offered to Michael O'Morough to take the lead part in the Christmas entertainment. The remaining £4200 is money owed to stage hands for the 2006 summer season.

(i) When Seamus set up in business, he invested £48 000 of his own money in it. He has recently received an offer of £200 000 from Lunatic Promotions Inc. to buy the business from him.

Required:
Prepare a 'corrected' balance sheet for the business as at 30 September 2007, explaining how (and why) you have treated the items described in (a) to (i) above.

7* Write a short explanation of the following concepts which have been discussed in this chapter:

(a) Fixed assets
(b) Current assets
(c) Depreciation
(d) Current liabilities
(e) Cash flow

8 Moors Ltd is a motor vehicle distributor, operating from premises in Canterbury, which has the following assets and liabilities. Identify which of them are current assets, which are fixed assets, which are current liabilities and which are long-term liabilities.

(a) A van used for the transport of spare parts and making deliveries to customers.
(b) Electronic engine testing equipment.
(c) Spare parts held in its service department stores.
(d) Petrol and diesel oil.
(c) Amounts due from credit customers.
(e) Amounts due to suppliers.
(f) A mortgage on its premises.
(g) Spanners, screwdrivers and socket sets.

9* Current trends in the regulation of the financial statements of companies are likely to lead to an increasingly legally driven system. Do you think that such a system will lead to a greater degree of comparability between the accounts of different companies? If so, why might this be the case?.

10* Given that the financial statements of commercial entities are supposed to communicate useful information to their readers, how could regulation help to improve the accessibility of the information contained in such statements to their intended readership?

11 It is often said that unsophisticated readers of financial statements do not appreciate the amount of judgement involved in the preparation of such statements. Identify the principal areas of such judgement in relation to:

(a) Fixed assets

(b) Stocks

(c) Debtors

(d) Trade marks.

12 Do you think that the international standardisation of financial reporting should be restricted to listed companies? Explain your answer.

APPENDIX Ch. 13

Groups of companies

There are some quite complex definitional issues about what constitutes a 'group' of companies and exactly how such a 'group' should prepare its financial statements. The IASB has issued standards regarding group accounts, in particular ISA 27 regarding the method of consolidation and IAS 28 regarding associate companies. The detailed requirements in this are beyond the scope of this book. The underlying issue, however, is a fairly straightforward one. This is that many companies, both large and small, have acquired ownership and control of other companies, and thereby of their resources and activities. For example, most of the major companies listed on the London Stock Exchange have a number of (sometimes many) subsidiary companies, which they have either acquired or formed over a number of years. In the case of acquisitions, subsidiaries may have been acquired on an amicable basis or as result of keenly contested 'takeovers'. From a financial reporting standpoint, whether it was a friendly or a hostile takeover does not matter. What is important is that in the financial statements of the parent company (the one which has carried out the acquisition), the investment in the subsidiary companies will simply be recorded at the cost of the acquisition, and the financial performance of the subsidiary companies will only be reflected in the accounts of the parent company as and when it receives dividends from them. The key issue is that the financial statements of the parent company alone will give a very incomplete picture of the financial performance and position of the totality of the resources and activities it controls (particularly when the subsidiary companies were acquired some years ago, or there is significant trading between the parent company and its subsidiaries). The larger the number and the greater the economic significance of the subsidiary companies, the bigger this problem will be.

APPENDIX Ch. 13 cont'd

Groups of companies—cont'd

The way out is to require the parent company to prepare 'consolidated' or 'group' accounts. These are intended to aggregate the financial performance and position of all the companies in the group (parent company and its subsidiaries). They aggregate all the resources and liabilities of the parent company and its subsidiaries (eliminating any commonality between these assets and liabilities, e.g. monies owed by one group company to another) and all the trading transactions between group companies. Their aim is to be a set of financial statements of the 'group' as a single commercial entity, rather than as a number of separate legal entities. Such 'group' accounts concentrate on the interface between the companies in the group, and the rest of the commercial world, to present a financial picture of the group, as opposed to its individual members.

The situation is complicated further by the fact that a 'parent' company may acquire significant of effective control/influence over the activities and resources of another company without owning the majority of the voting shares in such a company. In such a case the non-parent company is regarded as being an 'associated' company of the parent company and the 'parent company' needs to incorporate its share of the 'associated' company in its group accounts. The essence of the legal, and professional, requirements of reporting for groups of companies is that they should include:

- a 'consolidated' ('group') balance sheet which reflects all the assets controlled by the group and all its external liabilities;
- a 'consolidated' ('group') profit and loss account which reflects all the trading activities of the 'group' with external parties;
- a 'consolidated' ('group') cash flow statement which reflects all of the cash inflows and outflows of the 'group'.

Regulation, audit and taxation

14

Chapter preview

In this chapter we look at the regulation of corporate financial statements recognising the different sources of regulation, including:

- Legal regulation.
- Taxation requirements.
- Stock exchange requirements.
- The requirements of accounting standards with particular regard to those of the IASB.

Chapter introduction

There are four main sources for the regulation of financial reporting, and more generally of the reporting of corporate financial affairs. They are:

1 *Legal requirements*. These are imposed by the country in which the reporting entity is registered.

2 *Taxation requirements*. Most jurisdictions have different requirements for the computation of corporate taxation liabilities than the bases on which corporate annual reports are based.

3 *Stock exchange requirements*. The stock exchanges in a number of countries impose additional requirements, over and above the legal ones, on annual financial statements. This is particularly so where listed companies are required to comply with IASB requirements, e.g. EU member states and Australia.

4 *Professional statements.* Increasingly, although many countries have there own such statements, the trend is to require companies to comply with IASB requirements.

We will look at each of these in turn.

Legal requirements

Virtually every country which permits commercial activities to take place via 'companies' has detailed statutory provisions governing the activities of such organisations. The detail of such statute law is beyond the scope of this book, especially as the legal provisions vary from country to country. Readers who are interested in finding out more about national (local) legal requirements should consult locally oriented company law texts. Almost universally, the national (local) statutory requirements for the regulation of companies require that they prepare and publish annual (audited) financial statements. However, the nature of the detailed legal regulation regarding these statements varies significantly from country to country. In some countries, this regulation is very prescriptive; in others it is less so. Increasingly countries are requiring that companies use IASB financial reporting standards in the preparation of their annual financial statements, particularly for listed companies.

A widely held view is that (historically) there have been two main approaches to the legal regulation of the financial reporting of companies. These are often referred to as the 'Anglo-Saxon' approach and the 'Continental' approach. The 'Anglo-Saxon' approach is thought of as being one which limits the detailed legal requirements for company accounts to 'higher-level' ('macro') issues, e.g. a requirement to prepare and publish financial statements, a requirement for them to be audited, and some (limited) specification of their contents of these statements. This approach (implicitly) places a lot of reliance on the ability of the professionals (accountants) to ensure the 'fitness for purpose' of the resultant financial statements.

The 'Continental' approach is generally thought of as being one which imposes detailed legal requirements on the structure and content of financial statements, including the ways in which individual assets and liabilities are 'valued' in them. Broadly speaking, the 'Anglo-Saxon' approach holds in the UK and other English speaking countries, such as Australia, Canada, New Zealand and the USA, as well as in Hong Kong and Singapore; while the 'Continental' approach is employed in most European countries and those which previously had 'command' economies. In what follows, we will use the development of legal regulation of financial reporting in the UK as a 'case study' of the evolution of the 'Anglo-Saxon' approach.

Within the UK, the statutory requirements for financial reporting are contained in the *Companies Acts*, which date back to the middle of the nineteenth century when (for the first time) it became possible to form a company by a simple process of registration. From their earliest days the *Companies Acts* have recognised the need for companies to produce financial information about their activities (for the benefit of stakeholders) and to have such information audited.

Initially, the legal requirements for the provision of financial information (in the UK and elsewhere) focused on the balance sheet. This was regarded as the financial statement which provided information about the assets backing the company and thereby providing reassurance of its financial soundness and probity. Towards the end of the nineteenth century, and later in the early twentieth century, increasing emphasis began to be placed on the profit and loss account (income statement) and the importance of reporting financial performance. Later in the twentieth century, emphasis was also placed on the importance of financial reporting for groups of companies and of providing information on cash flows.

The mid- to late nineteenth century was also the era when the first professional accounting bodies, the precursors of the current professional institutes, were founded. The formation of these bodies was an important factor in the development of financial reporting because the requirements of the early *Companies Acts* in many ways reflected a traditional UK respect for the expertise of professional groups. Indeed, until relatively recently, the *Companies Acts* concentrated on specifying what types of financial statements companies had to produce and on requiring that specific items of information had to be disclosed. The detailed and practical implementation of these rather broad requirements was (in large part) left to the accounting profession to determine. This implementation was not always helped by the diversity of the accounting profession itself. Table 14.1 provides an overview of the current major professional accounting bodies in a number of countries.

In the UK, the detail of determining accepted accounting bases was not, unlike many other European countries, specified by the national legislature. There was, and

Table 14.1	Examples of professional accounting organisations
Country	**Professional organisation**
UK	The Institute of Chartered Accountants in England and Wales (ICAEW)
	The Institute of Chartered Accountants of Scotland (ICAS)
	The Institute of Chartered Accountants in Ireland (ICAI)
	The Chartered Association of Chartered Certified Accountants (ACCA)
	The Chartered Institute of Management Accountants (CIMA)
	The Chartered Institute of Public Finance and Accountancy (CIPFA)
Australia	CPA Australia (CPAA)
	The Institute of Chartered Accountants in Australia (ICAA)
	CMA Australia (CMAA)
	The National Institute of Accountants Australia (NIA)
New Zealand	The Institute of Chartered Accountants of New Zealand (ICANZ)
Canada	The Canadian Institute of Chartered Accountants (CICA)
	Certified General Accountants Association of Canada (CGAAC)
	Society of Management Accountants of Canada (CMAC)
USA	American Institute of Certified Public Accountants (AICPA)
	Association of Chartered Accountants in the U.S. (ACAUS)
	Institute of Management Accountants (IMA)
Hong Kong	Hong Kong Society of Accountants (HKSA)
Singapore	Institute of Certified Public Accountants of Singapore (ICPAS)
India	Institute of Chartered Accountants of India (ICAI)
	The Institute of Cost and Works Accountants of India (ICWAI)
	The National Institute of Certified Public Accountants (NICPA)
Nigeria	The Institute of Chartered Accountants of Nigeria (ICAN)

still is, no direct UK equivalent to the *Plan Comptable* of France or the Spanish *National Chart of Accounts*, which lay down in some detail the ways in which companies must report (in financial terms) on their activities. As a result differing accounting bases emerged in such important areas of financial reporting as depreciation, foreign currency translation and inventory valuation. This diversity was facilitated by the fact that the emergence of these differing practices – and their acceptability (in the circumstances of particular companies) was regarded as a matter for the exercise of the 'professional judgement' of individual accountants within the broad framework of what came to be known as GAAP. However, the previous freedom allowed to companies has been greatly restricted by the increasing use of IASB reporting standards for corporate financial statements.

The previous flexibility in the selection of accounting practices has for the last 40 or so years (and before that in the opinion of a number of informed commentators) been widely viewed as being a major problem for financial reporting, because of the scope that it affords to corporate management to select accounting representations of companies that suit their purposes, leading in some cases to *causes célèbres* such as recent ones in the USA, e.g. Enron, WorldCom and TimeWarner. This has led to strenuous efforts by regulators to reduce the range of choice open to entities in the preparation of their financial statements – the 'standardisation' movement, especially the increasingly important role of IASB statements.

In general, there is relatively little case law regarding the preparation of annual financial statements – such case law as does exist tends to be related to possibility of 'auditor negligence' in the audit of corporate financial statements, an issue we discuss later in this chapter with regard to auditor responsibility.

Taxation requirements

In most countries, local legislation is such that corporate taxation computations involve a number of adjustments being made to the reporting entity's financial statements, particularly its income statements. The principal such adjustments relate to:

- **Depreciation charges**. The choice of depreciation policy is a matter for the senior management of the reporting entity. However, their ability to make this choice effectively means that they can, in large part, determine their reported net income. From the perspective of taxation authorities this not acceptable. Thus, many countries do not accept this figure for the computation of corporate taxation liabilities. Instead, they substitute their own 'taxation depreciation' rules. These go by a variety of names – in the UK they are called **capital allowances**, of which there are three types: a **first year allowance** (the amount by which an asset can be depreciated for taxation purposes in the first year of ownership; annual **writing down allowances** (for each succeeding year the asset is owned); and finally a **balancing charge/allowance** (reflecting the gain/loss arising when the asset is disposed by the entity). Governments have considerable freedom of action in determining the rates of these allowances, and a major element in their decisions will be the state of the national economy, their desire to encourage inward investment or to promote the development of particular economic sectors.

  In addition to the above, many countries impose other forms of taxation on business entities. A very common one is **employment taxation,** based on the number of employees an entity has and the amount of their remuneration. In the UK, this form of taxation is called **national insurance** (NI) and it is intended to fund (at least in part) various elements of public sector provision, e.g. the national health service and state pensions. Many countries have some form of sales taxation, often called a purchase tax or in the EU **value added tax**. It is normal practice that business entities can recover this tax on their purchases but have to pay it on their sales revenues although such revenues will be stated net of tax in the income statement.

- **Bad and doubtful debt provisions.** Virtually every business will sell goods or services to customers on a credit sales basis and at the end of the day some of these customers will not pay for them. They will be bad debts and require provisions to be made against them. There are two forms of such provision, **specific provisions** and **general provisions**. In most countries specific provisions are deductible in computation of corporate taxation liabilities; general provisions are not so deductible.

Both the above mean that there will be differences between the timing of reported net income and its recognition for taxation purposes. These differences give rise to a phenomenon called **deferred taxation** which reflects these differences in timing. Depending on the nature and extent of these differences, deferred taxation can be either an asset or a liability to be included in the reporting entity's balance sheet.

Table 14.2	Timing differences – accountant's depreciation/UK Inland Revenue system		
Year	**1** **Straight-line deprecation (10%)** £	**2** **Written down allowance (25%)** £	**3** **Timing difference** £
1	100 000	250 000	−150 000
2	100 000	187 500	−87 500
3	100 000	140 625	−40 625
4	100 000	105 468	−5 468
5	100 000	79 102	+20 898
6	100 000	59 326	+40 674
7	100 000	44 495	+55 505
8	100 000	33 371	+66 629
9	100 000	25 028	+74 972
10	100 000	75 085	+24 915
	1 000 000	1 000 000	0

Note: These calculations relate to two methods of recognising the depreciation of assets purchased for £1 million. In column 1 the accountant's straight-line method is illustrated, the assumption being that the assets will last for ten years. In column 2 we have the capital allowance (depreciation) as determined by the Inland Revenue based on a reducing balance of 25% per year. Note that at the end of year 9 these assets have a written-down value of £75 085. If we assume that these assets have a zero disposable value, then this balance can be written off in year 10. In the third column we have the timing differences between these two methods. It can clearly be seen that in year 1 the accountant's profit is further reduced by an additional £150 000 of allowable expenditure, which, at 35%, reduces the corporation tax liability by £52 500. On the same principle, liability to corporation tax is reduced in the subsequent three years. Thereafter, this trend starts to be reversed as the revenue's recognition of depreciation becomes lower than that recognised by the accountant. These timing differences are credited and debited to a deferred taxation account but over the ten-year period net out to zero.

Stock exchange requirements

The principal interest of stock exchanges is that of ensuring that all stakeholders (present and potential) have reliable information on which to base their decisions. Hence the fact that many exchanges require that business entities use IASB standards in the preparation of their financial statements. In addition, many of them require listed companies to publish abbreviated 'interim financial statements' and report to the exchange any 'price sensitive' information as soon as they become aware of it. They also frequently require reporting entities to publish information not required by statute law, e.g. information on the performance of different segments of the business (the subject of IAS 14).

Professional statements

As we have already seen, increasingly stock exchanges require listed companies to use IASB standards in the preparation of their annual financial statements. The 2006 set of IASB standards contains the following ones:

International Financial Reporting Standards (IFRSs)

IFRS 1	First-time Adoption of International Financial Reporting Standards
IFRS 2	Share-based Payment
IFRS 3	Business Combinations
IFRS 4	Insurance Contracts
IFRS 5	Non-current assets Held for Sale and Discontinued Operations
IFRS 6	Exploration for and Evaluation of Mineral Resources
IFRS 7	Financial Instruments: Disclosures

International Accounting Standards (IASs)

IAS 1	Presentation of Financial Statements
IAS 2	Inventories
IAS 7	Cash Flow Statements
IAS 8	Accounting Policies, Changes in Accounting Estimates and Errors
IAS 10	Events after the Balance Sheet Date
IAS 11	Construction Contracts
IAS 12	Income Taxes
IAS 14	Segment Reporting
IAS 16	Property, Plant and Equipment
IAS 17	Leases
IAS 18	Revenue
IAS 19	Employee Benefits
IAS 20	Accounting for Government Grants and Disclosure of Government Assistance

Particular features of the regulation of corporate financial reporting

The detail of financial reporting requirements frequently varies, depending on the size of the company, the nature of its operations and its financing. The most common types of variation are:

1 *Exemptions for smaller companies*. Most countries do not impose the full rigour of financial reporting and auditing requirements on smaller companies. This is because it is thought that the burden involved would be out of proportion to the benefits gained by those associated with such companies. The most common approach employed is that of specifying thresholds which measure company size, and exempting those below these thresholds from at least some financial reporting requirements. Measures commonly used for determining these thresholds are: number of employees, capital employed sales turnover and number of shareholders.

2 *Additional requirements for groups of companies*. A group of companies is normally thought to exist when one company (a **parent company**) owns more than 50% of the voting share capital in another company (a **subsidiary company**), or otherwise controls such a subsidiary company. This ownership (control) means that the parent company is in a position to manage the affairs of the two (or more) companies as if they were a single economic entity, a **group of companies**. The view commonly taken is that not only should separate financial statements be prepared for the parent company and for each of its subsidiaries, but group (**consolidated**) financial statements should also be prepared and published. These group financial statements reflect the totality of the financial performance and state of affairs of the economic entity comprised

by the group of companies. The preparation of group financial statements is the subject of IAS 27 and IAS 28.

3 *Special requirements for particular types of companies.* It is common practice for special reporting requirements to be imposed on companies operating in economic sectors which put them into fiduciary relationships with the public. This is most commonly the case for financial institutions such as banks, insurance companies and building societies.

Auditing

Most countries require that the annual financial statements of all listed companies are subject to an annual audit. There are two principal types of audit: **external audit** and **internal audit.** The former is conducted by an independent external auditor from one of the professional practices approved by local legislation to carry out such audits. The latter is carried out by company employees who have the necessary expertise – some companies employ specialist staff to carry out this function. Both types of audit are normally carried out under the supervision of an entity's **audit committee,** which is normally staffed by a group of non-executive directors who both negotiate the auditor's remits and receive their final reports. Both types of audit are standard practice in both the private and public sectors, at least for larger entities. External audits are normally a legal requirement, although some countries offer some limitations on the scope of the external audit for smaller (private) entities.

The core auditing concepts for external audit are:

1 Auditor independence. The purpose of an external audit is to enhance the 'credibility' of the reporting entity's financial statements. These are normally prepared by management who may have reasons to overstate corporate performance. There is a body of economic theory, **agency theory**, which deals with the relationships between 'principals' (stakeholders) and their 'agents' (managers). Agency theory suggests that it is in the interests of both stakeholders and agents to employ auditors. However, it should be noted that are some circumstances which might lead to perceived threats to auditor independence. These include:

(i) **Fee income.** Auditors earn substantial sums of money from carrying out audits. For large listed groups of companies these fees can amount to millions of £s, $s or €s. Thus, there is a danger that an audit firm may not want to lose the income from a particular audit assignment and might because of this be tempted not to give a truly independent opinion. This problem is exacerbated by the fact that auditors are initially appointed by the directors of the entity, although their reappointment will be subject to the approval of shareholders at the entity's AGM. Because of this a number of countries have regulations which impose limits on the amount of fee income that an audit practice can derive from any client. These limits may be imposed by statute law or by the relevant professional bodies. In addition, a number of countries have considered the possibility of requiring business entities to rotate their auditors periodically, perhaps after every five years. The problem with this approach is that, following the demise of Arthur

Anderson after the Enron fiasco, there are now only four major international firms of auditors: *KPMG*, *PriceWaterhouseCoopers*, *Deloites*, and *Ernst and Young*. To some extent this dominance is being counteracted by the aggressive promotion of their services by a number of relatively smaller practices.

(ii) *Fees for other work*. Many audit firms provide their clients with services over and above their audit work. Typically these will involve taxation advice and consultancy services, corporate finance advice and specialist investigation services. The income from providing these services may be even greater than that they derive from their auditing income. The problem is that these other services may contribute significantly to the earnings of the auditing firm and thereby detract from their independence. This problem is reinforced by the fact that this other income is discretionary, i.e. the company's management may choose to employ a different firm of advisors, thereby threatening the income of their auditors. Again, some jurisdictions impose limits on these 'other' earnings, sometimes to the extent of banning them completely. However, in some countries the potential value of these other earnings has led to a phenomenon called 'low-balling'. This arises when an auditing firm deliberately quotes a very low (possibly uneconomic) fee to a potential client in the hope that the additional earnings will enable it to compensate for the low audit fee. The danger of course is that the auditing practice will concentrate on this other income at the expense of carrying out a 'competent' audit.

(iii) *Personal relationships*: These arise when a firm of auditors are closely linked with the senior staff of their client. This is not an uncommon problem. Most financial communities in all countries have close relationships of this type. Fund managers have links with insurance companies and with others such as banks. There is, undoubtedly, in all such communities, a broad set of personal relationships which may act so as to reduce auditor independence. However, such relationships are not normally the subject of legislation, although they are usually incorporated in 'codes of professional practice'.

(iv) *Financial involvement*. Both legislation and professional regulations tend to be quite specific regarding this. Broadly speaking, both of these require that auditing practices totally avoid accepting any audit assignments where they might have a financial involvement. This bar does not just relate to partners, it also relates to any staff who might be involved in the assignment. Most major auditing practices require that all staff declare whether or not they have any financial involvement with a client. The only exception to this requirement is where staff have a normal trading relationship with a client, e.g. a bank. Even then, they must not accept any preferential terms from the client, such as discounts.

(v) *Conflicting interests*. There are wide range of situations which might give rise to these, including offering other services to an audit client.

2 **Truth and fairness**. Depending on the country in which a company operates local legislation will require that its financial statements present either a 'true and fair view' or a 'fair' view of its financial position. Equivalent to the IASB,

there is another body which attempts to regulate auditing on an international basis. This is the **International Federation of Accountants (IFA)**. It has produced a number of statements on auditing standards. IAS 700 *The Auditor's Report on Financial Statements,* proposes the following structure for an unqualified audit report, i.e. one which confirms that the audited financial statements present 'a true and fair view' of the audited company's 'financial position and performance' – in other jurisdictions the phrase 'fairly present' is sometimes used. If the report is a qualified one, i.e. expressing some reservations about the contents of the financial statements, then different wording according to the nature of the reservations will be needed.

Report to the shareholders of Omega Plc

We have audited the accompanying balance sheet of Omega Plc as of 31 December 2007, and the related statements of income, cash flows, changes in equity and total realised gains and losses for the year then ended. These financial statements are the responsibility of the company's management. Our responsibility is to express an opinion on these financial statements based on our audit.

We have conducted our audit with International Standards on Auditing. These standards require that we plan and perform our audit to obtain reasonable assurance about whether the financial statements are free of material misstatement.

An audit includes examining, on a test basis, evidence supporting the amounts and disclosures in the financial statements. An audit also includes assessing the accounting principles used and significant estimates made by management, as well as evaluating the overall financial statement presentation. We believe that our audit provides a reasonable basis for our opinion.

In our opinion, the financial statements provide a true and fair view of the financial position of the company as of 31 December 2007, and of the results of its operations for that year, its cash flows for that year, its changes in equity for the year and its total recognised gains and losses for the year then ended in accordance with legal requirements.

Auditor's name: Date: Address:

---

3 **Auditor competence.** Most countries require that approved auditors have undergone a recognised period of professional training by an authorised training body, usually a recognised training practice of practising auditors. Some countries specify their requirements for this training, often including subjects such as: management accounting, financial reporting, business finance, auditing and professional ethics. Many also expect that qualified auditors undergo 'continuing professional development' on a regular basis, perhaps even to the extent of specifying how many hours per year must be spent on this. The purpose of this ongoing development is that of ensuring that approved auditors are fully up-to-date with modern auditing requirements.

4 **Auditor responsibility**. The ultimate responsibility of an auditor is that of providing an independent professional and expert opinion on an entity's financial statements in compliance with any relevant professional standards. There are two elements to this responsibility: for what the auditor is responsible and to whom the auditor owes a duty of responsibility.

(a) For what the auditor is responsible. The principal responsibilities are:

(i) To be familiar with all statutory duties, rights and powers.

(ii) To be familiar with all relevant professional obligations.

(iii) To maintain independence.

(iv) To plan the audit in such a way that sufficient relevant evidence is obtained to support the audit opinion.

(v) To ensure adequate supervision of all staff engaged on the audit.

(b) To whom the auditor is responsible. The key question here is who has a right of action against an auditor should the audit be negligently conducted? Traditionally the answer to this question has been the company itself and shareholders in the company. The company has a right of action because it is in a contractual relationship with the audit practice. The problem is that all too often audit deficiencies only come to light if a company becomes insolvent and they are identified by the company's liquidator. The shareholders are normally thought to have a right of action because they are thought to be the intended beneficiaries of the auditing contract via the enhanced credibility of the audited financial statements. Historically, the law has been disinclined to offer relief to other groups. In the words of Justice Cardozo in the case of Ultramares Corporation v. Touche (1931, 255, N.Y., 170, 174, N.E., 441, 74, A.L.R. 1139) the danger was one of 'creating liability in an indeterminate amount for an indeterminate period to an indeterminate class'.

In more recent years, a number of jurisdictions have relaxed this principle and allowed other parties to have a right of action on the grounds of a negligent audit having been carried out. In part, this has been on 'public policy' grounds based on the argument that if these other parties were not supposed to be beneficiaries of the audit process, why then do most countries require a compulsory annual audit? This is especially so when most countries require that entities file their annual financial statements with some statutory agency, in the UK the Registrar of Companies, where they are publicly available. Another factor in this trend is that virtually all auditing practices have professional indemnity insurance to cover them against potential legal action arising out of deficient audits. However, major audit firms find that insurers will impose quite restrictive terms on such insurance contracts, perhaps requiring large excesses (up to which level the auditing firm will have to pay for any losses), and quite low overall limits on the insurance cover they will provide. In part because of these limitations some countries have allowed auditing practices to have some degree of limited liability, in the UK such practices are identified by having the letters LLP after their name.

(c) For what is the auditor not responsible? Some users of financial statements, especially unsophisticated ones, fail to understand what an audit report (especially an unqualified report) means. Common misunderstandings include:

(i) The nature of the audit opinion: Some financial statement users interpret an unqualified audit opinion as meaning that the financial statements are 'correct'. This means that these users fail to appreciate the significant amounts of judgement that are involved in the preparation and auditing of such statements.

(ii) Ths scope of the audit report: Some users do not recognise that an audit report refers to the pages of the financial statements that it covers. Instead they think that the audit report covers the whole of the entity's annual report. This may be because many financial statement users do not actually read the audit report!

(iii) The economic well-being of the reporting entity: Evidence (e.g. Steen 1989) suggests that some users of financial statements believe that an unqualified audit report is a guarantee of the financial strength of the company. This may be because they fail to distinguish between information risk and economic risk. The audit report only deals with the former. The latter is ultimately a matter of stakeholder judgement.

(iv) The relative responsibilities of directors and auditors: The audit report should make these quite clear – it is unfortunate that it is not more widely read.

(v) Fraud detection: In recent times, detection of fraud is not seen as being an auditing priority. Instead its prevention is seen as a responsibility of management, with the entity's internal control systems being a major fraud prevention mechanism. Of course, if during the course of their audit the auditors detect fraud they will report it to management. They will also have to decide whether the extent of fraud is such as to prevent the financial statements presenting a 'true and fair view'.

(vi) Competence of management: This has never been regarded as an objective of auditing. However, research (e.g. Steen 1989; Humphrey, Moizer and Turley 1992) indicates many financial statement readers believe that auditors assess how well an entity has been managed. This is not the case.

5 **Audit evidence.** Ultimately, the value of an audit opinion will depend on the nature and quality of the evidence that an auditor has collected to justify the audit opinion. The planning of the collection of this evidence is a vital part of the audit process. Most actions for negligent audits are based on allegations that the auditor did not collect sufficient evidence to support the audit opinion. Included in the issues that an auditor should address in planning the collection and evaluation of audit evidence are:

(i) The cost of acquiring the evidence. Evidence, of whatever type, is costly to collect and evaluate.

(ii) The availability of evidence. The very concept of independent audit suggests that auditors will be able to collect evidence which will verify, or otherwise, the propositions contained in the financial statements. In many cases this assumption will be true: they can verify the existence of tangible assets by physical inspection (e.g. by attending an entity's physical inventory); and they can verify the amounts of receivables and payables by direct contact with debtors and creditors. However, some of the other issues involved in corporate financial reporting are largely matters of managerial judgment, e.g. the choice of accounting policies such as depreciation policies and the valuation of intangible assets. Sometimes it will be possible for auditors to obtain external advice on these issues, sometimes it will not. Ultimately however, it is the auditor's responsibility to assess managerial judgements in these regards. This is a difficult and demanding role, and one which is all too often judged with the benefit of hindsight.

(iii) Usefulness. Ideally an auditor will only want to collect evidence which will assist in the formulation of the final audit opinion, especially given the costs of acquiring audit evidence. In determining this, the auditor will have regard to factors such as: relevance, reliability, technicality, availability of supporting documentation and the source of the evidence.

The collection of audit evidence is normally a multi-stage process involving both an interim and a final audit. The former will normally take place towards the end of the entity's financial year and the latter after the end of the financial year.

1 *A review of an entity's internal control and operating procedures.* This will normally be part of an interim audit and will involve an assessment of these procedures, usually using a standard questionnaire, to assess the adequacy of them in the context of their being likely to lead to accurate financial reports.

2 **The sample testing of transactions.** As part of the interim audit the auditing firm will normally test a number of transactions to ensure that they have been correctly recorded. The choice of which transactions to test will be guided by the evaluation of the entity's internal control and operating procedures. This form of testing is often referred to as **compliance testing** and will help the auditor to plan the audit testing that will be required during the final audit.

3 **Analytic review.** This is normally part of the final audit and involves an analysis of the entity's draft financial statements. Its purpose is to help the auditor identify unexpected trends in these statements. It makes extensive use of the type of ratio analysis discussed in Chapter 6.

4 **Substantive testing.** The interim audit and the analytic review will help the auditor to plan the range and types of evidence that need to be collected during the final audit. The focus of these tests is that of confirmation of account balances by whatever evidence can be obtained, something we discussed earlier. Substantive testing is something of an iterative process, continuing until the auditor is satisfied that sufficient evidence has been collected to support an audit opinion.

At the end of the day, the auditor has to form an audit opinion. This will normally be discussed in advance with senior client management. Following these discussions, the auditor may well feel it appropriate to collect additional evidence, some of which may be suggested by client management. Only after all these processes have been completed can the auditor finalise the audit opinion and communicate it to client management.

Corporate annual reports and their contents

The outcome of all this regulation is an entity's annual financial statements, which are normally encapsulated in its **annual report**. The normal components of the annual report of a listed company in the UK having subsidiary companies will include the following (most of which are present, in one form or another, in annual corporate reports in a wide variety of other countries).

Chairman's statement (or equivalent). This will normally be a relatively brief (one or two page) statement giving an overview of the state of affairs of the company and the principal commercial factors affecting it during the financial year just ended, and those likely to affect it in the future. This statement is not (normally) subject to a formal audit, although auditors would be expected to ensure that it does not contain statements significantly at variance with the audited financial statements.

Chief executive's report (sometimes referred to as an **operating and financial review**). This will normally be a more detailed review of the company's operations, providing information about the performance of the principal operating units/segments and may run to several pages. Again, this report does not legally have to be audited, although prudent auditors will review it for consistency with the audited financial statements. Within a UK context, such a report will normally incorporate a commentary on (discussion of) issues such as:

- The entity's operating results for the period covering both the overall business and such segments of the business as are relevant to a proper understanding of the overall business.

- The dynamics of the business, i.e. those factors that may be influential in determining its future prosperity, including the main risks and uncertainties it faces and how management intend to deal with them.

- The investing activities of the business, both current and prospective, and the hoped for returns from such investments.

- Other activities which the business is undertaking to enhance its future prospects, e.g. marketing campaigns, training programmes, research.

- The results for the year from the perspective of the shareholders and the returns available to them.

- Areas where the reported performance of the company is particularly sensitive to the application of accounting judgement.

- The company's capital structure and treasury policy.

- Taxation charges and liabilities with a commentary on why they differ, if they do, from 'standard' charges.

- The business's cash flow sources and obligations and a commentary on its current liquidity.

- The company's resource structure, with particular reference to where the strengths of this structure may not be adequately reflected in the balance sheet, e.g. as regards intangible assets.

Report of the directors. In the UK this is a statutory requirement and while it does not form part of the audited accounts, the auditors have an obligation to ensure that its contents are in conformity with those accounts. Typically, it will contain the disclosure of information required by local (statute) law. Such disclosure requirements will normally (*inter alia*) include information regarding:

- Statement of the principal activities of the company.
- Details of directors.
- Information about the numbers and remuneration of employees.
- Changes in share capital.
- Charitable and political donations.
- Equal opportunities and disability policies.
- General meetings of the company.

Statement of directors' responsibilities. Recent debates, in the UK and elsewhere, on **corporate governance** (see Chapter 2) issues have led to the requirement for a clear statement of the responsibilities of directors, particularly with respect to the nature (and discharge) of their fiduciary duties. A report of this type will normally comment on issues such as:

(a) An overview of activities of major sub-committees of the Board of directors, including:

- the audit committee – in relation to the financial reporting of the company, its internal control systems and the external of the financial statements;
- the remuneration committee – in relation to remuneration of directors and senior management;
- the nomination committee – in relation to the constitution of the board of directors and the nomination of new directors.

(b) The board's responsibilities for:

- maintaining adequate systems of internal control;
- assessing and managing the risks facing the company;
- the financial statements presenting 'a true and fair' view.

Statement of auditor's responsibilities. Auditors (and others) have in recent years become increasingly concerned about the public's understanding (misunderstanding) of their role and responsibilities. This statement attempts to ensure that there is clarity about these and it is a counterpart to the statement of directors' responsibilities.

Report of the audit committee. It is now very common for stock exchanges to require listed companies to have audit committees. An audit committee is a committee of **non-executive directors** which is charged with managing a company's relations with its external auditors, and often with the supervision of its **internal audit** function. The original purpose of audit committees was that of reinforcing the independence of the external auditors from the company's executive directors.

Report of the remuneration committee. Increasingly a requirement of stock exchanges, a remuneration committee is a committee of non-executive directors which is charged with determining the appropriateness of the remuneration packages of executive directors and other senior employees.

Consolidated balance sheet. This is normally a legal (and stock exchange) requirement and is a statement which aggregates the external assets and liabilities of all the individual companies in the 'group' of companies, portraying them as if the group were a single economic entity.

Parent company balance sheet. Again a legal requirement and a statement which summarises the assets, liabilities and equity of the parent company in its own right.

Consolidated profit and loss account. Again a legal requirement and a statement which incorporates all the external trading transactions of companies within the group.

Consolidated cash flow statement. In the UK such a statement is required by financial reporting standards. In other countries it will either be a legal requirement or be required by financial reporting standards. It aggregates the external cash flows of all the individual companies within the group.

Notes to the accounts. These provide further details about the items contained in the primary financial statements, as well as other information required by law or quasi-law. They form part of the overall financial statements and are subject to audit. For listed companies they may be extensive, running to some tens of pages. In the UK the 4th Schedule to the 1985 *Companies Act* specifies a wide range of items which must be disclosed, either on the face of the accounts, or in notes to the accounts. These notes form part of the accounts and are subject to audit in the same way as the main body of the accounts. Increasingly companies include much of the statutorily required disclosures in the supplementary notes rather than on the face of the financial statements themselves. This has led to the notes, particularly for large companies, becoming both extensive (sometimes running to 20 or more pages) and technical (in accounting terms), because of the nature of the required disclosures. In addition to the statutory disclosures, further disclosures are required by accounting standards and stock exchange regulations. Notes to the accounts are a potentially very rich source of information to users. However, their length and complexity means that a large proportion of readers of accounts do not in fact read them, meaning that they at best will only acquire partial information and may perhaps misunderstand information contained on the face of the accounts. As a point of principle, the information contained in the notes to the accounts should serve to amplify the information contained in the body of the accounts – it should not restate, reinterpret or contradict such information. This is particularly important given the relatively limited readership of the notes.

Auditor's report. A statement from the company's auditors which is normally required by statute law. It states whether or not the financial statements, taken as whole (primary financial statements and notes to the accounts), provide a 'true and fair view' of the company's (group's) financial position and performance.

Other information. In addition to the foregoing, an annual report may (will) contain other information such as notification of the company's Annual General Meeting, five or ten year financial summaries and miscellaneous statements on such diverse topics as environmental performance and corporate citizenship.

Overall, the annual report may be very extensive. In some cases they provide over 100 pages of information. Some of this information is required by law and quasi-law, and as such is regulated to a greater or lesser extent. Some of it is subject to formal audit and some of it is not. Some of it is the result of the company and its management attempting to convey what they regard as being key messages to stakeholders and potential stakeholders, e.g. as regards concern for the environment. They may be more or less glossy and include promotional material (it is widely accepted that financial public relations has been a growth sector in recent years). Overall, they are a compendium of information, and one problem faced by users is knowing which parts are which, and which parts are audited (and hopefully more reliable as a result) and which parts are not.

Summary accounts

As has already been pointed out, the annual reports of major listed companies can be daunting documents. Accordingly, it is hardly surprising that many of their intended recipients, the archetypal private shareholders, read at best only part of them and that they tend to concentrate on the more accessible parts such as the chairman's statement and the operating review. This, of course, means that they may neglect the key financial information. In an attempt to remedy this problem, the 1989 Companies Act in the UK introduced the possibility of companies preparing much shorter 'summary accounts' to help the lay readers access the key information regarding the finances of companies. Taken in conjunction with the operating and financial reviews such accounts could provide a useful framework for such readers to get a core understanding of the company and its financial position and performance. At the very least, they could provide a basis for a discussion between a private shareholder and his/her financial advisor. The provisions introduced by the Act relate to listed companies and such of their members as wish to receive summary financial statements as opposed to the full set of accounts. Companies still have to prepare full accounts and file them with the Registrar of Companies and, prior to the issuing of summary as opposed to full accounts, they have to obtain the wishes of their shareholders. The key requirement for summary financial statements is that they must be consistent with the information in the full financial statements and that they must be accompanied by an auditor's report confirming this.

Conclusion

This chapter has covered a lot of material, ranging from legal issues to taxation issues, stock exchange requirements and auditing issues. The aim of the chapter has been to provide readers with an introduction to all of these issues. However, we recognise that a full understanding of all of them will require further reading, and we strongly advise readers to make full use of the recommended further reading shown below.

In this chapter we have looked at the regulation of corporate financial statements, paying particular attention to the different sources of regulation, reflecting the requirements, including those imposed by:

- Legal regulation
- Taxation requirements
- Stock exchange requirements
- The requirements of accounting standards with particular regard to those of the IASB.

Further reading

There is a wide range of further information available. The IASB website is a vital source about financial reporting issues. Davies, Paterson and Wilson (1999) provide a comparative perspective, while Alexander and Britton (2004) provide a broader discussion of financial reporting issues. Other useful sources are Elliot and Elliot (2003) and Sutton (2004). Useful material on corporate taxation is provided by all of these sources. Auditing is also covered by these texts, but readers are recommended to read the classic text by Mautz and Sharraf (1961), while Glynn (1993) provides a useful review of public sector issues.

Questions and exercises

Guide notes can be found at the back of the book for all questions marked with an asterisk*.

1* In what major respects does the role of external auditing in the public sector differ from external auditing in the private sector?

2 Why does taxable profit differ from accounting profit?

3 Should entities allow taxation to impact on their investment decisions?

4* What do 'lay' users expect that an unqualified audit report means?

5* To whom does an auditor owe a duty of care?

6* What sorts of internal control mechanisms would an auditor expect a company to have in place regarding its receivables?

7 Taxation is nothing more than an ordinary business expense. Discuss.

8 What forms of taxation are commonly used by governments other than corporation tax?

9 Should taxation planning be a central management responsibility?

10* Identify the auditable propositions inherent in including an amount for cash at bank in a company's financial statements.

11* Some commentators have stated that value-for-money (VFM) auditing is little different to management consulting. Do you agree?

12 Should taxation be an influence on business investment decisions?

Financial statement analysis

15

Chapter preview

This chapter focuses on interpretation of the accounting and related information contained in financial statements, concentrating on those published by private sector entities. The approach adopted is a review of the use of the information contained in the financial statements, in conjunction with information from other sources, to address key issues regarding past (and potential future) corporate performance.

The first part of the chapter concentrates on identifying potential users of accounting information about corporate entities and the key questions they want answering. It then goes on to review the sources of information available to help answer these questions, and the techniques that can be used to help interpret such information in a meaningful way. It stresses the fact that a full understanding of an entity's financial position requires integration of information drawn from a variety of sources, including, but not limited to, that contained in financial statements.

User group requirements

As discussed in Chapter 1, a wide range of individuals and organisations have financial and other links with companies. Despite this diversity of interests, there is a surprising degree of overlap in the information they need for assessing the benefits to be derived from continuing, or changing, these links. This is not to deny that different groups have their own specific interests, or that there may sometimes be a conflict between these interests. However, in one way or another, they are all concerned with the performance of the company, its continuing existence and its ability to provide them with a positive return in some form, most usually cash.

Ideally, each of these user groups would like information about the past performance of the entity; about its current state of affairs and, perhaps most importantly, about its future – with all of this information being directed to their specific concerns. In practice, with some exceptions, they have to make do with general purpose information and information about the future is only available in the form of estimates and forecasts, areas which accounting has traditionally fought shy of, at least as regards published financial statements. Thus, in practice great attention is paid to information about the past, and particularly the recent past. This information may be compared with prior expectations, whether formed by members of the user groups themselves, or by other interested parties, to help assess the progress of the company. Alternatively, it may be used to identify trends in the performance of the entity, as it is widely believed that identification of trends can help in the forecasting of future performance. Accountants recognise the fact that many users will attempt to identify trends and use these as a basis for forecasting future performance. This recognition underpins the concept of 'maintainable profit' and the emphasis on 'continuing operations' reflected in statements of financial performance.

A further concern of users is that the information typically available in financial statements does not directly address the questions to which they want answers. For example, investors (present and potential) want to know what they are likely to receive in dividends and what is the potential for capital appreciation of their investments; lenders are concerned with the servicing and due repayment of their loans; employees with the scope for increased remuneration and the security of their employment; suppliers and customers with the future of their business partnership with the enterprise and the community with the broader economic and societal impact of the enterprise. Traditional historical cost based financial statements provide little of this information directly. Users have to interpret the information that financial statements do in fact contain, in conjunction with that available from other sources to satisfy their information needs. Only rarely can they use the information contained in financial statements directly. However, as we have already suggested, there are a number of areas of interest common to all the different users of financial statements. These can be summarised under the following heads:

- **Economic sector.** No company can be appraised independently of the economic environment within which it operates. This environment both constrains the activities of the company and provides it with opportunities. Thus, the general state of the economy must be taken into account, as must issues specific to the sector(s) of the economy in which the company operates. Similarly, in a competitive market economy the activities and success of competitor companies must be considered.

- **Profitability.** The key issues here are whether or not the company's profit represents an adequate (however defined) return on the resources employed to generate it, and whether or not its profit performance can be sustained or improved in the future. There are many factors which need to be considered when making such an assessment, including: the company's ability to generate profits on the available resources; its profit margins; the levels of its sales and value added per employee; its gross profit margin and its cost structure.

- **Solvency.** The key issue here is whether or not the company is generating sufficient cash to meet its present, and likely future, obligations. In assessing this attention has to be paid to the balance between liquid assets and short-term liabilities, and to the effectiveness with which it manages its working capital. The company's management of its debtors, its stocks and its creditors has to be appraised. In doing this it, must be remembered that many businesses fail because they run out of money, even though they are in fact making profits.

- **Growth**. It is a truism that in the modern business world a company cannot stand still. However, although it is a truism, its importance for assessing the financial position of a company remains. A company's past growth record needs to be examined and an assessment of its future growth prospects made. Key indicators such as growth in sales and investment in plant and equipment need to be examined. However, the emphasis needs to be on real growth rather than apparent growth, resulting simply from inflation.

- **Financing**. The main issue here is whether or not the company has access to sufficient finance to enable it to meet its existing commitments and future expansion plans, and whether or not this finance is structured in an appropriate way. Attention needs to be paid to the maturity dates of debt finance; to the balance between debt and equity finance and to the burden which interest and the repayment of borrowing place on the company's profits and cash flows.

- **Investment performance**. Present and potential shareholders want to know how the company is going to perform as an investment. Will it be able to maintain or increase dividends; will they be likely to make capital gains; how do the capital markets rate the company and how does it compare with alternative investments?

Information sources

Corporate annual reports are only one of a wide range of sources of information about the activities and performance of companies available to decision makers. The main sources available can be classified as follows:

- **Publicly available information required by law or quasi-law**. A major source of this is a company's annual report and financial statements. In addition, most jurisdictions require that companies file additional detailed information with a statutory agency. In the UK, this is the Registrar of Companies via an annual return (which is available for inspection by the public). This return incorporates copies of the audited accounts, memorandum and articles of association, the address of the registered office, details of registered charges and other useful items. It should be noted that because this information is publicly available, those engaging in dealings with the company are deemed in law to be aware of it. Other sources of information in this category include the half-yearly reports required from listed companies, and the prospectuses and circulars issued by such companies when they are seeking to raise funds or are engaged in merger or de-merger activities.

- **Information which the company itself voluntarily discloses**. Information in this category includes that available from corporate magazines and newsletters, sales literature, press statements and the like. It can also include corporate advertising and press and television interviews with company executives.

- **Information available on a subscription or similar basis.** Summaries of company and sector data are available from sources such as Reuters, Bloombergs, Datastream and similar organisations. Increasingly this data is available via computer database systems. It is principally factual and incorporates summaries of the accounts, plus related financial ratios, together with other data such as details of dividends. Press cuttings and abstracting services are another useful source of information. Assessments of companies are regularly prepared by financial institutions and made available to their clients, and sometimes to wider audiences. In addition there is a wide range of trade associations generating information, as well as that published by organisations such as the CBI, the Institute of Directors and similar bodies.

- **Other informed comment.** The financial press (e.g *The Financial Times*, *The Wall Street Journal*, and *The Australian Financial Review*) is constantly producing comment and news about companies and the economy at large. In addition to this, governments produce a wide range of statistical publications, and organisations such as the Economist Intelligence Unit and specialised trade publications provide more detailed sources of information.

In many ways, the problem is not a lack of information – it is about determining which sources of information are the most relevant and reliable. These different sources have differing attributes with respect to the information needs of those seeking to make decisions about their links with companies. The information required by law and quasi-law tends to have a historical focus and is often the subject of some form of independent verification such as an audit. It is typically regarded as having more reliability than that from other sources, although some of the recent financial *cause célébrès* might indicate otherwise. Information from the other sources, as well as commenting on a company's past performance, will typically incorporate views on the future of the company and the economic sector in which it operates. Such information may be highly relevant to the decisions that people have to make but, because it concerns assessments of the future and is not normally subject to independent review, it may be less reliable. Stakeholders have to balance the relevance and reliability of the various sources of information and use a mix which matches their needs.

Analytic review and risk assessment

Stakeholders needing to make decisions about their financial involvement with companies are in a paradoxical situation. On one hand, because of the wide range of information sources available to them, they suffer from potential information overload; on the other hand they suffer from a lack of the information they really need. The key to this paradox is that the information with which they may be overloaded is all too often not really relevant to their needs (because of its historical focus), although it may be reliable (again because of its historical focus, and its being subject to audit or similar verification).

In some ways this is similar to the problem faced by auditors of corporate financial statements. When auditing the financial statements of a company, auditors are faced with a plethora of sources of potential information (evidence) relating to the 'truth and fairness' of the financial statements on which they have to report. Essential skills for auditors include the ability to identify the evidence they require to enable them to attest to the credibility of the accounts, and being able to evaluate sources of evidence available to them in terms of relevance and reliability to their needs. Stakeholders and their advisers need the same sort of skills. There is a great deal of information available to them, much (but not all) of it is helpful, and they need to develop strategies to help them identify what is relevant, what is reliable and what is useful to making their decisions.

One approach that auditors have developed to help them identify areas 'of concern' in corporate financial statements warranting their further attention, and justifying the need for corroborative evidence from independent sources, is that of analytic review. In the words of the International Auditing Practices Committee (IAPC: 1989, para 12):

> The application of analytical procedures is based on the expectation that relationships among data exist and continue in the absence of known conditions to the contrary.

The focus of analytic review procedures is the identification of relationships between aspects of financial information which might be expected to persist over time, and the use of these relationships to identify unexpected variances. The IAPC (1989, para 3) describe analytical procedures as including:

Comparison of financial information with

- comparable information for a prior period or periods,
- anticipated results such as budgets or other forecasts,
- similar industry information, such as a comparison of the entity's ratio of sales to accounts receivable with industry averages or with other entities of comparable size in the same industry.

Study of relationships

- among elements of financial information that would be expected to conform to a predictable pattern based on an entity's experience, such as a study of gross margin percentages, and;
- between financial and non-financial information, such as a study of payroll costs in relation to number of employees.

As the foregoing illustrates, the analytical review approach involves two distinct types of comparison. The first of these is an inter-temporal comparison, in which financial information for the same entity, but for different time periods, is compared to see whether or not it conforms to past trends and (or) expectations. The second is where financial information about the entity is compared with that for other entities, either on the basis of an individual entity by entity comparison or by the use of industry/sector averages. Such a comparison enables an assessment to be made of the performance of the entity in relation to its competitors.

In some ways, the first of these types of comparison should be easier because of the fundamental accounting concept of consistency. The application of this concept means that a user of financial statements should, at least in theory, be able to compare statements relating to different financial periods in the knowledge that events and transactions are always treated in the same way and that the accounting information is therefore truly comparable. Unfortunately this comparability may sometimes be more imagined than real. There are two main reasons for this:

1 An entity may, with justification, change its accounting policies from time to time, e.g. with respect to stock valuation methodologies or depreciation bases.

The impact of such changes, which must be disclosed in the financial statements, needs to be taken into account in any comparisons.

2 A more problematic issue relates to changes in price levels. Enterprises are not at present required to ensure that all the information they present is expressed in terms of a common dimension as regards price levels. Thus a user of accounting information will need to make their own adjustments to allow for the impact of changing prices.

Comparison with the financial performance of other entities, or with sectoral averages, also has its dangers. This is partly because different entities may not be sufficiently similar to allow a truly realistic comparison, and partly because different entities may adopt different accounting bases. Accordingly, care must be taken to ensure that the yardsticks being used for comparison are really suitable for that purpose.

As suggested above, an important use of the analytical review approach is in identifying areas where information about financial performance does not conform to expectations. This divergence may be the result of error, or it may be the result of truly differential performance. In the case of an audit, the auditor can (must) focus on identifying the reasons for the divergence and ensure that the financial statements do in fact properly portray the financial position of the reporting entity. The same obligation would, of course, apply to management if they use an analytical approach as part of their management control and performance evaluation systems. Whatever the cause, supplementary information needs to be obtained to explicate the differences if a proper assessment of corporate performance is to be made.

In general, external stakeholders (particularly individuals) are not in the privileged position of being able to obtain the supplementary information they need, although fund managers and analysts may have better access to such information – although this naturally has implications for the reality of corporate governance processes (see Chapter 2).

In general, the ordinary external stakeholders will only have access to publicly available information, and this is why the integration of the information in the financial statements with other sources of information is so important. However, we must query the extent to which such 'ordinary stakeholders' rely on the financial statements themselves, as opposed to relying on the commentaries and advice of the 'professionals'.

Another auditing concept of relevance to the external user of financial statements is that of audit risk – the risk that a set of financial statements will contain a material undetected error. Audit risk is a function of three different types of risk faced by an auditor:

1 **Inherent risk:** the risk that a material error will occur given the nature and activities of the client company.

2 **Control risk:** the risk that the client company's internal control systems will fail to detect and correct material errors.

3 **Detection risk:** the risk that any remaining undetected errors will fail to be detected during the audit.

The external user is not privy to the same range of information as the auditor and so cannot apply the audit risk concept in the same way as an auditor. However, the concept does suggest that external users of accounting statements should not approach them naively. They should consider the probable reliability of the different items of information contained in financial statements. While there would be little excuse for a misstatement in the amount for cash at bank or overdrafts (although this has been known), it would be foolish to believe that the amount shown in the balance sheet for stock and work in progress would be equally reliable. This is partly because of the inherent difficulties in valuing stocks, whatever the accounting bases used, and partly because of the range of accounting bases that may in practice be used for establishing inventory costs. Similarly, a user needs to be aware that financial statements relating to companies operating in some industrial and commercial sectors inevitably involve more significant judgements than do others, the dot-com boom and decline provides ample evidence of this. Equally, the financial statements of companies involved in long-term construction or similar contracts (where judgements have to be made about the cost of completing the contracts so that any necessary provisions against future losses can be made), insurance companies (which have to make estimates of future claims) and companies growing rapidly via the acquisition of other businesses (involving estimates of the value of such businesses) must all be subject to some question.

Ratio analysis

With this background, we can now look at accounting techniques which use ratio analysis to assist in interpretation of the information contained in financial statements. The essence of these techniques is that of linking significant items of accounting data to each other to compute a ratio and then comparing this ratio with a benchmark. Such benchmarks can be derived from a number of sources. They can be based on prior expectations; they can be based on budgets; they can be based on previous performance; they may be company specific or may relate to industry or wider economic averages. The scope is very wide. However, this scope can itself cause problems: of ensuring that the measurement bases of the items being compared are the same; of the reliability of the base data being used and of ensuring useful comparators are used. The user needs to exercise discretion in applying the approach of ratio analysis and, most importantly, needs to bear in mind that ratio analysis will only identify differences in performance. It cannot identify how or why those differences arose, and it is this which may be of prime importance. In many ways financial ratios need to be regarded as access routes to information, rather than providing information in their own right. However, comparison is the essence of ratio analysis – on its own a financial ratio means little.

Earlier we identified the key areas in which users require information as being: the economic sector in which the company operates; its profitability; its solvency; its growth record; its financing and its investment performance. The first of these is not an area in which ratio analysis of accounting information can help us. However, it does provide a context within which the information in the financial statements can be analysed. This context itself may well suggest questions which decision makers will need to ask, including the types of financial ratios they will want to calculate. The other key areas regarding which users want information are all, to a greater or lesser extent, susceptible to financial ratio analysis. In many ways, the ratios resulting from such analysis can be regarded as providing performance indicators, which summarise in quantitative terms the performance of the enterprise and its management in certain key areas.

To illustrate the use of financial ratio analysis we will use the case of Motors Ltd, a company which operates as a motor vehicle distributor in Sydney, Australia. It is a family owned company (and as such not listed) founded by Albert Johnston, who has recently died after a long illness. His son, James Johnston, who has been bearing an increasing responsibility for managing the company as a result of his father's illness, is now eager to sell it and has approached you as a possible purchaser. He has provided you with an abstract of the financial statements of Motors for the last two financial years, as presented in Table 15.1.

Before looking at the information contained in the financial statements in detail, a prospective purchaser should consider the context within which the offer for sale is being made. In the case of Motors issues such as the following would need to be considered:

- To what extent was the business dependent on the expertise of its late founder Albert Johnston for its success?

- Why does James Johnston want to sell the business?

- What type of motor vehicles does the company sell and what are its terms of trade with the manufacturer whose vehicles it distributes?

- What is the current, and likely future, state of trade in the motor industry in general, and as regards the type of vehicles that Motors is selling in particular?

These are just a few of the general commercial and business sector issues that a prospective purchaser would need to address. As such they are illustrative questions. In a real commercial situation there will be a wide range of commercial issues to be addressed and risk assessments to be made. These will be required whether or not a potential take-over is involved (as in the case of Motors) or any other financial involvement (e.g. an investment in the shares of a listed company, or a loan to a company) is being considered. Such broader considerations provide a framework within which the financial statements of the company can be examined to see how typical (of its type and business sector) is its financial performance, and to identify its particular financial strengths and weakness. With this background the financial statements of the company can be examined in more detail. However, before undertaking a detailed analysis using financial ratios, it would be sensible to formulate an overall 'helicopter' view of the company's financial performance and position from its financial statements. In the case of Motors such an overview would be likely to prompt the following questions:

- **Leasehold premises**. These have a historic cost value of $100 000 which has remained the same for 2006 and 2007. However, accumulated depreciation has risen from $38 000 to $40 000; i.e. an increase of $2000. Thus, the depreciation charge for the year 2002 relating to leasehold premises was $2000. Assuming a straight-line basis for depreciation, this indicates that a total of 20 years depreciation have been charged against the cost of the leasehold premises ($40 000/$2 000 = 20). This implies that the company purchased the premises 20 years ago at a cost of $100 000. From the viewpoint of a potential purchaser of the company, a key issue will be what the current value of these premises is. Even taking into account the uncertain state of the property market in recent years, it is likely that such a current value will be considerably in excess of the original cost.

Table 15.1	Financial statements of Motors Ltd

Balance sheets as at 31 December

	2007		2006	
	$000	$000	$000	$000
Fixed assets				
Leasehold premises:				
Cost	100		100	
Accumulated depreciation	40		38	
		60		62
Equipment:				
Cost	195		190	
Accumulated depreciation	110		80	
		85		110
		145		172
Current assets				
Stock	290		155	
Debtors	130		75	
Cash	20		90	
	440		320	
Current liabilities				
Creditors	235		130	
Net current assets		205		190
Long-term liabilities		(100)		(150)
Total net assets		250		212
Share Capital ($1 shares)		150		150
Retained profits		100		62
		250		212

Profit and loss accounts – Years to 31 December

	2007	2006
	$000	$000
Sales revenue	1700	1950
Cost of sales	1382	1575
Gross profit	318	375
Operating costs	201	225
Net profit	117	150
Taxation	43	47
Profit after taxation	74	103
Dividends	36	36
Retained profit	38	67

- **Equipment.** The recorded cost of equipment has increased from $190 000 to $195 000 and the accumulated depreciation has increased from $80 000 to $110 000. Although there is no specific information on disposals or purchases of equipment, these figures tend to suggest that there has not been any major investment in new equipment. Also they suggest that, on average, the equipment owned by the company is well past half its forecast useful life. This tends to indicate that the company has not been investing in new equipment, which might be a cause of concern to a potential purchaser.

- **Current assets.** There have been significant changes in these. Inventories have risen from $155 000 to $290 000, an increase of $135 000 or nearly 90%. This might indicate that the business is encountering difficulties in selling its vehicles. A related issue would be what exactly is the nature of these stocks, given that common practice in the motor trade involves the supply of vehicles from manufacturers to distributors on a consignment basis. Similarly, debtors have increased from $75,000 to $130 000, an increase of $55 000 or over 70%. This could indicate that the company is encountering difficulties in collecting money from its customers. A related issue might be why the business has debtors on this scale at all. Customary practice in the motor vehicle industry is that cars are sold either for cash or on credit terms provided via finance companies. In neither of these cases would the seller be involved in providing credit to its customers. Accordingly the source of the debtors would need investigation, as well as the increase. Cash has fallen from $90 000 to $20 000, a fall of $70 000. This is a major change, suggesting that careful attention should be paid to the business's cash flow position.

- **Current liabilities.** These have increased from $130 000 to $235 000, an increase of $105 000 or approximately 80%. This is a significant increase which might indicate that the business is encountering problems in meeting its short-term liabilities. Taken together with the decline in cash and the increases in stock and debtors, this increase in creditors indicates a potentially worrying situation.

- **Long term loans.** These have fallen from $150 000 to $100 000. This suggests that the company has repaid $50 000 during the year, and might further imply that it will need to repay a further $50 000 in each of the next two years. The terms of these long-term loans will need to be ascertained and, given the decline in cash balances mentioned above, a potential purchaser would need to look carefully at the cash flow position of the business to ensure that it has the capability to fund such repayments

- **Sales turnover.** This has declined from $1 950 000 to $1 700 000, perhaps reflecting difficult economic circumstances facing the motor trade as a whole. A prospective purchaser of Motors would want to know how this performance relates to that of competitors.

- **Profit after taxation.** This has declined from $103 000 to $74 000. Again, a prospective purchaser would want to know how much such a decline reflects the general economic circumstances facing the industry, and how much it reflects the particular circumstances facing Motors and the management responses to these.

- **Dividends.** These have remained the same, despite the decline in profit after taxation. There could be a number of reasons for this, including family members relying on dividends for their income. The exact reason would need to be ascertained.

To summarise, this overview of the financial statements indicates a company which may have a significantly undervalued property asset and is facing difficult trading circumstances which are impacting on its liquidity, while at the same time having to repay loans yet maintaining its dividend payments. With this background the financial performance of Motors can be analysed in more detail using financial ratios. However, before doing so it is important to note that we only have financial statements for two years. This is really not enough to identify trends with any degree of reliability. Ideally, we would need financial statements for earlier years as well. With this background we can proceed to look at ratio analysis techniques.

Profitability ratios

Profitability ratios focus on the relationship between the profit that an entity generates and the resources that it employs to generate this profit. There are two ratios that are commonly used to measure this relationship. These are:

- *Return on equity capital employed*. This ratio measures the effectiveness with which shareholders' funds have been employed in generating profits for the shareholders. It is calculated as follows:

$$\frac{\text{Profit after taxation}}{\text{Shareholders' funds}} \times 100 \qquad \textbf{(15.1)}$$

The profit after taxation provides a measure of the amount of profit the entity has generated which is attributable to the shareholders, and the shareholders' funds provide a measure of the resources attributable to the shareholders. The ratio provides a measure of how effectively management has deployed these resources in pursuit of a primary shareholder objective – profit.

There is, however, a technical difficulty in the computation of this ratio. This relates to the fact that we are comparing a flow of profit, which arises throughout the financial year, with a value of capital at a point in time. If the opening equity capital is used for this purpose then, for a profitable company, the value of the ratio will be overstated because, as the company generates profits throughout the year, the equity capital base will have increased but this increase will not have been reflected in the computation. Correspondingly, if the closing equity capital is used this will tend to understate the value of the ratio because management will not have had that closing value of resources available to them throughout the year. This problem is common to the computation of a number of financial ratios and a frequent response to it is to use averages instead of the point in time values. Thus, in the computation of the return on equity capital employed, the average value of the opening and closing equity capital could be used as the denominator. This would, however, require information about the opening and closing values to be available, which may not always be the case for external users of financial statements although it will normally be so for management. For simplicity, we will illustrate the use of the average method in relation to return on equity capital employed of Motors and in subsequent computations we will use year end values.

In the case of Motors the return on equity capital for the two years for which we have information available, and using the average method for the valuation of the capital, is:

$$2007: \frac{\$74\,000}{0.5\,(\$250\,000\,+\,\$212\,000)} \times 100 = 32.03\%$$

$$2006: \frac{\$103\,000}{0.5\,(\$212\,000\,+\,(\$212\,000\,-\,\$67\,000))} \times 100 = 57.70\%$$

There appears to have been a significant decline in the return on equity capital which Motors is achieving. However, in both years the return appears to be a relatively high one; this may be in part due to an understatement of the value of the leasehold premises. This is a reflection of a potentially significant problem – most financial statements are based on the historical cost method of accounting and record assets at the original cost of acquisition by the entity rather than their current value. For short-term (current) assets this may not be too great a problem, except in times of rapid price changes. It is more of a problem when it comes to long-term (fixed) assets. In this case, there may be significant divergences between the original cost of the asset and its current value. This seems to be the case in Motors where leasehold premises are shown in the financial statements at their original cost of 20 years ago. The current market value of this asset is likely to be significantly higher. The consequence of this is that any return on capital calculation using historical cost information is likely to show too high a return on capital. This is because the denominator in the calculation will be understated (being based on historical cost rather than current value) and the numerator will be overstated (insofar as it incorporates depreciation charges based on historical cost rather than current values). Thus, in times of price rises, return on capital calculations will tend to overstate rather than understate the true economic performance of entities by showing a higher return on capital employed than would be the case if true economic values were used. This misstatement will be the greater the more the divergence between historic cost and current economic value.

- *Return on total capital employed.* This ratio measures the effectiveness with which the totality of resources available to management have been deployed, irrespective of how those resources have been financed. It is calculated as follows:

$$\frac{\text{Operating profit}}{\text{Total long-term capital employed}} \times 100 \qquad \textbf{(15.2)}$$

Operating profit is defined as profit before the deduction of finance charges (interest) and taxation. This is a measure of corporate performance which is independent of the way in which resources are financed (by excluding the finance charges) and of taxation charges (which are outside the control of management). Thus, the focus of this ratio is on the economic efficiency and effectiveness achieved by management with the total resources available to them. As such it is a prime indicator of overall corporate performance, and is sometimes referred to as the master ratio.

In the case of Motors, assuming that the long-term loans bear interest at a rate of 10% per annum, the returns on total capital employed for the two years (using closing values for capital employed for simplicity of computation) were:

$$2007: \frac{\$7\,000 + \$10\,000}{\$250\,000 + \$100\,000} \times 100 = 36.28\%$$

$$2006: \frac{\$150\,000 + \$15\,000}{\$212\,000 + \$150\,000} \times 100 = 45.58\%$$

As with the return on equity capital employed, this ratio indicates a decline in financial performance, although not as great. This is, in part, the result of the repayment of £50 000 of the long-term loans.

Without having comparative figures from similar businesses and more information on the motor vehicle trade as a whole, it is not possible to comment on how good the financial performance of Motors has been during the two years for which we have financial statements. However, as suggested earlier, these return on capital ratios are perhaps higher than would normally be expected and this may well be due to the use of historic cost rather than current valuation for its leasehold premises.

Profitability ratios are the top of a pyramid of financial ratios, summarising overall corporate financial performance. There are numerous subsidiary ratios that can be calculated, each concentrating on a specific aspect of an entity's financial and commercial performance. The first tier of these ratios can be derived directly from the core notion of return on capital as follows:

$$\text{Return on capital} = \frac{\text{Profit}}{\text{Capital}} = \frac{\text{Sales revenue}}{\text{Capital}} \times \frac{\text{Profit}}{\text{Sales revenue}} \qquad \textbf{(15.3)}$$

Thus, return on capital can be analysed into two subsidiary measures. The first of these is the capital turnover rate (sales revenue/capital). This indicates the number of times that an entity turns over its capital in a financial period. In general terms businesses seek to turn over their capital as often as possible as by doing so they will be using such capital effectively. The second subsidiary measure is the rate of profit or profit margin. This relates the profit that an enterprise generates to the sales revenue from which this profit is derived. Different industrial and commercial sectors can have very different capital turnover rates and profit margins even though they may have similar returns on capital. A capital intensive industry such as heavy engineering may have a low capital turnover rate but a high profit margin. Correspondingly, a labour intensive company operating in the service sector may have a high capital turnover rate but a relatively low profit margin. Therefore, in analysing the information contained in corporate financial statements, it is not sufficient to look at the headline rate of return on capital, more detailed analysis is required. The first stage in such analysis frequently concerns an analysis of a company's profit as shown below.

Profit ratios

The next group of financial ratios concentrates on the relationships between the various components of profit and the balance between them. They enable decision makers to examine these relationships and detect changes in them. The highly aggregated nature of the annual financial statements of companies means that there is little scope for detailed analysis of the elements of profit by users of the statements. There is much more scope for such analysis by management who have access to detailed information about the various components of the profit and loss account. Management also have access to detailed budgetary information with which they can compare actual performance. Accordingly, profit ratios are potentially of much greater use to management than they are to external users of financial statements who can, at best, use them to make rather broad interpretations of corporate performance. Examples of the sorts of profit ratio that are commonly calculated include:

Gross profit margin. This ratio focuses on the relationships between sales revenues and the prime costs of providing goods or services to customers. It is concerned with the sharp end of the entity's activities and reflects the competitive pressures it faces, its market positioning and the effectiveness with which management are controlling prime costs. It is measured by:

$$\frac{\text{Gross profit}}{\text{Sales turnover}} \times 100 \tag{15.4}$$

A downward trend in this percentage may indicate that the entity is coming under increasing pressure from its competition. The possible reasons for such increased pressure are many, ranging from the entry of new direct competitors to the introduction of new products into the marketplace. Alternatively, it may be the result of a deliberate management decision to increase market share by an aggressive pricing policy. If this is the case, a user of the accounts would look for indications of sales growth. However, the ratio is not just a reflection of the market in which the enterprise operates. It also reflects the prime costs of supplying this market. Thus, a change in the ratio may be a function of changes in cost structures, the result perhaps of better management control of costs, or of changes in technology.

In the case of Motors the ratio for the two years was:

$$2007 : \frac{\$318\,000}{\$1\,700\,000} \times 100 = 18.71\%$$

$$2006 : \frac{\$375\,000}{\$1\,950\,000} \times 100 = 19.23\%$$

There has been a decline in this margin of 0.5%, which perhaps reflects competitive pressure in the motor industry. If this is the case, a fall of only 0.5% in the gross profit margin may represent very good performance by Motors, which has managed to (just about) maintain its gross profit margin despite a fall in sales turnover from $1 950 000 to $1 700 000.

Net profit margin. This concentrates on the proportion of the sales revenue of a business that net profit attributable to shareholders constitutes and it is calculated by:

$$\frac{\text{Net profit after taxation}}{\text{Sales turnover}} \times 100 \tag{15.5}$$

In the case of Motors, the ratios for the two years for which information is available are:

$$2007 : \frac{\$74\,000}{\$1\,700\,000} \times 100 = 4.35\%$$

$$2006 : \frac{\$103\,000}{\$1\,950\,000} \times 100 = 5.28\%$$

Thus, there has been a decline in Motors' performance over the two years in this key performance indicator, which reflects the net contribution that the sales of the business have made to generating profit attributable to shareholders and reflects the ultimate effectiveness of the entity's trading activities. The net profit margin percentage is potentially very helpful in the prediction of future profits, when combined with a sales forecast. However, it suffers from the disadvantage that it provides a very broad-brush overview. Profit after taxation is the net effect of many different cost and revenue elements under managerial control and of elements outside such control, e.g. taxation rates. Further analysis is needed, including the computation of the gross profit ratio as above.

Overhead costs percentage. Another area of corporate activity which impacts on net profit is that of support or overhead costs. A full understanding of the net profit margin, and changes in it, requires a review of the relationship between these support costs and the level of the entity's trading activities. There is a wide range of ratios that might be computed for this purpose. However, the information available to external users of financial statements means that only a few of them can in fact be calculated. Management, of course, can calculate many more because of their access to the whole range of financial information about the entity and its performance. The normal approach is one of measuring the percentage that overhead costs are of sales turnover.

$$\frac{\text{Overhead costs}}{\text{Sales turnover}} \times 100 \tag{15.6}$$

This ratio measures the relationship between the amount spent on overhead support costs and the level of activities being supported, as measured by sales turnover. The main use of the ratio is to provide an indication of the effectiveness with which management are controlling overhead costs relative to sales. The danger is that such ratios may provide a rather simplistic interpretation of the commercial activities of the enterprise, because of an implicit assumption that the overhead costs relate to activity in the same period. This may not be true. For example, management may have spent a great deal on a sales promotion campaign, the benefits of which may not arrive until the next financial period, or on the development of new computer systems, the benefit of which will not be achieved until future periods. The essence of the problem is that accounting requires such costs to be expensed because of the 'prudence' concept and as a result the benefits and the costs are not matched. A reader of the accounts should not simply rely on the ratios but link them with other available information to get a better understanding of such costs. Sources such as the Chairman's Report, brokers' circulars and press comment may be particularly helpful in this respect. In the case of Motors the ratio is:

$$2007 : \frac{\$201\,000}{\$1\,700\,000} \times 100 = 11.82\%$$

$$2006 : \frac{\$225\,000}{\$1\,950\,000} \times 100 = 11.54\%$$

Thus, there appears to have been little change in the proportion that overhead costs are of Motors' sales turnover. However, a more detailed analysis looking at the composition of these overhead costs, might prove instructive.

There is a 'standard set' of ratios which analysts tend to compute for all companies, irrespective of the industrial or commercial sector within which they operate and the ratios commented on above form part of this set. However, in addition to this standard set there are ratios which are more specific to particular industrial and commercial sectors. Examples of such sector specific ratios include:

- Sales (profit) per square metre of selling space – this a much used performance indicator in the retail trade.

- Research and development expenditure as a percentage of sales turnover – this is a much used indicator of the future viability of companies operating in high technology industries such as computing or pharmaceuticals.

The range of financial ratios that can be calculated is very wide. However, not all of them will provide users with useful additional information. A selection of those ratios which will in fact provide such information needs to be made, based on those elements of corporate performance which are the most important. The need for selectivity goes even further. There are standard formulae for the computation of financial ratios (which are described in this chapter). However, these standard formulae represent nothing more than the way in which such ratios are commonly calculated. They are not written in stone. If the application of the standard formulae will result in the provision of useful information, then they are worth using. However, there will be many occasions when more useful information can be obtained from the use of different formulae and different ratios. In such circumstances, the standard set of ratios should be departed from and different, more useful ratios, calculated. The standard set of ratios is the 'table d'hôte' menu and discerning decision makers may well find the 'a la carte' menu more beneficial.

Working capital ratios

These financial ratios concentrate on the solvency and liquidity of the company (in essence its ability to pay its liabilities as and when they fall due), and more generally on the effectiveness with which its working capital (short-term assets and liabilities) is being managed. They focus directly on areas which are crucial to corporate survival and which are the most susceptible to managerial action in the short term. The management of working capital is discussed in more detail in Chapter 6. The two most commonly calculated working capital ratios are:

Current ratio. This is an overall comparison of an entity's short-term (current) assets with its short-term liabilities. It is also known as the working capital ratio and is calculated by:

$$\frac{\text{Current assets}}{\text{Current liabilities}} \qquad \textbf{(15.7)}$$

In the case of Motors this ratio is:

$$2007 : \frac{\$4\,40\,000}{\$235\,000} = 1.87$$

$$2006 : \frac{\$320\,000}{\$130\,000} = 2.47$$

This indicates that there has been a considerable decline in the liquidity of Motors during the 2007 financial period. Declines in liquidity are generally regarded as being negative indicators of corporate performance. However, the importance of such declines depends, at least in part, on the base from which they result. In the case of Motors, although there has been a decline this has been from a very strong base, in which current assets covered current liabilities by more than a factor of two, to a position where they are still nearly covered twice.

Liquid ratio. This is a more focused ratio which compares an entity's **liquid** or **quick assets** with its short-term liabilities. Liquid assets are those assets which are readily convertible to cash which can then be used to settle liabilities. Other names for this ratio are the **acid test ratio** and the **quick ratio**. The normal formula for the calculation of this ratio is:

$$\frac{\text{Current assets} - \text{stocks}}{\text{Current liabilities}} \qquad \textbf{(15.8)}$$

The reason for deducting stocks from current assets is that they are generally regarded as being relatively illiquid short-term assets, because they are the most distant of these assets from being converted into cash. They may need to be transformed by some manufacturing process and they may then have to be sold on credit terms, resulting in a lengthy period before any cash is received. Thus, monies invested in stock may well not be available for settling short-term liabilities and should therefore be excluded from any assessment of the short-term solvency of an enterprise.

Prepaid expenses (such as insurance, rent and advertising) are other relatively illiquid assets. If a company has a significant proportion of prepaid expenses included in its current assets, it may be appropriate to deduct the amount of the prepaid expenses in addition to the value of the stocks in order to obtain the numerator for the quick ratio. In the case of Motors the liquid ratios are:

$$2007 : \frac{\$440\,000 - \$290\,000}{\$235\,000} = 0.64$$

$$2006 : \frac{\$320\,000 - \$115\,000}{\$130\,000} = 1.29$$

This portrays a dramatic shift in the liquidity position of Motors. At the end of 2006 its liquid assets covered its short-term liabilities by a factor of 1.29, while at the end of 2007 these assets were apparently insufficient to meet its short-term liabilities. Thus, on the face of it, Motors faces a potential solvency crisis. However, this might not in fact be the case because there are other issues to be taken into account when considering the solvency of an enterprise, and the normal way in which the liquid ratio is calculated does not take these into account. These include:

(a) **The actual, as opposed to the assumed, liquidity of assets.** All too often financial ratios are calculated on the assumption that current assets other than stocks represent the liquid assets of an entity. This may or may not be the case. Debtors, for example, may not in reality be liquid assets (defining liquidity as being readily convertible into cash). Typically, debtors take something of the order of 60 to 70 days to pay, which hardly represents immediate liquidity. In addition, accounting conventionally treats amounts receivable within twelve months as being a current asset. Thus debtors could include, for example, amounts due on 360 day bills of exchange where cash will not be received until nearly a year after the balance sheet date. If this were to be the case, then using the normal basis of computing financial ratios could lead to the liquidity of an entity being overestimated. The position is further complicated by the fact that an entity may have assets, other than current assets, which are in fact readily convertible into cash in the short term. This is particularly true of investments which are listed on a stock exchange, but may also apply to fixed assets such as property which can readily be sold for cash. In reality, the liquidity of an enterprise is much more a function of the realisability of its assets than it is of the accounting classification of those assets into long-term and short-term assets.

(b) **Access to finance.** The core question in assessing the liquidity/solvency of an entity is whether or not it has the resources to pay its liabilities as and when they fall due. One source of such resources is the assets of the entity, particularly its short-term assets and most importantly cash. However, equally important is the access that the entity has to borrowing. A company may have a deficit of liquid assets as compared to its short-term liabilities, but if it has access to sufficient borrowing facilities it will still be able to settle its short-term liabilities. Thus, a vital piece of information for people trying to assess the liquidity/solvency of an enterprise is information about borrowing facilities. Unfortunately, such information is not normally disclosed in annual financial statements.

There is a great deal of mythology regarding what are acceptable values for the current and liquid ratios of reporting entities. Many commentators suggest that a company should have a current ratio with a value between 1 and 2, and that companies with liquid ratios of less than 1 are facing liquidity problems. Such views fail to take into account the different circumstances which companies face, and the different patterns of cash flow persisting in different commercial sectors. Thus, for example, it is quite normal for successful retailers to have liquid ratios of less than 1 because their strong positive cash flows help to assure their solvency. Similarly, they fail to take into account the fact that investment in current/liquid assets by a company should be evaluated in the same way as any other investment, i.e. in terms of the returns that are generated. While large cash balances may ensure solvency, they may not be generating much profit for shareholders. Too large a cash balance may indicate that management are not using the resources available to them effectively. It may even indicate that the business is in decline. If a business's sales are declining then, at least in the short term, its cash resources may increase. This is the result of its receiving cash from previous credit customers while not having to pay out cash to suppliers for materials.

A company's cash position needs to be assessed in relation to its overall pattern of trade, rather than independently of it.

While the current and liquid ratios focus on the overall liquidity and solvency of an entity, there is another group of financial ratios which look in more detail at individual short-term assets and liabilities. These ratios are concerned with the specifics of working capital management. All of these ratios compare the 'stock' of a particular category of current asset or liability with the flows of costs or revenues associated with that asset or liability. Thus, debtors are compared with the credit sales which lead to the creation of debtors, and inventories are compared with cost of sales. There are two different ways of presenting these ratios. They can be presented as turnover rates, i.e. the number of times a particular class of asset/liability turns over each year. Alternatively, they can be presented in terms of the number of days' activity that the 'stock' of the particular asset or liability represents. These different presentations will be illustrated, using the example of Motors, for the most usually calculated ratios, which are as the following.

Stock (inventory) turnover. This ratio compares the amount that a company has invested in inventories with the cost of sales which this inventory supports. The money which a company invests in inventories is not available for other purposes, it is money which is 'tied up' and in general companies would prefer to have as little money 'tied up' in inventories as possible. Chapter 6 discusses the reasons why companies hold inventories in more detail. For the present, it is sufficient to recognise that it is generally accepted that efficient companies have lower levels of inventory relative to their cost of sales than do inefficient companies. Thus, a high stock turnover rate (or low stock turnover period) will usually be regarded as a sign of good management. Stock turnover rate is calculated by:

$$\frac{\text{Cost of sales}}{\text{Stock}} \qquad \textbf{(15.9)}$$

Stock turnover period is calculated by:

$$\frac{\text{Stock}}{\text{Cost of sales}} \times 365 \text{ (assuming 365 days in a financial year)} \qquad \textbf{(15.10)}$$

Both of these ratios combine a flow (cost of sales) with a position (stock), and as such are dependent on the choice of position that is made (opening stock, closing stock or average stock). As indicated earlier, for the purposes of simplicity, we will use the closing value for illustration. However, the implications of doing this need to be recognised. If the closing stock value is in any way atypical, then the resultant ratio may give an inappropriate portrayal of performance. It is widely accepted that some companies choose their financial year ends to reflect points in time when their stock levels are low. Thus, many retailers have financial periods ending on 31 January, i.e. after the busy Christmas periods and the January sales. In the case of Motors the stock turnover periods are:

$$2007 : \frac{\$290\,000}{\$1\,382\,000} \times 365 = 76.59 \text{ days}$$

$$2006 : \frac{\$155\,000}{\$1\,950\,000} \times 365 = 35.92 \text{ days}$$

There has been a dramatic increase in Motors' stock turnover period. *Prima facie*, this indicates that Motors has a major problem and has lost control of its stock levels. This could well be the case. However, the stock turnover period ratio simply tells us that there has been a change. It does not tell us the reason for the change. It might be that management have lost control of its stocks; equally the increase might be the result of deliberate management policies, e.g. stocking up to enable them to meet a large customer order due for delivery shortly after the financial year end, or the result of a large purchase made shortly before the year end at low prices. The ratio simply tells us that there has been a change in the relationship between inventories and cost of sales and therefore indicates that users should ask why this change has taken place. It does not, and cannot, tell users whether this change represents good or bad performance. Unfortunately, all too often analysts react to the change without further investigation and regard an increase in stock turnover period as being a negative performance indicator.

Debtor turnover. This ratio links the value of debtors with the credit sales that gave rise to these debtors. Companies would prefer to sell goods and services for cash rather than on credit, as by doing so they would avoid the risk of bad debts and not have to finance their customers' purchases. Unfortunately for them, credit sales are a well-established fact of life in the world of commerce and industry. Companies which insist on 'cash only' sales are likely to sell less than those which offer their customers credit facilities and therefore lose the profit that they could have made on these credit sales. However, the granting of credit to customers has a cost – the opportunity cost of the cash resources tied up in financing debtors, apart from the risk of non-payment by customers. When they offer customers credit facilities, companies will normally seek to obtain settlement as soon as possible. The debtor turnover ratios provide an indication of how successful they are in this respect. As with stock turnover, there are two versions of these ratios – the debtor turnover rate and the debtor turnover period. Debtor turnover rate is calculated by:

$$\frac{\text{Credit sales}}{\text{Debtors}} \qquad \text{(15.11)}$$

and debtor turnover period is calculated by:

$$\frac{\text{Debtors}}{\text{Credit sale}} \times 365 \text{ (assuming 365 days in a financial year)} \qquad \text{(15.12)}$$

As with stock turnover, debtor turnover involves a comparison between a flow (credit sales) and a position (debtors) and poses the same issues regarding how typical the position value is. For example, a large credit sale shortly before the year end could well distort the value of the ratio. A further difficulty is that corporate financial statements do not normally disclose the value of credit sales, instead they simply disclose the value of total sales. This means that external analysts can only base their calculations of debtor turnover on the total sales figure, and that the computation is susceptible to any changes in the balance between cash and credit sales. Management, of course, have access to the necessary information to enable to compute the ratio more precisely. In practice, some companies analyse their debtor turnover in rather more detail, e.g. by business sectors or customer groups, because they believe such analyses improve the quality of their decision taking.

In the case of Motors, the debtor turnover for the two years is as shown below, assuming that all sales were in fact credit sales because of a lack of information regarding the balance between credit and cash sales.

$$2007 : \frac{\$130\,000}{\$1\,700\,000} \times 365 = 27.91 \text{ days}$$

$$2006 : \frac{\$75\,000}{\$1\,950\,000} \times 365 = 14.04 \text{ days}$$

The period of credit being taken, on average, by Motors' customers has nearly doubled, and, *prima facie*, this is a bad sign, perhaps indicating either that the management of Motors has lost control of its debtor position, or that it is having to offer extended credit to secure business. Taken together with the earlier query about why Motors is selling on credit in the first place, this suggests that a prospective purchaser should raise a number of questions about its credit policies and credit management.

Creditor turnover. This ratio links the value of creditors with the amount of goods and services that a business is purchasing on credit terms. It suffers from exactly the same problems as any other financial ratio which links a flow (purchases) with a position (creditors) and, accordingly, needs to be viewed with some caution. A commonly held view is that creditors provide a source of free finance to a business and that payments to creditors should be deferred as long as practicable, suggesting that creditor turnover periods should be extended rather than reduced. This view ignores the value of any cash settlement discounts that may be offered by the supplier. As is demonstrated in Chapter 6, such cash settlement discounts can in fact be very valuable. Chapter 6 also discusses the fact that the speed with which creditors are paid is only one element in the relationships that a business has with its suppliers. Other elements include the prices paid for goods and services, the quality of these goods and services, and the willingness of the supplier to meet the precise requirements of the business. Excessive delay of payment to suppliers might lead to them ceasing to value the business being offered, and a reduction in the general terms of trade which they are prepared to offer, as well as the loss of cash settlement discounts. Creditor turnover rate is calculated by:

$$\frac{\text{Credit purchases}}{\text{Creditors}} \qquad \textbf{(15.13)}$$

The creditor turnover period is calculated by:

$$\frac{\text{Creditors}}{\text{Credit purchases}} \times 365 \text{ (assuming 365 days in a financial year)} \qquad \textbf{(15.14)}$$

Motors provides an example of the difficulties faced by external users of financial statements in evaluating the creditor management of companies. As is usually the case, no figures are provided for purchases by the business on credit terms. Accordingly, the ratios shown below are based on the (rather heroic) assumption that the cost of sales and other costs shown in the summary financial statements represent credit purchases.

$$2007 : \frac{\$235\,000}{\$1\,382\,000 + \$201\,000} \times 365 = 27.91 \text{ days}$$

$$2006 : \frac{\$130\,000}{\$1\,575\,000 + \$225\,000} \times 365 = 14.04 \text{ days}$$

This indicates that the period of credit that Motors is taking from its suppliers has more than doubled. This is a significant change and a potential purchaser would need to investigate the reasons for the change thoroughly. If it is the case that the change is a result of the business's inability to generate sufficient cash inflows to match its previous pattern of paying suppliers, this would be very worrying, both as regards its ability to meet its liabilities and as regards its future terms of trade with its suppliers. While a company's ability to meet its short-term liabilities will be significantly influenced by its short-term working capital management, it will also reflect its long-term capital structure

Financing ratios

The principal focus of these ratios is financial risk, i.e. the risk to those associated with a company which derives from the company's financial structure and, in particular, the risk introduced by a capital structure which involves debt and other forms of capital having preferential rights. There is a substantial body of research and literature regarding the implications of different types of capital structure for companies and their stakeholders. Corporate finance texts such as Watson and Head (2001) provide useful overviews of this area.

Broadly speaking, from a corporate perspective, debt capital is cheaper than equity capital because it enjoys greater security. This greater security relates to both annual interest payments and the repayment of capital. The annual interest payments are regarded as a cost of the company's operations and as such are a deduction in the computation of any profit out of which dividends can be paid to shareholders. Equally, debt capital ranks higher than shareholders' funds in entitlement for repayment of capital. The larger these prior claims of providers of debt finance the more risky is the investment of the equity holders, both as regards their entitlement to a share of the business's income and to repayment of their capital. There may also come a point where these prior claims are so large that they themselves become more risky. There are two financial ratios that attempt to measure this financial risk: one focuses on the capital values of debt and equity (the balance sheet gearing ratio) and the other on the income entitlements (the income gearing ratio). These ratios are sometimes referred to as leverage ratios rather than gearing ratios.

Balance sheet gearing ratio. There are a number of different variants of this ratio – some using financial statement values of debt and equity and some using capital market values. However, the principle is the same – a focus on the relative proportions of debt and equity capital. A common version of this ratio is:

$$\frac{\text{Debt capital}}{\text{Debt capital} + \text{Equity capital}} \times 100 \qquad \textbf{(15.15)}$$

This ratio provides a measure, albeit a fairly simplistic one, of the relative claims of debt holders and equity holders against the assets of the company. The higher the proportion of debt-holder claims, with their preferential status, the more risky become the shareholder claims. Thus, the ratio in this form is a basic indicator of financial risk. Its basic nature becomes even more apparent when the range of debt finance that companies can raise is considered. This includes mortgages, floating charge debentures, convertible loan stock and various types of preference shares, as well as more complex financial instruments. The situation is further complicated by the fact that different commercial sectors commonly have different patterns of capital structure. What might be an acceptable capital structure for a property company with a strong asset base, might be totally unacceptable for a company operating in the service sector with a strong but volatile cash flow. The capital markets tend to have quite strong views about the acceptable levels of gearing in different business sectors, and entities which exceed these levels may well find their share values being significantly downgraded. The Motors' balance sheet gearing ratio reveals the following:

$$2007 : \frac{\$100\,000}{\$100\,000 + \$250\,000} \times 100 = 28.57\%$$

$$2006 : \frac{\$150\,000}{\$150\,000 + \$212\,000} \times 100 = 41.44\%$$

This indicates that there has been a sharp decline in the proportion that debt finance provides of the overall long-term financing of Motors. This is principally the result of the repayment by the company of $50 000 of such long-term debt finance and this needs to be taken into account in the overall assessment of Motors' financial position, especially in the light of the apparent decline in its short-term liquidity position discussed earlier.

Although this ratio provides a useful indicator of financial risk, it does not cover an equally and perhaps more important risk issue – the terms on which the finance having priority claims have been made available, including maturity or repayment dates. Particular attention needs to be paid to the possible exposure of an entity to short-term claims for the repayment of such finance and whether or not the entity could fund such repayments, either out of existing funds or by access to alternative lines of credit. As is the case in most countries, company legislation in the UK requires extensive disclosure about the entitlements of debt and other finance providers having preferential rights. However, this disclosure is normally provided in the notes to the accounts, a part of corporate annual reports which research has shown to be read by relatively few people.

An important related consideration is the extent of a company's borrowing powers. It is common for a company's articles of association to empower its directors to borrow money and to pledge the company's assets as security for such borrowing. However, it is rare for this authority to be unfettered. Limits are often placed on the extent of this borrowing, and these limits are frequently expressed in terms of a proportion of the company's net assets, or equity. Debenture trust deeds often place similar restrictions on the borrowing powers of companies. Thus, the balance sheet gearing ratio, when looked at in conjunction with such restrictions, can provide a useful indicator of the extent to which a company is operating within its authorised borrowing limits.

Income gearing ratio. This ratio compares the amount of prior claim financing charges on corporate income to the amount of that income. The greater the proportion of these **prior charges,** the more that the residual (equity holders) share of corporate income is at risk. Relatively small declines in overall corporate income can lead to much greater declines in the income attributable to shareholders. The ratio is normally calculated as follows:

$$\frac{\text{Interest and other prior charges on income}}{\text{Operating profit}} \times 100 \qquad \textbf{(15.16)}$$

A common acronym for operating profit is **EBIT** (earnings before interest and taxation). In the case of Motors, assuming an interest rate of 10% per annum on the long-term debt, the income gearing ratios for the two years for which financial information is available are:

$$2007 : \frac{\$100\,000}{\$117\,000 + \$10\,000} \times 100 = 7.87\%$$

$$2006 : \frac{\$15\,000}{\$150\,000 + \$15\,000} \times 100 = 9.09\%$$

This indicates that the proportion that prior claim debt charges have on corporate income has declined. This would normally be regarded as a good thing from the point of view of the shareholders as it makes their share of corporate income more secure. However, security is not everything. Investment in the equity capital of companies is essentially a risk investment. Investors accept this risk in the expectation (hope) that they will receive a return which will compensate them for taking this risk. Given that debt finance is cheaper (from a corporate viewpoint) than equity finance, there may be advantages to shareholders in companies raising debt finance as this may enable them to undertake additional investment projects, thereby generating greater returns for the shareholders albeit that financial risk is increased. The question then becomes one of whether or not the potential upside for shareholders is sufficient, given the increments in business and financial risk associated with these investment projects. The key point is that there are no universally applicable benchmark values for financial ratios. They must always be assessed in the light of the prospects for the business sectors in which companies are operating and overall economic trends.

Investment performance ratios

This group of ratios concentrates on the performance of companies from the perspective of an equity investor (shareholder). They focus on the earnings attributable to shareholders, the balance between corporate earnings and dividend pay-outs, and the relationship between the market price of shares and the earnings and dividends attributable to shares. The most commonly computed ratios in this area are:

Earnings per share. This ratio measures the potential benefits available to shareholders from the profits generated by a company, irrespective of the extent to which such profits are in fact reflected in dividend distributions. As such, it is a key indicator of corporate performance from a shareholder perspective and, for listed companies, is widely quoted in the financial press. It is computed by:

$$\frac{\text{Earnings attributable to shareholders (i.e. profit after taxation)}}{\text{Number of shares in issue}} \qquad (15.17)$$

There are a number of technical issues associated with the computation of earnings per share, which are often caused by the (sometimes) complex financial instruments issued by companies to finance their activities. However, the focus is clear – measuring the financial performance of a company from the perspective of an individual share-holder. In the relatively straightforward case of Motors the earnings per share are:

$$2007 : \frac{\$74\,000}{\$150\,000} = 0.49 \text{ per share}$$

$$2006 : \frac{\$103\,000}{\$150\,000} = 0.69 \text{ per share}$$

This indicates that, from a shareholder perspective, the overall financial perform-ance of Motors was worse in 2007 than 2006 by quite a significant extent. This deterioration is principally the result of the decline in profits and profitability dis-cussed earlier. However, the amount of earnings per share does not on its own pro-vide a measure reflecting both the benefits and costs associated with investment in a company. To obtain such a measure, it is necessary to link the earnings attributable to ownership of a share with the cost of purchasing such a share.

Price earnings ratio. This ratio compares the benefits derived from the ownership of a share (in terms of participation in the profits) with the cost of purchasing such a share. It is calculated by:

$$\frac{\text{Market price of a share}}{\text{Earnings per share}} \qquad (15.18)$$

This ratio compares the earnings per share with the market price of a share. As such, it compares the profit that is generated by a company for its equity shareholders directly with the price that has to be paid (currently) to participate in those profits (by the pur-chase of shares). It provides a clear indication of the value that the capital market places on corporate earnings, reflecting its assessment of both the amount and the riskiness of these earnings, in the context of overall market and economic considerations. It is a ratio which is regularly calculated and reported in the financial press and is frequently invoked in takeover negotiations and the issue of new equity capital. However, it must be emphasised that the comparison is between historic earnings (as shown in the profit and loss account) and current market prices. There is no guarantee that this past per-formance will be repeated in the future, and yet it is in future earnings a new investor will participate. Past earnings are being used as a surrogate for future earnings.

As Motors is not a listed company it does not have a 'quoted' price per share. Accordingly, it is not possible to calculate a price-earnings ratio for it. However, price-earnings ratios are often used as one basis for the valuation of shares in unlisted companies. This is achieved by taking the average (typical) price-earnings ratio for similar, listed companies and multiplying it by the earnings per share for the company whose shares are to be valued. In the case of Motors and assuming a typical price-earnings ratio of 20:1, this approach would indicate a share value of $9.80 per share ($0.49 × 20). There are obvious difficulties with this approach, many of which relate to the difficulties inherent in identifying a suitable 'typical' price earnings ratio and the differences between a 'private' unlisted company and a 'public' listed company.

Dividend cover. This ratio focuses on the security of the current rates of dividends, and by doing so provides a measure of the possibility of those dividends being maintained in the future. It does this by measuring the proportion that current rates of dividends are of the profits from which such dividends can be declared without drawing on retained profits. The higher the ratio, the more that profits could decline without dividends being affected. This is particularly important in the light of the widely held view that the capital market places a very high premium on companies that maintain a steady, preferably expanding, rate of dividend payments rather than companies whose dividend rates fluctuate unpredictably. It is calculated by:

$$\frac{\text{Distributable profits for the year}}{\text{Dividend for the year}} \qquad \textbf{(15.19)}$$

In the case of Motors the dividend cover ratios are:

$$2007 : \frac{\$74\,000}{\$36\,000} = 2.06$$

$$2006 : \frac{\$103\,000}{\$36\,000} = 2.86$$

Motors has been able to maintain its rate of dividend to shareholders despite a fall in post tax profits from $103 000 to $74 000. However, the dividend payment is now only covered by profits by a factor of 2.06 rather than the 2.86 of the previous year. Future similar declines in profit would mean that the company would be unable to maintain its dividend rate without recourse to profits retained from earlier years.

Dividend yield. In many ways this is an acid test of corporate financial performance from an investor's point of view, focusing as it does on the relationship between a company's dividend pay-outs and the price that an investor has to pay to participate in these dividends. It is calculated by:

$$\frac{\text{Dividend per share}}{\text{Market price of a share}} \qquad \textbf{(15.20)}$$

In today's financial markets, an investor has a wide range of investment opportunities available and will want to assess the relative merits of these different opportunities. An important element in such an assessment will be the relative yields to be derived from different investment opportunities in the light of the relative risks involved, and this is where the dividend yield ratio comes into its own. It compares the amount of the dividend per share with the market price of a share, and provides a direct measure of the return on investment in the shares of an enterprise.

However, a note of caution must be sounded. This is because the dividends in the numerator of the dividend yield computation are historic dividends. They are the dividends that have been paid in the past and not those dividends which will be paid in the future and are the real basis of a return on investment. Equally, it must be recognised that stock market prices can be very volatile, being influenced by many factors, far from all of which have anything to with the performance of an individual company. Thus, while the ratio attempts to address something of crucial importance to an investor, it has to do so using past data on dividends in relation to what might be a rapidly changing market price. A further note of caution is that the dividend yield ratio ignores the possibility of capital appreciation resulting from increases in the market value of a company's shares. The earnings per share ratio attempts in part to rectify this by reflecting the fact that not all of an enterprise's profits are necessarily distributed as dividends. Some will almost certainly be retained and reinvested to secure future profits. A shareholder is, at least in theory, entitled to a share of both these retained profits and the future profits arising from reinvestment. The latter may of course be highly speculative. These will be important elements in the capital market's attitude to a company and the resultant market price of its shares.

Conclusion

As the foregoing indicates, there is a wide range of financial ratios that can be calculated from the financial statements of a reporting entity, even more so if the financial statements are used in conjunction with other sources of data. Such ratios can be of enormous help in gaining a fuller appreciation of an enterprise's financial performance. However, it is all too easy to calculate and use these ratios in a simplistic and trivial way. The ratios cannot be better than the information on which they are based – in the main financial statements are based on traditional historical cost concepts. While financial ratios do provide a useful structure for the interpretation of information contained in financial statements, they do not and cannot provide a complete basis for assessing the performance of companies and their management. This is because, while they can highlight changes in financial performance, they cannot identify the reasons for these changes and it is the reasons that are important. Instead, financial ratio analysis helps users of financial statements to identify the changes that have taken place and to ask more focused questions about such changes.

Chapter review

The data contained in the annual financial statements of enterprises is an important source of information for stakeholders. The technique of ratio analysis enables more effective use to be made of this information. It focuses on the relationships between key items of information, enabling important linkages to be established and analysis of trends to be undertaken. Care must be taken to ensure that ratios are not over-interpreted, and it must be recognised that the ratios depend on the reliability of the information contained in the underlying financial statements. The main areas where ratios can be of use in assessing and analysing the performance of enterprises are:

- profitability
- profit
- liquidity and working capital
- financial structure
- performance as investments.

Further reading

Holmes and Sugden (1996) provide a summary of how to interpret the information contained in published accounts, as do Alexander and Britton (1999), albeit in less detail. Griffiths (1995) and Smith (1996) show how to avoid a number of pitfalls in the interpretation of published financial statements. Alexander and Britton (2004) and Elliot and Elliot (2003) provide more-up-to date information.

Questions and exercises

Guide notes can be found at the back of the book for all questions marked with an asterisk*.

1* The draft accounts for Commentary Ltd for the year ended 31 December 2007 are shown below.

Commentary Ltd: Draft balance sheet as at 31 December 2007

	2007		2006	
	£000	£000	£000	£000
Fixed assets				
Freehold premises at cost		450		450
Motor vehicles:				
Cost	300		300	
Accumulated depreciation	180		120	
		120		180
		570		630
Current assets				
Stocks	260		180	
Debtors	160		120	
	420		300	
Current liabilities				
Creditors	120		140	
Bank overdraft	100		50	
	220		190	
Net current assets		200		110
Total net assets		770		740
Shareholders' interests				
Share capital (£1 shares)		400		400
Retained profits		170		140
		570		540
Long-term liabilities				
12% debentures		200		200
		770		740

Commentary Ltd: Draft income statement – year to 31 December 2007

	2007 £000	2007 £000	2006 £000	2006 £000
Turnover		1050		850
Cost of sales		710		580
Gross profit		340		270
Distribution costs	125		105	
Administration costs	81		66	
Debenture interest	24		24	
		230		195
Profit before taxation		110		75
Taxation		50		35
Profit after taxation		60		40
Dividends		30		25
Retained profit for year		30		15

Required:

When these draft accounts were laid before the board of directors (none of whom has had any training in accounting) the following points were raised by board members. Reply to each of these points in clear and simple terms, avoiding the use of unexplained accounting 'jargon'. Where appropriate, support your replies with calculations.

(a) 'It doesn't seem to do us much good to make profits; our cash position seems to go from worse to worse'.

(b) 'Why are our premises shown in the balance sheet at £450 000? It would cost us at least £1 000 000 to buy premises like ours today and we could easily sell them for that amount'.

(c) 'It is ridiculous to describe our motor vehicles as fixed assets. I never saw anything less fixed than our motor vehicles'.

(d) 'There is something wrong with the depreciation. For a start the figures in the balance sheet don't agree with the profit and loss account. Also I am sure that we are not providing enough depreciation to enable us to replace our vehicles at today's prices'.

(e) 'We seem to have let control over our debtors and stocks slip such that the amount we have tied up in these items has increased alarmingly. Is there any simple way of measuring how seriously we have strayed from our previous patterns?'

(f) 'What is our rate of return on capital employed? Does it make sense to compare that figure with those of other companies as a test of our performance?'

(g) 'I am told that financial analysts judge a company on its earnings per share. What is this figure for Commentary and what does it mean?'

2* Stargate Plc is a producer of electronic digital scanning equipment for both commercial and private photographers. The market for this type of equipment has expanded by 20% during the past year and the company claims that it has gained additional market share and improved its profit margins relative to its competitors during that period. The average gross profit margin has remained at 50% over the past two years and the net profit margin has improved from 30% to 35%. The company claims that the gains in its profit can be attributed to increased efficiency of the labour force and investment in new manufacturing technology. The number of employees has declined from 300 in the year 2006 to 250 in the year 2007.

Stargate's management has read in the local newspaper that a major customer has gone into liquidation. Stargate produces equipment for this customer to the customer's own design. The managers of Stargate have expressed surprise that no indication of the problem existed prior to the announcement, and are concerned about the possible impact of the liquidation on its own cash position.

The profit and loss accounts, balance sheets and cash flow statements for Stargate Plc for the last two years are shown below.

Stargate Plc
Profit and loss accounts for year to 31 December

	2007 £000	2006 £000
Sales	2880	3744
Cost of sales	1320	1950
Gross profit	1560	1794
Operating expenses	708	1040
Profit before interest and taxation	852	754
Interest	50	105
Profit before taxation	802	649
Taxation	321	260
Profit after taxation	481	389
Dividends	120	156
Retained profit for year	361	233

Stargate Plc
Cash flow statements for year to 31 December

	2007 £000	2006 £000
Net cash flow from operating activities	1067	413
Return on investments and servicing of finance		
Interest paid	(50)	(50)
Taxation: UK corporation tax	(250)	(314)
Capital expenditure		
Sale of fixed assets	90	20
Purchase of fixed assets	(900)	(928)
	(810)	(908)
Dividend paid	(80)	(120)
	(123)	(979)
Management of liquid resources		
Issue of share capital	150	401
New loan	0	550
Increase (decrease) in bank balances	27	28

Stargate Plc
Balance sheets as at 31 December

	2007 £000	2006 £000
Fixed assets		
Cost	1968	2496
Depreciation	(506)	(696)
	1462	1800
Current assets		
Stock	416	667
Debtors	600	1363
Bank	68	40
	1084	2070
Current liabilities		
Creditors: amounts falling due in less than one year	151	254
Dividends	120	156
Interest payable	50	105
Taxation payable	384	330
	705	845
Net current assets	379	1225
Creditors: amounts falling due after one year		
Debenture loans (10%, repayable 2015)	500	1050
Total net assets	1341	1975
Capital and reserves		
Ordinary shares of £1 each	500	860
Share premium	0	51
Retained profits	841	1074
	1341	1975

Notes to balance sheets

(a) Fixed assets that had originally cost £400 000 were sold during 2007 for £20 000, resulting in a loss on the sale of £40 000.

(b) The depreciation charge for the year 2007 was £530 000.

Required:
Assess the profitability, liquidity and efficiency of the company by analysing the financial statements using suitable accounting ratios.

3* Nemesis Ltd is a family owned electronics business which was founded by Josiah Nemesis some 30 years ago. He has recently died, leaving his 40% shareholding in the company to his son Henry. His two surviving sisters, Jemima and Henrietta, each own 10% of the shares in the company and ownership of the remaining shares is spread amongst the company's 50 employees. Henry Nemesis, who is a research chemist, wants to dispose of his shares and has approached JG Enterprises Plc, the listed holding company of a group of diverse manufacturing businesses, to ascertain if they will buy his shares for cash. To support his offer, he has provided JG with the following summary of the last four years' accounts of Nemesis.

Balance sheets as at 31 July (all figures in $000)

	2007	2006	2005	2004
Fixed assets:				
Freehold property (at cost)	300	300	300	300
Machinery – at cost	620	620	540	480
– accumulated depreciation	410	330	260	240
	210	290	280	240
Total net book value	510	590	580	540
Current assets:				
Stocks	440	410	370	360
Debtors	780	690	680	600
Cash	10	90	110	100
	1230	1190	1160	1060
Current liabilities:				
Creditors	570	650	580	530
Short-term bank loan	200	100	–	–
	770	750	580	530
Net current assets	460	440	580	530
Total assets	970	1030	1160	1070
Represented by:				
Share capital (£1 Ordinary Shares)	500	500	500	500
Retained profits	220	230	310	170
	720	730	810	670
Long-term loan	250	300	350	400
	970	1030	1160	1070

Profit and loss accounts (all figures £000)

	2007	2006	2005	2004
Sales	2400	2100	2250	2200
Operating profit	180	225	395	415
Interest charges	45	40	35	40
Net profit before taxation	135	185	360	375
Taxation	45	65	120	125
Net profit after taxation	90	120	240	250
Dividends	100	200	100	100
Retained profit	(10)	(80)	140	150

Required:

In your capacity as the financial advisor to JG, prepare a report for its senior management team regarding the potential acquisition of Nemesis. This report should not identify a possible price that JG might be prepared to pay. However, it should comment on any factors that JG might want to consider in determining such a price. It should also contain calculations of the following ratios:

(a) Return on total capital employed

(b) Return on equity capital employed

(c) Net profit margin %

(d) Current (working capital) ratio

(e) Liquid (quick) ratio

(f) Debtor turnover rate and period

(g) Balance sheet gearing (leverage) %

(h) Interest cover %

(i) Earnings per share

4 You are the accountant of a small family company called Mayday, and you have just prepared the draft accounts shown below for the year ended 31 August 2007, which are shown below.

Mayday Ltd: Draft balance sheet at 31 August 2007

	2007 $000	2007 $000	2006 $000	2006 $000
Fixed assets				
Freehold premises:				
Cost	600		600	
Accumulated depreciation	200		188	
		400		412
Equipment:				
Cost	640		460	
Accumulated depreciation	300		320	
		340		140
		740		552
Current assets				
Stock	370		290	
Debtors	410		320	
Cash	20		60	
	800		670	
Current liabilities				
Creditors	620		560	
Net current assets		180		110
10% debentures		(200)		–
		720		662
Shareholders' interests				
Share capital (£1 shares)		400		400
Retained profits		320		262
		720		662

Mayday Ltd: Draft income statement – year to 31 August 2007

	2007 $000	2006 $000
Sales	2400	1980
Cost of sales	1900	1600
Gross profit	500	380
Other costs	170	160
Net profit	330	220
Taxtion	110	80
Profit after taxation	220	140
Dividends	162	130
Retained profit	58	10

Required:

When you present these draft accounts to the board of directors for approval, Josiah Mayday, one of the directors who has recently returned from an extensive polar exploration trip, asks you the following questions:

(a) 'This is a well-established business with loyal staff and loyal customers. This is in part demonstrated by the increase in sales during the year to our existing customers. The business enjoys an enormous amount of goodwill – from our customers, our staff, and the local community. This might almost be our major asset. Why is this asset not reflected in the accounts?'

(b) 'I don't understand all this accounting jargon about depreciation and fixed assets. I knew the accounts would confuse me, except as regards our freehold property where I knew nothing had changed. That is why I asked you to tell me in advance of this meeting how much we had spent on acquiring new fixed assets, how much we had sold old assets for, and how much depreciation we had charged this year on our assets. You told me that we had spent $350 000 on new fixed assets, had sold old assets for $30 000 (and made a loss on the sale), and had charged depreciation of $60 000 during the year. This makes a nonsense of your draft accounts. If we charged £60 000 of depreciation during the year, how can the accumulated depreciation on our fixed assets, other than freehold property, have gone down?'

(c) 'As you know, I depend on the dividends on my shares for my income. I was against issuing the debentures that you advised us to issue. I am sure this makes my income more risky. Is there any way I can measure this increased risk?'

(d) 'On top of this, the money we are owed by our customers has gone up by nearly 30% over the year, and this in a time of recession. You must have lost control over the situation. What are you going to do about it?'

(e) 'All in all, I think I should sell my shares. I have been talking to my stockbroker and he tells me that companies like ours have a Price/Earnings ratio of about 15 to 1. What does this mean, and what does it indicate about the price I should sell my shares for?'

Required:

Provide Mr Josiah Mayday with answers to his questions, avoiding the use of technical jargon wherever possible.

5 The balance sheet and profit and loss account of Concentration SA for the years ending 31 August 2007 and 2006 are shown below:

Concentration Ltd: Balance sheet as at 31 August 2007

	2007		2006	
	€000	€000	€000	€000
Fixed assets				
Land and buildings:				
Cost	550		520	
Accumulated depreciation	90		80	
		460		440
Machinery:				
Cost	1340		1120	
Accumulated depreciation	750		580	
		590		540
		1 050		980
Current assets				
Stocks	980		830	
Debtors	570		650	
Cash	40		120	
	1590		1600	
Current liabilities				
Creditors	358		310	
Net current assets		1232		1290
Total net assets		2282		2270
Shareholders' interests				
Share capital (£1 shares)		1200		1200
Retained profits		282		270
		1482		1470
10% debentures		800		800
		2282		2270

Concentration Ltd: Income statement – year to 31 August 2007

	2007		2006	
	€000	€000	€000	€000
Turnover		3200		2200
Cost of sales		2590		1610
Gross profit		610		590
Distribution costs	320		260	
Administration costs	170		190	
		490		450
Profit before taxation		120		140
Taxation		48		56
Profit after taxation		72		84
Dividends		60		90
Retained profit		12		(6)

Note: Included in the distribution and administration costs is an amount of €180 000 (2006: €110 000) for depreciation charges.

Required:

A friend of yours, who has little knowledge of accounting, has asked you to comment on the company's performance as revealed by the above accounts, with particular reference to the use of accounting ratios, as he would like to know more about them. Provide your friend with a review of Concentration's financial performance and position, utilising such accounting ratios as you feel to be appropriate.

6   Shown below are extracts from the financial statements of Pressurised Plc for the three years ended 30 June 2004, 2005 and 2006 and for the year ended 30 June 2007, which are about to be issued. It can be noted that no dividend was paid by the company in 2005. In his statement accompanying the 2006 financial statements the chairman forecast the 'resumption of normal dividends' in the following year. The interim financial statements for the six months to December 2007 confirmed this expectation, although no interim dividend was declared.

   Within the last month there has been an unusually high level of trading in the company's shares and the share price has moved to a recent high of £0.70. The board of directors has recently received credible information that the main buyer of Pressurised shares is the Oz Conglomerate Group (OCG), and that an offer may shortly be made by that group to take over Pressurised. It is thought that the offer price will be about £1.08 per Pressurised share. This news is most unwelcome to the board of Pressurised, partly because it doubts the ability or willingness of OCG to carry through the development of the company which has been quietly planned over the past few years, and partly because the directors suspect their own prospects would be uncertain.

Extracts from the financial statements of Pressurised for the years ended 30 June are shown below:

	2004 £000	2005 £000	2006 £000	2007 £000
Extracts from income statements				
Sales	10 000	12 000	14 000	15 500
Profit before taxation[1]	2 000	1 400	100	840
Dividends	325	325	0	100
Extracts from balance sheets				
Ordinary share capital[2]	4 500	6 000	6 000	6 000
Share premium	0	630	630	630
Other reserves	860	1 060	1 110	1 380
10% debentures 2004	2 000	2 000	2 000	2 000
15% debentures 2015	0	0	2 000	2 000
Trade creditors	1 140	1 360	1 610	3 500
Bank overdraft	0	0	450	970
Land and buildings[3]	1 500	2 000	3 000	3 750
Other fixed assets[4]	3 900	4 000	3 900	4 030
Stocks	2 000	3 500	4 500	5 750
Debtors	1 400	2 250	3 000	3 250
Notes:				

1 The rate of corporation taxation over the relevant period has been 33%.

2 The ordinary shares have a nominal value of £1 each.

3 Land and buildings are stated at cost, originating back to 1990.

4 Other fixed assets are stated at cost less accumulated depreciation.

The following summarises the movements in the share price of Pressurised for the period under review:

	2004	2005	2006	2007
Share price (£) during year:				
Mean	3.50	1.80	0.60	0.63
High	3.70	2.44	1.40	0.70
Low	2.00	1.54	0.40	0.47

The following data relates to companies typical of high and low P/E ratio groups in the same industry as Pressurised:

	Company A	Company B
EPS	£0.08	£0.15
Dividend	£0.03	£0.08
Dividend cover	4	3
Most recent share price	£0.80	£2.25
P/E ratio	10	15
Dividend yield	4%	3%

Required:
The board of Pressurised has asked you to:

(a) Give your analysis of the recent performance and possible future prospects of the company based on the above information.

(b) Advise the chairman:

(i) As to the grounds, if any, on which to recommend that shareholders reject the expected bid, having regard to the figures in the accounts and to the results of comparable businesses.

(ii) What defensive measures the board might take to avoid this particular bid, or at least to obtain a higher offer. In this respect your attention is directed to the statistics for companies A and B which have been extracted from the financial press this week. A and B are typical of the two categories of company within the industry group to which Pressurised belongs.

7* Identify, from the perspective of a potential investor, the principal areas regarding which such an individual would like to have information to help assess whether or not to invest in the shares of a particular public listed company. Comment on the extent to which the annual financial statements of companies typically provide a source for such information.

8 You are the corporate loans officer in a high street branch of a bank. As such you have to decide on whether or not to make advances to corporate organisations. Jason's Ltd is a well established fashion store in Borchester and its directors have approached you with a view to your bank granting them loan facilities. What information would you ask them to provide to help you to assess the credit-worthiness of the company, and what sort of analysis would you carry out on this information?

9* 'Ratios on their own are fairly useless – they only become useful when they are compared with something'. What are the difficulties that might be encountered in making such comparisons by:

(a) a company's management

(b) a shareholder

(c) a banker

10 'There can be problems with using "Return on Capital Employed (ROCE)" as a measure of the economic performance of many companies. In fact, ROCE based on historic cost financial statements will typically overstate such performance'. Do you agree with this statement? Give reasons for your answer.

11 Ratio analysis can combine figures derived from the financial statements with figures from other sources (e.g. the price/earnings ratio). List some ratios which do this and might be useful for analysing the financial performance of:

(a) an airline

(b) a chain of retail stores

(c) a high technology manufacturing company.

12* 'Traditional financial ratios are of more use to management than to external stakeholders when it comes to assessing business performance'. Do you agree with this statement? If so, why?

PART 5

This final section contains three chapters. The first of these, 'Social responsibility and environmental accounting' concentrates on the increasing emphasis that companies and their stakeholders place on these issues and mechanisms for achieving this. The next chapter, 'Supply chain management' examines the importance of entities managing their logistics effectively and the techniques that they can employ to achieve this. The final chapter, 'Strategic business accounting' brings together the issues outlined in previous chapters to examine how a company can manage its operations to ensure the maximum benefit for its stakeholders.

Social responsibility and the environmental accounting

16

Chapter preview

Ever since the early 1980s there has been a growing concern to improve the level of social responsibility and environmental reporting in both the public and private sectors. While initial concerns tended to focus on issues such as the development of employee reports and value added statements, general social accounting disclosure has more recently focused on the reporting of environmental performance. At the same time, increasing emphasis has been placed on broader 'corporate governance' issues, particularly the roles and responsibilities of directors, as discussed in Chapter 2. Those who support greater social responsibility and environmental accounting by corporations see this in terms of a broader level of accountability owed to society as a whole, which should reveal the full impact of an enterprise's economic activities on a broader range of stakeholders.

This pressure for the development of a broader base of corporate accountability has arisen for various reasons. Incidents such as the *Exxon Valdez* oil spill and the Bhopal chemical leak received worldwide media attention. This led to a number of national and international initiatives in reaction to this new climate of public opinion. In addition to initiatives undertaken by individual companies, organisations such as the CBI, the British Institute of Management and the Institute of Directors have launched a series of initiatives designed to promote greater managerial social responsibility. The UK's Environmental Protection Act 1990 has also been recognised as an important step in implementing the 'polluter-pays' principle. Perhaps the most important accounting issue that arises as a result of this legislation, is in terms of costing out new pollution-control methods under the legal obligation imposed to minimise waste production, utilising what is called the 'best available technology not entailing excessive cost (BAT NEEC) principle' (see Owen 1992). At the same time, there is increasing concern about the responsibilities of corporations for their activities in developing countries (e.g. the use and remuneration of child labour) as part of the development of the ethical investment movement.

At the European Community level there has been the circulation of a draft Directive which has called for the compulsory environmental auditing of companies whose activities have a significant impact on the environment. There is also a resurgence of interest in the 'ethical behaviour' of businesses.

Introduction

Managers need to be well informed on the issues surrounding their organisation's broader social responsibilities. Touche Ross Management Consultants (1990) neatly sum up their attitude towards environmental issues in the title to their report: *Head in the Clouds or Head in the Sand*? Empirical evidence cited later in this chapter on the provision of information on social and environmental issues by UK companies tends to support the view that it is highly selective and largely public-relations driven. Roberts (1992) has, for example, indicated that UK companies are generally failing to keep up with best European, most particularly German, practice. No wonder pressure groups such as Friends of the Earth established the 'Green Con' award for companies making the most misleading claims. An oft quoted defence by companies has been that greater social disclosure could harm the interests of their investors, but this is now being challenged as investors, both individual and institutional, also demand that such information be provided.

It is not only managers who are under attack for their failure to be more socially responsible. By 'focusing on issues of profit and efficiency whilst ignoring the social and environmental dimensions of organisational performance, conventional accounting techniques are heavily implicated in the current environmental mess we've got ourselves into' (Owen 1992: 22). This observation is not necessarily new. Writing over 70 years ago, John Maynard Keynes (1939) observed that under 'the peculiar logic of accountancy' the men of the nineteenth century built slums rather than modern cities because slums paid more.

According to Epstein and Roy (1997) many companies cannot quantify their environmental costs and, in part because of this, cannot develop strategies to control (manage) such costs. This has obvious implications for potential externalities associated with environmental costs, and the need for the reporting of these. At the very least, management need to improve their control of environmental costs. Hanson and Mendoza (1999) draw an analogy here with the control of the costs of managing quality. They advocate an approach which prepares a management environmental report. This could usefully analyse environmental costs into four categories:

1 Prevention costs: these are the costs incurred to prevent the production of environmentally damaging waste. As such, they might include costs associated with the design of production process and the reduction of any resultant contaminants, recycling costs, and staff development costs.

2 Appraisal costs: these are the costs that an entity incurs in ensuring compliance with its national legal obligations regarding the inspection of processes and products, auditing processes and product and process testing.

3 Internal failure costs: these are the costs associated with production processes and the production of waste materials which are not discharged into the environment, so as to comply with regulatory requirements.

4 External failure costs: these are the costs of what might best be described as 'clean up' activities that a firm has to incur if it discharges unacceptable (by legal regulation) waste into the environment. Such activities might involve land reclamation, cleaning up of oil spills and recycling.

A report of this nature could be very valuable in helping management assess how much cost is being expended on environmental activities and focus their attention on optimising the quantum of such costs.

In the remainder of this chapter we continue our discussion by first reviewing the nature of social responsibility accounting. We then go on, in turn, to discuss the impact of social responsibility and environmental issues on management accounting, external financial reporting and external audit.

What is social responsibility accounting?

Any discussion on social responsibility accounting raises the spectre of some hard and challenging issues for management. As Estes (1976: v) has observed:

- What is the worth of corporate 'social responsibility' activities such as aid to minority businesses, recycling programmes, energy conservation, etc?

- Since social responsibility shows up in costs but not in revenues, how can the socially responsible corporation come out as good on the 'bottom line' as its irresponsible competitor? How can a company tell the story of its social contribution to the public?

- Will pollution control laws, by driving productive corporations out of business, cost society more than they save?

Social responsibility accounting is about trying to provide answers to questions such as these. It can be defined (Gray *et al.* 1987) as:

> The measurement and reporting of information on the impact that an organisation's activities are having on society as a whole. Such information may be used both internally and externally by management and as such extends beyond that traditionally prepared and reported upon.

Management increasingly needs information on its organisation's social responsibilities. It may need this in order to respond to critical media attention or to present to a government agency. Public interest groups, often referred to as pressure groups, continually lobby for greater social responsibility from corporations and this therefore has to be demonstrated. Such groups can range in diversity from consumer affairs organisations to environmental lobby groups and religious organisations. Concerns are raised about a diverse set of social issues, which can cover such topics as the impact of corporate activity on the environment, ethical investment strategies, the treatment of ethnic and disadvantaged groups in society and abroad, community involvement, and so on.

Often managers may not be entirely aware of the degree to which their organisation is in fact socially responsible, since much of this activity is devolved and not 'captured' centrally. While corporations are relatively well organised when it comes to deciding upon their reasons for general philanthropy – such as support of educational institutions or evaluating the benefits of its various human resource programmes – there is probably less appreciation of the 'social impact' arising more directly from the products and services that they provide. How much ethical effort and consequent financial resources are devoted to the completeness of product service information (in terms of packaging, labelling and advertising)? Are electrical goods energy (and, if appropriate, water) efficient? To what degree do products contain biodegradable parts? Social responsibility accounting can take various forms, ranging from simple and relatively inexpensive systems through to highly complex and costly ones. Depending upon the organisation, the degree of social responsibility accounting can cover all/some of the following approaches:

1 Periodic informal reviews of social responsibility activities at localised management meetings.
2 The preparation of cost estimates of the support of social programmes and activities.
3 Social impact analysis of the costs associated with the practice of socially undesirable activity (such as detrimental effects on the environment).

Practice varies as to the degree to which such information is reported externally. This can range from a couple of paragraphs outlining an organisation's 'attitudes' to its social responsibilities, largely devoid of related financial values, through to a very detailed outline of its responsibilities to society. However, as many researchers have observed, the selection and format of information reported is very much at the discretion of management and not in a regulated format as with the more traditional financial accounting information. As indicated earlier, the accounting profession has not entirely embraced the notion of social responsibility accounting. Jones (1990) conducted interviews with 57 accountants working in six large manufacturing and merchanting firms, and elicited the overwhelming responses that, in their view, profit is the prime, if not the only, goal of business and that social responsibilities were deserving of a very low level of priority.

The British Institute of Management has drawn up a charter for its members with respect to developing a policy for management and the environment (see Table 16.1). This policy promotes the idea that 'good management of the environment is good management', and that management and reporting systems will have to be modified or developed to provide this newly demanded information (Lester 1992).

The issue of social responsibility accounting is but part of a growing wider debate on the issue of corporate governance. As Carey (1992: 87) notes:

> For most companies the days when their valuable assets were mainly in the form of bricks and mortar and plant and machinery, 'things which you could see and kick' are gone. Consequently, if the business community and the economy in general are to continue to enjoy sustainable growth we must pay far greater attention in the future to maintaining and developing our stock of human and natural assets than has traditionally been the case. If we are to be successful it is essential that environmental problems should not be seen in isolation but placed in the context of the wider debate on corporate governance.

The impact of social responsibility and environmental issues on management accounting

In this section we consider how social responsibility factors and environmental factors can be incorporated into management accounting systems, with particular reference to investment appraisal and budgeting. Gray *et al.* (1993) carried out a survey that suggested that less than 40% of large UK companies have any environmental factors built into their financial-investment appraisal process, and less than 20% had environmental issues built into their budgeting systems. They also found that in only a minority of large companies are the accountants and accounting systems closely involved with central environmental questions as they relate to the company. One company which does this is the Body Shop. Burrit and Lehman (1995) discuss that company's evaluation of the investment appraisal of a wind farm for power generation. They conclude that 'environmental accountants can provide practical assistance through the disclosure of qualitative, attention directing facets of investment decision-making as part of the accountability process' (Burrit and Lehman 1995: 170).

While individual organisations are now developing different forms of environmental performance targets, their integration with the traditional accounting systems is still somewhat rare. Table 16.2 provides one such illustration, a voluntary list of performance indicators adopted by the UK chemical industry.

So long as performance indicators are kept separate from the more traditional financial criteria, the latter can always be expected to dominate when it comes to

Table 16.1	A policy for management and the environment

Management should:

- Recognise its obligations to owners, employees, suppliers, customers, users, society and the environment.
- Appoint directors or managers with responsibilities that include environmental issues.
- Educate and train all employees in environmental excellence.
- Make the most effective use of all natural resources and safe energy sources for the benefit of the organisation and the overall public interest.
- Promote the use of sustainable resources and minimise the use of finite resources.
- Reduce the amount of waste, avoid harmful pollution and find ways of reprocessing or converting waste materials into useful products and safely disposing of the residue.
- Actively seek to restore and protect the biosphere.
- Reduce environmentally related risks.
- Market products, services and processes which create the minimum environmental damage.
- Be willing to exercise influence and skill for the benefit of the society within which the organisation operates.
- Ensure that all public communications are true and unambiguous, with full disclosure of environmental, health and safety issues.
- Develop economic and financial models, where appropriate, which include the full cost compensation of damage or restoration to the environment.

Source: Lester (1992: 14).

evaluating performance. One key issue of concern to organisations is that it is invariably far easier to identify social responsibility impact cost than it is to identify benefit (environmental, financial or otherwise). However, this is not always the case, Eco Tec (1991) have reported that control of pollution costs in the quarrying and cement and in the paper and pulp industries resulted in savings of at least 7% of gross costs. Coopers & Lybrand, Deloitte (1992: 7) have also reported that:

> Although there are many other pressures at the moment on businesses of all sizes, those companies that take the trouble to investigate their environmental performance, and then start to make improvements, will gain a significant long-term advantage over their less-aware competitors. Businesses which are slow off the mark are likely to find it increasingly difficult to market their products, dispose of waste, obtain insurance, attract finance, keep within a new and much enhanced legal framework and recruit and retain the best staff.

Earlier in this book, we discussed the basic principles of investment appraisal and recognised that while, theoretically, there is one preferred basis, there are in practice a number of practical considerations that also need to be considered. Similarly, there are a number of problems concerning the incorporation of environmental and other social responsibility issues into investment decisions. Remember too that investment decisions are not solely concerned with new venture opportunities; the majority of such decisions actually relate to day-to-day operational issues such as the replacement of plant and equipment or the decision to invest in a particular research and development project. As would have been apparent from our earlier discussions, investment techniques such as ARR and payback have a tendency to favour short-term, less risky investment opportunities. When one considers the prospect of additional social-impact costs and the fact that benefits might be longer-term rather than shorter-term in coming and even less tangible to measure, it is easy to appreciate that

Table 16.2	Voluntary performance indicators adopted by the UK chemical industry

Health and safety
- fatalities
- non-fatal major accidents diseases
- accidents in relation to man-hours

Environment
- amount of 'special waste'
- discharges of 'red list' substances
- site specific data expressed in an 'environmental index'

Distribution
- number of transport incidents in relation to million tonne miles

Energy
- energy consumption per tonne of product

Complaints
- number of complaints made by public and regulators

Source: Adapted from *KPMG European Environment Briefing Note* (Winter 1991–2: 11).

the more traditional investment appraisal approaches have discouraged consideration of these issues. However, that is starting to change since environmental pressures (in the forms of legislation, technological development, societal attitudes, government regulations, etc.) now mean that management can no longer avoid such considerations. To this end, all organisations should always consider an environmental investment checklist such as that presented in Table 16.3.

Some organisations do take this response to environmental issues very seriously. An often quoted example is that of Alcan, where all capital expenditure proposals must include an environmental impact statement. Managers need to involve their accountants in such discussions; to do otherwise will lead to environmental considerations remaining marginalised.

When it comes to budgeting, Gray *et al.* (1993) found that lower than 15% of accountants in large UK companies had any explicitly environmental factors built into their budgeting process, and only another 4% had any plans to do so. Perhaps this is because a response to social responsibility accounting is not built into most organisations' appraisal systems. As Asher has aptly observed (Asher 1980: quoted in Chechile and Carlisle 1991: 54), there is a dilemma well known throughout management accounting:

> When managers see that their execution of socially responsible policies and programs is evaluated in promotional and compensation decisions, along with performance in meeting familiar profit, cost and productivity goals, they will believe and they will be motivated. For obvious and valid reasons middle managers concentrate their attention and skill on the accomplishment of performance objectives for which they know they are held responsible. They approve responsibility in terms of two familiar criteria. The first is what is measured and the second is what is rewarded.

The message is obvious: not only must social impact and environmental criteria be seen to be explicitly recognised in post-evaluation management reviews, it must also form part of the performance reward system. Table 16.4 is from a Chartered Institute of Management Accountants 1990 research study, and illustrates a useful list of action

Table 16.3	Ten-point checklist for more environmentally sensitive investment appraisal

1   Environmentally screen all investments.
2   Reconsider costs.
3   Reconsider benefits.
4   Reconsider the criteria applied.
5   Reconsider the possible options considered.
6   Consider the opportunity costs.
7   Reconsider the time horizon.
8   Reconsider the discount rate.
9   Consider the 'valuation of externalities'.
10 Consider sustainable costs.

Source: Gray *et al.* (1993: 160).

points for accountants and managers to consider in order to make their organisation more aware of a number of basic environmental issues.

The impact of social responsibility and environmental issues on external financial reporting

There have been numerous studies, both within the UK and elsewhere, that have reviewed the social responsibility and environmental disclosure policies of corporations and other forms of reporting entities. Guthrie and Parker (1989) undertook a

Table 16.4	Recommended action points

A management accountant, or indeed any other executive in a company, reading this report will quickly register possible action points. A checklist is set out below in the form of questions to be asked about any company. Some of them will not apply. For others, a positive response will be indicative of action already in hand. It is recommended that everyone should go through the questions after reading the report. There will be few cases where no possibilities to take positive steps emerge. Where action is indicated, it is vital that it is initiated.

In the context of your company ask the following questions and ensure answers are forthcoming:

1   Do we consistently monitor company practices and performance in terms of effects on the environment?
2   Do we systematically check that all public references to the company are picked up, particularly those with environmental dimensions?
3   Do we have a positive, proactive policy in respect of publicising positive environmental actions and policies?
4   Are all our company vehicles currently run on lead-free fuel?
5   For any that are not, can they be adjusted? If not, replacement should be considered.
6   Is the presence of catalytic converters taken into account when setting our policy for purchase/leasing of company cars? Is it possible to retrofit catalytic converters to any cars already in the fleet?
7   How large is our electricity bill and how is it built up? What is the largest constituent?
8   How can we make the use of lighting and heating more efficient without losses in its effectiveness?
9   Is a combined heat and power scheme feasible for our factory or office block?
10 Where and how soon can we set up schemes to recycle paper?
11 What other materials do we use in quantities that are sufficient to initiate collection schemes? How about cans or glass?
12 Do we already use recycled stationery or paper products? If so, what scope is there to extend the range? If recycled stationery is not in use, why not? Are we aware of the available range and quality of such recycled products?
13 Do we know what environmental audits are about? If not, how soon can we obtain information, particularly copies of two basic publications? If we are familiar with such audits, when will we be undertaking one?

Source: Chartered Institute of Management Accountants (1990).

comparative analysis of corporate social disclosure practices in the UK, the USA and Australia. The annual reports of the 50 largest listed companies in each country for the year 1983 were reviewed for evidence of disclosure relating to the environment, energy, human resources, products, community involvement and 'other'. The authors found that the mean corporate social disclosure in Australia (0.70 pages) was relatively low when compared to the USA (1.26 pages), while UK firms provided, on average, 0.89 pages of information. In relation to environmental disclosures, these authors found no company provided negative information about its activities. Within this survey it is perhaps worth saying a few more words about the UK data. Only two categories of information scored highly with UK companies, these being human resources (98%) and community involvement (96%). For other categories the scores were modest, with 14% for the environment, 10% for products and a miserly 2% for energy. The popularity of human resources and community involvement as disclosure categories is attributed by Guthrie and Parker (1989) to the fact that these were legal requirements. For example, companies must disclose information on numbers employed, remuneration and related benefits of dividends, etc.

Touche Ross Management Consultants (1990) conducted an in-depth survey into attitudes towards environmental issues on the part of 32 major UK companies. The survey indicated that, whereas more than half the companies studied claimed to devote some coverage, only a few dealt with the issues in any depth. As with the previous study, it was found that issues relating to human resources and community involvement rated far higher than those related to environmental issues. Gray *et al.* (1993) have summarised a number of general themes that have emerged from empirical research into the extent to which companies produce social responsibility information. This work is summarised in Table 16.5.

Roberts (1992) notes that the only European country with any specific disclosure requirements in the area of environmental impact is Norway. The Norwegian Enterprise Act 1989 requires corporations to include in the directors' report information on emission levels, contamination, and details of measures both planned and actually performed by the corporation with the objective of cleaning up the environment. Sadly, with few exceptions, the response of Norwegian corporations has been to provide brief statements that all relevant legislation has been complied with rather

Table 16.5 Conclusions from UK business/environment surveys
1 A significant minority of companies still fail to recognise the environment as a major business factor.
2 Not all companies recognise that the environment will increase in importance.
3 Between 20% and 50% of companies do not have environmental responsibility at bottom level.
4 About half of British companies still have no environmental policy.
5 There is widespread doubt about and resistance to environmental disclosure.
6 The majority of companies have not undertaken any environmental audit.
7 The principal motivation for taking environmental issues seriously is equally divided between legislation and personal, social familial or public opinion.
8 The primary areas of response are energy management, waste management, lead-free petrol and the use of recycled paper.
9 Investment appraisal is still conducted without environmental criteria.

Source: Gray *et al.* (1993: 35).

than the disclosure of detailed quantitative information. While acknowledging that there are generally increasing levels of disclosure across Europe, she recognises (Roberts 1992: 165) that much environmental disclosure remains generally voluntary:

> This means that corporations have almost complete discretion in deciding what information to provide and the form that the disclosure should take. This gives them the opportunity to present their activities in the best possible light by the judicious choice of what information to disclose and the reporting format used.

Few companies, it seems, are brave enough to follow the policy of Norsk Hydro of Norway, which states: 'We believe that the public has a right to information, and there is nothing that we want to hide. If we have a problem, it is also in our interest that it is brought to full public view.'

Jupe (1994, 1997) looked at the annual reports of large listed UK companies and found that the majority of disclosures were in the non-statutory sections of the report, but that there was an increasing trend of disclosure. However, he points out that these disclosures are selective, emphasising what might be seen as 'good' environmental performance, with a dearth of reports of failure. Again, most of the information disclosed is non-quantitative, and could be viewed as public relations type information. However, some progress does seem to be being made, and this is demonstrated by analyses of the reports submitted for the annual ACCA Environmental Reporting Awards.

The impact of social responsibility and environmental issues on external audit

Despite a Gallup survey commissioned by Coopers and Lybrand in 1990, which suggested that 58% of financial directors felt it would be useful for their auditors to comment on how satisfactory their company's management information systems and processes were in respect of environmental issues, social audit largely remains the prerogative of consumer and other pressure groups. In the UK social audits have been carried out by, among others, the Consumers' Association, Social Audit Ltd and Counter Information Services.

Gray *et al.* (1993) have reviewed the contributions of each of these three bodies. They note that commercial pressures in the late 1980s reduced the campaigning dimension of the Consumers' Association, leading it to focus narrowly upon product cost and efficiency. Social Audit Ltd's activities also faded in the 1980s but some of its earlier work can be found in *Social Audit Quarterly*. Counter Information Services was a radical group that referred to itself as a Marxist collective of journalists. Throughout the 1970s it targeted a number of prominent companies. For example, its report on Rio Tinto Zinc (RTZ) contained a number of serious observations, usually drawn from the *Ecologist* magazine, about the environmental performance of RTZ in general and one of its sites in particular.

Most commentators would agree that the 'social audit movement' is, was and remains, a largely diffuse and intermittent activity undertaken by groups that come and go.

Conclusion

There is a growing interest in corporate social and environmental reporting, not just from the well-established pressure groups, and there is some evidence that larger companies, in particular, are responding to this. The difficulty remains that such responses are still largely voluntary and unquantified. There is also the ongoing debate about broader corporate governance issues and the rights to information of the various stakeholders associated with corporations. Thus, while the indications of change are at least positive, it would not do to be over optimistic about the pace of such change. Perhaps changes in legislation are needed, in parallel with the development of explicit reporting standards for social and environmental reporting.

Chapter review

For various reasons, managements need to pay far greater attention to the increasing importance of social responsibility and environmental accounting. Those who support these moves see them in terms of a broader level of accountability owed by organisations and those who manage them to society as a whole. The importance of this area of discussion is revisited in the final chapter as part of the growing wider debate on corporate governance.

Further reading

For those new to this area we would suggest three useful books. The first is Estes's classic work Corporate Social Accounting (1976). Although published in 1976, it provides an excellent overview of how social accounting has been and may be applied in corporations, whether profit-seeking or not for profit. Rob Gray *et al.'s Accounting for the Environment* was published in 1993 and remains a popularly quoted reference for environmental accounting issues. Finally, we would suggest Dave Owen's *Green Reporting* (1992) as a text that provides the fundamental challenge to managers and accountants in the 1990s. It is a practical handbook that draws together the emerging issues in the environmental and social spheres, and addresses them in the context of that major medium of communication, the company report. Reference could also usefully be made to journals such as *Social and Environmental Reporting*.

Questions and exercises

As these questions are all of an investigative nature, no guide notes are provided.

1   For a company with which you are familiar, read the latest annual report and list as many references as you can to social responsibility issues. Consider whether these references are there purely because of legal requirements or because of other reasons.

2   Using the 12 points listed in Table 16.1, interview either (a) a small group of managers in the same organisation, or (b) a cross-company group of managers to solicit their views to the issues raised. What is your response to their replies?

3   Using the approach adopted in Table 16.1, attempt to develop some environmental performance indicators for an industry you are familiar with. To whom would these be most useful and why?

4   To what extent do you agree with the quotation from Owen (1992: 22) included in the introduction to this chapter? Can you give any examples to support or refute Owen's argument?

5   Suggest ways in which companies might be required to disclose greater information on environmental and other social responsibility performance, both in corporate annual reports and by any other forms of accountability you may consider useful.

6   One area of social responsibility covers employees, 'the human assets' of the enterprise. Discuss what issues of accountability and disclosure arise here, and what aspects of human assets might be routinely measured and reported (like other accounting information).

7   It has been suggested that companies report on environmental and social performance only when they have 'good news' to report. How might society ensure that there is full and objective reporting of such performance?

8   Some academics have suggested that 'human assets' (including aspects such as training and sculling) should be valued, or capitalised, and included in the financial balance sheet. Discuss the theoretical and practical arguments for and against this suggestion.

9   If you agree that most managers respond strongly only to performance objectives which they know about, which they understand, which are measurable and measured, and which affect their managerial performance assessment and rewards, then discuss how best to involve managers in achieving corporate environmental and other social responsibility objectives.

Supply chain management 17

Chapter preview

The focus of this chapter is how managers can manage their supply chain and logistics most effectively. The topics that we cover include:

- Principles and definitions
- Supply chain management accounting
- The financial reporting of the impact of logistics and supply chain management decisions.

Introduction

As never before, our global business environment is becoming more and more competitive, is subject to increasing technological change and has become much more customer orientated. Traditionally vertically integrated businesses have restructured and focused on core business activities, outsourcing to a variety of suppliers. Marketing strategies are changing; companies such as Dell were one of the first to recognise that there was a market for low-cost standardised computers. Like many of their competitors, they source the components for their computers from a wide cross-section of suppliers – cables, circuit boards, micro chips, casings, disc drives, screens, packaging – everything. There are numerous suppliers in this industry sector and year-by-year the pressure on them to provide components at reduced cost and to higher quality standards is ever increasing.

The innovation introduced by Dell was not to set up traditional distribution and sales channels but rather to market and sell direct to the customer, a strategy that was to prove even more cost-effective with the arrival of the Internet. Dell was therefore able to configure and assemble every PC to each customers' specification. This strategy also meant that, as technology and customers' preferences changed, Dell was not going to be left with millions of dollars worth of PC stocks that could become rapidly obsolete.

Retail giants such as Wal-Mart and Target aggressively changed the nature of their industry sector by pioneering supply chain practices such as bar-coding and cross-docking. A cross-docking operation is a flow-through warehousing solution designed to keep inventory at minimum levels, reduce turnaround times and to reduce distribution costs. Multiple suppliers deliver to a central warehouse, these loads are broken down, mixed with other products, re-loaded and shipped to the retail outlets. The standard set is that this cycle of operations happens within a 48-hour period. Cross-docking is a process that consolidates and stages inventory so that customer service levels can be raised while production and transportation economies of scale are obtained. As Fawcett *et al.* (2007: 189) have noted:

> In the 1980s, economic globalisation and the arrival of hugely successful Japanese companies such as Nippon Steel, Sony, and Toyota pressured US and European manufacturers to cut costs. The Japanese 'kieretsu', or buyer/supplier network, provided Japanese companies a competitive edge. Toyota and Honda relied on suppliers for approximately 80 per cent of a car's value. Sole sourcing arrangements with certified suppliers were often used. American carmakers, by contrast, maintained control of the production process, relying on suppliers for about 30 per cent of the assembled car .... The Japanese business model yielded superior quality matched by a US$2,000 per vehicle cost advantage, enabling Toyota and Honda to capture market share. This competitive disparity led US and European managers to rethink the desirability of arms-length, adversarial buyer-supplier relationships.

In all industry sectors, smart managers are looking for collaborative relationships up and downstream that deliver cost savings and flexibility as markets change in the never-ending quest to gain further market share and improve customer satisfaction. This recognition that the management of business suppliers, or intermediate customer relationships, was key to reducing costs across the chain of activities and operations from supply, through to process and distribution, to the ultimate consumer of the product or service, has led to the development of the concept of *supply chain management*.

In this chapter we discuss the importance that supply chain management is having on business practices and how such long-term collaborative relationships can benefit from information provided by management accounting techniques.

Principles and definitions

Supply chain management is a an approach to value adding at each stage of the supply network, a network that increasingly involves a number of independent, yet closely coordinated, players. The value a supply chain generates is the difference between what the final product or service is worth to the end consumer, or customer, and the effort the supply chain expends in filling the end customer's order. The Institute of Supply Management defines supply chain management as the:

> ... design and management of seamless, value-added processes across organisational boundaries to meet the real needs of the end customer.

Supply chain management, as a discipline, can be seen as an extension of logistics management. Christopher (2005: 4) defines logistics as the:

> ... process of strategically managing the procurement, movement and storage of materials, parts and finished inventory (and the related information flows) through the organization and its marketing channels in such a way that the current and future profitability are maximized through the cost-effective fulfilment of orders. Logistics is essentially a planning orientation and framework that seeks to create a single plan for the flow of product and information through a business.

His view is that supply chain management essentially builds upon this framework by seeking to develop strategies that achieve linkage and coordination between the processes of other entities in the pipeline, namely the chain of suppliers and customers, and the organisation itself. Successful supply chain management is about the management of relationships that leads to a high degree of cooperation and trust between the various internal and external players. It is an approach that attempts to break down the traditional arm's-length, often adversarial, approach to business relationships. Such an approach usually leads to the pooling of information and resources, often in terms of pooling manpower, assets and technologies.

One such approach, noted by Christopher (2005: 203) is the concept of 'Co-Managed Inventory'. The traditional business practice is that customers place orders with their suppliers; but this has a couple of distinct inefficiencies. Firstly, the supplier has no advanced warning of requirements and, despite all best efforts at trying to forecast demand usually carries unnecessary levels of safety stocks. Secondly, the supplier often has to face periods of unexpected short-term demand for products that result in frequent changes in production and distribution schedules, and leads to additional costs.

Such conditions can also lead to stock-out situations that impact on customer service and satisfaction. An alternative approach is to have the vendor managing inventory. This is possible when the customer shares information with the vendor. This information relates to the current level of sales, current on-hand inventory, and any details about forthcoming marketing activities, such as special promotions. It is then the supplier's responsibility to maintain the customer's inventory within specified upper and lower limits. The customer benefits because inventory levels can be significantly reduced and the risk of stock-outs is also significantly reduced. In this process it is also usually the case that the customer does not pay for inventory until just after it has been used or sold, so there are also significant savings in the required level of short-term working capital.

There are also significant advantages to the supplier because of the direct access to information on real demand, usually transmitted through Electronic Data Interchange (EDI) or web-based systems. The supplier is clearly better able to plan and schedule production and distribution, which in turn leads to better asset utilisation, a reduction in safety stocks, cost reductions, and, in turn, improved downstream relationships with its suppliers. EDI allows companies to place instantaneous, paperless orders with suppliers who are required to have a dedicated EDI link. Web-based solutions, on the other hand, require no dedicated solutions, only that both parties are linked to the Internet, which is a public channel.

Supply chain management has led to the development of other enabling technologies, such as enterprise resource planning (ERP) systems. ERP systems provide real-time tracking and global visibility of information that allows for intelligent decisions to be made. SAP, Peoplesoft, Oracle, JD Edwards, and Baan are some of the major

ERP developers. Whereas ERP systems show a company what is going on, there is also a higher order of technology supply chain management software which helps a company decide what it should do. One of the market leaders in this area is i2 Technologies.

Figure 17.1 provides a simple illustration of a supply chain network and Table 17.1 provides a succinct summary of how the concept of the supply chain changes a manager's perspective of key business decisions. Fawcett *et al.* (2007) believe that there are four decisions areas of strategy that supply chain managers must assess differently from the more conventional managers. The first of these decision areas is 'environment'. By scanning the environment effectively and then building the right supply chain team, these authors believe that important advantages, in terms of global market share, can be achieved. The second area is in the pooling or sharing of 'resources' by members of the supply chain. Some companies achieve benefits in this area by assisting suppliers to improve their production processes. Some suppliers to retailers manage the in-store inventory. Some manufacturers invite their suppliers to assist in new product design. The third area is in the area of defining competitive 'objectives'. As the only person who puts money into the chain is the end customer, it is vital that each company in the chain understands the end customer's expectations that up-stream suppliers feel that they are not supplying parts but are helping build the end product. The fourth area recognises that strategic advantage can be achieved in the supply chain by collaboratively improving information flows and providing feedback so that efficiency can be approved.

Supply chain management accounting

Those companies that adopt supply chain management look to achieve effective cost management decisions. Whilst traditional accounting systems tend to focus on product costs, relying upon fairly arbitrary methods of allocating shared and indirect costs, supply chain management tends to focus on measuring and monitoring customer costs. With supply chain management there is a different focus on cost accounting, one that attempts to concentrate on value-adding cost drivers and the elimination of non-value-adding cost drivers.

This can be simply illustrated by reference to the strategic cost management approach adopted by low cost short-haul airlines such as Southwest Airlines in the

| Figure 17.1 | Illustration of a Supply Chain Network |

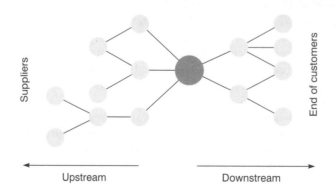

(ADAPTED FROM CHRISTOPHER, 2005, P. 5)

USA and Ryanair in Europe. Both airlines have adopted a similar strategy for competing against the major airlines, one that eliminates non-value-adding cost drivers from the design of their respective supply chains. These include:

- Use of secondary airports in order to save or eliminate landing charges, as well as achieving the benefits of reduced airport traffic and congestion to reduce time on the ground. Ryanair has a target turn around time of 25 minutes between landing and takeoff.

- Standardisation of aircraft type, in both cases using the Boeing 737, thereby securing efficiencies in the terms of the utilisation of on-board crews, maintenance, spare parts management, etc. Ryanair has achieved significant savings in maintenance by instituting relatively simple measures such as not having seats that recline or installing window blinds.

- Elimination of different classes of service and in-flight meal services, other than a basic pay snack service.

- Promoting on-line ticket purchasing and self-ticketing at check-in in order to further reduce costs.

The activities of airlines such as Southwest and Ryanair on short-haul routes have caused the major airlines to re-evaluate how they operate, and the beneficiary is the customer.

Table 17.1	SCM's influence on the four decision areas of strategy	
Strategy decision area	**Common strategic posture**	**Supply chain enabled perspective**
Environment	• React to environmental changes – view them as a threat • Independent environmental scanning.	• View change as a challenge and an opportunity. • Leverage relationships and technology to anticipate, define, and respond to changes in the competitive environment.
Resources	• Manage company-specific resources. • Buy the best inputs available. • Maintain good supplier relationships.	• Develop unique, boundary-spanning capabilities. • Develop and manage supplier capabilities. • Leverage customer resources when possible. • Build world-class supply chain team.
Objectives	• Deliver customer satisfaction. • Achieve sustainable competitive advantage. • Achieve profitability. • Achieve growth in stock price.	• Help the supply chain satisfy end-customer needs. • Help first-tier customers become more competitive. • Build continuous-improvement-based advantage. • Achieve sustained profitability.
Feedback	• Measure internal activity performance. • Monitor supplier performance. • One-way flow of information from customers to suppliers.	• Measure process and supply chain performance. • Share performance data to drive learning. • Two-way information and idea sharing with both customers and suppliers.

(*Source*: Fawcett *et al*. 2007, Table 1.1)

Supply chain and logistics management is about the management of activities across a series of pipelines, both internal and external. It is therefore desirable to have accounting systems in place that can measure the relevance costs so that overall financial performance can be assessed from an end-user perspective. This can lead to some cost reductions, but more importantly it leads to better cost-effectiveness. Traditional costing ignores cost trade-offs in the supply chain. An analysis of the cost chain might reveal that if total costs were to increase, thereby offering better end customer service, sales revenue might, as a consequence, increase to more than compensate for this cost increase.

A traditional costing approach would make it difficult to identify the extent to which particular trade-offs might be seen as beneficial. Traditional costing tends to be a 'black box' approach to monitoring costs. For example, a production manager might change production schedules to improve production efficiency and reduce the unit cost of production, but fail to realise that this has led to a diminution of customer satisfaction because this change has led to fluctuations in finished stock availability to the point that some customers have switched to competitor brands. What made sense to the production manager failed to take account of the company-wide ramifications. Traditional management accounting practices with regard to budgeting and standard-setting has tended to lead to what Christopher (2005: 97) terms as the 'compartmentalisation of company accounts'.

Supply chain management accounting is very much focused on measuring the incremental cost difference that occurs when there are changes in the supply chain. The introduction of the cross-docking warehousing system, discussed above, is a case in point, which led to a reduction not only in warehousing costs but additionally in transport costs, and the work capital requirements as stock levels were reduced. Traditional costing methods tend to concentrate on cost inputs, whereas the requirements of supply chain management require approaches that focus on costs attributable to activities undertaken across the pipeline of activities. Martinez Ramos (2004) provides a useful overview of the management accounting techniques most suitable for supply chain management. He identifies seven possible solutions, together with providing better accounting information for the management of supply chains:

- *Open-book accounting* – whereby the supplier shares internal accounting data with the buyer in order to identify critical activities that, jointly resolved, could lead to subsequent cost reductions. This is therefore a systematic process of sharing cost data between two legally independent organisations, a process of intra-corporate cost accounting. Mouritsen *et al.* (2001) would argue this process makes it easier to identify key cost drivers and that such information can be used to reorganise the entire supply chain, including the processes of business partners. Typical of such a process is the Japanese *keiretsu* corporate network where many suppliers are focused around a predominant specialised industry partner. It is a tradition in Japanese companies that suppliers provide the firm doing the assembly with strategic cost information. Munday (1992) found that 65% of all Japanese customers, in comparison to only 44% of US and 39% of British companies, expected information about the cost structure of products and other additional information on certain aspects of production. Open-book costing is also known as 'open-book transparency'. Such a process relies on trust, with a downside for the supplier if the buyer uses this data to press for further price reductions not linked to the agreed suggestions on how to reduce costs. Whilst this is likely to remain a risk for the supplier, the economic pressure from purchasers for such information is likely to intensify in the future.

- *Target costing* – which consists of three main processes: (i) deciding on the features of the product or service and estimating its selling price from them; (ii) establishing the desired profit target and then calculating the target cost; and (iii) achieving the previously established target cost. The target cost is required to cover all the company's producing and procuring costs of the product or service. Again this is a costing concept used very effectively by a number of leading Japanese manufactures. Lee (1994) considers that target costing, with its emphasis on market share and product leadership, is similar in some respects to activity based costing in that it relates profit to return on sales as opposed to return on investment, thereby allowing the company greater flexibility in production management and in production development. Increasingly once a product is designed and developed there is a limit to how much cost-cutting companies can do in the manufacturing stage. Target costing is therefore used and is most effective in the product development and design stage of the supply chain. Given a target price and a supplier's required return on sales, the question to be answered by target costing is what should a particular product cost, not what does it cost. To illustrate, suppose that a supplier was offered a contract to supply 10 000 items at $50. Further suppose that the supplier has a target return on sales of 30%, or $15 per unit in this case. Then this would suggest that the allowable unit cost is $35. If the supplier's management accountant estimated a cost per unit of $40 then there is a review of the costing structure and associated manufacturing processes to try to drive down the unit cost to the target of $35 as opposed to $40. If costs cannot be reduced by the full $5, management have to decide whether the contract is still worth undertaking for a lower target return on sales.

- *Kaizen costing* – an approach which is similar to target costing, but focuses on reducing costs during the manufacturing stage of the total pipeline of a product's development. It is based on the premise that after a product is introduced customers will tend to demand an increase in value over time from a combination of greater performance and lower cost. Indeed, the business plan or agreement between the supplier and purchaser may include a clause that anticipates an annual incremental reduction in cost. Whilst the cost reduction is, in effect, set by the market, the challenge for the supplier is to determine where such cost reductions are likely to come from. Some costs, for example, might come from new manufacturing methods. Other reductions might be anticipated once the production facility has settled down. Williamson (1997) notes that, in Japan, kaizen costing systems are run separately from the standard cost system, as the two systems have different uses. Standard costing systems are more geared towards financial accounting and reporting and monitoring performance against established standards. By contrast, kaizen costing drives changes in the way products are manufactured, which includes activities and reporting requirements that fall outside the standard cost system. Kaizen costing in Japan is typically found in the electrical, precision equipment and machinery industries, including the automotive industry. It is an approach being increasingly adopted by Western firms.

- *Activity based costing* – introduced in Chapter 5, is a technique whose origins date back to the US manufacturing sector in 1970s and 1980s and was first clearly defined by Kaplan and Bruns (1987). Instead of using broad brush approaches to allocate overhead costs to direct costs, ABC seeks to identify cause and effect relationships to objectively assign such costs by seeking out the various *cost drivers* in the supply chain. Overhead allocation is an extremely important issue when one considers that this represents around 37% and 66% of total costs in manufacturing and service firms respectively (Develin 1999). Lambert *et al.* (1998) categorise the major logistics costs in the supply chain as being inventory carrying costs; procurement costs; order processing costs; transportation costs and warehousing costs. Lin *et al.* (2001) discuss a seven-step strategy for the implementation of ABC for supply chain management. No costing system is perfect, however, and the ABC approach, by seeking to analyse the major resource-consuming activities in the supply chain, does assist in bringing the true costs of operation to management attention.

- *Balanced scorecard* – an approach that combines a mix of financial as well as non-financial measures, a concept focusing not only on financial outcomes but on the human issues that drive those outcomes. It is an approach attributed to Kaplan and Norton (1992). The balance scorecard is a management system, not a measurement system that assists companies to clarify their vision and strategy and translate them into action. The balanced scorecard views an organisation's vision and strategy from four perspectives: the learning and growth perspective; the business process perspective; the customer perspective and the financial perspective. The philosophy of this approach is that you cannot improve what you cannot measure. Metrics are therefore developed based on the priorities of the company's strategic plan. These provide the key business drivers and criteria for metrics that management need in order to direct the company's strategy. Performance criteria across a range of activities are produced, including: customer, product and service performance, operations, market, competitive comparisons, supplier, employee-related, and cost and financial. A search on the web will reveal a number of organisations who have developed the balanced scorecard concept for companies to adapt into their own organisation and supply chain.

- *Value chain analysis* – which breaks up the elements in the supply chain from the sourcing of basic raw materials through to the receipt of a product or service by the end customer in order to understand the behaviour of costs and the sources of differentiation. The concept of the value chain was introduced by Porter (1985). The primary value chains are seen as: inbound logistics; operations; outbound logistics; marketing and sales; and service. These activities are supported by the infrastructure of the firm (organisational structure, control systems, culture, etc.); human resource management (recruiting, training and development, compensation, etc.); technological capacity; and procurement strategy. The value chain model seeks to gain competitive advantage by cost advantage; minimising costs through value-adding activities and market differentiation; performing better than competitors. Porter identified ten drivers related to value chain activities: economies of scale; learning; capacity utilisation; linkages among activities; interrelationships among business units; degree of vertical integration; timing of market entry; company policy of cost or differentiation; geographical location; and institutional factors such as regulation, taxes, etc. A company develops a cost advantage by controlling these drivers better than their competitors. These drivers are not necessarily all derived in-house, some may be outsourced, with the company specialising in only two or three areas.

- *Total cost of ownership* – a structured approach for understanding the total costs associated with the acquisition and use of a given item or service over a period of time. This is an approach originally developed for the measurement of life-cycle assets with significant maintenance and operating costs. A total cost of operation statement includes not only the cost of purchase but all aspects associated with future use and maintenance. Costs that include: financing costs; staff training for operation and maintenance; installation; costs associated with failure or outage (planned and unplanned); output penalties; disaster recovery; associated utility costs; decommissioning and so on. In terms of a company's transport distribution fleet, these costs cover purchase, maintenance and sale as a used vehicle. When it comes to the purchase and management of a company's computer systems, the five year cost of ownership can be five to eight times the hardware and software acquisition costs (www.solutionmatrix.com).

Martinez Ramos (2004) suggests that the above techniques lend themselves to further development in order that the dynamics of the supply chain can more easily and relevantly be understood. These techniques, he argues, should lead to new accounting information systems that work across and outside traditional boundaries. However, as previously noted, for such developments to really work there requires a degree of trust between the various parties.

The financial reporting of the impact of logistics and supply chain management decisions

All managers are increasingly aware of the financial dimension of decision making, none more so than the new breed of supply chain managers. Effective supply chain solutions seek to maximise available resources and this inevitably has an impact on the use of both fixed and working capital. One approach considered in this regard is the impact that management decisions can have on the return on investment (ROI) ratio, a key financial indicator, originally discussed in Chapter 15. Recall that the ROI ratio can be broken down into two component ratios:

$$\text{ROI} = \frac{\text{Profit}}{\text{Sales}} \times \frac{\text{Sales}}{\text{Capital employed}}$$

As Christopher (2005: 84) notes:

Typically many companies will focus their attention to drive up ROI, yet it can often be more effective to use the leverage of improved capital turnover to boost ROI.
For example, many successful retailers have long since recognized that very small net margins can lead to excellent ROI if the productivity of capital is high, e.g. limited inventory, high sales per square metre, premises that are leased rather than owned and so on.

Figure 17.2 highlights the major elements determining ROI and the potential for improvement through effective logistics and supply chain management. Christopher (2005) also discusses the impact of logistics on the balance sheet; this is summarised in Figure 17.3. In terms of cash and receivables, of key importance is the imperative to shorten as much as possible the order cycle time, from when a customer places an order to when the goods are delivered, so that the invoice can be issued at the earliest opportunity. Working capital requirements can be significantly reduced through time compression across the various stages of the supply chain. Logistics and supply

Figure 17.2 Major elements that help determine ROI

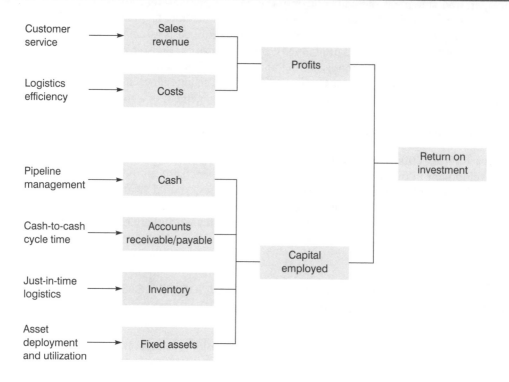

(SOURCE: CHRISTOPHER, 2005, FIGURE 3.2)

Figure 17.3 Logistics and supply chain management

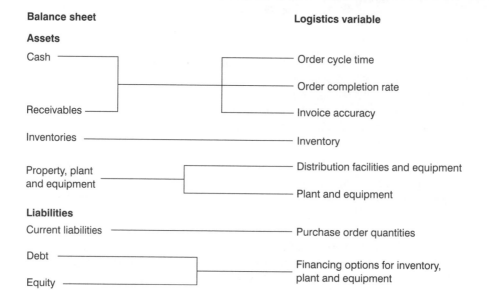

(SOURCE: CHRISTOPHER, 2005, FIGURE 3.3)

chain management policies and strategies clearly also have a material impact on all types of inventory levels and the types and locations of fixed assets (property, plant and equipment). The phasing of supplies to match the total logistics requirements of the system minimises current liabilities. Finally, the balance between debt and equity is also impacted by the various logistical and supply chain management strategies. By leasing, fixed assets can be converted into continuing expenses. Third-party suppliers of warehousing and transport represents a related issue – outsourcing. Such changes remove fixed assets from the balance sheet; that is, reduces fixed asset investment, and has a material impact on the funding requirements of a business.

Conclusion

The increasing recognition of the importance of logistics and supply chain management is having an impact on the type of accounting information managers require. Further work needs to be done to develop new management accounting techniques that meet the information requirements of managers who need to monitor the flow of costs that arise from the various lines in the supply chain. This is an alternative approach to the more traditional management accounting approach centred on input costs and budgets created along internal functional lines. Effective management accounting techniques have the potential to create considerable value for inter-organisational supply chains. Managers also need to recognise that the strategies they adopt for logistics and supply chain management also have a material impact on the way that profit is reported externally and the shape of the balance sheet presented in the annual report and financial accounts.

Chapter review

The goal of supply chain management is to strategically link the end customer, the supply and distribution network, the manufacturing/conversion process and the procurement processes in such a way as to better meet consumer satisfaction whilst, at the same time, seeking to keep costs to a minimum. Increased market share will increasingly go to those companies that have a supply chain superior to those of their competitors. Managers need to master the principles of effective logistics and supply chain management in order to remain competitive.

The need to have the ability to establish long-term relationships with their suppliers, relationships not based on arm's-length arrangements but partnerships based on trust and mutual dependency. Such relationships have demanded new thinking on the sorts of accounting information systems that need to be established in order to provide managers with relevant cost information for decision making. Supply chain management has now evolved beyond a mere cost-reducing business exercise into a core competency and source of competitive advantage for an increasing number of companies in an increasingly competitive global marketplace because of its impact on end customer service.

Further reading

Texts by Christopher (2005), Fawcett *et al.* (2007), Leenders *et al.* (2002) and Chopra and Meindl (2001) provide readers with a full overview of the development of the concept of supply chain management. The article by Martinez Ramos (2004) is a useful source for further references on the development of new techniques for the development of management accounting for supply chain managers.

Questions and exercises

1* Define the term 'supply chain management'. Illustrate the sorts of management initiatives that distinguish this concept from logistics management.

2* Critically review the four decision areas of strategy outlined by Fawcett *et al.* (2007). Describe, with illustrative examples, how supply chain thinking alters a manager's view of each decision area.

3* Use the web to source what you regard as a good example of a company that has a good reputation for implementing the concept of supply chain management. Describe what you consider to be particularly useful illustrations of how this company has used supply chain management to gain competitive advantage.

4 'Supply chain management is about the management of relationships, both internal and external to a company; relationships that require a high degree of cooperation and trust between the various parties'. Discuss.

5 What are the distinctive features that management accounting information systems have to adapt to in order to provide supply chain managers with relevant information with which to control and make business decisions? Why are traditional management accounting practices insufficient for the needs of supply chain managers?

6 By reference to the research paper of Martinez Ramos (2004), research and provide clear definitions of the following management accounting techniques: Open-book accounting; Target Costing; Kaizen Costing, Activity Based Costing; Balanced Score Card; Value Chain Analysis and Total Cost of Ownership.

7 With reference to question 6 above, critically discuss the practical issues associated with these techniques when adapting them to the needs of supply chain managers.

8* Discuss the ways in which logistics and supply chain management can impact on the reporting of financial performance and the balance sheet of companies. Illustrate your answer with relevant examples.

Strategic business accounting

18

Chapter preview

Much of what has been written so far in this text has recognised that managers (should) devote most of their energies to the planning and allocation of resources, and to motivating and controlling people in order to utilise the allocated resources to best effect. Senior management also finds itself involved in shaping and developing the strategic direction of the organisation as a whole.

In this final chapter we consider the importance of accounting in helping with the formulation and implementation of corporate strategy. In doing so, we will draw on some issues previously discussed, but re-emphasise their importance to strategy formulation. We will also introduce a few new accounting focused issues and we will set our overall discussion against the ongoing need for management to assess the organisation's strategic capability in a way that seeks always to 'add value'.

There are four main sections to our discussion. First, we quickly summarise what some authors have termed the four generic approaches to strategy. Second, we consider the importance of accounting to helping shape the strategic direction of an organisation. We then discuss how management can assess the strategic direction of an organisation. This section is in many ways an *audit*, in the broadest sense of the term, which should assist managers in reconsidering the value of some of the discussion in earlier chapters. Finally, we review a number of recent developments in management accounting which, taken together are sometimes dignified with the title of 'strategic management accounting'.

The four generic approaches to strategy formulation

In this section we seek to provide those not previously familiar with the literature on corporate strategy with a brief overview in order to place the remainder of our discussion in context. It is a section that summarises the explicit (normative) assumptions that underpin the four basic theories of strategy: classical, processual, evolutionary and systemic. For, as Whittington (1993: 10) reminds us:

> Theories are important. They contain our basic assumptions about key relationships in business life. They tell us what to look out for, what our first steps should be and what to expect as a result of our actions. Saving us from having to go back to first principles at each stage, they are actually short cuts to action. Often these theories are not very explicit or very formal. Whether building from experience or from books, we all tend to have our own private assumptions about how things work, how to get things done.

Each of the four theories to be discussed offers different views about our capacity as managers to think rationally and act effectively. It should be noted that they diverge widely in their implications for strategy formulation. Ultimately it is for each of us to finally decide which basic theory best aligns with our own experiences and needs.

The classical approach

Classicists see profitability as the key goal of any business, and rational planning as the means to achieve it. The economic framework on which this theory is based was mapped out in Chapter 9. It is a theory that states that management best serves the interest of *all* investors by undertaking all productive investment opportunities that yield a return greater than that available on the capital markets. Shareholders, in turn, borrow and lend on the capital markets to produce the cash flows that meet their own personal individual needs. In the 1960s authors such as Ansoff (1965), Chandler (1962) and Sloan (1963) wrote in support of the commitment to profit maximisation. Ansoff is credited with writing the first ever textbook on corporate strategy. He linked his strategic framework to a mix of military practice and normative economics. Chandler defined strategy as: 'The determination of the basic, long-term goals and objectives of an enterprise, and the adoption of courses of action and the allocation of resources necessary for those goals' (Chandler 1962: 13). His is an approach that favours a top-down, planned and rational approach to strategy formulation. It is based on a historical analysis of the development of four large North American corporations.

Sloan, a former president of General Motors (GM), stated that the strategic aim of business is to 'earn a return on capital, and if in any particular case the return in the long run is not satisfactory, the deficiency should be corrected or the activity abandoned' (Sloan 1963: 49). In over four decades with GM, Sloan helped pioneer the return on investment (ROI) criteria, the concept of divisionalised management structures and the separation of policy formulation from day-to-day operational management. More recently other writers, such as Porter (1980), in his industry structure analysis, have continued to favour the classical approach to strategy formulation.

The evolutionary approach

Proponents of the evolutionary approach see the attainment of a strategic framework as a dangerous delusion. There is much less confidence in senior management's ability to plan and act in a rational manner. They expect markets to secure profit maximisation and managers to be rational optimisers in a 'law of the jungle' view of the business world where only the best performers survive. As Henderson, founder of the Boston Consulting Group, (1989: 143) observes:

> Classical economic theories of competition are so simplistic and sterile that they have been less contributions to understanding than obstacles. These theories postulate rational, self-interest behaviour by individuals who interact through market exchanges in a fixed and static legal system of property and contracts…. Darwin is probably a better guide to business competition than economists are.

Hannan and Freeman (1988) support this proposition. They believe that the 'organizational selection process' is one that favours organisations with relatively inert structures, ones that cannot change their strategic direction and organisational structure at the same pace as their environments change. Williamson advises managers to seek always to be cost-effective and 'not to get distracted from the basics' (1991: 76). As Whittington (1993: 22) sums it up, the evolutionary advice is that it is better to let the environment do the strategy selection, not the managers.

The processual approach

Most processualists see strategy formulation as all about satisfying and settling for less than the optimal. They see the classicists as naive idealists, and though they share some common thinking with the evolutionists they are far less confident about the environment's ability to foster strategy selection.

To Cyert and March (1963) the notion of 'rational economic man' is a fiction, in practice, people are only 'boundedly rational'. By this they mean that managers are unable to handle more than a few factors at a time. Managers do not search unlimitedly for new information; rather, they are prone to accept the first satisfactory option that presents itself and they are easily biased by the information presented in support of that option. Organisations represent coalitions of individual managers, who each contribute their own personal objectives and value systems to the organisation. Managers bargain between themselves to arrive at a set of common goals more or less acceptable to them all. Bargaining involves compromise, which is just human nature. Strategic formulation is the result of 'political compromise' and has little to do with the concept of profit maximisation. Such an approach is by its very nature conservative, and hence is often slow to recognise the need for change, until some new 'dominant coalition' is recognised. Strategies represent ways in which managers attempt to simplify and bring order to the complex and chaotic daily environment in which our organisations exist.

Mintzberg (1987) proposes the metaphor of strategy as 'craft'. He likens the crafting of strategy to the potter who must use hands and mind together to shape the clay into a recognisable form. Crafting strategy is a continuous and adaptive process, with formation and implementation 'inextricably entangled'. Mintzberg argues that managers cannot be smart enough to think through strategy too far in advance. Managers should be honest with themselves and recognise that there is an inevitable logical incrementalism to the process, which will always involve a degree of experimentation and learning. Whittington (1993: 27) summarises the views of the processualists when he states that:

> Focus on the imperfections of organizational and market processes yields at least four conceptions of strategy radically different from the classical perspective: strategy may be a decision-making heuristic, a device to simplify reality into something managers can actually cope with; plans may just be managerial security blankets, providing reassurance as much as guidance; strategy may not precede action, but may only emerge retrospectively, once action has taken place; strategy is not just about carefully cultivating internal competencies. Many of the confident precepts of the Classicists are put into jeopardy; suddenly, it seems that goals are slippery and vague, long-term policy statements, vain delusions, and the separation of formulation from implementation a self-serving top management myth.

Systemic theory

Unlike the evolutionary and processual theorists, systemic theorists do retain some faith in the capacity of management to plan forward and to act effectively in the best interests of their investors. The central tenet of systemic theory is that decision makers are not simply detached, calculating individuals immersed in densely interwoven social systems. Granovetter (1985) suggests that behaviour that may appear irrational to the classicist may not appear so to systemic theorists, who believe that the performance of organisations differs according to the social and economic systems in which they are placed. Different kinds of enterprise structure become feasible and successful in particular social contexts. Hu (1992) has illustrated, for example, how successful multinational companies often have strong domestic roots. Nestle, with 96.5% of its employees outside of its home country, remains firmly in Swiss control by limited foreign shareholding voting rights to 3%. With the exception of Sony, most Japanese companies remain controlled by domestic senior management. As Whittington (1993) notes, the main message of the systemic theorists is that the formulation of strategy must be sociologically sensitive.

These four approaches to strategy offer different advice to management. Their main characteristics are summarised in Table 18.1. An appreciation of these alternative

Table 18.1	The four perspectives on strategy			
	Classic	*Processual*	*Evolutionary*	*Systemic*
Strategy	Formal	Crafted	Efficient	Embedded
Rationale	Profit maximisation	Vague	Survival	Local
Focus	Internal (plans)	Internal (politics/ cognitions)	External (markets)	External (societies)
Processes	Analytical	Bargaining/learning	Darwinian	Social
Key influences	Economics/military	Psychology	Economics/biology	Sociology
Key authors	Chandler	Cyert and March	Hannan and Freeman	Granovetter
	Ansoff	Mintzberg	Williamson	Marris
	Porter	Pettigrew		
Key period	1960s	1970s	1980s	1990s

Source: Whittington (1993).

approaches is useful since individual managers and organisations probably tend, more or less, to follow one of these directions. Managers should also appreciate that, for fairly obvious reasons, accountants by their training tend to see strategy through the eyes of the classicists, and hence their accounting systems tend to be somewhat rigid by conforming to fairly rigid norms.

The importance of the nature of the environment cannot be stressed enough when it comes to determining the organisational structure of a particular company. This structure tends to define the 'style' of management practised and, in turn, has profound influences on the way that accounting information is prepared and used. Table 18.2 provides an outline of environmental influence on organisational structure.

In environments that are simple and static, organisations tend to be more concerned with operational efficiency and their management styles, and accounting systems tend to be mechanistic and centralised. However, in environments that are simple and dynamic there is a real need to increase the extent to which managers are capable of sensing what is going on around them, identifying change and responding to it. A more organic style of management is therefore needed and this applies equally to the type of accounting models that are required. Increased complexity in stable environments is handled by devolving decision responsibility to specialists. At least for operational purposes, they tend to have more decentralised management structures and there is a need for interactive management accounting systems. Finally, where the environment is both complex and dynamic there is a need for speed and flexibility that only organic styles of management can provide; and the level of complexity is such that they must devolve responsibility and authority to specialists who either have a good level of financial management skills or dedicated accounting support.

Strategy evaluation and accounting

From the foregoing debate it is clear that accountants can work positively with managers if both parties are influenced by the underlying philosophy of either the classicist or the systemicist proponents of strategy evaluation. Elsewhere in this text we have examined accounting approaches to both short-term and long-term decisions. We have also recognised, from the outset, that it is cash that keeps organisations 'alive' and viable, and not accounting profit – companies become insolvent when they run out of cash to pay their bills (Chapter 6).

Table 18.2	Environmental influences on organisational structure	
	Stable	**Dynamic**
Complex	Decentralised bureaucratic (e.g. hospitals)	Decentralised organic (e.g. advanced electronics)
Simple	Centralised bureaucratic (e.g. mass production)	Centralised organic (e.g. retailing) *or* decentralised bureaucratic

Source: Adapted, with permission, from Mintzberg (1979: 268).

In this section we reconsider the value that certain accounting approaches can have in assisting managers to determine the strategic direction(s) that they wish to follow. The first issue is that of **added value** (Kay, 1993: 226):

> The creation of added value is governed by two factors – the value of the good or service to the customer and the cost of production to the firm. Added value is the difference between the two. The firm can never appropriate the whole of that added value. As the intensity of the competitive environment increases, prices will bid down the costs of other firms, and added value can only be the result of competitive advantages. In hot wars (i.e. unstable competitive environments), price is driven by the marginal cost of production. In cold wars (i.e. stable economic environments with markets in which firms have adopted compatible repeated game strategies), firms are generally able to earn some of the value of the goods and services they provide.

As Kay goes on to discuss, the costs which are relevant in measuring the value added from a particular productive activity are the **incremental** costs associated with that product or activity. These are the costs that arise from either increasing or decreasing activity as demand either rises or falls. Although every introductory economics textbook stresses the importance of marginal costs, in reality they play little role in business decisions. The cost estimates that form the background to pricing decisions tend to arise as a result of the allocations of accounting costs, in which virtually the whole of the business's expenses are attributed to some product or service. Activities are therefore monitored and driven by reference to their contribution – the amount which they yield over and above the direct (variable) costs associated with them. Most managers and accountants tend to see marginal cost pricing as a recipe for going broke. Recall, in relation to earlier discussions on contribution, that all too often management tends to see too high a proportion of the operational costs as fixed. While this may be true in the short term, it is folly necessarily to presume so into the longer term. In the long term every cost can be varied in line with the scale and operational requirements of the firm.

The more recent promotion of activity-based costing systems (see Chapter 5) can be seen as an approach to bridging the gap between the more mechanical approaches to cost allocation and the measurement of the direct costs associated with particular outputs. Again to quote Kay: 'Building up the structure of costs in this way links the value chain of the firm, the overall added value statement, and the incremental costs associated with individual products' (Kay 1993: 227). This is sound advice; the strategic imperative is to see such a cost structure as setting the basis for a pattern of minimum prices across all markets, with the additional recovery related to the value of products/services to customers/clients, and the state of competition in the variety of markets that exist from time to time.

Managers need also to understand the concept of **market segmentation**. This is particularly so in relation to the provision of services rather than to manufactured goods. Curiously, while from a marketing standpoint segmentation is almost seen as a nuisance – customers insisting that they be treated differently – from an economic perspective this presents an opportunity to enhance profitability and increase sales by distinguishing economic market opportunities and resisting the application of the law of one price. What managers need to appreciate is that market segmentation is a strategic imperative of economic survival. This can be achieved by individual pricing (one-on-one negotiation), group pricing (as often practised in the transport industry) and by product/service proliferation (similar but distinctive products/ services offered in different markets). However, underlying these strategies must be a clear recognition that the price must always cover relevant costs.

Supply-chain management (as discussed in Chapter 17) represents another strategic focus that managers and accountants should pay more attention to. Some writers describe this as either vertical relationships management or the life-cycle approach to product/service delivery. It is a concept which considers the whole supply chain from the sourcing of inputs through to processing and finally to customer delivery. All too often attention is too focused on internal processes. Many large organisations have to deal with too many suppliers and pay scant attention to the importance and mode of service/product delivery. Lateral thinking can radically improve cost reduction throughout all the links in the supply chain. For example, suppliers can be invited to send their personnel on to the shop floor to examine issues of quality and efficiency. Cost savings can then be shared pro rata. In Australia BHP Steel has various of its major suppliers provide personnel to work directly with its workers at identifying cost savings. It has also reduced its suppliers from thousands to only a few hundred by outsourcing some of its supply requirements to 'group' suppliers. As Baversox and Closs (1996) have noted, supply-chain relationships are among the most complex and least understood areas of logistics operations.

The final aspect that needs re-emphasis in this section is that of risk analysis. Again, we have already briefly introduced the contribution of portfolio analysis to the management of risk (Chapter 11). This is not the only approach to be considered. Simulation techniques such as Monte Carlo simulation analysis may also be useful in mapping out various probability-weighted scenarios. Pragmatic solutions such as insurance and the introduction of price-indexation clauses into contracts help to reduce the operational risks faced by both buyers and sellers. Hedging is also another strategy for adding value through contract design. In fact, management often does not spend enough time on good contract design and, while it may consult lawyers, it seldom discusses contract details with accountants. Contracts should be clear as to which party bears which risk. There are two basic principles (Kay 1993) of risk-sharing in contracts. Identifiable risks should be assigned to the party that has more control over them. If both have equal control (or if neither has control) risk should be assigned to whichever of the parties can manage it cheaply, often the larger of the parties. In the automobile industry the assembler invariably takes most of the risk associated with specific input costs. More general economic uncertainties, which neither party can particularly influence, tend to be shared between the parties in proportions that vary according to their current negotiating strength.

Assessing strategic direction

In this section we consider the information requirements that management needs to consider when carrying out a strategic assessment of the organisation. In many ways it is a review reflective of many of the issues earlier in this text. While it is formed around a strategic analysis of a private-sector organisation, those in the public sector will see obvious parallels with their own organisations.

As Kay (1993) has said, successful strategy requires a company to choose the market(s) in which its distinctive capabilities yield the greatest competitive advantage. How can this be achieved? First, it is important to collect appropriate quantitative and qualitative information on your own company, on the industry or sector it is in, and on a range of broader contextual (environmentally related) factors that have an impact on all companies in general. Ellis and Williams (1993) have set out a nine-cell table that defines this set of information needs (see Table 18.3). It should be recognised that there is considerable overlap between the different areas. A broad range of sources can be sought from which to compile this information, including annual reports, the business press, information-retrieval systems (such as FT Profile, Textline and Datastream) and industry/company-sponsored reports and books. It is important to remember that focusing on the non-financial components of the analysis and virtually ignoring the assessment of financial statements will give rise to a distorted picture. The same is also true in reverse, so it is important to ensure a balance in the information collected.

Careful attention should be paid to both the profitability and the cash-flow position of your own company as well as of your competitors. With respect to profitability, management needs to focus on:

- the extent to which turnover and profits/losses have been influenced by the various sectors/units of the company, and whether any of these business sectors/units have been acquired or disposed of during the year;
- significant notes to the accounts that might cover significant provisions and/or contingencies;
- change to or differences between accounting policies – key areas can relate to items such as depreciation, goodwill, pension–fund accounting and brand accounting;

Table 18.3	Key information requirements		
	Assessing strategic direction	*Financial statement analysis*	*Stock market assessment*
Company	1 Identify and assess corporate and business unit strategies, management resources, product market positions, etc.	2 Assess current and future outcomes of the company's strategies – sales, profitability, cash flow, etc.	3 Understand the market assessment and rating of the company
Industry/sector	4 Evaluate competitive forces and relative strengths and strategies of competitors Review key industry drivers and the likely future pattern of industry development	5 Make comparisons with other companies operating the same or similar product markets	6 Compare the company's rating with those of other in companies in the same sector Review performance of the sector against the overall market
Broad context	7 Assess key PEST change agents, i.e. political, economic, social and technological factors	8 Evaluate opportunities for raising funding (debt and equity), likely tax and interest-rate changes, etc.	9 Identify movements in the overall stock market and likely future pattern of share prices

Source: Ellis and Williams (1993).

- the identification of activities which are the key profit drivers and those areas/ units which are under performing;
- its strategies to improve areas of underperformance.

With respect to the company's overall cash position, management needs to focus on:

- assessing the cash-flow statement to see whether it is a generator or user of funds;
- establishing whether funds generated are from trading activities or are a result of restructuring – in both cases the use to which such funds have been put should be reviewed;
- considering whether the position in relation to the use of funds (if the company is a user of funds) has deteriorated or improved over the last 12 months and what has been done to improve matters;
- examining whether additional shares have been issued or borrowed funds raised, and for what purpose;
- identifying activities that are either cash-generators or cash-wasters;
- identifying strategies for maintaining or improving the cash-flow position.

Key financial ratio analysis should be undertaken to assess the company's position relative to its competitors. With this background management should endeavour to assess the extent to which the market is suggesting that future returns are likely to come from dividends or changes in share price and the basis on which this assessment is made. With respect to share prices, an analysis should be made of movements over the last 12 months and why these have occurred. Management needs to consider, for example, whether the market has already discounted certain future events in determining the share price. Management needs to consider the broader strategic future of the company. Is it, for example, a potential takeover target? If so, what is the management view on this? Is the takeover to be fought or should there be a concentration on what the company might be valued at? If management, to take another tack, believes the share price undervalues the company, what is it going to do to improve the company's standing? Financial-statement analysis and stock market assessment are critical to the assessment of strategic direction.

The work of Porter on the concept of gaining 'competitive advantage', and that of a number of authors on the development of the 'balanced scorecard' approach to the determination and evaluation of corporate strategy, has also been influential in the assessment of strategic direction. Both of these approaches to strategy determination derive, at least implicitly, from the classical approach to the development of business strategies.

Competitive advantage

A major stimulus to the examination of corporate strategies came from the work of Porter (1980 and 1985). The substance of Porter's argument is that there are three generic strategies a firm can adopt in seeking sustainable competitive advantage. These are:

1 **Cost leadership.** This entails the firm seeking to become the lowest cost producer within the industry in which it operates. In this context, competitive advantage comes before the potential 'super-profits' that the firm might be able to achieve from its cost leadership. This may involve the firm in assessing the potential

advantages that might be derived from economies of scale, better sourcing (or outsourcing) of productive inputs and the benefits of better technology.

2 **Differentiation.** Here the firm seeks to offer products (services) which are clearly perceived by customers as being of superior (unique) quality to those of its competitors. Effective use of product branding (e.g. Coca-Cola and Mercedes) may have much to offer in this regard, as may ongoing concern for consumers (e.g. by after-sales service) and a reputation for innovative product development (e.g. Apple Computers and the development of online banking services).

3 **Focus.** This is based on the firm seeking (obtaining) market advantage by focusing on areas where customers have special needs and who may be being neglected by other providers. Ultimately, the gains from such focus depend, at least in part, on achieving cost leadership or differentiation.

The types of competitive advantage that firms seek will, at least in part, depend on the commercial environment in which they find themselves. This has accounting and control system implications: a firm seeking cost leadership is likely to place great emphasis on cost control systems; a firm seeking differentiation may look to invest in the enhancement of its brands and the development of new products; a firm that seeks to obtain advantages from its focus may invest heavily in market research. Porter introduced the concept of value-chain analysis as a means of generating consumer satisfaction and managing costs effectively. This is a topic discussed in Chapter 16 as an important element of supply-chain management.

Porter also developed the 'Five Forces Model' of gaining competitive This model is illustrated in Figure 18.1.

According to this model, the five forces are:

1 *Intensity of rivalry among existing firms.* In large part, this depends upon the number and closeness of substitute products. The closer the substitutes (in terms of price and comparability) the more intense will be the competion.

Figure 18.1   Porter's Five Forces Model

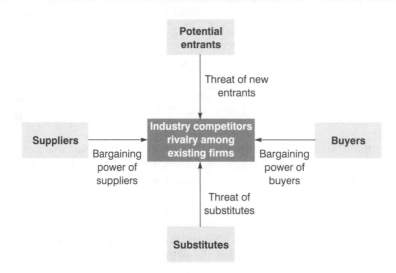

2 *Customers' bargaining power*. The stronger the market position of customers, the greater their bargaining power is likely to be. This is likely to have significant impacts on product pricing – the stronger the position of customers, the more likely they are to demand 'keen' prices.

3 *Suppliers' bargaining power*. This is the flip side of customer bargaining power. Suppliers are likely to be stronger and charge higher prices if there are high 'switching costs' of changing suppliers, or if there are no competitive products of equal quality or reputation – the role of established brand names may be important here.

4 *The likelihood of a substitute product emerging*. The more likely this is, in part because of new product development by competitors, then the greater will be the competitive forces the firm faces, particularly in a world of multinational competition.

5 *Barriers to entry:* The issue here is that of how easy it is for new competitors (local or international) to enter the marketplace with competing products. The role of trade barriers and of GATT is potentially important here.

The balanced scorecard

Another major stimulus to the development of corporate stategy was the work of Johnson and Kaplan (1987). This has been followed up in the UK by the work of people such as Bromwich and Bhimani (1989, 1994), and further work by Cooper and Kaplan (1991) and Kaplan and Norton (1992, 1993, 1996a, 1996b, 2001a, 2001b, 2001c and 2001d). The emphasis of all this work has been on the importance of *relevance* in the work of management accounting, on the need to integrate financial and operating information and, perhaps more importantly, on the need for a 'balanced scorecard', both for strategic planning and for the subsequent implementation and control of plans.

Kaplan and Norton identified four core features of a balanced scorecard approach, as outlined in Figure 18.2. These were:

1 **A financial perspective.** The focus of this perspective is the financial performance of the firm from a shareholder point of view. The core question is what do shareholders think about the firm's financial performance.

2 **An internal business process perspective.** This requires firms to ask themselves a question – at what business processes must we excel to satisfy our shareholders and our customers?

3 **A learning and growth perspective.** This perspective implies the notion of some form of corporate 'vision', perhaps something reflected in the firm's mission statement. This vision is likely (certain) to require the firm to be adaptable, responsive to change, and capable of learning from its past experiences.

4 **A customer perspective.** This follows on, at least in part, from the previous perspective. The question it is asking is – how successful are we in achieving our vision of customer service? Equally, how can we improve this service.

The requirements for the achievement of business success in these perspectives is well illustrated by Figure 18.3.

In Kaplan and Norton's view the factors which link all these perspectives together are the vision and strategy of the organisation. For each of the above perspectives, they suggest that success in their achievement should be assessed in four different dimensions. These are:

- the extent to which the organisation's vision and strategy are translated into specific strategic objectives;
- how successful the organisation is in communicating strategic objectives (and associated performance measures) throughout the organisation;
- the effectiveness of the organisation's planning and target setting processes, particularly at the strategic level;
- the effectiveness with which feedback and learning processes are embedded in the organisation.

There is no doubt that the balanced scorecard approach has been an influential one in recent years, although like many 'academic' concepts it has not become all-pervasive. It unquestionably has advantages in its meld of a variety of different corporate objectives and its emphasis on the need for effective processes to identify and monitor its success in the achievement of these objectives. Nevertheless, it is not an approach without its criticisms. These relate primarily to its mix of financial and non-financial performance measures, the absence of a specifically employee perspective, and the lack of a societal/environmental perspective. However, Kaplan and Norton stress that the balanced scorecard approach is meant as a framework for analysis and not as a straightjacket – it is open to organisations to add other perspectives specific to their needs. As with other approaches and facets involved in the development of corporate strategy, at the end of the day it is down to the organisation itself what approach it adopts – what matters is its success.

Figure 18.2   The balanced scorecard

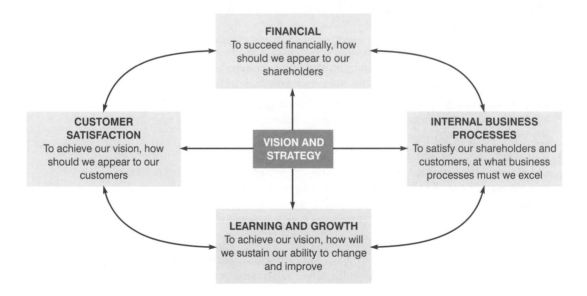

The 'new' accounting?

In recent years there has been a new, and emerging, feature of management accounting – that of companies, as part of their strategic management process, starting to use accounting concepts and techniques in the measurement of their external environment, and, in particular, assessing their own position *vis-à-vis* that of their competitors. This is indicative of a broader change in management accounting. Increasingly, accountants, in collaboration with managers, are starting both to measure new things and to measure existing things in different ways. The emergence of activity-based costing in recent years is one example of this. The drive behind this trend is the need for managers to have more relevant and more focused information in today's increasingly competitive environment. Closely associated with this 'new' accounting has been the emergence of new management techniques, a number of which have emerged either from Japan or as a response to changing technologies.

Thus, for example, increasing emphasis is placed these days on 'total quality management' concepts. There is an extensive and growing literature dealing with quality-management issues (see, e.g. Oakland 1994). Here, we are concerned with the impact of the quality movement on management accounting. Increasingly, the costs of quality (or the lack of it) are becoming significant to organisations; hence, they need to know what these costs are so that they can be managed. The following costs must be measured:

1 **Prevention costs.** These are the costs of the systems an organisation installs to prevent quality falling below the required level. They will typically include items such as staff training, preventative maintenance, planning and design costs, re-engineering and technical support costs.

2 **Appraisal costs.** These are the costs of ensuring that the required level of quality is being achieved. They will include items such as inspection and testing, supervisory and quality audit costs.

Figure 18.3   The balanced scorecard vector

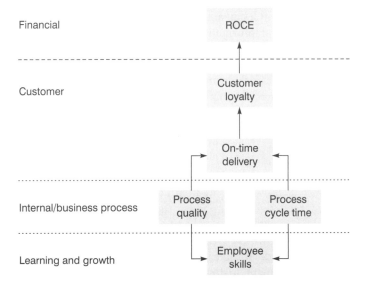

3 **Internal failure costs**. These are the costs that the organisation bears when quality standards are not achieved and this failure is recognised prior to delivery to the customer. They include items such as downtime, rework and scrap costs.

4 **External failure costs**. These are the costs that the organisation bears when quality standards are not achieved and sub-standard delivery is made to customers. Typically, they will include items such as warranty and product liability costs, as well as the opportunity costs of lost business as customers go elsewhere.

The costs of prevention and appraisal are normally referred to as the 'costs of conformance', and the internal and external failure costs as the 'costs of non-conformance'. The objective of management should be to minimise the total of these costs. To achieve this, it needs to understand the trade-offs between these two types of costs.

A related example of accounting seeking to measure costs that are directly relevant to management's information needs come with the assessment of supplier performance. There will be a trade-off between the price (per unit) charged by a supplier and the quality (broadly defined as 'fitness for purpose') of what is supplied. It is very tempting for management facing intense competition to go for the lowest price supplier, and traditional cost accounting systems may well encourage this. However, if the 'quality' is not right additional costs may well be incurred, and it becomes important to know what these costs are. There are a variety of ways this might be calculated but, in essence, they all involve approaches such as the computation of a 'supplier cost index', calculated by:

$$\frac{\text{Cost of purchased materials} + \text{Cost of non-value-adding activities}}{\text{Cost of purchased materials}}$$

Here, the cost of non-value-adding activities includes items such as the costs associated with inspection, rejection, reworking and non-scheduled delivery. The objective of the measurement is to help managers identify the lowest *total* cost suppliers rather than the lowest price suppliers. Of course, other issues (see Chapter 7) will be involved in the final selection of suppliers, but the cost will remain an important element.

Another area where accounting is starting to work more closely with management is that of production design and planning. Again, the thrust is that of providing managers with more relevant information. Two examples of this are 'target costing' and 'life-cycle costing'. The first of these completely reverses old-fashioned notions of 'cost-plus' pricing. In essence, cost-plus pricing involves designing a product (service), costing it (probably on a conventional absorption costing basis) and then trying to market it at a price which will produce an acceptable level of profit. Target costing involves assessing what the market is likely to be prepared to pay for a product (service) with a specified set of features and then, allowing for an acceptable profit margin, determining a target cost for it. The product design and subsequent manufacture is then focused on the achievement of this target cost. Partridge and Perren (1997) provide a good summary of the benefits of target costing, emphasising its links with notions of 'continuous improvement', such as those associated with the introduction of 'lean production techniques'. However, they rightly emphasise the fact that the real opportunity of continuous improvement is at the pre-production stage (Partridge and Perren 1997).

This is where life-cycle costing comes into play. Life-cycle costing recognises that the decisions made at the early stages of product design and specification frequently commit management to future patterns of cost, giving only restricted freedom of

Figure 18.4 Typical market life cycle

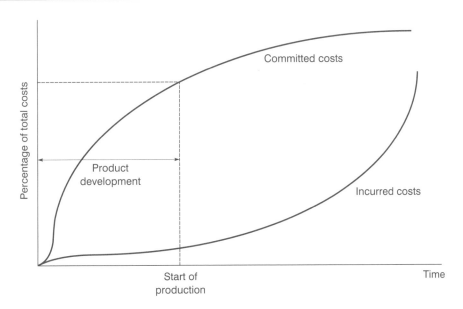

Figure 18.5 Elements of strategic planning

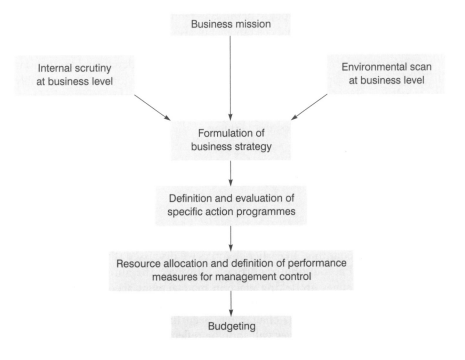

choice (and cost management) once production starts. Thus, great emphasis needs to be placed on managerial understanding of decisions being made during product development. Figure 18.4 illustrates the impact of such decisions. Accountants have a major role to play here as part of a multi-disciplinary team which works to produce product designs that will meet target costs over the life-cycle of the product.

Figure 18.4 illustrates a typical pattern of the commitment and incurring of costs over the life-cycle of a product. The decisions made during the design phase of the product effectively commit the organisation to certain costs being incurred during the production process. Subsequently, during the production phase, costs are actually incurred (and recorded in the costing records of the organisation). It is only at the end of the production (and after sales) phase that the two curves shown in Figure 18.4 come together – showing the total cost of the production process – from inception to final completion. The costs which are committed during the design and development phase (i.e. engineered into the product) can be very substantial – in Figure 18.4 they represent over 70% of overall final costs that will be incurred. This is why management, with the support of accountants, need to monitor the design phase closely.

At the same time, new production techniques, such as 'advanced manufacturing technologies' and 'just-in-time' management, are reinforcing the need for change in traditional management and cost accounting systems. Fortunately, there is evidence that management accountants are responding to these challenges (see, e.g. Bromwich and Bhimani 1989, 1994; Green and Amenkheinan 1992; Shank and Govindarajan 1992; Drury and Dugdale 1996).

Similar moves are taking place with regard to customers. For too long, management accounting's emphasis has been on the profitability of product (service) lines. Little attention has been paid to the profitability of servicing individual customers. In part, this issue is addressed by activity-based costing, with its questioning of the costing of small bespoke batches of product. It is now also being addressed by 'customer-profitability' analysis. This involves looking not just at the sales (and contribution generated therefrom) that are being made to individual customers, but also at the costs of generating those sales. Thus it looks at issues such as the number of orders (and the cost of processing them), the balance between standard and non-standard product ordered (and the associated costs), and the costs of support and servicing for individual customers. A commonly found result when customer-profitability analysis is first introduced is that servicing some customers (even quite large ones) costs money rather than makes money.

Figure 18.5 provides an overview of the core elements in the overall formulation of a business strategy.

Conclusion

In this chapter we have been able to give only a flavour of the changes that are taking place in accounting. In earlier chapters we discussed the changes that are taking place in financial accounting (reporting). However, the authors believe that the most significant changes are taking place in management accounting and financial management. The pace of change in these areas over the last decade has been significant, although much of this change has been limited to large multinational companies. Hopefully these changes will soon be reflected in the practices of smaller enterprises and the public sector. The core elements of this change have been a renewed focus on the need for management accountants to provide management with *relevant* information. This has led them to seek to measure old things differently; to measure new things; to break away from the dominance of financial accounting; and to integrate financial and operating information. Greater emphasis is being placed on the role of performance indicators and involvement in the whole value-chain of business, and on the need to integrate accounting practices with strategic planning (Wilson 1995).

Chapter review

At the beginning of this book we stated that its focus would be primarily on the contribution that accounting and accountability systems can make towards the more efficient and effective management of business enterprises, because of the rapidly changing nature of the financial consequences of the activities of organisations and individuals.

Following the two introductory chapters, the book moved on to look in some detail at management accounting principles and practices, focusing on the role of management accounting in providing relevant information to help them fulfil their planning, deciding and controlling responsibilities.

The book then spent some time looking at ways in which organisations finance their activities and the costs of such finance, moving on to look at capital investment decisions and business reorganisation decisions.

We then looked at a range of financial reporting issues. In this context, the areas covered included the importance and bases of accounting records, a review of the key financial statements and their interpretation, together with the legal and regulatory requirements associated with their publications. Financial reports are important because they provide outsiders with financial information on the organisation's performance. They are also an important means by which management understands how competitors are doing.

When we wrote the third edition we highlighted our concerns over the reliability of the financial information provided to investors and analysts in financial statements. Over time there have been many examples of a lack of reliability, ranging from cases such as Polly Peck, Coloroll, British and Commonwealth and Maxwell Communications in the 1970s and 1980s. Regrettably, this lack of reliability has continued with later examples such as Enron, WorldCom and Rank Xerox.

Directors owe statutory duties to their companies and shareholders. These duties include a duty of care, skill and diligence as well as a duty not to inflate or make secret profits. In all the cases cited above it was clear that certain directors misused their powers and that other bodies, such as firms of accountants and the banks, were either complicit or negligent in not preventing such abuse.

One of the major confusions with financial reporting for many 'ill-informed' users of annual financial statements is the basic fact that profit does not equal cash. This confusion, regrettably, often also resides with sections of management, and many so-called 'profitable' companies have gone bust in recent years. Shareholders have lost their investment, their interests being failed by the professionals, management and the regulators who were employed to protect them. Even in the stock market it remains the case that far too much attention is given to the 'magic' earnings-per-share number (see Smith 1996). Financial reports should be read only if due attention is given to the accounting policies and footnotes that accompany the main financial statements. Always remember:

PROFIT REPRESENTS AN OPINION(S); CASH IS FACT

It is cash that pays wages, invoices, dividends and funds reinvestment. The need to generate cash effectively came to the fore in those parts of the book dealing with management accounting and investing activities. The basics of costing, having been considered, attention was paid to both short- and long-term investment strategy. All the time we considered the contribution, in cash terms, that was likely to arise from following a particular course of action. Despite recognising that the basic economic objective of maximising shareholder wealth underpins much of the theory of decision making, we also had to recognise that the behaviourai sciences also have much to offer us in this area. In reality, managers tend not to be maximisers; they tend to be risk-averse satisfiers. By examining aspects of behavioural accounting we were then able to consider aspects of financial control and issues associated with the measurement of management accountability. Time and again we pointed out that often, financial control systems fail because the means by which management is evaluated are not necessarily congruent with overall organisational objectives. This was particularly illustrated when we considered the evaluation of managers in a divisionalised organisation. What became clear was that there was no ideal way of measuring management's performance.

Corporate strategy develops as a result of compromise; organisations tend to develop multiple objectives rather than a unitary objective. Multiple objectives tend to mean that managers have to trade on the importance of one priority relative to another. The quality of information, including accounting information, is critical to aiding our understanding of whether, overall, the organisation is achieving its targets. Managers tend to operate in a market or quasi-market environment. As such, all have to be commercially accountable. It is important that they demand and use good-quality accounting information when they make decisions and monitor performance. If they are to use this information they must understand the principles and assumptions that underlie its presentation. They must also be prepared to help to make decisions on the underlying assumptions that will have an impact on the quality and relevance of the accounting information provided.

Further reading

In the last few years a number of texts have been published that have sought more closely to combine accounting and strategic management. There are also some excellent tests that deal with strategy in a way that is very accessible for managers. Whittington's *What is Strategy?* (1993) is an excellent, short and stimulating read which challenges basic assumptions of management orthodoxy. Johnson and Scholls's *Exploring Corporate*

Strategy (1999) is a popular standard text on corporate strategy. Ellis and Williams, in *Corporate Strategy and Financial Analysis* (1993), uniquely seek to interface managerial accounting and stock-market perspectives in terms of strategies that companies follow. Kaplan and Norton's work on the 'Balanced Scorecard' (e.g. 1996a, 1996b, 2001a) focuses on the implementation of strategies and the role of performance measurement. Kay's *Foundations of Corporate Success* (1993) integrates organisation and financial perspectives on the performance of successful firms. In addition, journals such as *Journal of Management Accounting Research* and *Management Accounting* are replete with articles reflecting changes in management accounting practice.

Questions and exercises

Guide notes can be found at the back of the book for all questions marked with an asterisk*.

1* To compete and cooperate in a dynamic business environment we need to be sensitive to the diverse textures of different business systems. Discuss.

2* To what extent is it fair to state that the success of Far East economies, the entry of the Eastern European countries into the capitalist world and the closer interaction of Western European countries are compelling a proper appreciation of the diversity of practice within capitalist economies?

3* Marginal cost pricing is seen by most firms and accountants as a recipe for going broke, yet every elementary economics textbook stresses the importance of marginal costs. Who is right, the accountants or economists?

4* Why is it that activity-based costing helps build up the structure of costs in ways which link the value-chain of the firm, the overall added-value statement and the incremental costs associated with individual products?

5* For an organisation with which you are familiar, define its value-chain and associated competitive advantages and disadvantages?

6* Using the structure set out in Table 18.2, analyse a company with which you are familiar both in relation to its industry sector and against the broader economic framework of the your home economy.

7 How useful are companies' annual reports in assessing their strategic direction?

8 'Analysts should be focusing their energies on reviewing the cash position of companies rather than focusing on levels of profit and balance sheets'. Do you agree?

9 Assume that your analysis of your company's share price leads you to believe it is undervalued in the market. Why would this be of concern and how would you endeavour to promote its revaluation upwards?

10 To what extent do you believe that all managers also need to be competent financial managers?

11 Directors owe statutory duties to their companies. Do you know what those duties are and the penalties involved for non-compliance?

12 In the light of recent corporate scandals such as Enron, WorldCom and Rank Xerox, what measures should be taken to try and assure that such example of financial report manipulation are prevented in the future.

GLOSSARY OF TERMS

AASB (1) Australian Accounting Standards Board.

AASB (2) An accounting standard issued by the Australian Accounting Standards Board.

abridged accounts (UK) The Companies Acts exempt small and medium sized companies from the full financial reporting requirements specified in the Acts. In particular, small companies can file an abbreviated balance sheet with the Registrar of Companies and do not have to file a profit and loss account. Medium sized companies can file an abbreviated profit and loss account. Full accounts are still required for shareholders and an audit is still required. The qualifying criteria for these exemptions are specified in section 247 of the Companies Act 1989

absorption costing A method of determining the unit cost of products, normally on a full-cost basis inclusive of direct costs and indirect costs or overheads. The overhead charges are proportional to some measure of direct work done on the product, rather than to a measure of actual work done in the support services (as under activity-based costing).

accelerated depreciation An approach to depreciation in which the cost of the asset being depreciated is written off over a period of time shorter than its forecast useful life.

acceptance credit An arrangement via which a bank allows a customer to issue bills of exchange up to an agreed limit. Normally used by enterprises in place of overdrafts where large amounts are involved.

account As a noun, the generic name of the subdivisions of an entity's accounting records used for the purposes of analysis. As a verb, the generic name for the process whereby an entity (individual) renders a statement about its actions, and their outcomes, to those having a right to such a statement.

accountability The generic name for the relationship which subsists between an entity (individual) which has to account for its actions and the entity (person) to whom the account is rendered.

accountant A person suitably trained to prepare, update and analyse accounts.

accounting The setting-up, maintenance and analysis of financial records and the preparation of financial reports from such records. (also referred to as accountancy).

accounting bases The accounting measurement methods that are available to entities in the preparation of their financial statements. The range of accounting bases is very wide and there is frequently more than one recognised accounting basis for dealing with a particular item, e.g. depreciation.

accounting entity An entity, whether a person, partnership, company or other economic unit, which prepares financial statements. A distinction may need to be made between an accounting entity and a legal entity, e.g. the business of an individual is an accounting entity, but the legal entity includes both the person's business and personal affairs.

accounting period The period of time spanning the date between two consecutive balance sheets and to which the profit and loss account relates. For companies it is normally 12 calendar months.

accounting policies These are the specific accounting bases adopted by an enterprise in the preparation of its financial statements. Companies have to disclose significant accounting policies as part of the notes to their financial statements.

accounting rate of return A technique for the evaluation of investment projects which compares the potential average annual increase in profit which would result from a project to the amount of the investment required by the project. This technique is analogous to the return on capital employed measure of corporate and divisional performance.

accounting reference period The period by reference to which accounts have to be prepared and submitted to members of the company. In the UK, section 3 of the Companies Act 1989 lays down the regulations for determining the accounting reference period.

accounting standards The generic name given to the statements issued by professional bodies (and others) in an attempt to standardise (regulate) the preparation of financial statements by companies. The International Accounting Standards Board's statements have increasingly major acceptance, e.g. within the EU for listed companies.

accounting standards board In the UK, a sub-committee of the Financial Reporting Council which was set up in 1990 and has taken over the work previously carried out by the Accounting Standards Committee in relation to the issuing of authoritative statements on accounting standards.

accounting standards committee Originally set up in 1970, when it was called the Accounting Standards Steering Committee, the Accounting Standards Committee sought by the issue of Statements of Standard Accounting Practice to narrow the range of accounting bases that could be adopted in accounts and to ensure greater comparability between the accounts of different enterprises. Its work has been taken over by the Accounting Standards Board.

accounts payable An alternative term to creditors for describing amounts owed by an entity to third parties.

accounts receivable An alternative term to debtors for describing amounts owed to an entity by third parties.

accrual An amount included in the creditors of an entity in the preparation of its financial statements to allow for expenditure which has not yet been recorded in the accounting records of the entity.

accruals basis The normal basis of preparing accounts for trading enterprises. On this basis the income and expense effects of transactions are incorporated into the entity's financial statements, whether or not they have as yet resulted in cash flow consequences, and matched with one another so far as a relationship can be established. This is the basis of accounting required by the IASB (*See* below).

accumulated depreciation The cumulative amount of depreciation charged against an asset during the period from its acquisition to the date of the financial statements.

acid test ratio The ratio of an enterprise's liquid assets to its short-term liabilities. Also referred to as the liquid ratio and the quick ratio, it provides a measure of the enterprise's liquidity.

acquisition Normally refers to one company obtaining control of another by means of purchasing at least 50% of the voting shares in the company being acquired. Often referred to as a takeover.

acquisition cost The original historical cost of acquiring an asset.

activity based costing An approach to the costing of individual products and services which focuses on the identification of 'cost drivers', i.e. those activities which lead to indirect production costs being incurred, and which charges the individual products or services with these indirect costs on the basis of their demand for these 'cost drivers'.

activity based management The use of information derived from activity-based costing in order to improve cost control, work and value-added analysis, pricing and product-mix decisions, etc.

added value The difference, e.g. at each stage of production, between the value of a product and the cost of the materials used to make it.

administration A part of the corporate insolvency process whereby it is possible for qualified insolvency practitioners (administrators) to take over the management of a failing company with a view to reviving it and avoiding receivership or liquidation.

advanced corporation tax The income tax paid by a company on behalf of its shareholders in relation to dividend payments. Later, subject to certain restrictions, it can be offset against the company's mainstream corporation tax in the UK.

affiliate A company which holds less than a majority of voting shares in another company, or which is a subsidiary of another company.

agency theory This theory pertains to the relationship between the owners of a firm and the managers of the firm, whereby management has the responsibility for acting as the agent of the owners in pursuing their best interests, and which raises the question of how well management performs this role.

agreed bid A takeover offer which has obtained the support of the directors of the target company, who recommend to their shareholders that the offer should be accepted.

allocation The process via which costs or revenues are assigned to a business segment, responsibility centre, product or service. There are numerous different bases on which this process can be conducted. However, wherever possible an attempt should be made to carry it out according to logical measures of production or use.

allotment The process via which shares in a new issue are allotted to those who have applied for such shares. Frequently, the terms of the offer will specify the basis of such allotment in the event of the offer being oversubscribed.

amortisation The writing off over a number of accounting periods of the original (historical) cost of an asset or a liability. It is sometimes used as a synonym for depreciation. In the context of assets it is most commonly used to describe the writing off of intangible rather than tangible assets.

analytic review The process of analysing ratios and trends and then comparing the amounts recorded for measured quantities with the amounts predicted for these quantities in order to assess the completeness, accuracy and and validity of data produced by an organisation's accounting systems.

annual general meeting A meeting which (in the UK) a company must hold each year and which all shareholders are entitled to attend. The business to be conducted at this meeting normally includes: consideration of the directors' report and accounts; election of directors; appointment of auditors and the declaration of dividends. Shareholders must be given 21 days' notice of the meeting in writing.

annual report A report made each year by the directors to the shareholders. *Inter alia*, it contains the directors' report and accounts. It normally contains a statement by the chairman and a range of information on the company's activities. Such a report is required by the Companies Acts, which also specify a number of specific items of information that it must contain. Accounting standards and stock exchange regulations (for listed companies) also specify disclosure requirements.

annual return A report lodged by a company with the registering authority within a specified time after the company's annual general meeting and in a form prescribed by company law. It contains, *inter alia* (in the UK), the address of the company's registered office, a list of the company's directors, and may include a report on the company's accounts. Such a report is normally available for public inspection.

annuity An annuity is a cash flow of a contractually agreed amount which lasts for a specified number of years. A common form of annuity is where individuals pay an insurance company a lump sum in exchange for annual (monthly) payments from the insurance company for the rest of their life.

APB A professional body formed in 1991 to take over the work of the APC for the issue of Auditing Standards and Guidelines.

arbitrage The purchase or sale of securities on one stock market together with an almost simultaneous offsetting sale or purchase of those securities on another stock market to obtain a profit from any difference in prices.

Articles of Association Every company (in the UK) requires a set of Articles of Association which are in effect part of the constitution of the company. They specify how the company shall conduct its affairs and the rights and obligations of various parties involved with the company.

ASB A sub-committee of the Financial Reporting Council which has taken over the work of the ASC in relation to the issuing of authoritative statements on accounting standards.

ASC Originally set up in 1970 (as the ASSC) to issue authoritative statements on accounting standards. Its work has now been taken over by the ASB.

asset Assets are rights or other access to future economic benefits controlled by an entity as a result of past transactions or events.

asset-turnover ratio The ratio of the sales turnover of the enterprise to the net assets employed. It is commonly regarded as a measure of the efficiency with which the assets are employed in generating sales.

associated companies An associated company is a company in which another company has a participating interest and over which it has significant influence but not control. The consolidated accounts of a group of companies must account for their share of the associated company's profits.

attest function The function of certifying or confirming the validity of an assertion or representation of actions or events.

attributable cost The cost per unit (or, sometimes, per product line or per organisational unit) which could be avoided or escaped if a particular product or other segment of a business was discontinued while leaving the supporting organisational structure (and costs) intact.

audit The systematic examination of financial statements for the purpose of determining the 'truth and fairness' of their presentation.

audit committee A committee of the board of directors, normally composed of non-executive directors, which has responsibility for monitoring the relationships between the company and its auditors.

audit committee report An annual report of the audit committee which (in the UK) forms part of the annual financial statements of a company.

audit evidence The outcomes of those (evidence gathering) procedures carried out by an auditor to enable an opinion on the 'truth and fairness' of the annual financial statements to be expressed.

auditing The process of carrying out an audit.

auditing standards Authoritative statements on auditing (in the UK) from the Auditing Practices Board (APB) which issues them as Statements of Auditing Standards. On an international basis, similar statements are issued by the International Federation of Accountants.

auditor The person who carries out an audit. To carry out an audit of the accounts of a company in the UK such a person must be a member of one of the professional bodies approved for this purpose by the Secretary of State and hold a current practising certificate. The 1989 Companies Act in the UK introduced a number of changes regarding the activities of auditors pursuant to the 8th Directive of the European Union. In practice, most auditors are partnerships of qualified accountants rather than individuals.

auditor independence The requirements imposed on auditors, in the UK and elsewhere, to ensure that they are able to give an unbiased view in their audit report.

auditor responsibility Those things for which an auditor can (cannot) be held responsible and the process via which such responsibility can be enforced.

Australian Accounting Standards Board A body established under the Australian Securities Commission Act of 1989 to take over the role of the previous Accounting Standards Review Board and to develop and review proposed accounting standards.

authorised share capital The maximum amount of share capital which the company is (in the UK) authorised by its Memorandum of Association to issue at any point in time. The amount can be altered by means of a resolution of the company in general meeting and is disclosed each year in the accounts.

average rate The average price of a security on a trading day.

avoidable cost That amount of cost which will not continue to be incurred if an existing activity ceases, or that amount of cost that will not be incurred if a potential activity is not undertaken.

bad debts The amount of money owed to an entity by its debtors which will not be collectable from them.

balance sheet One of the primary financial statements, being a statement of an entity's assets, liabilities and equity at a particular date. In the case of companies it is normally a statutory annual requirement and the Companies Acts (in the UK) specify its form and content in some detail, and require that it presents a true and fair view of the state of the company's affairs at the relevant date. The IASB's statements contain a number of pronouncements regarding the format of balance sheets.

balance sheet equation The relationship that holds in double-entry bookkeeping at any given time between assets (A), liabilities (L) and owners' equity (OE), i.e. that $A = L + OE$.

balance sheet gearing The relationship between an entity's debt finance and its total sources of finance. It can also be expressed in terms of the prior claims of the debt finance.

bankruptcy The state of an individual being unable to pay his/her debts. There are various legal rules dealing with bankruptcy, most notably (in the UK) the Insolvency Act of 1986.

bearer securities A security (e.g. share or bond) where simple possession of the certificate is proof of ownership, as ownership of the security is not registered.

beta factor A measure of the volatility of returns on an individual stock relative to the market as a whole. Stocks with a beta of 1.0 are said to have a risk equal to that of the market as a whole (equal volatility). Stocks with a beta greater than 1.0 have more risk than the market; while those with a beta less than 1.0 have less risk than the market as a whole.

bill of exchange 'An unconditional order in writing addressed by one person to another signed by the person giving it requiring the person to whom it is addressed to pay on demand, or at some fixed or determinable future time, a sum certain in money to or to the order of a specified person or to the bearer.' Section 3(1), Bills of Exchange Act, 1882.

bill of materials A schedule of the direct materials required for the manufacture of a specified type and quantity of product.

bonds Documentation evidencing medium or long-term borrowing by an enterprise, a government or other organisation.

bonus shares An issue of fully paid shares to shareholders by way of a dividend out of a company's undistributed profits.

bookkeeping equation *See* balance sheet equation.

book value The amount at which an asset is stated in an entity's balance sheet as opposed to its market value. It is sometimes referred to as carrying value.

Break-even point That volume of activity at which the revenues an entity generates are just equal to the costs that it incurs, and it accordingly makes neither profit nor loss.

budget A formal quantified statement (normally expressed in financial terms) of a plan of action.

budget appropriation An authorisation made via a budgetary process to spend a specified amount of resources for a specified purpose.

budget variance The difference between the amount contained in a budget and the corresponding actual cost or revenue.

budgetary control The continual comparison of budget forecasts with actual performance.

buffer stocks Stocks of raw materials or finished goods which have been purchased so as to tide an organisation over during a period of uncertainty.

call A demand by a company for additional capital from its shareholders, most commonly where shares have been issued on a part-paid basis and the company wants the whole, or part, of the unpaid balance to be paid.

called-up share capital The amount of the issued share capital that the shareholders have been 'called upon' to pay. It is equal to the amount of the issued share capital in the absence of calls in advance or in arrears.

capital allowances The amounts which an entity is permitted under taxation legislation to charge against its earnings in lieu of depreciation of its fixed assets. As part of computing an entity's taxable profit, the accounting depreciation is added back to profit and the capital allowances deducted. Capital allowances and accounting depreciation may differ significantly.

capital asset pricing model An economic model for determining the required rate of return on an investment, taking into account the required rate of return on a risk-free investment, the difference between the risk-free rate of return and that for the capital market as a whole, and the relationship between the risk of the investment in question and that of the market as a whole.

capital budgeting The process via which an enterprise formally plans its capital investment programme. It incorporates, but is not restricted to, the appraisal of individual capital investment projects.

capital employed The resources utilised by a business in the conduct of its trading activities to generate profit. Its two main components are working capital and fixed assets.

capital expenditure on fixed assets Company legislation normally has a number of disclosure requirements relating to such expenditure, whether already made or for which future commitments have been entered into or authorised by the directors.

capital gains tax A tax on surpluses made on the disposal of capital (fixed) assets. It applies to individuals and not to companies which pay corporation tax on all gains.

capital gearing The relationship between the amount of debt finance and the amount of equity finance of an entity. The relationship can be either in terms of the capital amounts of the finance or in terms of its consequences for income distribution. It is sometimes referred to as leverage.

capital investment appraisal The process of determining whether or not it is worthwhile investing in longer term capital projects. There are a range of accounting techniques available to assist in this process. It is one part of capital budgeting.

capital maintenance A concept stating that an enterprise cannot be regarded as having made a profit in an accounting period unless the value of its capital at the end of the period is at least equal to the value of its capital at the start of the period after allowing for any equity distributions or contributions. The different approaches to measuring capital for this purpose are the subject of much debate in accounting, especially because of the effects of price level changes on capital values.

capital markets Competitive markets for equity securities or debt securities with maturities of more than one year.

capital redemption reserve A non-distributable reserve created on the redemption of redeemable preference shares, other than by the issue of new shares.

capital reserves These are either legally not available for distribution (e.g. unrealised revaluation reserves and share premiums) or are not regarded as being available for distribution by the directors for other reasons.

capital structure theory A theory that addresses the relative importance of debt and equity in the overall financing of the firm.

carrying value *See* book value.

cash basis A method of accounting under which transactions are only recognised at the time they lead to the payment or receipt of monies.

cash book The prime accounting record in which the receipt and disbursement of cash is recorded.

cash budget A plan, covering a specific period of time, summarising the anticipated future receipts and payments of an enterprise, i.e. its forecast cash flow.

cash conversion period The period of time that it takes an entity to recoup its cash expenditure. It is normally thought of as being the elapsed time between the payment of creditors and the receipt of cash from debtors.

cash flow The actual cash receipts and payments of an enterprise for a particular accounting period.

cash flow accounting A system of accounting based on actual cash flows as opposed to the accruals basis of accounting.

cash flow forecast A forecast, covering a specific period of time, of the estimated receipts and payments of an enterprise.

cash flow statement One of the primary financial statements, being a statement which summarises the principal components of an entity's receipts and payments during a specified financial period.

chairman's report A report by the chairman on the activities of the enterprise which is normally included as part of its annual report.

charge to secure debentures A form of security, with similarities to a mortgage, offered to lenders whereby the enterprise pledges assets as security for repayment of loans. A charge issued by a company can be a fixed charge, in which case specific assets are the subject of the charge, or a floating charge over all assets of the company. Charges have to be registered with the Registrar of Companies to be effective. The lender has a prior claim for repayment out of the proceeds of selling the charged assets.

chart of accounts A schedule listing the titles of all the accounts contained in a ledger system, together with an appropriate numbering system for such accounts.

chief executive's report See chairman's report.

circulating assets Assets produced or purchased by an entity for the purpose of conversion into cash or profit in the short term – also known as floating assets.

closing rate (or price) method The price of a security at the end of a trading day.

collateral Commonly used to refer to security given to secure a loan. More precisely, it refers to security given by a third party rather than the borrower.

commitment accounting A system of accounting which records the expenditure which an entity has committed itself to making as opposed to the expenditure it has actually incurred. It enables management of the entity better to assess the extent of 'free' resources available for fresh initiatives.

committed costs Costs which have not yet been incurred but which are the subject of a contract such that they will be incurred in the future.

common costs A cost the benefits of which are enjoyed by a number of different segments of an entity and which cannot be logically allocated to the individual segments.

Companies Acts Statute law regulating the affairs of companies. In the UK the most recent is the 1989 Companies Act which updates the 1985 Companies Act, which itself was a consolidation of previous Acts.

company An entity with a legal personality separate from its members registered under and subject to the requirements of the company legislation..

compliance testing That part of an audit which checks that a company's internal control system is operating as specified.

conglomerate A large company, often with numerous subsidiary companies, which operates in a number of different, and apparently unrelated, commercial and industrial sectors.

conservatism An accounting concept, rooted in nineteenth-century ideas of creditor and investor protection, which requires accounts to be prepared on a cautious rather than an optimistic basis as regards the valuation of assets and liabilities and the measurement of revenues and expenses. It is similar to the fundamental accounting concept of prudence.

consistency A fundamental accounting concept which requires that a company should follow the same accounting policies each year in the preparation of its annual financial statements. It is important for the purposes of inter-temporal comparison.

consolidated accounts Consolidated accounts are accounts which incorporate the accounts (balance sheet, profit and loss account, statement of total recognised gains and losses and cash flow statement) of the parent company and those of its subsidiary undertakings. These accounts normally are required by company legislation to give a true and fair view, relating to the undertakings included in the consolidation as a whole, so far as concerns the members of the parent company.

consolidated balance sheet *See* consolidated accounts.

consolidated income statement (profit and loss account) *See* consolidated accounts.

consolidated cash flow statement *See* consolidated accounts.

contingencies A condition of the situation at balance sheet date, the ultimate financial effect of which will only be confirmed on the occurrence (or not) of one or more uncertain future events.

contingent liability A liability the crystallisation of which is contingent on some future event occurring or not occurring (*See* contingencies). Corporate legislation normally requires disclosure of such contingent liabilities in the accounts.

continuity convention Another name for the 'going concern' convention.

continuous budget Also called a rolling budget, this is a budget which constantly covers a specified future period of time by adding another accounting period at the conclusion of each accounting period completed.

contracting out The process of taking a service/function previously provided by a public sector organisation (such as a local authority) and, via a tendering process, offering it to alternative providers on very carefully specified contractual terms (both operational and financial). It is sometimes referred to as outsourcing.

contribution The difference between the variable revenues and the variable costs attaching to a particular course of action.

contribution approach A method of preparing profit and loss accounts which separates variable from fixed costs and emphasises the difference between variable revenues and variable costs (contribution). The object of the approach is to emphasise the dynamics of cost and revenue behaviour for planning and control purposes.

contributions from owners The amount of equity capital invested in the firm.

contribution margin The difference between sales revenues and variable costs.

controllable cost A cost that can be directly controlled at a given level of management.

convertible loan stock Loan stock which carries the option of being converted into shares on specified

terms at some future date, or on the occurrence of some future event.

corporate governance Those processes which a company (normally listed) is expected to have in place to ensure the appropriate and orderly conduct of its affairs.

corporate report The annual report of an enterprise intended to give useful information to its recipients.

corporation tax The taxation that companies pay on their taxable profits.

cost The sacrifice that is entailed in acquiring or using goods or services. There are a number of different bases for measuring cost, most notably acquisition cost and opportunity cost.

cost accounting That part of accounting which deals with the collection, allocation and control of the costs of producing a product or service.

cost-benefit analysis An approach, derived from economics, for appraising the overall costs and benefits (including ones not normally measured in financial terms, and particularly public ones) of a particular activity or set of activities.

cost centre A responsibility centre within an enterprise, the performance of which is assessed in terms of the service it provides and the costs that it incurs in providing that service.

cost driver A measurable characteristic of work activity (e.g. number of transactions, or time devoted to a particular beneficiary product, service, client, etc.) which can be recorded and used as the basis for the assignment of costs (especially in activity-based costing).

cost-effectiveness analysis The process of determining whether the profits that are on offer are deemed to be satisfactory in the light of the costs involved.

costing The process whereby the cost of a business activity or product is measured and analysed.

cost-plus A pricing mechanism whereby some (usually predetermined) mark-up or profit margin is added to cost (whether direct/variable cost, full production cost or total cost).

cost of capital The cost to an enterprise of its sources of finance. It is normally expressed as an annual percentage of the finance and reflects the relative costs and proportions of debt (provided by lenders) and equity (provided by shareholders) finance.

cost of sales The cost to an enterprise of the goods or services it supplies to its customers. In financial accounts, it is normally calculated on an absorption-costing basis.

cost-volume-profit analysis An accounting technique based on analysing the cost and revenue structure of an enterprise into component elements based on their variability relative to the volume of activity. This form of analysis, which is sometimes referred to as 'break-even' analysis, is most commonly used as an aid to budgeting and profit planning.

costing The process whereby the cost of a business activity or product is measured and analysed.

creative accounting The use of accounting techniques or procedures to mislead intended users of financial statements by presenting a 'rosy view' of corporate performance. It takes advantage of those accounting ambiguities which may allow differing accounting presentations.

credit An amount entered on the right-hand side of a ledger account, or the offering of credit terms (deferred payment) to customers.

creditors The amounts owed by an enterprise to those who have supplied it with goods or services for which they have not as yet been paid, or to those who have lent the enterprise money.

credit limit The maximum amout of credit that is supposed to be offered to a customer.

credit rating An evaluation of the creditworthiness of an individual or firm.

cum div (cum dividend) A term signifying that a quoted share price includes the right to receive a declared dividend.

cumulative preference shares Preference shares on which arrears of dividends have to be paid before any dividend can be paid to ordinary shareholders. The amount of any arrears of such dividends has to be disclosed in the accounts.

currency conversion The process of exchanging an amount in one currency for the equivalent amount in another.

currency translation The calculation of the equivalent of an amount in one currency in terms of another for accounting purposes. Unlike currency conversion, it does not involve the actual exchange of an amount in one currency for the equivalent amount in another.

current assets Assets which are held by an enterprise for the short term and are expected to be converted to cash within that term, normally regarded as being within 12 months of the date of the accounts. They are sometimes referred to as circulating assets.

current cost accounting A basis of preparing accounts under which non-monetary items in the accounts are valued at their current cost equivalent (i.e. market or replacement cost valuation) rather than their historical cost. This system of accounting, intended to allow for high rates of inflation, has proved highly contentious..

current liabilities Liabilities which are due for settlement within the short term, which is normally regarded as being within 12 months.

current operating performance concept An accounting concept describing which items should be included in the net income for a given accounting period. Non-recurring items (i.e. extraordinary items) are excluded and instead are shown after the determination of net income or as adjustments to retained earnings.

current purchasing power accounting A basis of preparing accounts under which items in the accounts are stated in terms of their equivalent purchasing power as at the end of the accounting period.

current ratio The ratio of an entity's current assets to its current liabilities. The ratio is regarded as being a measure, albeit a relatively crude one, of an enterprise's liquidity.

dawn raid An unexpected acquisition of shares in a company by a potential acquirer – such activity often takes place as soon as a stock market opens, to prevent rumours spreading.

debentures A debenture is a document issued by a company to a lender as evidence of a debt due to the lender. Such debts usually arise out of a loan and are normally the subject of a fixed and/or floating charge. There are various kinds of debentures but commonly they involve more than one lender and involve the creation of a deed of trust charging the property of the company in favour of a trustee for the debenture holders. Debenture holders, or their trustee, have various legal rights to ensure the value of their security.

debit An amount entered on the left-hand side of a ledger account – often (in common parlance) thought of as a negative performance indicator.

debtor ageing analysis The analysis of debtors (accounts receivable) according to the age of outstanding debtors. It is used for control purposes as part of an entity's credit management processes, and to assess any requirement for a provision for bad debts.

debtors Amounts owing to an enterprise, normally arising from the sale of goods or services on a non-cash (credit) basis.

debtor turnover The ratio between an entity's debtors and its sales on a credit basis. It is usually expressed in terms of the number of days' credit sales represented by debtors or in terms of the multiple that credit sales are of debtors. It is commonly regarded as an indicator of the efficiency of an entity's debtor collection practices.

decision package Documentation used in the implementation of zero-base budgeting (typically involving the use of pro formas). It describes the decision unit involved (typically a cost or profit centre with delegated authority for its actions) and the costs/revenues of its operation.

deferral method A tax effect accounting method under which the tax effects of current timing differences are deferred and allocated to future accounting periods when the timing differences will be reversed.

deferred asset An asset the worth of which is contingent upon some reasonably certain future event. Most commonly encountered in the case of a deferred taxation asset.

deferred taxation A provision for taxation which recognises the differences in timing in the recognition of profit for accounting and taxation purposes.

depletion A means of computing depreciation for an asset the economic life of which is limited by the speed at which it is used up. It is most commonly applied in the extractive industries and involves depreciating the asset in line with the rate of extraction.

depreciation The process of allocating the net cost (original acquisition cost less estimated scrap value) of a long-lived asset over its estimated life. There are a number of accounting techniques for doing this, including straight-line depreciation, the reducing-balance method and usage-based methods.

depreciation charge This is the amount of depreciation included in an entity's profit and loss account for a particular accounting period and represents that accounting period's share of the total depreciation of the asset(s) in question.

deprival value A basis of valuing assets based on the loss that an enterprise would suffer if it were to be deprived of those assets. This idea of value was an important element in the development of the current cost accounting methodology.

differential cost The difference in future costs that an enterprise will incur depending on what courses of action it chooses to pursue, compared to the continuation of present policy.

dilution Refers to the decrease in earnings per share and/or control that existing shareholders suffer when new shares are issued wholly or in part to parties other than themselves.

direct cost A cost which is specifically and measurably identified with a particular product or activity within an enterprise. Such costs are sometimes referred to as separable costs.

direct labour organisation (DLO) That part of a local authority responsible for undertaking maintenance and construction work for which separate annual accounts and reports are required. Extension of this into office and other non-manual local authority work has led to the further and related concept of the direct service organisation (DSO).

direct taxation Taxes on individuals and organisations based on their income or profits, e.g income tax and corporation tax. It is a tax on income rather than spending.

directors' emoluments The amounts that directors receive from a company. Corporate legislation usually requires extensive and detailed disclosure of these amounts.

directors' report An annual report from the directors of a company to its shareholders. Corporate legislation usually specifies its minimum contents. Such a report usually accompanies the company's annual accounts.

discounted cash flow A method of investment appraisal based on the present value, after allowing for the cost of capital and timing, of the future cash flows associated with an investment project. There are two principal variants of the method (net present value and the internal rate of return).

discretionary costs Costs, the incurring of which, is a matter of discretion for management. Typically, they relate to items of expenditure which are not an essential part of the entity's short-term activities, e.g. research and development, advertising, staff development, etc. Thus, they are clearly matters for management policy decisions.

distributions to owners See dividends.

dividend That part of the profits of a company that is distributed to the shareholders of the company in proportion to the numbers of shares that they hold and the respective rights attaching to those shares. Local corporate legislation normally contains regulations relating to dividend payments and there have been a number of legal cases dealing with them.

Generally, dividends can only be paid out of realised profits, whether from the current trading year or previous years.

dividend cover The multiple that the profits available for paying a dividend are of the actual amount of the dividend paid.

dividend policy Relates to the policy of the company (directors) on how it divides its profits between paying dividends to shareholders and retaining them for reinvestment.

dividend valuation model A model for determining the value of a share by using the present value of an expected stream of future dividends.

dividend yield The ratio between the dividend per share and the market price of a share. Effectively it is a measure, albeit fairly crude, of the return on investment in shares, ignoring any possible capital gains.

division A major responsibility centre within an enterprise which has devolved responsibility for a particular activity or set of activities, the performance of which is appraised in terms of the profitability of these activities.

double-entry bookkeeping The principle that every transaction affects two or more components of the accounting equation.

drawings The amount of money a sole trader, or the partners in a partnership, withdraw from their business for their personal use.

earnings A synonym for profit. However, like profit, earnings can be measured at a variety of different levels, e.g. operating earnings (profit), earnings (profit) before taxation, earnings (profit) after taxation, earnings (profit) per share depending on the purpose for which it is being measured.

earnings per share The profit for an accounting period attributable to ordinary shareholders divided by the number of ordinary shares in issue.

earnings yield The ratio of the earnings per share of a company to the market price of an ordinary share. It is the inverse of the price-earnings ratio.

economic order quantity (EOQ) The size of an inventory order that minimises the total cost of ordering and carrying inventory.

efficient markets hypothesis (EMH) A hypothesis to the effect that the capital market efficiently imputes all available information into the market prices of securities. There are three variants of the hypothesis: the weak version; the semi-strong version and the strong version. The hypothesis is relevant to accounting as annual accounts are a source of information available to the market.

However, the hypothesis is the subject of some contention.

entity That set of activities having an independent existence for which accounts are prepared.

equity Ownership interest in the entity.

equity share capital That part of the share capital of a company which has unfettered rights to share in the distribution of dividends or in the capital of a company after all preferential and prior claims have been met. In effect it is the pure risk capital.

EU directives The mechanism via which the European Commission has attempted to achieve harmonisation within the Community with regard to the regulation of corporate entities. After due process, and with some flexibility, member states are expected to incorporate the contents of these directives into local legislation.

exceptional item Material items which derive from events or transactions that fall within the ordinary activities of the reporting entity and which individually or, if of similar type, in aggregate need to be disclosed by virtue of their size or incidence if the financial statements are to give a true and fair view.

ex div (ex dividend) A term signifying that the share price excludes the right to receive a declared dividend.

exercise price The price at which a warrant (or other similar security) allows the investor to purchase ordinary shares.

expectations gap The gap between what the public expects of external auditors and what the auditors believe they are accountable for.

expense An amount of money or other asset used up or consumed, or a liability incurred, in the ordinary course of an organisation's activities.

exposure draft Part of the process of formulating and promulgating accounting standards. An exposure draft is a preliminary draft of the text of a proposed standard issued for comment by interested parties prior to standard being finalised..

external audit An audit (typically) of the financial statements of a corporate organisation carried out by independent auditors.

external financial limits The limits imposed by central government on the annual use of external finance by public sector organisations.

extraordinary items Material items possessing a high degree of abnormality which arise from events or transactions that fall outside the ordinary activities of the reporting entity and which are not expected to recur. They do not include exceptional items nor do they include prior period items merely because they relate to a prior period.

factoring A generic term to describe the raising of finance by the 'sale' of debtors to a financial institution. There are a number of different forms of factoring, ranging from ones involving the 'sale' of individual large invoices to ones involving whole sales ledgers, and ones with differing entitlements in the case of bad debts.

fair value A feature of the acquisition method of accounting for business combinations which requires that valuation of assets acquired should be at their fair (arm's-length) values at the date of the combination.

FIFO An approach to valuing stocks in which it assumes that those items remaining in stock at the end of the accounting period are those that were purchased most recently. The acronym stands for 'first in, first out'.

finance lease A finance lease is a lease which effectively transfers the risks and rewards associated with ownership of the leased asset from the lessor to the lessee. Thus, the substance of the arrangement is a purchase transaction rather than a rental one and it is accounted for as such.

financial management The responsibility for the allocation of funds to current and fixed assets, to obtain the best mix of financing alternatives, and to develop an appropriate dividend policy within the overall context of the firm's objectives.

financial management initiative An initiative introduced by central government (in the UK) in the 1980s aimed at developing better management information systems.

financial ratio A generic term for the comparison of related figures in financial statements so as to assess corporate performance.

financial statements Statements showing the financial position of an enterprise at a given date (the balance sheet); the profit for the accounting period ended on the given date (the income statement); the gains and losses recognised in the accounting period (statement of total recognised gains and losses); the statement of changes in equity and the flow of funds through the enterprise in that accounting period (cash flow statement). The statements are normally supported by explanatory notes.

first in, first out method *See* FIFO.

fixed assets Assets owned by an enterprise for long-term use in its activities rather than for resale.

fixed assets register A schedule of fixed assets owned by an enterprise, showing date of purchase, cost and accumulated depreciation.

fixed capital Items such as premises or equipment.

fixed charge The charge of a specific asset(s) as security for a debt.

fixed costs Costs the amount of which are not expected to vary in the period being considered, typically one year, whatever the level of activity engaged in by an enterprise.

fixed overheads Costs, other than direct costs, the amount of which is not expected to vary in the period being considered by an enterprise.

fixtures and fittings A term used to describe things which are attached to premises, and articles of furniture, etc. which did not form part of the original building.

floating charge A charge on all the assets of an enterprise, to the extent that individual assets or groups of assets are not the subject of a fixed charge, as security for a debt.

flotation Introduction of a company to the stock exchange by the offering of its securities for sale to the 'public' and its inclusion in the stock exchange list; also known as an initial public offering (IPO).

flow-of-funds statement A financial statement summarising the principal sources of funds and the applications of funds of an entity during an accounting period.

formats of accounts Local corporate legislation normally specifies the formats that companies must adopt in preparing their annual accounts.

franked investment income Income consisting of dividends previously charged to corporation tax in the hands of the company paying the dividend.

full costing *See* absorption costing.

functional budget A budget which charges costs (resource inputs) to individual functions or activities. It is sometimes referred to as a programme budget.

fundamental accounting concepts The broad basic assumptions underlying periodic financial accounts. In the absence of a clear statement to the contrary in the accounts it is assumed that these basic assumptions (the going concern concept; the accruals concept; the consistency concept and the prudence concept) have been applied in the preparation of the accounts.

fundamental accounting identity *See* balance sheet equation.

gains Gains are increases in ownership interest, other than those relating to contributions from owners.

gearing The relationship between the amount of debt finance and the amount of equity finance of an enterprise. The relationship can be expressed either in terms of the capital amounts of the finance or in terms of its consequences for income distribution. It is sometimes referred to as leverage.

general reserve A reserve which has not been appropriated by the directors for any specific purpose.

generally accepted accounting practice The body of accounting principles which (over time) has come to be accepted as bases for the preparation of financial statements. Accounting standards are generally based on a 'preferred' subset of these principles.

going concern One of the four fundamental accounting concepts. The essence of the concept is an assumption that an enterprise will continue in existence throughout the foreseeable future and that there is no necessity to reflect 'break-up' or liquidation values in the financial statements.

goodwill The value of the commercial advantages that an entity enjoys because of its prior existence. It reflects such things as the entity's particular expertise and trade reputation. In the case of some entities, particularly ones in the service/knowledge sectors, it may represent the major trading 'asset' of the enterprise. However, as it is not separable/saleable from the enterprise, is very difficult to place a value on, and is not normally valued in corporate financial statements, other than consolidated statements.

goodwill on consolidation Appearing only in a consolidated balance sheet, this is the excess of the amount paid to acquire an interest in a subsidiary over the corresponding proportion of the fair value of net assets of the subsidiary at the date of acquisition.

gross profit The difference between the selling price of an article and the cost of the materials and labour which are required to produce it.

group A parent company together with its subsidiary undertakings. The parent company of a group is normally required, under local corporate legislation, to publish consolidated accounts.

group accounts The accounts of a group of companies. The format of such accounts is normally determined by local corporate legislation. In the UK and Australia, group accounts may only be presented in a consolidated format. Some other countries have different requirements.

harmonisation Commonly thought of as the movement to have financial statements prepared in different countries having a common basis for their preparation. The EU has been influential in this regard.

historical cost The traditional measurement basis employed in accounting under which assets and liabilities are recorded at their original transaction value and revenues and costs are recorded at their monetary values. The historical cost basis does allow for some deviations from the foregoing, particularly with regard to revaluations of fixed assets and the substitution of market value for cost in the case of current assets where market value is lower than historical cost.

holding company Another name for the parent company of a group of companies.

IASC A grouping of professional accountancy bodies from over 80 countries which attempts to standardise/harmonise international financial reporting practices.

IFAC A grouping of professional accounting bodies which is trying to harmonise accounting practice.

imputation system A system under which shareholders are compensated for the tax which companies have effectively paid on their behalf.

income The money, or other valuable benefits, received or the amount expected to be received by an accounting entity, whether from its trading activities or other sources, with the exception of contributions of capital and loans made to the entity.

income statement Another name for a profit and loss account.

incremental budgeting An approach to the preparation of budgets which uses the previous budget as the starting point and concentrates on changes (increments/decrements) from that budget. Such an approach does not challenge the relevance of the volume/cost assumptions on which the previous budget was based.

independence The ability by auditors to act with integrity and objectivity, having no bias and remaining neutral in the conduct of their professional services.

indirect costs Costs which are not directly identifiable or measurable with the individual products or activities of an enterprise.

indirect taxation Where the tax is not collected directly from the taxpayer, e.g. VAT. It is a tax on spending rather than income.

insider trading This occurs when someone has information that is not available to the public and uses this privileged information to profit from trading in a company's shares.

insolvency The state of an entity being unable to meet its liabilities. The legal regulations dealing with insolvency in the UK are contained in the Insolvency Act 1986.

intangible assets These are assets which have no underlying physical substance. Examples include: goodwill, trade marks, copyrights and, more controversially, brand names.

integrated accounting package A computer package consisting of several modules, each performing a separate accounting function, in which entries made in one module are recorded automatically in other modules.

interim accounts Financial information about an enterprise which relates to a period shorter than a financial year.

interim dividend A dividend distributed prior to approval of dividends by a company's annual general meeting.

interim report A report issued by a company during the course of a financial year. Such reports are usually a stock exchange requirement for listed companies.

internal audit The ongoing investigation of compliance with established policies and procedures (internal control systems) of a business by its internal audit staff.

internal control The whole system of methods and procedures adopted by the management of an entity to assist it in achieving, as far as possible, the orderly and efficient conduct of its business affairs.

internal rate of return A method of discounted cash flow analysis which involves calculating that discount rate which just equates the present value of the cash inflows attaching to an investment project with the present value of the cash outflows attaching to it. This discount rate, the internal rate of return, is then used as a basis for deciding whether or not the investment project should be undertaken on the basis of comparing it with the entity's cost of capital.

inventory An overall term, of US origin, for describing an enterprise's holding of raw material stocks, work in progress and finished goods.

investment centre A responsibility centre, the performance of which is assessed in terms of the rate of return on the capital invested in its resources.

Used especially in association with a divisional management structure and transfer pricing.

issued share capital The nominal value of the share capital actually issued at any point in time. It is disclosed in the accounts.

job order costing A costing system under which product costs are charged, allocated and apportioned on the basis of individual jobs or contracts.

joint costs Broadly the same concept as common costs. To be distinguished from joint product costs, which arise where a single set of resources becomes transformed in a joint process into two or more main products and/or by-products (often with separate additional processing).

journal entry The format in which a transaction is entered in the general journal.

just-in-time management An approach to the management of inventories which attempts to ensure that inventories are delivered just as they are required for production purposes.

lead time The period it takes to acquire inventories in time for them to be used in production.

leasing A method under which the use of assets for a specified period of time is secured by an entity, the lessee, entering into a contract for hire with another party, the lessor.

ledgers A collection of accounting records which (in a manual system) are usually on separate pages of the ledger. In a computer based system equivalent information is also recorded, albeit in a different format.

leverage See capital gearing.

leveraged buyout Existing corporate management, or a third party, makes an offer to take the business 'private' with necessary finance being (largely) obtained by borrowing.

liabilities Liabilities are the obligations of an entity to transfer economic benefits as a result of past transactions or events.

liability method A method of accounting for taxation under which the expected tax effects of current timing differences are reported, either as liabilities, or as assets representing advance payment of future taxes.

life-cycle costing/pricing The process of planning a product's development, production and marketing over its (economic) lifetime, costing all this, and pricing it. If prices seem non-viable, all cost elements will be reiterated to obtain a profitable outcome, or the product will be abandoned.

LIFO An approach to valuing stocks which assumes that those items remaining in stock at the end of the accounting period are those that were the first to be purchased. The acronym stands for 'last in, first out'.

limited-liability company A company incorporated with limited liability under the provisions of the relevant corporate legislation. The limited liability typically relates to the liability of the members of the company in case of insolvency. The limitation may be determined by the nominal value of the shares in the company or by the amount of a guarantee given by the members.

limited partnership A partnership in which the liability of some of the partners for the debts of the partnership is limited. However, limited partners are not permitted to engage in the management of the affairs of the partnership and there must be at least one unlimited partner.

limiting factor A 'bottleneck' or point in the production or distribution cycle at which volume becomes capped while other resources are still not fully utilised. It is important to identify this, both for feasible removal, and meanwhile to analyse which products maximise profit contribution while fully utilising the capacity of the limiting factor.

line-item budgets Budgets which detail income/ costs in terms of individual categories of revenue/ expenditure (e.g. rents, salaries, printing, telephones, etc.).

liquid assets Assets which are either cash or readily convertible to cash.

liquidation The process by which the assets of a company are realised into cash, its liabilities paid off and any surplus distributed to the shareholders.

liquidity A term referring to the net short-term funding position of an enterprise. A 'liquid' enterprise is one which has sufficient short-term funding to meet its financial obligations and, perhaps, a sufficient surplus of funding to engage in new opportunities as they present themselves.

listed company A company whose shares are listed on a stock exchange and can be traded on that exchange.

loan capital Long-term finance which an entity obtains by borrowing.

loan stock Tradeable interests in loan capital.

losses Losses are decreases in ownership interest, other than those relating to distributions to owners.

management accounting That part of accounting which involves the provision of information to management for planning, control and decision making.

management auditing An examination of the performance of various levels of management over a period of time.

management buyout *See* leveraged buyouts.

management information system A system, often computerised, designed to provide the management of an organisation with the information required for decision making.

marginal cost A concept derived from economics which measures the increase in total costs associated with an increase in output/activity levels (normally of one unit).

margin of safety The difference, in units or as a percentage of sales, between actual (forecast) sales volume, and the volume at which profit break-even is achieved. Used in evaluating alternative products or production methods, etc., often in association with cost-volume-profit analysis.

market value The amount obtainable, or reasonably expected to be obtainable, from the sale in an active market of an asset.

master ratio *See* return on capital employed.

matching Another name for the accruals concept derived from the principle of 'matching' the costs and the revenues for transactions included in the accounts of a particular accounting period.

materiality An accounting concept recognising that accounts cannot report with complete accuracy every minute detail of an enterprise's affairs on the grounds of practicality and of limited potential benefit to the readers of the accounts. However, accounts should contain all material information. Information is regarded as being material if its omission or misstatement could influence the economic decisions of users taken on the basis of the financial statements.

Memorandum of Association Part of the constitution of a company registered under the Companies Acts in the UK. The memorandum of association is a legal requirement and its minimum contents are specified in the Companies Acts.

merger A combination of two business enterprises conducted in such a way that one enterprise is not in substance acquiring the other. Normally, corporate legislation and accounting standards specify conditions which must be met if a business combination is to be treated as a merger.

minority interest Arises when one company acquires another but acquires less than 100% of the shares. The remaining shareholders in the company acquired are referred to as the minority shareholders and their interests in the assets and profits of the acquired company are referred to as minority interests.

mixed costs   Costs which contain both fixed and variable elements (which often cannot easily be separately measured). *See* semi-fixed costs and semi-variable costs.

monetary assets   Assets which are cash or whose value in cash terms is fixed.

NASDAQ   National Association of Securities Dealers Automated Quotation System. An electronic network on which the OTC market in the US operates.

national insurance   In the UK, the system whereby the government takes money from employers and employees and makes payments to persons who are sick, unemployed or retired, etc. The amount of the contribution is related to income.

net assets   The value of assets less liabilities which equals the amount of the ownership interest.

net current assets   The difference between an entity's current assets and its current liabilities.

net present value   The current equivalent value of the net of the future cash inflows and cash outflows of an investment project discounted at the enterprise's cost of capital. The net present value technique is one of the discounted cash flow techniques for investment appraisal.

net profit ratio   The relationship between the net profit for a period and the sales turnover for that period.

net realisable value   The amount which an asset would realise, net of selling expenses, if it were to be sold.

net worth   The book value of an enterprise's equity, i.e. the book value of its assets less the book value of its liabilities.

neutrality   The absence of bias. Neutrality is a desirable feature of financial information.

nominal share capital   Another name for a company's authorised share capital, i.e. the maximum amount of share capital that a company is authorised by its Memorandum of Association to issue at a point in time.

nominal value   *See* par value.

non-executive directors   Members of the Board of Directors who do not play a part in the day-to-day management of the business.

non-voting shares   Shares which do not carry any entitlement to vote at general meetings of the company.

notes to financial statements   These may run to many pages and are intended to amplify the information contained in the financial statements themselves.

objectivity   *See* neutrality.

off-balance-sheet finance   Arises where entity secures the use (control) of assets in such legal forms as does not constitute ownership.

operating lease   Any lease other than a finance lease, i.e. one which does not substantially transfer all the risks and rewards of ownership to the lessee.

operating profit   Profit for an accounting period before charging taxation and interest. It is widely regarded as indicating the profit generated by management on the resources under their control, independently of how those resources are financed.

opportunity cost   An economic concept which regards the cost of utilising a resource as being the benefit forgone by not using it in its best alternative use.

ordinary shares   Those shares entitled to participate in the profits and capital of a company after all prior claims against profits and capital have been met.

output measures   Measures of the quantity of service/product produced. Such measures are often used in the performance appraisal of managers responsible for the provision of particular services/products.

overdraft   An arrangement which an individual or company has with a bank to enable them to borrow money on a short-term basis up to an agreed overdraft limit. Interest is only chargeable on the amount that is actually borrowed rather on the total of the facility. Accordingly, overdrafts can offer a flexible means of short-term borrowing. However, the interest rates that are charged are often relatively high and the borrowing may be repayable on demand.

overhead costs   Costs which are not directly identified with a particular product or activity. They are also referred to as indirect costs. However, many indirect costs are variable costs, whereas many 'true' overhead costs are relatively fixed.

over-trading   Expansion by a trading entity of its sales and production without sufficient financial resources to back-up this expansion.

ownership interest   The residual interest in net assets of an entity.

paid-up share capital   The amount of a company's share capital which has actually been subscribed by the shareholders.

par value The currency amount (e.g. pounds, dollars, euros) nominally attached to each of a company's shares.

parent company A company which has subsidiary companies or undertakings. Also sometimes referred to as a holding company.

participating preference shares Preference shares which, in addition to their preferential rights, also have some rights to participate in profits and capital after other prior claims have been met.

partnership A form of business entity involving two or more owners (partners) or 'The relation which subsists between persons carrying on a business in common with a view of profit'. (Section 1, *Partnership Act 1890* (UK)). Except in the case of a limited partnership, all partners carry a joint and several liability for the debts of the partnership.

payback period The amount of time it will take for the cash inflows arising from an investment project to repay the cash investment that was made in the project.

perpetuity An investment without a maturity date for the returns on the investment.

placement Issuance of stock at a particular market price.

planning, programming, budgeting (PPB) A budgetary approach, initially developed for the public sector within the USA, which attempts to establish clearly defined goals and objectives for each area of an organisation's operations. These are then linked with quantification of the benefits and costs of operations and used for identifying, and subsequently monitoring, the most desirable programmes.

ploughing back The retention of profits for further investment in the enterprise as opposed to distributing profits to the equity owners.

post-completion audits The audit of investment projects after their completion, comparing budget estimates with actual results and analysing any variances such as to facilitate better planning in the future.

pre-acquisition profits Profits earned and retained by a subsidiary prior to its acquisition.

preference shares Shares which have prior claims over those of ordinary shares as regards either or both dividends and repayment of capital. The rights of different types of share capital are normally contained in a company's articles of association.

preferential creditors Creditors who have a prior claim over other creditors as regards the settlement of their debt out of the assets of the company. Their

prior claim may be established by statute law or by contract.

prepayments Payments for goods or services where the payment has been made prior to the end of the accounting period but the goods or services are not received or completed until after the end of the period. Shown as an asset in an enterprise's accounts, they are the counterpart to accruals.

present value The current discounted value of a future sum. *See* net present value.

price-earnings ratio The relationship between the earnings per share and the market price of a share. Effectively it shows how many years' earnings, at the last reported rate, will be needed to cover the cost of buying a share.

primary market The market for the raising of new funds as opposed to the trading of securities already in existence.

primary ratio *See* return on capital employed.

prime documents *See* source documents.

prime records Those records which contain the first recording of a transaction (e.g. the cashbook).

prior charges Claims against the assets or profits of a company that have a right to settlement before other claims.

private company A company which is not a public company.

profit The difference between an enterprise's revenues and its expenses.

profit and loss account A primary financial statement giving details of an enterprise's revenues and expenses. In the case of companies a profit and loss account is required to show a true and fair view of the profit, or loss, for the accounting period.

profit centre A responsibility centre within an enterprise, the performance of which is assessed in terms of the profit that it generates from its activities. It may incorporate subsidiary cost and revenue centres.

prospectus An invitation to subscribe to the share or debenture capital of a company. The contents of prospectuses are normally closely regulated by legislation.

provision An amount put aside in the accounts relating to an anticipated liability or to a reduction in value of an asset where the amount cannot be identified with a high degree of accuracy.

prudence concept A fundamental accounting concept stating that whenever accounting judgement is required it is preferable to understate rather than overstate assets, income, profits, etc. and to overstate liabilities. Income and profits are only ultimately realised when they result either in cash or the receipt of future cash is relatively certain. Excessive prudence may lead to misguided decisions.

public company In the UK, a public limited company which has the designation 'plc' after its name. To be a public company, a company's memorandum of association must permit this and it must have a minimum authorised capital of £50,000 (or such higher amount as the Secretary of State may determine) and comply with certain other legal regulations. Only a public company may offer its shares and debentures to the public or have its shares listed on a stock exchange.

purchase method This is a method of consolidating the accounts of subsidiary companies with the parent company. The basis of this method is that the assets and liabilities of the subsidiaries are aggregated with those of the parent company and that the cost of the parent company's investment in the subsidiary company is eliminated. Any differences between the book value of the subsidiaries' net assets at the time of acquisition and the cost of the parent company's investment, allowing for minority interests, is treated either as purchased goodwill or as a capital reserve on acquisition. One consequence of this method of consolidation is that the pre-acquisition profits of the subsidiaries are frozen and are not available for distribution. It is also known as the acquisition method.

quick assets Another name for liquid assets. Essentially these are assets that can be readily and rapidly converted into cash. A common way of defining them is current assets less stocks and work in progress. However, for some purposes this approach may be inadequate and an alternative one is to regard liquid assets as being debtors, excluding prepayments, plus cash and marketable securities.

quick ratio The relationship between the liquid assets of an enterprise and its short-term (current) liabilities. Also referred to as the acid test and the liquid ratio.

quoted company A company whose shares are listed on a stock exchange.

rate of return The relationship between profit and the resources (net assets) employed to generate those profits.

ratio analysis An approach to interpreting the information contained in financial statements based on relating significant figures to each other.

receivables Another term, of US origin, for debtors.

reducing-balance depreciation An approach to calculating depreciation in which the depreciation charge for a period is based not on the original cost of the asset but on its net book value at the beginning of the relevant financial period.

remuneration committee Normally, for a listed company, a sub-committee of non-executive directors having responsibility for the determination of the financial rewards payable to directors and other senior management.

replacement cost The amount it would cost to replace an asset with a similar one.

reserve accounting The accounting practice of passing extraordinary and prior-year items through reserves rather than through the profit and loss account.

reserves *See* capital reserves.

residual value An estimate of the net amount recoverable on the ultimate disposal of an asset at the end of its useful life.

responsibility accounting The process whereby managers are held accountable for decisions that they make, and not for centrally controlled costs or decisions.

retained profits Profits earned by an enterprise but not distributed to owners.

return on capital employed (ROCE) The relationship between the profit of an enterprise and the capital employed in generating that profit. The most common variants are return on equity capital employed (which relates profit attributable to equity owners to equity capital) and return on total capital employed (which relates operating profit to total-long-term capital). It is commonly regarded as a measure of the effectiveness with which management have utilised the capital available to them.

return on equity capital employed *See* return on capital employed.

return on total capital employed *See* return on capital employed.

return on investment (ROI) A measure analogous to return on capital employed but relating to units within a business (e.g. divisions), or to specific projects or capital outlays.

revaluation The process whereby an asset (normally a fixed asset) is stated in the accounts at its current value rather than its historical cost. The difference between the two is shown as a reserve arising on revaluation and, as it is not realised, it is not distributable.

revenue *See* income.

sales The revenues an entity generates from its trading activities.

secondary market The market for securities that have already been issued. It is a market in which individual investors trade back and forth with each other.

segmental reporting An aspect of financial reporting in which the overall profits and revenues of an entity (or group of entities) are disaggregated into significant business or geographical segments to provide more detailed information about activities.

semi-fixed costs Costs which are not permanently fixed for all volumes. They arise, and therefore become fixed, at intermediate stages in the volume range, and are sometimes termed 'step costs'.

semi-variable costs Costs which change with variation in volume of work or activity, but whose rate of change is not constant, linear or necessarily always predictable for any given volume.

sensitivity analysis Any method which takes alternative data on costs, sales (demand), the timing of events, etc., to check the possible consequences of failure to achieve the target (or most probable) outcome of a decision. May be combined with profitability analysis.

share capital The amount of a company's capital, divided into shares of a fixed amount the rights of which are determined by the company's articles of association.

shareholder A member of a company by virtue of ownership of a share(s).

shareholders' funds The total of share capital and reserves. Also referred to as equity capital.

share premium This arises when shares are issued at an amount exceeding their nominal value. This excess is a non-distributable reserve.

statement of auditing standards Standards that prescribe the basic principles for the conduct of an audit and which govern the professional responsibilities of an auditor.

statement of directors' responsibilities That part of an annual corporate report which highlights those matters for which directors are responsible.

statement of financial performance See profit and loss account.

statement of recommended practice These are statements of accounting practice prepared by recognised 'industry groups' dealing with current and best accounting practice specific to their industry.

statement of standard accounting practice These are authoritative statements on accounting practice intended to narrow areas of difference and variety in financial reporting. In the UK, these are now issued by the Accounting Standards Board (ASB) and are intended to apply to financial statements intended to present a 'true and fair view'.

statement of total recognised gains and losses A supplementary statement to the profit and loss account intended to show all those gains/losses for the financial period not recorded in the profit and loss account.

stock (1) See inventory.

stock (2) A financial asset representing a share of the ownership of a corporation. Entitles the owner to dividends, if any are paid.

stock exchange A place in which stocks are traded on behalf of investor clients.

stock market That network of exchanges on which stocks are traded on behalf of investor clients.

stock turnover An accounting ratio which measures the relationship between an entity's inventories and its cost of sales. In general, it is thought that efficient management of inventories (stocks and work-in-progress) will result in inventory holdings which are relatively low in relation to cost of sales. The ratio is expressed either as the number of day's cost of sales represented by inventories or as the multiple that cost of sales are of inventories.

straight-line depreciation A method of calculating depreciation based on subtracting a fixed asset's forecast salvage value from its original cost and dividing the result by the estimated life of the asset.

strategic management accounting The development of management accounting information to facilitate the development of a sustainable competitive position.

subsidiary company A company which is under the control of another company (its parent company).

substance over form An accounting doctrine, which is the subject of some debate, stating that accounting statements should reflect the underlying economic substance of an event or transaction rather than its precise legal form.

substantive testing Part of the audit process which involves the direct confirmation of account balances (e.g. counting cash, inspection of fixed assets, etc.).

systematic risk The element of an investment asset's risk that cannot be eliminated, no matter how diversified an investor's portfolio.

tangible assets Assets that are not intangible. See intangible assets.

tangible fixed assets   Fixed assets having an underlying physical substance.

target costing/pricing   Prices are taken or forecast from the market, in the light of market share/volume sought. Profit margin is deducted to determine allowable total costs. Products and production methods/efficiency are then designed/engineered/adapted to be completed within allowable cost. May be used with life-cycle costing/pricing.

temporal method   A method of translating the financial statements of an overseas operation into local currency.

timing differences   Differences in the accounting periods within which an item is recognised for taxation purposes as opposed to accounting purposes.

transfer pricing   The internal mechanisms via which goods or services transferred from one part of an enterprise to another are charged for.

trial balance   A statement listing all the account balances in the general ledger. A trial balance is prepared to verify the equality of debit and credit balances (as required by the accounting equation).

true and fair view   The requirement imposed by the Companies Acts in the UK on the accounts of companies is that they should present a 'true and fair view' of the state of affairs at balance sheet date and of the profit, or loss, for the period ending on that date.

turnover   Sales revenues.

two-part tariff   A method of transfer-pricing, or other pricing or charging, in which a fixed or time-related charge is used for resources committed, and a variable-cost-plus charge is used to cover the direct and variable costs (with some profit contribution usually added) of the actual volume of goods or services supplied/transferred.

unit cost   The total (full) cost of producing one unit of a good or service.

unquoted company   A company the shares of which are not listed on a stock exchange.

unlimited company   An unusual type of company where the liability of the members of the company is not limited, either by shares or by guarantee.

variable costs   Costs the total amount of which vary as the level of an entity's activity changes.

variance   The difference between a budgeted amount and the corresponding actual outturn.

venture capitalist   Organisations (often investment banks) that invest money in high-risk, newly established enterprises or provide funding for the acquisition of established enterprises (e.g. via management buyouts).

warrant   An option to buy securities at a set price for a given period.

weighted average cost of capital   The cost of capital computed by multiplying the cost of each item in the capital structure of an organisation by the proportion that it is of that capital structure.

window dressing   A pejorative term referring to the practice of companies trying to put the 'best gloss' on their financial position (as reported in their financial statements) by the incorporation of 'questionable' elements.

working capital   Current assets less current liabilities.

zero-base budgeting (ZBB)   A system of budgeting, originally developed in the USA for non-trading organisations. Its approach is a 'bottom-up' one involving the ranking of the contribution that differing activities make to the achievement of organisational objectives in cost/benefit terms.

REFERENCES AND FURTHER READING

Accounting Principles Board (1966), *Reporting the Results of Operations*, American Institute of Certified Public Accountants.

Alchian, A. and Demesetz, H. (1972), 'Production, information costs and economic organisation', *American Economic Review*, 62, 777–95.

Aldis, J. and Renshall, M. (1990), *The Companies Acts 1985 and 1989: Accounting and Financial Reporting Requirements*, London, KPMG Peat Marwick McLintock and Institute of Chartered Accountants of England and Wales.

Alexander, D. and Britton, A. (2004), *Financial Reporting*, 7th edn, London, International Thomson Publishing.

Alexander, D. and Nobes, C. (1994), *A European Introduction to Financial Reporting*, Hemel Hempstead, Prentice–Hall International (UK).

American Accounting Association (1966), *A Statement of Basic Accounting Theories*, New York, AAA.

American Accounting Association (1972), *Report of the Committee on Concepts of Accounting Applicable to the Public Sector*, Sarasota, USA.

American Law Institute (1983, 1984), List of Board Duties available at http://www.ali.org/.

Amey, L.R. and Egginton, D.A. (1975), *Management Accounting: A Conceptual Approach*, London, Longman.

Ansoff, H.I. (1965), *Corporate Strategy*, Harmondsworth, Penguin.

Ansoff, H.I. (1968), *Administrative Behaviour*, Harmondsworth, Penguin.

Argenti, J. (1980), *Practical Corporate Planning*, London, Allen and Unwin.

Argyris, C. (1964), *Integrating the Individual and the Organisation*, Chichester, John Wiley & Sons.

Arnold, D. and Turley, S. (1996), *Accounting for Management Decisions*, 3rd edn, Hemel Hempstead, Prentice-Hall.

Audit Commission (1986), *Performance Review in Local Government*, London, Audit Commission.

Australian Accounting Standards Board (1990), *Statement of Accounting Concepts*, Melbourne, AASB.

Bailes, J.C. and Kleinsorge, I.K. (1992), 'Cutting waste with JIT', *Management Accounting*, May.

Baversox, D.J. and Closs, D.J. (1996), *Logistical Management*, New York, London, McGraw-Hill.

Bebbington, J., Gray, R. and Laughlin, R. (2001), *Financial Accounting Practice and Principles*, 3rd edn, London, Thomson Learning.

Bebchuk, L.A. (2004), 'Designing a Shareholder Access Rule', Discussion Paper No. 461 2/2004, *Harvard Law School*, MA 02138, available at http://www.law.harvard.edu/programs/onlin_center/.

Black, F. (1986), 'Noise', *Journal of Finance*, 41, pp. 529–34

Block, S.B. and Hirt, G.A. (2002), *Principles of Corporate Finance*, New York, McGraw-Hill.

Brearley, R.A. and Myers, C.M (2003), *Principles of Corporate Finance*, 7th edn, London, McGraw-Hill.

Bright, J., Davies, R.E., Downes, C.A. and Sweeting, R.C. (1992), 'The deployment of costing techniques and practice: a UK study', *Management Accounting Research*, 3(3), 201–11.

Bromwich, M. (1976), *The Economics of Capital Budgeting*, Harmondsworth, Penguin.

Bromwich, M. and Bhimani, A. (1989), *Management Accounting: Evolution not Revolution*, London, Chartered Institute of Management Accountants.

Bromwich, M. and Bhimani, A. (1994), *Management Accounting: Pathways to Progress*, London, Chartered Institute of Management Accountants.

Brownell, P. (1982), 'The role of accounting data in performance evaluation, budgetary participation and organisational effectiveness', *Journal of Accounting Research*, Spring, 12–27.

Burrit, R.L. and Lehman, C. (1995), 'The Body Shop wind farm: an analysis of accountability and ethics, *British Accounting Review*, 27(3): 167–86.

Butterworths (1997), *Butterworths UK Tax Guide*, 1997–98, London, Butterworth & Co.

Butler, R. (1993), *Strategic Investment Decisions: Theory and Practice*, London, Routledge.

Canadian Institute of Chartered Accountants (1988), *Handbook Section 1000 – Financial Statement Concepts*, Canadian Institute of Chartered Accountants.

Carey, A. (1992), 'A questioning approach to the environment', in D. Owen (ed.), *Green Reporting: Accountancy and the Challenge of the Nineties*, London, Chapman and Hall.

Carsberg, B.V. (1969), *Introduction to Mathematical Programming for Accountants*, London, George, Allen & Unwin.

Chandler, I. (1962), *Strategy and Structure*, Cambridge, MA: MIT Press.

Chartered Institute of Management Accountants (1990), *Corporate Reporting: The Management Interface*, London, Chartered Institute of Management Accountants.

Chechile, R.A. and Carlisle, S. (eds) (1991), *Environmental Decision Making: A Multidisciplinary Perspective*, New York, Van Nostrand Reinhold.

Chopra, S. and Meindl, P. (2001), *Supply Chain Management – Strategy, Planning and Operation*, Prentice-Hall, ISBN 0–13–026465–2.

Christopher, M. (2005), *Logistics and Supply Chain Management: Creating Value-Adding Networks*, FT Prentice-Hall, ISBN 0–273–68176–1.

Clarke, T. (2004), *Theories of Corporate Governance*, Routledge, ISBN 0–415–32307–X.

Collier, P.M. (2003), *Accounting for Managers: Interpreting Accounting Information for Decision–Making*, Chichester, John Wiley & Sons.

Collier, P.A., Cooke, T.E. and Glynn, J.J. (1988), *Financial and Treasury Management*, Oxford, Heinemann Professional Publishing.

Colley, J. (Jnr), Doyle, J.L., Logan, G.W., Stettinius, W. (2003), *Corporate Governance*, McGraw-Hill, ISBN 0–07–140346–9.

Cooke, T.E. and Glynn, J.J. (1991), 'Fixed asset replacement in a recession', *Accountancy*, November: 83–5.

Cooper, R. (1990), 'Cost classification in unit-based and activity-based manufacturing cost systems', *Journal of Cost Management*, Winter, 4–13.

Cooper, R. and Kaplan, R.S. (1988), 'Measure costs right: make the right decisions', *Harvard Business Review*, September/October: 96–103.

Cooper, R. and Kaplan, R.S. (1991), *The Design of Cost Management Systems: Text, Cases and Readings*, Hemel Hempstead, Prentice-Hall.

Coopers and Lybrand, Deloitte (1992), 'Industry briefing', London, Coopers and Lybrand, Deloitte. In-house publication for clients.

Cyert, R.M. and March, J.G. (1963), *A Behavioural Theory of the Firm*, New York, Prentice-Hall.

Davies, M., Paterson, R. and Wilson, A. (1999), *UK GAAP: Generally Accepted Accounting Practices in the UK*, 6th edn, London, Butterwoths Tolley.

DePaula, F.C. and Attwood, F.A. (1982), *Auditing Problems and Practice*, London, Pitman.

Deakin, S. (2003), 'After Enron: An age of enlightment?', *Organisation*, 10(3), 583–87.

De George, R.T. (2006), 'The relevance of philosophy to business ethics', *Business Ethics Quarterly*, 16, 3.

Dean, J. (1951), *Managerial Economics*, New York, Prentice-Hall.

Davies, A. (1999), *A Strategic Approach to Corporate Governance*, Gower, ISBN 0–566–08074–5.

Develin, N. (1999), 'Unlocking overhead value', *Management Accounting*, 77(11); 22.

Dominiak, G.F. and Louderback, J.G. (1988), *Managerial Accounting*, 5th edn, Boston, MA, Kent Publishing Company.

Duska, R.F. and Duska, B.S. (2003), *Accounting Ethics*, Cambridge MA: Blackwells, ISBN 0–631–21650–2.

Drury, C. (2004), *Management and Cost Accounting*, 6th edn, London, Thomson Learning.

Drury, C. and Dugdale, D. (1996), 'Surveys of management accounting practice', in C. Drury (ed.), *Management Accounting Handbook*, London, Butterworth-Heinemann.

Drury, C., Braund, S., Osbourne, P. and Tayles, B. (1992), *A Survey of Management Accounting Practices in UK Companies*, London, Chartered Association of Certified Accountants.

Eco Tec (1991), *Industry Costs of Pollution Control*, Birmingham.

Ellis, J. and Williams, D. (1993), *Corporate Strategy and Financial Analysis*, London, Pitman Publishing.

Elliot, B. and Elliot, J. (2003), *Financial Accounting and Reporting*, 7th edn, London, FT Prentice-Hall.

Emmanuel, C. and Otley, D. (1985), *Accounting for Managerial Control*, New York, Van Nostrand Reinhold.

Emmanuel, C., Otley, D. and Merchant, K. (1995), *Accounting for Management Control*, 2nd edn, London, Chapman and Hall.

Epstein, M. and Roy, M.J. (1997), 'Environmental management to improve corporate responsibility, *Journal of Cost Management*, 16(2), 190–203.

Estes, R. (1976), *Corporate Social Reporting*, New York, John Wiley & Sons.

Fama, E., Fisher, I., Jensen, M. and Roll, R. (1969), 'The adjustment of stock prices to new information', *International Economic Review*, February.

Fawcett, S.E., Ellram, L.M., and Ogden, J.A. (2007), *Supply Chain Management – From Vision to Implementation*, Pearson Prentice-Hall, ISBN 0–13–101504–4.

Fayol, H. (1949), *General and Industrial Management*, London, Pitman.

Financial Accounting Standards Board (1980), *Statement of Financial Accounting Concepts (SFAC) 2: Qualitative Characteristics of Accounting Information*, Stanford, CT, FASB.

Financial Accounting Standards Board (1985), *Elements of Financial Statements*, Financial Accounting Standards Board, Stanford, CT, FASB.

Firth, M.A. (1977), 'An empirical investigation of the impact of the announcement of capitalized issues on share prices', *Journal of Business, Finance and Accounting*, Spring.

Fisher, I. (1907), *The Rate of Interest*, London, Macmillan.

Fisher, I. (1930), *The Theory of Interest*, London, Macmillan.

Francis, R.D. (2000), *Ethics & Corporate Governance*, New South Wales University Press, ISBN 0–868–40682–1.

Freeman, M.A. (1985), 'The implications of agency theory for behavioural research' *AAANZ Conference Paper.*

Glynn, J.J. (1985), *Value for Money Auditing in the Public Sector*, Hemel Hemstead, Prentice-Hall.

Glynn, J.J. (1993), *Public Sector Accounting and Control,* 2nd edn, Oxford, Blackwell.

Glynn, J.J., Gray, A. and Jenkins, W.I. (1992), 'Auditing the three Es: the Challenge of Effectiveness', *Public Policy and Administration*, Winter.

Glynn, J.J. and Perkins, D. (1997), 'Control and accountability in the UK NHS market', *International Journal of Public Sector Management*, 10(1–2), 62–75.

Goetz, H. (1949), *Management Planning and Control*, Maidenhead, McGraw-Hill.

Goldman, A. and Barlev, B. (1974), 'The auditor-firm conflict of interest: its implications for independence', *Accounting Review*, October, 707–18.

Gordon, M.J. (1959), *The Investment, Financing and Valuation of the Corporation*, London, Irwin.

Granovetter, M. (1985), 'Economic action and social structure: the problem of embededdness', *American Journal of Sociology*, 93(1), 485–510.

Gray, R.H., Owen, D.L. and Maunders, K.T. (1987), *Corporate Social Reporting: Accounting and Accountability*, Hemel Hempstead, Prentice-Hall.

Gray, R., Bebbington, J. and Walters, D. (1993), *Accounting for the Environment*, London, Paul Chapman Publishing.

Green, F.B. and Amenkheinan, F.E. (1992), 'Accounting innovation: a cross-sectional survey of manufacturing firms', *Journal of Cost Management for the Manufacturing Industry*, Spring.

Griffiths, I. (1995), *New Creative Accounting*, London, Macmillan.

Guthrie, J. and Parker, L.D. (1989), 'Corporate social disclosure practice: a comparative international analysis', in M. Neimark (ed.), *Advances in Public Interest Accounting*, JAI Press.

Hannan, M.T. and Freeman, J. (1988), *Organisational Ecology*, Cambridge, MA, Harvard University Press.

Hanson, D.R. and Mendoza, R. (1999), 'Costos de Impacto Ambiental: Su Medicion, Asignation, y Control', *INCAE Revisita*, Vol X, No. 2.

Hatry, H.P. (1979), *Efficiency Measurement for Local Government Services*, Washington DC, Urban Institute.

Henderson, B.D. (1989), 'The origin of strategy', *Harvard Business Review*, November–December: 139–43.

Hendriksen, E.S. (1982), *Accounting Theory,* 4th edn, Illinois, Richard D. Irwin Inc.

Henley, D., Likeirman, A. Perrin, J. *et al.* (1992), *Public Sector Accounting and Financial Control*, London, Chapman and Hall.

Herzberg, F.B. (1959), *The Motivation to Work*, Chichester, John Wiley & Sons.

HIH Royal Commission, The (2003), chaired by Justice Neville Owen, available at http://www.hihroyalcom.gov.au/, Commonwealth of Australia publication, April.

Hill, N.C. and Sartoris, W.L. (1995), *Short-term Financial Management,* 3rd edn, Englewood Cliffs, NJ, Prentice-Hall.

Hirshleifer, J. (1958), 'On the theory of optimal investment decisions', *Journal of Political Economy*, 66(4), 329–52.

HM Treasury (1984), Investment Appraisal in the Public Sector: A Technical Guide for Government Departments, London, HMSO.

HM Treasury (1988), *Output and Performance Measurement in Central Government: A Technical Guide*, HMSO.

Hodgson, P. (2004), 'The Wall Street example: Bringing excessive executive compensation into line', *Ivy Business School Journal*, May/June, pp.1–6.

Hofstede, G.H. (1968), *The Game of Budget Control*, London, Tavistock Publications.

Holmes, G. and Sugden, A. (1994), *Interpreting Company Reports and Accounts,* 5th edn, Hemel Hempstead, Woodhead-Faulkner.

Hopwood, A.G. (1988), 'Accounting and Organisational Action', *Accounting from the Outside: The Collected Papers of Anthony G. Hopwood*, New York, Garland.

Horngren, C.T., Bhimani, A., Datar, S.M. and Foster, G. (2002), *Management and Cost Accounting,* 2nd edn, Prentice-Hall.

Horngren, C.T., Bhimani, A., Datar, S.M. and Foster, G. (2005), *Management and Cost Accounting,* 3rd edn, Prentice-Hall.

Hu, Y.S. (1992), 'Global or stateless corporations: national firms win operations', *Management Review*, Winter, 115–26.

Humphrey, C.G., Moizer, P. and Turley, S.W. (1992), *The Audit Expectations Gap in the United Kingdom*, London, Institute of Chartered Accountants in England and Wales.

Inflation Accounting Committee (1975), Cmnd 6225 (The Sandilands Report), London, HMSO.

Innes, J. and Mitchell, F. (1995), *Activity-based Costing: A Review with Case Studies*, London, Chartered Institute of Management Accounting.

Institute of Chartered Accountants of New Zealand (1991), *Statement of Concepts for General Purpose Financial Reporting*, ICANZ.

International Accounting Standards Board (2006), *Presentation of Financial Statements*, London, IASB. Other statements of the IASB are summarised in Chapters 12 and 13.

International Federation of Accountants (1987), *Preface to Statements on International Management Accounting*, New York, IFAC.

International Federation of Accountants Committee (1998), *Statements of auditing standards*, IFAC, New York.

International Organisation of Securities Commissions (2000), *IASC Standards: Report of the Technical Commission of the International Organisation of Securities Commissions*, IOSC.

Jensen, M.C. and Meckling, W.H. (1976), 'Theory of the firm, managerial behaviour, agency costs and ownership structure, *Journal of Financial Economics*, October, 305–60.

Johnson, G. and Scholes, K. (1993), *Exploring Corporate Strategy: Text and Cases*, London and New York, Prentice-Hall.

Johnson, G. and Scholes, K. (1999), *Exploring Corporate Strategy: Text and Cases,* 5th edn, London and New York, Prentice-Hall.

Johnson, H.T. and Kaplan, R.S. (1987), *Relevance Lost: The Rise and Fall of Management Accounting*, Boston, MA, Harvard Business School Press.

Jones, R. (1985), *Local Government Audit Law*, London, HMSO.

Jones, C. (1990), 'Corporate social accounting and the capitalist enterprise', in D. Cooper and T.M. Hopper (eds), *Critical Accounts*, Macmillan.

Jupe, R. (1994), 'How green are UK company accounts? An exploration of changing corporate environmental disclosures', *Social and Environmental Accounting*, 14(2): 2–4.

Jupe, R. (1997), 'How green are UK company environmental reports? An exploration of corporate voluntary disclosures', *Social and Environmental Accounting*, 17(1): 5–8.

Kaplan, R.S. and Bruns, W. (1987), *Accounting and Management: A Field Study Perspective*, Harvard Business School Press, ISBN 0–875–84186–4.

Kaplan, R.S. and Norton, D.P. (1992), 'The balanced scorecard measures that drive performance', *Harvard Business Review*, Jan-Feb, 71–9.

Kaplan, R.S. and Norton, D.P. (1993), 'Putting the balanced scorecard to work', *Harvard Business Review*, Sept–Oct, 134–47.

Kaplan, R.S. and Norton, D.P. (1996a), 'Using the balanced scorecard as a strategic management system', *Harvard Business Review*, Jan–Feb, 75–85.

Kaplan, R.S. and Norton, D.P. (1996b), *The Balanced Scorecard: Translating Strategy into Action*, Boston, MA, Harvard Business School Press.

Kaplan, R.S. and Norton, D.P. (2001a), *The Strategy-focused Organisation*, Boston, MA, Harvard Business School Press.

Kaplan, R.S. and Norton, D.P. (2001b), 'Balance without profit', *Financial Management*, January, 23–26.

Kaplan, R.S. and Norton, D.P. (2001c), 'Transforming the balanced scorecard from performance measurement to strategic management: Part 1', *Accounting Horizons*, March, 87–104.

Kaplan, R.S. and Norton, D.P. (2001d), 'Transforming the balanced scorecard from performance measurement to strategic management: Part 2', *Accounting Horizons*, June, 147–60.

Katz, D. and Khan, R.L. (1966), *The Social Psychology of Organisations*, Chichester, John Wiley & Sons.

Kay, J. (l993), *Foundations of Corporate Success*, Oxford, Oxford University Press.

Kay, J.A. and King, M.A. (1978), *The British Tax System*, Oxford, Oxford University Press.

Keasey, K., Thompson, S. and Wright, M. (1997), *Corporate Governance – Economic, Management and Financial Issues*, Oxford: Oxford University Press.

Kendall, A. and Kendall, N. (1998), *Real World Corporate Governance*, FT Prentice-Hall, ISBN 0–566–08074–5.

Keynes, J.M. (1939), 'National self-sufficiency', *Yale Law Review*, Vol. 22: 755–63.

Lambert, D.M., Stock, J.R., Ellram, L.M. (1998), *Fundamentals of Logistics Management*, Irwin/McGraw-Hill, Boston, MA.

Lapsley, I. (1986), 'Investment appraisal in UK non-trading organisations', *Financial Accountability and Management*, 2(2), Summer, 135:51.

Lee, T.A. (1986), *Company Auditing,* 3rd edn, New York, Van Nostrand Reinhold.

Lee, J.Y. (1987), *Managerial Accounting: Changes for the 1990s*, Wokingham, Addison-Wesley.

Leenders, M.R., Fearon, H.E., Flynn, A.E., and Johnson, P.F. (2002), *Purchasing and Supply Management*, McGraw-Hill Irwin, ISBN 0–07–237060–2.

Lester, K. (1992), 'Protecting the environment: a new managerial responsibility', in D. Owen (ed.), *Green Reporting: Accountancy and the Challenge of the Nineties*, London, Chapman and Hall.

Levy, H. and Sarnatt, M. (1986), *Capital Investment and Financial Decisions*, 2nd edn, Hertfordshire, Prentice-Hall.

Likert, R. (1961), *New Patterns of Management*, New York, McGraw-Hill.

Lin, B., Collins, J. and Su, R.K. (2001), 'Supply chain costing: an activity-based perspective', *International Journal of Physical Distribution & Supply Chain Management*, 31(10): 702–13, ISSN 0–960–003 5.

Lintner, J. (1956), 'Distribution of incomes of corporations among dividends, retained earnings and taxation', *American Economic Review*, May.

Lorsch, J. and MacIver, E. (1989), *Pawns or Potentates: The Reality Of America's Corporate Boards*, Boston, MA: Harvard University Press.

Lumby, S. (1991), *Investment Appraisal and Financing Decisions*, London, Chapman and Hall.

Marsh, P. (1977), Ph.D Dissertation, London Graduate School of Business.

Martinez Ramos, M. (2004), 'Interaction between management accounting and supply chain management', *Supply Chain Management: An International Journal*, 9(2):134–8, Emerald Group Publishing Ltd., ISSN 1 359 854 6.

Maslow, A.H. (1954), *Motivation and Personality*, London, Harper & Row.

Mautz, R.K. and Sharaf, H.A. (1961), *The Philosophy of Auditing*, Sarasota, FL, American Accounting Association.

Mayo, E. (1933), *The Human Problems of a Civilisation*, London, Macmillan.

McGregor, D. (1960), *The Human Side of Enterprise*, New York, McGraw-Hill.

McInnes, W. (1993), *Auditing into the Twenty-first Century*, Edinburgh, Institute of Chartered Accountants of Scotland.

McIntyre, A.D. and Coulthurst, N.J. (1986), *Capital Budgeting in Medium Sized Businesses*, London, Chartered Institute of Management Accountants.

Mepham, M. (1980), *Accounting Models*, Stockport, PolyTech Publishers.

Mintzberg, H. (1987), 'Crafting strategy', *Harvard Business Review*, July–August, 65–75.

Mishan, E. (1971), *Cost-Benefit Analysis*, London, George, Allen & Unwin.

Modigliani, F. and Miller, M.H. (1958), 'The cost of capital, corporate finance and the theory of investment', *American Economic Review*, June.

Modigliani, F. and Miller, M.H. (1961), 'Corporate income taxes and the cost of capital', *Journal of Business*, October.

Modigliani, F. and Miller, M.H. (1963), 'Corporate income taxes and the cost of capital: a correction', *American Economic Review*, June.

Moore, P.C. (1976), *Basic Operational Research*, London, Pitman.

Mouritsen, J., Hansen, A. and Hansen, C.O. (2001), 'Inter-organizational controls and organizational competencies: episodes around target cost management/functional analysis and open book accounting', *Management Accounting Research*, 12(2): 221–44.

Munday, M. (1992), 'Accounting cost data disclosure and buyer-supplier partnerships: a research note', *Management Accounting Research*, 3(3): 245–50.

Murphy, M.P. (1996), 'Management audit', in J.J. Glynn, D.A. Perkins and S. Steward (eds), *Achieving Value for Money in the NHS*, London, Saunders.

Nobes, C. and Parker, R.H. (1995), *Comparative International Accounting*, 4th edn, Hemel Hempstead, Prentice-Hall International (UK).

Oakland, P. (1994), *Total Quality Management*, Oxford, Butterworth-Heinemann.

OECD (1999), *Principles of Corporate Governance*, Paris, OECD.

Mace, M. (1971), *Directors: Myth and Reality*, Boston, MA: Harvard University Press.

Otley, D. (1977), *Behavioural Aspects of Budgeting: Accountants' Digest No. 49*, London, Institute of Chartered Accountants in England and Wales.

Otley, D. (1980), 'The contingency theory of management accounting: achievement and prognosis', *Accounting, Organisations & Society*, 5(1): 194–208, reprinted in C. Emmanuel, D. Otley and K. Merchant (eds), *Readings in Accounting for Management Control*, London, Chapman & Hall.

Owen, D. (ed.) (1992), *Green Reporting: Accountancy and the Challenge of the Nineties*, London, Chapman and Hall.

Parker, R.H. (1984), *Macmillan Dictionary of Accounting*, London, Macmillan.

Partridge, M. and Perren, L. (1997), 'Vice-versa', *Accountancy*, November, 54.

Perkins, D. (1996), 'Control and VFM', in J.J. Glynn, D. Perkins and S. Stewart (eds), *Managing Healthcare: Achieving Value for Money*, London, Van Nostrand Reinhold and Chapman and Hall.

Perrow, C. (1970), *Organisational Analysis*, Tavistock, Wadsworth.

Pike, R.H. and Wolfe, M.B. (1988), *Capital Budgeting in the 1990s*, London, Chartered Institute of Management Accountants.

Pinches, G.E. (1982), 'Myopia, capital budgeting and decision making', *Financial Management*, Autumn.

Porter, M.E. (1980), *Competitive Strategy: Techniques for Analysing Industries and Firms*, New York, Free Press and Macmillan.

Porter, M.E. (1985), *Competitive Advantage*, New York, Free Press.

Power, M. (1997), *The Audit Society: Rituals of Verification*, Oxford, Oxford University Press.

Price Waterhouse (1990), *Value for Money Auditing*, London, Gee & Co.

Report of the Select Committee on Corporation Tax (HCP 622).

Roberts, C. (1992), 'Environmental disclosures in corporate annual reports in Western Europe', in D. Owen (ed.), *Green Reporting: Accountancy and the Challenge of the Nineties*, London, Chapman and Hall.

Ross, S.A., Thompson, S.C., Christensen, M.T., Westerfield, R.W. and Jordan, B.D. (2001), *Fundamentals of Corporate Finance*, 2nd Australian edn, Sydney, McGraw-Hill.

Samuels, J.M., Wilkes, F.M. and Brayshaw, R.E. (1995), *Management of Company Finance*, 6th edn, London, International Thomson Press.

Samuels, J.M., Wilkes, F.M. and Brayshaw, R.E. (1999), *Management of Company Finance*, 7th edn, London, International Thomson Press.

Shank, J.K. and Govindarajan, V. (1992), 'Strategic cost management and the value chain', *Journal of Cost Management*, 5(4): 5–21.

Sharpe, W.K. (1964), 'Capital asset prices: a theory of market equilibrium under conditions of risk', *Journal of Finance*, September, 10–18.

Shillinglaw, G. (1963), 'The concept of attributable cost', *Journal of Accounting Research 1(1)*: Reprinted in D. Solomons (ed.), *Studies in Cost Analysis*, 2nd edn, London, Sweet & Maxwell.

Simon, H.A. (1957), *Administrative Behaviour*, New York, Free Press.

Sloan, A.P. (1963), *My Years with General Motors*, Sidgewick & Jackson.

Smith, T. (1996), *Accounting for Growth: Stripping the Camouflage from Company Accounts*, 2nd edn, London, Century Business.

Solomons, D. (1952), *Studies in Costing*, London, Sweet & Maxwell.

Solomons, D. (1983), *Divisional Performance: Measurement and Control*, New York, Marcus Weiner Publishing.

Stacey, R.D. (1993), *Strategic Management and Organisational Dynamics*, London, Paul Chapman.

Stedry, R.C. (1960), *Budget Control and Cost Behaviour*, New York, Prentice-Hall.

Steen, D.C.M.E. (1989), *Audits and Auditors: What the Public Thinks*, London, KPMG Peat Marwick McLintock.

Taylor, F.W. (1947), *Scientific Management*, London, Harper & Row.

Taylor, P.A. (1996), *Consolidated Financial Reporting*, London, Paul Chapman.

Tobin, J. (1958), 'Liquidity preference as a behaviour towards risks', *Review of Economic Studies*, February, 65–86.

Touche Ross Management Consultants (1990), *Head in the Clouds or Head in the Sand? UK Managers Attitudes to Environmental Issues: A Survey*, London, Touche Ross & Co.

Walter, J.E. (1967), *Dividend Policy and Enterprise Evaluation*, London, Wadsworth.

Watson, D. and Head, T. (2001), *Corporate Finance: Principles & Practice*, London, Financial Times Pitman Publishing.

Whittred, W.Z.T., Zimmer, I. and Taylor, S. (2000), *Financial Accounting: Incentive Effects and Economic Consequences*, 5th edn, London, Harcourt, Brace Johanovic.

Whittington, R. (1993), *What is Strategy – And Does It Matter?*, London and New York, Routledge.

Wilson, R.M. (1995), 'Strategic management accounting', in D. Ashton, T. Hopper and R.W. Scapens (eds), *Issues in Management Accounting*, Hertfordshire, Prentice-Hall.

Wilson, R.M.S. and Chua, W.F. (1993), *Managerial Accounting: Method and Meaning*, 2nd edn, London, International Thomson Business Press.

Williamson, O.E. (1991), 'Strategising, economizing and economic organisation', *Strategic Management Journal*, 12: 75–94.

Williamson, A. (1997), 'Target and kaizen costing', *Manufacturing Engineer*, February: 22–4.

WEBSITES

Note: These website addresses are correct at the time of writing. However, they may be subject to change in the future. Accordingly users are advised to make use of the website supporting this text which is updated on a regular basis and incorporates the relevant hypertext links.

AAA	www.rutgers.edu/Accounting/raw/aaa
AASB	www.aasb.com.au
ACCA	www.acca.co.uk
AICPA	www.aicpa.org
APB	www.apb.co.uk
ASB	www.asb.org.uk
ASE	www.asx.com.au/asx/homepage/index.jsp
CBI	www.cbi.org.uk
CICA	www.cica.com
CIMA	www.cima.org.uk
CIPFA	www.cipfa.org.uk
DTI	www.dti.gov.uk
EU	www.europa.eu.int
FASB	www.fasb.org
FRC	www.frc.org.uk
FRRP	www.frrp.org.uk
FSA	www.fsa.gov.uk
FT	www.ft.com
IASB	www.iasb.co.uk
IASC	www.isac.org.uk
ICAEW	www.icaew.co.uk
ICAI	www.icai.ie
ICAS	www.icas.org.uk
IFAC	www.ifac.org
IIA	www.theiia.org
IOSCO	www.iosco.org
LSE	www.londonstockexchange.com
NAO	www.nao.gov.uk
NASDAQ	www.nasdaq.com
NHS	www.nhs50.nhs.uk
NYSE	www.nyse.com
UITF	www.asb.org.uk/uitf
IBE	www.ibe.org.uk

GUIDE NOTES FOR THE ANSWERS TO THE EXERCISES

Chapter 1

1* Many students will answer this question in the context of a simple club. Such simple club may have only cash receipts (income) and cash payments (expenditure) accounts, perhaps with a balance sheet. Often this may provide adequate 'disclosure', but not necessarily good 'accountability'. Students should be clear that disclosure and accountability are not the same, although good disclosure is one requirement of good accountability. Even in the case of a simple club, good accountability may require not just disclosure in the accounts of relevant categories of information, but also: an audit and an auditor's report, a report of the chairman at an AGM, encouragement of questioning the chairman and auditor at the AGM, and making the books and records of the accounts available for the inspection of members. Students with experience of more complex organisations should give more advanced answers. Students may (and should) query the lack of accrual-type information – even for clubs, where the lack of a depreciation (i.e. annualised use cost) charge for a substantial asset, such as a computer or a DJ music system, could seriously reduce the relevance, and in a sense the accountability, of each separate year's accounts viewed in isolation (as they usually are, both for accountability and for operational decision taking). Students should be encouraged to think imaginatively in suggesting 'improvements', even if at this stage of the course their ideas may not be clearly formulated or realistic, or use professional terminology.

3* The question refers to Table 1.3 in this chapter, and it relates at least indirectly to all the discussion in this chapter focused on the listed characteristics of financial accounting reports. The answer to this question is speculative; there is no 'absolute' correct answer. A simplistic answer would be that 'Accounting reports are not sufficiently accurate to be truthful, and vice versa: hence, they are neither accurate nor truthful'. More usefully, one may speculate that neither of these two characteristics was included by any of the four expert bodies cited in the table, for the reason that the experts recognise that there is necessarily too much estimation or approximation in accounting information and measurements, and too many areas of judgement, as to justify such fairly absolute terms of certainty and virtue as 'accurate' and 'truthful'. It is essential for students to understand that the apparent precision or preciseness of accounting does not of itself guarantee accuracy or truth, or indeed even other less absolute characteristics such as comparability, relevance and reliability.

4* Ideally students should think about other possible 'trade-offs' between pairs of the 'desirable characteristics of accounting reports', to compare them to the trade-off between 'Relevance' and 'Reliability' even if they do not write about them. The importance of the cited trade-off depends on the argument that often improving the degree of 'relevance' in reports can only be achieved by reducing their degree of 'reliability', and vice versa. Relevance relates to meeting the needs of particular users for particular types of decisions, and often this implies estimations and choices of information helpful for forecasting the future.

Reliability, in contrast, is not concerned with report users, but rather with the integrity, consistency and auditability of the data and information inputs to reports and of the disclosure in the reports themselves. Reliability looks to the past and may minimise estimation and use of judgement, while relevance may involve the opposite behaviour and lead to different conclusions on profits and balance sheet values.

6* The management accountant's role is to contribute to the management process by supplying useful information and advice. This involves interaction with managers at all levels. If accountants are to supply useful information, this must be based on activity data which is as relevant and accurate as possible. Typically, it is the managers who control or at least oversee the collection of the raw data on the use of resources which the management accountant must have in order to calculate and report costs, expenditure, and performance as compared to budgets and other plans. It is pointed out in the chapter that costs comprise the volumes of resources consumed, multiplied by the unit prices of those resources. In general the accountant has easy access to the prices, but must depend on managers for the accurate collection and recording of the data on the uses of resources, and the volumes consumed in those uses. Even in the discipline of the business world, it can be difficult to achieve a high quality of data recording and collection, but the problem is even greater in the public sector, where many 'managers' see themselves primarily as nurses, doctors, teachers, social workers, etc., and see data collection and recording as a distraction and waste of precious professional time. Accountants need to exercise leadership and the arts of education and persuasion to help build up understanding, cooperation and assistance from managers. Especially is this so where the management accountant is responsible for an active system of budgeting and budgetary control over managers, where behavioural problems and attitudes become very important for successful cooperation, as will be discussed in some detail in Chapter 7. Students should have reread the chapter section on 'Accounting and Management Information Systems'. However, this question requires students to use a little imagination, and perhaps to draw on other courses of study, to obtain a balanced view in their answers. In an ideal world a MIS comprises an integrated information system holding all data and processing all information needed in support of all aspects of corporate management. This is technically very difficult to achieve, very expensive, and few if any enterprises have achieved it. The accounting function may claim to lead the entire MIS programme on the grounds that it is numerate, that it must use computers for its work, and that the accounting function is (because of legal and contractual commitments) the most important information system to have controlled access to processing capacity and time. These arguments may not carry strong conviction with other management functions, perhaps notably personnel and marketing management, who may see their information needs as equally important to the enterprise's success and survival. An organisational alternative is to view MIS as a management function in its own right, with its own specialist head reporting to the chief executive or his deputy. This alternative has been tried in business and the public sector, but the result frequently appears to have been an MIS unit which becomes introspective, more concerned with the continuing evolution of its software and hardware than with the immediate information needs and timetable deadlines of operational functions such as accounting and production. In the real world, the decision on who controls MIS may need to depend on the quality of senior management and leadership available within the enterprise at any given point in time.

8* The essence of the difference between the private and the public sector is that businesses in the private sector have as their primary objective the generation of profit by supplying goods and services to their customers – frequently they will seek to make as much profit as possible. In the public sector, the primary objective of organisations is the provision of services to the public to as great an extent as possible, while remaining within budgetary limits. Thus, in the private sector, financial management is, in large part, about helping the business generate (and collect) revenues in excess of the associated costs; identifying investment and other projects which help in this and ensuring the availability of the necessary financial resources to support these activities. In these circumstances financial budgets and forecasts provide targets, but often the aim is to exceed these targets (e.g. revenue budgets). Traditionally, in the public sector an organisation's revenue has been largely fixed (e.g. by the amount of taxation or other revenue that is allocated to it by local or central government). Thus, the emphasis is very much on the regularity of expenditure, on cost control and on developing performance measures to replace the use (in the private sector) of profit and revenue.

In essence, these differences arise from the different accountabilities in the two sectors – in the private sector for the use of owners' (shareholders') resources in the generation of profits; in the public sector the efficient and effective use of public funds. There are obviously areas of similarity in these two accountabilities. Both require the maintenance of suitable financial (and other) records; both require the preparation and monitoring of budgets and other financial reports; both require the effective management of cash flows; both require information about the costs of products and services, and both require internal control systems. Thus, a great deal of accounting is very similar across the two sectors. The differences relate to the context within which the organisation operates – its accountabilities, its objectives, and (to some extent) its culture and values.

Accounting as a discipline is (or should be) inherently neutral – as such it is able to serve the needs of both sectors.

11* This is a question designed to make you think ahead to issues in other chapters. In this chapter we discussed the desirable characteristics of accounting information. In terms of these 11 characteristics, you might wish to reflect upon how it was that some of these accounting scandals took so long to come to light. In the case of companies such as Enron and Worldcom, was their financial statement objective, comparable, realistic and reliable, for example? How was it possible for such frauds to occur? Was it the failure of the regulatory system or the system of accounting/auditing regulation? As this is the first chapter we want you to speculate. As you progress through the text you might like to revisit this question and see how your thoughts have further developed.

12* The reference to 'different truths' was referred to earlier in the text. Accounting is not a precise science. Even though financial accounting is subject to regulatory processes, there are still a number of options available when it comes to matters of valuation for example. Some firms periodically revalue their freehold assets, as they are probably the most significant assets on their balance sheets. Some firms may depreciate a particular class of assets over, say, five years whilst other firms might choose a larger or shorter period. Management accounting has no regulatory framework and so it can often be the case that different firms have very different approaches to, for example, the recognition of overheads. This is important for the determination of issues such as pricing or departmental performance. Managers need to have a real appreciation that different costing regimes can produce quite markedly different results. Again this question is designed to get you thinking about issues we will be discussing in subsequent chapters.

13* This question relates to the first introductory pages of this chapter. Clearly it is not practicable to regulate the provision of what is after all internal information. What is important is that dear principles are incorporated into any management accounting information system and this is better done by education rather than regulation via standards etc.

14* This question calls for students to be able to illustrate the importance of cash rather than accounting profit in management accounting. Cash flows are what keep organisations in business. As we progress through the rest of the book this is stressed time and time again. Illustrations similar to that used in the chapter should demonstrate the student's understanding of this important distinction.

16* Students will probably need to refer to the reference to Stedry. This is clearly a behavioural issue. Does the notion of 'tight yet achievable' have more to do with the scientific management model? Are such issues more to do with the overall corporate culture of the organisation?

18* Agency theory is useful because it is based on well argued economic principles which are translated into this notion of contractual relationships. However its does remain mainly of academic interest.

20* Clearly there needs to be ways in which internal information reconciles with external information. In fact, in many organisations, the dominance of the need to publish externally has often led to a very poor level of internal (management) accounting information. This question does also call to mind issues such as timing differences, the need to keep certain information out of the public arena etc.

Note that in the public sector there was a tendency to concentrate more on cost statements than external reports. Nowadays however there is a convergence of external reporting requirements between the public sector and private sector. This is principally to do with government's market approach to public service provision.

Chapter 2

1* The basic responsibilities of the board of directors in the governance of a company can be found at http://www.businesslink.gov.uk for UK director responsibilities. Similar links are easily searchable for other jurisdictions. For example, in Australia the relevant link is http://asic.gov.au where there is both information on director responsibilities and, additionally, a series of related papers, such as 'Director's Responsibilities: The reality vs. the myths', an address by the ASIC Chairman to the Australian Institute of Company Directors, 17 August, 2006 in Melbourne. Students should note the broad comparability of responsibilities across jurisdictions such as Australia, the UK and the USA, particularly when related to the key role of non-executive directors and the tightening of the definitions of responsibilities of the CEO and CFO.

2* Classically, governments tend to prefer self-regulation rather than direct intervention in the governance of companies. Governments prepare the legislative frameworks for the governance and management of corporate bodies through the various company law acts of individual countries. Groups such as stock exchanges establish review bodies and have commissioned reports from which guidance or codes of practice are prepared. Internationally, groups such as the OECD have attempted to influence individual countries as they seek to improve upon their supervision of governance. Governments also expect professional bodies to also oversee the role that their members play in the monitoring and supervision of governance codes of practice. One of the key concerns of governments is to ensure that companies not only act in the best interest of shareholders but in fact act in the interests of all stakeholders. The UK can be regarded as an international leader in non-regulatory activism in promoting boards to be more corporately responsible. There is a Minister for Corporate Social Responsibility (CSR), as well as initiatives to raise the profile of CSR and to undertake research into CSR. Also see http://www.mises.org/journals/Padilla7.pdf 'Government regulation, Unintended Consequences, and the Rise of Omnipotent Management', Alexandre Padilla and Andrei Kerptul.

3* For an in-depth review of the findings of the HIH Insurance Royal Commission, and the lessons that can be learnt, download http: //www.cbs.curtain.edu.au/ teachingareas/businesslaw/research/business-law-working-paper-series, 'The demise of HIH: what part did failed corporate governance policies play', John D. Motais, Business Law Working Paper Series 05.0.

8* This question can be fully answered by reference to The Institute of Business Ethics website at http://www.ibe.org.uk.

11* This question requires students, firstly, to consult the websites of major corporations and to download their codes of corporate governance and business ethics. Secondly, these codes should be compared with appropriate frameworks as developed by groups such as the Institute of Business Ethics, http://www.ibe.org.uk. This site also provides links to a number of relevant corporate websites.

12* The key to this question is that, in principle, there is little difference between the roles of board members in corporate boards and not-for-profit boards. However, there can be tensions in needing to have a board that understands good management practice as opposed to being composed of members who feel that they wish to link with the organisation and is not really prepared or skilled at understanding their statutory responsibilities, etc. A web search of large charitable organisations will provide examples of the duties of their board members. Also sites such as http://www.boardsource.org and http://cqcapd.state.ny.us/Bestpractices/boardroom/htm provide directions to other relevant material to answer this question.

Chapter 3

1* This question requires the preparation of journals to record the content of prime records into the ledger accounts of Suppliers Ltd. These should be as follows:

(a)   Credit sales to customers amounting to $60 000 of merchandise that originally cost $30 000.

Date	Description	Code	Debit $	Credit $
7/1	Product sales	004-001		60 000
	Trade debtors	002-101	60 000	
	Cost of goods sold	005-001	30 000	
	Finished goods stock	002-003		30 000
			90 000	90 000

(b)   Cash sales to customers amounting to $7000 of merchandise which originally cost $3700:

Date	Description	Code	Debit $	Credit $
7/1	Product sales	004-001		7 000
	Cash at bank	002-202	7 000	
	Cost of goods sold	005-001	3 700	
	Finished goods stock	002-003		3 700
			10 700	10 700

(c)   Purchase of materials from suppliers on credit terms amounting to $35 000:

Date	Description	Code	Debit $	Credit $
7/1	Raw material stock	002-001	35 000	
	Creditors	003-001		35 000
			35 000	35 000

(d)   Payments to suppliers for materials supplied on credit terms amounting to $18 000

Date	Description	Code	Debit $	Credit $
7/1	Creditors	003-001	18 000	
	Cash at bank	002-202		18 000
			18 000	18 000

(e)   Payments to staff of salaries and wages amounting to $6000

Date	Description	Code	Debit $	Credit £
7/1	Wages	005-002	6000	
	Cash at bank	002-202		6000
			6000	6000

2* The question requires us to calculate the annual depreciation charges for a new machine acquired by Jehosophat Ltd on three alternative bases.

(a)   The straight line basis

This is the most straightforward computation as by definition the depreciation charge will be the same for each of the five years. It is calculated by:

$$\text{Annual depreciation charge} = \frac{\text{Original cost} - \text{Expected residual value}}{\text{Forecast life of the asset}}$$
$$= (\$244{,}000 - \$24{,}000)/5$$
$$= \$44{,}000 \text{ per annum.}$$

(b)   The reducing balance method

Here a separate depreciation charge has to be calculated for each of the five years. The first stage in the process is the calculation of the annual rate of depreciation using the formula given in the text

i.e.: Annual depreciation rate $= 1 - \sqrt[n]{(S/C)}$

where: n = life of the asset

S = expected residual value

C = cost of the asset

Inserting the data for Jehosophat gives:

Annual depreciation rate $= 1 - \sqrt[n]{(\$24\,000/\$244\,000)} = 0.371$

We can then apply this annual percentage as follows:

Year	Opening balance	Depreciation charge	Closing balance
One	$244 000	$90 624	$153 476
Two	153 476	56 939	96 537
Three	96 537	35 815	60 722
Four	60 722	22 528	38 194
Five	38 194	14 170	24 024

(c)   The usage basis

This basis requires us to compute a depreciation cost per operation, allowing for any residual value. The forecast number of operations is:

$$8000 + 12\,000 + 10\,000 + 5000 + 5000 = 40\,000$$

Thus the cost per operation $= (\$244\,000 - \$24\,000)/40\,000 = \$5.50$

Therefore the annual depreciation charges are:

Year one:	8 000 × $5.5	= $44 000
Year two:	12 000 × $5.5	= $66 000

Year three:	10 000 × $5.5	= $55 000
Year four:	5 000 × $5.5	= $27 500
Year five:	5 000 × $5.5	= $27 500

The question then asks us to plot the year-end values of the equipment on the differing depreciation bases:

6* The question requires the design of a cash book layout to record transactions using the chart of accounts in Table 3.2, in the main text. Table 3.2 is only an extract from a potential chart of accounts for an enterprise. It does not, for example, include any account titles/codes relating to the analysis of costs. Accordingly, some extensions of the chart of accounts shown in Table 3.2 are needed. With this proviso in mind, the following analysis is required in the cashbook to cope with the specified transactions:

Code	Account Title
001-003	Fixed Assets: Motor vehicles – cost
002-101	Trade debtors
003-001	Current Liabilities: Materials suppliers
005-004	Marketing costs
005-002	Payroll costs
007-001	Long term loans
007-001	Share capital

Some of the required analysis relates to receipts and some to payments. Accordingly, for convenience and in line with common practice, the cashbook needs to be divided into two sections: one dealing with receipts and one dealing with payments. Suggested formats for this are shown below.

Cash Receipts

Date	Reference	Amt €	002-101 €	006-601 €	XXX €	XXX €	XXX €
XXX	Customer receipt	2 000	2 000				
XXX	Share capital	20 000		20 000			

Cash Payments

Date	Reference	Amt €	001-003 €	005-004 €	003-001 €	007-001 €	005-002 €
XXX	Van	10 000	10 000				
XXX	Advertisement	200		200			
XXX	Supplier	2 500			2 500		
XXX	Loan	10 000				10 000	
XXX	Wages	6 000					6 000

8* The requirement is to design a chart of accounts for a new newsagent business operating from rented premises. As ever, in designing a chart of accounts for a business a trade-off needs to be made between the extent of the analytic information provided via the use of a chart of accounts and the costs associated with maintaining a very comprehensive analytic accounting system. In the case of a sole trader operating as a newsagent the analysis could be very detailed, e.g. down to the level of the sales of each newspaper, magazine or brand of cigarettes. However, this would be expensive to operate and the value of the information to John Smith, the proprietor, is dubious. It is not practical to produce a definitive answer to the question. However, some general principles can be identified and these can then be applied in producing an actual chart of accounts. These principles are illustrated below:

Assets

The chart of accounts will need to distinguish between:

(i) Fixed assets – there should be provision for the separate analysis of the major categories of fixed assets. In the case of Smith, occupying rented premises, the major categories are likely to include:

- Shop fixtures and fittings
- Office equipment
- Motor vehicles

(ii) Current assets – there should be provision for the following:

- Stocks – the extent of the detailed analysis needs to be closely integrated with the analysis that is going to be made of sales and purchases. For a newsagent using a traditional form of till/cash register it might be practical to analyse stock movements in terms of perhaps half a dozen categories, e.g. newspapers, magazines, tobacco products, soft drinks, confectionery and books.

- Debtors – a newsagent is essentially a cash sales business, apart from newspaper deliveries. Thus the core requirement would relate to amounts owing for newspaper deliveries, unless there were any corporate organisations which were offered credit facilities.

- Cash – as a newsagent is primarily a cash sales business, particular attention would need to be paid to this area. At a minimum, there would need to be separate ledger accounts for each bank account the business operates, and for cash registers/tills in use, as well as for any petty cash floats. Particular attention would need to be paid to internal control systems surrounding the cash movements within the business.

Liabilities

The core requirement here is that Smith has adequate information about to whom the business owes money and when it is due. This will obviously require detailed records dealing with each credit terms supplier. However, some general categories of liabilities are likely to be needed. These include:

- Taxation liabilities.
- Customs and Excise (for VAT, etc.)
- Suppliers (particularly the wholesalers from whom supplies are purchased)
- Utilities (e.g. gas, electricity, telephone)
- Loan creditors (if applicable)

Revenues

The extent of the analysis here ties in closely with that relating to stocks and purchases. In the case of Smith it is likely to be limited to the categories shown above. However, other larger retailers may have a much more extensive analysis of their activities.

Retailers such as Sainsbury's, Safeways and Tesco's have stock/sales/purchases systems that analyse activities down to individual product lines and each individual store location. In the case of Smith this level of detail is likely to be unnecessary. However, an analysis into cash and credit sales could be helpful.

Costs

The main need here will be an analysis that mirrors that for stock and revenues, at least as regards merchandise. However, a chart of accounts will also need to recognise the various support (overhead) costs such as:

- Wages and salaries
- Rent
- Heat, light and power
- Printing and stationery
- Depreciation charges
- Maintenance

The extent of the analysis will depend on the relative scale of expenditure in the different areas.

9* The number and range of prime documents that a business like Makeit will need to have will depend in part on how detailed an analysis of its activities it requires, and how formal a system of internal control the proprietor of the business requires. Typically, smaller businesses tend to have more informal systems of internal control than larger businesses. However, one important principle that should be adhered to is that wherever possible the prime documents should be pre-numbered. This pre-numbering will enable a check to be made that all prime documents are accounted for and recorded in the prime records (books of prime entry and supporting records, e.g. stores ledgers). Subject to this, a business such as Makeit would probably have prime documents that would include the following:

Asset movements

- Stocks and work-in-progress: the core issues here are the need to record the movement of raw materials and finished goods through the business, and to record the costs of the jobs that are carried out for customers. Typically, the sort of prime documents that will be needed to do this will include:
- Goods received notes to record the receipt of goods from suppliers
- Stores requisitions to record the issue of materials to particular customer jobs
- Goods returned notes to record the return of defective goods to suppliers
- Time sheets to record the time that the blacksmiths spend on each job
- Delivery notes to record the delivery of goods to customers, and their acceptance by the customers, and to facilitate the raising of sales invoices

- Debtors: the core issues here are firstly to record the negotiation and acceptance of customer orders and then to record the completion of these orders and the subsequent payment by the customers. Typically, the types of prime documents that will be needed to achieve this include:

- Customer order/acceptance forms to record the details of the order (specification, delivery details, price and any other relevant details of the customer's order)

- Sales invoices to record the invoicing of the customers. Frequently these are part of a multi-part document of which the delivery note is another part.

- Credit notes to record errors and exceptions in the invoicing of customers, e.g. when an error is made in the price invoiced to a customer.

- Cash receipt records that represent the interface between debtor management and cash management. The prime documents in this area need to cater for actual cash receipts (pre-numbered cash receipt books) and postal receipts (listings of cheques received in each day's posts).

- Cash: here Makeit will need to cater for both cash at bank and actual cash transactions. The core issue is to have prime documents that ensure all cash transactions are recorded. Typically this will need:

- Petty cash vouchers to record any direct cash payments.

- Cheque requisitions to record the need for and the issue of cheque payments.

- Cash receipt records as described above.

- Cheque books to record cheques actually issued.

- Bank paying-in books to record monies deposited in bank accounts.

Liabilities movements

The core issue here is the recording of the incurring and the settlement of liabilities. Some of the necessary prime documents have already been referred to earlier; e.g. chequebooks and goods received notes. Other prime documents that will be needed include:

- Purchase orders to record the goods ordered from suppliers and the terms on which they are ordered e.g. price, discounts and delivery.

- Purchase invoices from suppliers showing what suppliers are actually asking for and which can be authenticated from the purchase orders.

- Debit notes which record claims against suppliers, e.g. for defective or short deliveries.

- Demands from other creditors, e.g. utilities for services consumed.

- Contracts and similar documents, e.g. rental agreements.

- Loan agreements

Revenues

The core issue here is to ensure the recording of all revenues accruing to the business. Thus the range of prime documents will need to reflect the types of income enjoyed by the business. Some of these have already been identified, principally the revenues due from customers from work carried out on their behalf. However, there may be other sources of revenue for which prime documents need to be provided, e.g.:

- Vending machine takings
- Consultancy services
- Advertising space
- Rental from accommodation

Costs

The core issue here is ensure the correct recording of the costs incurred by Makeit in carrying out its activities. Many of the prime documents needed for this purpose have already been referred, e.g. those dealing with movements in liabilities. Perhaps the major core area not yet referred to is that of the payroll. There needs to be a system of prime documents recording who is employed and what terms, what overtime is worked, and what payroll taxes are incurred. This will require employment contracts, authorised timesheets and the use of PAYE and NI records for employees.

As in virtually all business enterprises, there will be transactions affecting Makeit which will not be recorded by the normal system of prime documents, e.g. depreciation of fixed assets, accruals/prepayments and any exceptional/unusual transactions. Thus, the prime documents will need to be supplemented by an effective system of journal entries.

10* Unification has a well-established accounting and internal control system. As such it can reasonably be assumed that this system will record all the normal transactions that the company enters into during its financial year. However, as with most organisations, it is likely that adjustments to these accounting records will be necessary for the preparation of the financial statements. These adjustments will have asset/liability (i.e. balance sheet consequences) and revenue/cost (i.e. profit and loss account) consequences and most will be the result of applying the accruals/matching concept and the prudence concept. The most probable areas where such adjustments might be required, concentrating on the balance sheet consequences, are:

Assets:

Fixed assets:

(a) Processing of the depreciation charges for the year

(b) Elimination of any time expired fixed assets

(c) Changing the basis of the valuation of fixed assets from historical cost to current market values

Current assets:

Stocks:

(a) Reduction of value of excess and obsolete stocks to current market value from original cost

(b) Reconciliation of stock value as shown by the accounting system to that revealed by a physical verification of stock to allow for e.g. shrinkage and recording errors

Debtors:

(a) Provision against potential bad debts

(b) Prepayments

Cash:

(a) Items recorded on the bank statements but not yet recorded in the cash book, e.g. bank charges, interest, and direct debits

(b) Any differences between cash balances recorded by the accounting system and those verified by physical inspection

Liabilities:

(a) Accruals for goods received where purchase invoices have not yet been processed

(b) Accruals for other costs where invoices have not yet been received, e.g. utilities costs and interest charges

11* Annual depreciation of fixed assets as charged in the profit and loss account is the mechanism via which accountants apply the matching principle to long-lived assets, i.e. those which span multiple accounting periods. Effectively it is the mechanism via which the net cost of ownership of the asset (i.e. original cost less estimated residual value) is apportioned to the individual accounting periods during which the asset is owned. Thus, depreciation itself has no direct cash flow consequences. The cash flows relating directly to the asset take place when it is acquired and when it is disposed of (except of course for those assets acquired on instalment terms).

The focus of depreciation is the allocation of the net cost of ownership. Accordingly it has no direct linkage to providing for the replacement of the assets in question. It certainly does not provide cash to fund the replacement of assets.

However, there is an indirect effect of depreciation. The amount of depreciation charged in the profit and loss account reduces the amount of profit that is available for distribution to shareholders, as does any other cost. Thus it does have an indirect cash flow impact insofar as it reduces the amount of cash that can be paid out as dividends. This is not, however, the same as saying that it saves cash as there are many other factors affecting companies' dividend distribution policies, including the availability of cash with which to pay dividends.

There is a particular form of depreciation which takes this even further – replacement cost depreciation. In this type of depreciation the replacement cost of the asset is used in calculating depreciation rather than the original cost. In times of rising prices this means that depreciation charges will be higher than under the normal method, and that as a result the amount of distributable profit will be reduced, forcing the company to retain more resources. However, even replacement cost depreciation does not provide an identifiable separate fund with which to purchase replacement assets.

Chapter 4

1* (a) Calculation of works overhead absorption rates:

– for Direct Materials (DM):	TWO/DM	= £10 000/£8000	= 125%
– for Direct Labour Cost (DLC):	TWO/DLC	= £10 000/£13 000	= 77%
– for Direct Labour Hours (DLH):	TWO/DLH	= £10 000/3150	= £3.175
– for Machine Hours (MH):	TWO/MH	= £10 000/900	= £11.11
– Prime Cost (PC):	TWO/PC	= £10 000/£22 800	= 44%

Applying the above-calculated overhead absorption rates on the five bases would result in the following alternative total works overhead burdens for the three jobs, for the month of September:

	Job No 1	Job No 2	Job No 3	Total absorbed
DM basis	£6 250	£2 500	£1 250	£10 000
DL	5 775	3 850	385	10 010
DLH	4 763	4 763	476	10 002
MH	5 555	3 333	1 111	9 999
PC	5 720	3 520	792	10 032

(b) Students were asked only to calculate four bases for overhead absorption – it would be interesting to know which of the five bases above they omit: probably Prime Cost, as it was not recommended in the text. The authors dislike it, normally, on grounds that it is a figure of compromise, or averaging, whereas the general goal is to find and use the 'most appropriate basis', defined as the basis which most closely matches the causative influence on the level and particularly the variability in the overheads total from period to period. In this exercise we cannot establish the main causative influence.

We can note that Job No. 3's resource use pattern is out of line from the other two jobs, especially on Direct Materials and Machine Hours. We can note that there is variability in labour cost per labour hour and per machine hour. We note that total works overhead seems very high in proportion to the direct costs. But if the overhead is confirmed as genuinely that, the information we would seek ought to include data for a larger number of jobs (and months) to search for a pattern, and also data on the cost elements comprised in works overhead. For example, does TWO contain a large element of depreciation and/or machine maintenance, suggesting machine hours as the most appropriate basis? Or is there a large element of design and drawing office charges and can complexity here be linked to the grade (i.e. costliness) of labour used, and thus to direct labour cost as the most appropriate basis?

2* Elite Shoe Company statement of production, sales and profit

	A Shoes		B Shoes		Company
	$/unit	$000	$/unit	$000	$000
Manufacturing costs					
DM	10	400	5	600	1000
DW	5	200	3	360	560
VPO	1.25	50	0.75	90	140
FPO	1	40	1	120	160
Total mfg. costs	17.25	690	9.75	1170	1860
Admin. o/hd	2.5	100	1.5	180	280
Total cost prod/ops	19.75	790	11.25	1350	2140
Less finished stock		79		112.5	191.5
Cost of goods sold	19.75	711	11.25	1237.5	1948.5
Plus selling costs	1.75	63	1.75	192.5	255.5
Cost of sales	21.50	774	13	1430	2204
Sales revenue	25	900	15	1650	2550
Profits	3.50	126	2	220	346

Students might choose a different format for the solution to that shown above, and different captions. The treatment above departs a little from the model shown in Figure 4.5 partly because here we lack a breakdown between the fixed and variable portions of administration overhead (and selling cost). The solution shown represents a liberal absorption view on what overhead may be capitalised into finished stocks. A more rigorous view would exclude any administration overhead from finished stocks: this would reduce company profits for the year by $25 000. A purist period costing viewpoint would further disallow any fixed production overhead (FPO) and finished stocks: and this would reduce company profits by a further $14 000. The balance sheet values of finished stock (shown above as "Less finished stock") would be reduced by the amounts of period costs deducted from profits.

3* (a) Summary of Hi-Tech Ltd Accounts, latest year, variable costing basis

	€000
Closing stock	(480)
Cost of sales	1270
Fixed admin. and sales overheads	(300)
Fixed production overheads	(400)
Gross profit (variable basis)	1030
Net profit (variable cost basis)	180
Offset sales	2300
Opening stock	150
Prime cost	1,400
Variable admin. and sales overheads	(150)
Variable production overhead	200

The above summary of accounts on the variable costing basis could of course be set out with alternative formats and captions. Under variable costing the net profit has been reduced by €70 000 (28%). This is reconciled by the elimination of €120 000 of fixed production overheads removed from the closing stock and now charged fully to current year net profits, offset by €50 000 removed from the opening stock (and cost of sales) to correct the closing stock in last year's accounts on the variable costing (or, period costing) basis.

(b) Both sets of accounts disclose the large increase in stocks over the year. This should alert users (and students) to turn to the balance sheet (and the cash flow or sources and applications of funds statements if available) to examine the working capital position and the general financial risk exposure of the company. *Prima facie*, the company has produced too much, relative to its current market, so questions need asking as well regarding management competence.

From the variable/period cost perspective, this is an example where full absorption costing overstates current net profits, opening the possibility of relatively larger dividends being paid out, to the detriment of company liquidity and financial stability. The variable costing approach offers the advantage of greater prudence in the timing of profit recognition, against the disadvantage of profits which may vary more from the norm or trend from year to year (i.e. variable costing reduces income smoothing in financial disclosure).

7* Students should have referred to the 'opportunity cost' subsection near the beginning of the chapter. Opportunity cost, the net benefit, contribution or saving forgone by following one course of action instead of the next best alternative course of action, cannot normally appear in cost reports because, of course, it is a measure of what the firm is not doing, but rather might have done. Indeed it is not easy to see how opportunity cost could be included in routine cost and budget reporting, or that it would even be useful to do so. Where the opportunity cost concept is useful, and indeed important if not essential to success, is in managerial planning and decision making. Opportunity cost is about alternative courses of action, about choice. Any planning and decision situation involves choice, including the alternative (implicit) decision to do nothing, or to change nothing.

The more costly the change contemplated, especially if new capital outlay is involved with a lengthy period required for the 'recovery' of the capital through operating revenues, the more important it is for all feasible alternative courses of action to be explored, the opportunity costs assessed (together with associated risks and uncertainty), and the optimal choice of action identified. The opportunity cost concept can be given explicit recognition and use in preparing reports for management at the stage of evaluating the net costs, savings or gains from adopting alternative plans or decisions. This can be applied for decisions affecting production methods, product choice, marketing methods, etc., and for major capital outlays whose evaluation methods are discussed in later chapters.

8* In preparing this graph, students should refer to the chapter section on 'costs related to time and activity'. This graph is similar to Figure 4.3, but with the added complication of how to display step-type mixed costs, or semi-fixed costs (S-FC on graph). Pure variable cost (VC is by definition constant per unit of activity), regardless of volume. Pure fixed cost (FC) is a curving function showing unit fixed cost reducing as volume increases. S-FC per unit rises as each step activates, then falls per unit in a curve because it behaves as a fixed cost until the next step is reached.

OX identifies the volume of lowest (average) total unit cost. OY is the volume at which major new fixed costs arise (presumably involving major capital expenditure on plant and possible building space). Beyond OY we are into a new strategic situation requiring review of capital policy, markets, prices and marketing. From this graph we cannot tell what is the optimum (i.e. profit-maximising) volume for the firm, because we lack a unit-revenue (or, price) line on the graph (NB. Remember that the feasible market price itself may vary at different volumes.)

Regarding the second part of the question set, except when mixed costs are step costs arising at infrequent volume intervals, but quite large in scale when they arise, it does not appear that the existence of mixed costs significantly limits the usefulness of the conventional simplification of all costs into the two categories of fixed and variable. This assumes that often semi-fixed cost increases typically occur in frequent small steps. This generalisation will be the more probable, the larger and more diverse is an organisation and its activities. While simplification to just fixed and variable costs may be acceptable for routine cost measurement and reporting, however, it should be said also that for planning and decision making on specified changes in volume or product mix it will be more accurate to attempt to isolate main individual mixed costs for separate inclusion in the cost analysis.

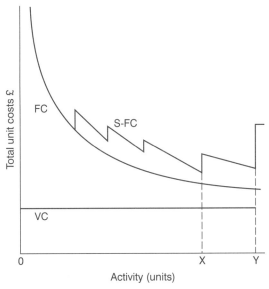

Activity (units)

9* Fixed costs are constant or fixed for a period of time. They tend to be the costs of keeping an organisation in being, of providing the infrastructure to enable operations. As such, these costs have to be shared among various operations, activities and outputs, to which they are likely individually to relate only indirectly. In contrast, the variable costs tend mainly to comprise the direct costs incurred in the actual operation, for labour and material, etc. However, running the core and infrastructure of the organisation (e.g. services such as central administration and building maintenance and heating, etc.) also involves variable costs for consumables, bought-in services, etc., although these costs are indirect rather than direct, at least for the purposes of routine, traditional costings and cost reporting. But yet, if these same core services are viewed differently, as control centres internally, then their variable costs represent direct costs to their own cost centres even while they remain indirect costs from the perspective of classifying costs for charging to the final units, and departments providing outputs marketable outside the enterprise.

As often occurs, assigning costs to categories must depend on the purpose for which the cost information is to be used. For example, most fixed costs will be indirect for purposes of routine control reporting of production department costs and product costs. But if the purpose of cost analysis is to study the effects of change – of products, of volume, of production technology, or whatever – then any cost which could change becomes potentially direct and variable in that particular analysis. This complication is best left for full discussion with students after Differential Cost Analysis is introduced in a later chapter.

Chapter 5

1* The answers to parts (a), (b) and (c) can be found more quickly by numerical methods than the use of CVP graphs, but the latter have the advantage of helping students visualise the relationships with which they are dealing. The graphs may be orthodox, with TFC shown as a horizontal band at the base, the variant with TVC as a wedge at the base and TFC as a diagonal band, or as profit-graphs. Students should of course clearly label their axes, with money values on the vertical axis and unit volumes on the horizontal.

(a)   BEV = TFC/CU = £700 000/£30 = 23 333 units

10% profit volume = TFC/(CU-unit profit) = £700 000/£20 = 35 000 units.

(NB. The logic of this solution is that the 10% target profit, or £10 per unit, becomes a first charge on contribution and reduces the net contribution per unit by that amount.)

(b)   In this dual price variation, the first 20 000 units at a £30 per unit contribution will cover £600 000 of fixed costs. That leaves FC of £100 000 to be covered at the lower CU of £10. Hence: BEV = FC/CU = £100 000/£10 = 10 000 units at the lower price. Thus, the overall BEV = 20 000 + 10 000 = 30 000 units.

(c)   IV = differential TFC/differential UVC = £200 000/£20 = 10 000 units.

This same solution applies to both (c) versus (a), and (c) versus (b). However, this solution is restricted by the assumption that the same contribution per unit (CU) will be maintained under each alternative. For an optimal solution we need to know the most probable prices and sales volumes under each alternative. But at the least the relatively low indifference volume suggests a fairly low level of risk in moving to alternative (c).

(d)   Alternative (c) looks attractive, but we need firm information on the realistic market sales at alternative prices. Cutting prices greatly and suddenly can arouse suspicion about motives and quality. Smaller price cuts, better dealer margins and extra spending on marketing and promotion could be the best strategy to combine with (c). (NB. The authors cheated a little here. Ideally, this should be treated as a long-term capital expenditure decision, if the new equipment lease involves continuing financial commitments and cancellation penalties. This question could be adapted for Chapter 9). Ideally students will suggest use of sensitivity analysis to this decision.

2*   (a)   Unit costs

	Normal sales	Special order	Differential costs*
Variable and other direct costs:	€80	€90	€45 000
Direct labour plus overtime (averaged to units)	12	6 000	–
Direct materials	75	90	45 000
Variable production overheads	30	30	15 000

Variable admin. and sales overheads	15	15	7 500
plus transport for special orders	–	35	17 500
Direct tooling costs for special order	–	20	10 000
	200	292	146 000
Normal sales price			350
Normal unit contribution			150
Normal unit contribution lost on 200 units forgone to fill special order			30 000
Special order revenue needed to break-even on the special order, i.e. no change in total profit before tax			€176,000

* The differential costs are for the 500-unit special order, 200 units in normal time and 300 units in overtime. Added to the direct costs of the special order is the 'opportunity cost' of the contribution forgone by displacing 200 units of normal sales to make time for the special order.

(b) The tender price leaving profits for the six months unaltered is as calculated above, €176 000. The tender price to retain the same overall profit margin on the enlarged volume of 2700 units in six months, requires calculation of the total costs on the new basis: these are the same costs used in the new budget in (c) below, €802 000 in total. The target tender price is then found by first using the equation €840k / €696k = x / €802k to find x, this being total sales including the special order. x = €967 931. From x is deducted sales for 2200 units at normal prices, €770 000, leaving special order tender price of €197 931. The recalculated six-month budget on this tender basis is as follows:

Sales (22 000 × €350, + €197 931 special order)		€967 931
Direct labour (€176 000 + €45 000 + €6000 O.T.)	€227 000	
Direct materials (€165 000 + €45 000)	210 000	
Variable production o/hd (2700 × €30)	81 000	
Fixed production o/hd (€120 000 + €10 000 tooling)	130 000	
Variable admin. & sales o/hd (€33 000 + €25 000)	58 000	
Fixed admin. & sales o/hd	96 000	802 000
Budgeted profit before tax, for six months		€165 931

(c) The above tender prices ignore risk and uncertainty. A higher tender might be sought, subject to market competition and the prospects for repeat business and wider exports. Unknown is if cutting normal sales by 200 units for six months will lose goodwill/future sales, or alternatively, if some of the 200 lost sales units can be clawed back in overtime in next six months.

3* (a) The numbers required to complete the blanks in the assigned list involve no conceptual or computational difficulty. Filling in the blanks is intended simply to arouse some curiosity in students regarding why the relative percentages and rankings differ so much between the products, and between alternative cost or performance measures. The numbers for the blanks are as follows:

Products: (values in £000s)	A	B	C	D
Value added (sales less purchases)	100	60	20	10
Value added (% of sales)	55.5	50	33.3	10
Absorption net profit (margin)	30	15	5	4

Absorption net profit to sales, %	16.7	12.5	8.3	4
ABC net profit (margin)	15	30	10	–1
ABC net profit to sales, %	8.3	25	16.7	–1
Product contribution	40	40	20	7
Product contribution ratio, %	22.2	33.3	33.3	7
Capital turnover ratio, %	85.7	133.3	75	333.3
Absorption-cost based ROCE	14.3	16.7	6.3	13.3
Activity-based-costing (ABC) ROCE	7.1	33.3	12.5	–3.3

Product D stands out for its low value added, low variable cost other than purchase cost, and comparatively low capital employed. D is presumably a bought-in finished product, perhaps requiring only painting, labelling, packaging and perhaps some distinctive gadget or finishing touch. D is not significantly profitable, but it might contribute indirectly to other products' sales by rounding out a range. Tinbrass's other products are manufactured, with C standing out on some but not all tests as being the least profitable/desirable. The divergence of margins between the absorption basis and the ABC basis suggests either that one of the costing bases is misleading, or that the products are quite different in batch size, amount of support services, etc., i.e. circumstances in which ABC (if well executed) is likely to be more accurate.

(b) Assuming spare capacity, especially if long-term, products A and B with the highest value added should be preferred because they make the greatest use of internal resources (for stability), with product B having the edge because of higher contribution ratio. However, if the firm is instead at full capacity, then the contribution ratio becomes even more important at the margin – with existing fixed costs largely irrelevant – and B and C are to be preferred. B appears to be better by ROCE criteria, but ROCE can be misleading especially for short-run volume change decisions, for the reasons that capital employed allocations can be misleading on allocation and historical-cost grounds, and that marginal capital needs for incremental sales are likely to be relatively low; i.e. marginal return on marginal capital may be high even when long-term ROCE seems unfavourable.

4* Below are calculations and comments for use in the report for the chief executive of Chippers Ltd. Individual Lecturers may wish to suggest or require that students adopt a particular layout or style for the report.

(a) Cost absorption/driver rate for overhead allocation

	Absorption costing	*ABC*
Purchasing	0.03 of Materials value	£25 per ABC hour
Production control	£0.18 per dir. lab. hr.	£22.50 per ABC hr.
Inspection and testing	0.015 of materials value	£37.50 per ABC hr.
Design services	£0.25 per dir. lab. hr.	£50 per ABC hr.

NB. The given data did not make clear if 'cost in month' was actual, budgeted, or standard, cost. Given that overhead allocations should be made and monitored on a continuous (or even 'real-time') basis, the cost measure used should clearly be either budgeted cost, or else standard cost multiplied by normal (or, sometimes forecast) volume levels.

Cost allocations by absorption costing compared to ABC:

	Product A		Product B	
	Absorption	ABC	Absorption	ABC
Purchasing	£ 3 000	£ 2 500	£ 1 500	£ 2 000
Production control	2 700	2 475	900	1 575
Inspection and testing	1 500	1 500	750	1 125
Design services	3 750	1 000	1 250	300
Total OH charge for month	10 950	7 475	4 400	5 000

(b) The calculations suggest that both Products A and B are established products making little call on Design Services, and that under absorption costing they are effectively cross-subsidising other products by carrying a level of design services charges greatly above their fair or economic share. However, the differences in other service overheads are not very material, especially as the total of the portion of overhead costs studied here does not represent a really large proportion of total product cost/value. It is when the proportion of total cost expended on support service/overheads becomes large, that ABC becomes potentially extremely helpful in respect of obtaining more relevant and accurate end-product costs.

There is a *prima facie* case to expect that the ABC costs, if correctly structured and accurately collected, will provide management information which is 'more true' than under absorption costing. It may be 'more helpful' to management, also, both as regards end product costs (see above, and also (c) below), and certainly as regards the potential for more accurate and rigorous control of the costs, efficiency, scale and focus of the support-service-activities included in the ABC system. But, two caveats. First, use of ABC for tight control of service overheads may cause conflict in Chippers, between ABC accountability and normal functional (and budget) accountability, because of the way the various production support services have been fragmented among the main operational departments for reasons of quality and policy control. And, second, an ABC system would be significantly more expensive to use than the existing simple absorption costing system, so there remains the eternal question of justifying the 'cost of costing'.

(c) The limited variations between absorption and ABC overhead charges (other than design services), combined with the low proportion of total service charges to total costs, suggests that in practice the adoption of ABC might have little impact on pricing, where the firm is a price maker. However, where it is a price taker and especially if a product involves more or less than normal design, testing, etc. the ABC information may help the firm to judge better what are acceptable minimum prices to ensure recovery of differential costs.

5* It may assist the discussion below if we first make some attempt to estimate (i) the extent to which the overhead cost allocation/apportionment methods used may have overstated the 'fair' overhead share of Countess, and (ii) the likely portion of the overheads charged which may be fixed and not probably amenable to be avoided or escaped if the Countess is discontinued:

	Overstatement	Fixed costs
Selling expenses	€50+	€75+
Workshop (indirect) labour	?	–
Energy, rent, rates, premises, etc.	10+	75+
Transport	–	25+
Administration	?	25+
Totals	€60+	€200+

(a) On the evidence available, I would not discontinue the Countess ~~immediately~~, but I would pursue the problem for additional information and analysis. Some change(s) in product, costs and/or selling price is/are clearly needed. The reason for taking no precipitate action is that the ability to offer a bedroom package at under the psychological price barrier of €2000 must have some (possibly substantial) commercial value in attracting customers through advertising, window displays, etc. Discontinuance may be argued on grounds that no product should fail to earn profit in its own right, regardless of any indirect contribution it makes to overall company profitability. However, the accountant's overhead charges may overstate the loss by €60 or more, per sale (see above, and (b) below). Moreover, the overhead charges may include fixed costs that may be unavoidable to the continuing business, and which are independent of the cash flow associated with Countess sales: these could amount to €200 or more, so that the cash-flow costs of each Countess sale might be €1840 (€2100 – 60 – 200) or even less, leaving a cash-flow profit contribution of at least €150 from each Countess sale.

(b) Selling expenses based on the average of all packages may overstate fair cost to the extent that less sales time may be 'invested' in Countess sales, and any salesman's bonus will be less than average, and perhaps much less. ~~Much~~ sales expense will be fixed, and common to the selling of the package range.

Workshop labour can be fairly charged on sampled job sheets provided the latter are just for Countess: but if the average is for all packages, then it will overstate fair cost for a simple, low-specification package. One may query if this cost should not be dealt with as direct-labour, rather than as an overhead?

Energy, rent, rates, etc. is a ragbag overhead which has no obvious link of causation or explanation with direct labour as an apportionment basis. Possibly pro-rata to sales value would be the least unfair basis. This category contains high fixed costs, unavoidable if Countess is abandoned.

Transport may be fairly charged as an overhead function of direct labour. Administration expense might be more a function of number of sales, than of proportional sales revenue, so here the accountant's figures might actually slightly understate 'true' overhead costs for Countess.

(c) It follows that one would like the accountant to supply a breakdown of overhead costs between fixed and variable, and between avoidable and unavoidable (or, common-cost) overheads, and also to provide justification (or reform) for his apportionment methods. (NB. This is a situation where

Shillinglaw's attributable cost principles and method could be applied.) Other information required is as regards the pricing and product range behaviour of competitors, and any market research or other information available regarding customer attitudes to price and the importance of a low price or loss leader to attract shoppers.

Finally, can the specification or quality of purchases and/or the amount of direct labour used for the Countess be cut to save costs and yield some profit, without going so far as to damage the firm's repute or to transgress business ethics?

7* Students should have referred to the chapter section on 'differential cost and revenue analysis'. Differential cost is similar to what is termed incremental/ decremental cost in some texts; however, the term 'incremental cost' is preferably avoided lest students are led to think the approach is in some way related to 'incremental budgeting', a process discredited for tending to perpetuate any existing waste of resources. Differential cost is similar in concept to the economist's marginal cost, but the differential cost approach is the more realistic and accurate because it does not restrict itself to small unit changes in output, and it can and should take step costs into account.

As regards the principles and method of differential cost analysis, this approach is used to study future costs (and revenues) to aid decision making in planning activities as distinct from routine control. It is used to study the consequences of change from present product-mix or volumes (or technology, or markets or distribution systems, etc.), to one or more alternative states of resource use. The particular concern is with costs that change, or that will be different: therefore existing historical costs are irrelevant except as a framework of reference to what costs to check, and what costs to include if the change options are to be compared directly to the status quo.

As regards the comparison with 'CVP studies derived from historical absorption costs', differential cost analysis has the advantage, if it is conscientiously and expertly applied, of using cost and revenue figures which are relevant and realistic for future operations, which must be clearly specified. The greater the amount of change being considered for future operations, the greater the advantage of differential cost analysis.

11* The first part of this question is simply a factual 'revision' type question for which students should draw upon the relevant sections in both this chapter and Chapter 1.

The final paragraph of comment for Q1 (above) set out a *raison d'être* for interest in ABC, i.e. the need to improve understanding and control of overheads/indirect costs. The second need is for more accurate end product costs. Although ABC can be installed and operated in somewhat different ways, in general it is arguable that there are three main differences from absorption costing. Firstly, whereas absorption costing distributes indirect costs and other overheads on a basis proportional to some chosen basis of workload in the production function itself (e.g. machine hours), ABC distributes such costs to production (and other end users) on the basis of measuring and costing actual service resources used for each order/batch/service traceable to end products (or to other intermediate cost centres receiving benefit). Secondly, whereas absorption costing does not necessarily involve detailed cost analysis within the indirect-cost service departments, to enable cost absorption transfers to take place, under ABC such analysis is necessary (in the matching of workload and cost drivers, and its costing) and such analysis can and should be exploited to improve understanding and control of efficiency within the service departments (and indeed of the efficacy and value-for-money of the service outputs provided). And thirdly, whereas absorption costing normally works for cost centres based on the conventional functional organisational structure of the firm, ABC can and should pool costs on the basis of interdependent activities, thus sometimes bringing together costs from more than one functional service department.

Chapter 6

1* The first step is to calculate the forecast pattern of daily receipts:

Forecast weekly receipts = £25 480 000/52 = £490 000

If we assume that £x is the amount that is expected to be received each day from Wednesday to Friday, then we calculate x as follows:

$$2x + 2x + x + x + x = £490\ 000,\ \text{i.e.}\ x = £70\ 000$$

Thus, the forecast daily receipts are:

Monday	£140 000
Tuesday	£140 000
Wednesday	£ 70 000
Thursday	£ 70 000
Friday	£ 70 000

With this background we can investigate the three options being considered:

(a)   daily banking

(b)   banking twice per week (on Tuesdays and Fridays)

(c)   continuing the existing practice of banking once per week, on Fridays

Under the current policy Torment is incurring additional interest charges as a result of being more overdrawn than it would be if it were to bank daily. There would be a similar, albeit smaller, additional interest charge if the banking twice per week option were to be adopted. The number of '£ days' of extra interest incurred can be calculated as follows:

		Option (b)		Option (c)	
	Receipts	Days interest charged	'£ days'	Days	'£ days'
Monday	140	1	140	4	560
Tuesday	140	0	0	3	420
Wednesday	70	2	140	2	140
Thursday	70	1	70	1	70
Friday	70	0	0	0	0
			350		1190

Thus option (b) is equivalent to Torment having an additional overdraft, as compared to a daily banking, of £350 000 outstanding for one day each week. The approximate extra annual interest charge of this is:

$$£350\ 000 \times (10\%/365) \times 52 = £4985$$

A similar calculation can be done for option (c):

$$£1\ 190\ 000 \times (10\%/365) \times 52 = £16\ 949$$

The other factor to consider is cost of making the bankings. Each banking costs Torment £50. Thus the banking costs of the options are:

(a) $5 \times £50 \times 52 = £13\ 000$
(b) $2 \times £50 \times 52 = £5200$
(c) $1 \times £50 \times 52 = £2600$

Accordingly we can summarise the costs of the three options as follows:

	Option (a)	Option (b)	Option (c)
Interest costs	0	4 985	16 949
Banking costs	13 000	5 200	2 600
	13 000	10 185	19 549

Thus, the lowest cost option from Torment's point of view is for option (b), i.e. banking twice per week on Tuesdays and Fridays.

2* This is a typical question on the cash-operating problem. The solution in terms of the length of the cash operating cycle for years 20X1 and 20X2 is shown below.

20X1	20X2

Raw materials stock:

$365 \times 80\ 000/384\ 000 = 76$ days	$365 \times 108\ 000/520\ 000 = 76$ days

Credit from suppliers:

$365 \times 64\ 000/384\ 000 = \underline{\quad 61\quad}$	$365 \times 78\ 000/384\ 000 = \underline{\quad 55\quad}$
15 days	21 days

Work-in-progress:

$365 \times 56\ 000/560\ 000 = 37$	$365 \times 72\ 000/720\ 000 = 37$

Finished goods:

$365 \times 64\ 000/560\ 000 = 42$	$365 \times 92\ 000/720\ 000 = 47$

Debtors:

$365 \times 128\ 000/640\ 000 = \underline{\quad 73\quad}$	$365 \times 192\ 000/800\ 000 = \underline{\quad 88\quad}$
167 days	193 days

Comments could include:

(a) increase in length of operating cycle is 26 days, i.e. 16%

(b) reason for this increase is:

(i)	creditors receiving payment more quickly	6 days
(ii)	finished goods staying in stock longer	5
(iii)	debtors taking longer to pay	15
		26 days

(c) operating cycle could be improved by:

(i) quicker collection of accounts

(ii) reducing level of raw material stock

(iii) shorter production period

(iv) extending credit taken from suppliers

(v) reducing level of finished goods stock

Each of the above may have other implications, lost discounts, lost sales, lost goodwill, etc. and decisions should be taken only after considering the total situation.

3* There are three main elements here:

(a) the increase in profit generated by the additional sales. This can be calculated by:

$$£2 \text{ mill} \times 0.05 \times 0.2 = £20\ 000$$

(b) the cost of the discount. This can be calculated by:

$$£2.1 \text{ mill} \times 0.25 \times 0.025 = £13125$$

(c) the saving in bank interest. This can be calculated by:

(i) current debtors: $£2 \text{ mill} \times 73/365 = £400\ 000$

(ii) new debtors $(£2.1 \text{ mill} \times 0.75 \times 73/365)$

$$+ (£2.1 \text{ mil} \times 0.25 \times 7/365) = £325\ 068$$

Thus there will a saving in bank interest of $(£400\ 000 - £325\ 06) \times 0.12 = £8\ 992$

Taking all these factors into account, Jason will be better off as a result off offering the discount by:

$$£20\ 000 + £8\ 992 - £13125 = £15\ 867$$

8* Over-trading occurs when a company is trading at a level of activity beyond that which its capital base can support. It typically happens when companies expand their sales rapidly as a result of which they have to support larger levels of stock and debtors but are unable to obtain more credit from their suppliers. As a result of this they can very rapidly run out of cash. It is a phenomenon which is quite common amongst smaller and medium sized companies with poor working capital management and little access to finance.

9* Classically these motives are derived from the trading motive, the speculative motive, the precautionary motive and the budgetary motive. High levels of stock can reduce uncertainty, increase the possibility of quantity discounts from suppliers, purchase in advance of anticipated price rises and have longer production runs. Although the question does not ask specifically for this it would probably be useful to ask students to identify the disadvantages of holding large levels of stock.

Chapter 7

1* (a) The authors' preferred method for showing the flexible budget for the Metalfab exercise is shown below. It is not the only 'correct' solution, and not necessarily the best. Alternative solutions may differ both in format or presentation, and in some of the 'numbers' generated, depending on assumptions made (and students should state their assumptions where conscious that alternative interpretations or treatments may be possible). The budget solution shown below needs to be understood by reading jointly with the statements of assumptions and explanations that follow below the budget.

Metalfab machine shop – four-week flexible budget

Productive machine hours	1000 hrs	1089 hrs	1633 hrs	2000 hrs
	£	£	£	£
Productive time: direct labour				
Supervisor (FC)	1 600	1 600	1 600	1 600
F/t operators, normal time	7 000	7 616	7 616	7 616
Casual operators, normal time	0	7	3 808	3 808
Overtime supervisor	0	0	12	372
operators	0	0	9	312
Set up, maint. & stopped time				
– in normal time	1 235	1 345	2 016	2 016
– in overtime	0	0	9	585
Idle time (no production)	725	0	0	0
Heating and lighting (FC)	320	320	320	320
Power	500	545	817	1 000
Breakdown and repair costs	600	653	980	1 200
Lubricants and sundries	400	436	653	800
Depreciation (FC)	2 917	2 917	2 917	2 917
Materials wastage and spoilage	2 000	2 178	3 266	4 000
Total machine shop costs	£17 297	£17 617	£24 023	£29 546
Unit machine shop costs	£17.30	£16.18	£14.71	£14.77

Assumptions: That productive labour time exactly equals productive machine time; that all full-time labour is employed at all output levels, leading to idle time below 1089 productive machine hours; that the supervisor is chargeable full time to productive hours, even though in practice much of his time will be given to managing set-ups, routine maintenance, and putting 'idle time' to good use in extra maintenance, clean ups, machine painting, training, etc.

(b) The solution might have been improved if clear separation had been made between fixed and variable costs, and/or between controllable and non-controllable costs. The format used was chosen to keep all labour costs together, as being the main concentration of controllable cost and management interest.

The solution shown uses columns for four different activity levels. Students may have used more columns and different activity levels. The authors' choice includes 1000 and 2000 productive machine hours because these were the ends of the range cited in the given data. The figure 1089 was used because this is the point at which the full-time operators are fully productive, and where the first unit of casual labour is employed. And 1633 hours was used because this is the point where the first unit of overtime has to be employed. Students could have used up to 2200 hours to extend the range of the budget, as calculations show (after allowing that 15% of total paid operator time is on set-up and maintenance, etc.) that the maximum productive hours available, using all the machines and all allowed labour overtime, is 2203 per four-week budget period.

The justification for including the 1089 and 1633 hours columns is to help signal to the supervisor (or other budget holder) where are the critical control points for bringing in the casual labour, and for organising for overtime. The total figures at the bottom of the budget are not of great significance to the budget holder for control; his main focus should be held to the direct/variable/controllable items represented in individual subheadings. Similarly, the unit cost figures will not be of importance to the budgetholder, but may be of use to higher management planning production levels, sales and prices. The unit cost falls as production rises because fixed costs are diluted over a larger number of units, while from 1633 to 2000 hours the unit costs rise slightly because the increase from overtime use is greater than the reduction from the further dilution of fixed costs.

2* A suitable form of budget for next year, for Tweedshire Libraries, might be as follows (and some lecturers/students might wish additionally to include a column for the past year's total budget, and even a budget change column):

Operating budget for Tweedshire Libraries (year XXXX)

	Books & Periodicals Dept.	Customer Services Dept.	Totals
Controllable expenditure:			
Staff costs	£155 925	£103 950	£259 875
Books, periodicals, bindings, etc.	126 175		126 175
CDs, records, tapes, software, etc.		61 800	61 800
FFE, including computer hardware, etc.	28 480	43 260	72 100
Total controllable expenditure	310 940	209 010	519 950
Allocated costs (overheads):			
Rent for space used in library buildings	36 050	15 450	51 500
Maintenance and energy costs	28 840	12 360	41 200
Total allocated costs	64 890	27 810	92 700
Total budgeted expenditure and costs	375 830	236 820	612 650
Total budget authorised			612 850
Budget reserves; unallocated			200
Target contribution from services (10%)		23 682	
Target customer revenue from services		260 502	

Notes to budget: Depreciation on assets (other than premises), based on start-of-year asset valuations, is estimated to be £120 000. Any net contribution from Customer Services Dept. is to be carried forward, divided equally between the departmental budget and the overall library budget.

Some students might produce a slightly different budget in which maintenance and energy costs are included in the controllable budget section. With suitable advice, and guidelines, this could be ideal for devolved budget management and responsibility; but there is a risk of local management cutting maintenance to cover for failure to control staff numbers/costs, etc. There may be a case here for dividing responsibility (and budget) between local and central management, but we have no data given in this exercise to allow this.

The total budget reserves of £200 shown arise as a balancing figure because the cut backs in staff hours and book and periodical purchases saved slightly more than the cost increases imposed by the pay rise of 2% greater than the budget inflation uplift to staff costs. Strictly, the £200 is an unappropriated balance, rather than a formal budget reserve. Many budgetholders would seek to retain a higher proportion of budget 'in reserve' (if allowed reasonable discretion on 'virement'), but most senior budget officers will prefer to retain any reserves centrally, and to see all departmental expenditure fully allocated and justified before budgets are finally agreed.

Under full accrual accounting, 'depreciation' charges on the non-premises assets (unless auditors agree that these short-lived assets can be 'expensed' in year of purchase) would presumably be calculated and charged (in lieu of cash purchase) to controllable budget or allocated-cost budget so as to best match accountability with controllability in the overall budget.

3* (a) **Set up fixed and flexed budgets and compare to actual:**

	Fixed Budget	Flexed Budget	Actual	Variance
Units	100 000	80 000	80 000	
	£	£	£	£
Sales	540 000	432 000	392 000	(40 000)
Material: A	80 000	64 000	57 600	6 400
Material: B	100 000	80 000	115 200	(35 200)
Material: C	120 000	96 000	76 800	19 200
	300 000	240 000	249 600	(9 600)
Labour	75 000	60 000	54 400	5 600
Variable expenses	25 000	20 000	18 400	1 600
	400 000	320 000	322 400	(2 400)
Contribution	140 000	112 000	69 600	42 400
Fixed costs	80 000	80 000	82 000	(2 000)
Profit	60 000	32 000	(12 400)	44 400

(b) **Analyse the operational variances**

Materials:

A Total variance $= $ £6 400 favourable

Price variance $= 128\ 000 \times (£0.45 - £0.40) = $ £6 400 unfavourable

Quantity variance $= (128\ 000 - 160\ 000) \times £0.40 = $ £12 800 favourable

B   Total variance   = £35 200 unfavourable

     Price variance   = 256 000 × (£0.45 – £0.50) = £12 800 favourable

     Quantity variance   = (256 000 – 160 000) × £0.50 = £48 000 unfavourable

C   Total variance   = £19 200 favourable

     Price variance   = 256 000 × (£0.30 – £0.30) = nil

     Quantity variance = (256 000 – 320 000) × £0.30 = £19 200 favourable

Labour:

     Total variance   = £5600 favourable

     Rate variance   = 16 000 × (£3.40 – £3.00) = £6400 unfavourable

     Efficiency variance = (16 000 – 20 000) × £3.00 = £12 000 favourable

Variable expenses:

     Total variance   = £1600 favourable

     Expenditure   = £18 400 – (80 000 × £0.25) = £1600 favourable
     variance

Fixed expenses:

     Total variance   = £2000 unfavourable

     Sales price variance:

     Sales price variance   = 80 000 × (£4.90 – £5.40) = £40 000 unfavourable

(c) **Summary report**

Original budgeted profit		£60 000
Planning variance		28 000
Flexed budget		32 000
Price variances:		
Material A	£(6 400)	
Material B	12 800	
Labour rate	(6 400)	nil
Usage variances:		
Material A	£ 12 800	
Material B	(48 000)	
Material C	19 200	
Labour	12 000	(4 000)
Expenditure variances:		
Variable overheads	£ 1 600	
Fixed overheads	(2 000)	(400)
Sales price variance		(40 000)
		(12 400)

7* This is a revision-type question, for which students may find it helpful to draw together points from the subsections on 'Budget administration', 'Budget reports' and 'Behavioural problems', as well as from the text more generally. The question is intended to focus on the ex post aspects of reporting and control as two separate features of budgeting, as distinct from the ex ante aspects of budgetary planning and budget setting.

The features of effective **budgetary reporting** which students should include in their comments comprise at least the following:

- Promptness: reports should be available before the mid-point of the next reporting period, to allow motivation and time for corrective action before the next reporting date.

- Accuracy: reports need to be accurate for the information both to be useful and to carry conviction and authority for the application of budget discipline and any needed sanctions.

- Relevance: clearly the data and information in reports must be relevant to managers' responsibilities, and authority, and to the work and resources involved, in order to carry conviction.

- Clarity: budget reports need to use a format, classification system and captions which are clearly understandable to non-accountants (and, NB, too much detail is as undesirable as excessive aggregation of accounts).

- A more debatable feature is the routine provision of copies of budget reports to each manager's superior manager: the authors favour that practice as a way of signalling that the budget is a form of 'contract' for performance within line management, not with the accountants.

As regards features of effective **budgetary control**, these include:

- Credibility: for credibility the basic need is that the original budget targets or allocations should be realistic, or reasonably attainable, and that preferably they should have been agreed between the manager and his line boss.

- Controllability: all items in the budget should be controllable by the budget holder, or at the least only those items which are controllable should be included in performance assessment of the manager (as distinct from the activity or process); some points made in comment on Question 2 are also relevant here.

- Explanation: budget or other accounting staff should be willingly and helpfully available to explain budget detail and (within reason) to investigate or double check budget report detail which managers think inaccurate or unfair.

- Follow-up: the managerial culture and administrative arrangements should ensure that significant unfavourable budget performance (variances) are pursued both by the budget officer and the manager's own boss (as needful), as well as favourable performance being praised or rewarded.

8* Students must defend the statement cited, unless they disagree with the proposition that everything that goes wrong is ultimately due to human weakness or to acts of God or nature, and the latter can hardly be blamed for failings in budgetary planning and control.

Some students may wish to structure their response around the three categories outlined in the 'Behavioural problems' subsection in the chapter: i.e. budget slack, pumping and overreaction. Of course that categorisation is not sacrosanct, or even all-inclusive, so that the question gives students an opportunity to display insight or imagination as regards budgetary control relationships – which in the real world can often be fraught indeed.

Perhaps of more interest is if students explore where the 'weakest link' can manifest itself, why, and (time permitting) what to do about it. Regrettably the weakest link of human behaviour can be within the accounting department itself. The cause may be lack of enterprise in analysing costs or in reporting them promptly and fully, or it may be lack of confidence in dealing with other professions, lack of ability or training to communicate with non-accountants, or, worst of all, the desire to preserve professional mystique or power by less than full and clear disclosure.

Alternatively the weakest link in the working of budgetary systems may lie within management, particularly top management – especially given the presumption that managerial failings of junior management are ultimately the responsibility of top management. If top management creates or tolerates the wrong culture of budgetary management, then the system will not work. The major function of budgets should be to help every manager do his or her job better. Their use as a basis for schemes of rewards and sanctions should be secondary, and arguably may even undermine the major function of helping managers manage better. It may sound like a platitude, but top management should ensure that the budget system operates in an open manner and as part of a teamwork context, and not as an outlet for individual managers' gamesmanship and mouse-and-cat conflict with the budget accountant.

9* Much of the student response to this question will be drawn from the subsection on 'top-down or bottom-up?' and the section on 'budgets and behaviour'. So in these notes we take the alternative approach of what are the arguments *against*. After all, in the real world it too often occurs that alleged disadvantages are allowed to outweigh possible advantages, especially under uncertainty or where extra effort is needed to effect change before advantages can be realised.

The disadvantages of top-down budgeting include the risk that managers will feel no proprietary interest in the budget system, and limited personal responsibility for the budgets set. Managers may suspect that some strategic and other planning information is being kept from them, and that budgets proposed from the top may include unreasonable and hidden targets for improved efficiency. These disadvantages can be minimised by open channels of communication with managers about strategic and other factors being built into their draft budgets, but it is all too easy to make excuses and slip back into a process where budgets are prepared in a 'backroom' atmosphere and delivered to managers on a 'take it or leave it' basis.

The disadvantages of bottom-up budgeting obviously include the risks of 'waste' of time of managers, and the time of budget accountants as well in explaining costs and the budget process to individual managers, rectifying mistakes and unreasonable assumptions in managers' drafts, watching out for built-in budget slack, etc. More legitimately, there is concern that even with a genuine effort to make managers informed about strategy and more detailed forecasts and targets for sales and production, the generation of many separate, individual budgets may not add up to a coherent, let alone optimal, overall master budget plan for the corporate enterprise as a whole. This can be a particular problem in the public sector, where the organisation provides a wide range of services/outputs and there has been a tradition of 'incremental budgeting'.

Often the best practical solution may be a compromise, where budgets are drafted centrally on a 'pencilled in' basis, with individual managers given time to think and a genuine opportunity to challenge and influence final budget decisions.

Chapter 8

1* (a) ROI

Income/sales × sales/investment = £1.8mill/5mill × 5mill/8mill = 22.5%

RI:

Profit budgeted	£1.8mill
Minimum required return (£8mill × 20%)	£1.6mill
Residual income	£0.2mill

(b) RI would increase by £50 000. This can be calculated in two ways – either by considering the changes in the variables or by preparing a revised statement of total operations.

(i) considering the changes in the variables:

Increase in sales (10 000 × £45)	450 000
Increase in variable costs (10 000 × £20)	200 000
Increase in contribution margin	250 000
Increase in fixed costs	100 000
Increase in profit	150 000
Increase in minimum required return (£500 000 @ 20%)	100 000
Increase in RI	50 000

(ii) revised statement of operations:

Sales (£5mill + £0.45mill)	5 450 000
Variable costs (110 000 × £20)	2 200 000
Contribution margin	3 250 000
Fixed costs (£1.2mill + £0.1mill)	1 300 000
Divisional profit	1 950 000
Minimum required return (£8.5mill @ 20%)	1 700 000
RI	250 000

The new £250 000 RI is £50 000 more as a result of this special order.

(c) (i) If Invicta accepts the lower transfer price, revenue, and hence contribution margin, will be reduced by £8 per unit for 20 000 units, i.e. a total of £160 000. With no change in fixed costs this means a similar drop in Invicta's profit. This will be balanced by a corresponding increase in Wessex's profit, resulting in no overall change in the group profit of PFF Plc.

(ii) If Invicta does not accept the lower price, revenue, and hence contribution margin, will decline by £30 per unit for 20 000 units, i.e. a total of £600 000. However, they would save avoidable fixed costs of £250 000, leading to a net decline in profit of £350 000. From Wessex's point of view buying externally will lead to an increase in contribution margin of 20 000 units @ £8 per unit, i.e. an increase of £160 000. From the point of view of the company as a whole this results in a net decrease in profit of (£350 000 – £160 000) = £190 000, illustrating some of the dysfunctional effects of full-cost-plus internal transfer pricing.

2* (a) Would a manager of Carlton accept or reject the proposal? – Contribution is £150 000 × 60% = £90 000 less fixed costs of £70 000 gives an annual profit of £20 000. This represents an ROI of 20%, i.e. in excess of the projected rate of return of the company (15%) and the cost of capital (12%). However, inspection of Carlton's profit plan indicates an ROI of 25%, i.e. the proposed investment would lower Carlton's prospective ROI. Accordingly a manager of Carlton whose performance is assessed on the basis of the division's ROI would be tempted to reject the investment on this basis.

(b) Would a board member of Harkness want Carlton to accept or reject the proposal? – The best alternative investments proposed by other divisions have prospective ROIs of approximately 15%, i.e. below that for Carlton's project. Accordingly, a board director would want Carlton to proceed with the project, assuming that there were no broader strategic implications.

(c) The foregoing demonstrates the basic problem with ROI as a performance measure, that it is based on overall average. Most commentators would favour the use of some form of RI approach. In this case if RI was used, and was based on the firm's cost of capital (12%), any marginal increase would be to the good of the management.

3* (a) The key circumstances at Foolem, as affecting both internal and external pricing, are that both operational divisions have spare capacity and external markets lacking clear/fixed market-price guidelines. Accepting that the objective of maximising the plc's overall profit must be more important than protecting the real or notional independent profit/investment centre status of separate divisions, the above all combines to suggest that the company should adopt transfer prices which will improve the quality of information for both divisions to make profit-increasing decisions for the firm as a whole. In pure theory, given the imperfect markets, all internal costs should be passed to pricing and contract decision makers on a marginal/variable cost basis. However, such costs could be uplifted slightly for some (incentivising) target contribution, or planned and optimising transfer prices could be adopted on a negotiated basis using the two-part tariff system (to preserve some substantial element of divisional profit-investment-centre credibility).

(b) Possible transfer prices (per chargeable hour) for Division B may be calculated as follows:

	Full-cost-plus	Relevant-cost-plus	Two-part tariff
Divisional variable costs	$100	$100	$100
Depreciation charged by Division C	50		
Rent charges for allocated space	200		
Other central transfer service charges	50	50(?)	50(?)
Divisionally controlled fixed costs	50		
Target return on divisionally controlled capital	18	18	18
Transfer price, per prime labour hour	468	168	168

Notes: 'Relevant costs' are to be determined 'in the eye of the beholder': here I have equated them with marginal/variable costs so far as determinable. Although we are told that the central services are block/fixed charges, space rent and depreciation are charged separately, so the remaining service charges may be largely variable (for the plc), and thus they have been treated above as if variable. Here the 'Plus' element in the transfer price has been calculated as the target return on division-controlled capital: students may choose and justify some other basis for setting the 'Plus' (and see below).

(c) A purist might argue that the plc's weighted cost of capital should have been used in the above capital-charge, not the target rate. Alternatively, it may be argued that in a labour-skill-intensive business such as Foolems, ROCE or ROI on physical assets is secondary, almost irrelevant. A good return should be being earned on the plc's human capital and expertise/goodwill, so that target returns should be expressed as a function of sales/revenue/volume, not physical capital employed. This would lead to setting substantially higher profit targets (and higher pricing targets, subject to the state of competition).

Most of the plc's money/physical capital is tied-up in its (possibly unnecessarily expensive) head-office premises, facilities and services: this is the likely justification for having the separate Division C, but a result appears to be the imposition of uncompetitive space-based transfer-cost burdens on Division B. A review of head-office investment, use and charging is needed.

Existing transfer prices between Division B and A are on a 'negotiated' basis. Detail of this is unspecified, but based on most common practice, one may expect the negotiation consists of 'haggling down' from full-cost-plus transfer prices supplied by the accountant. Arguably, use of marginal or relevant cost, or a negotiated two-part tariff, would greatly benefit the plc.

7* This question calls for the student to be clear of the advantage of RI over ROI, yet recognising that many of the problems associated with ROI apply to RI. The RI target is usually set at, or in excess of, the organisation's overall required rate of return. The key advantage of RI is that it relates return to a capital base. An illustration of the use of RI, as outlined in the chapter, would clearly demonstrate the student's understanding of RI.

8* This question call for an analysis of the merits and demerits of ROI and RI together with an understanding of the key principles required when measuring and monitoring management accountability. Issues such as controllable expenditure, the sharing of joint costs and control over capital expenditure all feature in this question.

9* Despite the attributes that might be obtained from a divisionalised organisation there are a number of potential conflicts that can arise. Recall the Valletta case in the chapter. As stated in the text, no division should be able to increase its own reported performance at the expense of others.

Chapter 9

1* The core points to be made in response to the managing director's statement are:

(a) The £1 million already spent on research and development is a sunk cost and thus not relevant to any future decision.

(b) The inclusion of Corporation Tax in investment appraisal is rather more complex than he suggests. Such tax is leviable on corporate rather than project profits and the amount of such tax is at least in part dependent on how the company is financed (debt vs. equity, as interest is tax deductible).

(c) Acceptance, at least in general terms, of his view that every product should pay its own way, cover its own costs and give a decent return. To some extent, however, this begs the question of how such costs and returns are to be measured. A preferable assessment of the new product would be as follows:

Time	Cash flow		Factor	PV
t_0	Investment	£(2 000 000)	1.000	(2 000 000)
t_{10}	Scrap value	£100 000	0.247	24 700
t_0	Working capital	£(1 800 000)	1.000	(1 800 000)
t_{10}	Working capital release	£1 800 000	0.247	444 600
t_{1-10}	Annual sales	£90 × 40 000	5.019	18 068 400
t_{1-10}	Direct costs	(£28 + £12) × 40 000	5.019	(8 030 400)
t_{1-10}	Manufacturing o'hds	(£22 × 40 000) – £300 000	5.019	(2 911 020)
t_{1-10}	Selling etc. costs	£4 × 40 000	5.019	(803 040)
	Net present value			2 993 240

Thus the new product appears to have a positive prospective net present value and therefore is worth undertaking.

2* (a) Graph – possible points for plotting on graph:

Present values (all figures in $000s)

Project A	@10%	@15%	@20%	@25%
Investment	(1000)	(1000)	(1000)	(1000)
Year 1	727	696	666	640
Year 2	413	378	347	320
Year 3	225	197	174	154
	365	271	187	114

Project B	@10%	@15%	@20%	@25%
Investment	(1000)	(1000)	(1000)	(1000)
Year 1	91	87	83	80
Year 2	248	227	208	192
Year 3	1126	987	869	768
	465	301	160	40

Students can plot the required graph using the above information.

(b) Internal rate of return

The B line should intersect the axis at approximately 27.2%.

(c) Different costs of capital

(i) At 10% project B has the higher NPV
(ii) At 20% project A has the higher NPV

3* (a) Establishing in-house pathology services

Time	Cash flow	Amount	PV factors		P.V.s	
			6%	12%	6%	12%
t_0	Capital cost	250 000	1.000	1.000	250 000	250 000
t_1	Running cost	650 000	0.943	0.893	612 950	580 450
t_2	Running cost	750 000	0.890	0.797	667 500	597 750
t_3	Running cost	800 000	0.840	0.712	672 000	569 600
	Sale of lease	100 000	0.840	0.712	(84 000)	(71 200)
					2 118 450	1 926 600

(b) St Bottomley's

Time	Cash flow	Amount	PV factors		PVs	
			6%	12%	6%	12%
t_0	Charge	750 000	0.943	0.893	707 250	669 750
t_2	Charge	850 000	0.890	0.797	756 500	677 450
t_3	Charge	900 000	0.840	0.712	756 000	640 800
t_{1-3}	Rent	15 000	2.673	2.402	(40 100)	(36 030)
					2 179 650	1 951 970

Thus, on both interest rate assumptions the in-house facility appears preferable:

@ 6% by £61 200
@12% by £25 970

However, in both cases this difference is less than the present value of the amount it is assumed can be raised from the sale of the lease.

There are also questions about the relative certainty of the other cash flows and the in-house option makes no allowance for revenues from, e.g., GP fundholders. Similarly there are questions about the comparability of the range and quality of the services.

6*
- Actual results should be compared with estimated results and significant variances analysed so as to make better informed decisions in the future.
- Often projects are unique and thus some of their implementation problems are likewise fairly unique.
- All project appraisals are made with a degree of uncertainty.
- Some state that rigid post-mortems can discourage initiative and produce a policy of overcaution.
- Audits do possibly check management from being overly optimistic.
- Research has shown that around two-thirds of UK companies undertake post-audits. In the UK public sector this figure is around 50%.

8* The government, principally the Treasury, has never really had much problem with the concept of net present value (NPV). It sees the benefits of NPV as being the main economic appraisal technique in both the public and private sectors. As we know, the rationale in the private sector is to maximize the long-term value of the shareholders' investment. In the public sector there is now increasing awareness that capital cost is not a free good, that funds principally derive, via taxation, from the private sector, and that as funds are in limited supply, there is an opportunity capital cost. It is also true that cost minimisation is analogous to profit maximisation except that in the public sector cost minimisation leads to greater and/or alternative service delivery. Students working in the public sector should be aware of the growing emphasis to cover capital costs and to adopt sound appraisal techniques. The discount rate is determined by the Treasury, the test discount rate (TDR), and is based on the net of tax return earned by relatively low risk medium sized private sector enterprises.

12* Taxation is a business expense. We have taxable profits which are negative cash flows and we have certain expenses that are tax deductible, thereby saving tax. Tax only features in an appraisal decision if we have taxable profits against which benefits can be offset. Many texts highlight the fact that we should discount net of tax cash flows by a net of tax discount factor. However, we are of the opinion that gross cash flows discounted by a gross discount rate makes more sense to most managers since it is out of gross funds that taxation has to be paid. Nevertheless, the incorporation of tax into a DCF calculation is not too difficult, as illustrated by the chapter example of Strathmore PLC.

Chapter 10

1* (a) Overreaction with the price returning to its 'true' value.

(b) This is how an efficient market might be expected to behave.

(c) Evidence of an inefficient market. Reaction should be quicker.

2* Day 1 – the total value of each firm is:

$$X: \$1 \times 4 \text{ million} = \$4 \text{ million}$$
$$Y: \$2 \times 10 \text{ million} = \$20 \text{ million}$$

Y appears to be making an offer of $6 million for X which appears to be worth $4 million. This will reduce the value of Y by $2 million to $18 million, or $1.80 per share. When it is known that the takeover will result in savings, the total value of Y will rise to $21.2 million, which is $2.12 per share.

(i) If the market is semi-strong form efficient, the market reacts only as information becomes publicly available:

	Value per share	
	X	Y
Day 2	$1.00	$2.00
Day 4	$1.50	$1.80
Day 10	$1.50	$2.12

(ii) If the market is strong-form efficient, all information is reflected in the share price, even if not in the public domain. This would suggest the possibility of insider-trading.

	Value per share	
	X	Y
Day 2	$1.50	$2.12
Day 4	$1.50	$2.12
Day 10	$1.50	$2.12

3* (a) $$\frac{0.275}{0.20 - 0.10} = €2.75$$

(b) $$€2 = \frac{(0.10)1.08}{(i - 0.08)}$$
$$i = 13.4\%$$

8* This question requires an understanding of the term 'insider-trading' and why such an activity can destabilise market trading. In most companies insider-trading is subject to both statutory and non-statutory legislation – reference should usefully be made to such regulation. Insider information can be defined as specific price-sensitive information relating to particular securities which have not been made public. The aim of such legislation is to ensure that the market operates freely on a basis of equality between buyers and sellers.

Examples:

- Goodman, as chairman of Unigroup Plc (1987), who sold shares to his girlfriend for her to resell just days before the announcement of a significant loss (UK example).
- Levine, managing director of Diessel Burnham Lambert Inc (1986), charged with providing information to Ivan Boesky. Boesky fined $100 million by SEC (US example).

9* This question is well covered in the text. The key issue is the difficulty in valuing and selling the shares in a non-listed company. Also listed companies find it easier to raise debt capital than non-listed companies. Non-listed companies have to benchmark against listed companies in order to arrive at approximate prices for their shares. Note that this is far from being a precise science.

11*

Advantage	Comment
• Immediate finance at low cost	Because of the conversion option, loans can be raised at below normal interest rates.
• Attractive, if share prices depressed	Where firms wish to raise equity finance, but share prices are currently depressed, convertibles offer a 'back-door' share issue method.
• Self-liquidating	Where loans are converted into shares, the problems of repayment disappear.
• Exercise of warrants related to need for finance	Options would normally be exercised where the share price has increased. If the options involved the payment of extra cash to the company, this creates extra funds when they are needed for expansion.

Chapter 11

1* (a) Nominal value of debentures: $10m × 100/80 = $12.5m.

Market cost of debt: $750 000/$10 000 000 × 100 = 7.5%.
(Actual interest paid: $12.5m × 6% = $750 000)
Market cost of equity: ($3.60m − $0.75m)/$20m × 100 = 14.25%.
(Return available to equity is equal to annual profit less interest paid)

(b) WACC: (20/30 × 14.25%) + (10/30 × 7.5%) = 12%.

(c) Overall cost of capital: $3.6m/$30m × 100 = 12%.

Note the answers to (b) and (c) are the same, illustrating the point that the overall cost of funds is the WACC using market values as weights.

2* (a) *Exe Ltd*

Return on equity = £250 000/£1 750 000 × 100 = 14.29% = WACC

Wye Ltd

Return on debt = 8%, as given in question.

Return on equity = $\dfrac{£250\,000 - 80\,000(\text{interest}) \times 100}{£1\,000\,000}$ = 17%

WACC = (17% × 0.5) + (8% × 0.5) = 12.5%.

The total value of Wye exceeds that of Exe, despite the operating cash flows of both firms being equal and both firms being in the same risk class. In an MM world the value of both firms should be the same and therefore the ordinary shares of Exe and Wye must be misvalued; Exe shares being undervalued and Wye shares being overvalued.

(b) As a holder of 4% of the shares in Wye Ltd, Liam's strategy should be to sell at market value, take on personal borrowing to maintain the financial risk faced by shareholders in Wye and invest this total sum in the shares of Exe Ltd.

4% of Wye shares sell for		£40 000
Personal borrowing (8%)		40 000
Sum to be invested in Exe		80 000
Income from Exe shares (£80k/£1.75m × £250k)	11 429	
Less interest (£40k × 8%)	3 200	8 229
Previous income from Wye shares (£40k × 0.17)		6 800
Gain from arbitrage		1 429

4* (a) Before the board took this decision, the value of the shares would have been:

$$V_o = d_1/(r\text{-}g) = [0.10\,(1+0.06)]/(0.08 - 0.06) = €5.30$$

After the board's decision is made known, and given the assumptions made, the market should rise to:

$$\dfrac{\dfrac{(0.125)}{(0.08-0.07)}}{(1.08)^3} = \dfrac{12.5}{(1.08)^3} = €9.92$$

(b) Under the assumptions made, Arthur could sell shares at the end of each of the next three years to earn an income of (approx.) €100 per annum, as follows:

		Year 1	Year 2	Year 3
Sell	10 shares at €10.715	€107.15		
Sell	9 shares at €11.575		€104.175	
Sell	~~8~~ shares at €12.50			€100
	27			

At the end of year 3 Arthur should have 973 shares remaining, valued at €12.50 each, or €12 162.50.

If the project had not been undertaken then Arthur would have 1000 shares valued at €6.3125* = €6312.50.

(* Being, €5.30 × 1.06³ = €6.3125)

7* This is a question that requires a sound knowledge of the M & M propositions, together with a discussion of what happens when their various, restrictive, assumptions are relaxed. If M&M's propositions were to hold true then their basic proposition that there is no ideal mix of debt and equity would be correct. However, in the real world, there are market distortions that clearly do show that it is possible to have a capital structure that is preferable to other structures. This is a question that can also draw upon perceived practice in particular markets. For example, firms in Australia tend to be lowly geared and pay substantial taxes. This would suggest that there is a limit to the use of debt financing to generate tax shields. We can also observe that firms in similar industries tend to have similar capital structures, suggesting that the nature of their assets and operations is an important determinant to capital structure. To stay with the Australian context, this could be easily observed by contrasting the annual reports of Woolworths, the supermarket chain, with Bluescope Steel, the largest Australian manufacturing firm. Students in other countries could follow a similar line of discussion and choose two contrasting companies of similar comparison.

8* This question basically requires a reprise of M & M's three propositions regarding the optimal capital structure debate. This can be done either by researching the original articles or other books devoted to financial theory, or, as in this text, using an illustration to explain the theory. The real issue is that M & M used normative economies to provide an artificial view of how markets operate. As such their theory is flawless. The real discussion is much to do with the constraints that they introduced in order for their theory to work. Given that, apart from M & M, we only have empirical evidence to observe and analyse, we can see the true value of what M & M have to offer. In other words, the mirror image to their theoretical argument provides managers with a list of variables that they need to consider when attempting to determine their firm's optimum capital structure.

9* The quotation in this question is taken from *Principles of Corporate Finance*, Brearley and Myers (2000), first Australian edition (p. 459), published by McGraw-Hill. This is a well-known text published in many countries, principally the UK and USA. It is a useful text for those seeking a more detailed introduction to financial theory. This quotation refers to the 1961 paper of M & M. It was a theoretical paper showing the irrelevance of dividend policy in a world without taxes, transaction costs or other market imperfections. Even today M & M's proof is generally accepted as correct, and the argument has shifted to whether taxes or other market imperfections alter the situation. To fully answer this question requires an understanding of M & M's argument. That is, once you fix the firm's investment policy, you fix its total expected future free cash flow and the risk of that cash flow. These are factors that determine a firm's value. The present value of the dividends must be equal to the present value of the firm's free cash flow. Discussion on M and M also requires a clear understanding of their separation theorem. M and M's views on the irrelevance of dividend policy is in contrast to those that argue that dividend policy is important as it communicates important information to the market.

Chapter 12

1* The total value of Firm B to Firm A is the pre-merger value of B plus the anticipated synergetic gain of $400 from the merger:

500 shares @ $6 = $3000 plus anticipated gain $400   = $3400
The price to be paid is: 500 shares @ $7   = $3500
Net loss should merger proceed $ 100

2* (a)   After the merger, Firm C will have 1250 shares on issue. If the revised value of this firm is $22 000, the price per share is $22 000/1250 = $17.60 which is a rise of $1.60 compared to its pre-merger price.

Since Firm D's shareholders end up with 250 shares in the merged firm, the cost of the merger is 250 × $17.60 = $4400, not 250 × $16.00 = $4000.

(b) The combined firm has earnings of $2000 ± $800 = $2800, so EPS is $2800/1250 = $2.24, up from $2000/1000 = $2.00. The old P/E ratio was $16/$1 = 8. The new P/E ratio is $17.60/$2.24 = 7.6%.

3* (a)   A 60% holding

(i)   The normal basis of valuing a holding of this size is by reference to assets and to earnings. Assuming the purchaser wished to continue the business of the company, the earning basis is more relevant.

(ii)   Assets basis, allowing for full liability of 30% on a chargeable gain:

Net assets per balance sheet	£1 414 000
Revaluation of freeholds (£1 200 000 – £860 000) × 0.7	238 000
	£1 652 000
Value per share (£1 652 000/150 000)	£11.01

(iii) P/E basis, subjective as non-quoted, say 5.

EPS: (£410 000) 0.7/150 000 = £1.91
Value per share (EPS × P/E) = £1.91 × 5 =   £9.56

(iv) Current and liquid ratios are satisfactory.

(v) As firm will continue trading and assets not realised their price is closer to £10 per share.

(b) A 5% holding

(i) The normal basis of valuing a holding of this size is by reference to dividends.

(ii) High asset backing, favourable ratios and profit trends also are factors that will influence valuation.

(iii) The yield on similar quoted securities is 8.1%. It is normal to uplift this by 25% – 50% for the unmarketability of unquoted securities. Let us assume therefore a yield of 10%.

(iv) Yields quoted in the FT are gross, whenever the percentage dividend declared is net. Thus the 12% dividend declared for 2006 needs to be grossed up. Assuming ACT 20/80 = ¼, we get:

Dividend per share = (12% × £1 × 100/80) = 15 pence.

(v) The dividend yield valuation would thus be:

$$100/10 \times 15 \text{ pence} = £1.50 \text{ per share.}$$

This is considerably lower than the value per share of the majority holdings.

(vi) With more information we could have applied a dividend valuation approach; i.e. including growth, but cost of equity figures are not given (Note: dividend yield is not the cost of equity as it does not include the growth factor.)

7* This is a question concerning the defences that can be employed against unwelcome takeover bids. The question also implies that directors must carefully consider their motives for recommending the rejection of an offer. As such, directors are duty bound to present all relevant facts to shareholders so that they can make informed decisions. They need to point out issues related to price of the offer relative to the real value of their current holdings as well as issues related to the terms of the takeover (e.g. cash versus a share exchange).

Defences include: securing an offer from a friendly company such as under a defensive merger (White Knight); poison pills (existing shareholders being granted 'rights' to be exercised at a later date); sale of key assets (Crown Jewels); golden parachutes for senior executives, revaluation of assets and profit forecasts and so on.

Directors owe a duty of care to shareholders and, in the end, must/should advise shareholders to accept a bid, even if unsolicited, where they are clearly better off. In most cases the shareholders of the acquired company tend to gain more than the shareholders of the acquiring company.

8* From the point of view of the bidding firm's shareholders a cash offer has a number of advantages; e.g. it represents an easily understood approach when resistance is expected, no alteration of shareholder control – maintain the status quo. On the other hand, a possible advantage for the bidder of a share-for-share exchange is the effect of the relatively high price-to-earnings ratio of the bidding company on the earnings of the target company. From the point of view of the shareholders of the target company a share-for-share exchange delays the imposition of capital gains tax. In addition, they retain a financial interest in the fortunes of the firm they have sold. Other issues include – the bidder, in a share-for-share exchange, has no real call on immediate cash flow, although in the longer term additional dividends will need to be paid. In the long run, for the bidder, equity is the most expensive form of capital.

10* MBOs vary in scale and size. There is a need to understand the motives of the seller, the potential attractiveness to the MBO team and the financial terms (especially with respect to the possible involvement of a venture capitalist). Against this analysis, it is possible to have a discussion on the advantages and disadvantages. The funding of an MBO is usually very complicated. In the early years the bought-out firm will be very highly geared and the venture capitalist will also expect to gain additional benefit by taking up a proportion of the equity. Whilst the long-term benefits appear attractive, the buyout team are under a degree of stress and may sell out to a competitor rather than staying the pace.

Chapter 13

1* The question requires the preparation of a balance sheet and a profit and loss account (income statement) using the account balances shown in the question.

Hendy Ltd
Balance sheet
As at 31 December 2007

	£	£
Fixed assets:		
at cost	65 098	
less accumulated depreciation	16 751	48 347
Current assets:		
Cash and bank balances	1 000	
Debtors	17 158	
Stocks	19 431	
	37 589	
Current liabilities:		
Bank overdraft	7 423	
Creditors	9 538	
	16 961	
Net current assets		20 628
Loan (repayable 31 December 2012)		(10 000)
Total net assets		58 975
Share capital	30 000	
Retained profits	28 975	58 975

Hendy Ltd
Income statement
For the year ended 31 December 2007

	£	£
Credit sales		89 649
Cash sales		57 053
		146 702
Cost of goods sold		76 030
Gross profit		70 672
Depreciation charge for the year	6 984	
Operating costs	41 582	48 566
Net profit for the year		22 106
Retained profit as at 1 January 2007		6 689
Retained profit as at 31 December 2007		28 795

As the information given in the question only relates to 2007 it is not possible to include comparative figures in either the balance sheet or the income statement. It should also be noted that the accounts contain no provision for taxation, or for a distribution to shareholders. As such they should be regarded as draft accounts.

2* The cash flow statement for liquidity for the year ended 31 December 2007 is as shown below:

	2007
	£000
Net cash flow from operating activities	
Operating profit	748
Depreciation charged	764
Loss on sale of fixed assets	20
Increase in stocks	(216)
Increase in debtors	(139)
Increase in creditors	70
	1 247
Returns on investment and servicing of finance	
Interest paid	(38)
Taxation paid	
UK Corporation Tax	(58)
Capital expenditure	
Sale of fixed assets	80
Purchase of fixed assets	(1 673)
	(1 593)
Dividend paid	(84)
Management of liquid resources	
Issue of share capital	500
Long term loans	20
	520
Decrease in cash in hand and at bank	(6)

7* The question asks for short explanations of a number of concepts which have been introduced in Chapter 3.

(a) *Fixed assets*

These are assets which an enterprise intends to hold for the long term, at least 12 months beyond the date to which accounts are being prepared, and to use in its activities as part of its productive/service delivery capacity. Whether an asset is classified by accountants as a fixed asset or not has little to do with the physical nature of the asset. The focus is the purpose for which the enterprise acquired the asset and the period of time for which it expects to keep it. Examples of fixed assets could include: land and buildings, plant and machinery, fixtures and fittings, motor vehicles, etc.

(b) *Current assets*

These are the short-term assets of the enterprise which it does not intend to own beyond the next 12 months. An alternative name for assets of this type is circulating assets as they circulate through the business in line with its trading cycle. Thus a business might start off with cash which it uses to buy stock; it then sells the stock on credit terms creating a different current asset (a debtor); the debtor then pays the debt and the business ends up with cash again (hopefully more than it started with). Current assets are in many ways the subject of an enterprise's trading operations. Careful attention needs to be paid to the management of these assets, and this is the subject of discussion in chapter 6.

(c) *Depreciation*

Depreciation results from the fact that an enterprise holds fixed assets for the long term. Thus the use of fixed assets will span a number of different account-ing periods and this needs to be reflected in accounts of these different accounting periods. The matching principle, one of the fundamental account-ing principles, requires that revenues be matched with the costs incurred in generating these revenues. Part of such costs will relate to the use of the pro-ductive/service delivery capacity provided by the fixed assets. Depreciation is the reflection of such costs. Effectively what depreciation does is to apportion the original cost of a fixed asset (less any anticipated residual value) to the different accounting periods comprising the useful life of the asset. There are a number of different techniques for doing this, the most notable being: the straight-line method, the reducing balance method and various usage based methods. The depreciation for any particular accounting period is included as a cost in the profit and loss account, while the balance sheet summarises the accumulated depreciation, i.e. the total depreciation charged against the exist-ing fixed assets of an enterprise since they were first acquired.

(d) *Current liabilities*

These are the counterpart of current assets, i.e. they are the short-term liabil-ities of an enterprise. They represent all the present obligations of an enter-prise which it expects that it will have to settle during the coming 12 months. The major component of current liabilities will probably be the amounts owed to suppliers for goods/services supplied on credit. Other types of current liabilities might be taxation, bank overdrafts and dividends.

(e) *Cash flow*

The cash flow of an enterprise during a period of time is simply the net of the amount of cash that it has received and any cash that it has paid out. Cash in this sense includes banking transactions. Cash flow differs from profit in that profit is typically calculated on the accruals basis, i.e. recognising the impact of transactions other than ones resulting in the exchange of cash, e.g. credit sales. A suitable pattern of cash flow is essential for the financial health of an enterprise. Unless it is generating sufficient cash inflows from its activities it will be unable to meet its liabilities as they fall due. Thus effective cash flow management is essential for the financial health of an enterprise and is an important element of the concept of financial adaptability.

9* The first part of this question requires agreement/disagreement with the proposition that current trends in legislation are likely to lead to an increasingly legally driven system of financial reporting. Issues that should be considered here include:

(i) the influence of EU Directives on UK legislation and the 'legalistic' tradition of financial reporting in much of Europe

(ii) the need to give 'teeth' to accounting standards (IASs) and the role (and legal status) of the IASB

(iii) a general trend towards increasing regulation in the financial sector (broadly defined)

(iv) increasing regulation of the accountancy profession (e.g. via implementation of the 8th EU Directive)

The second part of the question relates to whether or not a legally driven system of financial reporting will lead to greater comparability. The easy answer to this is yes – because all financial statements will be prepared in accordance with the same rules. However, a little thought should reveal that this is rather a 'glib' answer – the comparability may be more of form than of substance. There are at least three reasons for this:

(i) how can the financial statements of companies engaging in vastly different areas of economic activity ever be truly comparable, consider e.g. an oil exploration company vs. an insurance company vs. a supermarket. The economic environments and activities involved are so different that it is difficult to see how any one unified (legally driven) system of financial reporting can ever lead to true comparability.

(ii) the role of judgement – the preparation of all financial statements, even if there are detailed legal regulations, involves the exercise of an enormous amount of judgement. Such judgement may be honest but erroneous, or even biased.

(iii) the age structure of corporate assets – unless some system of 'current value' accounting is adopted (and legally driven systems tend to shy away from this) then in times of changing prices the age of assets will affect financial statements, perhaps significantly.

Perhaps we ought to accept that there are limits to the extent of comparability that can be achieved between the financial statements of companies, particularly ones in different business sectors.

10* This is, at least on the face of it, a rather simplistic question, masking a number of important issues which tutors could explore at a number of levels, depending on the courses they are teaching and the learning objectives they are trying to achieve. Issues that might usefully be debated include:

(i) why does the question restrict itself to commercial enterprises – do not stakeholders in other enterprises have similar interests?

(ii) what is meant by useful information and who determines what is useful? Should this be the prerogative of the preparers of financial statements and the regulators (e.g. the IASB) or should users play a part? If so how are the user groups and their representatives to be identified? How are conflicts between their interests/needs to be resolved?

(iii) is it possible that representatives of stakeholder groups involved in determining financial reporting issues will be financially sophisticated – this raises the question of how representative such representatives are likely to be. Also is it not possible that there will be a bias towards the 'professionals'?

(iv) what is meant by 'accessibility' – is it availability or does it go further – involving issues of understandability/usability? How does this relate to the question of simplified/abbreviated accounts (such as those envisaged by the 1989 Companies Act)?

(v) can 'accessible' (particularly in the context of abbreviated/simplified accounts) provide an adequate basis for decision making by stakeholders?

(vi) to what extent can (should) legislation make financial statements less opaque by identifying key issues which should be disclosed in clear and understandable language as opposed to hieratic language?

(vii) should commentary on apparently factual (accounting) information be subject to audit?

There is a wealth of issues that could be explored here, with a primary focus on the purpose of financial reporting and how this can best be achieved.

Chapter 14

1* The objectives of external auditing in the private sector have evolved over time, leading to the present emphasis on enhancing the credibility of the information contained in financial statements. At various times in this evolution emphasis has also been placed on the detection of fraud and verification of the accuracy of the financial records. In addition, the Companies Acts specify the primary responsibilities of an external auditor in the private sector (principally stating whether or not the financial statements present 'a true and fair view').

Historically, the emphasis of external audit in the public sector was on 'financial regularity', i.e. ensuring that monies were only expended on 'approved' (e.g. by Parliament) purposes, that all revenues were properly collected and that the records of this expenditure/revenue were accurate, i.e. the emphasis was on 'regularity'.

In the case of private sector external audits regularity was also important as auditors need(ed) to verify the reliability of underlying accounting records on which financial statements were based. It is possible to argue that this distinction (credibility vs. regularity) was more apparent than real because of the different nature of public sector (cash based) and private sector (accruals based) financial reporting. In both instances the end product was intended to be reliable (credible) accountability statements, albeit in different forms.

However, in recent years a more substantive difference has emerged between the activities of public and private sector external auditors. Although the then Comptroller and Auditor General had long had some responsibility for ensuring that public monies were not wasted, the changes introduced in the early 1980s with the formation of the National Audit Office and the Audit Commission placed much greater emphasis on their commenting whether or not public sector organisations were achieving 'value for money'. This is not a responsibility that the generality of external auditors in the private sector would willingly accept. They would argue that 'value for money' is the responsibility of the company's management and its internal audit department, unless they are specifically asked to look at 'value for money' issues over and above their responsibilities under the Companies Acts and for an additional fee!

4* The focus of this question is the 'expectations gap'; i.e. the difference between what the 'professionals' think an audit is and their responsibilities are and the evidence that many readers of financial statements have rather greater expectations of the audit process. There is no 'right' answer to the question. Instead it invites students to explore the 'expectations gap'. The depth to which this can/should be explored obviously depends on the type of course the students are pursuing.

However, we would expect that students would at least refer to the following issues:

(i) why auditors might maintain that their responsibilities are limited to truth and fairness, including reference to the Companies Act requirements and professional statements

(ii) the evolution of auditors' responsibilities, in the minds of auditors and readers of audit reports

(iii) research into readers' perceptions of the responsibilities of auditors and the meaning of 'unqualified' audit reports

(iv) why the 'expectations gap' is of concern to the accountancy/auditing profession

(v) the debate about the 'new format' audit reports which attempt to spell out the relative responsibilities of directors and auditors

(vi) recent statements on the responsibilities of auditors relating to illegal acts by their clients

(vii) the implications of the 'expectations gap'; e.g. as regards the legal/moral responsibilities of auditors

(viii) potential future developments regarding auditors' responsibilities in the light of the 1989 Companies Acts and related developments such as the work of the Auditing Standards Board.

5* The responsibility of auditors is governed in part by company law (insofar as it sets out what they are responsible for), in part by contract law (because there is a contract between the auditor and the company) and in part by the law of tort. It is not the purpose of this book to go into great detail regarding the liability of auditors – students who wish to do this could usefully refer to a specialist auditing text (e.g. Lee). However, students ought to be aware that despite financial statements being public documents (filed with the Registrar of Companies) there are limitations on the extent to which the law affords users of them action against auditors for negligent performance of the audit. This was vividly illustrated in the Caparo case. The objective of the question is principally to provoke a debate about breadth and depth of auditors' responsibilities to third parties (i.e. parties other than the company itself and the shareholders) in the light of the discussion about stakeholders in earlier chapters.

6* There are obviously a wide range of internal controls that an auditor (and management) would want to see in place in this context. Students should be encouraged to look at both general credit approval procedures and ones that are specific to the scenario posed by the question. Reference might also be made to the discussion of debtor management in Chapter 15.

Amongst the general controls that would normally be expected to be in place are:

(i)   definition and documentation of credit policies by senior management

(ii) initial credit vetting and its appropriate documentation as standard practice; e.g. the taking up of bank and trade references

(iii) definition and documentation of credit terms; e.g. the maximum amount of credit to be allowed and settlement terms

(iv) accounting records which identify amounts owed by debtors and how long individual amounts have been outstanding; i.e. aged analysis of debtors

(v)   procedures for ensuring that customers adhere to their credit terms

(vi) follow up procedures relating to collection of overdue debts

(vii) procedures for the authorisation of credit sales, having reference to the credit terms and performance of individual customers

10* Auditable propositions in this respect would include:

(a) The company claims to have bank accounts

(b) The relevant banks acknowledge the existence of these bank accounts

(c) There are duly authorised bank mandates in relation to these accounts

(d) The amount(s) shown in the balance sheet are in agreement with the company's accounting records (cash books, etc.)

(e) The amount(s) included in the balance sheet can be confirmed by the relevant banks (after due allowance is made for items in transit and other reconciling items)

(f) The amount(s) shown in the balance sheet are available to the company at its order

11* This question gets to the heart of the relationships involved in the accountability process and the role(s) of the auditor in this process. It invites students to distinguish between the roles of an auditor and a management consultant. This requires them to analyse these roles and ask themselves for whose benefit the activity is being undertaken. In the case of an audit, the emphasis will normally be on the auditor reporting to the 'owner' of the resources on the extent to which the auditee(s) (stewards/directors) have fulfilled their responsibilities according to the terms of the accountability relationship. A management consultancy exercise, on the other hand, would normally be thought of as being commissioned by management (however defined) to appraise their activities with a view to improving them, if possible.

Thus, the authors suggest, the distinction between a 'value for money' audit and a similar management consultancy assignment is not so much the processes involved in carrying out work. In both cases it should involve an appraisal of the extent to which 'value for money' is being achieved. Instead the distinction relates to declared objectives of the exercise. Is it an appraisal intended to assist managers (stewards) improve their 'value for money' performance (with the appraisers/auditors and their terms of reference being specified by the managers/stewards) or is it an evaluation of managerial performance being carried out for the owners/providers of the resources to reassure them that the stewards/directors are fulfilling their obligations adequately.

Chapter 15

1* The question requires the explanation of various elements in the draft accounts of Commentary Ltd using clear and simple terms, and avoiding the use of unexplained jargon.

(a) The questioner is querying the value of making profits when the company's cash (bank balance) position 'seems to go from bad to worse'. In fact Commentary made a profit after taxation of £60 000 during 2007. However, its balance sheet reveals an increase in the bank overdraft from £50 000 to £100 000 and no cash at bank or in hand. Thus on the face of it the questioner is correct. The company has made a profit but has seen a worsening in its cash position.

However, the question reveals a misunderstanding of the relationship between cash and profit. When a company makes a profit during a financial period this is associated with an increase in its overall net assets. Cash is only one element in these net assets. Thus it is perfectly possible for a company to be profitable and incur a deterioration in its cash position. This is because the accounts are prepared on the accruals basis, which recognises the existence of assets and liabilities other than cash. However, if the cash basis of accounting were to be used this would not happen. Under this basis of accounting surpluses (profits) are automatically equalled by increases in cash.

It should, however, be noted that under the accruals basis of accounting it is perfectly possible for a company to be profitable and yet become insolvent, i.e. have insufficient cash resources to meet its liabilities as and when they fall due. Thus management have to have regard both to profit that their activities generate and to the timing of the cash flow consequences of those activities.

(b) The normal basis of accounting is the historical cost basis under which assets are recorded at their cost of acquisition. In the case of fixed assets this is justified on the grounds that they are acquired for long-term use in the business and therefore their current market value is not a relevant piece of information. They are stated in the balance sheet at historical cost, less any accumulated depreciation.

However, it has been recognised for some time that doing this may have a number of undesirable consequences. In particular it can lead to the current value of the resources employed in the business being significantly understated. This will lead to distortions in the computation of profitability ratios, and may impose unnecessary limitations on the company's borrowing powers. Accordingly, it is now quite common practice for companies to periodically revalue their fixed assets, most notably their land and buildings, to current market value. When this is done the balance sheet values of the fixed assets are amended to reflect the current value and a non-distributable revaluation reserve is created in the capital section of the balance sheet.

Unfortunately, companies seem happier to revalue their fixed assets upwards in times of rising prices than they are to revalue them downwards in times of falling prices. Also a great deal of judgement may be involved in the determination of the current market value. Accordingly, the process of revaluation is not without its dangers.

(c) Accountants regard a fixed asset as being an asset acquired for long term use (typically regarded as being more than 12 months) with a view to using it in the generation of future profits. Thus the word 'fixed' relates to the economic purpose for which the asset was acquired and not to its physical nature. Accordingly, it is perfectly possible for fixed assets to highly mobile. Apart from motor vehicles, other examples of 'mobile' fixed assets might include trains, aeroplanes and ships.

(d) This question relates first to the depreciation figures shown in the income statement and balance sheet and, secondly, by implication, the purpose of depreciation.

As regards the first part of the question. the depreciation figures in the income statement and balance sheet have different purposes. The depreciation figure in the income statement is the depreciation charge for the year. It represents the allocation to that financial year of the anticipated lifetime depreciation of the assets employed by the business during that year. Thus it is a cost. The balance sheet figure, on the other hand, might be seen more properly as accumulated depreciation. It represents the total amount of depreciation that has been charged, in the current and earlier years, against all the fixed assets that the company owned at the end of the year. To summarise, the income statement contains the charge for the current year while the balance sheet records current and prior year charges.

As regards the second part of the question, the purpose of accounting depreciation is not to provide a fund with which to purchase replacement fixed assets. Rather, it is to apportion the net lifetime ownership cost of a fixed asset (original cost – salvage value) to the various financial years during which the asset is owned. This is an application of the fundamental accounting concept of 'matching'. Indirectly depreciation leads to the retention of resources within a company as it reduces the amount of distributable profit. There is, however, no guarantee that these resources will be in a form which can be used to purchase replacement assets. Some companies, recognising this, go a stage further and calculate replacement cost depreciation (this is based on the anticipated replacement cost of an asset rather than its original cost). This further reduces the distributable profit, but again there is no guarantee that the resources retained within the company will actually be able to be used to purchase replacement assets.

(e) Stocks and debtors have certainly increased during the year – from £180 000 to £260 000, and from £120 000 to £160 000 respectively, i.e. increases of 44.4% and 33.3%. These are undoubtedly significant increases. However, increases like this do not necessarily indicate a loss of managerial control. Amongst other things they may simply be a reflection of an increase in the level of business activity or changes in price levels. This can be checked by comparing the values of stocks and debtors which indicate the level of activity and prices. These are the cost of sales and sales turnover figures.

Looking first at stocks, we can calculate the stock turnover period which measures how long, on average, stocks are held before being sold. The relevant calculations for Commentary are:

2006: $365 \times 180/580 = 113.3$ days
2007: $365 \times 260/710 = 133.7$ days

This indicates that the average stockholding period has increased by 20 days (17.7%). On the face of it this is a significant change from the previous pattern and warrants further investigation, although it does not necessarily indicate loss of control. There could be other explanations, e.g. a bulk purchase of stock shortly before the year-end at favourable prices, or a build-up of stock for a large customer order to be despatched shortly after the year end.

Turning to debtors the corresponding calculations are:

2006: $365 \times 120/850 = 51.5$ days
2007: $365 \times 160/1050 = 55.6$ days

Here the average period debtors takes to pay has increased by five days (9.8%). This is not as dramatic an increase as for stocks but should still be investigated. As for stocks the increase does not automatically indicate a loss of control – there could be other explanations.

(f) Rate of return on capital employed compares the profit that an enterprise has generated with the value of the resources employed in generating that profit. There are a number of different ways of measuring it, depending on how the profit and capital are defined. There are two variants that are relevant in the case of Commentary.

Return on total long-term capital employed. This compares operating profit (profit before the deduction of interest and taxation) with total long-term capital (equity capital and debt capital). This provides a measure of how effectively the resources of the company have been employed in the generation of profit independently of how those resources have been financed. The relevant calculations for Commentary are:

2006: $(75 + 24)/(540 + 200) \times 100 = 13.4\%$
2007: $(110 + 24)/(570 + 200) \times 100 = 17.4\%$

Thus there appears to have been an increase in the profitability of Commentary.

Return on equity capital employed. This compares the return to equity shareholders (profit after taxation) with equity capital (share capital and reserves). It provides a measure of how effectively the resources provided by the equity shareholders have been used. The relevant calculations are:

$$2006: 40/540 \times 100 = 7.4\%$$
$$2007: 60/570 \times 100 = 10.5\%$$

Again an increase in profitability.

Thus it appears that Commentary is doing better than last year with regard to the returns it is generating from the resources it is employing. However, this does not address the question of whether it is doing better than its competitors. To find this out it is necessary to compare its returns with those being generated by competitors and this is a perfectly sensible thing to do. Nevertheless, some caution needs to be exercised. In particular, care should be taken to ensure that the businesses being compared are truly comparable. It would not make sense to compare the return being generated by a major retailer such as Marks & Spencer or David Jones with that of a corner shop. Similarly, care should be taken to ensure that the accounts of companies have been based on similar accounting policies, as differences in these policies will lead to the reporting of different profit and capital figures. Finally, care should be taken to ensure that the age structure of the assets of the companies is comparable as this could be reflected in different asset values and depreciation charges being reflected in the accounts.

(g) Earnings per share are calculated as follows:

Earnings per share (EPS) = (Profit attributable to shareholders)/(No. of shares in issue)

There are a number of technical considerations in calculating, e.g. those arising when a company issues new shares during the course of a financial year or when it has issued convertible loan stock and, in the UK, are the subject of Statement of Standard Accounting Practice No. 1. The essence of EPS is that it computes the 'ultimate' measure of profit performance – how much the company has earned during the year for each shareholder. However, as it is a composite figure it does not give any indication of the factors that have contributed to these earnings – it is very much a 'bottom-line' figure. This is something the ASB is keen to avoid – it believes that stakeholders need to look not just at the bottom-line but also at the elements that contribute to this. Hence, the importance it places in FRS3 on disclosing the important elements that go to make up the 'bottom-line'.

2* The following ratios can be calculated:

Ratio	2006	2007
Gross profit	54.2%	47.9%
Net profit before interest and taxation	29.6%	20.1%
Return on total capital employed	46.3%	24.9%
Debtor collection period	76.0 days	132.9 days
Creditor payment period	41.7 days	47.5 days
Stock turnover period	115.0 days	124.8 days
Current ratio	1.54:1	2.45:1
Quick ratio	0.95:1	1.66:1
General expenses ratio	25%	28%
Return on shareholders' capital	36%	20%
Gearing	37%	53%
Interest cover	17.0:1	7.2:1
Sales growth	N/A	30%
Sales per employee	£9 600	£14 976
Profit per employee	£2 840	£3 016

Stargate Plc has outperformed the market in terms of sales growth (30% v. 20%) and by implication has gained market share, but the claims made in relation to profitability gains are not supported by the ratios. Overall gross profit has increased by £234 000 over the period but the gross profit % has declined (47.9% v. 54%) – this might be due to price reductions to gain additional market share. The net profit % has declined (20% v. 30%) against an industry trend of strengthening margins (35% v. 30%).

Return on capital has declined: for return on total capital (25% v. 46%) and for return on shareholders' funds (20% v. 36%). The general expenses ratio has deteriorated (28% v. 25%). Unfortunately no industry comparative data is available.

The company has invested heavily in new equipment in both years and there has been an improvement in efficiency, as measured by sales and profits per employee. However, the levels being achieved seem rather poor (e.g. £15 000 sales per employee). Again benchmark data would be helpful.

There is evidence from the accounts that debtor collections have deteriorated sharply (133 days v. 76 days) as has stock turnover (125 days v. 115 days). These trends should have been revealed by management accounts and should not have come as a surprise. To what extent might these changes have been caused by the impending failure of the major customer?

The major problem appears to be poor liquidity: current and acid test ratios have risen (2.45:1 v. 1.54:1 and 1.66:1 v. 0.95:1). However, this is primarily due to the increased size of the numerator (largely caused by the increases in debtors and stocks). It is likely that these increases are a major factor in the decrease in 'net cash flow from operating activities').

Taken together, these changes may have serious implications for a business operating in what appears to be a 'high-tech' industry with increasing customer expectations and short product life-cycles. A clear danger is that of product obsolescence. Equally, the (significant) increase in the debtor collection period is worrying – how much was caused by the failure of the major customer, is proper attention being paid to credit control procedures, has a thorough bad debt review been carried out? It seems likely that these changes have been a major factor in the need to raise additional long-term finance (share capital and debentures).

Overall, the position is worrying – apparent loss of control over stock and debtors, failure of a major customer, apparently low levels of productivity, declining profit margins. Management have some serious questions to answer.

3* The question requires a report in your capacity as financial adviser to JG. Such a report could take a number of forms. However, a useful approach is to structure it as follows:

(a) General commercial considerations

(b) Overview of the financial statements

(c) Detailed financial ratio calculations

(d) Conclusions

Using this approach, the following would appear relevant:

(a) *General commercial considerations:*

- Why might JG be interested in acquiring Nemesis? How does it fit with its existing portfolio of activities? Does it have the management skills to manage an electronics firm?

- To what extent would JG want to control Nemesis? Would the other shareholders be willing to sell their shares? What impact might this have on employee commitment?

- Would Henry Nemesis be willing to consider a share exchange rather than a cash sale? What about the other shareholders? If so, on what terms? Would the shareholders be willing to consider a price conditional on future earnings rather than a fixed price?

- Was the business really dependent on the deceased Josiah Nemesis? If so what is its future potential?

- Does the business have any competitive advantage, e.g. intellectual property? Who are its competitors/customers? What is the future for its type of products, etc?

(b) *Overview of the financial statements:*

- What is the market value of the freehold properties?

- The machinery is quite heavily depreciated (approximately two-thirds of cost) – does this indicate that significant future investment is required in this area?

- Cash balances appear to have been declining steadily over the period in question

- Short-term loans were first taken out in 2006 and increased in 2007. Long-term loans appear to be being repaid at $50 000 per annum. What are the terms (interest, repayment, etc.) of these loans?

- In the last two years dividends have exceeded post-tax profits, most notably in 2006. Does this indicate that existing shareholders have been 'milking' the company?

- The year 2006 appears to have been a bad year – the year in which sales declined and dividends significantly exceeded profits. Was this the year that Josiah Nemesis died?

Both the commercial considerations and the overview of the financial statements raise a number of questions. With the information available it is not possible to provide answers to these questions (and they are not as such required). However, identifying these questions indicates an appreciation of core issues involved in a potential acquisition and helps to focus attention on that results of the financial ratio calculations.

(c) *Financial ratio calculations:*

(i) Return on total capital employed:

This is calculated by:

$$\frac{\text{Profit before interest and taxation}}{\text{Total long term capital employed}} \times 100$$

There are a number of issues involved here as at what date, and in what way this capital employed should be calculated (e.g. start/mid/end of year; balance sheet values; current market values; etc.). Here, and in the rest of the solution notes, for simplicity, end of year balance sheet values are used. On this basis, the relevant calculations are:

2007:	$(135+45)/970 \times 100$	= 18.6%
2006:	$(185+40)/1030 \times 100$	= 21.8%
2005:	$(360+35)/1160 \times 100$	= 34.1%
2004:	$(375+40)/1070 \times 100$	= 38.8%

These figures indicate a significant, albeit slowing, decline in this rate of return, i.e. resources are being employed less effectively in the generation of profit.

(ii) Return on equity capital employed:

This is calculated by:

$$\frac{\text{Profit attributable to shareholders}}{\text{Equity capital employed}} \times 100$$

The relevant calculations are:

2007:	$90/720 \times 100$	= 12.5%
2006:	$120/730 \times 100$	= 16.4%
2005:	$240/810 \times 100$	= 29.6%
2004:	$250/670 \times 100$	= 37.3%

These provide a similar, even more dramatic, picture of significantly declining performance than above.

(iii)   Net profit margin %:

This calculated by:

$$\frac{\text{Profit after taxation}}{\text{Sales turnover}} \times 100$$

The relevant calculations are:

2007:	90/2400 × 100	= 3.8%
2006:	120/2100 × 100	= 5.7%
2005:	240/2250 × 100	= 10.7%
2004:	250/2200 × 100	= 11.4%

These calculations reinforce the early picture, i.e. a steadily, and rapidly declining net profit margin percentage.

(iv)   Current (working capital ratio):

This is calculated by:

$$\frac{\text{Current assets}}{\text{Current liabilities}}$$

The relevant calculations are:

2007:	1230/770	= 1.60
2006:	1190/750	= 1.59
2005:	1160/580	= 2.00
2004:	1060/530	= 2.00

Again, this shows an adverse trend.

(v)   Liquid (quick) ratio:

This is calculated by:

$$\frac{\text{Current assets} - \text{stock}}{\text{Current liabilities}}$$

The relevant calculations are:

2007:	790/730	= 1.08
2006:	780/750	= 1.04
2005:	790/580	= 1.36
2004:	700/530	= 1.32

On the face of it these ratios indicate an adequate, albeit tightening, level of liquidity. However, the increase in short-term loans is a concern.

(vi)   Debtor turnover period:

These are calculated by:

$$\frac{\text{Debtors}}{\text{Sales turnover}} \times 365$$

The relevant calculations are:

2007:	780/2400 × 365	= 118.6 days
2006:	690/2100 × 365	= 119.9 days

2005: 680/2250 × 365 = 110.3 days
2004: 600/2200 × 365 = 99.5 days

Again, these show a deteriorating trend with debtors taking longer, on average, to collect.

(vii) Balance sheet gearing (leverage):

This is calculated by:

$$\frac{\text{Long-term debt}}{\text{Total long-term capital employed}}$$

The relevant calculations are:

2007: 250/(720+250) = 25.8%
2006: 300/(730+300) = 29.1%
2005: 350/(810+350) = 30.2%
2004: 400/(670+400) = 37.4%

These show an overall decline over the four years, principally because of the long-term loan repayments.

(viii) Interest cover:

This is calculated by:

$$\frac{\text{Operating profit}}{\text{Interest payable}}$$

The relevant calculations are:

2007: 180/45 = 4 times
2006: 225/40 = 5.6 times
2005: 395/35 = 11.3 times
2004: 415/40 = 10.4 times

Again, these figures show a declining trend with interest payments absorbing a higher proportion of operating profits.

(ix) Earnings per share:

This is calculated by:

$$\frac{\text{Profits attributable to shareholders}}{\text{No. of shares in issues}}$$

The relevant calculations are:

2007: 90/500 = $0.18
2006: 120/500 = $0.24
2005: 240/500 = $0.48
2004: 250/500 = $0.50

Again these show a declining trend over the period.

(d) *Summary*: the commercial considerations and overview of the financial statements raise a number of questions that need further investigation. The financial ratios indicate a declining business with erratic sales growth, declining profitability and liquidity, albeit with not-unacceptable levels of return on capital employed. The core question is whether or not the decline could be arrested and reversed by new owners who could acquire the business without paying an excessive price.

7* As is pointed out in the chapter, there are six principal areas in which a potential investor is likely to be interested, although obviously the degree of interest will vary from investor to investor and from company to company. The core issue is that a potential investor wants to be able to assess the potential risk of and the potential reward from an investment. Subject to this, the areas are likely to be:

(i) *Economic sector* – the annual financial statements have relatively little to offer here, apart, perhaps, from the operating and financial review.

(ii) *Solvency* – the annual financial statements do provide some information here, most notably the cash flow statement, current assets and current liabilities. However, this is of course ex-post rather than ex-ante information.

(iii) *Growth* – the provision of comparative information is of some, limited, assistance here. Of perhaps more use would be a five or ten year summary of the type most listed companies provide, although this is of course unaudited and is unlikely to be adjusted for price level changes.

(iv) *Financing* – again the financial statements do provide some information here, albeit of an ex-post nature.

(v) *Profitability* – similar comments apply as to solvency and financing.

(vi) *Investment performance* – the financial statements do provide some information, e.g. about earnings, but this has to be combined with information from other sources, e.g. market prices.

To summarise, the financial statements do provide a range of useful information but the utility of this information is restricted by its ex-post orientation. In addition there is a much broader set of information needed by potential investors, which they do not provide, e.g. economic sector prospects, alternative investments, etc.

9* The starting point here is asking with what sort of information the three groups might want to make comparisons. To the extent that this information is publicly available, then in principle there is no real difference between the groups, except perhaps in terms of financial sophistication. However, beyond such publicly available information there are significant differences. Management, for example, have access to all the information of the company, perhaps most notably its budgets and plans. Bankers may be able to use their relationships with a company to obtain the corporate information they require, e.g. aged lists of debtors. In general terms, the shareholder is the one who is likely to encounter the greatest difficulties in carrying out a meaningful ratio analysis.

12* Frequently, the computation of financial ratios and their comparison with benchmarks (budgets, competitor organisations, time-series data, etc.) will indicate the need for additional information to enable variations to be understood properly. This may include the computation of more detailed, disaggregated, ratios..

Chapter 17

1* Supply chain management is, in effect, the economic theory of comparative advantage applied at the firm or agency level. As defined by Fawcett *et al.* (2007: 8): 'Supply chain management is the design and management of seamless, value-added processes across organisational boundaries to meet the real needs of the end customer'. Historically, organisations have failed to realise that they are part of a chain or network that could work more effectively if they were open-minded to breaking down organisational boundaries in order to reduce inventory levels and a range of operational and overheads costs up and down the chain. Supply chain management is an approach to value adding at each stage of the supply chain network, a network that starts externally with suppliers, progresses internally through the various departments within the firm and then externally again through various distribution channels to the end customer or user. Supply chain management, as a discipline, is an extension of logistics management. Whilst logistics is essentially a planning orientation and framework that seeks to create a single plan for the flow of a product or service, supply chain management builds upon this framework by managing the basis on which the relationships in the chain should be managed. Supply chain management is therefore a specialised form of relationship management. Successful supply chain management leads to the pooling of information and resources, often in terms of pooling manpower, assets and technologies.

2* This question requires an understanding of Table 17.1 in this chapter, which is reproduced from Fawcett *et al.* (2007). The four decision areas are: environment, resources, objectives and feedback. The table contrasts the more traditional view of each decision area with a supply chain enabled perspective. Astute managers need to be acutely aware of the environment within which they operate – their competitive, legal and 'political' environments. Resources include both tangible and intangible resources. Whilst a textbook approach to setting key objectives tends to focus on key financial goals, a supply chain view would consider that long-run financial goals are only met when the firm efficiently satisfies its customers. Feedback loops help managers to adapt strategy to meet changing conditions. In order to proceed, management need to design what Fawcett describes as a 'supply chain road map'. Such a map relies on the answers to four questions: Who are we? How do we fit? How should we fit? How do we get there? Supply chain managers understand the need for innovation and collaborative arrangements. Such initiatives include the pooling of warehousing, the sharing of business systems, inviting suppliers to comment on new product development, inviting suppliers onto the production shop floor so that they can contribute to efficiency savings, the sharing of financial information.

3* The object of this exercise is to search the web for illustrative examples of how companies have embraced the notion of supply chain management. Such examples can include manufacturers such as BlueScope Steel or companies that offer transport and freighting solutions such as Toll Holdings or DHL.

8* This question is easily answered by reference to Figures 17.2 and 17.3 in the text. These are taken from Christopher (2005). When it comes to improving financial performance measures such as ROI, supply chain management strategies such as customer service, logistics efficiency, just-in-time inventory approaches, etc. are key to improving both the numerator and denominator elements of the ratio. Balance sheet performance is also improved by logistical solutions that improve supply order cycle times, completion rates and inventory management. Supply chain strategies can also impact on the way in which a firm determines the long-term funding of its fixed assets.

Chapter 18

1* This question requires a discussion of the variety of business systems established, including accounting systems. In terms of their influence on the organisation, it is still generally the case that accounting information systems dominate the forward direction of corporate ability. This question could well be tackled by reference to a specific organisation.

2* This question should provide for an interesting discussion given (at the time of writing) the collapse of so many of the so-called tiger economies. There still is a diversity of accounting practice. In the areas of management accounting many of the approaches adopted are fairly unsophisticated and concentrate on control issues. It is hardly surprising therefore that issues appear to occur on a fairly cyclical basis.

3* This answer takes students back to the earlier introduction to the principles of costing and short-term decision making (refer to Chapters 4 and 5).

4* This question simply requires students to provide an understanding of the technique of ABC costing and instances of when its application is most useful.

5* This is a general question designed to allow students to consider the strategic direction(s) adopted by an organisation with which they are familiar.

6* This is similar in context to that required in question 5 but utilises an analysis approach developed by Mintzberg (1979).

INDEX

Page numbers for figures have suffix **f**, those for tables have suffix **t**, those for equations have suffix **e**.